Contents

II Are you making the most of your SatNav?

VI Distance table

1 Key to road map pages, key to road map symbols

2 Road maps of Great Britain at 10 miles to 1 inch

24 M25 and routes into London

25 M6 and routes into Birmingham

26 M60 and routes into Manchester and Liverpool

27 Key to city plan and approach map symbols

28 City plans and **NAVIGATOR**® approach maps

28 Aberdeen
29 Aberystwyth
30 Ashford (Kent)
31 Ayr
32 Bangor (Gwynedd)
33 Barrow-in-Furness
34 Bath
35 Berwick-upon-Tweed
36 Birmingham
38 Blackpool
39 Bournemouth
40 Bradford
41 Brighton
42 Bristol
44 Bury St Edmunds
45 Cambridge
46 Cardiff (Caerdydd)
48 Canterbury
49 Carlisle
50 Chelmsford
51 Cheltenham
52 Chester
53 Chichester
54 Colchester
55 Coventry
56 Croydon
57 Derby
58 Dorchester
59 Dumfries
60 Dundee
61 Durham
62 Edinburgh
64 Exeter
65 Fort William
66 Glasgow
68 Gloucester
69 Grimsby
70 Hanley
71 Harrogate
72 Haywards Heath
73 Hull (Kingston upon)
74 Inverness
75 Ipswich
76 Kendal
77 King's Lynn
78 Lancaster
79 Leicester
80 Leeds
82 Lewes
83 Lincoln
84 Liverpool
86 Llandudno
87 Llanelli
88 London
96 Luton
97 Macclesfield
98 Manchester
100 Maidstone
101 Merthyr Tydfil
102 Middlesbrough
103 Milton Keynes
104 Newcastle-upon-Tyne
106 Newport (Casnewydd)
107 Newquay
108 Northampton
109 Norwich
110 Nottingham
111 Oban
112 Oxford
113 Perth
114 Peterborough
115 Plymouth
116 Poole
117 Portsmouth
118 Preston
119 Reading
120 St Andrews
121 Salisbury
122 Scarborough
123 Shrewsbury
124 Sheffield
126 Southampton
127 Southend-on-Sea
128 Stirling
129 Stoke-on-Trent
130 Stratford-upon-Avon
131 Sunderland
132 Swansea (Abertawe)
133 Swindon
134 Taunton
135 Telford
136 Torquay
137 Truro
138 Wick
139 Winchester
140 Windsor
141 Wolverhampton
142 Worcester
143 Wrexham (Wrecsam)
144 York

145 Index to road maps

153 County and unitary authority boundaries

154 Using GPS with **NAVIGATOR**® mapping

First published in 2007 by

Philip's, a division of
Octopus Publishing Group Ltd,
2–4 Heron Quays, London E14 4JP

www.philips-maps.co.uk

First edition 2007
First impression 2007

ISBN-10 0-540-09080-8
ISBN-13 978-0-540-09080-8

Cartography by Philip's

Data for the speed cameras provided by PocketGPSWorld.com Ltd.

Information for Tourist Attractions shown on the mapping supplied by VisitBritain.

Information for National Parks, Areas of Outstanding Natural Beauty, National Trails and Country Parks in Wales supplied by the Countryside Council for Wales.

Data for Regional parks, Long Distance Footpaths and Country Parks in Scotland provided by Scottish National Heritage.

Data for National Scenic Areas in Scotland provided by the Scottish Executive Office. Crown copyright material is reproduced with the permission of the Controller of HMSO and the Queen's Printer for Scotland. Licence number C02W0003960.

Information for National Parks, Areas of Outstanding Natural Beauty, National Trails and Country Parks in England supplied by the Countryside Agency.

Information for canal bridge numbers supplied by GEOprojects (UK) Ltd.

Printed by Toppan, China

Photographic acknowledgements

Cover and Page II – Adrian Muttitt / Alamy • **Page IV** Hugh Threlfall / Alamy **Page V** Monteverde / Alamy • **Aberdeen** – Shenval / Alamy **Aberystwyth** – David Newham / Alamy • **Ashford** – Image Advertising **Ayr** – Ayrshire and Arran Tourist Board • **Bangor** – Rob Rayworth / Alamy **Barrow-in-Furness** – David Martin Graphics / Alamy **Bath** – James Hughes • **Berwick-upon-Tweed** – curved-light / Alamy • **Birmingham** – Birmingham City Council • **Blackpool** – Chris Parker • **Bournemouth** – Bournemouth Borough Council • **Bradford** – Bradford Council • **Brighton** – Leonardo Media BV • **Bristol** – James Hughes • **Bury St Edmunds** – East of England Tourist Board **Cambridge** – East of England Tourist Board • **Cardiff** – James Hughes • **Canterbury** – Canterbury City Council • **Carlisle** – Justin Kase / Alamy • **Chelmsford** – East of England Tourist Board • **Cheltenham** – Cheltenham Tourism / David Sellman • **Chester** – Iconotec / Alamy **Chichester** – James Hughes • **Colchester** – Colchester Image Library **Coventry** – CV One Ltd • **Croydon** – Croydon Design • **Derby** – Derby City Council • **Dorchester** – Jack Sullivan / Alamy • **Dumfries** – Allan Devlin • **Dundee** – Purestock / Alamy • **Durham** – James Hughes **Edinburgh** – Iconotec / Alamy • **Exeter** – James Hughes • **Fort William** – The Highlands of Scotland Tourist Board • **Glasgow** – Greater Glasgow and Clyde Valley Tourist Board • **Gloucester** – James Hughes **Grimsby** – North East Lincolnshire Council • **Hanley** – Travel and Places / Alamy • **Harrogate** – Harrogate International Centre • **Haywards Heath** – Keith Shuttlewood / Alamy • **Hull** – Hull City Council • **Inverness** – The Highland Council • **Ipswich** – Ipswich Borough Council **Kendal** – South Lakeland District Council • **King's Lynn** – Borough Council of King's Lynn and West Norfolk • **Lancaster** – Lancaster City Council • **Leicester** – Ian Francis / Alamy • **Leeds** – GothMeister Imaging / Alamy • **Lewes** – Lewes District Council • **Lincoln** – Justin Kase / Alamy • **Liverpool** – The Mersey Partnership • **Llandudno** – Rob Rayworth / Alamy • **Llanelli** – Carmarthenshire County Council • **London** – James Hughes; Coaster / Alamy • **Luton** – TK Stock / Alamy • **Macclesfield** – Macclesfield Borough Council • **Manchester** – North West Tourist Board • **Maidstone** – imagebroker / Alamy • **Merthyr Tydfil** – Richard Naude / Alamy • **Middlesbrough** – Shenval / Alamy • **Milton Keynes** – Justin Kase / Alamy • **Newcastle-upon-Tyne** – Andrew Siddens / Alamy • **Newport** – James Hughes • **Newquay** – Restormel Borough Council • **Northampton** – David Burton / Alamy • **Norwich** – East of England Tourist Board • **Nottingham** – Joe Fox / Alamy • **Oban** – images-of-france / Alamy • **Oxford** – Tourism South East • **Perth** – Shenval / Alamy • **Peterborough** – East of England Tourist Board • **Plymouth** – James Hughes • **Poole** – Poole Tourism **Portsmouth** – Worldwide Picture Library / Alamy **Preston** – Lancashire Tourism Partnership • **Reading** – Neil McAllister / Alamy • **St Andrews** – Kingdom of Fife Tourist Board • **Salisbury** – James Hughes **Scarborough** – Scarborough Borough Council • **Shrewsbury** – Shropshire Tourism • **Sheffield** - Pete Hill / Alamy **Southampton** – James Hughes • **Southend** – David Burton / Alamy **Stirling** – David Gowans / Alamy • **Stoke** – Rolf Richardson / Alamy • **Stratford-upon-Avon** – David Newham / Alamy • **Sunderland** – curved-light / Alamy • **Swansea** – James Hughes • **Swindon** – Paul Heinrich / Alamy • **Taunton** – James Hughes • **Telford** – Borough of Telford and Wrekin • **Torquay** – English Riviera Tourist Board • **Truro** – James Hughes • **Wick** – P Tomkins / Visit Scotland / Scottish Viewpoint **Winchester** – James Hughes • **Windsor** – Royal Borough of Windsor and Maidenhead • **Wolverhampton** – Wolverhampton City Council **Worcester** – James Hughes • **Wrexham** – Wrexham County Borough Council • **York** – James Hughes

Are you making the most of your SatNav?

A recent survey discovered that 14 per cent of British drivers never use a paper road map. Instead they put their trust entirely in their satellite navigation system.

Others, even fervent SatNav buffs, won't set out without a paper map. This is not just because the papers are full of scare stories about drivers ending up on cliff tops or stuck down a muddy lane. They want to 'know where they are', and not just get where they want to go.

Then there are those who just don't like gadgets, or don't trust them. A commonly heard complaint from such drivers is that the data coming out of the SatNav goes out of date – and with factory-installed sytems can sometimes be past their sell-by date even before the car has hit the showroom. The result is frustration as drivers are ordered to drive into cul de sacs or the wrong way up one-way streets.

But the SatNav is a smooth operator and the statistics in its favour are persuasive. One digital map company, Teleatlas, boasts that it has 20 million kilometres of road and 787 million addresses in 64 countries thoroughly researched. All this information is available at the touch of a button from the comfort of the driver's seat. You couldn't get all that in a road atlas.

So is the best solution to have a SatNav and a paper map?

It seems that it is – or you wouldn't be reading this now.

The spy in the sky

There's some very meaty space hardware out there that feeds information down to motorists whenever their system requests it. It's not just one satellite, of course, but a working total of 24 in the Global Positioning Satellite (GPS) system. They are operated by the US military, but don't let that put you off. The US is committed to keeping the system up and running for its commercial users in times of peace and war. Anyway, for now there are no other options until 2010, when the 30 satellites of the European Galileo system come on line.

Each satellite, operating under solar power, measures just six metres (20 ft) across and travels 12,000 miles above the planet at a speed of 7,000 miles per hour, achieving two total orbits every 24 hours. When a SatNav system is operating it is seeking data from at least three satellites to pinpoint its position – although often it uses more - and claims accuracy to within ten metres on the ground. (The European Galileo system promises to provide accuracy to within one metre). When it has made a satellite connection it may take the in-car system fewer than 30 seconds to cough up a location. The process is called Time To Fix or TTF.

That's how a SatNav knows where it is. But to know where it's going and how to get there it also needs software in the form of a digital map and, at the moment, just two companies dominate the market. They are the rapidly expanding Tele Atlas, based in Belgium, and the giant Chicago-based Navteq.

Perfecting the digital map

Although digital mapping began in the 1980s it is only in the last decade that the technology has really taken off. About 1m SatNavs were sold in the UK in 2005, in a market that has gone up five fold in two years. Now the number of SatNav users in Britain is closing on five million. It's still far from saturation point and, say market analysts, the only way is up.

But SatNav software is only as good as the data it contains so it's vital for digital map makers to keep their road information up to date. New carriageways are being opened while existing roads might become one way streets, for example. It doesn't take long for a dataset to become degraded.

Both Navteq and Tele Atlas gain update information from office-based researchers who scan local authority papers and the internet for snippets about road changes. They also work with on-the-road organisations whose employees can report back alterations in the road network. These might be courier companies or even pizza deliverers. Tele Atlas has a programme called MapInsight that allows anyone to report inaccuracies or changes they encounter, via an internet website. It helps to flag up changes that are occurring worldwide on a daily basis.

Finally there are mapmakers who take to the road to find out first hand what's going on. Working in pairs, they use a car specially equipped with a GPS receiver on its roof that's wired to a laptop computer. The passenger is linked to the same computer via a headset and records remarks about the journey, for example, the speed limit, significant landmarks or the siting of a petrol station. These are known as Points of Interest or POIs. Think of the road network as a base layer with other information laid in strata across the top.

Other mobile mapping vehicles used by Tele Atlas are equipped with six digital cameras that capture both still and moving images, with at least two configured as stereo-pair; precisely tuned positioning devices, including a GPS receiver, gyroscope and odometer; and computer equipment for ultra efficient data collection, storage, and processing.

Then there's Object Acquisition Stereo Image Station (OASIS), an application that enables accurate identification and precise location of objects in three-dimensional space. Add to that Automatic Road Signs Acquisition (AROSA), more advanced still. This gizmo automates the processing of captured signage data. Further, there's Data Integration and Management Tools (DIAMENT), in effect a set of tools that automates the process of transforming captured features data into a spatial (navigation) database.

If you prefer to put it another way, the systems up and running to collect information for digital maps have an awful lot of bells and whistles. Once captured and processed, all this information is downloaded into a mainframe and crunched through the mapping software. That's how the information is kept up-to-date.

Safety hazards

One negative aspect to SatNavs which is getting increasing publicity is the level of distraction they provide for drivers. Motorists who need to read a paper map read tend to pull over and turn off their engines. Those with SatNav are tempted to tinker with their system while they are on the move, despite recommendations to the contrary made by manufacturers. For very sound reasons, using a mobile telephone while driving is against the law. Should not SatNav operations really fall into the same category?

Dr Gary Burnett has been conducting research into 'Human Computer Interaction' at Nottingham University. 'Visual distraction is clearly an issue when you are bringing a computer display into a car next to people who may look at it while driving.

'(Human computer interaction) affects your ability to respond to unexpected events like a car stopping suddenly in front of you, or a pedestrian walking out into the road. All those things have been found in our research and others. It is absolutely critical that SatNav design minimizes distraction.'

In September, Department of Transport figures on the causes of accidents revealed 32 per cent were caused by a failure to look properly. Could it be, as safety campaigners fear, that in-car auto-pilots are causing a loss of concentration among as many as a third of the nation's drivers? The warnings are writ large and government officials are beginning to take notice.

The Department for Transport is consulting manufacturers, motoring groups and safety organisations on how to get the best and eliminate the worst from the SatNav revolution.

Its paper, called In-Vehicle Information Systems Consultation, states: 'There is a definite need to change the status quo, either through increased regulation or a deregulatory approach'.

'The key general considerations include ensuring the human-machine interface of the device is not unduly distracting and ensuring the routing algorithms favour the most appropriate roads.'

In the meantime, there are genuine fears that SatNavs are dangerously fallible. They have been accused of conducting both ambulances and police cars on emergency calls

10 good things about SatNav

1 With spoken instructions there's nothing to dent driver concentration. Complaints that SatNav voices are monotone or even patronising are a thing of the past too, as voices can be imported into the gadget in the same way as ringtones into mobile telephones.

2 SatNav can help you save money. By flagging up short cuts SatNav can save petrol costs and help cut carbon emissions, a growing consideration for drivers in our ecology conscious world.

3 SatNavs are more than one trick ponies and their capabilities are only going to get greater. If they are not yet must-have gadgets then they soon will be.

4 By using addresses or postcodes, SatNavs can get you door-to-door. Paper maps only bring you to the road you need, not to the exact location.

5 Journey planning only takes seconds with SatNav. No more poring over the atlas or heated debates about whether that thin blue line on the map is a road or a canal.

6 Many SatNavs have maps of Europe as well as Britain. No more wrestling with several different maps when you drive to Spain or the Alps.

7 Portable SatNav systems are getting better all the time. Complaints about flimsy or awkward box mountings, inadequate volume and reception problems are all being fixed.

8 Smartphone technology will allow you to check for upcoming cafes, pubs and restaurants – even browsing the menus in advance and texting an order en route.

9 SatNav can find you a parking space or toilets in a strange city – no more frustration in the final stages of your journey.

10 SatNav will help you survive road pricing. If your usual route becomes chargeable (and there could be fees of up to 90 pence per mile on major trunk roads at peak times) SatNav will find you the shortest – and cheapest – detour.

10 good things about an atlas

1 With an atlas you can visualise your journey and drive with more confidence that you are heading the right way.

2 With an atlas you can easily plan a journey with several stops, and check if there are places near your route that you would like to visit.

3 An atlas costs much less than a SatNav. Even the most rudimentary gadget will cost you ten times as much as an atlas – and probably more.

4 Updates for atlases are much cheaper and more straightforward to use. (Simply buy a new one and throw away the old one.)

5 No one will break into your car to steal your dog-eared atlas. Let's face it, no matter how useful they are, the resale value just isn't there.

6 You can rely on an atlas to show you the quickest or shortest route. SatNav often doesn't. One on-line car dealer reckons SatNav could be adding as much as 600 miles a year to car journeys.

7 Atlases don't lose signal or 'hang'. If a SatNav system crashes, it can leave its hapless user high and dry.

8 Drivers using road atlases don't need to follow the herd. When SatNav gives prior warning of a traffic hold-us, hundreds of vehicles can be re-directed down the same narrow lanes.

9 When you read a paper map, you don't give up your common sense. It's usually SatNav drivers, not map readers, who drive into rivers or get stuck in farm tracks.

10 It's quicker and easier to use a map when two people are travelling together. According to Computing Which? magazine a driver and navigator covering a set route using an atlas went a distance of 67 miles in one hour and thirty five minutes. Using SatNav a different car took eight minutes longer and covered more than 70 miles to complete the same journey.

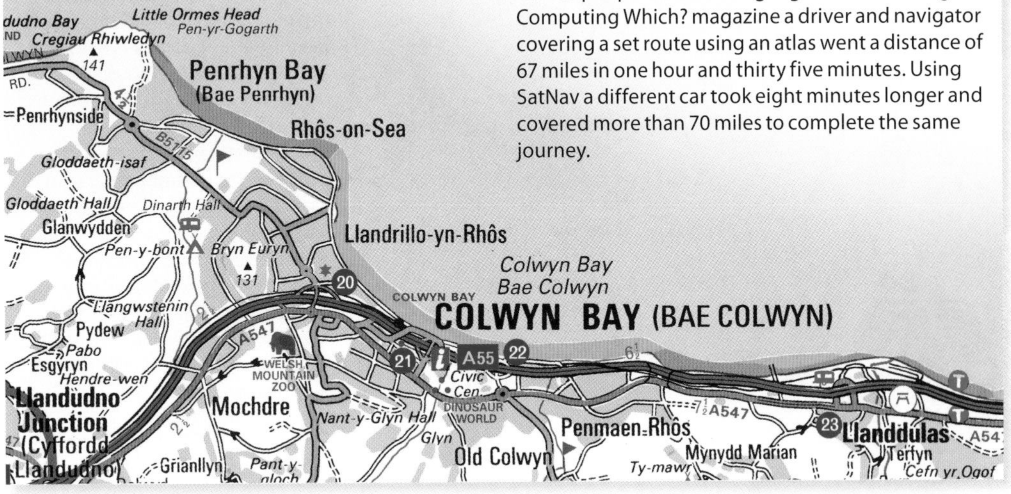

around the houses, causing crucial delay to their arrival. Thus far, though, the consequences have not been disastrous.

Navigating the market

Back in the 1990s, when portable GPS devices first appeared on the shelves of your friendly local electrical retailer, it was all so simple. Choice was limited, friends were easily impressed and you whiled away the commuter run flicking casually at your prominently-mounted screen to the envy of hapless, gadget-less drivers sitting alongside in the grid-lock. With a look of relief, and knowing smile, you'd swing off down some unlikely rat-run leaving the uninitiated to fume at your hi-tech know-how. Being SatNav savvy was a doddle and it was even easier to feel smug.

Unfortunately, the combination of advancing technology, intense competition and slick marketing has made everything that bit trickier. As every SatNav owner considering an upgrade will know, it's easier to do Cardiff to Hull on the back-roads than navigate your way through the dizzying array of devices, operating systems, service providers and pricing structures that bombard potential purchasers from every direction. In negotiating this maze you need to know exactly what you're buying. Just because new services exist, doesn't make them right for your needs.

Essentially, motorists have three types of SatNav platforms to choose from – fixed or portable stand-alones, hand-held 'smart phones' or PDAs (personal digital assistants), and real-time traffic monitoring systems. Each does a perfectly decent job but, as always, the devil's in the detail. Here's a look at the current options plus a peek into the future.

The Stand-alones

These devices work 'straight from the box' and typify most people's understanding of what the technology is all about. You might have to connect them to a PC for software and map updates, or new information on accident black spots, but essentially you charge up, switch on, tap in a destination postcode or address and follow verbal instructions linked to a map stored on the SatNav's hard drive and displayed on a dashboard-mounted digital screen. Battery life may be low – perhaps 2-4 hours – but you can easily re-charge via your car's lighter socket.

Tom Tom is far and away the market leader in this sector. According to research analysts Canalys it bagged almost a third of all European sales in 2006, ahead of Garmin (17%) and Mio Technology (10%). Much of the company's success has been built on the Tom Tom One (under £200 by early 2007) which has been widely praised for simple, intuitive touch-screen controls and clear instructions.

The One has evolved over the years into an ever sleeker form – almost of credit card dimensions. It boasts useful extras such as the ability to save locations as favourites, a 'recent-destinations' browser, and sound volume that increases at speed to overcome ambient noise. The device can be paired via a Bluetooth receiver with a mobile phone to receive real-time traffic news (more of this later). You can instruct it to avoid known trouble spots and manually add in 'points of interest' such as speed camera sites, greasy spoon cafes and petrol stations.

Tom Tom's higher-end products now include the portable Go 910 World GPS Navigation Unit (around £350), a good example of how

SatNav devices are fast morphing into PDA territory. As well as full map coverage of Europe, the USA and Canada, all pre-installed on the 20GB hard drive, the Go 910 also offers hands-free phone calls via Bluetooth, an MP3 player, and iPod interface. For an additional annual subscription, you can also have real-time weather and traffic information.

Subscription services such as these are seen as the Next Big Thing in SatNav. They generate an additional income stream which users can easily take for granted. Whether you get value for money depends on your circumstances. If you have an hour's drive across London to get to work each day, real-time information about an accident on the Hammersmith flyover could save you from hours stuck in a jam. On the other hand if you're a country vet toiling the backroads of rural Devon you might wait years before receiving a warning of trouble ahead.

Getting to the nub of subscription and software packages is therefore crucial to wringing out value. The Garmin Nuvi 350, for instance, at around £200, is an excellent device if you frequently travel abroad. It offers genuinely useful extras such as a language guide. This allows the strictly English-speaking tourist travelling through foreign backwaters to translate text to speech (and vice versa) using a bank of 17,000 words and 20,000 phrases. Six languages are supported – including French, Italian and Spanish - and there's a handy guide to pronunciation. The Nuvi even includes a world travel clock, currency converter, calculator, measurement converter and JPEG photo viewer. But if real-time traffic monitoring is what you really need, think again. Garmin will charge an extra £150 per year for this single service.

There are obviously variations on the stand-alone SatNav theme. Some devices, like the Becker Cascade 7944, must be fitted permanently into the hi-fi slot on your dashboard. That makes it less easy to steal, but is a dubious advantage if you plan to change cars regularly. The Cascade is a very accurate piece of kit – it can even tell whether you're in the correct lane as you approach a roundabout – and some drivers regard its narrow, map-free display as less distracting. But whatever the handbook says about easy fitting, most of us would need to spend around £75 on a professional installation.

At least with the Cascade you can see from the packet what's involved. Not so with the AA's Navigator system, which requires two manuals and two rather tiresome set-up processes. It demands the use of a touch-screen stylus, even in SatNav mode, which is hardly conducive to sensible driving. But the Navigator does also gives you Microsoft's natty Pocket PC operating system, which can run office software, and so encourages you to keep it with you, not leave it in your vehicle as a target for thieves.

The main problem with traditional stand-alone devices using built-in digital maps is the update chore. You need to regularly plug into your PC or Mac and hook up to an internet website which downloads new mapping information, software updates, bug fixes, and the latest information about roadworks and bottlenecks. Tom Tom's 910 Go, for instance, seeks updates on almost a weekly basis and although it's not the end of the world if you log-in late it is one more thing to remember in a busy lifestyle.

Why can't you have a SatNav permanently connected to the internet, which downloads only the section of map it currently needs, and so saves large chunks of memory space? And why can't you also download live online traffic and weather reports, hotel and restaurant information and updates on air or ferry delays? The answers are that you can. All you need is a smartphone or PDA (Personal Digital Assistant).

Smart thinking

So, what are smart phones? Sometimes called 3G (third generation) phones they're part of a new wireless technology which has massively improved mobile access to the internet. Of the estimated 5 million SatNav systems on British roads at the end of 2006, something like a million were installed on smart phones – that's at least a million travellers open to suggestions for nearby hotels, coffee shops, pizza parlours, shopping centres, car parks – the list is constantly growing.

Between now and 2009 analysts expect this 'location-based' service market will double to around £110 million in the UK. There will be a tidal wave of products designed to make us feel the internet is as crucial to stress-free motoring as a SatNav, hi-fi, MP3 and DVD player, all of which will have to make space for the smart phone (or at least work with it). To some extent this process has already happened; as mentioned above it's possible to pair the latest stand-alone SatNavs

Don't let thieves 'go home' with your SatNav

While in-car SatNav systems are usually secure, portables have become a top target for thieves. SatNavs are being stolen in London alone at a rate of 450 a month. Remember, if the SatNav has a 'go home' button the thief could reach your place and ransack it before you return. There are simple precautions you can take to thwart the snatchers.

Close all windows and lock the doors when you leave your car, even if it's only for a short while.

Don't leave anything on display in your car. Make sure you remove all parts of the system, including any support cradles and suction pads fitted to the windscreen. Be sure to erase the distinctive suction pad mark, as this flags up potential booty to a passing thief.

Don't leave the SatNav in your glove compartment – it's the first place a thief will look. Instead, leave your glove compartment open to show there is nothing inside and take the system and components away with you.

If it's not possible to take the navigation system away with you, then lock it safely in your boot.

Keep a record of the make, model and serial number of the equipment. Store this somewhere safe, separately from the vehicle.

Mark your system with your postcode and house number or vehicle registration using a special security marker such as an ultra-violet pen or SmartWater. This will make it difficult for thieves to sell your property, and enable police to return the items to you if they are recovered.

with a phone, via a Bluetooth connection, to use internet services. However this isn't necessarily cheap and Bluetooth is still an emerging, occasionally temperamental, technology. It begs the question: why buy a separate SatNav at all if your smartphone or PDA will do the job?

One of the first UK phone networks to embrace the smart phone SatNav revolution is Orange. It has launched a business service allowing subscribers to download maps and traffic information direct to their phones from a central server via 3G, Wifi (broadband), GPRS (that's 'old' phone technology) or its own EDGE radio network. The GPS software comes from a dedicated provider called Webraska while the maps are supplied by Navteq. Driving directions backed by pictograms are displayed on the phone or PDA screen. It means information is always up to date, bugs are eliminated and users can change cars whenever they like, taking their SatNav with them.

The Orange system costs a one-off £150 for a licence, GPS receiver and in-car charger. There's then an annual charge for real-time traffic information and additional maps of Europe (around £27 each). You pay for any data downloaded at your phone's standard rate, so you need to tailor your mobile phone package accordingly. But, given that you're saving the cost of a stand-alone SatNav, and a lot of time plugging it in and out of your computer, the Orange looks attractive. With manufacturing giant Nokia now also a player – its 330 Auto Navigation device was launched at the end of 2006 – phone companies are viewing the SatNav market hungrily.

If you want a smartphone or PDA solution to SatNav there are a couple of health warnings. Check your phone is compatible by logging in to the software provider's website before you part with cash. The Navicore Personal has had some good reviews – you simply insert a memory card into your mobile which links via Bluetooth to a separate GPS receiver on the dashboard – but it only works with phones using the Symbian operating system. Secondly, bear in mind that phone screens are generally small and can get hopelessly busy when you're being told several things at once. If you like clear visual aids, a PDA such as Blackberry might be the better option And don't forget that many traditional stand-alone manufacturers, such as Tom Tom, can themselves offer a smartphone-based system.

Real-time traffic monitoring systems

The real-time SatNav camp is dominated in the UK by Trafficmaster, the company which maintains a network of more than 7,500 traffic sensors on motorways and trunk roads. Trafficmaster sells this data to commercial rivals – ie the phone networks – but also sells its own fixed device and Smart Nav. This type of system doesn't have the full road network that you get with both the high-end in-car systems and the portables. So there's a temptation to dismiss these as neither fish nor fowl. But there are some definite advantages, not least in cost, if you want a dedicated, permanently installed system, but don't want to pay the £2000 or so that an in-car system might cost.

Essentially you install the software and GPS receiver into your car and pay a subscription fee. Before starting your journey you tap your destination postcode on to a touch screen (or dial a control centre) and instructions are automatically downloaded. Your route will depend on prevailing traffic conditions at the time and is constantly monitored – and changed if necessary – every three minutes by a computer which calculates the time advantages of any detour. All downloaded data is part of the deal.

The basic package for the fixed device works out at around £500 plus £100 for installation, £120 annual subscription and £25 connection fee. You also have to pay extra for a screen. You can bolt on extras such as speed camera warnings (£8 per month) or Stolen Vehicle Tracking (£10 per month). This package looks, and is, expensive compared with the portable competition but it has a good reputation for accuracy and is much loved by users. Best of all, if anything does go wrong you can talk to a real live person as opposed to a digital keypad. In times of stress, such details can matter.

Future Trends

The next generation of SaNav systems will not only plan routes and send verbal warnings of delays; they'll even beam you live pictures of the road ahead. Provided the Highways Agency, police and other bodies agree, footage from their cameras will be collated and organized into a series of still photos. So, travelling westbound on the M4, you'll be able to check instantly how traffic is moving at the next three junctions and get a preview of any trouble at Bristol. For city drivers this could be particularly useful as the software will work out which cameras are most relevant to possible routes.

The aim is to deliver all this via the internet and mobile phone / PDA , together with a dashboard screen to display photos. Aside from phone data charges the estimated cost is likely to be surprisingly cheap – as little as £100 – although if the camera-owning agencies charge Siemens for footage there's likely to be an additional subscription. Watch this space.

Philip's map on an *i-mate* smart-phone
For details see www.anquet.co.uk

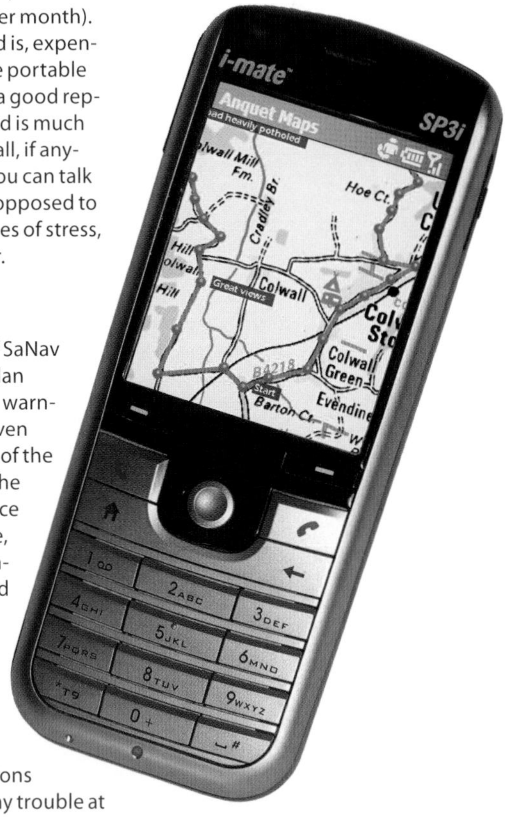

Distance table

Distances are shown in miles and, in italics, kilometres. For example, the distance between Birmingham and Brighton is 163 miles or 262 kilometres.

	Swansea	Stranraer	Southampton	Shrewsbury	Sheffield	Portsmouth	Plymouth	Oxford	Oban	Nottingham	Norwich	Newcastle upon Tyne	Manchester	Liverpool	Lincoln	Leicester	Leeds	Land's End	Kyle of Lochalsh	Kingston upon Hull	John o' Groats	Inverness	Holyhead	Harwich	Great Yarmouth	Gloucester	Glasgow	Fort William	Fishguard	Exeter	Edinburgh	Dundee	Dover	Doncaster	Carlisle	Cardiff	Cambridge	Bristol	Brighton	Braemar	Bournemouth	Blackpool	Birmingham	Berwick-upon-Tweed	Ayr	Aberystwyth	Aberdeen	London
London																																																
Aberdeen																																															517 / *832*
Aberystwyth																																														445 / *716*	211 / *340*
Ayr																																													317 / *510*	183 / *295*	394 / *634*
Berwick-upon-Tweed																																												134 / *216*	311 / *501*	182 / *293*	352 / *567*
Birmingham																																											274 / *441*	289 / *465*	114 / *183*	420 / *676*	117 / *188*
Blackpool																																										123 / *198*	181 / *291*	180 / *290*	153 / *246*	308 / *496*	226 / *364*
Bournemouth																																									270 / *435*	147 / *237*	412 / *663*	436 / *702*	207 / *333*	564 / *908*	107 / *172*
Braemar																																								524 / *843*	281 / *452*	385 / *620*	148 / *238*	143 / *230*	405 / *652*	59 / *95*	482 / *776*
Brighton																																							534 / *859*	92 / *148*	286 / *460*	163 / *262*	409 / *658*	446 / *718*	253 / *407*	573 / *922*	52 / *84*
Bristol																																						147 / *237*	477 / *768*	82 / *132*	204 / *328*	81 / *130*	362 / *583*	370 / *595*	125 / *201*	493 / *793*	122 / *196*
Cambridge																																					169 / *272*	116 / *187*	438 / *705*	154 / *248*	208 / *335*	100 / *161*	306 / *493*	357 / *575*	214 / *344*	471 / *758*	54 / *87*
Cardiff																																				190 / *306*	45 / *72*	182 / *293*	483 / *778*	117 / *188*	209 / *336*	103 / *166*	368 / *592*	382 / *615*	105 / *169*	505 / *813*	157 / *253*
Carlisle																																			289 / *465*	264 / *425*	277 / *446*	370 / *596*	196 / *316*	343 / *552*	87 / *140*	196 / *315*	87 / *140*	93 / *150*	224 / *360*	221 / *356*	301 / *484*
Doncaster																																		142 / *229*	209 / *336*	116 / *187*	175 / *282*	236 / *380*	310 / *499*	235 / *378*	94 / *151*	94 / *151*	184 / *296*	235 / *378*	176 / *283*	344 / *554*	171 / *275*
Dover																																	242 / *390*	389 / *626*	238 / *383*	125 / *201*	202 / *325*	82 / *132*	553 / *890*	174 / *280*	312 / *502*	194 / *312*	424 / *683*	478 / *769*	297 / *478*	588 / *947*	71 / *114*
Dundee																																523 / *842*	275 / *443*	152 / *245*	441 / *710*	406 / *654*	430 / *692*	517 / *832*	52 / *84*	495 / *797*	239 / *385*	349 / *562*	113 / *182*	117 / *188*	376 / *605*	67 / *108*	448 / *721*
Edinburgh																															56 / *90*	462 / *744*	219 / *352*	96 / *154*	385 / *620*	345 / *555*	373 / *600*	456 / *734*	91 / *146*	439 / *707*	183 / *295*	292 / *470*	57 / *92*	73 / *117*	320 / *515*	125 / *201*	390 / *628*
Exeter																														450 / *724*	518 / *834*	248 / *399*	251 / *404*	353 / *568*	121 / *195*	249 / *401*	76 / *122*	184 / *296*	550 / *885*	82 / *132*	282 / *454*	157 / *253*	428 / *689*	446 / *718*	201 / *323*	569 / *916*	181 / *291*
Fishguard																													230 / *370*	399 / *642*	460 / *740*	331 / *533*	247 / *398*	297 / *478*	112 / *180*	270 / *435*	154 / *248*	291 / *468*	493 / *794*	222 / *357*	209 / *336*	170 / *274*	371 / *597*	373 / *600*	56 / *90*	504 / *811*	260 / *418*
Fort William																												486 / *782*	560 / *901*	144 / *232*	127 / *204*	596 / *959*	357 / *575*	206 / *332*	485 / *781*	479 / *771*	486 / *782*	575 / *926*	125 / *201*	539 / *867*	296 / *476*	392 / *631*	190 / *306*	133 / *214*	430 / *692*	149 / *240*	510 / *821*
Glasgow																											101 / *163*	376 / *605*	449 / *723*	44 / *71*	83 / *134*	488 / *786*	249 / *401*	96 / *154*	385 / *620*	372 / *599*	373 / *600*	468 / *753*	110 / *177*	439 / *707*	183 / *295*	292 / *470*	101 / *163*	33 / *53*	320 / *515*	145 / *233*	397 / *639*
Gloucester																										346 / *557*	454 / *731*	153 / *246*	111 / *179*	349 / *562*	410 / *660*	191 / *307*	150 / *241*	247 / *398*	56 / *90*	123 / *198*	35 / *56*	159 / *256*	443 / *713*	99 / *159*	174 / *280*	56 / *90*	318 / *512*	330 / *531*	102 / *164*	468 / *753*	109 / *175*
Great Yarmouth																									225 / *362*	419 / *674*	527 / *848*	366 / *589*	335 / *539*	386 / *621*	484 / *779*	185 / *298*	167 / *269*	320 / *515*	284 / *457*	82 / *132*	275 / *443*	180 / *290*	477 / *768*	240 / *386*	252 / *406*	180 / *290*	345 / *555*	402 / *647*	294 / *473*	517 / *832*	128 / *206*
Harwich																								82 / *132*	196 / *316*	432 / *695*	543 / *874*	337 / *542*	279 / *449*	413 / *665*	469 / *755*	125 / *201*	194 / *312*	336 / *541*	246 / *396*	67 / *108*	217 / *349*	128 / *206*	504 / *811*	187 / *301*	275 / *443*	167 / *269*	372 / *599*	425 / *684*	281 / *452*	535 / *861*	76 / *122*
Holyhead																							349 / *562*	334 / *538*	191 / *307*	330 / *531*	438 / *705*	167 / *269*	282 / *454*	333 / *536*	394 / *634*	360 / *580*	181 / *291*	231 / *372*	216 / *348*	270 / *435*	206 / *332*	334 / *538*	426 / *686*	288 / *463*	141 / *227*	148 / *238*	311 / *501*	305 / *491*	111 / *179*	439 / *707*	269 / *433*
Inverness																						474 / *763*	569 / *916*	553 / *890*	504 / *811*	166 / *267*	66 / *106*	542 / *872*	618 / *995*	158 / *254*	132 / *212*	622 / *1001*	383 / *617*	262 / *422*	549 / *884*	505 / *813*	539 / *867*	617 / *993*	75 / *121*	597 / *961*	348 / *560*	458 / *737*	215 / *346*	199 / *320*	486 / *782*	105 / *169*	550 / *885*
John o' Groats																					129 / *208*	603 / *970*	693 / *1116*	677 / *1090*	628 / *1011*	295 / *475*	195 / *314*	671 / *1080*	744 / *1197*	285 / *459*	259 / *417*	746 / *1201*	507 / *816*	391 / *629*	680 / *1094*	630 / *1014*	668 / *1075*	741 / *1193*	202 / *325*	724 / *1165*	478 / *769*	574 / *924*	342 / *550*	328 / *528*	601 / *967*	232 / *373*	663 / *1067*
Kingston upon Hull																				518 / *834*	394 / *634*	231 / *372*	196 / *316*	207 / *333*	169 / *272*	254 / *409*	369 / *594*	280 / *451*	309 / *497*	234 / *377*	295 / *475*	256 / *412*	47 / *76*	158 / *254*	244 / *393*	139 / *224*	233 / *375*	245 / *394*	327 / *526*	264 / *425*	127 / *204*	134 / *216*	185 / *298*	251 / *404*	223 / *359*	364 / *586*	184 / *296*
Kyle of Lochalsh																			445 / *716*	189 / *304*	84 / *135*	514 / *827*	611 / *983*	602 / *969*	528 / *850*	179 / *288*	79 / *127*	567 / *913*	628 / *1011*	216 / *348*	186 / *299*	671 / *1080*	432 / *695*	275 / *443*	564 / *908*	555 / *893*	552 / *888*	651 / *1048*	159 / *256*	618 / *995*	372 / *599*	471 / *758*	263 / *423*	212 / *341*	499 / *803*	189 / *304*	586 / *943*
Land's End																		763 / *1228*	421 / *678*	868 / *1397*	741 / *1193*	405 / *652*	390 / *628*	446 / *718*	235 / *378*	573 / *922*	686 / *1104*	353 / *568*	123 / *198*	574 / *924*	642 / *1033*	381 / *613*	374 / *602*	477 / *768*	245 / *394*	374 / *602*	200 / *322*	308 / *496*	665 / *1070*	205 / *330*	405 / *652*	281 / *452*	552 / *888*	570 / *917*	313 / *504*	692 / *1114*	297 / *478*
Leeds																	405 / *652*	394 / *634*	55 / *89*	487 / *784*	360 / *579*	176 / *283*	223 / *359*	196 / *315*	174 / *280*	215 / *346*	329 / *530*	237 / *381*	270 / *435*	202 / *325*	258 / *415*	260 / *418*	29 / *47*	119 / *192*	232 / *373*	145 / *233*	194 / *312*	260 / *419*	293 / *472*	255 / *410*	72 / *116*	113 / *182*	156 / *251*	212 / *341*	169 / *272*	327 / *526*	189 / *304*
Leicester																95 / *153*	320 / *515*	500 / *805*	102 / *164*	588 / *947*	461 / *742*	190 / *306*	147 / *237*	140 / *225*	85 / *137*	314 / *505*	422 / *679*	209 / *336*	196 / *315*	296 / *476*	349 / *562*	185 / *298*	74 / *119*	206 / *332*	154 / *248*	68 / *109*	120 / *193*	166 / *267*	389 / *626*	158 / *254*	140 / *225*	39 / *63*	252 / *406*	299 / *481*	153 / *246*	414 / *666*	97 / *156*
Lincoln															51 / *82*	68 / *109*	371 / *597*	476 / *766*	44 / *71*	554 / *892*	427 / *687*	216 / *348*	155 / *249*	128 / *206*	159 / *256*	291 / *468*	399 / *642*	272 / *438*	247 / *398*	258 / *415*	314 / *505*	202 / *325*	39 / *63*	191 / *307*	208 / *335*	85 / *137*	183 / *295*	197 / *317*	357 / *575*	209 / *336*	128 / *206*	90 / *145*	224 / *360*	274 / *441*	199 / *320*	383 / *616*	131 / *211*
Liverpool														129 / *208*	130 / *209*	75 / *121*	361 / *581*	407 / *655*	130 / *209*	511 / *822*	382 / *615*	102 / *164*	265 / *427*	240 / *386*	140 / *225*	216 / *348*	329 / *530*	160 / *257*	237 / *381*	216 / *348*	286 / *460*	299 / *481*	86 / *138*	120 / *193*	169 / *272*	194 / *312*	161 / *259*	272 / *438*	318 / *512*	234 / *377*	49 / *79*	93 / *150*	219 / *352*	213 / *343*	104 / *167*	341 / *549*	202 / *325*
Manchester													35 / *56*	84 / *135*	92 / *148*	40 / *64*	361 / *581*	406 / *654*	95 / *153*	500 / *805*	373 / *600*	124 / *200*	228 / *367*	212 / *341*	126 / *203*	215 / *346*	329 / *530*	197 / *317*	236 / *380*	215 / *346*	285 / *459*	276 / *444*	61 / *98*	119 / *192*	183 / *295*	165 / *266*	161 / *259*	257 / *414*	318 / *512*	227 / *365*	48 / *77*	80 / *129*	196 / *315*	212 / *341*	129 / *208*	340 / *547*	185 / *298*
Newcastle upon Tyne												132 / *212*	168 / *270*	159 / *256*	187 / *301*	92 / *148*	498 / *802*	318 / *512*	132 / *212*	395 / *636*	268 / *431*	272 / *438*	308 / *496*	281 / *452*	266 / *428*	148 / *238*	253 / *407*	329 / *529*	364 / *586*	110 / *177*	166 / *267*	358 / *576*	114 / *183*	57 / *92*	325 / *523*	241 / *388*	299 / *481*	352 / *567*	201 / *323*	347 / *558*	129 / *208*	207 / *333*	64 / *103*	149 / *240*	257 / *414*	235 / *378*	286 / *460*
Norwich											264 / *425*	185 / *298*	220 / *354*	105 / *169*	119 / *192*	176 / *283*	421 / *678*	582 / *937*	149 / *240*	654 / *1053*	529 / *852*	311 / *501*	73 / *117*	20 / *32*	204 / *328*	385 / *620*	504 / *811*	343 / *552*	308 / *496*	366 / *589*	422 / *679*	174 / *280*	147 / *237*	289 / *465*	262 / *422*	62 / *100*	252 / *406*	175 / *282*	457 / *735*	214 / *344*	232 / *373*	166 / *267*	328 / *528*	382 / *615*	276 / *444*	496 / *798*	114 / *183*
Nottingham										130 / *209*	157 / *253*	73 / *118*	98 / *158*	35 / *56*	25 / *40*	70 / *113*	345 / *555*	479 / *771*	90 / *145*	557 / *896*	430 / *692*	185 / *298*	150 / *241*	153 / *246*	110 / *177*	293 / *472*	401 / *646*	220 / *354*	221 / *356*	262 / *422*	328 / *528*	205 / *330*	43 / *69*	194 / *312*	172 / *277*	83 / *134*	145 / *233*	193 / *311*	353 / *568*	183 / *295*	111 / *179*	50 / *80*	221 / *356*	274 / *441*	164 / *264*	393 / *633*	122 / *196*
Oban									390 / *628*	492 / *792*	233 / *375*	307 / *494*	308 / *496*	387 / *623*	419 / *674*	307 / *494*	665 / *1070*	128 / *206*	346 / *557*	244 / *393*	117 / *188*	427 / *687*	524 / *843*	515 / *829*	441 / *710*	92 / *148*	49 / *79*	481 / *774*	549 / *884*	123 / *198*	117 / *188*	585 / *942*	346 / *557*	188 / *303*	477 / *768*	468 / *753*	465 / *748*	565 / *910*	141 / *227*	530 / *853*	285 / *459*	384 / *618*	180 / *290*	94 / *151*	412 / *663*	178 / *286*	499 / *803*
Oxford								462 / *744*	109 / *175*	145 / *233*	260 / *418*	144 / *232*	172 / *277*	137 / *221*	73 / *117*	168 / *270*	274 / *441*	550 / *885*	192 / *309*	656 / *1056*	532 / *856*	238 / *383*	145 / *233*	200 / *322*	52 / *84*	356 / *573*	472 / *760*	205 / *330*	156 / *251*	372 / *599*	433 / *697*	141 / *227*	145 / *233*	260 / *418*	108 / *174*	83 / *134*	74 / *119*	108 / *174*	465 / *749*	90 / *145*	187 / *301*	64 / *103*	324 / *521*	353 / *568*	154 / *248*	483 / *777*	57 / *92*
Plymouth							199 / *320*	587 / *945*	267 / *430*	343 / *552*	410 / *660*	283 / *455*	283 / *455*	293 / *472*	242 / *389*	316 / *509*	89 / *143*	674 / *1085*	355 / *571*	790 / *1271*	664 / *1069*	328 / *528*	309 / *497*	365 / *588*	157 / *253*	495 / *797*	595 / *958*	264 / *425*	46 / *74*	496 / *798*	552 / *888*	300 / *483*	297 / *478*	399 / *642*	167 / *269*	293 / *472*	122 / *196*	224 / *361*	587 / *945*	128 / *206*	328 / *528*	203 / *327*	474 / *763*	492 / *792*	237 / *382*	615 / *990*	218 / *351*
Portsmouth						176 / *283*	77 / *124*	545 / *877*	191 / *307*	207 / *333*	337 / *542*	236 / *380*	254 / *409*	201 / *323*	162 / *261*	257 / *414*	259 / *417*	633 / *1019*	269 / *433*	737 / *1186*	613 / *987*	311 / *501*	166 / *267*	221 / *356*	119 / *192*	448 / *721*	555 / *893*	251 / *404*	135 / *217*	453 / *729*	514 / *827*	130 / *209*	234 / *377*	348 / *560*	142 / *229*	144 / *232*	97 / *156*	48 / *77*	547 / *881*	52 / *84*	264 / *425*	141 / *227*	401 / *645*	430 / *692*	222 / *357*	560 / *901*	70 / *113*
Sheffield					230 / *370*	283 / *455*	135 / *217*	339 / *546*	37 / *60*	146 / *235*	125 / *201*	38 / *61*	72 / *116*	46 / *74*	62 / *100*	33 / *53*	361 / *581*	427 / *687*	65 / *105*	520 / *837*	393 / *632*	168 / *270*	187 / *301*	166 / *267*	126 / *203*	248 / *399*	348 / *560*	215 / *346*	237 / *381*	235 / *378*	291 / *468*	245 / *394*	18 / *29*	152 / *245*	194 / *312*	120 / *193*	161 / *259*	226 / *364*	320 / *515*	216 / *348*	86 / *138*	76 / *122*	190 / *306*	245 / *394*	159 / *256*	360 / *579*	159 / *256*
Shrewsbury				82 / *132*	207 / *333*	225 / *362*	106 / *171*	364 / *586*	93 / *150*	205 / *330*	201 / *323*	69 / *111*	58 / *93*	133 / *214*	84 / *135*	109 / *175*	303 / *488*	451 / *726*	169 / *272*	567 / *912*	438 / *705*	113 / *182*	240 / *386*	225 / *362*	77 / *124*	272 / *438*	382 / *615*	145 / *233*	179 / *288*	274 / *441*	330 / *531*	251 / *404*	109 / *175*	176 / *283*	111 / *179*	159 / *256*	103 / *166*	226 / *364*	371 / *597*	185 / *298*	98 / *158*	45 / *72*	265 / *426*	269 / *433*	77 / *124*	399 / *642*	160 / *258*
Southampton			185 / *298*	199 / *320*	21 / *34*	151 / *243*	64 / *103*	530 / *853*	176 / *283*	206 / *332*	324 / *521*	221 / *356*	239 / *385*	204 / *328*	137 / *220*	232 / *373*	228 / *367*	618 / *995*	256 / *412*	723 / *1164*	598 / *963*	293 / *472*	164 / *264*	220 / *354*	105 / *169*	433 / *697*	541 / *871*	233 / *375*	105 / *169*	438 / *705*	500 / *805*	143 / *230*	209 / *336*	324 / *521*	121 / *195*	148 / *238*	76 / *122*	61 / *98*	532 / *856*	31 / *50*	251 / *404*	128 / *206*	388 / *624*	417 / *671*	201 / *323*	547 / *880*	77 / *124*
Stranraer		445 / *716*	277 / *446*	263 / *423*	461 / *742*	500 / *805*	379 / *610*	148 / *238*	290 / *467*	403 / *649*	158 / *254*	220 / *354*	221 / *356*	298 / *480*	330 / *531*	220 / *354*	585 / *942*	263 / *423*	259 / *417*	379 / *610*	262 / *422*	338 / *544*	410 / *660*	426 / *686*	343 / *552*	84 / *135*	195 / *314*	392 / *631*	454 / *731*	124 / *200*	167 / *269*	496 / *798*	257 / *414*	101 / *163*	390 / *628*	379 / *610*	378 / *608*	475 / *765*	194 / *312*	444 / *715*	188 / *303*	297 / *478*	170 / *274*	51 / *82*	325 / *523*	228 / *367*	402 / *647*
Swansea	417 / *671*	161 / *259*	118 / *190*	217 / *349*	182 / *293*	206 / *332*	141 / *227*	506 / *815*	192 / *309*	301 / *485*	347 / *559*	187 / *301*	195 / *314*	233 / *375*	177 / *285*	248 / *399*	285 / *459*	594 / *956*	264 / *425*	696 / *1120*	572 / *921*	184 / *296*	267 / *430*	329 / *530*	89 / *143*	409 / *658*	496 / *798*	67 / *108*	161 / *259*	412 / *663*	473 / *761*	274 / *441*	232 / *373*	309 / *497*	41 / *66*	227 / *365*	85 / *137*	222 / *357*	505 / *813*	167 / *269*	216 / *348*	119 / *192*	383 / *616*	379 / *610*	73 / *117*	507 / *816*	194 / *312*
York	272 / *438*	222 / *357*	258 / *415*	133 / *214*	52 / *84*	278 / *448*	333 / *536*	181 / *291*	309 / *497*	77 / *124*	181 / *291*	84 / *135*	64 / *103*	99 / *159*	75 / *121*	108 / *174*	24 / *39*	411 / *661*	407 / *655*	37 / *60*	479 / *771*	352 / *566*	204 / *328*	228 / *367*	201 / *323*	189 / *304*	217 / *349*	330 / *531*	261 / *420*	287 / *462*	194 / *312*	250 / *402*	282 / *454*	34 / *55*	121 / *195*	244 / *393*	165 / *266*	222 / *357*	275 / *443*	285 / *459*	269 / *433*	96 / *154*	130 / *209*	148 / *238*	214 / *344*	195 / *314*	319 / *513*	207 / *333*

Abbreviated local authority names

BD	Bridgend
BF	Bracknell Forest
BG	Blaenau Gwent
BL	Blackpool
BM	Bournemouth
BN	Blackburn with Darwen
CB	City and County of Bristol
CBH	City of Brighton and Hove
CE	City of Edinburgh
CF	Cardiff
CM	Clackmannanshire
CN	City of Nottingham
CY	Caerphilly
DD	Dundee City
DE	Derby City
DN	Darlington
ED	East Dunbartonshire
ER	East Renfrewshire
FK	Falkirk
GC	Glasgow City
HL	Hartlepool
HN	Halton
IC	Inverclyde
KH	Kingston upon Hull
LE	Leicester City
LU	Luton
MB	Middlesbrough
MR	Merthyr Tydfil
NEL	North East Lincolnshire
NL	North Lanarkshire
NP	Newport
NPT	Neath Port Talbot
PL	Plymouth
PM	Portsmouth
PO	Poole
RC	Redcar and Cleveland
RD	Reading
RF	Renfrewshire
RT	Rhondda Cynon Taff
SD	Southend-on-Sea
SL	Slough
SN	Stockton-on-Tees
SO	Southampton
ST	Stoke-on-Trent
SW	Swindon
TB	Torbay
TF	Torfaen
TK	Thurrock
TW	Telford and Wrekin
WA	Warrington
WD	West Dunbartonshire
WK	Wokingham
WL	West Lothian
WM	Windsor and Maidenhead

Key to road map pages

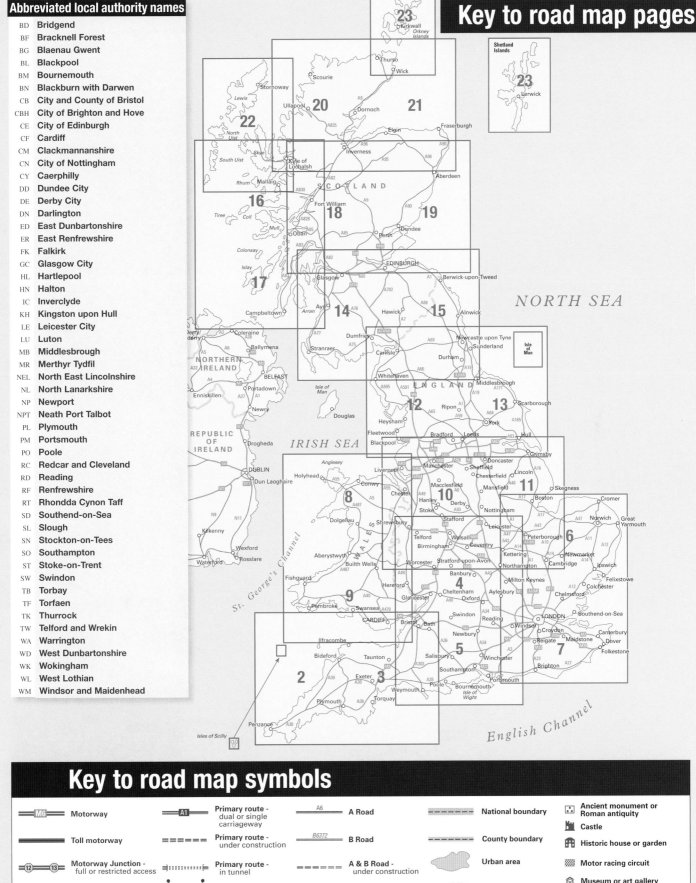

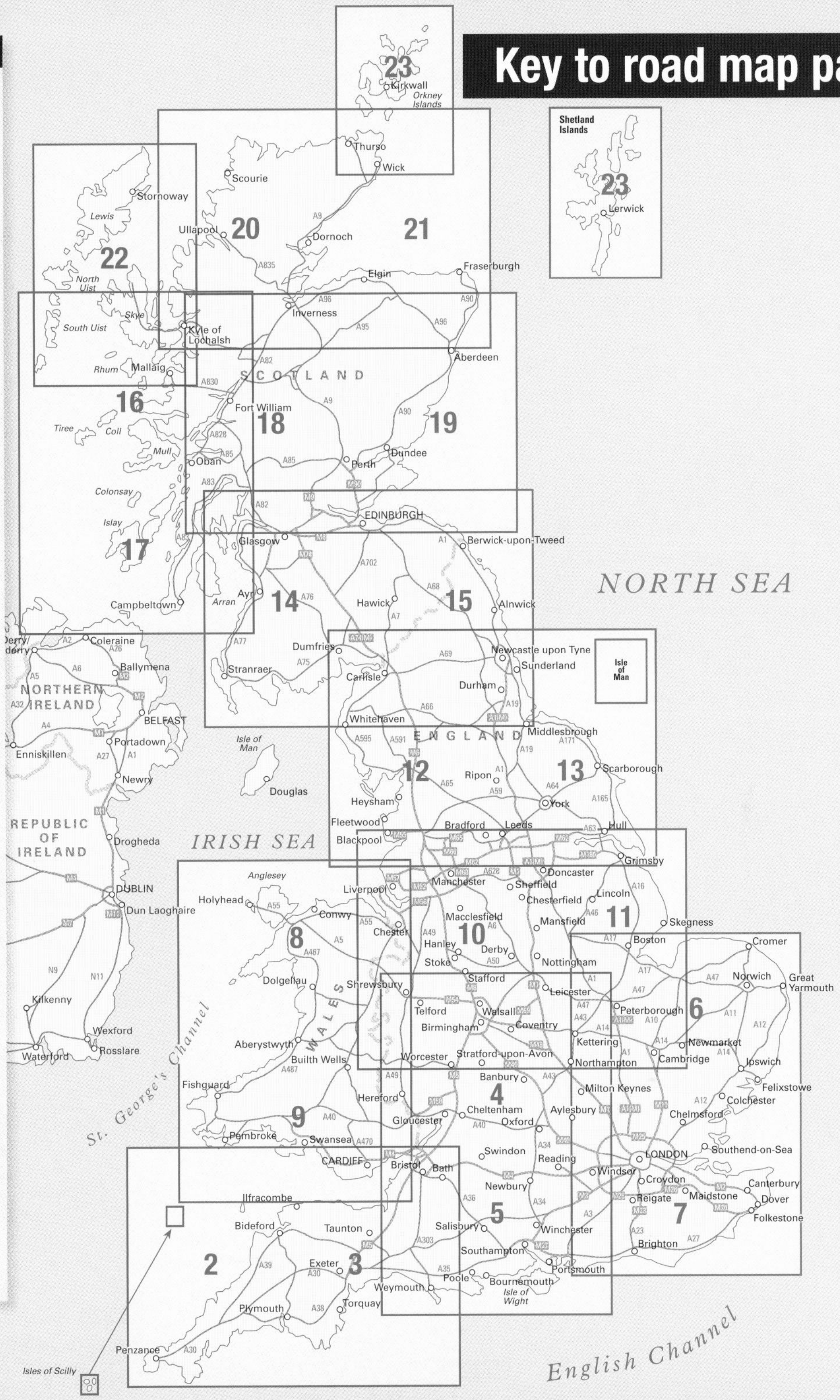

Key to road map symbols

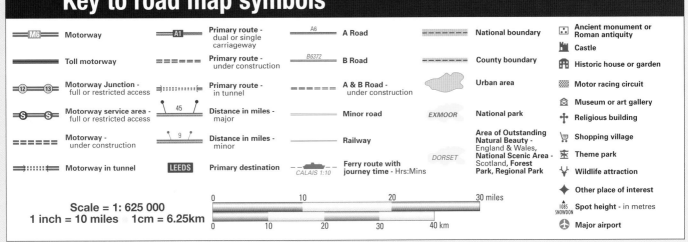

Motorway	Primary route - dual or single carriageway	A Road
Toll motorway	Primary route - under construction	B Road
Motorway Junction - full or restricted access	Primary route - in tunnel	A & B Road - under construction
Motorway service area - full or restricted access	Distance in miles - major	Minor road
Motorway - under construction	Distance in miles - minor	Railway
Motorway in tunnel	Primary destination	Ferry route with journey time - Hrs:Mins

National boundary	Ancient monument or Roman antiquity
County boundary	Castle
Urban area	Historic house or garden
EXMOOR National park	Motor racing circuit
DORSET Area of Outstanding Natural Beauty - England & Wales, National Scenic Area - Scotland, Forest Park, Regional Park	Museum or art gallery
	Religious building
	Shopping village
	Theme park
	Wildlife attraction
	Other place of interest
	Spot height - in metres
	Major airport

M6 A1 A6 B6372 45 9 LEEDS CALAIS 1:10 1085 SNOWDON

Scale = 1: 625 000
1 inch = 10 miles 1cm = 6.25km

0 10 20 30 miles
0 10 20 30 40 km

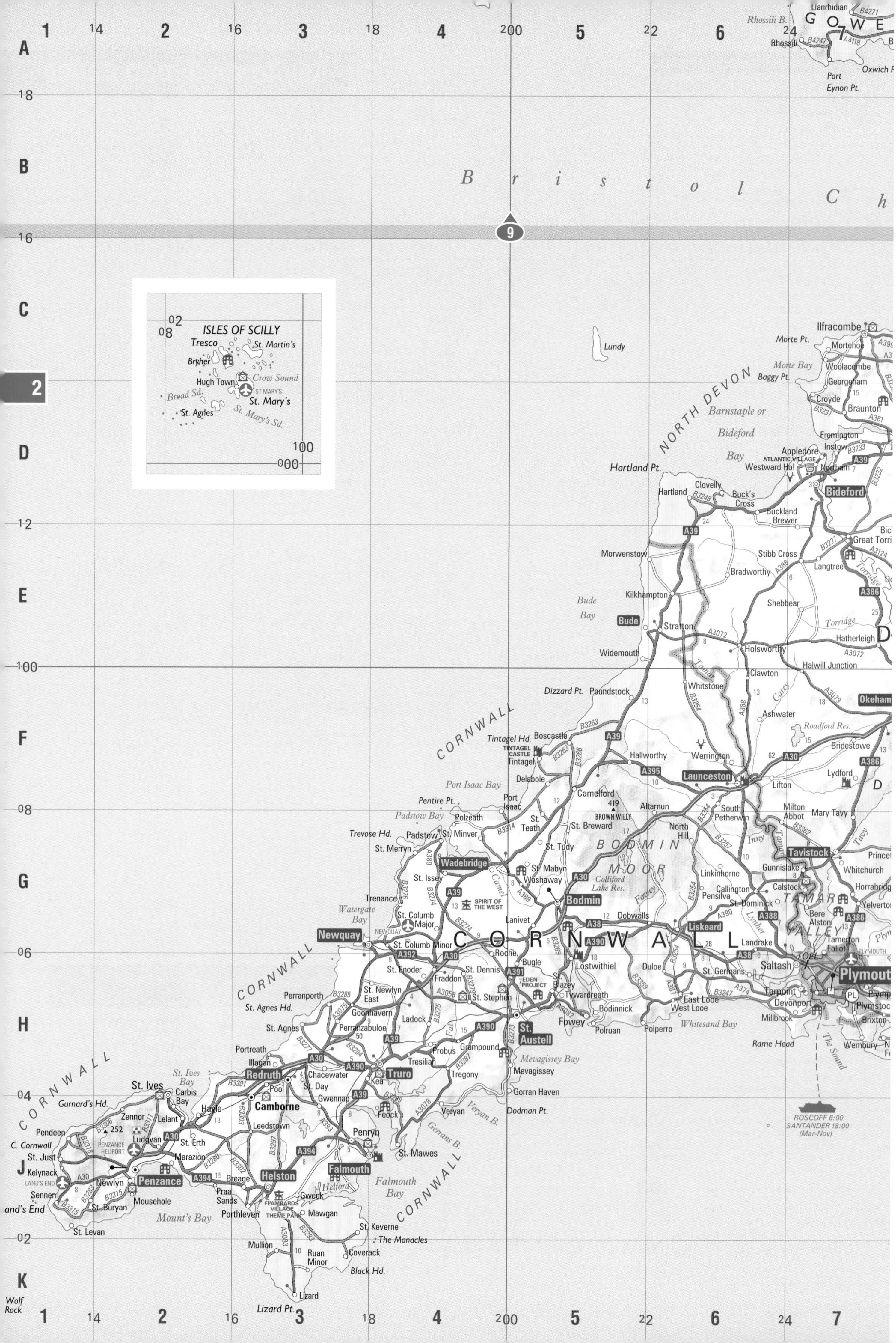

2
Bristol Channel
ISLES OF SCILLY
Tresco
St. Martin's
Bryher
Hugh Town
Crow Sound
St. Mary's
Broad Sd.
St. Agnes
St. Mary's Sd.
Lundy
NORTH DEVON
Barnstaple or Bideford Bay
Hartland Pt.
Hartland
Clovelly
Buck's Cross
Buckland Brewer
Bideford
Northam
Westward Ho!
Appledore
Instow
Fremington
Braunton
Croyde
Georgeham
Woolacombe
Mortehoe
Morte Pt.
Morte Bay
Baggy Pt.
Ilfracombe
Great Torrington
Langtree
Stibb Cross
Bradworthy
Shebbear
Morwenstow
Kilkhampton
Bude Bay
Bude
Stratton
Widemouth
Holsworthy
Hatherleigh
Halwill Junction
Okehampton
Clawton
Whitstone
Ashwater
Dizzard Pt.
Poundstock
Roadford Res.
Bridestowe
Lydford
Lifton
Launceston
Werrington
Hallworthy
Tintagel Hd.
Boscastle
Tintagel Castle
Tintagel
Delabole
Camelford
Port Isaac Bay
Port Isaac
Pentire Pt.
Polzeath
Padstow Bay
Trevose Hd.
Padstow
St. Minver
St. Merryn
St. Teath
St. Breward
419 Brown Willy
Altarnun
South Petherwin
North Hill
Milton Abbot
Mary Tavy
Tavistock
BODMIN MOOR
St. Tudy
Wadebridge
St. Mabyn
Washaway
Colliford Lake Res.
Linkinhorne
Gunnislake
Calstock
Callington
Pensilva
St. Dominick
Tamar Valley
Bere Alston
Whitchurch
Horrabridge
Yelverton
St. Issey
Trenance
Spirit of the West
Bodmin
Lanivet
Dobwalls
Liskeard
Watergate Bay
St. Columb Major
Newquay
St. Columb Minor
CORNWALL
Roche
Landrake
Tamerton Foliot
Saltash
Plymouth
St. Enoder
St. Dennis
Bugle
Lostwithiel
Duloe
St. Germans
Fraddon
St. Newlyn East
Eden Project
St. Blazey
Tywardreath
East Looe
West Looe
Torpoint
Devonport
Plymstock
Perranporth
St. Stephen
Ladrock
Goonhavern
Perranzabuloe
Bodinnick
Fowey
Polruan
Polperro
Whitesand Bay
Millbrook
Rame Head
Wembury
The Sound
St. Agnes Hd.
St. Agnes
St. Austell
Portreath
Illogan
Probus
Grampound
Tresillian
Mevagissey Bay
Mevagissey
Redruth
Chacewater
St. Day
Truro
Kea
Tregony
Gorran Haven
Dodman Pt.
St. Ives
St. Ives Bay
Carbis Bay
Gurnard's Hd.
Zennor
Lelant
Hayle
Pool
Camborne
Gwennap
Feock
Veryan
Veryan B.
Roscoff 6:00
Santander 18:00
(Mar-Nov)
Pendeen
252
Ludgvan
Penzance Heliport
St. Erth
Leedstown
Penryn
Gerrans B.
C. Cornwall
St. Just
Marazion
St. Mawes
Falmouth
Kelynack
Land's End
Newlyn
Penzance
Breage
Helston
Helford
Falmouth Bay
Sennen
St. Buryan
Mousehole
Praa Sands
Gweek
Land's End
Mount's Bay
Porthleven
Flambards Village Theme Park
Mawgan
St. Keverne
St. Levan
The Manacles
Mullion
Ruan Minor
Coverack
Black Hd.
Lizard
Lizard Pt.
Wolf Rock
Rhossili B.
Rhossili
Llanrhidian
GOWER
Oxwich Pt.
Port Eynon Pt.
9

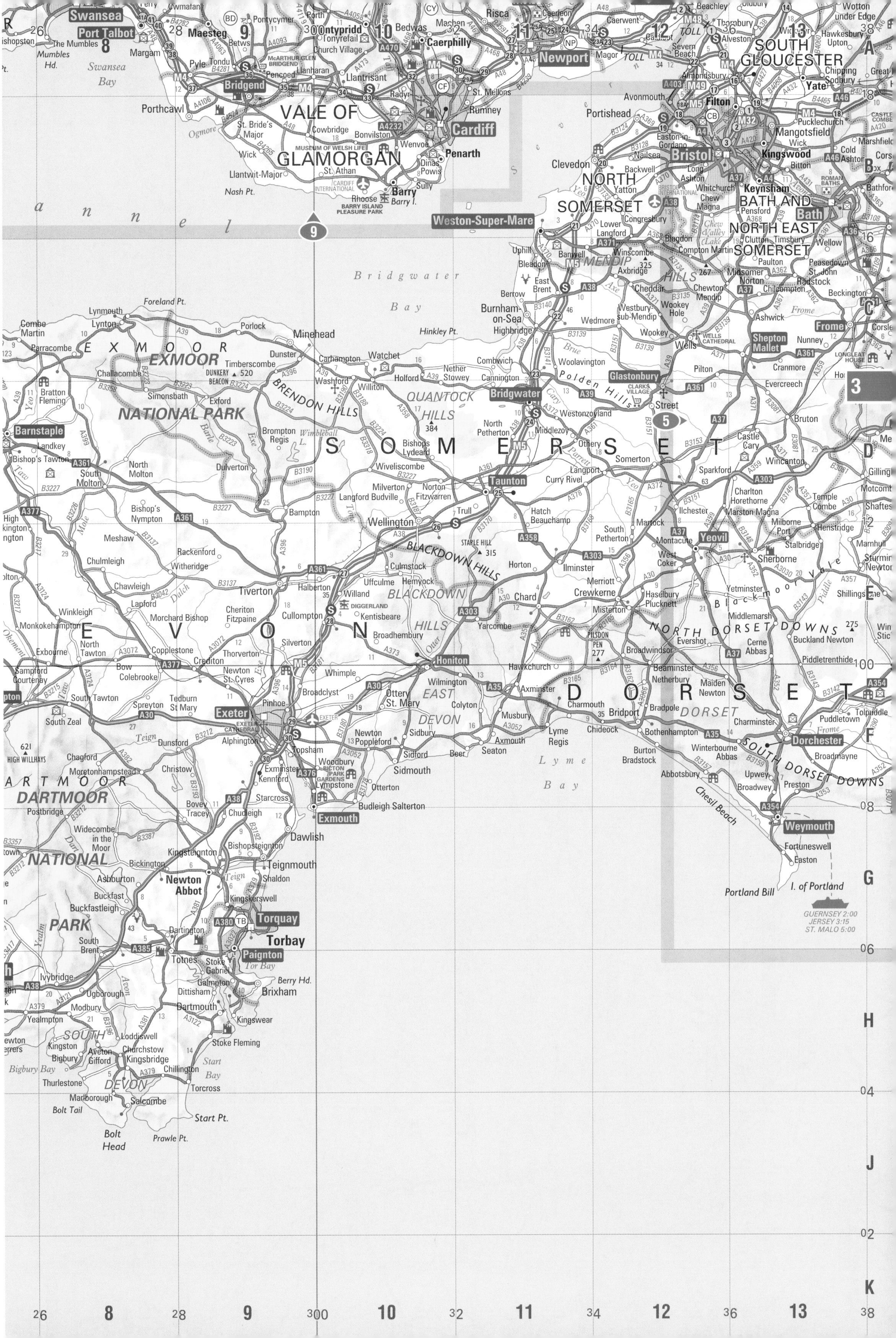

Swansea
Port Talbot
The Mumbles
Mumbles Hd.
Swansea Bay
Margam
Maesteg
Pontycymer
Betws
Pyle
Tondu
Pencoed
Bridgend
McARTHUR GLEN BRIDGEND
Porthcawl
Ogmore
St. Bride's Major
Wick
Llantwit-Major
Nash Pt.
Pontypridd
Tonyrefail
Church Village
Llanharan
Llantrisant
Cowbridge
Bonvilston
MUSEUM OF WELSH LIFE
VALE OF GLAMORGAN
St. Athan
CARDIFF INTERNATIONAL
Rhoose
BARRY ISLAND PLEASURE PARK
Barry
Barry I.
Bedwas
Machen
Caerphilly
Radyr
Cardiff
Wenvoe
Penarth
Dinas Powis
Sully
St. Mellons
Rumney
Risca
Caerleon
Newport
Magor
Caerwent
TOLL
Beachley
Thornbury
Alveston
Severn Beach
Almondsbury
Avonmouth
Portishead
Filton
Bristol
Easton-in-Gordano
Nailsea
Clevedon
Backwell
Long Ashton
Whitchurch
Keynsham
Yatton
NORTH SOMERSET
BRISTOL INTERNATIONAL
Chew Magna
Pensford
Weston-Super-Mare
Congresbury
Lower Langford
Blagdon
Chew Valley Lake
Compton Martin
Winscombe
Banwell
Uphill
Bleadon
MENDIP
Axbridge
Cheddar
HILLS
East Brent
Berrow
Burnham-on-Sea
Highbridge
Wedmore
Westbury-sub-Mendip
Wookey Hole
Wookey
Wells
WELLS CATHEDRAL
SOUTH GLOUCESTER
Hawkesbury Upton
Wotton under Edge
Chipping Sodbury
Yate
Pucklechurch
Mangotsfield
Wick
Kingswood
Cold Ashton
Bitton
Bath
ROMAN BATHS
Bathford
BATH AND NORTH EAST SOMERSET
Clutton
Timsbury
Paulton
Midsomer Norton
Radstock
Peasedown St. John
Wellow
Chewton Mendip
Chilcompton
Beckington
Frome
Ashwick
Shepton Mallet
Nunney
LONGLEAT HOUSE
Cranmore
Evercreech
Pilton
Glastonbury
CLARKS VILLAGE
Street
Bruton
Castle Cary
Wincanton
Sparkford
Charlton Horethorne
Marston Magna
Temple Combe
Milborne Port
Henstridge
Yeovil
Sherborne
Stalbridge
Marnhull
Ilchester
Montacute
West Coker
Martock
South Petherton
Merriott
Crewkerne
Haselbury Plucknett
Misterton
Yetminster
Middlemarsh
Blackmoor Vale
Evershot
Cerne Abbas
Buckland Newton
Piddletrenthide
NORTH DORSET DOWNS
Broadwindsor
Beaminster
Netherbury
Maiden Newton
PILSDON PEN 277
Bradpole
Bridport
Chideock
Charmouth
Bothenhampton
Burton Bradstock
Abbotsbury
Chesil Beach
Winterbourne Abbas
Charminster
Dorchester
Puddletown
Tolpuddle
Broadmayne
SOUTH DORSET DOWNS
Upwey
Broadwey
Preston
Weymouth
Fortuneswell
Easton
Portland Bill
I. of Portland
GUERNSEY 2:00
JERSEY 3:15
ST. MALO 5:00
DORSET
D O R S E T
Lyme Bay
Lyme Regis
Axminster
Hawkchurch
Musbury
Axmouth
Seaton
Beer
Colyton
Honiton
Wilmington
EAST DEVON
Ottery St. Mary
Sidbury
Sidford
Sidmouth
Newton Poppleford
Otterton
Budleigh Salterton
Exmouth
Lympstone
Woodbury
BICTON PARK GARDENS
Topsham
Exminster
Kennford
Starcross
Dawlish
Exeter
EXETER CATHEDRAL
Alphington
Pinhoe
Broadclyst
Whimple
Newton St. Cyres
Crediton
Thorverton
Silverton
Cullompton
Broadhembury
Kentisbeare
DIGGERLAND
Willand
Halberton
Uffculme
Culmstock
Hemyock
BLACKDOWN HILLS
Yarcombe
Chard
Ilminster
Horton
STAPLE HILL 315
Hatch Beauchamp
Trull
Taunton
Wellington
Langford Budville
Milverton
Norton Fitzwarren
Wiveliscombe
Bishops Lydeard
Curry Rivel
Langport
Somerton
Othery
Middlezoy
Westonzoyland
North Petherton
Bridgwater
Polden Hills
Woolavington
Cannington
Combwich
Nether Stowey
Holford
QUANTOCK HILLS
384
Williton
Watchet
Carhampton
Washford
Dunster
Minehead
Hinkley Pt.
Bridgwater Bay
Porlock
Timberscombe
DUNKERY BEACON 520
BRENDON HILLS
Brompton Regis
Wimbleball L.
Dulverton
Bampton
S O M E R S E T
Exford
Simonsbath
Challacombe
EXMOOR
E X M O O R
NATIONAL PARK
Lynmouth
Lynton
Foreland Pt.
Combe Martin
Parracombe
Bratton Fleming
Barnstaple
Landkey
Bishop's Tawton
North Molton
South Molton
Bishop's Nympton
Meshaw
Rackenford
Witheridge
Tiverton
Chulmleigh
Chawleigh
Lapford
Morchard Bishop
Cheriton Fitzpaine
Winkleigh
Monkokehampton
North Tawton
Exbourne
Copplestone
Bow
Colebrooke
Sampford Courtenay
South Tawton
Spreyton
Tedburn St Mary
South Zeal
Dunsford
Christow
Chagford
Moretonhampstead
HIGH WILLHAYS
621
DARTMOOR
D A R T M O O R
Postbridge
Bovey Tracey
Chudleigh
Widecombe in the Moor
NATIONAL PARK
Kingsteignton
Bishopsteignton
Teignmouth
Shaldon
Newton Abbot
Bickington
Ashburton
Buckfast
Buckfastleigh
Kingskerswell
Torquay
Torbay
Paignton
Tor Bay
Dartington
Totnes
Stoke Gabriel
Galmpton
Brixham
Berry Hd.
Dittisham
Dartmouth
Kingswear
Stoke Fleming
South Brent
Ivybridge
Ugborough
Modbury
Yealmpton
Loddiswell
Kingston
Bigbury
Aveton Gifford
Churchstow
Kingsbridge
Chillington
Start Bay
Torcross
SOUTH DEVON
Bigbury Bay
Thurlestone
Marlborough
Salcombe
Bolt Tail
Bolt Head
Prawle Pt.
Start Pt.
M4
M5
M32
M48
M49
A30
A35
A37
A38
A39
A303
A358
A361
A377
A380
A385
26
28
30
32
34
36
38
8
9
10
11
12
13
A
B
C
D
E
F
G
H
J
K
3
5

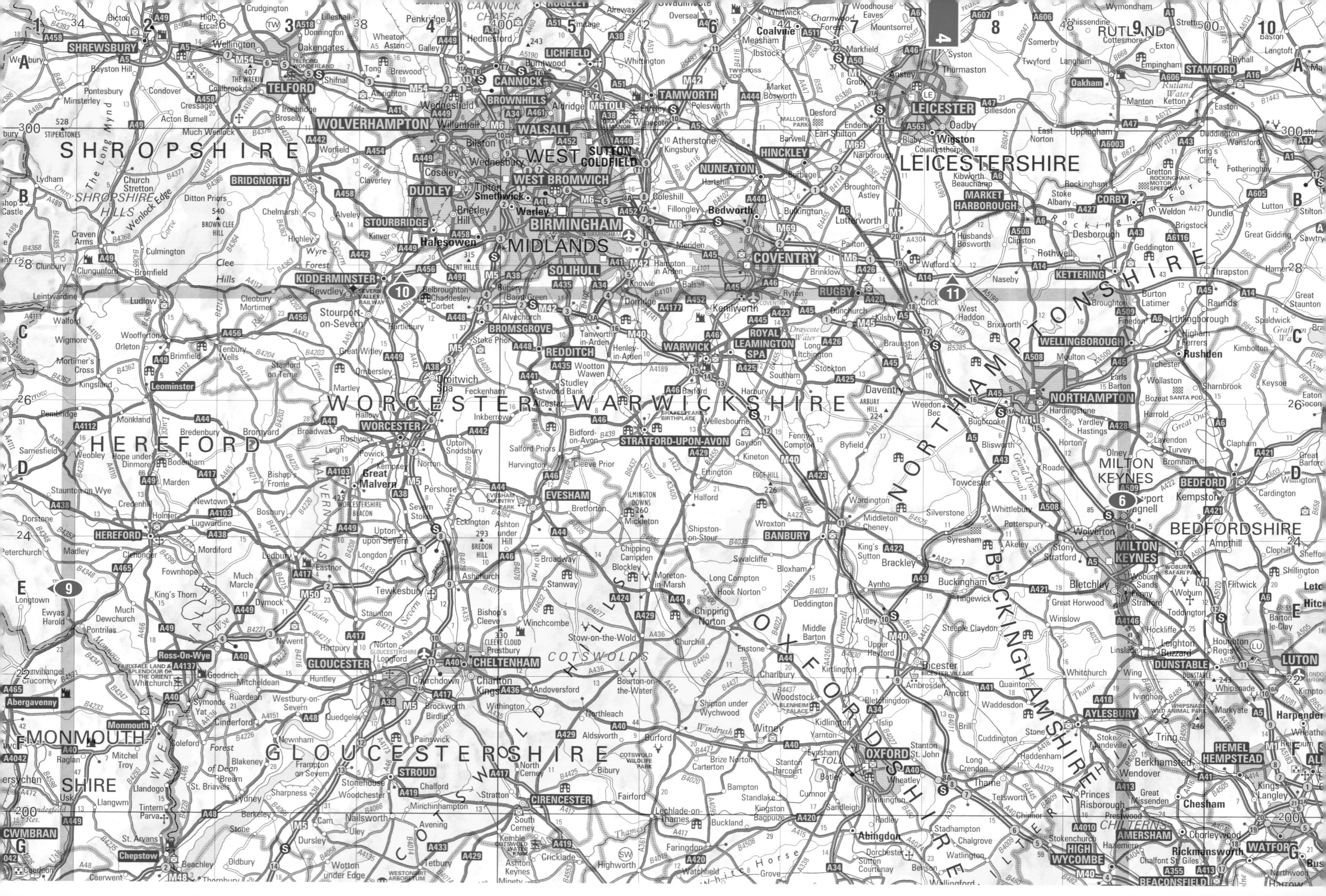
4
SHROPSHIRE
HEREFORD
WORCESTER
WARWICKSHIRE
WEST MIDLANDS
LEICESTERSHIRE
NORTHAMPTONSHIRE
BUCKINGHAMSHIRE
BEDFORDSHIRE
OXFORDSHIRE
GLOUCESTERSHIRE
MONMOUTHSHIRE
RUTLAND
MILTON KEYNES
COTSWOLDS
SHREWSBURY
TELFORD
WOLVERHAMPTON
WALSALL
BIRMINGHAM
COVENTRY
LEICESTER
NORTHAMPTON
KETTERING
WELLINGBOROUGH
RUGBY
NUNEATON
HINCKLEY
TAMWORTH
LICHFIELD
CANNOCK
BROWNHILLS
SUTTON COLDFIELD
WEST BROMWICH
DUDLEY
STOURBRIDGE
KIDDERMINSTER
BRIDGNORTH
SOLIHULL
REDDITCH
BROMSGROVE
WARWICK
ROYAL LEAMINGTON SPA
STRATFORD-UPON-AVON
WORCESTER
EVESHAM
HEREFORD
GLOUCESTER
CHELTENHAM
STROUD
CIRENCESTER
BANBURY
OXFORD
BEDFORD
DUNSTABLE
LUTON
AYLESBURY
HEMEL HEMPSTEAD
AMERSHAM
HIGH WYCOMBE
WATFORD
BEACONSFIELD
STAMFORD
Oakham
CORBY
MARKET HARBOROUGH
Leominster
Ross-On-Wye
Abergavenny
Chepstow
CWMBRAN

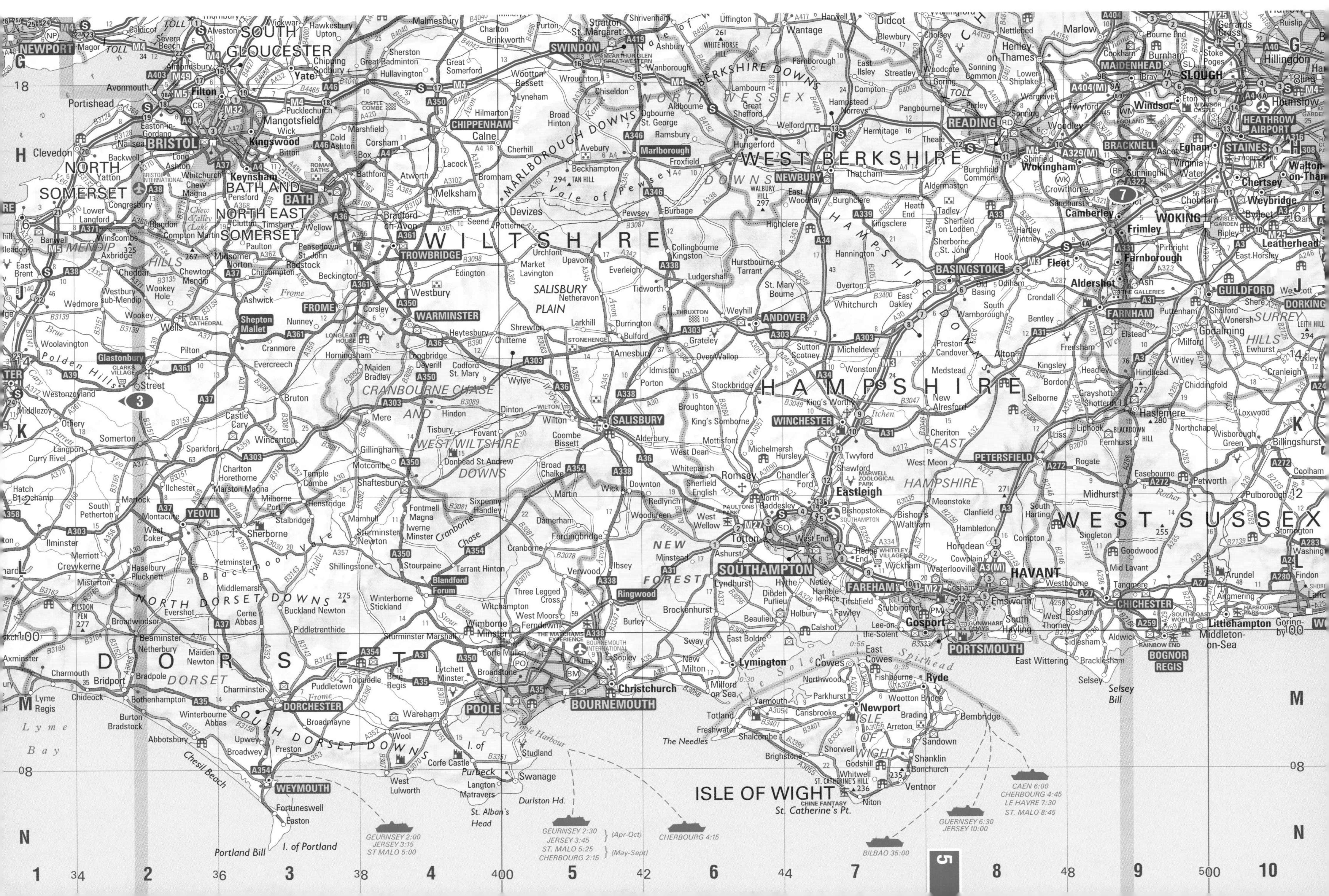

5
WEST BERKSHIRE
HAMPSHIRE
WILTSHIRE
DORSET
WEST SUSSEX
SOUTH GLOUCESTER
BATH AND NORTH EAST SOMERSET
NORTH SOMERSET
SALISBURY PLAIN
NEW FOREST
BRISTOL
BATH
SWINDON
READING
BASINGSTOKE
SALISBURY
SOUTHAMPTON
PORTSMOUTH
BOURNEMOUTH
POOLE
WINCHESTER
ANDOVER
NEWBURY
GUILDFORD
SLOUGH
MAIDENHEAD
BRACKNELL
FARNHAM
CHICHESTER
PETERSFIELD
HAVANT
FAREHAM
DORCHESTER
WEYMOUTH
YEOVIL
FROME
TROWBRIDGE
WARMINSTER
CHIPPENHAM
Marlborough
Ringwood
Glastonbury
Shepton Mallet
ISLE OF WIGHT
St. Catherine's Pt.
The Needles
Portland Bill
I. of Portland
Chesil Beach
Selsey Bill
CAEN 6:00
CHERBOURG 4:45
LE HAVRE 7:30
ST. MALO 8:45
GUERNSEY 6:30
JERSEY 10:00
BILBAO 35:00
CHERBOURG 4:15
GEURNSEY 2:30
JERSEY 3:45
ST. MALO 5:25
CHERBOURG 2:15
(Apr-Oct)
(May-Sept)
GEURNSEY 2:00
JERSEY 3:15
ST MALO 5:00

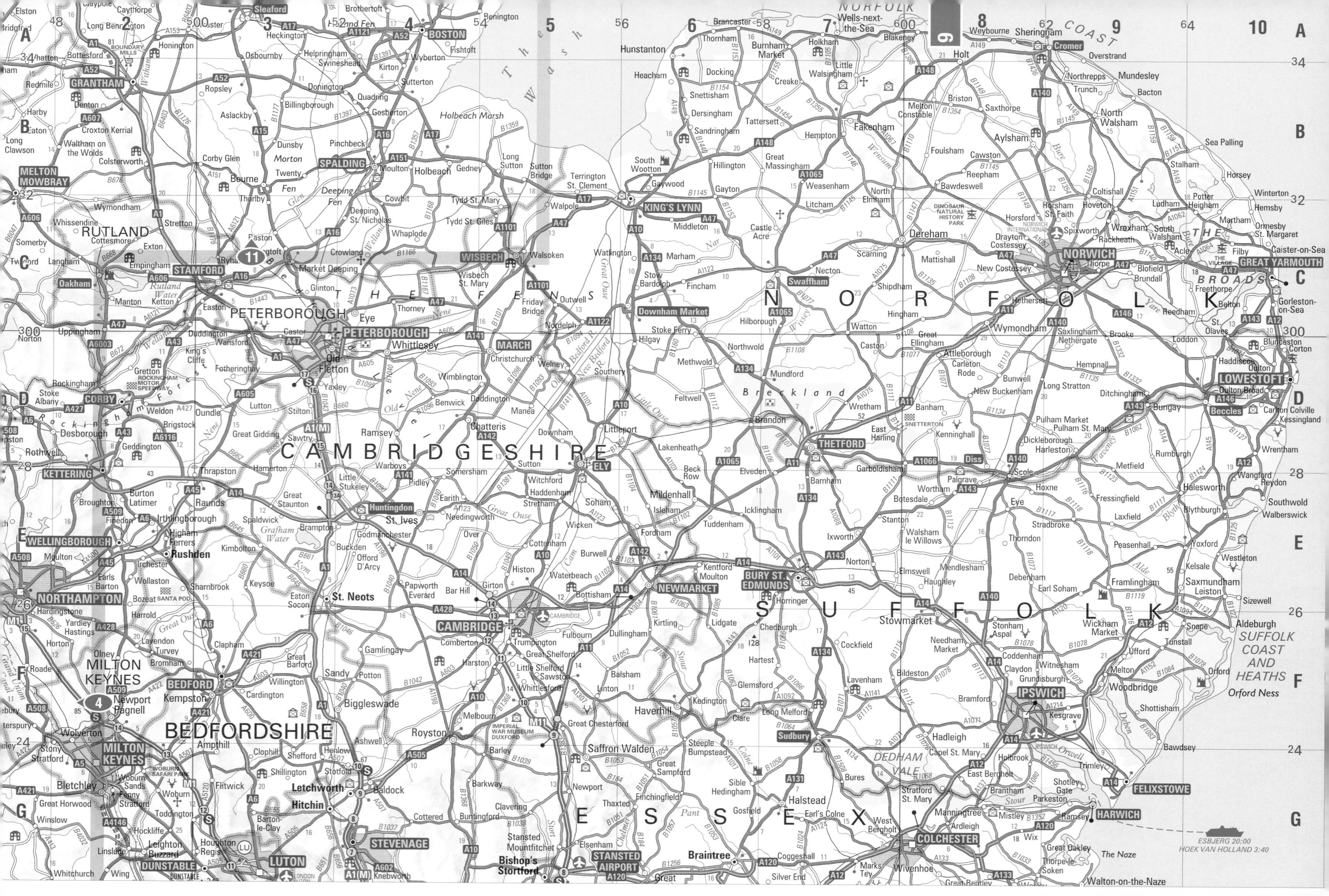

NORFOLK
SUFFOLK
ESSEX
CAMBRIDGESHIRE
BEDFORDSHIRE
RUTLAND
MILTON KEYNES
THE FENS
The Wash
NORFOLK COAST
THE BROADS
SUFFOLK COAST AND HEATHS
DEDHAM VALE
Breckland
NORWICH
GREAT YARMOUTH
LOWESTOFT
KING'S LYNN
PETERBOROUGH
CAMBRIDGE
IPSWICH
COLCHESTER
FELIXSTOWE
HARWICH
BURY ST. EDMUNDS
NEWMARKET
THETFORD
ELY
WISBECH
MARCH
SPALDING
BOSTON
GRANTHAM
STAMFORD
MELTON MOWBRAY
KETTERING
CORBY
WELLINGBOROUGH
NORTHAMPTON
BEDFORD
LUTON
DUNSTABLE
STEVENAGE
STANSTED AIRPORT
Sudbury
Swaffham
Downham Market
Huntingdon
Cromer
Diss
Beccles
ESBJERG 20:00
HOEK VAN HOLLAND 3:40

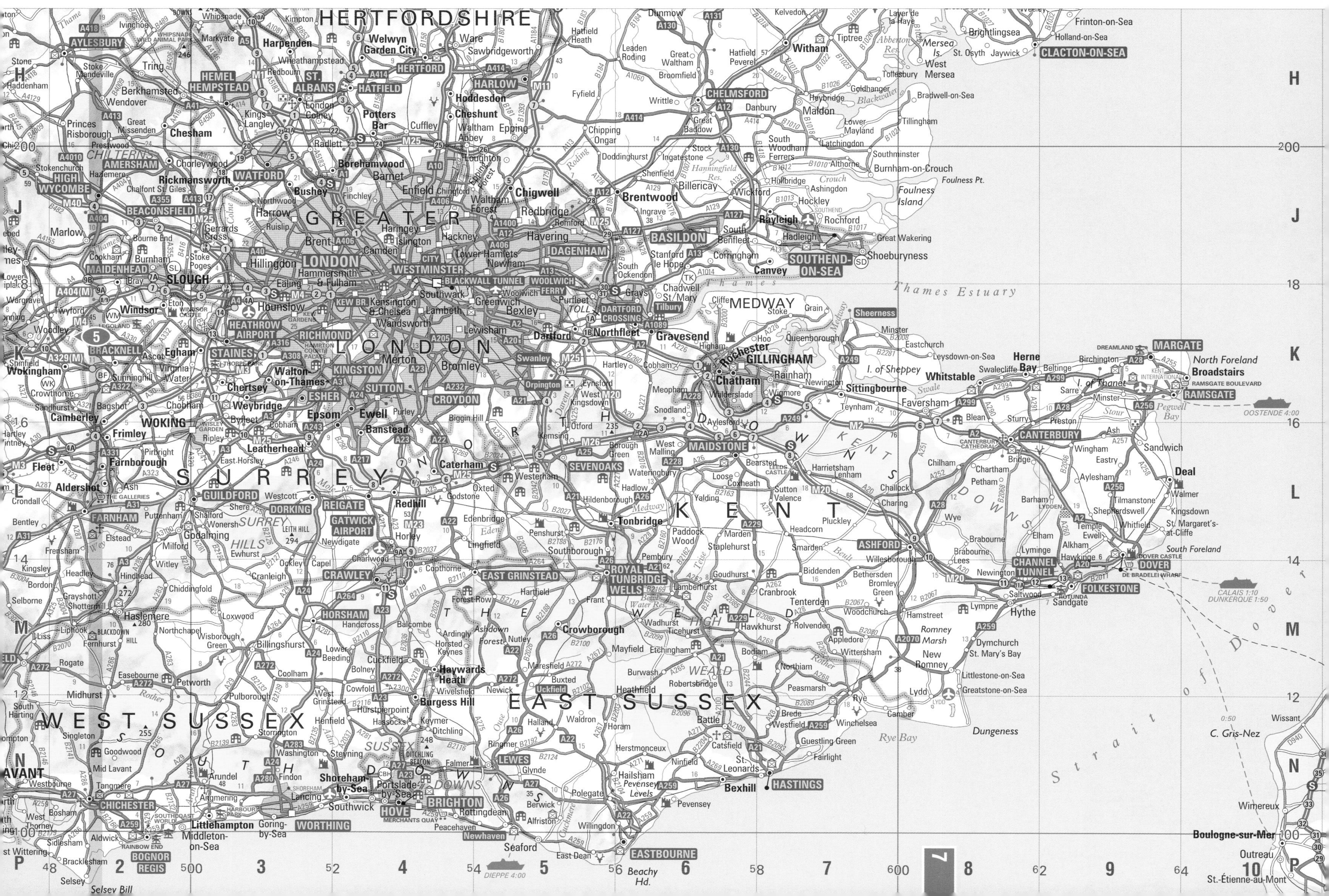

HERTFORDSHIRE
GREATER LONDON
SURREY
KENT
WEST SUSSEX
EAST SUSSEX
NORTH DOWNS
SOUTH DOWNS
WEALD
MEDWAY
Thames Estuary
Strait of Dover
LONDON
WESTMINSTER
CITY
CROYDON
DAGENHAM
BASILDON
CHELMSFORD
SOUTHEND-ON-SEA
CLACTON-ON-SEA
GILLINGHAM
MAIDSTONE
CANTERBURY
MARGATE
RAMSGATE
DOVER
FOLKESTONE
ASHFORD
HASTINGS
EASTBOURNE
BRIGHTON
HOVE
LEWES
WORTHING
CHICHESTER
BOGNOR REGIS
HORSHAM
CRAWLEY
GATWICK AIRPORT
REIGATE
DORKING
GUILDFORD
FARNHAM
WOKING
SLOUGH
WATFORD
HEMEL HEMPSTEAD
ST. ALBANS
HATFIELD
HERTFORD
HARLOW
AYLESBURY
HIGH WYCOMBE
AMERSHAM
BEACONSFIELD
MAIDENHEAD
BRACKNELL
HEATHROW AIRPORT
STAINES
KINGSTON
SUTTON
ESHER
RICHMOND
SEVENOAKS
ROYAL TUNBRIDGE WELLS
EAST GRINSTEAD
CHANNEL TUNNEL
Boulogne-sur-Mer
C. Gris-Nez
Wissant
Wimereux
Outreau
St.-Étienne-au-Mont
Dungeness
Beachy Hd.
Selsey Bill
Foulness Island
North Foreland
South Foreland
Rye Bay
Pegwell Bay
OOSTENDE 4:00
CALAIS 1:10
DUNKERQUE 1:50
DIEPPE 4:00

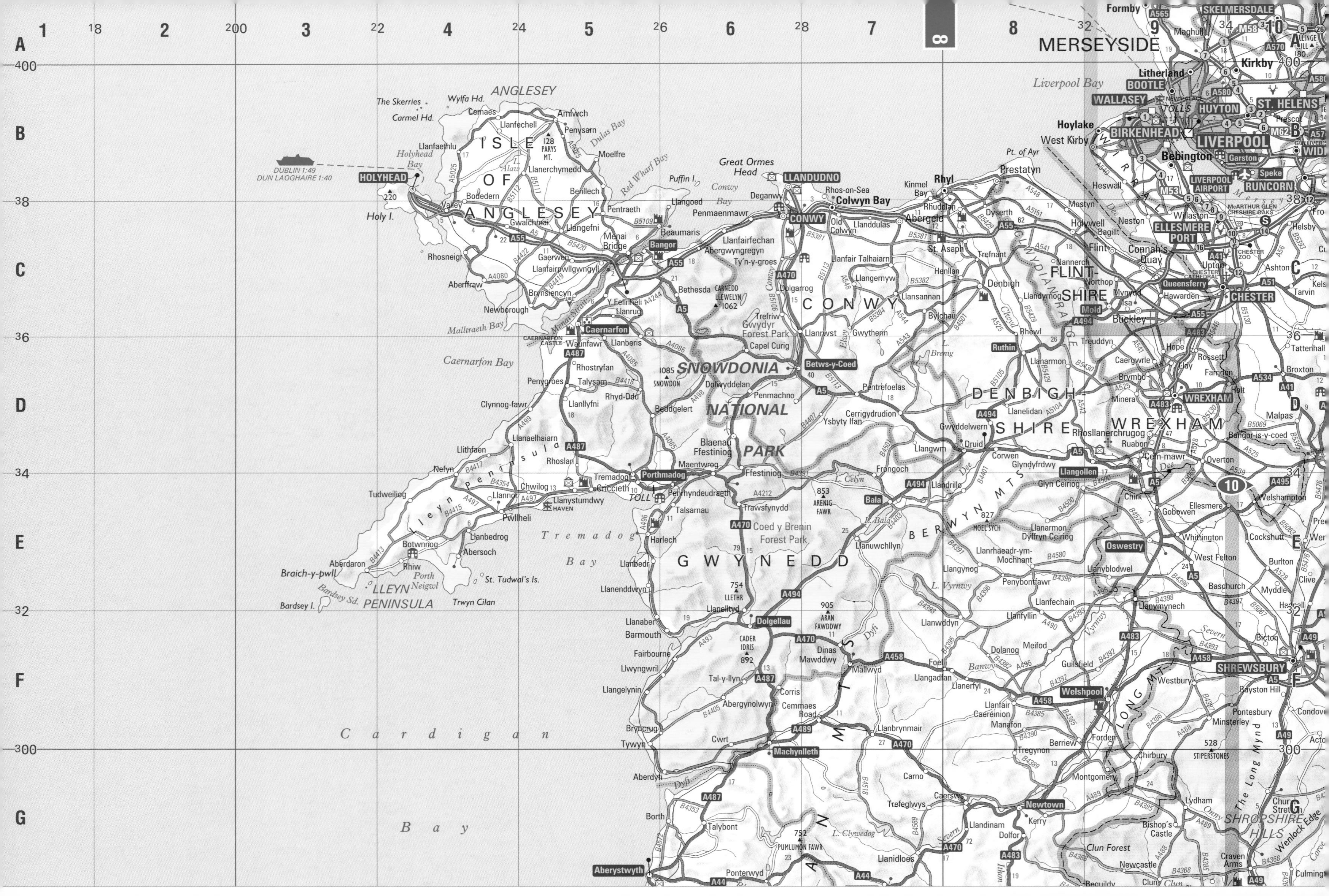

8
MERSEYSIDE
Liverpool Bay
ANGLESEY
ISLE OF ANGLESEY
HOLYHEAD
Holy I.
The Skerries
Carmel Hd.
Wylfa Hd.
Cemaes
Amlwch
Llanfechell
Penysarn
Dulas Bay
Moelfre
Llanerchymedd
Benllech
Pentraeth
Red Wharf Bay
Puffin I.
Beaumaris
Menai Bridge
Bangor
Llangefni
Gwalchmai
Bodedern
Valley
Rhosneigr
Aberffraw
Newborough
Malltraeth Bay
Brynsiencyn
Llanfairpwllgwyngyll
Gaerwen
Caernarfon
Caernarfon Bay
Llanberis
Waunfawr
Rhostryfan
Penygroes
Talysarn
Clynnog-fawr
Llanllyfni
Llanaelhaearn
Llithfaen
Nefyn
Tudweiliog
Lleyn Peninsula
LLEYN PENINSULA
Aberdaron
Braich-y-pwll
Bardsey I.
Bardsey Sd.
Rhiw
Botwnnog
Porth Neigwl
Llanbedrog
Abersoch
St. Tudwal's Is.
Trwyn Cilan
Pwllheli
Llannor
Chwilog
Llanystumdwy
Criccieth
Tremadog Bay
Porthmadog
Tremadog
Penrhyndeudraeth
Talsarnau
Harlech
Llanbedr
Llanenddwyn
Llanaber
Barmouth
Fairbourne
Llwyngwril
Llangelynin
Tywyn
Bryncrug
Aberdyfi
Borth
Aberystwyth
Talybont
Cardigan Bay
LLANDUDNO
Great Ormes Head
Conwy Bay
CONWY
Deganwy
Penmaenmawr
Llanfairfechan
Abergwyngregyn
Llangoed
Bethesda
CARNEDD LLEWELYN 1062
SNOWDONIA NATIONAL PARK
SNOWDON 1085
Beddgelert
Capel Curig
Betws-y-Coed
Dolwyddelan
Penmacho
Blaenau Ffestiniog
Ffestiniog
Maentwrog
Trawsfynydd
Coed y Brenin Forest Park
GWYNEDD
Dolgellau
CADER IDRIS 892
LLETHR 754
ARENIG FAWR 853
ARAN FAWDDWY 905
Dinas Mawddwy
Mallwyd
Corris
Machynlleth
Cwrt
Bala
Frongoch
Llandrillo
Corwen
Llangollen
BERWYN MTS
MOEL SYCH 827
Rhos-on-Sea
Colwyn Bay
Old Colwyn
Llanddulas
Abergele
Kinmel Bay
Rhyl
Rhuddlan
Prestatyn
Pt. of Ayr
Dyserth
St. Asaph
Trefnant
Denbigh
Henllan
Llanfair Talhaiarn
Llangernyw
Llansannan
Dolgarrog
Trefriw
Gwydyr Forest Park
Llanrwst
Gwytherin
Bylchau
Pentrefoelas
Cerrigydrudion
Ysbyty Ifan
CONWY
Ruthin
DENBIGHSHIRE
Llanelidan
Gwyddelwern
Druid
Llangwm
FLINTSHIRE
Mold
CLWYDIAN RANGE
Flint
Holywell
Mostyn
Connah's Quay
Buckley
Hawarden
Queensferry
CHESTER
WREXHAM
Ruabon
Rhosllanerchrugog
Chirk
Cefn-mawr
Overton
Oswestry
Ellesmere
Whittington
Welshampton
Llanarmon Dyffryn Ceiriog
Llanrhaeadr-ym-Mochnant
Penybontfawr
Llangynog
Llanfyllin
Llanfechain
Llanymynech
Welshpool
Meifod
Dolanog
Guilsfield
Llanfair Caereinion
Llanerfyl
Foel
Llangadfan
Manafon
Tregynon
Berriew
Montgomery
Newtown
Carno
Caersws
Llanidloes
Trefeglwys
Llanbrynmair
Llandinam
Dolfor
Kerry
PUMLUMON FAWR 752
SHREWSBURY
LONG MT.
The Long Mynd
SHROPSHIRE HILLS
STIPERSTONES 528
Clun Forest
Bishop's Castle
Craven Arms
Wenlock Edge
BIRKENHEAD
LIVERPOOL
WALLASEY
BOOTLE
HUYTON
ST. HELENS
RUNCORN
ELLESMERE PORT
Hoylake
West Kirby
Bebington
Heswall
Neston
LIVERPOOL AIRPORT
Formby
SKELMERSDALE
Kirkby
DUBLIN 1:49
DUN LAOGHAIRE 1:40

POWYS
CEREDIGION
CAMBRIAN
CARMARTHENSHIRE
PEMBROKESHIRE
MYNYDD PRESCELLY
MYNYDD EPPYNT
MYNYDD DU
BRECON BEACONS
NATIONAL PARK
PEMBROKESHIRE COAST NATIONAL PARK
BLACK MOUNTAINS
MONMOUTHSHIRE
VALE OF GLAMORGAN
GOWER
SWANSEA
NORTH SOMERSET
MENDIP HILLS
Bristol Channel
Carmarthen Bay
Swansea Bay
St. Brides Bay
Cardigan
Fishguard
Haverfordwest
Milford Haven
Pembroke Dock
Pembroke
Tenby
St. Clears
Carmarthen
Llandeilo
Llandovery
Llanelli
Swansea
Port Talbot
Neath
Bridgend
Cardiff
Newport
Cwmbran
Chepstow
Abergavenny
Monmouth
Brecon
Builth Wells
Llandrindod Wells
Rhayader
Llangurig
Hereford
Leominster
Merthyr Tydfil
Weston-super-Mare
Aberystwyth
Aberaeron
New Quay
Lampeter
Tregaron
St. David's
Aberdare
Pontypridd
Caerphilly
Pontypool
Ebbw Vale
Barry
Penarth
Rhondda
ROSSLARE 3:30
ROSSLARE 3:45
H
J
K
L
M
N
P
1
2
3
4
5
6
7
8
9
10
18
200
22
24
26
28
32
16

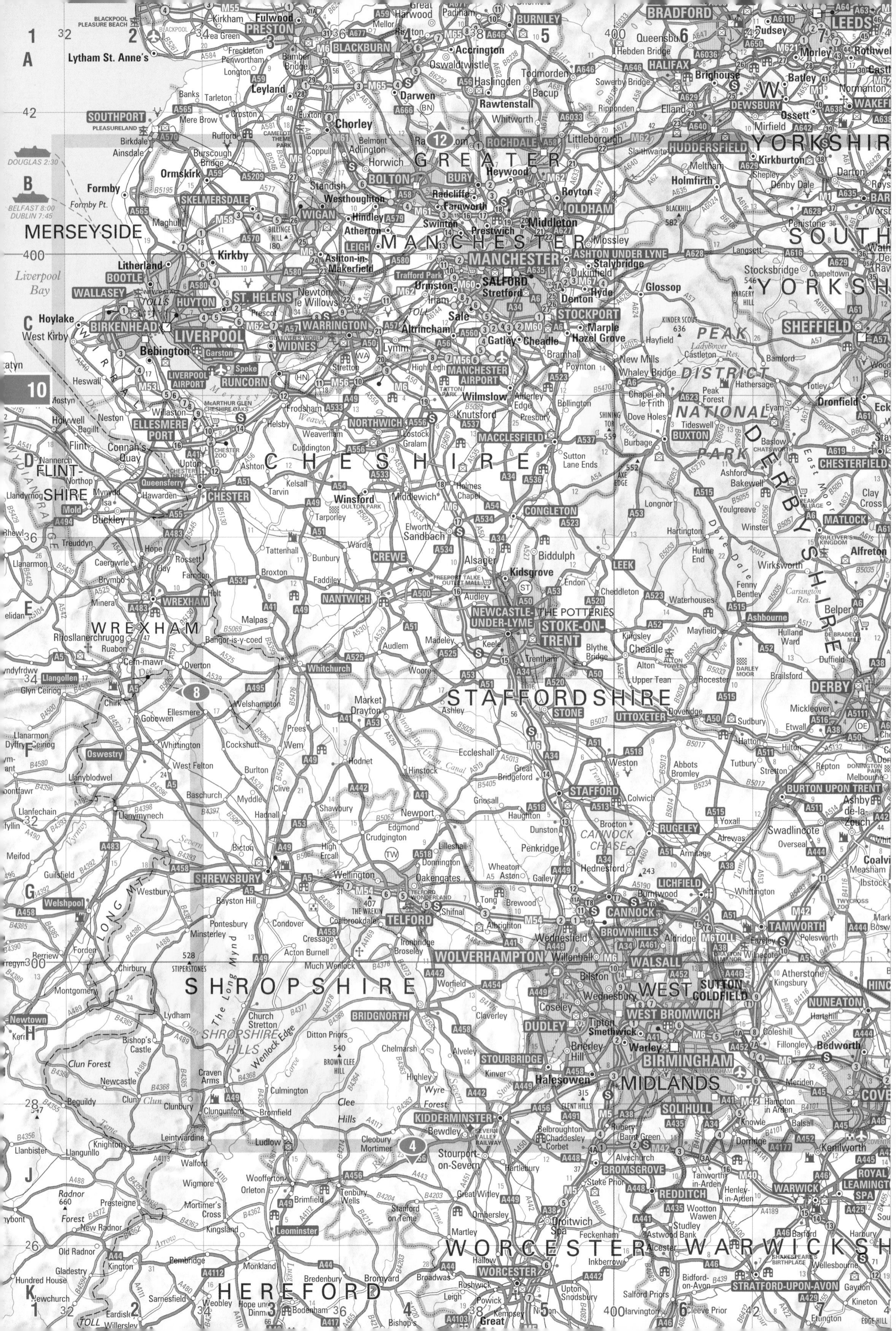

MERSEYSIDE
Liverpool Bay
GREATER MANCHESTER
WEST YORKSHIRE
SOUTH YORKSHIRE
CHESHIRE
PEAK DISTRICT NATIONAL PARK
DERBYSHIRE
FLINTSHIRE
WREXHAM
STAFFORDSHIRE
SHROPSHIRE
SHROPSHIRE HILLS
WEST MIDLANDS
WORCESTER
WARWICKSHIRE
HEREFORD
Clun Forest
Cannock Chase
The Long Mynd
Clee Hills
DOUGLAS 2:30
BELFAST 8:00
DUBLIN 7:45
PRESTON
BLACKPOOL PLEASURE BEACH
Lytham St. Anne's
SOUTHPORT
BLACKBURN
BURNLEY
BRADFORD
LEEDS
HALIFAX
HUDDERSFIELD
DEWSBURY
WAKEFIELD
ROCHDALE
BOLTON
BURY
WIGAN
OLDHAM
SKELMERSDALE
MANCHESTER
SALFORD
STOCKPORT
ASHTON UNDER LYNE
MANCHESTER AIRPORT
BOOTLE
WALLASEY
BIRKENHEAD
LIVERPOOL
LIVERPOOL AIRPORT
HUYTON
ST. HELENS
WARRINGTON
WIDNES
RUNCORN
ELLESMERE PORT
NORTHWICH
MACCLESFIELD
SHEFFIELD
CHESTERFIELD
BUXTON
CHESTER
Queensferry
Mold
CONGLETON
CREWE
NANTWICH
LEEK
MATLOCK
NEWCASTLE-UNDER-LYME
STOKE-ON-TRENT
WREXHAM
Llangollen
Oswestry
Whitchurch
Ashbourne
DERBY
UTTOXETER
STONE
STAFFORD
BURTON UPON TRENT
RUGELEY
LICHFIELD
CANNOCK
TAMWORTH
SHREWSBURY
Welshpool
TELFORD
WOLVERHAMPTON
WALSALL
BROWNHILLS
SUTTON COLDFIELD
NUNEATON
WEST BROMWICH
DUDLEY
BIRMINGHAM
STOURBRIDGE
SOLIHULL
BRIDGNORTH
Newtown
KIDDERMINSTER
BROMSGROVE
REDDITCH
WARWICK
ROYAL LEAMINGTON SPA
Leominster
WORCESTER
STRATFORD-UPON-AVON

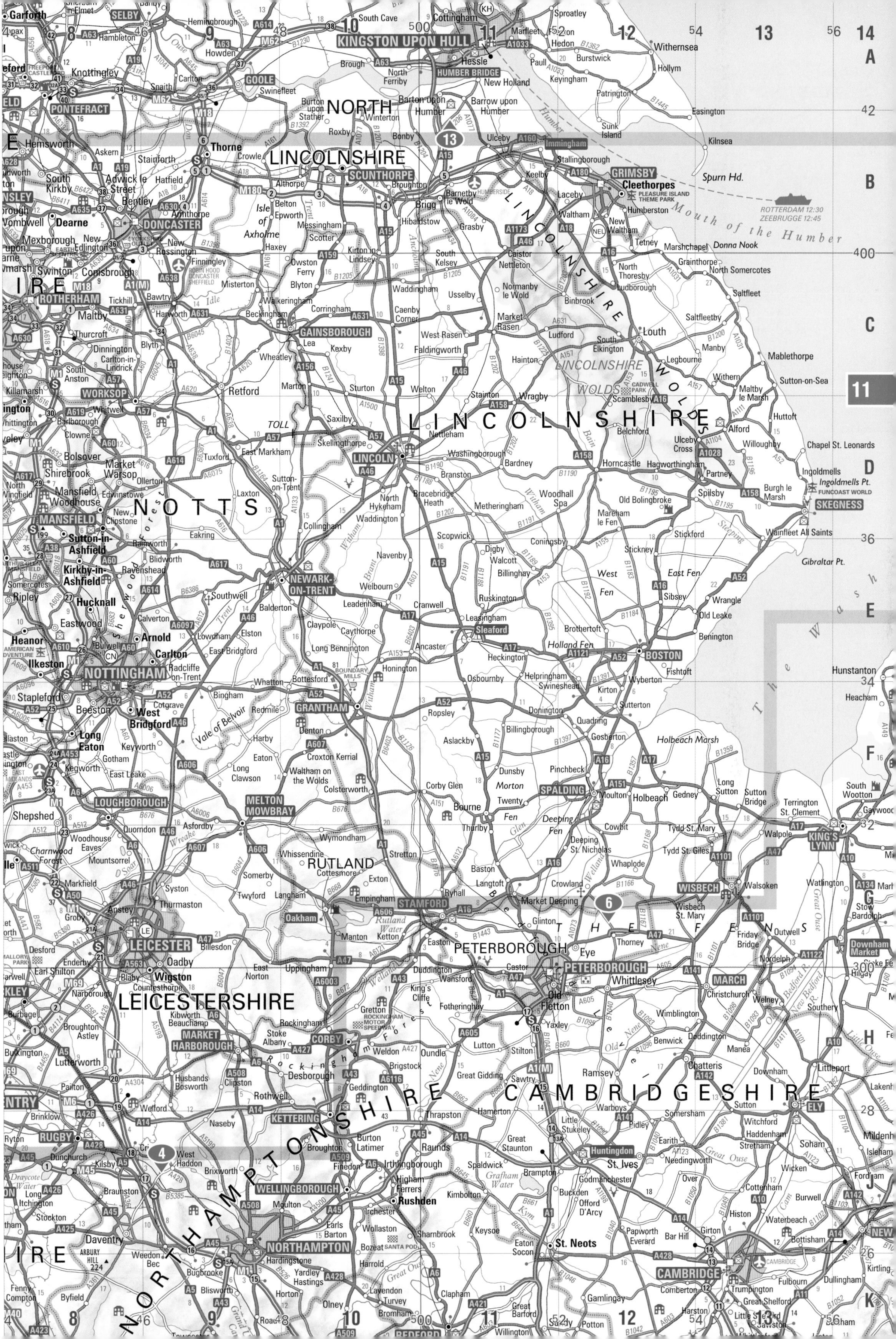

KINGSTON UPON HULL
HUMBER BRIDGE
NORTH LINCOLNSHIRE
SCUNTHORPE
GRIMSBY
Cleethorpes
Immingham
Spurn Hd.
ROTTERDAM 12:30
ZEEBRUGGE 12:45
Mouth of the Humber
Withernsea
Easington
Kilnsea
SELBY
GOOLE
PONTEFRACT
DONCASTER
ROTHERHAM
GAINSBOROUGH
WORKSOP
Retford
LINCOLNSHIRE WOLDS
LINCOLNSHIRE
LINCOLN
Louth
Mablethorpe
Sutton-on-Sea
Alford
Chapel St. Leonards
Ingoldmells
SKEGNESS
Horncastle
Spilsby
NOTTS
MANSFIELD
NEWARK-ON-TRENT
NOTTINGHAM
Sleaford
BOSTON
The Wash
Hunstanton
GRANTHAM
Vale of Belvoir
LOUGHBOROUGH
MELTON MOWBRAY
SPALDING
KING'S LYNN
RUTLAND
Oakham
STAMFORD
WISBECH
THE FENS
PETERBOROUGH
LEICESTER
LEICESTERSHIRE
MARKET HARBOROUGH
CORBY
KETTERING
MARCH
CAMBRIDGESHIRE
ELY
Huntingdon
St. Ives
St. Neots
CAMBRIDGE
RUGBY
WELLINGBOROUGH
NORTHAMPTONSHIRE
NORTHAMPTON
Daventry
Rushden
Downham Market
11

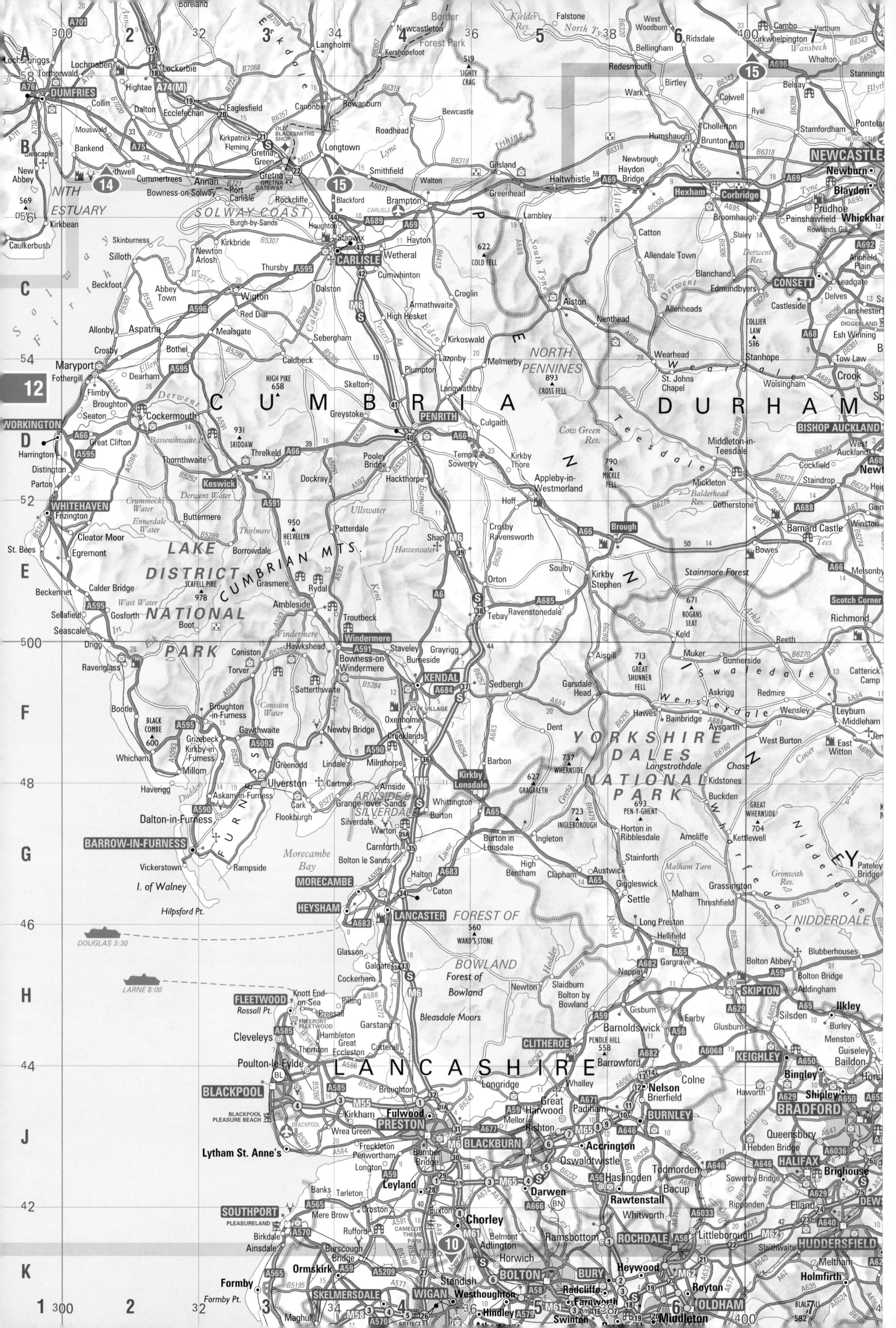

CUMBRIA
DURHAM
LANCASHIRE
LAKE DISTRICT NATIONAL PARK
CUMBRIAN MTS.
NORTH PENNINES
YORKSHIRE DALES NATIONAL PARK
FOREST OF BOWLAND
Forest of Bowland
Bleasdale Moors
NIDDERDALE
Stainmore Forest
SOLWAY COAST
NITH ESTUARY
Solway Firth
Morecambe Bay
FURNESS
ARNSIDE & SILVERDALE
Eskdale
Teesdale
Weardale
Swaledale
Wensleydale
Wharfedale
Nidderdale
Kielder Res.
North Tyne
South Tyne
Derwent Res.
Cow Green Res.
Ullswater
Haweswater
Windermere
Coniston Water
Derwent Water
Bassenthwaite L.
Thirlmere
Crummock Water
Ennerdale Water
Wast Water
Malham Tarn
Grimwith Res.
Balderhead Res.
I. of Walney
Hilpsford Pt.
Formby Pt.
Rossall Pt.
DOUGLAS 3:30
LARNE 8:00
DUMFRIES
Lockerbie
Annan
Gretna Green
Langholm
Longtown
CARLISLE
Brampton
Haltwhistle
Hexham
Corbridge
NEWCASTLE
Newburn
Blaydon
Prudhoe
Whickham
CONSETT
Stanhope
Crook
Wolsingham
BISHOP AUCKLAND
Alston
Wigton
Silloth
Aspatria
Maryport
WORKINGTON
Cockermouth
Keswick
WHITEHAVEN
Egremont
St. Bees
Seascale
Ravenglass
PENRITH
Appleby-in-Westmorland
Kirkby Stephen
Brough
Barnard Castle
Middleton-in-Teesdale
Richmond
Windermere
Ambleside
Grasmere
Coniston
Hawkshead
KENDAL
Sedbergh
Kirkby Lonsdale
Ulverston
Dalton-in-Furness
BARROW-IN-FURNESS
Millom
Grange-over-Sands
Carnforth
MORECAMBE
HEYSHAM
LANCASTER
Settle
Hawes
Leyburn
Aysgarth
Ingleton
Skipton
Ilkley
KEIGHLEY
Bingley
Shipley
BRADFORD
HALIFAX
Brighouse
HUDDERSFIELD
FLEETWOOD
Cleveleys
Poulton-le-Fylde
BLACKPOOL
Lytham St. Anne's
Garstang
Clitheroe
PRESTON
Fulwood
BLACKBURN
Accrington
BURNLEY
Nelson
Colne
Leyland
Chorley
SOUTHPORT
Ormskirk
Formby
SKELMERSDALE
WIGAN
BOLTON
BURY
ROCHDALE
OLDHAM
Heywood
Middleton
Todmorden
Rawtenstall
Darwen
HIGH PIKE 658
SKIDDAW 931
HELVELLYN 950
SCAFELL PIKE 978
CROSS FELL 893
MICKLE FELL 790
BLACK COMBE 600
WHERNSIDE 737
INGLEBOROUGH 723
PEN-Y-GHENT 693
GREAT SHUNNER FELL 713
ROGANS SEAT 671
GREAT WHERNSIDE 704
WARD'S STONE 560
PENDLE HILL 558
COLD FELL 622
SIGHTY CRAG 519
M6
M55
M65
M61
M62
M58
A74(M)
A66
A69
A6
A590
A595
A65
A59
12
14
15
10

ISLE OF MAN
Pt. of Ayre
Andreas
Bride
Ramsey Bay
JURBY SOUTH
Sulby
Ramsey
Ballaugh
Maughold
Maughold Hd.
Kirk Michael
SNAEFELL 620
Peel
Laxey
St. John's
Glenmaye
Onchan
SOUTH BARRULE 483
Foxdale
Douglas
HEYSHAM 3:30
Bradda Hd.
Colby
Ballasalla
Port Erin
RONALDSWAY
Castletown
BELFAST 2:45
DUBLIN 2:45
(Apr-Oct)
LIVERPOOL 2:30
Port St. Mary
BILLOWN
Calf of Man
Langness
STAVANGER 20:45
HAUGESUND 23:00
AMSTERDAM 15:00
ASHINGTON
Pegswood
Newbiggin-by-the-Sea
MORPETH
Bedlington
Cowpen
Blyth
Cramlington
Hartley
Seaton Delaval
Earsdon
Whitley Bay
TYNEMOUTH
Longbenton
Wallsend
SOUTH SHIELDS
TYNE & WEAR
Jarrow
Hebburn
Boldon
GATESHEAD
SUNDERLAND
Birtley
Washington
Penshaw
Ryhope
Stanley
Chester-le-Street
Houghton-le-Spring
Seaham
Hetton-le-Hole
Murton
Easington Colliery
DURHAM
Easington
Haswell
Peterlee
Horden
Wheatley Hill
Wingate
Willington
JACKSONS LANDING
HARTLEPOOL
Trimdon
Ferryhill
Chilton
Sedgefield
Tees Bay
Shildon
Greatham
Wolviston
Teesside
REDCAR
Billingham
Eston
Marske-by-the-Sea
Saltburn-by-the-Sea
Brotton
STOCKTON-ON-TEES
MIDDLESBROUGH
Skelton
Loftus
Staithes
Thornaby on Tees
Guisborough
Kettle Ness
DARLINGTON
Stainton
Hinderwell
Lythe
Hurworth-on-Tees
Eaglescliffe
Yarm
WHITBY
Barton
Stokesley
Great Ayton
Sneaton
Hawsker
Dalton
Hutton Rudby
Castleton
Egton
CROFT
Great Broughton
Sleights
Robin Hood's Bay
East Cowton
CLEVELAND HILLS
Goathland
Fylingdales Moor
Staintondale
Scorton
Catterick
Osmotherley
NORTH YORK MOORS NATIONAL PARK
Brompton
Rosedale Abbey
Cloughton
NORTH YORKSHIRE
Patrick Brompton
Leeming Bar
Northallerton
HAMBLETON HILLS
Burniston
Bedale
Hawnby
Hutton-le-Hole
Lockton
Scalby
WATERSPLASH WORLD
SCARBOROUGH
South Otterington
Knayton
Kirkbymoorside
NORTH YORKSHIRE MOORS RAILWAY
VALE OF YORK
Rievaulx
Ayton
Eastfield
Sutton-under-Whitestonecliffe
Thornton-le-Dale
Ebberston
Thirsk
Pickering
Seamer
Masham
Carlton Miniott
Helmsley
Snainton
Vale of Pickering
Filey
Sowerby
Ampleforth
FLAMINGO LAND
Staxton
LIGHTWATER VALLEY
Topcliffe
Hovingham
The Carrs
Sherburn
Hunmanby
Filey Bay
YORKSHIRE WOLDS
HOWARDIAN HILLS
Malton
Rillington
Burton Fleming
RIPON
Easingwold
Terrington
Norton
Flamborough
Flamborough Hd.
Weaverthorpe
FOUNTAINS ABBEY
Helperby
Stillington
Sheriff Hutton
Rudston
Boroughbridge
BRIDLINGTON
Bishop Monkton
Aldborough
Langtoft
Acklam
Sledmere
Kilham
Burton Agnes
Ripley
Strensall
Garton-on-the-Wolds
Bridlington Bay
Whixley
Fridaythorpe
Nafferton
Knaresborough
Haxby
Wetwang
Driffield
Lissett
Killinghall
New Earswick
HARROGATE
Green Hammerton
Upper Poppleton
Rawcliffe
Stamford Bridge
EAST RIDING OF YORKSHIRE
Skipsea
Beeford
Marston Moor
YORK
Dunnington
Bainton
Hutton Cranswick
North Frodingham
Spofforth
CITY OF YORK
Acomb
Fulford
Elvington
Barmby Moor
Pocklington
Hornsea
FREEPORT HORNSEA
Wetherby
Collingham
Boston Spa
Wheldrake
Middleton on the Wolds
Otley
HAREWOOD HOUSE
Harewood
Bramhope
Tadcaster
Escrick
Hayton
Market Weighton
Leven
LEEDS/BRADFORD
Beverley
Holme-on-Spalding-moor
Skirlaugh
HOLDERNESS
Aldbrough
Yeadon
WEST
LEEDS
Cawood
Riccall
North Newbald
Sherburn in Elmet
Barlby
Bubwith
Garforth
SELBY
South Cave
Cottingham
Sproatley
Pudsey
Kippax
Hemingbrough
KINGSTON UPON HULL
Marfleet
Preston
Withernsea
Morley
Rothwell
Hambleton
Howden
Hessle
Hedon
Burstwick
Hollym
Brough
North Ferriby
HUMBER BRIDGE
Paull
Keyingham
Batley
Castleford
Knottingley
Carlton
GOOLE
New Holland
Normanton
Snaith
Swinefleet
Barton-upon-Humber
Barrow upon Humber
Patrington
Ossett
WAKEFIELD
PONTEFRACT
Burton upon Stather
NORTH
Winterton
Humber
Easington
Mirfield
Sunk Island
YORKSHIRE
Hemsworth
Thorne
Roxby
Bonby
Ulceby
Immingham
Kilnsea
Kirkburton
Askern
Stainforth
Crowle
LINCOLNSHIRE
Stallingborough
Darton
Cudworth
Royston
South Kirkby
Adwick le Street
Hatfield
SCUNTHORPE
Keelby
GRIMSBY
Spurn Hd.
Shepley
Denby Dale
BARNSLEY
Bentley
Althorpe
Broughton
Barnetby le Wold
HUMBERSIDE
Cleethorpes
PLEASURE ISLAND THEME PARK
Laceby
Worsbrough
Armthorpe
Belton
Brigg
Penistone
Wombwell
Dearne
DONCASTER
Isle of Axholme
Messingham
Hibaldstow
Grasby
New Waltham
Humberston

NORTH AYRSHIRE
SOUTH LANARKSHIRE
EAST AYRSHIRE
SOUTH AYRSHIRE
DUMFRIES & GALLO
SOUTHERN UPLANDS
COWAL
CUNNINGHAME
KYLE
CARRICK
GALLOWAY
THE MACHARS
THE RHINS
BUTE
NORTH ARRAN
14
16
19
GLASGOW
GREENOCK
PAISLEY
ERSKINE BRIDGE
KINCARDINE BRIDGE
FORTH ROAD BRIDGE
STIRLING
EAST KILBRIDE
KILMARNOCK
IRVINE
AYR
DUMFRIES
STRANRAER
WORKINGTON
WHITEHAVEN
Dumbarton
Clydebank
Bearsden
Milngavie
Renfrew
Johnstone
Barrhead
Rutherglen
Uddingston
Hamilton
Motherwell
Wishaw
Airdrie
Coatbridge
Cumbernauld
Kirkintilloch
Kilsyth
Denny
Falkirk
Grangemouth
Bo'ness
Linlithgow
Bathgate
Livingston
Whitburn
Shotts
Alloa
Dunfermline
Helensburgh
Alexandria
Gourock
Dunoon
Rothesay
Largs
Ardrossan
Saltcoats
Stevenston
Kilwinning
Troon
Prestwick
Maybole
Girvan
Cumnock
Lanark
Carluke
Larkhall
Strathaven
Biggar
Moffat
Sanquhar
Kirkconnel
Thornhill
Castle Douglas
Dalbeattie
Kirkcudbright
Gatehouse of Fleet
Newton Stewart
Wigtown
Whithorn
Isle of Whithorn
Glenluce
Portpatrick
Port Logan
Drummore
Mull of Galloway
Burrow Hd.
Luce Bay
Wigtown Bay
Solway Firth
Firth of Clyde
Sound of Bute
Holy I.
Pladda
Ailsa Craig 334
Heads of Ayr
Brodick
Lamlash
Great Cumbrae Is.
Little Cumbrae Is.
Lochmaben
Lockerbie
Annan
Maryport
Cockermouth
Silloth
Aspatria
NITH ESTUARY
LARNE 1:49 (Mar-Sept)
LARNE 1:45
BELFAST 1:45
Queen Elizabeth Forest Park
Galloway Forest Park
Clyde-Muirshiel Regional Park
Pentland Hills Regional Park
Argyll Forest Park
Campsie Fells
Lennox Hills
Lowther Hills
Rhinns of Kells
The Glenkens
Nithsdale
Annandale
Clydesdale
MERRICK 844
CAIRNSMORE OF FLEET 710
GREEN LOWTHER 733
BROAD LAW 840
CULTER FELL 748
WHITE COOMB 822
GOAT FELL 874
BEN LOMOND
Loch Lomond
1 2 3 4 5 6 7
A B C D E F G H J

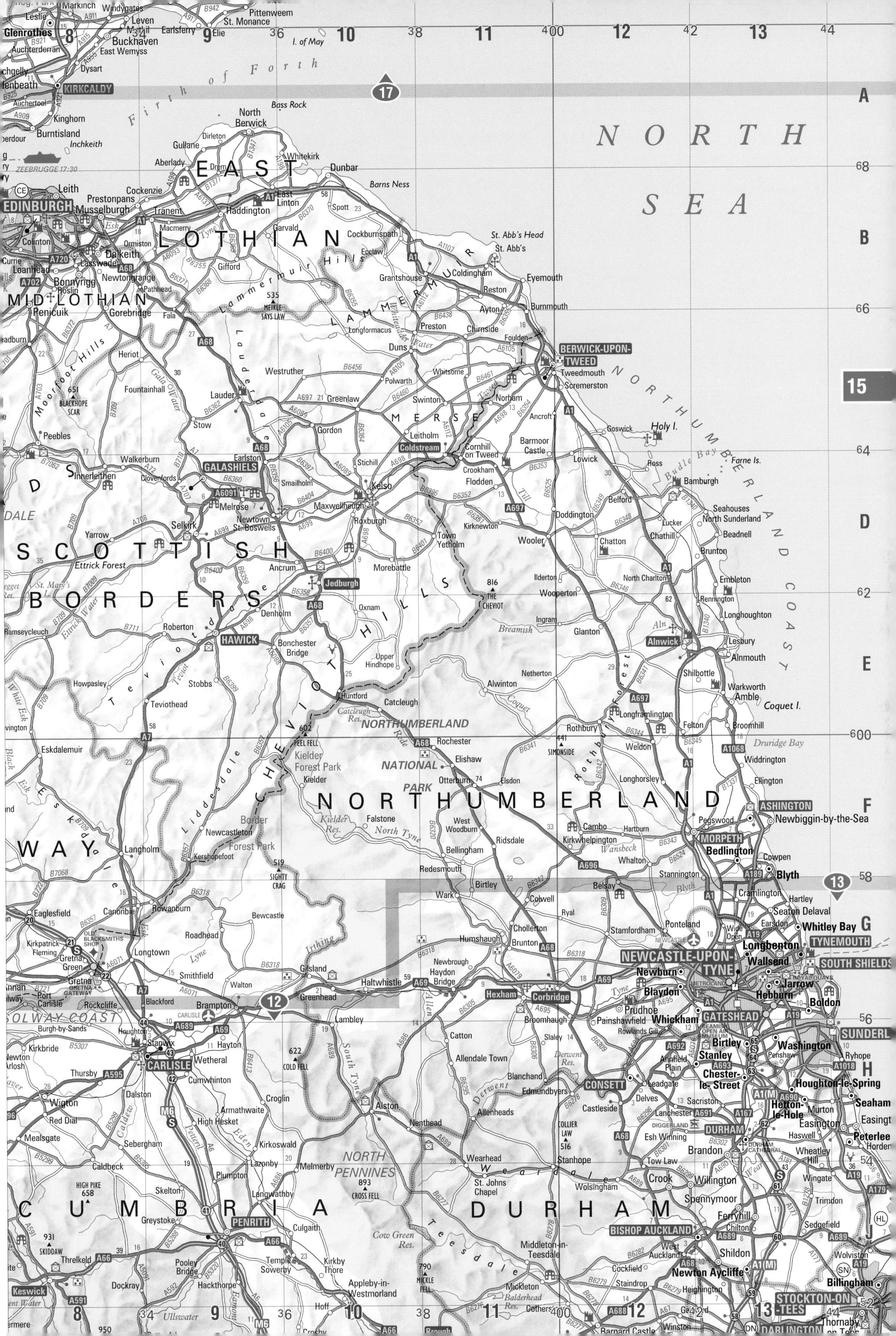

NORTH SEA
Firth of Forth
EAST LOTHIAN
MIDLOTHIAN
SCOTTISH BORDERS
NORTHUMBERLAND
NORTHUMBERLAND NATIONAL PARK
CUMBRIA
DURHAM
NORTH PENNINES
SOLWAY COAST
NORTHUMBERLAND COAST
CHEVIOT HILLS
LAMMERMUIR
Lammermuir Hills
Moorfoot Hills
MERSE
Lauderdale
Teviotdale
Liddesdale
Eskdale
Weardale
Teesdale
Redesdale
Ettrick Forest
Kielder Forest Park
Border Forest Park
Rothbury Forest
EDINBURGH
Leith
Musselburgh
Prestonpans
Dalkeith
Lasswade
Loanhead
Bonnyrigg
Penicuik
Gorebridge
Colinton
Currie
Glenrothes
Leslie
Leven
Methil
Buckhaven
East Wemyss
Dysart
KIRKCALDY
Kinghorn
Burntisland
Inchkeith
Elie
Earlsferry
St. Monance
Pittenweem
I. of May
Bass Rock
North Berwick
Dirleton
Gullane
Aberlady
Drem
Whitekirk
Dunbar
East Linton
Haddington
Tranent
Cockenzie
Macmerry
Ormiston
Gifford
Garvald
Spott
Barns Ness
Cockburnspath
St. Abb's Head
St. Abb's
Coldingham
Eyemouth
Reston
Burnmouth
Ayton
Grantshouse
Chirnside
Preston
Duns
Longformacus
Foulden
BERWICK-UPON-TWEED
Tweedmouth
Scremerston
Holy I.
Goswick
Ross
Budle Bay
Farne Is.
Bamburgh
Seahouses
North Sunderland
Beadnell
Lucker
Chathill
Belford
Lowick
Ancroft
Barmoor Castle
Norham
Swinton
Whitsome
Polwarth
Westruther
Greenlaw
Gordon
Leitholm
Coldstream
Cornhill on Tweed
Crookham
Flodden
Kelso
Stichill
Smailholm
Maxwellheugh
Roxburgh
Town Yetholm
Kirknewton
Doddington
Wooler
Chatton
Ilderton
Wooperton
North Charlton
Embleton
Rennington
Longhoughton
Lesbury
Alnmouth
Alnwick
Shilbottle
Warkworth
Amble
Coquet I.
Broomhill
Druridge Bay
Widdrington
Ellington
Felton
Longframlington
Weldon
Rothbury
Longhorsley
Glanton
Ingram
Netherton
Alnwinton
Breamish
THE CHEVIOT
SIMONSIDE
ASHINGTON
Newbiggin-by-the-Sea
Pegswood
MORPETH
Bedlington
Cowpen
Blyth
Stannington
Cramlington
Hartley
Seaton Delaval
Earsdon
Whitley Bay
TYNEMOUTH
SOUTH SHIELDS
Longbenton
Wallsend
Jarrow
Hebburn
Boldon
NEWCASTLE-UPON-TYNE
GATESHEAD
Newburn
Blaydon
Prudhoe
Whickham
Ponteland
Stamfordham
Belsay
Whalton
Hartburn
Cambo
Kirkwhelpington
Wansbeck
SUNDERLAND
Washington
Penshaw
Ryhope
Birtley
Stanley
Chester-le-Street
Houghton-le-Spring
Hetton-le-Hole
Seaham
Murton
Easington
Peterlee
Horden
Haswell
Wheatley Hill
Wingate
Trimdon
Sedgefield
DURHAM
Brandon
Sacriston
Lanchester
Esh Winning
Tow Law
Crook
Willington
Spennymoor
Ferryhill
Chilton
Shildon
West Auckland
BISHOP AUCKLAND
Newton Aycliffe
Heighington
Cockfield
Staindrop
Barnard Castle
Winston
Gainford
DARLINGTON
STOCKTON-ON-TEES
Thornaby-on-Tees
Billingham
Wolviston
CONSETT
Leadgate
Delves
Castleside
Annfield Plain
Stanhope
Wolsingham
Middleton-in-Teesdale
Mickleton
Cotherstone
Balderhead Res.
Cow Green Res.
CROSS FELL
MICKLE FELL
St. Johns Chapel
Wearhead
Allenheads
Nenthead
Alston
Allendale Town
Catton
Blanchland
Edmundbyers
Derwent Res.
Slaley
Hexham
Corbridge
Broomhaugh
Riding Mill
Haydon Bridge
Newbrough
Haltwhistle
Greenhead
Gilsland
Humshaugh
Chollerton
Brunton
Colwell
Ryal
Wark
Birtley
Bellingham
West Woodburn
Ridsdale
Otterburn
Elsdon
Elishaw
Rochester
Catcleugh
Catcleugh Res.
Kielder
Kielder Res.
Falstone
North Tyne
PEEL FELL
SIGHTY CRAG
Kershopefoot
Newcastleton
Bewcastle
Roadhead
Lambley
COLD FELL
Brampton
Walton
Smithfield
Longtown
Canonbie
Rowanburn
Langholm
Eskdalemuir
Teviothead
Stobbs
Howpasley
Hawick
Roberton
Denholm
Bonchester Bridge
Upper Hindhope
Huntford
Jedburgh
Oxnam
Morebattle
Ancrum
Newtown St. Boswells
Melrose
Galashiels
Selkirk
Clovenfords
Innerleithen
Walkerburn
Peebles
Earlston
Stow
Lauder
Heriot
Fala
Fountainhall
MEIKLE SAYS LAW
BLACKHOPE SCAR
Yarrow
St. Mary's Loch
Ramseycleuch
Eaglesfield
Kirkpatrick-Fleming
Gretna Green
Gretna
Gretna Gateway
Port Carlisle
Rockcliffe
Blackford
Burgh-by-Sands
Houghton
Stanwix
CARLISLE
Wetheral
Hayton
Cumwhinton
Kirkbride
Thursby
Wigton
Red Dial
Dalston
Mealsgate
Sebergham
Caldbeck
HIGH PIKE
Armathwaite
High Hesket
Croglin
Kirkoswald
Lazonby
Melmerby
Plumpton
Langwathby
Skelton
Greystoke
PENRITH
Culgaith
Temple Sowerby
Kirkby Thore
Appleby-in-Westmorland
Hoff
Pooley Bridge
Dockray
Hackthorpe
Threlkeld
SKIDDAW
Keswick
Ullswater
Eamont
Eden
Caldew
Petteril
South Tyne
Irthing
Lyne
Coquet
Allen
Derwent
Wear
Tyne
Tweed
Till
Aln
Whiteadder Water
Gala Water
Teviot
White Esk
Black Esk
Ettrick Water
ZEEBRUGGE 17:30
OLD BLACKSMITHS SHOP
BEAMISH OPEN AIR MUSEUM
DURHAM CATHEDRAL
METROLAND
ROYAL QUAYS
DIGGERLAND
15
17
13
12

Coulags
Monar Forest
1052
SGURR A' CHOIRE GHLAIS 1083
Beauly
Beauly Firth
Kessock
Culloden
Balloch
Cawdor
INVERNESS
Ferness
H I G H L A N D
Lochcarron
L. Monar
Monar Lodge
Struy
THE AIRD
Craggie
GLEN STRATHFARRAR
SGURR NA LAPAICH 1150
Stromeferry
L. Mullardoch
Liatrie
Cannich
Strath Glass
Drumnadrochit
Dores
Farr
Moy
Lettoch
Dornie
Elchaig
1182 CARN EIGE
Glen Affric
Affric Lodge
Lewiston
L. Duntelchaig
Torness
Tomatin
659 CARN GLAS-CHOIRE
Grantown-on-Spey
Dulnain Bridge
Inverinate
KINTAIL
MEALFUARVONIE 696
Errogie
Carrbridge
Nethy Bridge
Glenelg
Shiel Bridge
GLEN AFFRIC
FIVE SISTERS 1068
Foyers
Boat of Garten
1120 A'CHRALAIG
Invermoriston
Loch Ness
Strath Dearn
1012 THE SADDLE
Glen Shiel
Glen Moriston
White Bridge
810 CARN NA SAOBHAIDHE
Aviemore
Glen More Forest Park
Arnisdale
L. Cluanie
Fort Augustus
Coignafearn Lodge
Alvie
Glenmore Lodge
L. Loyne
GLEN MOR
MONADHLIATH MTS.
Kincraig
STRATH SPEY
CAIRN GORM 1245
L. Quoich
Coille Mhorgil
Tomdoun
941 CARN BAN
Kingussie
KNOYDART
Glen Garry
Invergarry
L. Garry
Newtonmore
Ruthven
CAIRNGORM MTS.
1295 BRAERIACH
1309 BEN MACDHUI
1040 SGURR NA CICHE
16
Laggan
Carnachuin
Murlaggan
L. Lochy
Laggan
Drumgask
L. Arkaig
Brae Roy Lodge
CREAG MEAGAIDH 1128
LOCHABER
983 CULVAIN
Clunes
Glen Roy
Glen Spean
L. Laggan
BADENOCH
Gairlochy
Gaick Lodge
MOUNTAIN
Dalwhinnie
Glenfinnan
Kinlocheil
Roybridge
Spean Bridge
L. Eil
Corpach
Caol
Achaphubuil
FORT WILLIAM
1342 BEN NEVIS
L. Treig
GRAMPIAN
1148 BEN ALDER
L. Ericht
Dalnaspidal
1008 BEN DEARG
Forest of Atholl
1121 BEINN A' GHLO
Spittle of Glenshee
LOCH SHIEL
ARDGOUR
Achriabhach
BEN NEVIS
PERTH
Corran
Onich
Kinlochleven
L. Errochty
Glen Garry
Blair Atholl
Strontian
888
KINGAIRLOCH
L. Leven
Blackwater Res.
Tay Forest Park
Glencoe
Ballachulish
Rannoch Station
Kinloch Rannoch
Tummel Bridge
L. Tummel
Kirkmichael
Pitlochry
Glen Coe
1148 BIDEAN NAM BIAN
L. Laidon
L. Rannoch
1081 SCHIEHALLION
AND
APPIN
Tay Forest Park
Rannoch Moor
RANNOCH
LOCH RANNOCH
Strath Tay
Ballinluig
Portnacroish
Glen Etive
1098 CLACH LEATHAD
GLEN COE
Keltneyburn
Aberfeldy
RIVER TAY
BENDERLOCH
L. Creran
L. Tulla
1079
Glen Lyon
Bridge of Balgie
Fearnan
Kenmore
Dalguise
LYNN OF LORN
Achnacroish
BEN LAWERS 1214
GLEN LYON
KINROSS
Dunkeld
Bridge of Orchy
1074 BEN DORAIN
Lawers
L. Tay
Ardtalnaig
Garrow
Loch Etive
BREADALBANE
Glen Orchy
Amulree
Connel
Taynuilt
BEN CRUACHAN 1126
Killin
Bankfoot
Oban
Glen Almond
LORN
Tyndrum
Ardchyle
930 BEN CHONZIE
Harrietfield
Kilbride
Dalmally
1130 BEN LUI
Crianlarich
1174 BEN MORE
Lochearnhead
L. Earn
St. Fillans
Methven
Kilchrenan
Cladich
Balquhidder
Comrie
Gilmerton
Crieff
Kilninver
983 BEN VORLICH
Strath Earn
Bridge of Earn
Inverlochlarig
L. Voil
LOCH LOMOND AND THE TROSSACHS NATIONAL PARK
Ardlui
Strathyre
Muthill
L. Avich
STIRLING
Auchterarder
Dunning
Kilmelford
Cairndow
1011 BEN IME
Stronachlachar
Gleneagles
Blackford
Inveraray
Inversnaid
L. Katrine
THE TROSSACHS
Callander
Greenloaning
729 BEN VENUE
Tarbet
973 BEN LOMOND
Arrochar
Kinbuck
Sheriff Muir
Ford
ARGYLL
Furnace
Strachur
Lochgoilhead
Argyll Forest Park
Aberfoyle
Doune
Dunblane
720
OCHIL HILLS
BEINN BHEULA 779
Queen Elizabeth Forest Park
Thornhill
Bridge of Allan
Menstrie
Alva
Dollar
Kilmartin
Garbhallt
Loch Lomond
Kippen
STIRLING
Alloa
Tillicoultry
Dunans
COWAL
Carrick
Luss
Buchlyvie
Gargunnock
KNOCKHILL
Saline
Lochgair
Garelochhead
Faslane
Drymen
Balfron
Bannockburn
Clackmannan
Kincardine
Dunfermline
Ardentinny
Coulport
Killearn
Fintry
Lennox Hills
Plean
Airth
Culross
KINCARDINE BRIDGE
Otter Ferry
Helensburgh
Balloch
Campsie Fells
Carron Valley Res.
Dunipace
Stenhousemuir
Larbert
Grangemouth
Rosneath
Jamestown
578
Denny
Kilfinan
Sandbank
Strone
Kilcreggan
Alexandria
Bonhill
Strathblane
Kilsyth
Falkirk
Bo'ness
Glenstriven
Cove
Gourock
Cardross
Lennoxtown
Bonnybridge
Tighnabruaich
Kames
Colintraive
Rhubodach
Dunoon
GREENOCK
Dumbarton
Milngavie
Kirkintilloch
Cumbernauld
Linlithgow
Port Glasgow
ERSKINE BRIDGE
Bearsden
Bishopbriggs
Broxburn
Portavadie
Innellan
Wemyss Bay
Clydebank
Muirhead
Slamannan
Bathgate
Tarbert
Kilmacolm
Erskine
Airdrie
Armadale
Port Bannatyne
Kelmorlie
Clyde-Muirshiel Regional Park
Bridge of Weir
Renfrew
Caldercruix
Rothesay
Craigmore
PAISLEY
GLASGOW
Coatbridge
Harthill
Whitburn

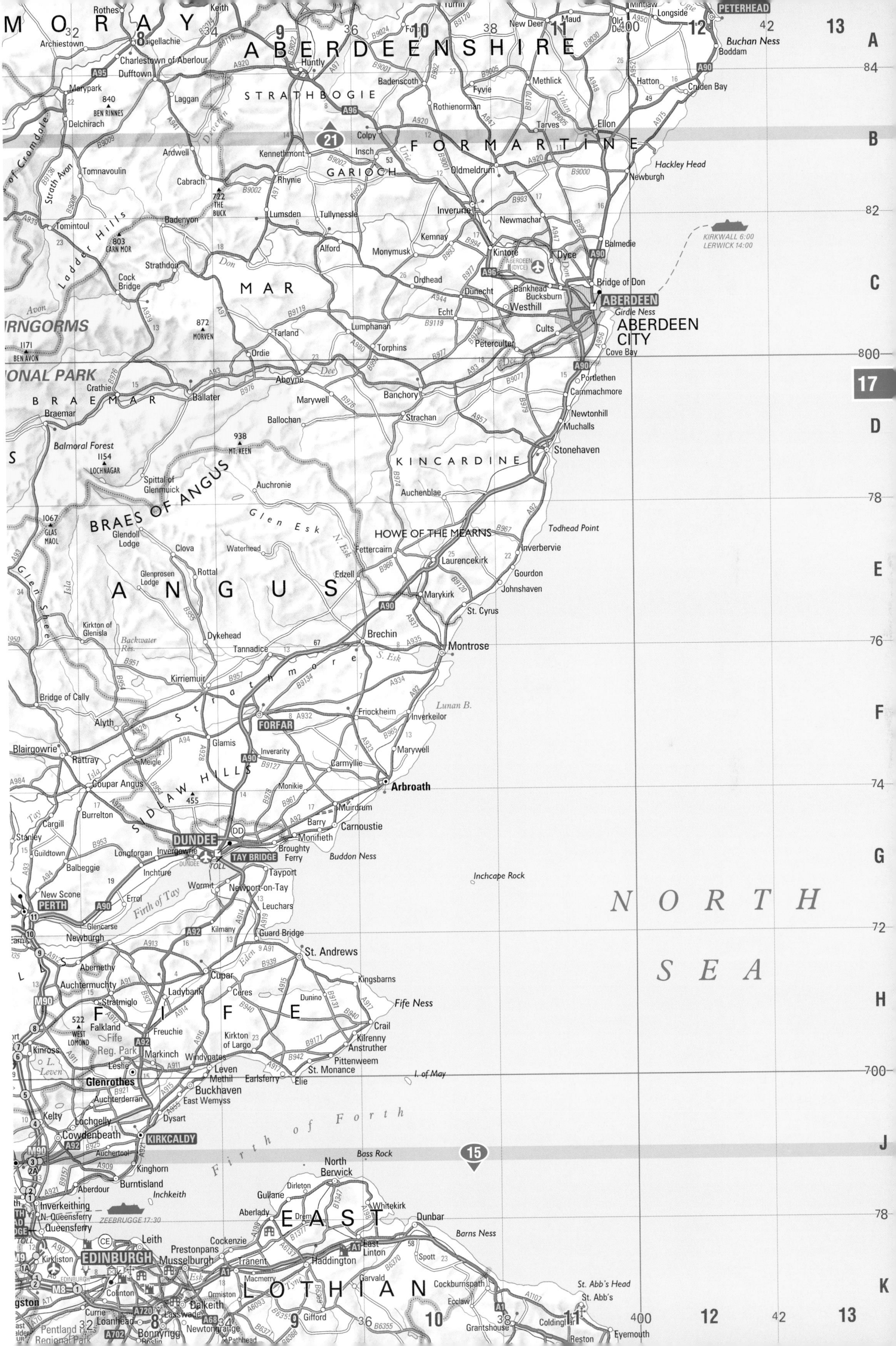

MORAY
ABERDEENSHIRE
PETERHEAD
Buchan Ness
Boddam
Rothes
Keith
Archiestown
Craigellachie
Charlestown of Aberlour
Dufftown
Huntly
STRATHBOGIE
Marypark
840 BEN RINNES
Laggan
Delchirach
Badenscoth
Fyvie
Methlick
Rothienorman
Hatton
Cruden Bay
New Deer
Maud
Longside
Tarves
Ellon
FORMARTINE
Colpy
Insch
Kennethmont
Ardwell
Tomnavoulin
Cabrach
722 THE BUCK
Rhynie
GARIOCH
Oldmeldrum
Hackley Head
Newburgh
Strath Avon
Tomintoul
Ladder Hills
803 CARN MOR
Badenyon
Lumsden
Tullynessle
Inverurie
Newmachar
Kemnay
Balmedie
KIRKWALL 6:00
LERWICK 14:00
Alford
Monymusk
Kintore
Dyce
ABERDEEN (DYCE)
Strathdon
Cock Bridge
Ordhead
Bankhead
Bucksburn
Bridge of Don
ABERDEEN
ABERDEEN CITY
Girdle Ness
MAR
Dunecht
Westhill
Echt
CAIRNGORMS
872 MORVEN
Tarland
Lumphanan
Cults
Peterculter
Cove Bay
1171 BEN AVON
Ordie
Torphins
NATIONAL PARK
Crathie
Ballater
Aboyne
Dee
Banchory
Portlethen
Cammachmore
BRAEMAR
Braemar
Marywell
Strachan
Newtonhill
Muchalls
Ballochan
Balmoral Forest
938 MT. KEEN
Stonehaven
1154 LOCHNAGAR
KINCARDINE
Spittal of Glenmuick
BRAES OF ANGUS
Auchronie
Auchenblae
1067 GLAS MAOL
Glen Esk
Glendoll Lodge
Todhead Point
HOWE OF THE MEARNS
Fettercairn
Inverbervie
Clova
Waterhead
Laurencekirk
Gourdon
Glenprosen Lodge
Rottal
Edzell
Johnshaven
ANGUS
Glen Shee
Marykirk
St. Cyrus
Kirkton of Glenisla
Backwater Res.
Dykehead
Brechin
Montrose
Tannadice
Kirriemuir
Strathmore
Bridge of Cally
Lunan B.
Friockheim
Inverkeilor
Alyth
FORFAR
Blairgowrie
Rattray
Glamis
Inverarity
Marywell
Meigle
Carmyllie
Coupar Angus
SIDLAW HILLS
Monikie
Arbroath
455
Cargill
Burrelton
Muirdrum
Barry
Carnoustie
Stanley
DUNDEE
Monifieth
Broughty Ferry
Guildtown
Longforgan
Invergowrie
TAY BRIDGE
TOLL
Buddon Ness
Balbeggie
Inchture
Tayport
Inchcape Rock
New Scone
PERTH
Errol
Wormit
Newport-on-Tay
Firth of Tay
Leuchars
NORTH SEA
Glencarse
Newburgh
Kilmany
Guard Bridge
St. Andrews
Abernethy
Cupar
Kingsbarns
Auchtermuchty
Ladybank
Ceres
Dunino
Fife Ness
Strathmiglo
FIFE
522 WEST LOMOND
Falkland
Freuchie
Crail
Fife Reg. Park
Kirkton of Largo
Kilrenny
Anstruther
Kinross
Markinch
Windygates
Pittenweem
L. Leven
Leslie
Glenrothes
Leven
Methil
Earlsferry
Elie
St. Monance
I. of May
Buckhaven
East Wemyss
Auchterderran
Kelty
Lochgelly
Dysart
Firth of Forth
Cowdenbeath
KIRKCALDY
Bass Rock
Auchtertool
Kinghorn
North Berwick
Burntisland
Aberdour
Inchkeith
Dirleton
Gullane
Whitekirk
Inverkeithing
N. Queensferry
Queensferry
ZEEBRUGGE 17:30
Aberlady
Drem
EAST
Dunbar
Barns Ness
Leith
Cockenzie
Prestonpans
East Linton
EDINBURGH
Musselburgh
Tranent
Haddington
Spott
Kirkliston
Garvald
Macmerry
LOTHIAN
Cockburnspath
St. Abb's Head
St. Abb's
Colinton
Ormiston
Ecclaw
Currie
Dalkeith
Lasswade
Loanhead
Pentland Hills Regional Park
Bonnyrigg
Newtongrange
Pathhead
Gifford
Grantshouse
Coldingham
Reston
Eyemouth
A
B
C
D
E
F
G
H
J
K
84
82
800
78
76
74
72
700
78
17

18
SOUTH UIST
HECLA 605
620 BEN MHOR
Tobha Mor
Rubha Ardvule
L. Eynort
Dalabrog
Loch Baghasdail (Lochboisdale)
L. Boisdale
SOUTH UIST MACHAIR
Cille Bhrighde
Sound of Barra
Sd. of Eriskay
Eriskay
Greian Hd.
BARRA
HEAVAL 384
Bruernish Pt.
Bagh a Chaisteil (Castlebay)
Vatersay
Sandray
Pabbay
Mingulay
Berneray
Neist Pt.
Roskhill
HEALAVAL BHEAG
L. Bracadale
Bracadale
Coillore
Fernilea
Carbost
MINGINISH
Drynoch
Sligachan
Glenbrittle
THE CUILLIN HILLS
CUILLIN HILLS
1009
775 GLAMAIG
928 BLA BHEINN
Rubh' a Dunain
Soay
Soay Sd.
L. Scavaig
Elgol
L. Eishort
Portree
Sconser
Narrows
Clachan
Brochel
RAASAY
Scalpay
Crowlin Is.
Toscaig
App
Broadford
Breakish
Kyleakin
Kyle of Lochalsh
Kylerhea
Tarskavaig
Teangue
Armadale
Ardvasar
Eilean Iarmain
Sd. of Sleat
Pt. of Sleat
Canna
Sanday
Sd. of Canna
Kilmory
Kinloch
RÙM
810
Harris
THE SMALL ISLES
Sound of Rùm
Cleadale
Eigg
394
Galmisdale
Sd. of Eigg
Muck
INNER HEBRIDES
Cuillin Sound
HIGHLAND
SKYE
Kishorn
L. Carron
Ardarroch
Stromemore
Plockton
Stromeferry
Lochcarron
Coulags
Auchtertyre
L. Alsh
Dornie
Inverinate
KINTAIL
Glenelg
Shiel Bridge
FIVE SISTERS 1068
1012 THE SADDLE
Glen Shiel
Arnisdale
L. Hourn
Airor
LADHAR BHEINN 1019
KNOYDART
Inverie
L. Nevis
Mallaig
Morar
L. Morar
Tarbet
1040 SGURR NA CICHE
Arisaig
Sd. of Arisaig
Lochailort
Glenfinnan
MORAR, MOIDART & ARDNAMURCHAN
882 RHOIS-BHEINN
MOIDART
Shona I.
L. Moidart
Kinlochmoidart
LOCH SHIEL
Loch Shiel
Pt. of Ardnamurchan
Achosnich
Kilmory
ARDNAMURCHAN
Acharacle
Kilchoan
527 BEN HIANT
Mingary
Salen
Glenborrodale
L. Sunart
Polloch
SUNART
Strontian
888
ARDGOUR
Corran
Sorisdale
COLL
Clabhach
Arinagour
Acha
TIREE
Caoles
Scarinish
Middleton
Hynish B.
Hynish
Passage of Tiree
Caliach Pt.
Treshnish Is.
Tobermory
Calgary
Dervaig
L. Frisa
Drimnin
MORVERN
Claggan
Lochaline
Sound of Mull
L. Tuath
Ulva
Gometra
Oskamull
LOCH NA KEAL, ISLE OF MULL
Staffa
Salen
Fishnish
MULL
966 BEN MORE
Craignure
Lochdon
L. Spelve
Croggan
L. Scridain
Pennyghael
Lochbuie
L. Buie
Carsaig
Iona
Fionnphort
Bunessan
ROSS OF MULL
Lismore I.
LYNN OF LORN
KINGAIRLOCH
Loch Linnhe
Achnacroish
Kerrera
Oban
Kilbride
Kilninver
LORN
ARGYLL
Connel
Taynuilt
BENDERLOCH
L. Creran
Portnacroish
APPIN
BEN CRUACHAN 1126
Loch Etive
Kilchrenan
Cladich
Dalmally
1130 BEN LUI
Glen Orchy
Bridge of Orchy
L. Tulla
Glen Etive
GLEN COE
1098 CLACH LEATHAD
1148 BIDEAN NAM BIAN
Glen Coe
Glencoe
Ballachulish
Kinlochleven
L. Leven
Onich
BEN NEVIS
Achriabhach
1342 BEN NEVIS
FORT WILLIAM
Achaphubuil
Corpach
Caol
L. Eil
Kinlocheil
Caledonian Canal
Gairlochy
L. Lochy
Clunes
Spean Bridge
Royb
LOCHABER
L. Arkaig
983 CULVAIN
Murlaggan
Glen Garry
L. Garry
Invergarry
Coille Mhorgil
Tomdoun
L. Quoich
L. Loyne
L. Cluanie
Glen Moriston
1120 A' CHRALAIG
GLEN AFFRIC
Glen Affric
Affric Lodge
1182 CARN EIGE
L. Mullardoch
Ling
Elchaig
SGURR NA LAPAICH 1150
Liatrie
Monar Forest 1052
L. Monar
Monar Lodge
SGURR A' CHOIRE GHLAS 1083

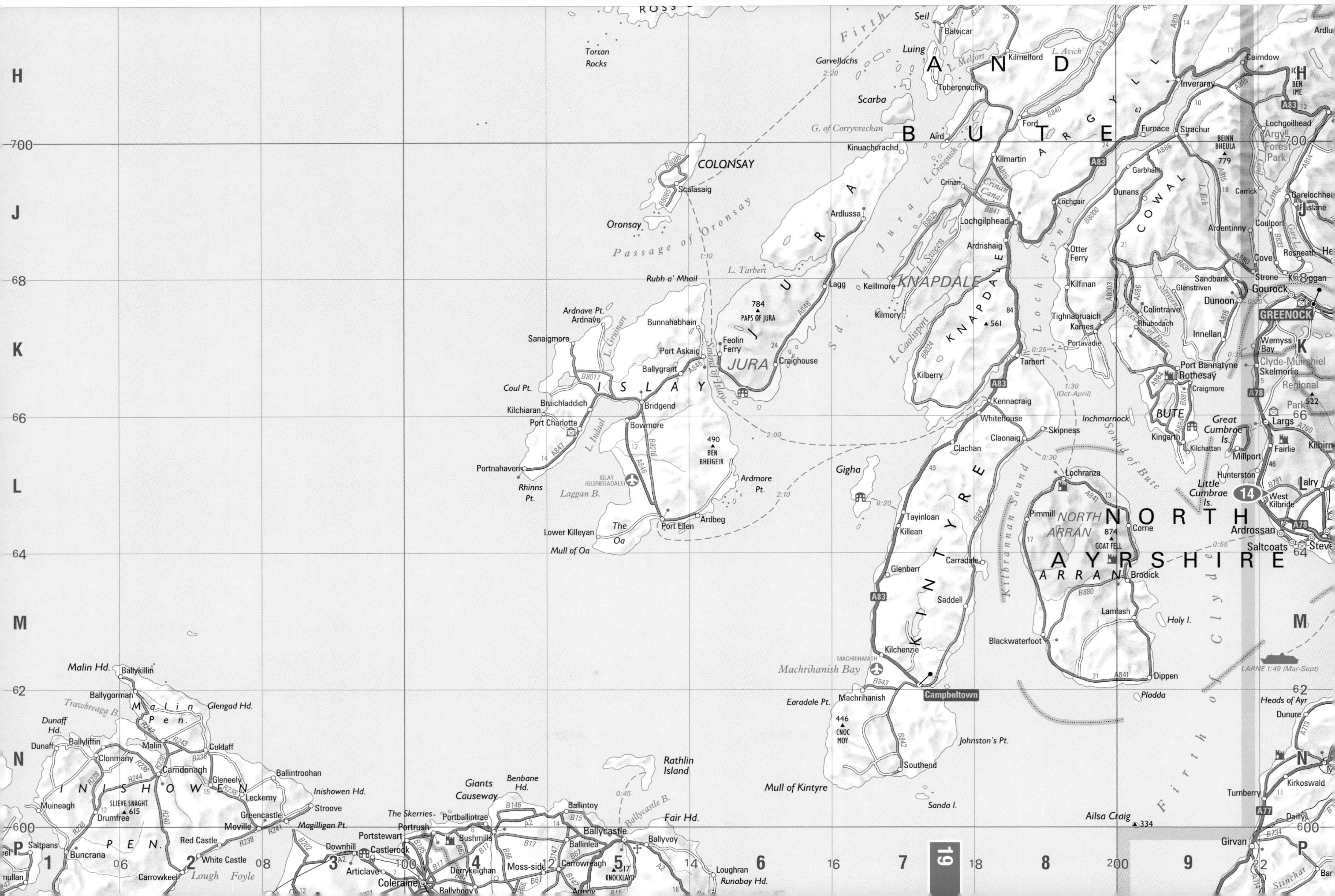

ARGYLL AND BUTE
NORTH AYRSHIRE
COWAL
KNAPDALE
KINTYRE
JURA
ISLAY
ARRAN
NORTH ARRAN
INISHOWEN PEN.
Malin Pen.
COLONSAY
Oronsay
Scalasaig
Passage of Oronsay
Torran Rocks
Seil
Balvicar
Luing
Garvellachs
Firth of Lorn
Scarba
G. of Corryvreckan
Kilmelford
L. Melfort
L. Avich
Toberonochy
Ford
Aird
Kinuachdrachd
Inveraray
Cairndow
Furnace
Strachur
BEINN BHEULA 779
BEN IME
Lochgoilhead
Argyll Forest Park
L. Goil
L. Long
Carrick
Garelochhead
Lisiane
Coulport
Ardentinny
Cove
Rosneath
Strone
Kilcreggan
Gourock
GREENOCK
Sandbank
Dunoon
Glenstriven
L. Striven
Innellan
Colintraive
Rhubodach
Kyles of Bute
Wemyss Bay
Clyde-Muirshiel Regional Park
522
Skelmorlie
Port Bannatyne
Rothesay
Craigmore
BUTE
Kingarth
Kilchattan
Great Cumbrae Is.
Millport
Little Cumbrae Is.
Largs
Fairlie
Kilbirnie
Hunterston
West Kilbride
Dalry
Ardrossan
Saltcoats
Stevenston
Garbhallt
Dunans
L. Eck
Otter Ferry
Kilfinan
Tighnabruaich
Kames
Portavadie
Lochgair
Loch Fyne
Kilmartin
Crinan
Crinan Canal
L. Craignish
Lochgilphead
Ardrishaig
L. Sween
Keillmore
Kilmory
L. Caolisport
Kilberry
561
Tarbert
Kennacraig
Whitehouse
Claonaig
Skipness
Inchmarnock
Sound of Bute
Ardlussa
Lagg
784 PAPS OF JURA
L. Tarbert
Rubh a' Mhail
Sound of Jura
Feolin Ferry
Craighouse
Sound of Islay
Bunnahabhain
Port Askaig
Ballygrant
Bridgend
Bowmore
Ardnave Pt.
Ardnave
Sanaigmore
L. Gruinart
Coul Pt.
Bruichladdich
Kilchiaran
Port Charlotte
L. Indaal
Portnahaven
Rhinns Pt.
ISLAY (GLENEGADALE)
Laggan B.
490 BEN BHEIGEIR
Ardmore Pt.
The Oa
Port Ellen
Ardbeg
Lower Killeyan
Mull of Oa
Gigha
Clachan
Tayinloan
Killean
Carradale
Glenbarr
Saddell
Kilbrannan Sound
Kilchenzie
MACHRIHANISH
Machrihanish Bay
Machrihanish
Campbeltown
Earadale Pt.
446 CNOC MOY
Johnston's Pt.
Southend
Sanda I.
Mull of Kintyre
Lochranza
Pirnmill
Corrie
874 GOAT FELL
Brodick
Lamlash
Holy I.
Blackwaterfoot
Dippen
Pladda
Firth of Clyde
Ailsa Craig 334
LARNE 1:49 (Mar-Sept)
Heads of Ayr
Dunure
Kirkoswald
Turnberry
Girvan
Stinchar
Malin Hd.
Ballykillin
Ballygorman
Trawbreaga B.
Glengad Hd.
Dunaff Hd.
Dunaff
Ballyliffin
Clonmany
Malin
Culdaff
Carndonagh
Gleneely
Ballintroohan
Inishowen Hd.
Leckemy
Muineagh
SLIEVE SNAGHT 615
Drumfree
Greencastle
Stroove
Moville
Magilligan Pt.
Saltpans
Buncrana
Red Castle
White Castle
Carrowkeel
Lough Foyle
Downhill
Castlerock
Articlave
Coleraine
Portstewart
Portrush
The Skerries
Portballintrae
Bushmills
Giants Causeway
Benbane Hd.
Derrykeighan
Moss-side
Ballintoy
Ballycastle
Ballinlea
Carrowreagh
Ballycastle B.
Ballyvoy
Fair Hd.
517 KNOCKLAYD
Rathlin Island
Loughran
Runabay Hd.
Armoy
Ballybogy
1:10
2:00
2:10
2:20
1:30 (Oct-April)
0:25
0:30
0:20
0:35
0:45
0:55
H
J
K
L
M
N
P
700
68
66
64
62
600
1
06
2
08
3
100
4
12
5
14
6
16
7
18
8
200
9
22
14

1
18
2
200
3
22
4
24
5
26
6
28
7
A
B
C
D
E
F
G
H
J
K
98
96
94
92
900
88
86
84
82
20
C. Wrath
Kyle of Durness
Faraid Hd.
Durness
Achiemore
Whiten Hd.
Strathan
Kyle of Tongue
Strathy Pt.
Portskerra
Strathy
Bettyhill
A836
25
Craigtown
Dalhalvaig
Forsinain
Sheigra
L. Inchard
Kinlochbervie
B801
A838
18
L. Eriboll
Heilam
A838
28
Eriboll
Tongue
A836
Borgie
KYLE OF TONGUE
Rhiconich
L. Laxford
908
FOINAVEN
L. Hope
927
BEN HOPE
763
BEN LOYAL
Strathmore
Handa I.
Scourie
A894
Laxford Bridge
Reay Forest
NORTH-WEST SUTHERLAND
L. Loyal
B871
Strath Naver
Naver
721
BEN STACK
L. More
A838
Eddrachillis Bay
Pt. of Stoer
Kylestrome
Unapool
Kinloch
873
BEN HEE
Altnaharra
B873
L. Naver
L. nan Clar
B871
36
Kinbrace
Culkein
Drumbeg
B869
ASSYNT
809
QUINAG
A894
961
BEN KLIBRECK
36
L. Choire
Strath of Kildonan
Stoer
A837
L. Assynt
SUTHERLAND
36
Altanduino
Inchnadamph
28
Lochinver
998
BEN MORE ASSYNT
Enard B.
Inverkirkaig
847
CANISP
A836
A838
Black Water
Rubha Coigeach
ASSYNT-COIGACH
Glen Oykel
Duchally
Loch Shin
Dalnessie
HIGHLANDS
N o r t h   M i n c h
Reiff
A837
Ledmore
Elphin
STORNOWAY 2:40
Summer Is.
Cromalt Hills
A836
Langwell
Brora
L. Brora
Achiltibuie
L. Lurgainn
A835
Sallachy
Lairg
Achavraie
COIGACH
16
14
A839
Rogart
Torroble
Strathkanaird
A837
Lubcroy
18
Rosehall
A839
9
B864
10
Greenstone Pt.
Gruinard B.
L. Broom
Oykel Bridge
Oykel
Altass
A837
Fleet
Golspie
Inveran
Shin
L. Fleet
Cove
L. Ewe
Mellon Charles
Laide
39
Badrallach
Alt na h'Airbhe
Ullapool
Culrain
Bonarbridge
DORNOCH FIRTH
Embo
Aultbea
B8057
Ardessie
Ardcharnich
Freevater Forest
Croick
Ardgay
Kincardine
A949
Clashmore
11
Dornoch
A949
Melvaig
A832
12
Carron
13
A836
Dornoch Firth
B8021
1062
AN TEALLACH
A835
EASTER ROSS
Edderton
Tain
L. na Sealga
1081
BEN DEARG
A9
Longa I.
Poolewe
Fionn L.
A832
Braemore
710
BEN THARSUINN
B9176
14
L. Gairloch
Gairloch
L. Maree
WESTER ROSS
Fearn
Port Henderson
B8056
Kerrysdale
Balintore
Kilmuir
1109
SGURR MOR
L. Glascarnoch
L. Glas
Alness
A9
Nigg B.
B9175
Red Point
Talladale
18
981
SLIOCH
56
20
1045
BEN WYVIS
Alness
Invergordon
Balnapaling
22
L. Fannich
A835
B817
Cromarty Firth
Balblair
L. Torridon
A832
Evanton
B9163
Cromarty
Rona
WESTER ROSS
Cullicudden
Diabaig
Kinlochewe
Achanalt
Garve
BLACK ISLE
A832
B9160
LIATHACH 1053
8
9
A832
L. Luichart
Strathpeffer
A834
Dingwall
B9169
Rosemarkie
Nairn
Fasag
Torridon
Achnasheen
Milton
Contin
Fortrose
B9092
Inner Sound
Shieldaig
A890
Strathconon
Cononbridge
22
Avoch
Ardersier
17
24
Munlochy
INVERNESS AIRPORT
B9091
B9101
Applecross Forest
A896
23
Achnashellach
Scardoy
Glen Orrin
Muir of Ord
A832
A9
North Kessock
B9039
A96
B9006
Cawdor
Carron
Monar Forest
1083
SGURR A' CHOIRE GHLAIS
Beauly
Beauly Firth
Culloden
Balloch
Applecross
Coulags
1052
L. Monar
A831
Beauly
INVERNESS
L. Kishorn
HIGHLAND
Monar Lodge
THE AIRD
Struy
Toscaig
Ardarroch
Lochcarron
GLEN STRATHFARRAR
A833
B861
Nairn
Craggie
Crowlin Is.
Strathcarron
Stromemore
A890
Ling
SGURR NA LAPAICH 1150
Strath Glass
Caledonian Canal
B862
B9154
Plockton
13
Liatrie
Dores
Moy
L. Carron
Stromeferry
L. Mullardoch
27
27
Scalpay
Cannich
A831
Drumnadrochit
A82
Farr
Kyle of Lochalsh
5
Auchtertyre
Elchaig
18
Affric
Lewiston
L. Duntelchaig
16
659 CARN GLAS-CHOIRE
Kyleakin
L. Alsh
Dornie
1182
CARN EIGE
Glen Affric
B852
Torness
B862
B851
Tomatin
A87
A87
Loch Ness
MEALFUARVONIE 696
A9
Broadford
Breakish
Inverinate
Affric Lodge
L. Affric
Errogie
Dulnain
Strath Dearn
54
82
Kylerhea
KINTAIL
Foyers
A851
Glenelg
Shiel Bridge
FIVE SISTERS 1068
GLEN AFFRIC
Invermoriston
13
810
CARN NA SAOBHAIDHE
Eilean Iarmain
1120
A'CHRALAIG
30
52
A887
17
White Bridge
Coignafearn Lodge
Aviemore
1012
THE SADDLE
Glen Moriston
L. Hourn
Arnisdale
Glen Shiel
L. Cluanie
Fort Augustus
B862
MONADHLIATH MTS.
10
Alvie
Teangue
Snd. of Sleat
Airor
LADHAR BHEINN 1019
L. Quoich
L. Loyne
Coille Mhorgil
Tomdoun
A87
14
A82
941
CARN BAN
Kincraig
Kingussie

21
Tor Ness
Hurliness
South Walls
Swona
South Ronaldsay
Burwick
Cleat
Pentland Firth
STROMNESS 1:30
Dunnet Hd.
Stroma
Muckle Skerries
John o' Groats
Duncansby Head
Duncansby
Brough
Mey
Canisbay
Holborn Hd.
Scrabster
Thurso
Dunnet
Dunnet B.
Dounreay
Castletown
Freswick
Reay
Nybster
L. Calder
Sordale
Sortat
Keiss
Halkirk
Hastigrow
Sinclair's B.
Olgrinmore
Reiss
Noss Hd.
Watten
Staxigoe
Mybster
Wick
Strath Halladale
CAITHNESS
Forsinard
Thrumster
Achavanich
Ulbster
Halberry Head
Lybster
Latheron
Braemore
Dunbeath
MORVEN
Kildonan
Berriedale
Ousdale
Ord of Caithness
Helmsdale
BEN DHORAIN
Brora
Tarbat Ness
Portmahomack
Moray Firth
Branderburgh
Lossiemouth
Burghead
Hopeman
Burghead B.
Findhorn
ELGIN
Garmouth
Spey B.
Buckie
Findochty
Portknockie
Cullen
Portsoy
Troup Hd.
Rosehearty
Kinnairds Hd.
FRASERBURGH
Kinloss
Lhanbryde
Portgordon
Fordyce
Banff
Macduff
Gardenstown
Pennan
New Aberdour
Inverallochy
St. Combs
Rathen
Forres
Barnhill
Fochabers
Craibstone
Weachyburn
Strichen
Crimond
Rattray Hd.
Auldearn
Kellas
Dallas
Newmill
Aberchirder
Newbyth
New Pitsligo
St. Fergus
Littlemill
Mulben
Cuminestown
Rothes
Keith
Turriff
BUCHAN
Mintlaw
PETERHEAD
MORAY
Longside
Old Deer
Maud
New Deer
Fortrie
Buchan Ness
Boddam
Ferness
Archiestown
Craigellachie
Charlestown of Aberlour
ABERDEENSHIRE
Dufftown
Huntly
Methlick
Fyvie
Badenscoth
Hatton
Cruden Bay
Marypark
BEN RINNES
Laggan
STRATHBOGIE
Rothienorman
Lettoch
Delchirach
Tarves
Ellon
Grantown-on-Spey
Ardwell
Kennethmont
Insch
Colpy
FORMARTINE
Hackley Head
Dulnain Bridge
Tomnavoulin
Cabrach
Rhynie
GARIOCH
Oldmeldrum
Newburgh
Carrbridge
SPEY
Hills of Cromdale
Strath Avon
THE BUCK
Inverurie
KIRKWALL 6:00
LERWICK 14:00
Nethy Bridge
Tomintoul
Badenyon
Lumsden
Tullynessle
Newmachar
Boat of Garten
CAIRNGORMS
CARN MOR
Ladder Hills
Alford
Monymusk
Kemnay
Balmedie
Glen More
Forest Park
Strathdon
Kintore
Dyce
ABERDEEN (DYCE)
Glenmore Lodge
NATIONAL PARK
Cock Bridge
MAR
Ordhead
Dunecht
Bankhead
Bucksburn
Bridge of Don
ABERDEEN
Avon
Echt
Westhill
Tarland
Lumphanan
Cults
MORVEN
GORM

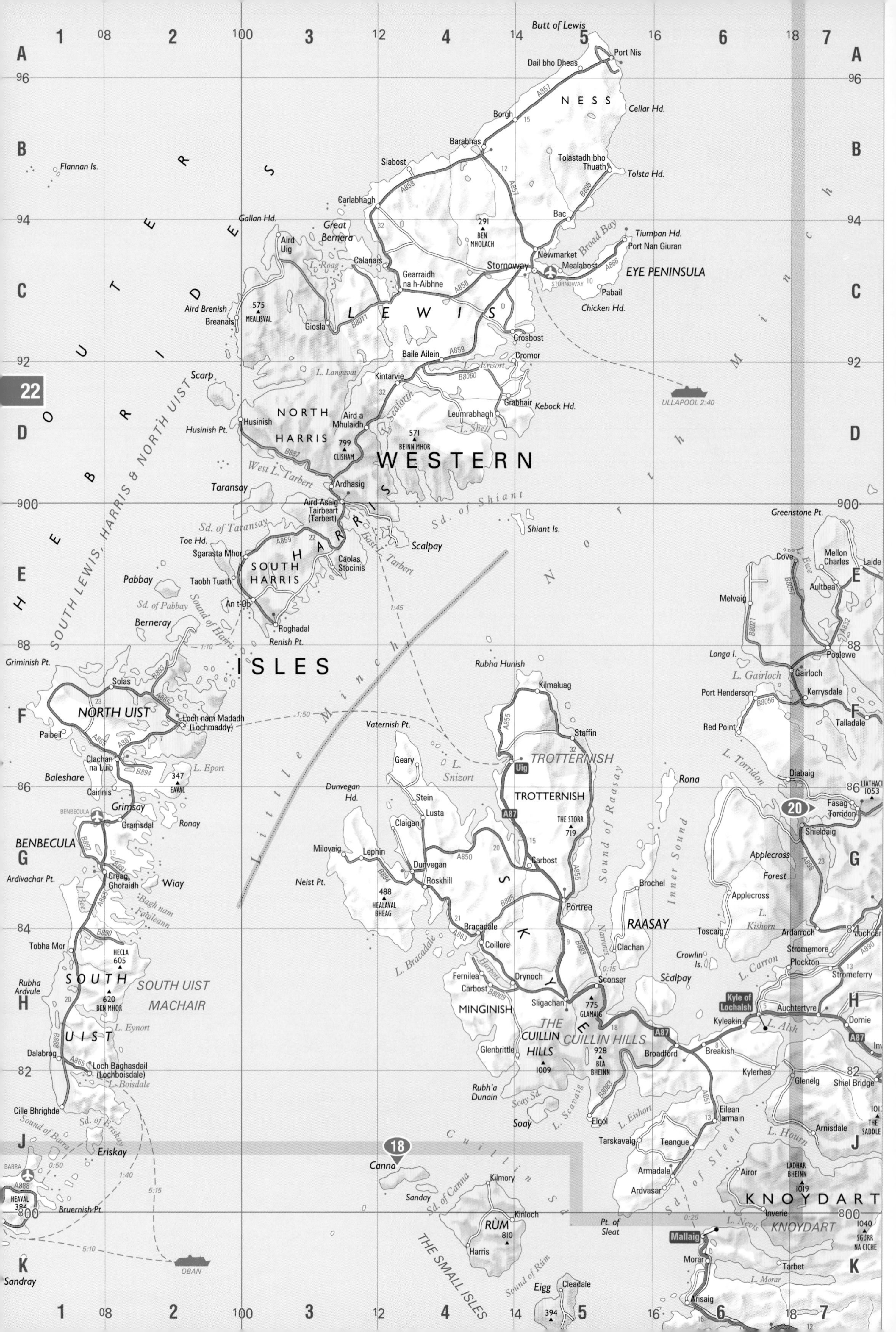

1
2
3
4
5
6
7
A
B
C
D
E
F
G
H
J
K
08
100
12
14
16
18
96
94
92
900
88
86
84
82
800
22
20
18
Butt of Lewis
Port Nis
Dail bho Dheas
NESS
Cellar Hd.
Borgh
Barabhas
Siabost
Tolastadh bho Thuath
Tolsta Hd.
Flannan Is.
Carlabhagh
Bac
Gallan Hd.
Great Bernera
Aird Uig
L. Roag
Calanais
291 BEN MHOLACH
Broad Bay
Tiumpan Hd.
Port Nan Giuran
Newmarket
Mealabost
Stornoway
STORNOWAY
EYE PENINSULA
Gearraidh na h-Aibhne
Pabail
Chicken Hd.
Aird Brenish
Breanais
575 MEALISVAL
Giosla
LEWIS
Crosbost
Baile Ailein
Cromor
L. Erisort
L. Langavat
Kintarvie
Scarp
Grabhair
Kebock Hd.
ULLAPOOL 2:40
L. Seaforth
Leumrabhagh
L. Shell
Aird a Mhulaidh
NORTH HARRIS
Husinish
Husinish Pt.
799 CLISHAM
571 BEINN MHOR
WESTERN
West L. Tarbert
Ardhasig
Taransay
Aird Asaig
Tairbeart (Tarbert)
Sd. of Shiant
Shiant Is.
Sd. of Taransay
East L. Tarbert
Scalpay
Toe Hd.
Sgarasta Mhor
HARRIS
Caolas Stocinis
SOUTH HARRIS
Pabbay
Taobh Tuath
Sd. of Pabbay
An t-Ob
Sound of Harris
Roghadal
Renish Pt.
Berneray
1:45
1:10
ISLES
OUTER HEBRIDES
SOUTH LEWIS, HARRIS & NORTH UIST
North Minch
Little Minch
Griminish Pt.
Solas
Rubha Hunish
Kilmaluag
NORTH UIST
Loch nam Madadh (Lochmaddy)
1:50
Paibeil
Vaternish Pt.
Staffin
Uig
TROTTERNISH
Clachan na Luib
L. Eport
Geary
L. Snizort
Baleshare
347 EAVAL
Dunvegan Hd.
Cairinis
Stein
Lusta
Rona
BENBECULA
Grimsay
Gramsdal
Ronay
Claigan
THE STORR 719
Sound of Raasay
Inner Sound
Milovaig
Lephin
Dunvegan
A850
Garbost
Ardivachar Pt.
Creag Ghoraidh
Wiay
Roskhill
Neist Pt.
488 HEALAVAL BHEAG
SKYE
Portree
Brochel
Bagh nam Faoileann
Bracadale
RAASAY
Coillore
L. Bracadale
Narrows
Clachan
Tobha Mor
HECLA 605
L. Harport
Fernilea
Carbost
Drynoch
Crowlin Is.
Scalpay
Rubha Ardvule
SOUTH UIST
SOUTH UIST MACHAIR
620 BEN MHOR
MINGINISH
Sconser
Sligachan
775 GLAMAIG
L. Eynort
THE CUILLIN HILLS
CUILLIN HILLS
928 BLA BHEINN
1009
Glenbrittle
Broadford
Dalabrog
Loch Baghasdail (Lochboisdale)
L. Boisdale
Rubh'a Dunain
Soay Sd.
L. Scavaig
Cille Bhrighde
Sound of Barra
Sd. of Eriskay
Soay
Elgol
L. Eishort
Eriskay
0:50
1:40
5:15
5:10
BARRA
HEAVAL 384
Bruernish Pt.
Canna
Cuillin Sd.
Sanday
Sd. of Canna
Kilmory
RUM
Kinloch
810
Harris
THE SMALL ISLES
Sound of Rum
Eigg
Cleadale
394
OBAN
Sandray
Pt. of Sleat
Sd. of Sleat
Tarskavaig
Teangue
Armadale
Ardvasar
Mallaig
Morar
Arisaig
0:25
L. Nevis
Inverie
KNOYDART
Tarbet
L. Morar
Airor
LADHAR BHEINN 1019
Arnisdale
L. Hourn
1040 SGURR NA CICHE
Eilean Iarmain
Kylerhea
Glenelg
Shiel Bridge
Breakish
Kyleakin
Kyle of Lochalsh
L. Alsh
Auchtertyre
Dornie
Stromeferry
Plockton
Stromemore
L. Carron
Ardarroch
Lochcarron
Toscaig
Applecross
L. Kishorn
Applecross Forest
Shieldaig
Fasag
Torridon
Diabaig
L. Torridon
LIATHACH 1053
Red Point
Port Henderson
L. Gairloch
Gairloch
Kerrysdale
Talladale
Longa I.
Poolewe
Melvaig
Cove
L. Ewe
Aultbea
Mellon Charles
Laide
Greenstone Pt.
A857
A858
A859
A866
B895
B8011
B8060
B887
A865
A867
B893
B894
A855
A87
B884
A863
B885
B883
B892
B891
B890
B888
B8083
A851
A888
B8021
B8057
A832
B8056
A896
A890

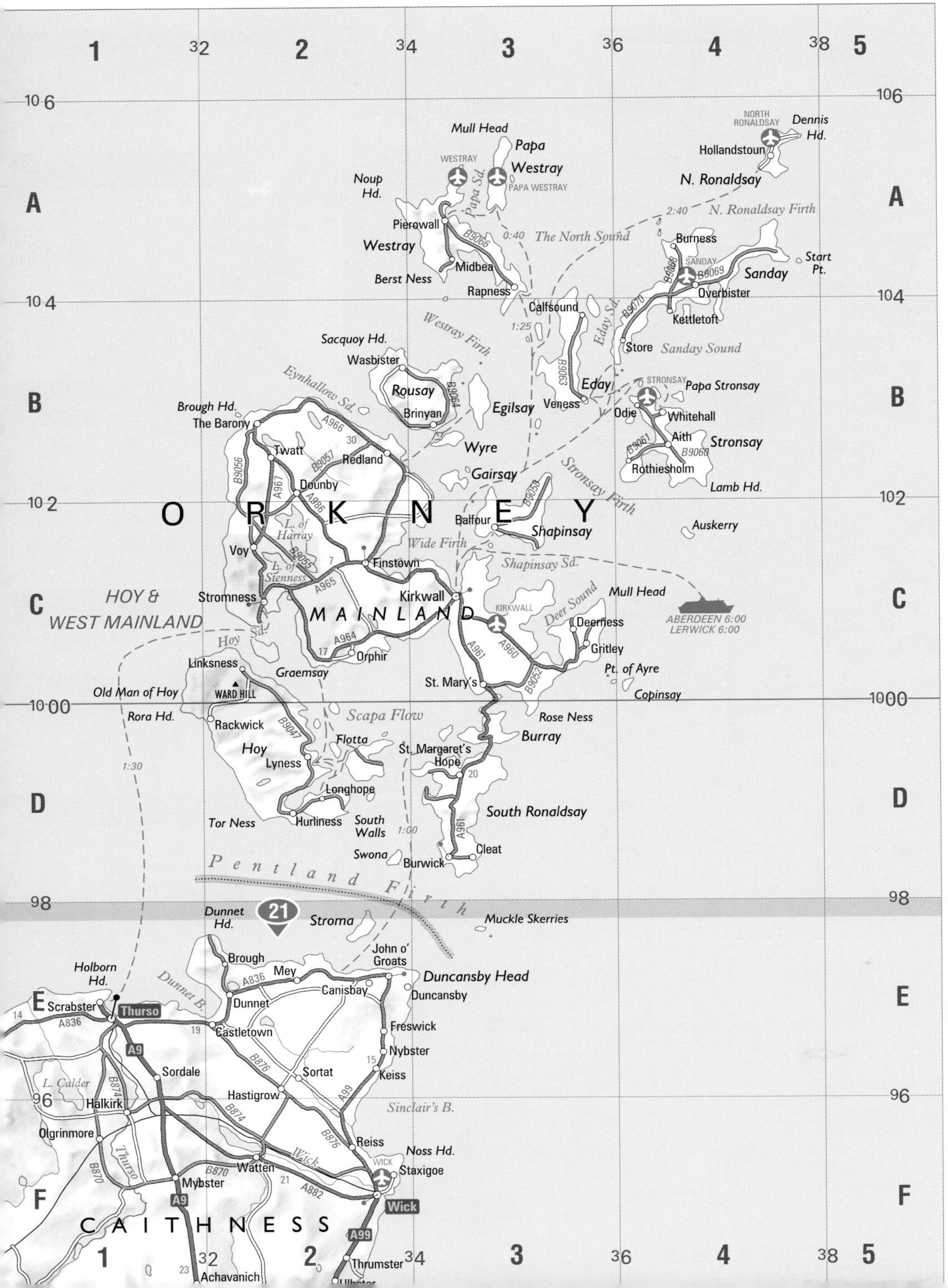
ORKNEY
HOY & WEST MAINLAND
MAINLAND
CAITHNESS
Mull Head
Papa Westray
Westray
Noup Hd.
Pierowall
Midbea
Berst Ness
Rapness
N. Ronaldsay
Hollandstoun
Dennis Hd.
N. Ronaldsay Firth
The North Sound
Burness
Sanday
Start Pt.
Overbister
Kettletoft
Calfsound
Westray Firth
Eday Sd.
Store
Sanday Sound
Sacquoy Hd.
Wasbister
Rousay
Brinyan
Egilsay
Eday
Veness
Papa Stronsay
Odie
Whitehall
Aith
Stronsay
Rothiesholm
Lamb Hd.
Eynhallow Sd.
Brough Hd.
The Barony
Twatt
Redland
Dounby
Wyre
Gairsay
Stronsay Firth
Balfour
Shapinsay
Auskerry
L. of Harray
Voy
Finstown
Wide Firth
L. of Stenness
Stromness
Kirkwall
Shapinsay Sd.
Mull Head
Deer Sound
Deerness
Gritley
Pt. of Ayre
Copinsay
ABERDEEN 6:00
LERWICK 6:00
Orphir
Hoy Sd.
Linksness
Graemsay
Old Man of Hoy
WARD HILL
St. Mary's
Rora Hd.
Rackwick
Scapa Flow
Rose Ness
Burray
Hoy
Flotta
Lyness
St. Margaret's Hope
Longhope
South Ronaldsay
Tor Ness
Hurliness
South Walls
Swona
Burwick
Cleat
Pentland Firth
Dunnet Hd.
Stroma
Muckle Skerries
John o' Groats
Duncansby Head
Duncansby
Holborn Hd.
Brough
Mey
Canisbay
Dunnet
Dunnet B.
Scrabster
Thurso
Castletown
Freswick
Nybster
Keiss
Sordale
Sortat
L. Calder
Halkirk
Hastigrow
Sinclair's B.
Olgrinmore
Reiss
Noss Hd.
Staxigoe
Watten
Wick
Mybster
Thrumster
Achavanich
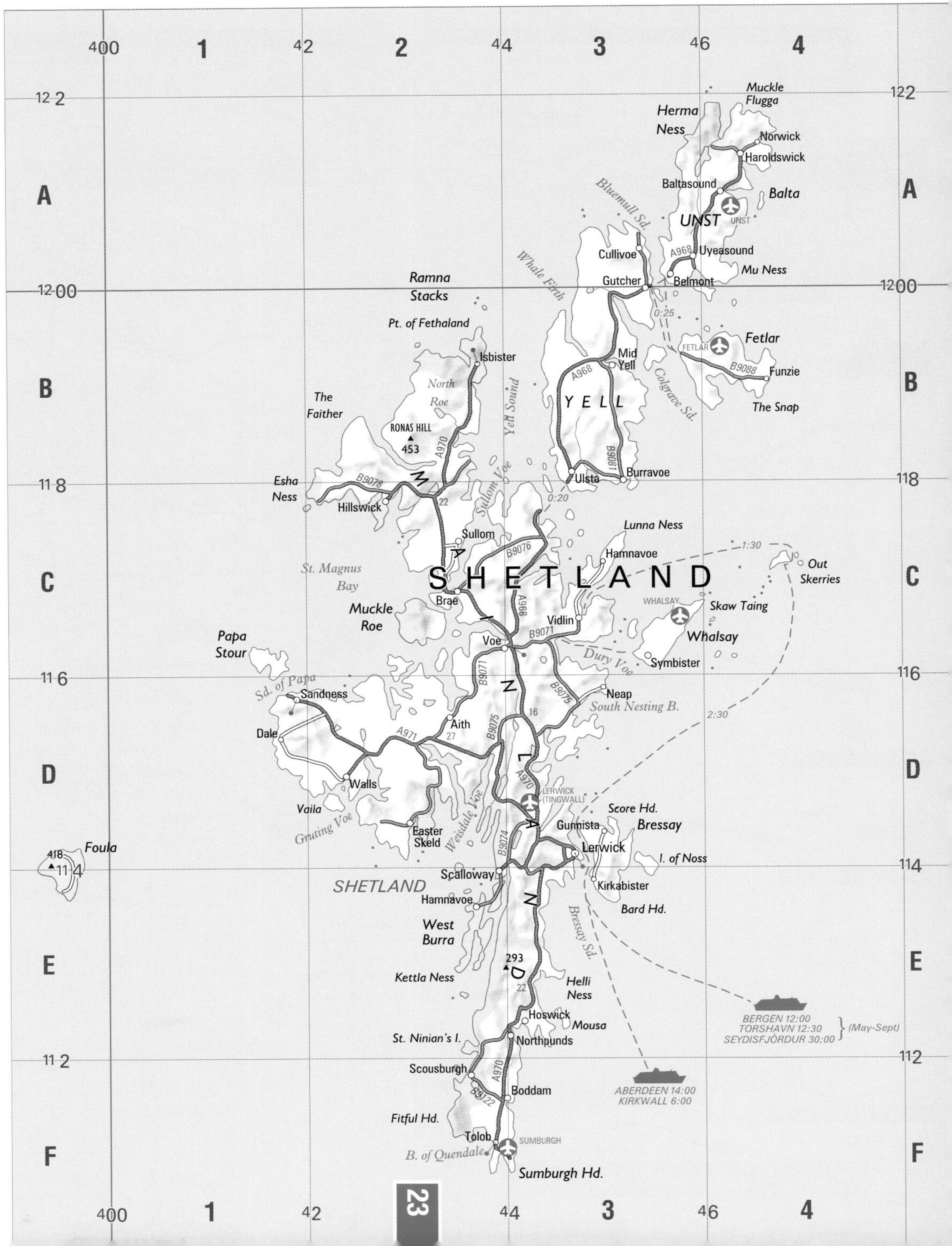
SHETLAND
UNST
YELL
Muckle Flugga
Herma Ness
Norwick
Haroldswick
Baltasound
Balta
Bluemull Sd.
Cullivoe
Uyeasound
Mu Ness
Gutcher
Belmont
Ramna Stacks
Pt. of Fethaland
Whale Firth
Fetlar
Funzie
Isbister
Mid Yell
North Roe
Yell Sound
Colgrave Sd.
The Snap
The Faither
RONAS HILL
453
Ulsta
Burravoe
Esha Ness
Hillswick
Sullom Voe
Sullom
Lunna Ness
Hamnavoe
Out Skerries
St. Magnus Bay
Brae
Muckle Roe
WHALSAY
Skaw Taing
Whalsay
Vidlin
Papa Stour
Voe
Dury Voe
Symbister
Sd. of Papa
Sandness
Neap
South Nesting B.
Dale
Aith
Walls
Vaila
Gruting Voe
Weisdale Voe
Easter Skeld
LERWICK (TINGWALL)
Score Hd.
Bressay
Gunnista
Lerwick
I. of Noss
Foula
418
Scalloway
Kirkabister
Bard Hd.
Hamnavoe
West Burra
Bressay Sd.
293
Kettla Ness
Helli Ness
Hoswick
Mousa
St. Ninian's I.
Northpunds
BERGEN 12:00
TORSHAVN 12:30
SEYDISFJÖRDUR 30:00
(May-Sept)
Scousburgh
Boddam
ABERDEEN 14:00
KIRKWALL 6:00
Fitful Hd.
Tolob
SUMBURGH
B. of Quendale
Sumburgh Hd.

M25 *and routes into London*

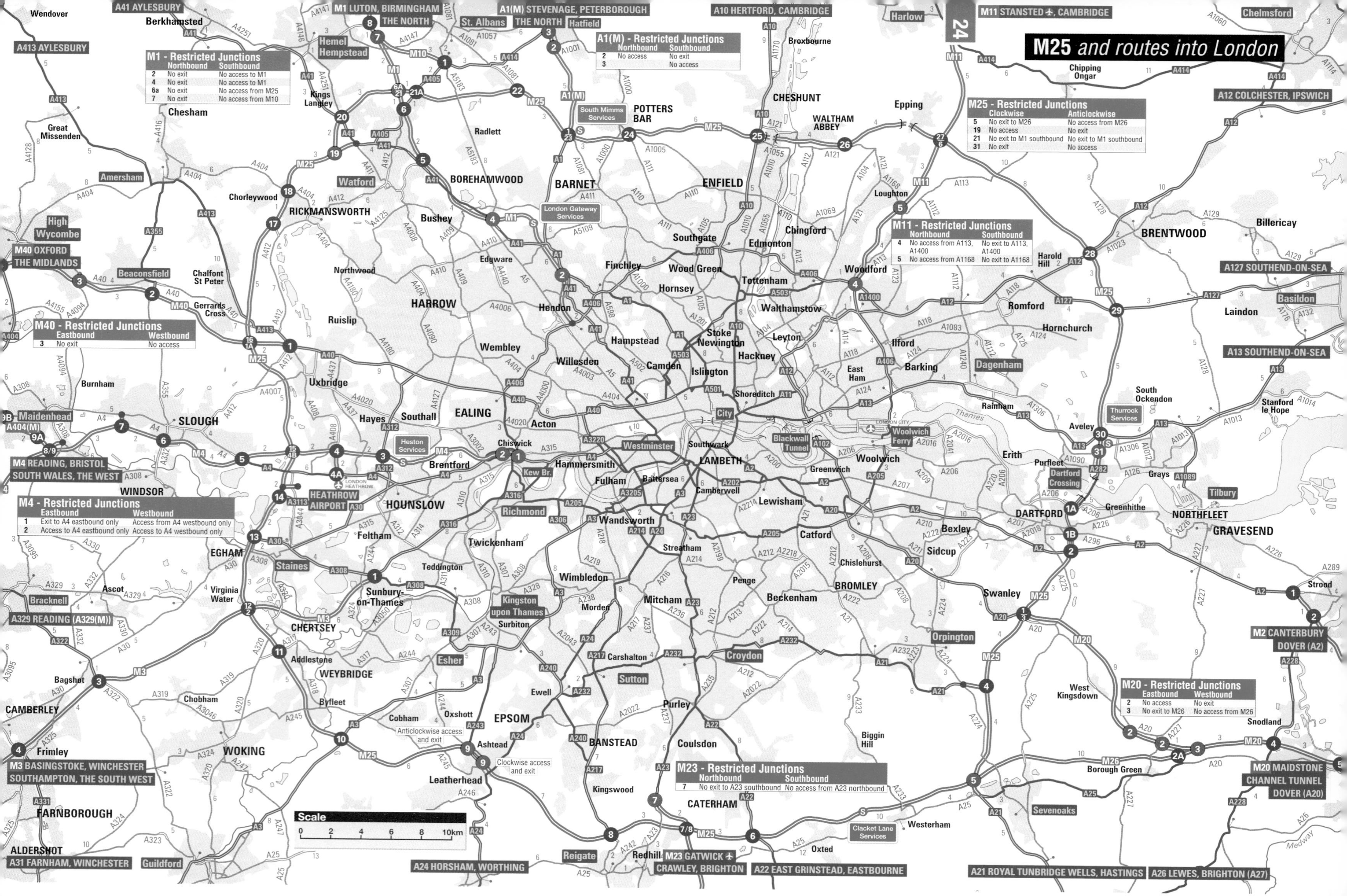

M1 - Restricted Junctions

	Northbound	Southbound
2	No exit	No access to M1
4	No exit	No access to M1
6a	No exit	No access from M25
7	No exit	No access from M10

A1(M) - Restricted Junctions

	Northbound	Southbound
2	No access	No exit
3		No access

M25 - Restricted Junctions

	Clockwise	Anticlockwise
5	No exit to M26	No access from M26
19	No access	No exit
21	No exit to M1 southbound	No exit to M1 southbound
31	No exit	No access

M11 - Restricted Junctions

	Northbound	Southbound
4	No access from A113, A1400	No exit to A113, A1400
5	No access from A1168	No exit to A1168

M40 - Restricted Junctions

	Eastbound	Westbound
3	No exit	No access

M4 - Restricted Junctions

	Eastbound	Westbound
1	Exit to A4 eastbound only	Access from A4 westbound only
2	Access to A4 eastbound only	Access to A4 westbound only

M20 - Restricted Junctions

	Eastbound	Westbound
2	No access	No exit
3	No exit to M26	No access from M26

M23 - Restricted Junctions

	Northbound	Southbound
7	No exit to A23 southbound	No access from A23 northbound

M6 and routes into Birmingham

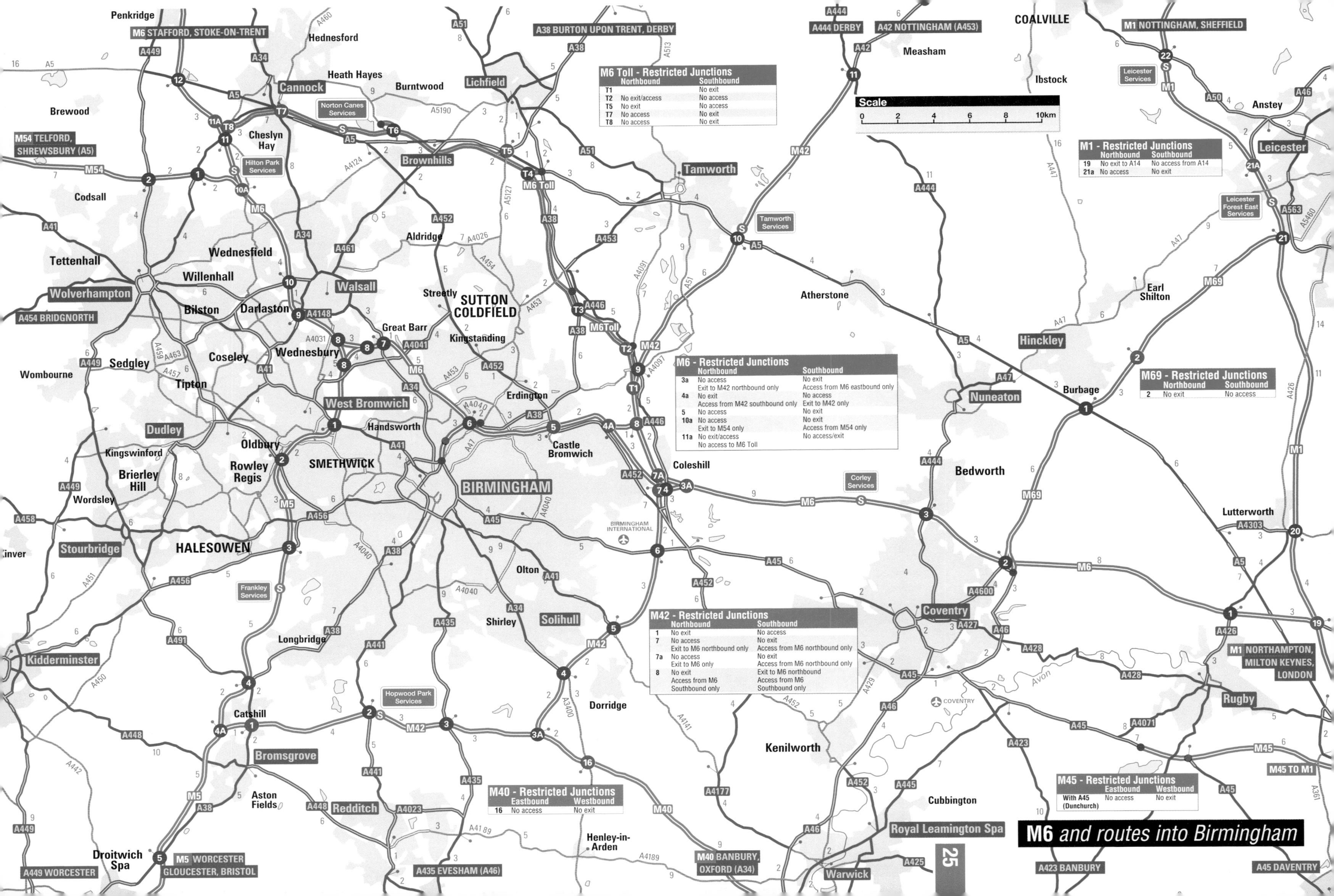

M6 Toll - Restricted Junctions

	Northbound	Southbound
T1		No exit
T2	No exit/access	No access
T5	No exit	No access
T7	No access	No exit
T8	No access	No exit

M1 - Restricted Junctions

	Northbound	Southbound
19	No exit to A14	No access from A14
21a	No access	No exit

M6 - Restricted Junctions

	Northbound	Southbound
3a	No access Exit to M42 northbound only	No exit Access from M6 eastbound only
4a	No exit Access from M42 southbound only	No access Exit to M42 only
5	No access	No exit
10a	No access Exit to M54 only	No exit Access from M54 only
11a	No exit/access No access to M6 Toll	No access/exit

M69 - Restricted Junctions

	Northbound	Southbound
2	No exit	No access

M42 - Restricted Junctions

	Northbound	Southbound
1	No exit	No access
7	No access Exit to M6 northbound only	No exit Access from M6 northbound only
7a	No access Exit to M6 only	No exit Access from M6 northbound only
8	No exit Access from M6 Southbound only	Exit to M6 northbound Access from M6 Southbound only

M40 - Restricted Junctions

	Eastbound	Westbound
16	No access	No exit

M45 - Restricted Junctions

	Eastbound	Westbound
With A45 (Dunchurch)	No access	No exit

M60 *and routes into Manchester and Liverpool*

Restricted Junctions

M6	Northbound	Southbound
20	No exit to M56 eastbound	No access from M56 westbound
24	No exit	No access
25	No access from A49	No exit

M53	Northbound	Southbound
11	No exit to M56 westbound	No exit to M56 westbound

M56	Eastbound	Westbound
2	No exit	No access
4	No exit	No access
7		No access
8	No exit or access	No exit
9	No access from M6 northbound	No access to M6 southbound
15	No exit to M53	No access from M53 northbound

M57	Northbound	Southbound
3	No exit	No access
5	No exit	No access

M58	Eastbound	Westbound
1	No exit	No access

M60	Clockwise	Anticlockwise
2	No exit	No access
3	No exit to A34 northbound	No exit to A34 northbound
4	No access to M56	No exit to M56
5	No exit to A5103 southbound	No exit to A5103 northbound
14	No exit to A580	No access from A580
16	No exit	No access
20	No access	No exit
22		No access
25	No access	
26		No exit or access
27	No exit	No access

M61	Northbound	Southbound
2	No access from A580 eastbound	No exit to A580 westbound
3	No access from A580 eastbound No access from A666 southbound	No exit to A580 westbound

M66	Northbound	Southbound
1	No access	No exit

M67	Eastbound	Westbound
1a	No access	No exit
2	No exit	No access

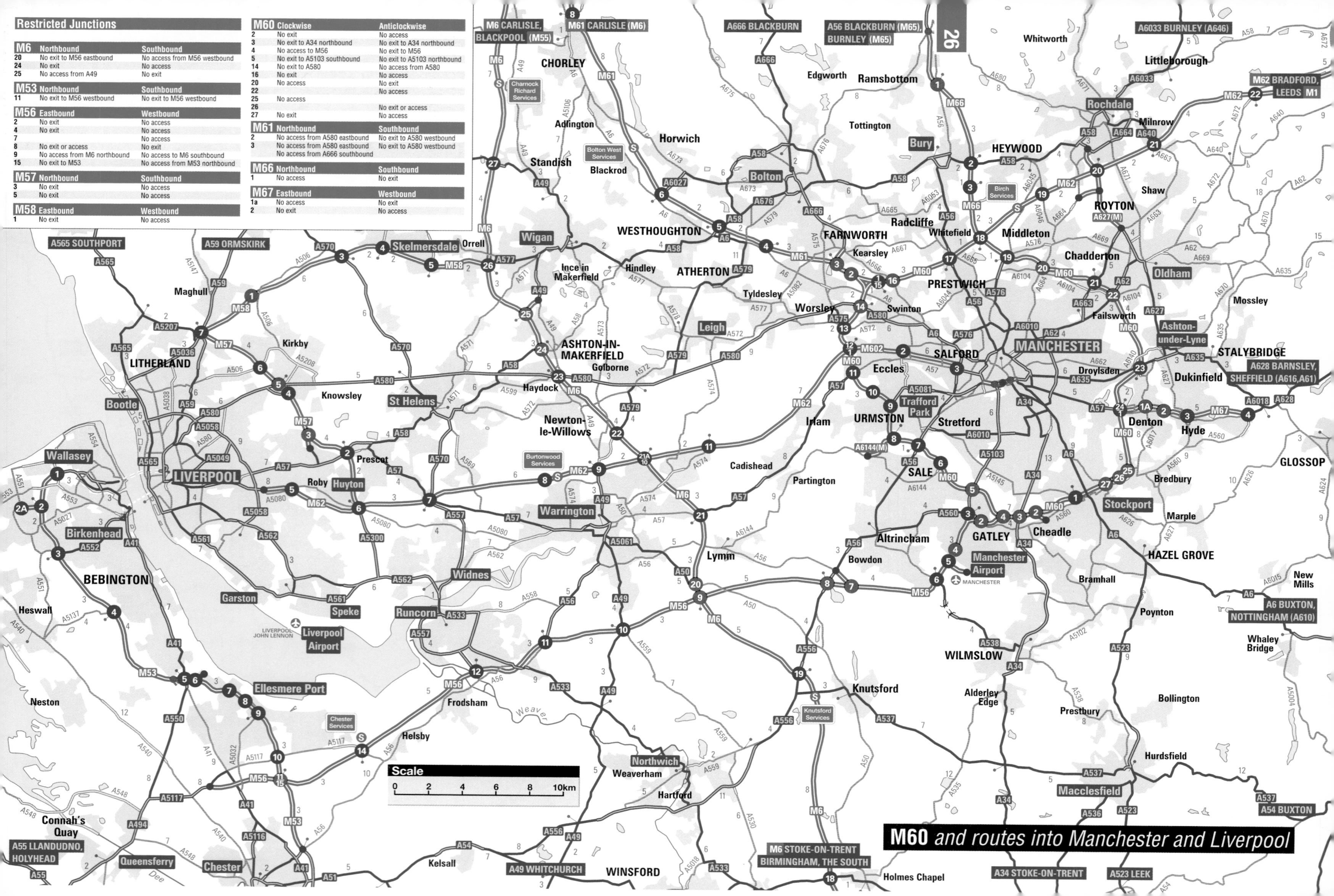

Key to map symbols

NAVIGATOR® city approach maps

Motorways

M6 · 1 · 2 · Pease Pottage Services · Toll

Junction · Restricted junction · Services · Toll motorway

- **Primary route** – dual, single carriageway, service station
- **Numbered junctions** – full, restricted access
- **under construction, narrow**
- **Primary destination** (LEEDS)
- **A road** – dual, single carriageway (A1031)
- **under construction, narrow**
- **B road** – dual, single carriageway (B1200)
- **Minor road, drive or track**
- **Ring road**
- **Distance in miles**
- **Tunnel, multi-level junction**
- **Toll, steep gradient** – points downhill
- **Speed camera** – single, multiple
- **National trail** – England and Wales
- **Long distance footpath** – Scotland
- **Railway with station, level crossing, tunnel** (FAIRFIELD)
- **Preserved railway with station, tramway** (ALRESFORD)
- **National boundary**
- **County or unitary authority boundary**
- **Car ferry, catamaran**
- **Passenger ferry, catamaran**
- **Hovercraft, freight ferry**
- **Internal ferry** – car, passenger
- **Principal airport, other airport or airfield**
- **Area of outstanding natural beauty** – England and Wales; **Forest park, National park, National scenic area** – Scotland; **Regional park**
- **Woodland**
- **Beach** – sand, shingle
- **Linear antiquity**
- **Navigable river or canal** (R. SEVERN)
- **Lock, flight of locks, canal bridge number**
- **Viewpoint, motoring organisation phone box**
- **Site and date of battle, spot height** – in metres (1066, 965)
- **National nature reserve, national sport venue**
- **Shopping village, park and ride** (P&R)
- **Caravan site, camping site**

- Abbey / priory
- Ancient monument
- Aquarium / dolphinarium
- Art gallery
- Art collection or museum
- Bird sanctuary or aviary
- Castle
- Cathedral
- Church
- Country park
- Country park – Scotland
- County show ground
- Farm park
- Garden
- Golf course
- Historic ship
- House
- House and garden
- Local museum
- Marina
- Maritime or military museum
- Motor racing circuit
- Museum
- Picnic area
- Preserved railway
- Racecourse
- Roman antiquity
- Safari park
- Theme park
- Tourist Information Centre
  - – open all year
  - – seasonal
- Transport collection
- Viewpoint
- World Heritage Site
- Youth hostel
- Zoo
- Historic feature
- Other place of interest

City and town plans

- **Motorway**
- **Primary route** – dual, single carriageway
- **A road** – dual, single carriageway
- **B road** – dual, single carriageway
- **Minor through road, one-way street**
- **Pedestrian roads**
- **Shopping streets**
- **Congestion Charge zone**
- **Streets exempt from Congestion Charge**
- **Railway with station**
- **Underground station, metro station** (Bank, West St)
- **Tramway with station** (City Hall)
- **Railway or bus station, park**
- **Shopping precinct or retail park**
- **Hospital, parking,** (H, P)
- **Police station, post office, youth hostel** (PO)

- Abbey or cathedral
- Ancient monument
- Aquarium
- Art gallery
- Bird garden
- Building of public interest
- Castle
- Church of interest
- Cinema
- Garden
- Historic ship
- House
- House and garden
- Museum
- Preserved railway
- Roman antiquity
- Safari park
- Shopmobility
- Theatre
- Tourist Information Centre open all year
- Tourist Information Centre open summer only
- Zoo
- Other place of interest

Approach map scale 1:90900 • 1cm = 0.9km • 1inch = 1.4 miles

0 · 1 · 2 · 3 · 4 miles

0 · 1 · 2 · 3 · 4 · 5 · 6 kilometres

Aberdeen

Known chiefly as the Granite City (granite is still used in all forms of building, even the roads), Aberdeen is the oil capital of Europe and the floral capital of Scotland with 45 parks and two miles of sandy beach. Places of interest include St Machar's and St Andrew's Cathedrals, the Winter Gardens, Provost Skene's House and the university, which was founded in 1495. The shopping hub for north-east Scotland, the city boasts five shopping centres – the Bon Accord, the Academy, St Nicholas, the Trinity and the Galleria, as well as a large indoor Market Hall. There is a good selection of bars and restaurants as well as theatres, music venues and cinemas.

▲Aberdeen harbour Lighthouse at dawn

Aberdeen Visitor Centre, 23 Union Street, Aberdeen AB11 5BP Tel 01224 288828

BBC Radio Scotland 92.4-94.7 FM and 810 AM • **Northsound 1** 96.9 FM **Northsound 2** 1035 MW

www.aberdeencity.gov.uk

★ Do not miss

★**Aberdeen Art Gallery**, Schoolhill – Modern Art, Impressionists, Scottish Colourists

★**Aberdeen Maritime Museum**, Shiprow – shipbuilding, fishing industry and North Sea oil

★**Satrosphere**, The Tramsheds, Constitution Street – interactive science and technology museum

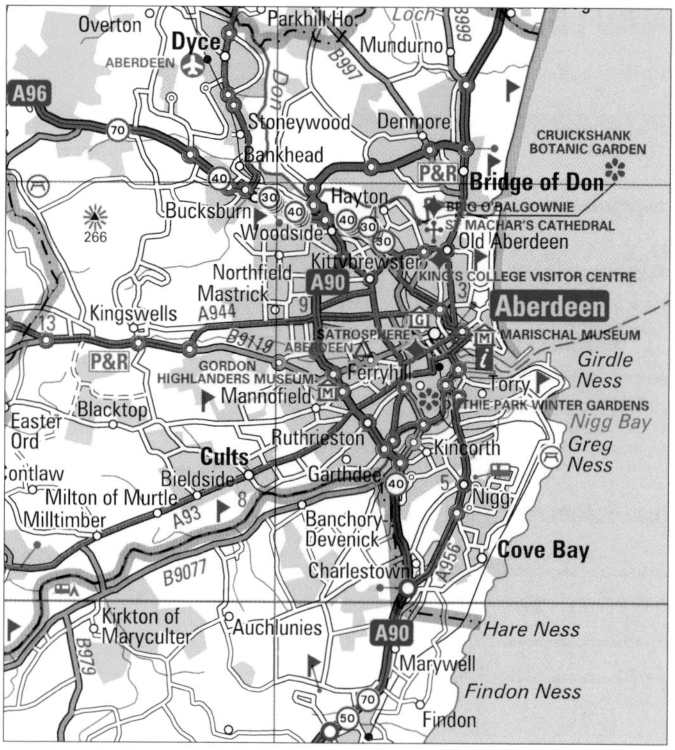

¼ mile
¼ ½ km

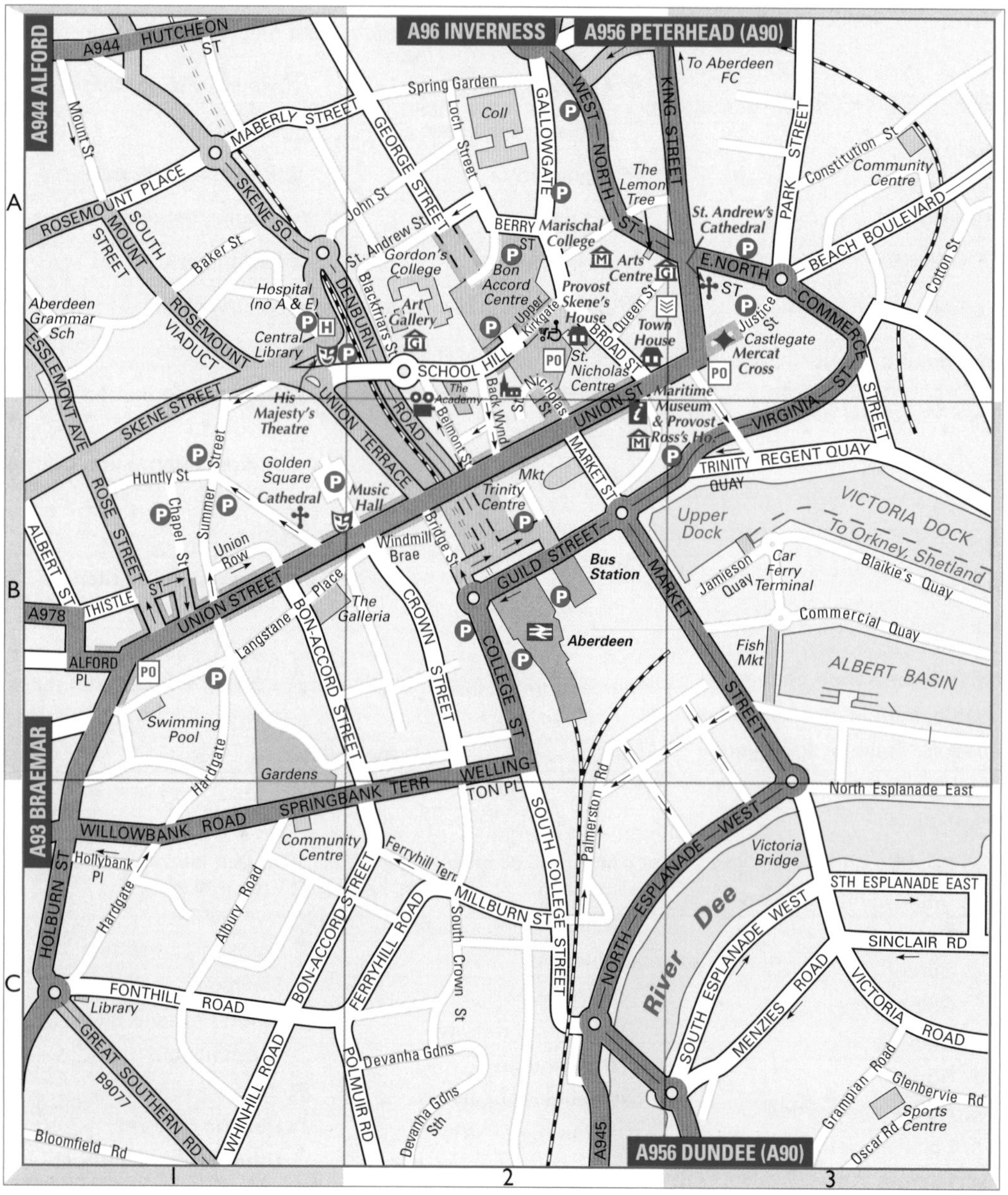

Aberdeen

Aberdeen ⇄ B2
Aberdeen Grammar School A1
Academy, The. B2
Albert Basin. B3
Albert St. B1
Albury Rd C1
Alford Pl B1
Art Gallery 🏛 . . . A2
Arts Centre 🏛 . . . A2
Back Wynd A2
Baker St A1
Beach Blvd. A3
Belmont St. B2
Berry St A2
Blackfriars St. . . . A2
Blaikie's Quay B3
Bloomfield Rd . . . C1
Bon-Accord Ctr. . A2
Bon-Accord St . . .B1
Bridge St B2
Bus Station B2
Car Ferry Terminal. B3
Castlegate A3
Cathedral † B1
Central Library . . A1
Chapel St B1
College St B2
Commerce St. . . . A3
Commercial Quay .B3
Community Centre. A3/C1
Constitution St . . A3
Cotton St A3
Crown St B2
Denburn Rd A2
Devanha Gdns . . . C2
Devanha Gdns South C2
East North St. . . . A3
Esslemont Ave. . . A1
Ferryhill Rd C2
Ferryhill Terr C2
Fish Market B3
Fonthill Rd. C1
Galleria, The. B1
Gallowgate. A2
George St. A2
Glenbervie Rd . . . C3
Golden Sq B1
Gordon's College A2
Grampian Rd C3
Gt Southern Rd . . C1
Guild St B2
Hardgate B1
His Majesty's Theatre 🎭 A1
Holburn St C1
Hollybank Pl C1
Hospital Ⓗ A1
Huntly St B1
Hutcheon St. A1
Information Ctr ℹ.B2
Jamieson Quay . . .B3
John St. A2
Justice St. A3
King St A2
Langstane Pl B1
Library C1
Lemon Tree, The . A2
Loch St. A2
Maberly St A1
Marischal College 🏛 A2
Maritime Museum & Provost Ross's House 🏛 B2
Market St B3
Menzies Rd C3
Mercat Cross ✦. . A3
Millburn St. C2
Miller St A3
Market B2
Market St B2
Mount St A1
Music Hall 🎭 B1
North Esp East . . C3
North Esp West . . C2
Oscar Rd. C3
Palmerston Rd . . C2
Park St A3
Police Station 🏢. A2
Polmuir Rd. C2
Post Office PO. A2/A3/B1
Provost Skene's House 🏠 A2
Queen St A2
Regent Quay B3
Rose St. B1
Rosemount Pl . . . A1
Rosemount Viaduct. A1
St Andrew St A2
St Andrew's Cathedral † A3
St Nicholas Centre. A2
St Nicholas St . . . A2
School Hill. A2
Sinclair Rd. C3
Skene Sq A1
Skene St. B1
South College St. C2
South Crown St. . C2
South Esp East . . C3
South Esp West. . C3
South Mount St. . A1
Sports Centre . . . C3
Spring Garden. . . A2
Springbank Terr . C1
Summer St. B1
Swimming Pool. . .B1
Thistle St B1
Town House 🏠 . . A2
Trinity Centre. B2
Trinity Quay B3
Union Row B1
Union St. B1
Union Terr B2
Upper Dock B3
Upper Kirkgate . . A2
Victoria Bridge . . C3
Victoria Dock. B3
Victoria Rd. C3
Virginia St A3
Wellington Pl. B2
West North St . . . A2
Whinhill Rd C1
Willowbank Rd . . C1
Windmill Brae B2

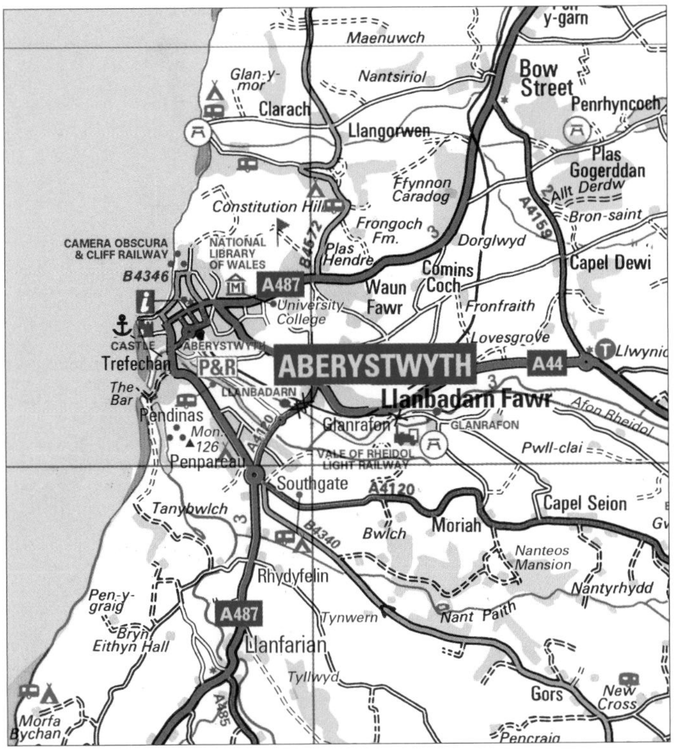

Aberystwyth

Aberystwyth exists on the site of a prehistoric hillfort called Pen Dinas – the earthworks of which are still visible. The town was established more than 700 years ago by charter from Edward I and is now an important seat of learning and the main town and holiday resort of Cardigan Bay with a one-mile-long promenade to rival Brighton. There are many places of interest such as the remains of the castle, Aberystwyth Cliff Railway, the National Library of Wales, Dyfi Furnace, the pier and the marina. There is a regular market on Saturdays and a farmers' market once or twice a month.

▲Aberystwyth from Constitution Hill

★Do not miss

★**Aberystwyth Arts Centre**, Penglais – film, theatre, music, exhibitions

★**Coliseum Gallery Ceredigion Museum**, Terrace Road – historical artefacts

★**Vale of Rheidol Railway**, Park Avenue – a steam railway

Tourist Information Centre, Lisburne House, Terrace Road, Aberystwyth SY23 2AG
Tel 01970 612125

BBC Radio Wales 95.3 FM • **Radio Ceredigion** 96.6, 97.4, 103.3 FM

www.aberystwyth-online.co.uk

Aberystwyth

Aberystwyth RFC. C3
Aberystwyth Station B2
Aberystwyth Town Football Ground B2
Alexandra Rd.....B2
Ambulance Station C3
Baker St.........B1
Banadl Rd B2
Bandstand A1
Bath St......... A2
Boat Landing Stage A1
Boulevard St Brieuc C3
Bridge St B1
Bronglais Hospital B3
Bryn-y-Mor Rd .. A2
Buarth Rd.........B2
Bus Station B2
Cae Ceredig..... C3
Cae Melyn A2
Cae'r-Gog B3
Cambrian St.......B2
Caradoc Rd B3
Caravan Site C2
Castle (Remains of) .B1
Castle St.........B1
Cattle Market.....B2
Cemetary B3
Ceredigion Museum A1
Chalybeate St B1
Cliff Terr........ A2
Club House A2
Commodore .. A1
County Court..... A2
Crown Buildings ..B2
Dan-y-Coed....... A3
Dinas Terr........ C1
Eastgate..........B1
Edge-hill Rd B2
Elm Tree Ave B2
Elysian Gr........ A2
Felin-y-Mor Rd .. C1
Fifth Ave......... C2
Fire Station C1
Glanrafon Terr B1
Glyndwr Rd B2
Golf Course A3
Gray's Inn Rd.....B1
Great Darkgate St..............B1
Greenfield St.....B2
Heol-y-Bryn A2
High St...........B1
Infirmary Rd..... A2
Information Ctr .B1
Iorwerth Ave B3
King St...........B1
Lauraplace.......B1
Library B1
Lifeboat Station . C1
Llanbadarn Rd.....B3
Loveden Rd A2
Magistrates Court A1
Marina C1
Marine Terr A1
Market B1
Mill St...........B1
Moor La B2
National Library of Wales........B3
New Promenade ..B1
New St B1
North Beach A1
North Parade.....B2
North Rd......... A2
Northgate St B2
Parc Natur Penglais A3
Parc-y-Llyn Retail Park..... C3
Park & Ride......B2
Park Ave.........B2
Pavillion.........B1
Pendinas C1
Penglais Rd B3
Penparcau Rd C1/C2
Penrheidol...... C2
Pen-y-Craig A2
Pen-yr-angor ... C1
Pier St B1
Plas Ave B3
Plas Helyg C2
Plascrug Ave . B2/C3
Police Station . C2
Poplar Row B2
Portland Rd B2
Portland St A2
Post Office .B1/B3
Powell St B1
Prospect St B1
Quay Rd B1
Queen St B1
Queen's Ave...... A2
Queen's Rd A2
Riverside Terr ...B1
St Davids Rd B3
St Michael's ...B1
School of Art......B2
South Beach B1
South Rd B1
Sports Ground.....B2
Spring Gdns..... C1
Stanley Rd B2
Swimming Pool & Leisure Centre.. C3
Tanybwlch Beach C1
Tennis Courts B3
Terrace Rd.......B1
The Bar.......... C1
Town Hall....... A2
Trefechan Bridge .B1
Trefor Rd A2
Trinity Rd B2
University Campus B3
University of Wales (Aberystwyth) ..B1
Vaenor St.........B2
Vale of Rheidol Railway C3
Victoria Terr..... A1
Viewpoint ✦ . A2/A3
War Memorial ...B1
Y Lanfa......... C1

¼ mile
¼ ½ km

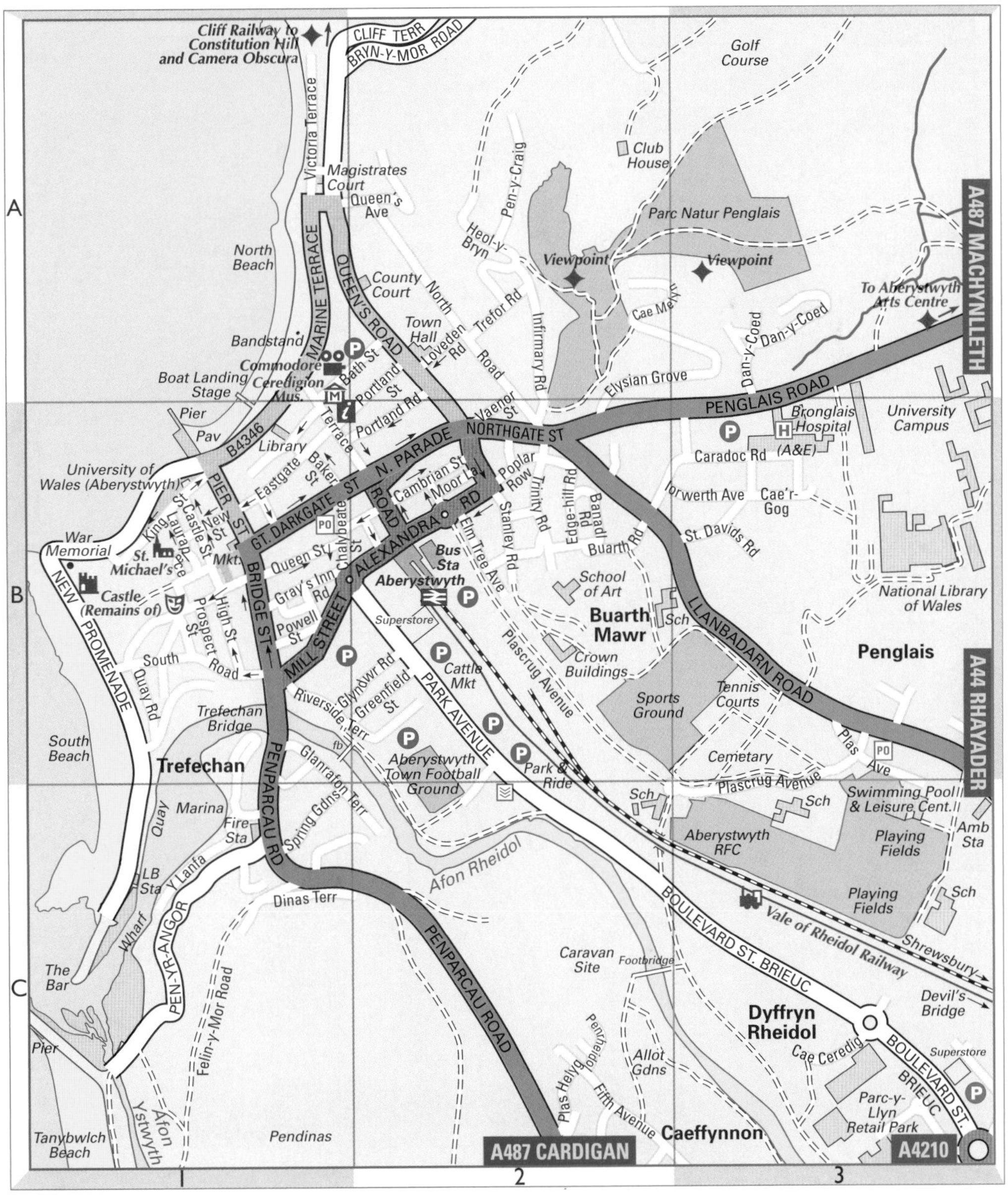

Ashford

A Kent town believed to date back to the Danish invasion of the country in 893. By 1600, it had become a substantial market town, with numerous picturesque medieval and Tudor buildings; local history is traced in the Ashford Borough Museum. Today it's best known as a stopping point on the Eurostar route to the Continent and for its large designer clothes outlet. Nearby attractions include the Agricultural Museum at Brook, the awardwinning South of England Rare Breeds Centre and neighbouring Yonsea Farm, the Woodchurch Village Life Exhibition, Woodchurch Windmill, the Port Lympne Wild Animal Park and Historic Mansion and Gardens, Swanton Hill watermill at Mersham, Church Hill Cottage Gardens at Charing Heath, Beech Court Gardens at Challock, the Romney, Hythe and Dymchurch railway towards the coast, Kipp Cottage Garden at Biddenden Green, and Biddenden Vineyards and Ciderworks. The town is on the doorstep of the North Downs, with its many walks, and activities such as golf, cycling, gliding and fishing.

▲North Street

Ashford Tourist Information Centre, 18 The Churchyard, Ashford TN23 1QG Tel 01233 629165

BBC Radio Kent 96.7, 97.6, 104.2 FM • **Invicta** 96.1 FM

www.ashford.gov.uk

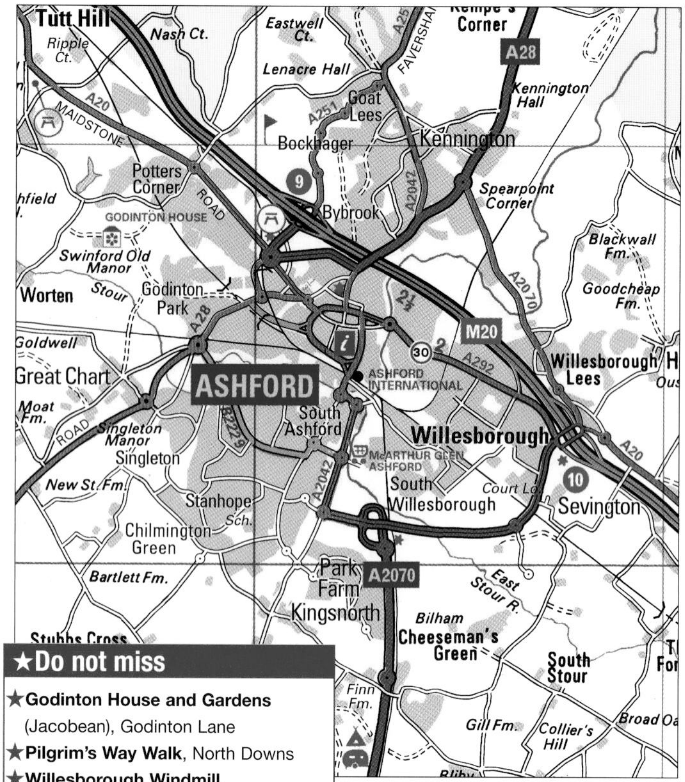

★Do not miss

★**Godinton House and Gardens** (Jacobean), Godinton Lane

★**Pilgrim's Way Walk**, North Downs

★**Willesborough Windmill**, Willesborough

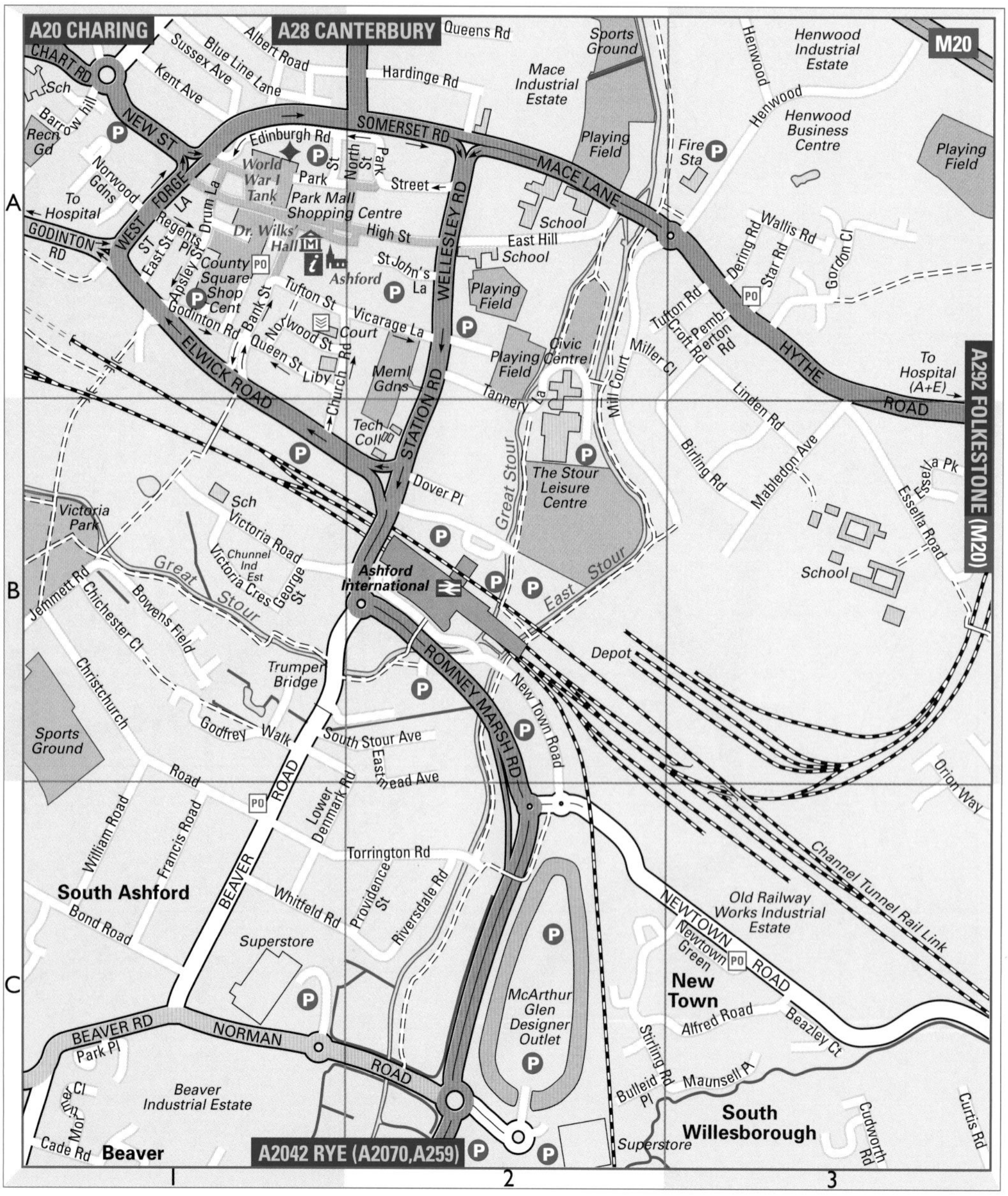

Ashford

Albert Rd A1
Alfred Rd C3
Apsley St A1
Ashford A1
Ashford International Station B2
Bank St A1
Barrow Hill Gdns. A1
Beaver Industrial Estate C1
Beaver Rd C1
Beazley Ct C3
Birling Rd B3
Blue Line La. A1
Bond Rd C1
Bowens Field B1
Bulleid Pl C2
Cade Rd C1
Chart Rd A1
Chichester Cl. B1
Christchurch Rd B1
Chunnel Industrial Estate B1
Church Rd A1
Civic Centre A2
County Square Shopping Centre A1
Court A1
Croft Rd A3
Cudworth Rd C3
Curtis Rd C3
Dering Rd A3
Dover Pl B2
Dr Wilks' Hall A1
Drum La A1
East Hill A2
East St A1
Eastmead Ave B2
Edinburgh Rd A1
Elwick Rd A1
Essella Pk B3
Essella Rd B3
Fire Sta A3
Forge La A1
Francis Rd C1
George St B1
Godfrey Walk B1
Godinton Rd A1
Gordon Cl A3
Hardinge Rd A2
Henwood A3
Henwood Business Centre A3
Henwood Industrial Estate A3
High St A2
Hythe Rd A3
Information Ctr A1
Jemmett Rd B1
Kent Ave A1
Library A1
Linden Rd B3
Lower Denmark Rd C1
Mabledon Ave B3
Mace Industrial Estate A2
Mace La A2
Maunsell Pl C3
McArthur Glen Designer Outlet C2
Memorial Gdns A2
Mill Ct A2
Miller Cl A2
Mortimer Cl C1
New St A1
Newtown Green C3
Newtown Rd B2/C3
Norman Rd C1
North St A2
Norwood Gdns A1
Norwood St A1
Old Railway Works Industrial Estate C3
Orion Way C3
Park Mall Shopping Centre A1
Park Pl C1
Park St A1/A2
Pemberton Rd A3
Police Station A1
Post Office A1/A3/C1
Providence St C2
Queen St A1
Queens Rd A2
Regents Pl A1
Riversdale Rd C2
Romney Marsh Rd B2
St John's La A2
Somerset Rd A2
South Stour Ave B2
Star Rd A3
Station Rd B2
Stirling Rd C2
Stour Leisure Centre, The B2
Sussex Ave A1
Tannery La A2
Technical College B2
Torrington Rd C2
Trumper Bridge B1
Tufton Rd A3
Tufton St A1
Vicarage La A2
Victoria Cres B1
Victoria Park B1
Victoria Rd B1
Wallis Rd A3
Wellesley Rd A2
West St A1
Whitfeld Rd C1
William Rd C1
World War I Tank ✦ A1

¼ mile
¼ ½ km

PRESTWICK

AYR

Ayr

A resort on the west coast of Scotland, the birthplace of poet Robert Burns, with a c.1491 bridge, a 1650s church where Burns was christened, the 15th-century Greenan Castle built on the site of an Iron Age fort, Loudoun Hall, a fine early-16th-century townhouse, Miller's Folly, an observation house converted from a sentinel post on Cromwell's citadel, and the thatched Tam O'Shanter public house. Among the many traditional seaside entertainments and recreational facilities are some long sandy beaches, sea-angling trips, Firth of Clyde cruises aboard the *Waverley* (the world's last seagoing paddlesteamer), a leading racecourse, the Heads of Ayr Farm Park, and Haven Holiday Park. There's a wide range of both specialist and chain shops in its centre.

▲Ayr with Arran in the distance

★Do not miss

★ **Belleisle Estate**, south Ayr

★ **Burns National Heritage Park and Cottage and Tam O'Shanter Experience**, Alloway

★ **Rozelle House and Maclaurin Gallery**, south Ayr

31

Ayr

Ailsa Pl B1	Alloway Pl C1	Auld Kirk ⛪ B2
Alexandra Terr . . . A3	Alloway St C2	Back Main St B2
Allison St B2	Arran Terr B1	Back Peebles St . . A2
Alloway Pk C1	Arthur St B2	Back Hawkhill Ave A3

Ashgrove St C2	Barns Cres C1	Bath Pl B1
Auld Brig B2	Barns Pk C1	Bellevue Cres . . . C1
Ayr Academy B1	Barns Street La . . C1	Bellevue La C1
Ayr Harbour A1	Barns St C1	Beresford La C2
Ayr Station ⇌ . . . C2		Beresford Terr . . . C1
Ayr United FC A3		Borderline 🎭 B2

Boswell Pk B2	Cassillis St B1	Mill Wynd C2
Britannia Pl A3	Cathcart St B1	Miller Rd C1
Bruce Cres B1	Charlotte St B1	Montgomerie Terr . B1
Burns Statue ✦ . . C2	Citadel Leisure Centre B1	New Bridge B2
Bus Sta C2	Citadel Pl B1	New Bridge St B2
Carrick St C2	Civic 🏛 C3	New Rd A2
	Compass Pier . . . A1	Newmarket St B2
	Content Ave C3	Newton-on-Ayr Station ⇌ A2
	Content St B2	North Harbour St . B1
	Craigie Ave B3	North Pier A1
	Craigie Rd B3	Odeon 🎬 C2
	Craigie Way B3	Oswald La A1
	Cromwell Rd B1	Park Circus C1
	Crown St A2	Park Circus La . . . C1
	Dalblair Rd C2	Park Terr. C1
	Dam Park Sports Stadium C3	Pavilion Rd C1
	Damside A2	Peebles St A2
	Dongola Rd C3	Philip Sq B1
	Eglinton Pl B1	Police Station 🚔 . . B2
	Eglinton Terr B1	Post Office 🏤 A2/B2
	Elba St B2	Prestwick Rd A2
	Elmbank St A2	Princes Ct A2
	Esplanade B1	Queen St B3
	Farifield Rd C1	Queen's Terr B1
	Fort St B1	Racecourse Rd . . . C1
	Fothringham Rd . . C3	River St B2
	Fullarton St C1	Riverside Pl B2
	Gaiety 🎭 C2	Russell Dr A2
	Garden St B2	St Andrews Church ⛪ C2
	George St B2	St George's Rd . . . A3
	George's Ave A3	Sandgate B2
	Glebe Cres A2	Savoy Park C1
	Glebe Rd A2	Seabank Rd B1
	Gorden Terr B3	Smith St C2
	Green St A2	Somerset Rd A3
	Green Street La . . A2	South Beach Rd . . B1
	Hawkhill Ave A3	South Harbour St . B1
	Hawkhill Avenue La B3	South Pier A1
	High St B1	Strathaye Pl B2
	Holmston Rd C3	Taylor St A2
	Information Ctr ℹ . . B1	Town Hall B2
	James St B3	Tryfield Pl A3
	John St B2	Turner's Bridge . . . B2
	King St B2	Union Ave. A2
	Kings Ct B2	Victoria Bridge . . . C3
	Kyle Centre C2	Victoria St B3
	Kyle St C2	Viewfield Rd A2
	Library B2	Virginia Gdns A2
	Limekiln Rd A2	Waggon Rd A2
	Limonds Wynd . . . B2	Walker Rd A3
	Loudoun Hall 🏛 . . B2	Wallace Tower ✦ . . B2
	Lymburn Pl B3	Weaver St A2
	Macadam Pl B2	Weir Rd A2
	Main St B2	Wellington La C1
	Mcadam's Monument C1	Wellington Sq C1
	Mccall's Ave A3	West Sanouhar Rd A3
	Mews La B1	Whitletts Rd B3
	Mill Brae C3	Wilson St A3
	Mill St C3	York St A1
		York Street La B1

¼ mile
¼   ½ km

Newton-on-Ayr

A79 KILMARNOCK (A77)

A719 KILMARNOCK (A77)

Dock

North Pier
Compass Pier
South Pier
Dock
Ayr Harbour
Esplanade

Newton Trading Estate

Stabling Point

Ayr United FC Somerset Park

Taylor Street

Waggon Road

Weir Road
Glebe Road
Elmbank St

Limekiln Road

PRESTWICK RD

To Prestwick Airport
Alexandra Ave
Union Ave
McCALL'S AVENUE
Britannia
St

Virginia Coll

NEW ROAD

Weaver St

Allison Street

Princes Ct
Russell

Back Hawkhill Avenue
Hawkhill Avenue
Hawkhill Avenue La

Viewfield Road

Drive Sch

Cemy

WHITLETTS ROAD → To Racecourse

ST GEORGE'S RD
George's Ave
West Sanouhar Rd

WALKER RD

Somerset Street

Wilson Street

KING STREET

Wallacetown

George St
Queen St

Elba St
James St
Victoria St

Craigie Park

Sch

Race Course

CRAIGIE ROAD

Oswald Lane
York Street
York Street Lane
Green Street
Green Street Lane
Crown St
North Harbour Street
Back Peebles St
Peebles St
Back Main St
Damside

Ind Est
Borderline 🎭
Liby
Garden St

New Bridge
River St

Kings Ct
Limonds Wynd

Content St

MAIN ST

Philip Sq

Seabank Rd
Montgomerie Terr
Arran Terr
Eglinton Pl
Ayr Academy
Loudoun Hall
Town Hall
Court
Newmarket St
Auld Brig
Bruce Cres
Citadel St
Cromwell Rd
Ailsa Pl
Eglinton Terr
Queen's Terr
Charlotte Street
Mews La
Bath Pl
South Ayrshire Council HQ

FORT ST
SANDGATE
NEW BRIDGE ST
Cathcart St

Bus Sta
Boswell Pk
Fullarton St
Gaiety 🎭

Wellington Sq
McAdam's Mon
WELLINGTON SQUARE
Wellington La
Park Terr
Pavilion
PAVILION RD

Low Green

ESPLANADE

Farifield Rd

RACECOURSE RD
ALLOWAY PL

BARNS ST
Barns St La
Barns Pk
Alloway Pk
Barns Cres

DALBLAIR ROAD
MILLER ROAD

Burns Statue
Park Circus Lane
Park Circus
Bellevue La
St Andrews Church ⛪
Bellevue Cres
Beresford Terr
To Burns Cottage Museum, Alloway

Savoy Park

Auld Kirk
Wallace Tower
High Street
Arthur St
Strathaye Pl
MacAdam's Wynd
JOHN STREET
Craigie Avenue
Fothringham Rd

Kyle Centre
Carrick St
Mill Wynd
Mill Street

SMITH STREET
KYLE ST
ALLOWAY ST

Fire Sta
Content Ave
Civic
Victoria Bridge
Weir
Coll
Dam Park Sports Stadium
Bowling Green
Allot Gdns
Lymburn Pl
Caravan Park
Craigie Estate
CRAIGIE WAY
Gorden Terr
Riverside Pl

River Ayr
Turner's Bridge

Odeon 🎬
Beresford Terr
Ashgrove Street
To Hosp, A+E
Superstore
Dongola Street
Sch
Mill Brae

River Ayr

Cemetery

A719 TURNBERRY   **A79, A77**   **A713 DALMELLINGTON**   **A70 CUMNOCK**

1   2   3

ℹ **Ayr Tourist Office**, 22 Sandgate, KA7 1BW Tel 01292 288688

📻 **BBC Radio Scotland** 92.4-94.7 FM and 810 AM • **West FM** 96.7 FM

💻 www.south-ayrshire.gov.uk

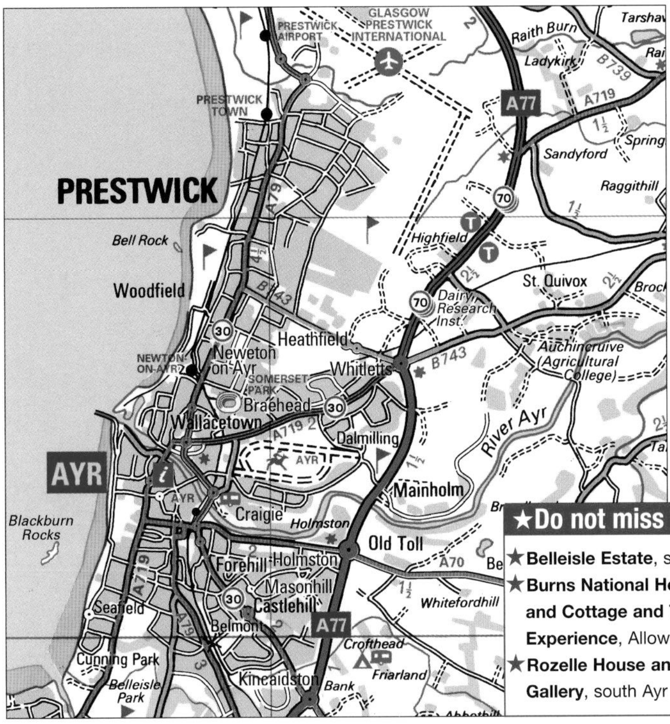

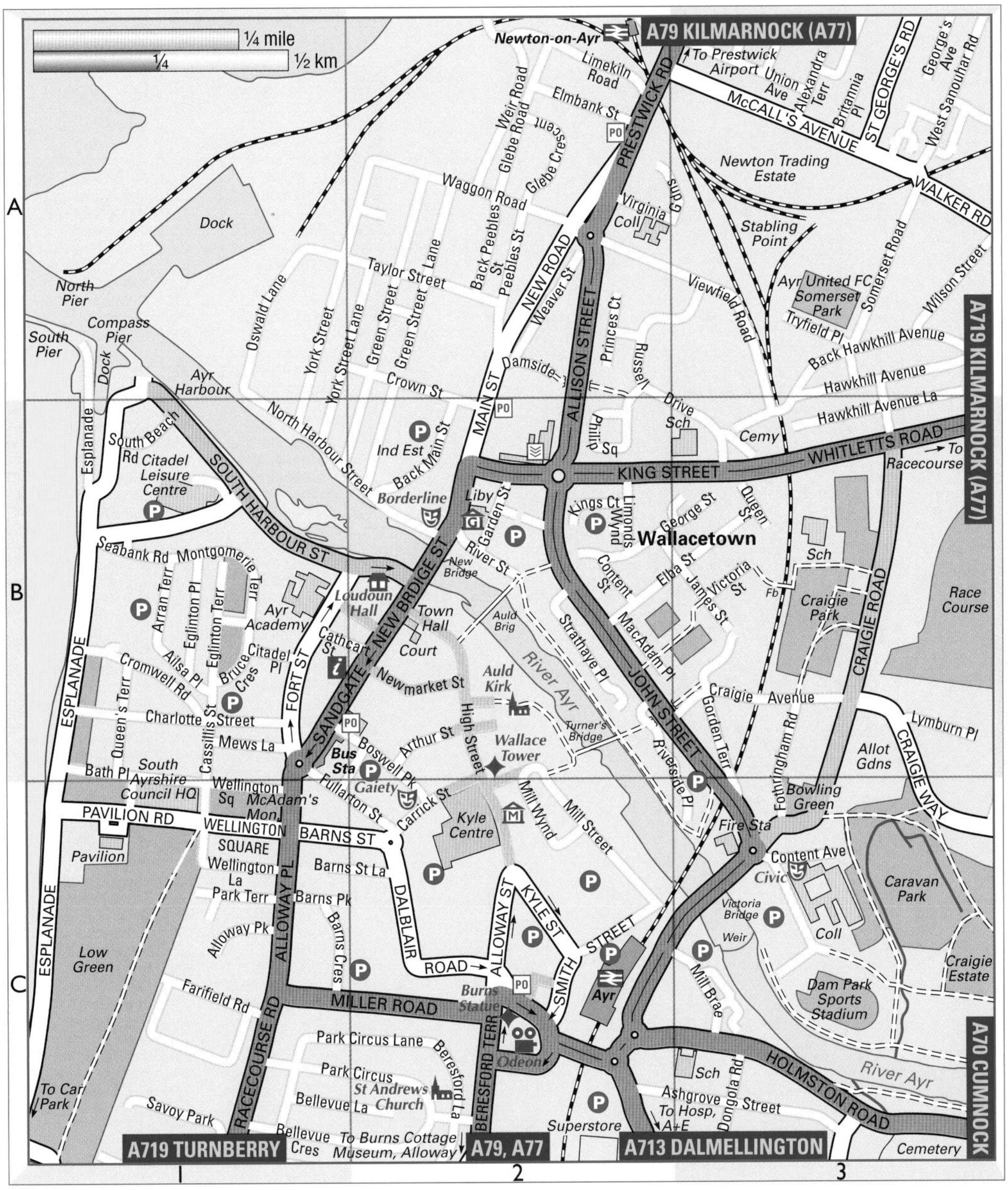

Bangor

An historic university and cathedral city, one of Wales' oldest, Bangor is first recorded as the site of a monastery built by Bishop Deiniol in about AD 525. The tomb of Welsh prince Owain Gwynned lies in the cathedral, and the city was the starting point for pilgrimages to Bardsey Island. The Museum and Art Gallery details the city's history as a major seaport from which local slate was shipped around the world. Situated across the Menai Strait from Anglesey and offering panoramic views, Bangor has an elaborate Victorian pier and Wales' longest high street, with good shopping facilities. The Gorsedd Circle was used for a previous Eisteddfod.

▲Penrhyn Castle

Bangor Tourist Information Centre, Town Hall, Deiniol Road, Bangor LL57 2RE Tel 01248 352786

BBC Radio Wales 94.8 FM
Champion 103.0 FM

www.nwt.co.uk

★Do not miss

★**Bangor Cathedral**, Cathedral Close
★**Cochwillan Old Hall**, Tal-y-Bont
★**Penrhyn Castle**, east Bangor

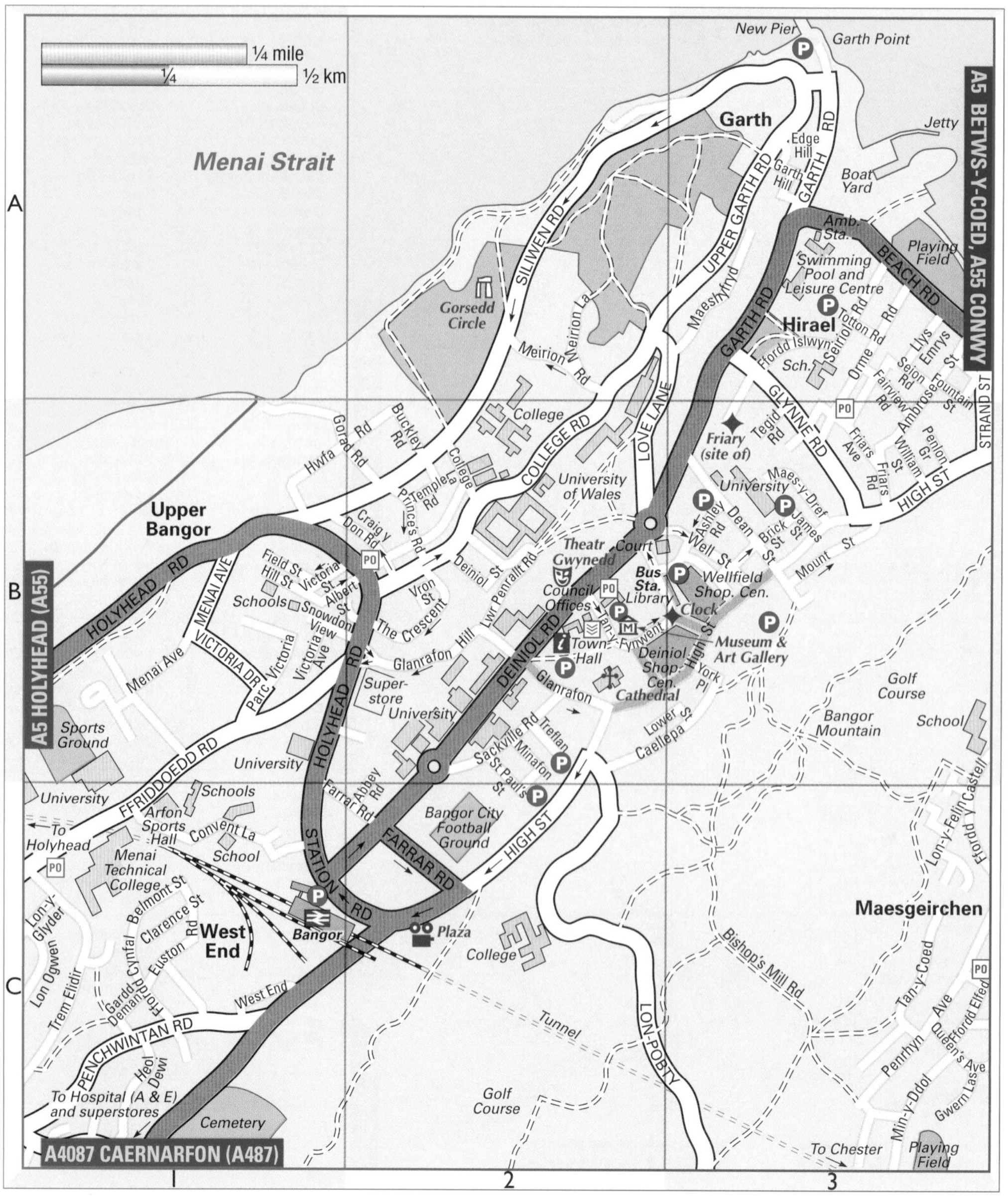

Bangor

Abbey Rd C2
Albert St. B1
Ambrose St A3
Ambulance Station A3
Arfon Sports Hall C1
Ashley Rd. B3
Bangor City Football Ground C2
Bangor Mountain .B3
Bangor Station C1
Beach Rd A3
Belmont St. C1
Bishop's Mill Rd . C3
Boat Yard A3
Brick St. B3
Buckley Rd. B2
Bus Station B3
Caellepa B2
Caernarfon Rd. . . C1
Cathedral ✝ B2
Cemetery C1
Clarence St C1
Clock ✦ B3
College. B2/C2
College La B2
College Rd B2
Convent La. C1
Council Offices . . .B2
Court. B2
Craig y Don Rd . . .B2
Dean St. B3
Deiniol Rd B2
Deiniol Shopping Centre. B2
Deiniol St. B2
Edge Hill A3
Euston Rd. C1
Fairview Rd A3
Farrar Rd C2
Ffordd Cynfal. . . . C1
Ffordd Elfed. C3
Ffordd Islwyn. . . . A3
Ffordd y Castell. . C3
Ffriddoedd Rd B1
Field St. B1
Fountain St A3
Friars Ave. B3
Friars Rd B3
Friary (Site of) ✦ .B3
Gardd Deman . . . C1
Garth Hill A3
Garth Point A3
Garth Rd. A3
Glanrafon. B2
Glanrafon Hill B2
Glynne Rd B3
Golf Course B3
Golf Course C2
Gorad Rd B1
Gorsedd Circle A2
Gwern Las C3
Heol Dewi C1
High St B3/C2
Hill St B1
Holyhead Rd B1
Hwfa Rd B1
Information Ctr .B2
James St B3
Library B2
Llys Emrys A3
Lon Ogwen. C1
Lon-Pobty C2
Lon-y-Felin C3
Lon-y-Glyder. . . . C1
Love La. B2
Lower Penrallt Rd.B2
Lower St. B2
Maes-y-Dref B3
Maeshyfryd A3
Meirion La A2
Meirion Rd. A2
Menai Ave B1
Menai Technical College. C1
Min-y-Ddol C3
Minafon B2
Mount St B3
Museum & Art Gallery B2
New Pier A3
Orme Rd. A3
Parc Victoria B1
Penchwintan Rd . C1
Penlon Gr. B3
Penrhyn Ave C3
Plaza C2
Police Station . .B2
Post Office B2/B3/C1/C3
Prince's Rd B2
Queen's Ave. C3
Sackville Rd. B2
St Paul's St B2
Seion Rd. A3
Seiriol Rd. A3
Siliwen Rd A2
Snowdon View B1
Sports Ground. . . .B1
Station Rd C1
Strand St B3
Swimming Pool & Leisure Centre. . A3
Tan-y-Coed C3
Tan-y-Fynwent . . .B2
Tegid Rd. B3
Temple Rd B2
The Crescent B2
Theatr Gwynedd B2
Totton Rd A3
Town Hall B2
Treflan B2
Trem Elidir. C1
University of Wales B2
Upper Garth Rd. . A3
Victoria Ave B1
Victoria Dr B1
Victoria St B1
Vron St B2
Well St B3
Wellfield Shopping Centre. B3
West End C1
William St B3
York Pl B3

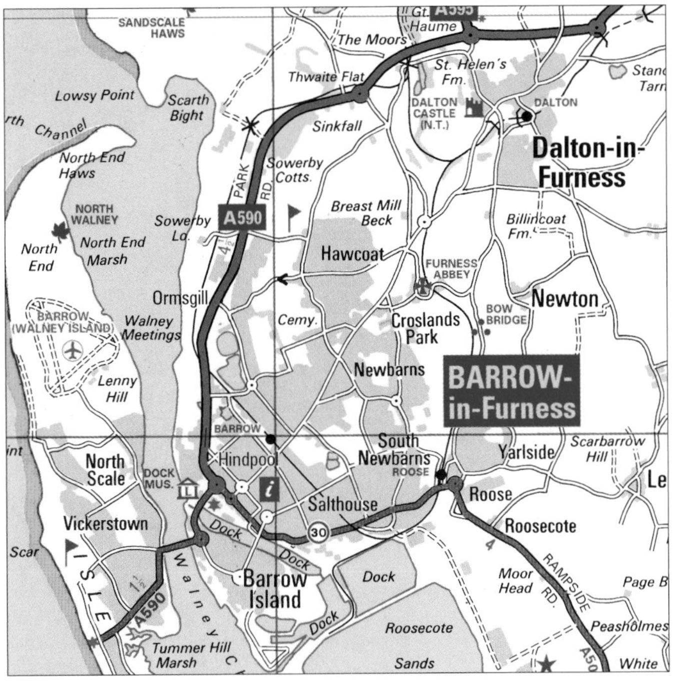

Barrow-in-Furness

A Victorian market town with a proud shipbuilding history, focused around its handsome red sandstone modern Gothic town hall and set within easy reach of several good beaches and against the backdrop of the mountains of the Lake District (20 minutes away). The large indoor market has more than 80 independent stalls selling local produce and more. Nearby are South Lakes Wild Animal Park, a leading conservation zoo, Bardsea Country Park with its woodland areas and picnic areas, Dalton Castle (National Trust), once a courthouse and dungeon for Furness Abbey, two nature reserves on the Isle of Walney and the characterful villages of Askam and Ireleth on the Duddon Estuary. The annual summer Festival of the Sea is one of the best times to visit.

▲Furness Abbey

Barrow Tourist Information, Duke Street, Barrow-in-Furness LA14 1HU Tel 01229 894784

BBC Radio Cumbria 96.1 FM and 837 AM • **The Bay** 96.9 FM

www.barrowbc.gov.uk

★Do not miss

★**Dock Museum**, North Road

★**Furness Abbey and Custodian's Cottage** (English Heritage), just north of town

★**Piel Castle** (English Heritage), Piel Island

Barrow-in-Furness

Abbey Rd A3/B2
Adelaide St A2
Ainslie St A3
Albert St........ C3
Allison St B3
Anson St......... A2
Argyle St B3
Arthur St B3
Ashburner Way .. A1
Barrow Raiders RLFC...........B1
Barrow Station A2
Bath St...... A1/B2
Bedford Rd...... A3
Bessamer Way... A1
Blake St A1/A2
Bridge Rd....... C1
Buccleuch Dock . C3
Buccleuch Dock Rd C2/C3
Buccleuch St.....B2
Byron St......... A2
Calcutta St...... A1
Cameron St C1
Carlton Ave A3
Cavendish Dock Rd C3
Cavendish St . B2/B3
Channelside Walk.B1
Channelside Haven C1
Chatsworth St... A2
Cheltenham St .. A3
Church St....... C3
Clifford St B2
Clive St..........B1
Collingwood St ..B2
Cook St......... A2
Cornerhouse Retail Park......B2
Cornwallis St.....B2
Courts.......... A2
Crellin St B3
Cross St C3
Dalkeith St.......B2
Dalton Rd.... B2/C2
Derby St B3
Devonshire Dock. C2
Dock Museum, The B1
Drake St........ A2
Dryden St....... A2
Duke St... A1/B2/C3
Duncan St B2
Dundee St C2
Dundonald St B2
Earle St......... C1
Emlyn St.........B2
Exmouth St A2
Farm St......... C2
Fell St...........B3
Fenton St B3
Ferry Rd C1
Forum 28 ......B2
Furness College ..B1
Glasgow St.......B3
Goldsmith St A2
Greengate St B3
Hardwick St..... A2
Harrison St B3
Hartington St.... A2
Hawke St B2
Hibbert Rd A2
High Level Bridge C2
High St..........B2
Hindpool Park Retail Park......B2
Hindpool Rd......B2
Holker St A2
Hollywood Retail & Leisure Park ..B1
Hood St A2
Howard St B2
Howe St A2
Information Ctr .B2
Ironworks Rd. A1/B1
James St B3
Jubliee Bridge... C1
Keith St..........B2
Keyes St A2
Lancaster St..... A3
Lawson St B2
Library B2
Lincoln St....... A3
Longreins Rd A3
Lonsdale St C3
Lord St B3
Lorne Rd B3
Lyon St......... A2
Manchester St....B2
Market B2
Market St B2
Marsh St.........B3
Michaelson Rd .. C2
Milton St A2
Monk St B2
Mount Pleasant...B3
Nan Tait Centre ..B2
Napier St B2
Nelson St B2
North Rd.........B1
Open Market B2
Parade St B2
Paradise St B3
Park Ave........ A3
Park Dr......... A3
Parker St A2
Parry St A2
Peter Green Way. A1
Phoenix Rd A1
Police Station ..B2
Portland Walk Shopping Centre.B2
Post Office . A3/B2/B3
Princess Selandia C2
Raleigh St A2
Ramsden St.......B3
Rawlinson St B3
Robert St B3
Rodney St........B2
Rutland St A2
St Patrick's Rd .. C1
Salthouse Rd..... C3
School St B3
Scott St..........B2
Settle St A3
Shore St C3
Sidney St B2
Silverdale St B3
Slater St.........B2
Smeaton St B3
Stafford St A3
Stanley Rd C1
Stark St C3
Steel St..........B1
Storey Sq B3
Strand.......... C3
Sutherland St B3
TA Centre A2
The Park........ A3
Thwaite St B3
Town Hall B2
Town Quay C3
Vernon St........B2
Vincent St B2
Walney Rd A1
West Gate Rd.... A2
West View Rd.... A3
Westmorland St . A3
Whitehead St.... A3
Wordsworth St .. A2

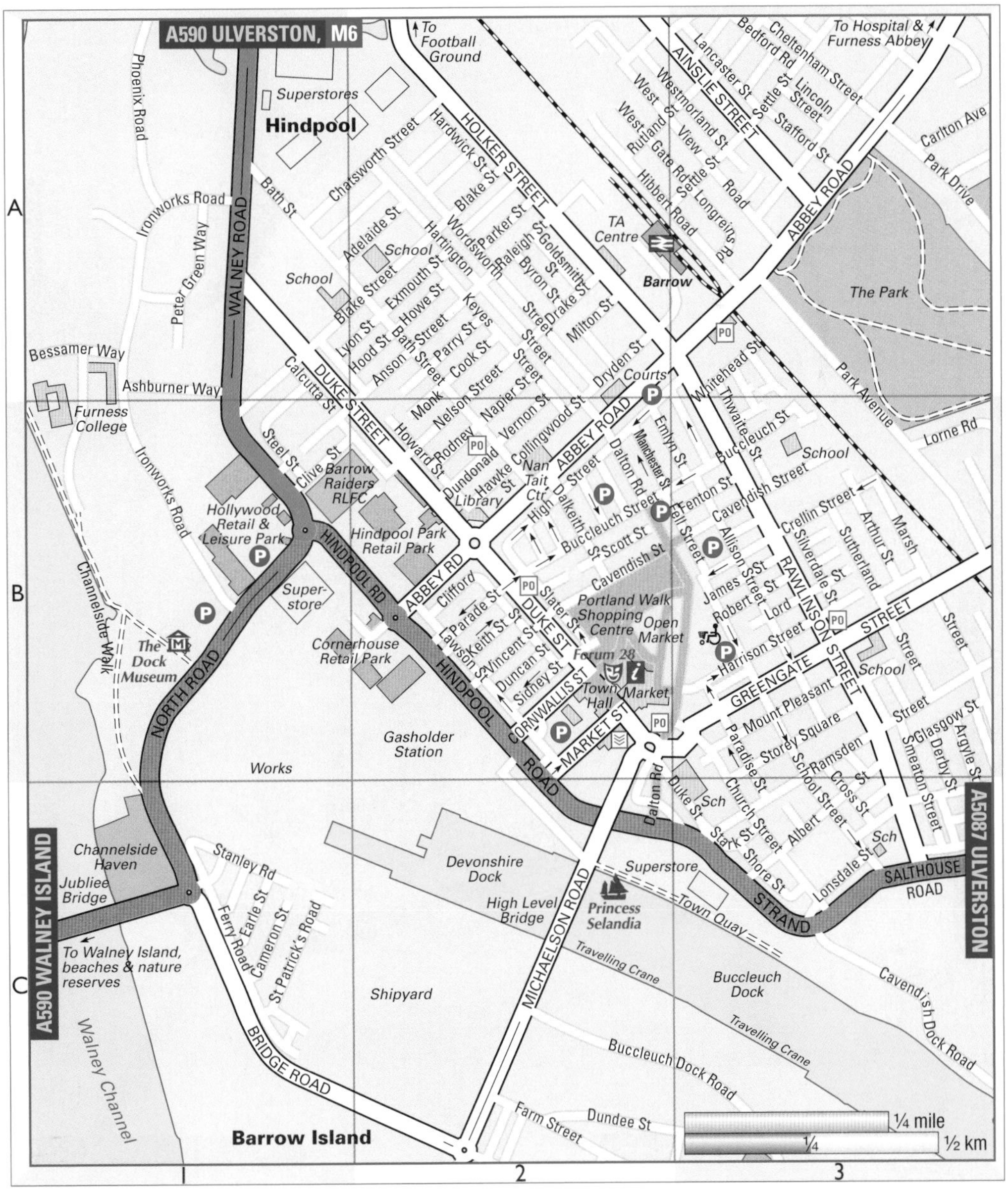

Bath

▲Pulteney Bridge

★Do not miss

★**Bath Abbey and Heritage Vaults**, York Street

★**Roman Baths Museum and Pump Room**, Stall Street

★**No.1 Royal Crescent –** 18th-century townhouse with period furnishings

A UNESCO World Heritage site on the site of thermal springs, boasting a host of important architectural sites, including the Royal Crescent and the Circus. Historical museums and galleries include the Building of Bath Museum, Museum of Bath at Work, Museum of Costume, Postal Museum, Bath Aqua Theatre of Glass, the William Herschel Museum, the Museum of East Asian Art and the Victoria Art Gallery in the Guildhall. The Theatre Royal is one of the country's oldest and most impressive drama venues and the 18th-century Assembly Rooms are still used for concerts and balls. Jane Austen's life and times are explored in the Jane Austen Centre. Green spaces include the Georgian Garden, the Royal Victoria Park and Prior Park Land-scape Garden. The town is a major centre for shopping with specialist shops lining Robert Adam's Pulteney Bridge and plenty of high street shops. As a university town there are many great pubs and restaurants for all tastes.

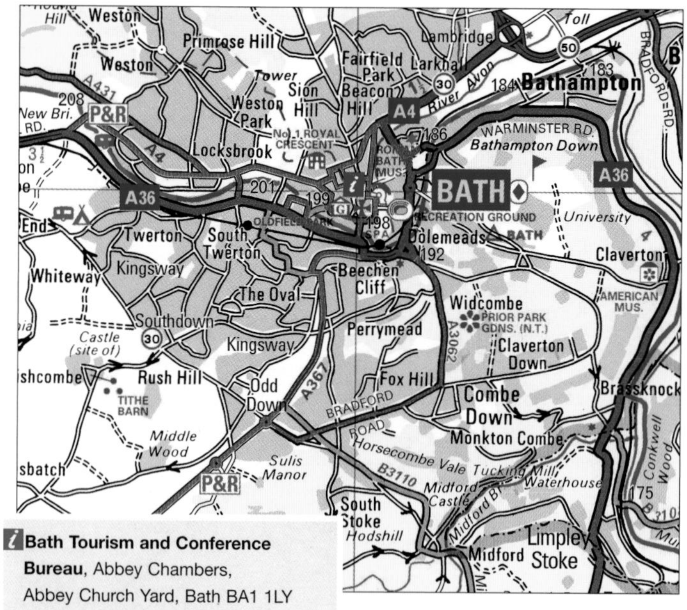

ℹ Bath Tourism and Conference Bureau, Abbey Chambers, Abbey Church Yard, Bath BA1 1LY
Tel 0906 711 2000 (60p per min)

BBC Somerset Sound 1566 AM
Bath FM 107.9 FM • **Classic Gold** 1260 AM • **GWR** 103.0 FM

www.visitbath.co.uk

¼ mile
½ km

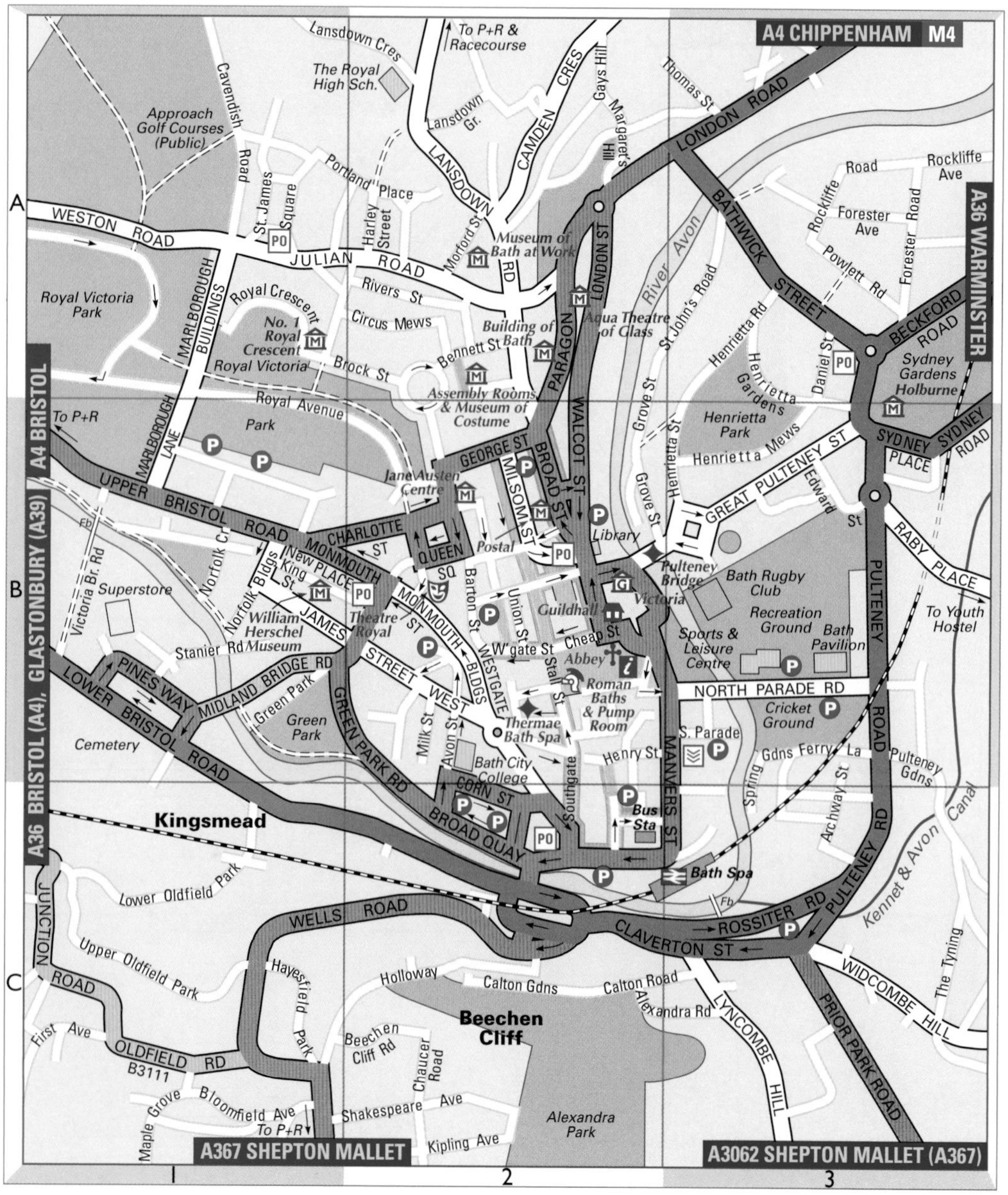

Bath

Alexandra Park C2
Alexandra Rd C2
Approach Golf Courses (Public) A1
Aqua Theatre of Glass A2
Archway St C3
Assembly Rooms & Museum of Costume A2
Avon St B2
Barton St B2
Bath Abbey B2
Bath City College B2
Bath Pavilion B3
Bath Rugby Club B3
Bath Spa Station C3
Bathwick St A3
Beechen Cliff Rd C2
Bennett St A2
Bloomfield Ave C1
Broad Quay C2
Broad St B2
Brock St A1
Building of Bath Museum A2
Bus Station C2
Calton Gdns C2
Calton Rd C2
Camden Cr A2
Cavendish Rd A1
Cemetery B1
Charlotte St B2
Chaucer Rd C2
Cheap St B2
Circus Mews A2
Claverton St C2
Corn St C2
Cricket Ground B3
Daniel St A3
Edward St A3
Ferry La B3
First Ave C1
Forester Ave A3
Forester Rd A3
Gays Hill A2
George St B3
Great Pulteney St B3
Green Park B1
Green Park Rd B2
Grove St B2
Guildhall B2
Harley St A2
Hayesfield Park C1
Henrietta Gdns A3
Henrietta Mews B3
Henrietta Park B3
Henrietta Rd A3
Henrietta St B3
Henry St B2
Holburne Mus B3
Holloway C2
Information Ctr B2
James St West B1/B2
Jane Austen Centre B2
Julian Rd A1
Junction Rd C1
Kipling Ave C2
Lansdown Cr A1
Lansdown Gr A2
Lansdown Rd A2
Library B2
London Rd A3
London St A2
Lower Bristol Rd B1
Lower Oldfield Park C1
Lyncombe Hill C3
Manvers St B3
Maple Gr C1
Margaret's Hill A2
Marlborough Buildings A1
Marlborough La B1
Midland Bridge Rd B1
Milk St B2
Milsom St B2
Monmouth St B2
Morford St A2
Museum of Bath at Work A2
New King St B1
No. 1 Royal Crescent A1
Norfolk Bldgs A1
Norfolk Cr B1
North Parade Rd B3
Oldfield Rd C1
Paragon A2
Pines Way A1
Police Station B3
Portland Pl A2
Post Office A1/A3/B2/C2
Postal Mus B2
Powlett Rd A3
Prior Park Rd C3
Pulteney Bridge B2
Pulteney Gdns B3
Pulteney Rd B3
Queen Sq B2
Raby Pl B3
Recreation Ground B3
Rivers St A2
Rockliffe Ave A3
Rockliffe Rd A3
Roman Baths & Pump Room B2
Rossiter Rd C3
Royal Ave A1
Royal Cr A1
Royal High School, The A2
Royal Victoria Park A1
St James Sq A1
St John's Rd A3
Shakespeare Ave C2
Southgate C2
South Pde B3
Sports & Leisure Centre B3
Spring Gdns C3
Stall St B2
Stanier Rd A1
Sydney Gdns A3
Sydney Pl B3
Theatre Royal B2
Thermae Bath Spa B2
The Tyning C3
Thomas St A3
Union St B2
Upper Bristol Rd B1
Upper Oldfield Park C1
Victoria Art Gallery B2
Victoria Bridge Rd B1
Walcot St B2
Wells Rd C1
Westgate St B2
Weston Rd A1
Widcombe Hill C3
William Herschel Museum B1

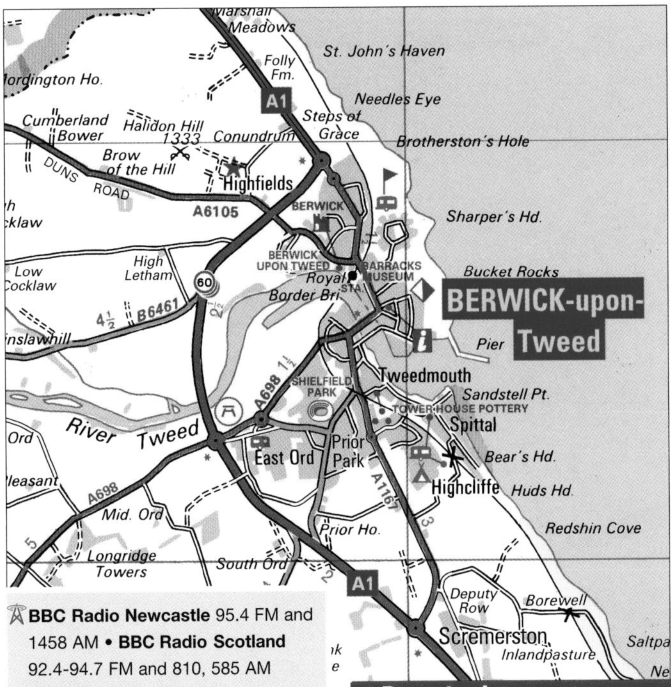

Berwick-upon-Tweed

England's most northerly town, which began life as an Anglo-Saxon settlement and changed hands between the Scottish and English 13 times. It has retained part of its walls, erected by Edward I against Scottish attack in the 14th century (little remains of its border castle), and the 1611 Old Bridge over the Tweed. Set amidst its many attractive Georgian buildings are a mid-18th-century spired town hall and a rare Cromwellian church, Holy Trinity, with some 16th-century Flemish stained glass and a reredos by Lutyens but minus a steeple, tower or church bell. The country's oldest purpose-built barracks now house an art gallery containing part of the Burrell Art Collection, two military museums and local-history displays. Just south of Berwick, Holy Island has a 7th-century priory that was the cradle of Christianity in the north, a Heritage Centre, and a miniature 16th-century castle converted into an Edwardian country house by Lutyens. Nearby you will find 14th-century Etal Castle with an exhibition of border warfare and weaponry, some relating to the Battle of Flodden. The town is also home to many arts and crafts shops. The Maltings arts centre and several pubs provide entertainment.

▲ Lindisfarne Priory

BBC Radio Newcastle 95.4 FM and 1458 AM • BBC Radio Scotland 92.4-94.7 FM and 810, 585 AM
Radio Borders 97.5 FM

Tourist Information Centre,
106 Marygate, Berwick-upon-Tweed
TD15 1BN Tel 01289 330733

www.berwick-upon-tweed.gov.uk

★Do not miss

★**Berwick Art Gallery**, Berwick Barracks
★**Lindisfarne Priory**, Holy Island
★**Paxton House & Picture Gallery** (Palladian), just west of town

Berwick-upon-Tweed

Bank Hill B2
Barracks 🏛 A3
Bell Tower ✦ A3
Bell Tower Pl A2
Berwick Bridge ...B2
Berwick Infirmary 🅷 A3
Berwick Rangers F.C. C1
Berwick-upon-Tweed ⇌ A2
Billendean Rd ... C3
Blakewell Gdns ...B2
Blakewell St......B2
Brass Bastion ✦ . A3
Bridge St B3
Brucegate St A2
Castle (Remains of) ♜ A2
Castle Terrace ... A2
Castlegate A2
Chapel St A3
Church Rd C2
Church St........B3
Court............B3
Coxon's La A3
Cumberland Bastion ✦ A3
Dean Dr C2
Dock Rd C2/C3
Elizabethan Walls....... A2/B3
Fire Station B1
Flagstaff Park B3
Football Ground . C3
Foul Ford B3
Gallery 🏛 A3
Golden Sq B2
Golf Course A3
Greenwood C1
Gunpowder Magazine 🏛 B3
Hide Hill.........B3
High Greens..... A2
Holy Trinity ⛪ ... A3
Information Ctr 🛈 A2
Kiln Hill B2
King's Mount ✦ ..B3
Ladywell Rd..... C2
Library A3
Lifeboat Station . C3
Lord's Mount ✦ . A3
Lovaine Terrace.. A2
Low Greens A3
Main Guard 🏛....B3
Main St...... B2/C2
Maltings Art Centre, The B3
Marygate B3
Meg's Mount ✦.. A2
Middle St C3
Mill St.......... C2
Mount Rd....... C2
Museum 🏛 B3
Ness St..........B3
North Rd........ A2
Northumberland Ave A2
Northumberland Rd C2
Ord Dr...........B1
Osborne Cr B2
Osborne Rd B1
Palace Gr B3
Palace St B3
Palace St East....B3
Pier Rd B3
Playing Field C1
Police Station 🅿 B3
Post Office 🅿 A2/B2/B2
Prince Edward Rd B2
Prior Rd C2
Quay Walls.......B3
Railway St A2
Ravensdowne B3
Records Office... A3
Riverdene........B1
Riverside Rd B2
Royal Border Bridge......... A2
Royal Tweed Bridge..........B2
Russian Gun ✦ ...B3
Scots Gate ✦..... A2
Scott's Pl A2
Shielfield Park... C1
Shielfield Terr ... C2
Silver St B3
Spittal Quay..... C3
Superstores C2
The Avenue B3
The Parade A3
Tower Gdns A2
Tower Rd C2
Town Hall B3
Turret Gdns C2
Tweed Dock.......B2
Tweed St A2
Tweedside Trading Estate.. C1
Union Brae.......B2
Union Park Rd....B2
Walkergate...... A3
Wallace Gr...... A3
War Memorial ... A2
Warkworth Terrace........ A2
Well Close Sq ... A2
West End B2
West End Pl B1
West End Rd B1
West St..........B3
West St......... C3
Windmill Bastion ✦ B3
Woolmarket......B3

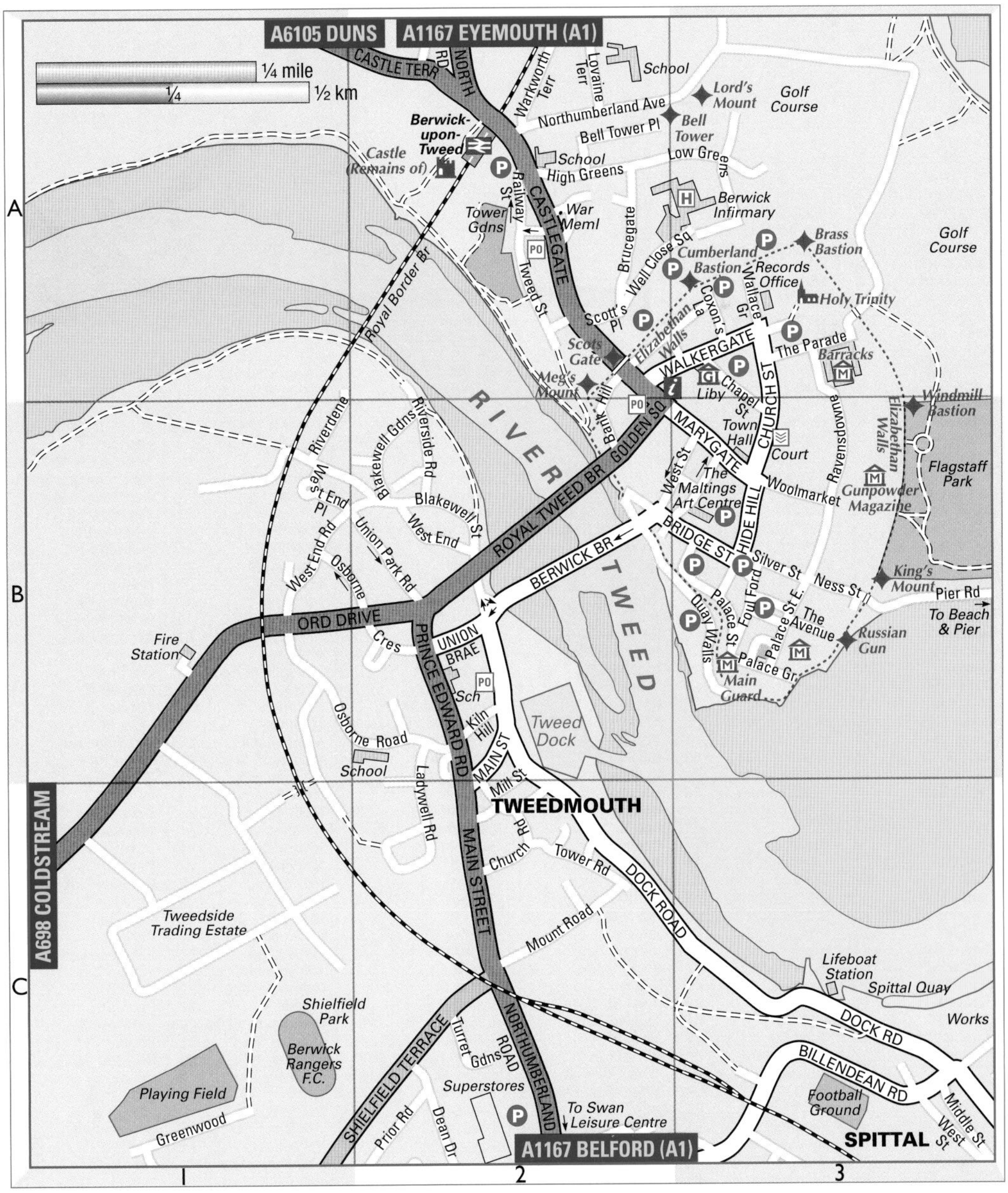

Birmingham

Abbey St A2
Aberdeen St A1
Acorn Gr B2
Adams St A5
Adderley St C5
Albert St B4/B5
Albion St B2
Alcester St C5
Aldgate Gr A3
Alexandra Theatre C3
All Saint's St A2
All Saints Rd A2
Allcock St C5
Allesley St A4
Allison St C4
Alma Cr B6
Alston Rd C1
Arcadian Centre C4
Arthur St C6
Assay Office B3
Aston Expressway A5
Aston Science Park B5
Aston St B4
Avenue Rd A5
BT Tower ✦ B3
Bacchus Rd A1
Bagot St B4
Banbury St B5
Barford Rd B1
Barford St C4
Barn St C5
Barnwell Rd C6
Barr St A3
Barrack St B5
Bartholomew St C4
Barwick St B4
Bath Row C3
Beaufort Rd C1
Belmont Row B5
Benson Rd A1
Berkley St C3
Bexhill Gr C3
Birchall St C5
Birmingham City F.C. (St Andrew's) C6
Birmingham City Hospital (A&E) A1
Bishopsgate St C3
Blews St A4
Bloomsbury St A6
Blucher St C3
Bordesley St C4
Bowyer St C5
Bradburne Way A5
Bradford St C5
Branston St A3
Brearley St A4
Brewery St A4
Bridge St A3
Bridge St C3
Bridge St West A4
Brindley Dr B3
Broad St C3
Broad St UGC C2
Broadway Plaza ✦ C2
Bromley St C5
Bromsgrove St C4
Brookfield Rd A2
Browning St C2
Bryant St A1
Buckingham St A3
Bullring C4
Bull St B4
Cambridge St C3
Camden Dr B3
Camden St B2
Cannon St C4
Cardigan St B5
Carlisle St A1
Carlyle Rd C1
Caroline St B3
Carver St B2
Cato St A6
Cato St North A6
Cattell Rd C6
Cattells Gr A6
Cawdor Cr C1
Cecil St B4
Cemetery A2/B2
Cemetery La A2
Centre Link Industrial Estate A6
Charlotte St B3
Cheapside C4
Chester St A5
Children's Hospital B4
Church St B4
Claremont Rd A2
Clarendon Rd C1
Clark St C1
Clement St B3
Clissold St B2
Cliveland St B4
Coach Station C5
College St B2
Colmore Circus B4
Colmore Row B4
Commercial St C3
Constitution Hill B3
Convention Centre C3
Cope St B2
Coplow St B1
Corporation St B4
Council House B3
County Court B4
Coveley Gr A2
Coventry Rd C6
Coventry St C5
Cox St B3
Crabtree Rd A2
Cregoe St C3
Crescent Ave A2
Crescent Theatre C3
Cromwell St A6
Cromwell St B3
Curzon St B5
Cuthbert Rd B1
Dale End B4
Dart St C6
Dartmouth Circus A4
Dartmouth Middleway A5
Dental Hospital B4
Deritend C5
Devon St A6
Devonshire St A1
Digbeth Civic Hall C5
Digbeth High St C4
Dolman St B6
Dover St A1
Duchess Rd C2
Duddeston ⇄ B6
Duddeston Manor Rd B5
Duddeston Mill Rd B6
Duddeston Mill Trading Estate B6
Dudley Rd B1
Edgbaston Shopping Centre C2
Edmund St B3
Edward St B3
Elkington St A4
Ellen St B2
Ellis St C3
Erskine St B6
Essex St C4
Eyre St B2
Farm Croft A3
Farm St A3
Fazeley St B4
Felstead Way B5
Finstall Cl B5
Five Ways C2
Fleet St B3
Floodgate St C5
Ford St A2
Fore St C4
Forster St B5
Francis Rd C2
Francis St B5
Frankfort St A4
Frederick St B3
Freeth St C1
Freightliner Terminal B6
Garrison La C6
Garrison St B6
Gas St C3
Geach St A4
George St B3
George St West B2
Gibb St C5
Gillott Rd B1
Gilby Rd C2
Glover St C5
Goode Ave A2
Goodrick Way A6
Gordon St B6
Graham St B3
Granville St C3
Gray St C6
Great Barr St C5
Great Charles St B3
Great Francis St B6
Great Hampton Row A3
Great Hampton St A3
Great King St A3
Great Lister St A5
Great Tindal St C2
Green La C6
Green St C5
Greenway St C6
Grosvenor St West C2
Guest Gr A3
Guild Cl C2
Guildford Dr A4
Guthrie Cl A3
Hagley Rd C1
Hall St B3
Hampton St B3
Handsworth New Rd A1
Hanley St B4

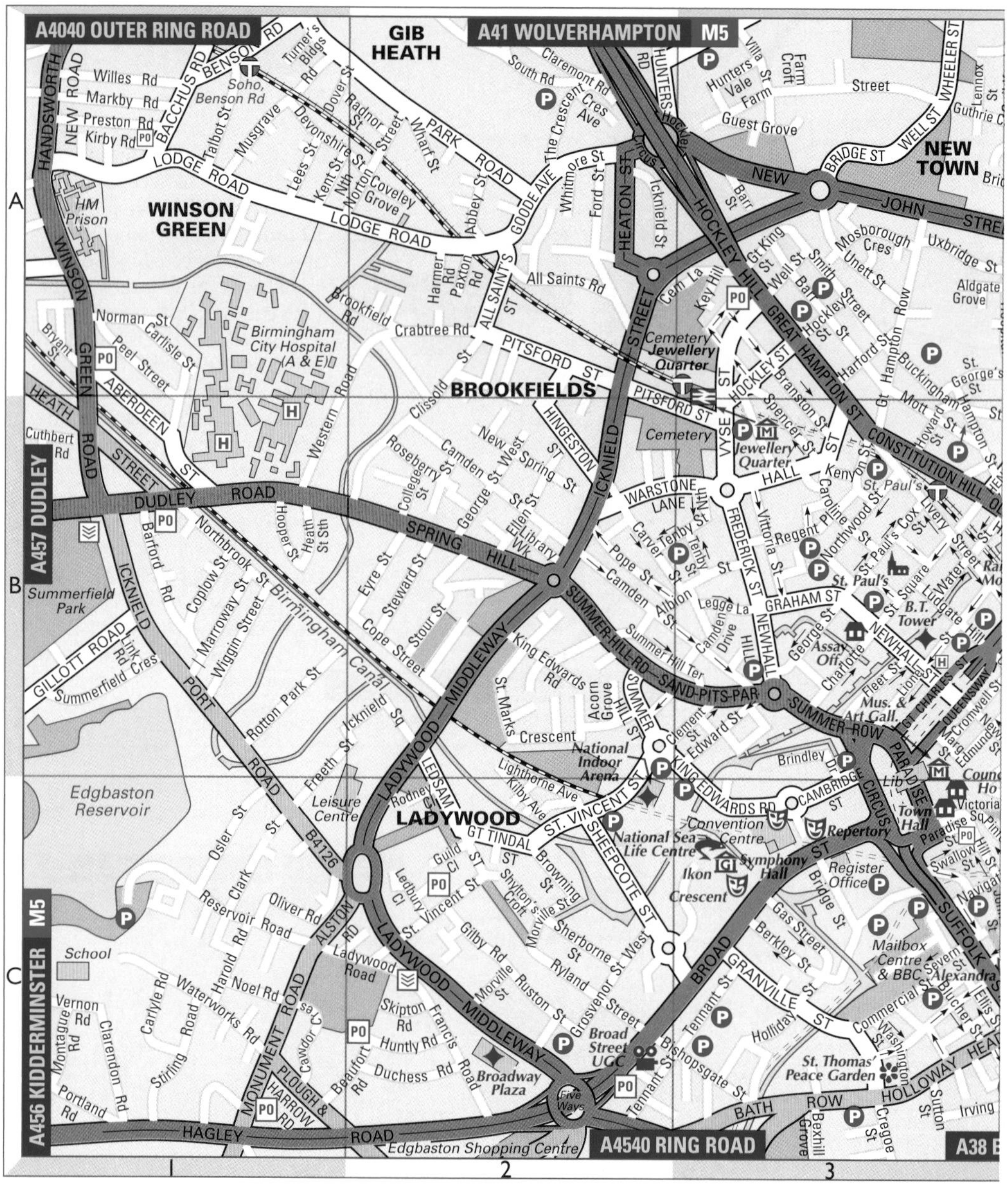

Harford St A3
Harmer Rd A2
Harold Rd C1
Hatchett St A4
Heath Mill La C5
Heath St B1
Heath St South B1
Heaton St A2
Heneage St B5
Henrietta St B4
Herbert Rd C6
High St C4
High St C5
Hilden Rd B5
Hill St C3
Hindlow Cl B6
Hingeston St B2
Hippodrome Theatre C4
HM Prison A1
Hockley Circus A2
Hockley Hill A3
Hockley St A3
Holliday St C3
Holloway Circus C4
Holloway Head C3
Holt St B5
Hooper St B1
Horse Fair C4
Hospital St A4
Howard St B3
Howe St B5
Hubert St A5
Hunters Rd A2
Hunters Vale A3
Huntly Rd C2
Hurst St C4
Icknield Port Rd B1
Icknield Sq B2
Icknield St A2
Ikon Gallery C3
Information Ctr C4
Inge St C4
Irving St C3
Ivy La C5
James Watt Queensway B4
Jennens Rd B5
Jewellery Quarter ⇄ A3
Jewellery Quarter Museum B3
John Bright St C4
Keeley St C6
Kellett Rd B5
Kent St C4
Kent St North A1
Kenyon St B3
Key Hill A3
Kilby Ave C2
King Edwards Rd B2
King Edwards Rd C3
Kingston Rd C6
Kirby Rd A1
Ladywood Middleway C2
Ladywood Rd C1
Lancaster St B4
Landor St B6
Law Courts B4
Lawford Cl B5
Lawley Middleway B5
Ledbury Cl C2
Ledsam St B2
Lees St A1
Legge La B3
Lennox St A3
Library A6/C3
Library Walk B2
Lighthorne Ave B2
Link Rd B1
Lionel St B3
Lister St B5
Little Ann St C5
Little Hall Rd A6
Liverpool St C5
Livery St B3
Lodge Rd A1
Lord St A5
Love La A5
Loveday St B4
Lower Dartmouth St C6
Lower Loveday St B4
Lower Tower St A4
Lower Trinty St C5
Ludgate Hill B3
Mailbox Centre & BBC C3
Margaret St B3
Markby Rd A1
Marroway St B1
Maxstoke St C6
Melvina Rd A6
Meriden St C4
Metropolitan (R.C.) ✝ B4
Midland St B6
Milk St C5
Mill St A5
Millennium Point B5
Miller St A4
Milton St A4
Moat La C4
Montague Rd C1
Montague St C5
Monument Rd C1
Moor Street ⇄ C4
Moor St Queensway C4
Moorsom St A4
Morville St C2
Mosborough Cr A3
Moseley St C4
Mott St B3
Museum & Art Gallery B3
Musgrave Rd A1
National Indoor Arena ✦ B2
National Sea Life Centre C3
Navigation St C3
Nechell's Park Rd A6
Nechells Parkway A5
Nechells Pl A6
New Bartholomew St C4
New Canal St B5
New John St West A3
New Spring St B2
New St C4
New Street ⇄ C4
New Summer St A4
New Town Row A4
Newhall Hill B3
Newhall St B3
Newton St B4
Newtown A4
Noel Rd C1
Norman St A1
Northbrook St B1
Northwood St B3
Norton St A2
Old Crown House C5
Old Rep Theatre, The C4
Old Snow Hill B4
Oliver Rd C1
Oliver St A5
Osler St C1
Oxford St C5
Pallasades Centre C4
Palmer St C5
Paradise Circus C3
Paradise St C3
Park Rd A2
Park St C4
Pavilions Centre C4
Paxton Rd A2
Peel St A1
Penn St B5
Pershore St C4
Phillips St A4
Pickford St C5
Pinfold St C4
Pitsford St A2
Plough & Harrow Rd C1
Police Station A4/B1/B4/C2/C4
Pope St B2
Portland Rd C1
Post Office A1/A3/A5/B1/B5/C1/C2/C3/C5
Preston Rd A1
Price St B4
Princip St B4
Printing House St B4
Priory Queensway B4
Pritchett St A4
Proctor St A5
Queensway B3
Radnor St A2
Railway Mosaics ✦ B4
Rea St C4
Regent Pl B3
Register Office C3
Repertory Theatre C3
Reservoir Rd C1
Richard St A5
River St C5
Rocky La A5
Rodney Cl C2
Roseberry St B2
Rotton Park St B1
Rupert St A5
Ruston St C2
Ryland St C2
St Andrew's Industrial Estate C6
St Andrew's Rd C6
St Andrew's St C6
St Bolton St C6
St Chads Circus B4
St Chads Queensway B4
St Clements Rd A6
St George's St A3
St James Pl B5
St Marks Cr B2
St Martin's C4
St Paul's B3
St Paul's (Metro station) B3
St Paul's Sq B3
St Philip's ✝ B4
St Stephen's St A4
St Thomas' Peace Garden ✽ C3
St Vincent St C2
Saltley Rd A6
Sand Pits Pde B3
Severn St C3
Shadwell St B4
Sheepcote St C2
Shefford Rd A4
Sherborne St C2
Shylton's Croft C2
Skipton Rd C2
Smallbrook Queensway C4
Smith St A3
Snow Hill ⇄ B4
Snow Hill Queensway B4
Soho, Benson Rd (Metro station) A1
South Rd A2
Spencer St B3
Spring Hill B2
Staniforth St B4
Station St C4
Steelhouse La B4
Stephenson St C4
Steward St B2
Stirling Rd C1
Stour St B2
Suffolk St C3
Summer Hill Rd B2
Summer Hill St B2
Summer Hill Terr B2
Summer La A4
Summer Row B3
Summerfield Cr B1
Summerfield Park B1
Sutton St C3
Swallow St C3
Sydney Rd C6

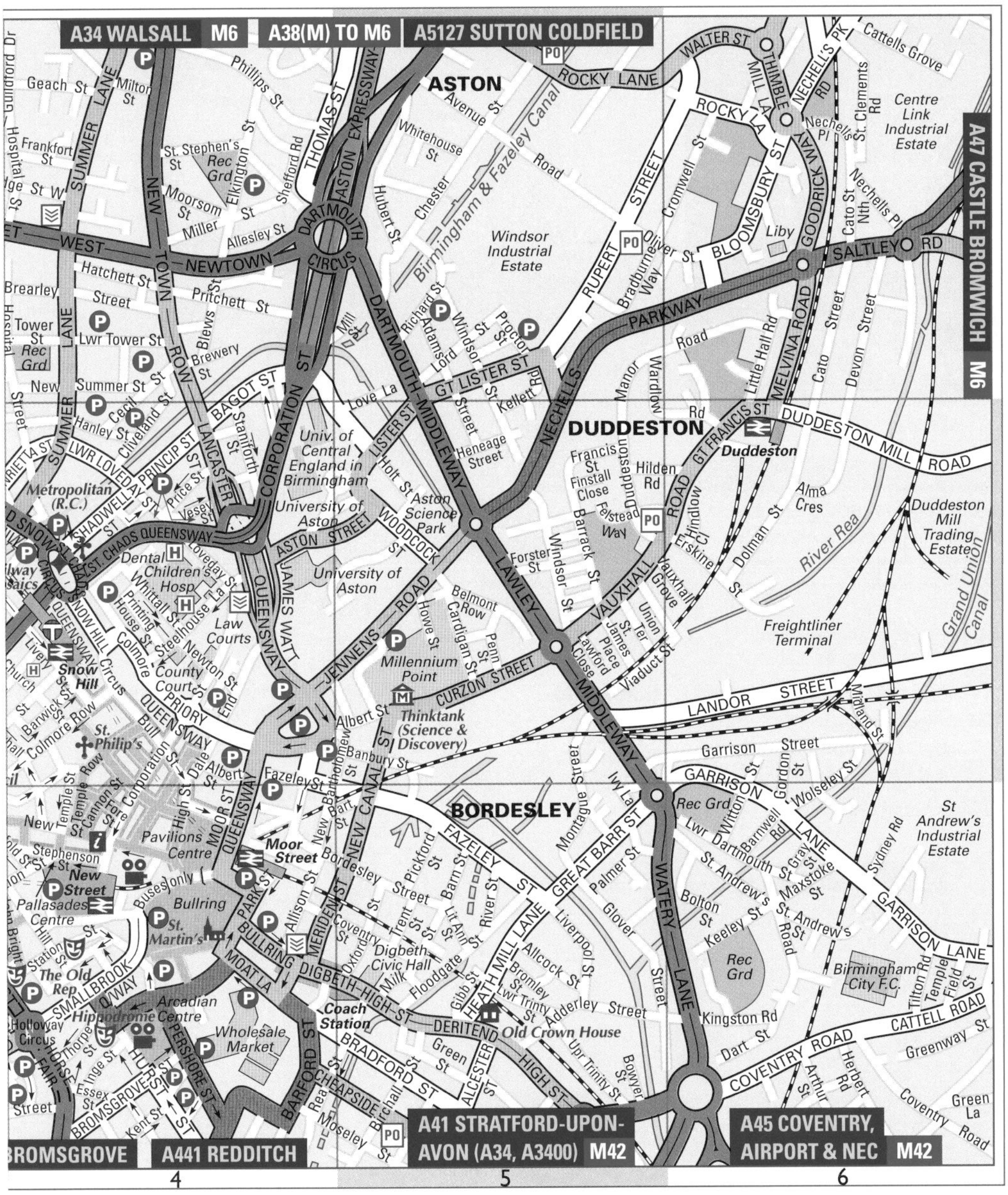

Birmingham

▲Chamberlain Square

Birmingham has recently undergone major regeneration in the centre with the redevelopment of the Bullring Shopping Centre to house luxury shops and boutiques, restaurants and glass-covered pedestrian streets, and to include the landmark Selfridges building. There are also many different street markets. The extensive canal network has also been improved and there are more acres of parks and open spaces than in any other city in the UK, including the Botanical Gardens in Edgbaston. The Barber Institute of Fine Arts is within University campus. There is a wealth of choice of entertainment, from theatres and cinemas to international cuisine and a fine array of pubs and bars. The city is also known as the capital of Balti – chiefly in the area between the A34 and the A435 to the south of the centre.

Symphony Hall C3
Talbot St. A1
Temple Row. C4
Temple St. C4
Templefield St. . . C6
Tenby St B3
Tenby St North . . B2
Tennant St C2
The Crescent A2
Thimble Mill La. . A6
Thinktank (Science & Discovery) . . . B5
Thomas St A4
Thorpe St. C4
Tilton Rd C6
Tower St. A4
Town Hall C3
Trent St. C5
Turner's Buildings A1
Unett St A3
Union Terr B5
University of Central England in Birmingham . .B4
University of Aston B4/B5
Upper Trinity St . . C5
Uxbridge St A3
Vauxhall Gr B5
Vauxhall Rd B5
Vernon Rd C1
Vesey St B4
Viaduct St B5
Victoria Sq C3
Villa St A3
Vittoria St. B3
Vyse St B3
Walter St A6
Wardlow Rd A5
Warstone La. B2
Washington St. . . C3
Water St B3
Waterworks Rd . . . C1
Watery La. C5
Well St A3

¼ mile
¼ ½ km

Tourism Centre and Ticketshop, The Rotunda, 150 New Street, Birmingham B2 4PA
Tel 0870 225 0127

BBC WM 95.6 FM • **BRMB** 96.4 FM
Heart 100.7 FM • **Saga** 105.7 FM

www.birmingham.gov.uk

★Do not miss

★**Birmingham Museum and Art Gallery**, Chamberlain Square – fine art, archaeology, local and industrial history

★**Millennium Point**, Curzon Street – The Hub, University of the First Age • Thinktank (the Birmingham Museum of Science and Discovery) • Young People's Parliament • IMAX

★**National Sea Life Centre**, Brindley Place – aquarium

Western Rd B1
Wharf St. A2
Wheeler St. A3
Whitehouse St. . . A5
Whitmore St A2
Whittall St B4
Wholesale Market C4
Wiggin St B1
Willes Rd A1
Windsor Industrial Estate A5
Windsor St. A5
Windsor St B5
Winson Green Rd A1
Witton St C6
Wolseley St C6
Woodcock St. B5

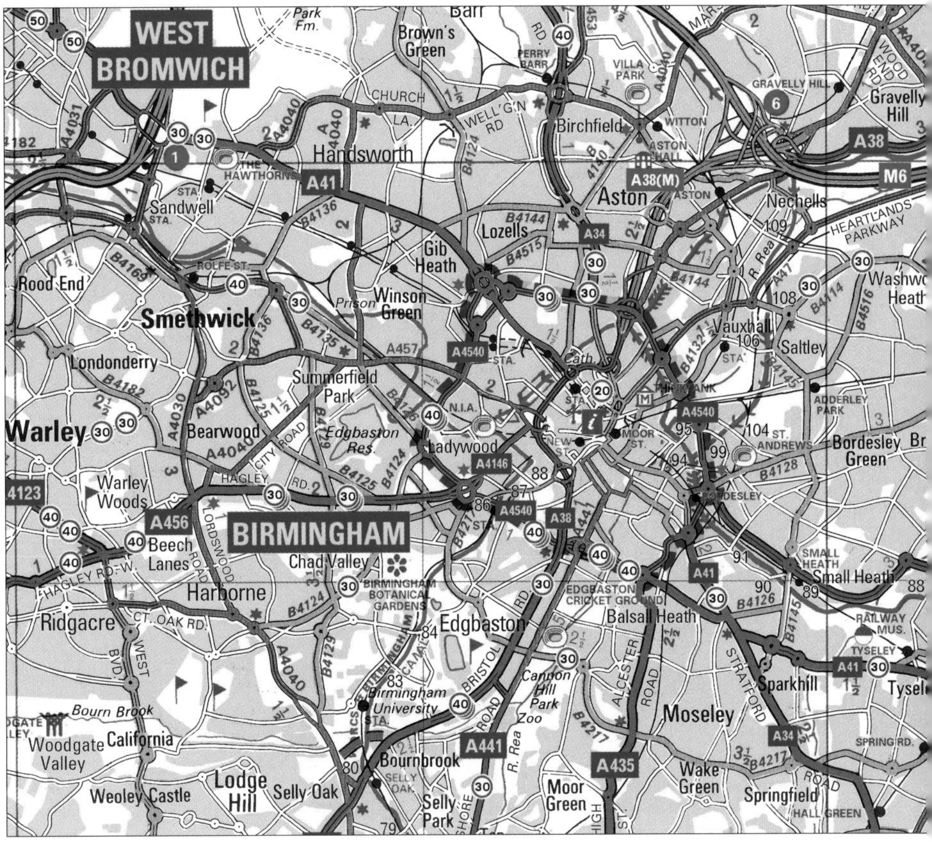

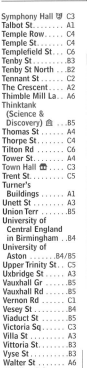

Blackpool

38

A popular holiday resort since mid-Victorian times, with a 10-mile promenade decorated by the Illuminations for part of the year and along which trams run. The Pleasure Beach has more than 145 rides and attractions, including the tallest, fastest rollercoaster in Europe, and the famous 518ft tower, opened in 1894 and based on the Eiffel Tower, with a circus and ballroom. The town has 3 piers, the 32-acre Zoo Park and Dinosaur Experience, the Lifeboat Station and Visitor Centre, the Model Village and Gardens, Louis Tussaud's Waxworks, and the Sandcastle – one of the UK's largest waterworlds. Green relief is afforded by the Blackpool Countryside Experience, a series of nature walks starting at Stanley Park, and temporary exhibitions are held at the Grundy Art Gallery.

▲Blackpool Tower and Illuminations

★Do not miss

- ★**Blackpool Tower**, The Promenade
- ★**Sea Life Centre**, The Promenade
- ★**Stanley Park**, near town centre

Tourist Information Centre, 1 Clifton Street, Blackpool, Lancashire FY1 1LY Tel 01253 478222

BBC Radio Lancashire 103.9 FM
Magic 999 AM • **Radio Wave** 96.5 FM • **Rock FM** 97.4 FM

www.visitblackpool.com

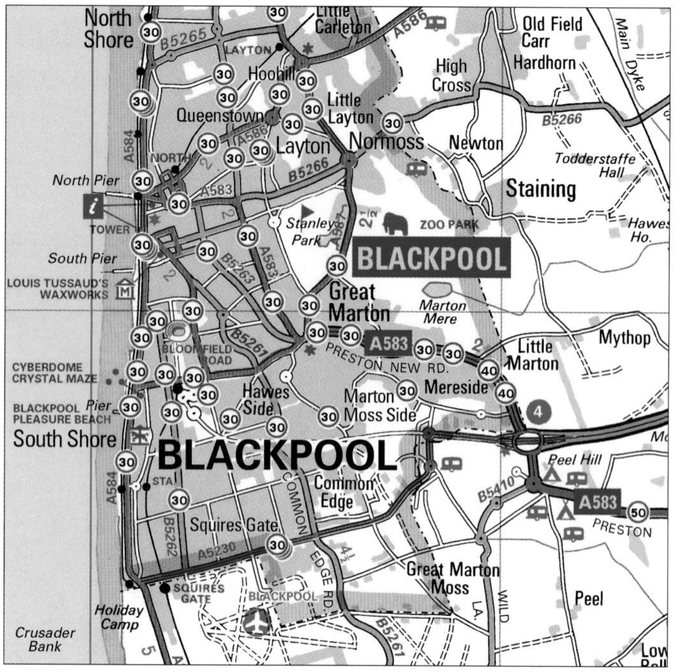

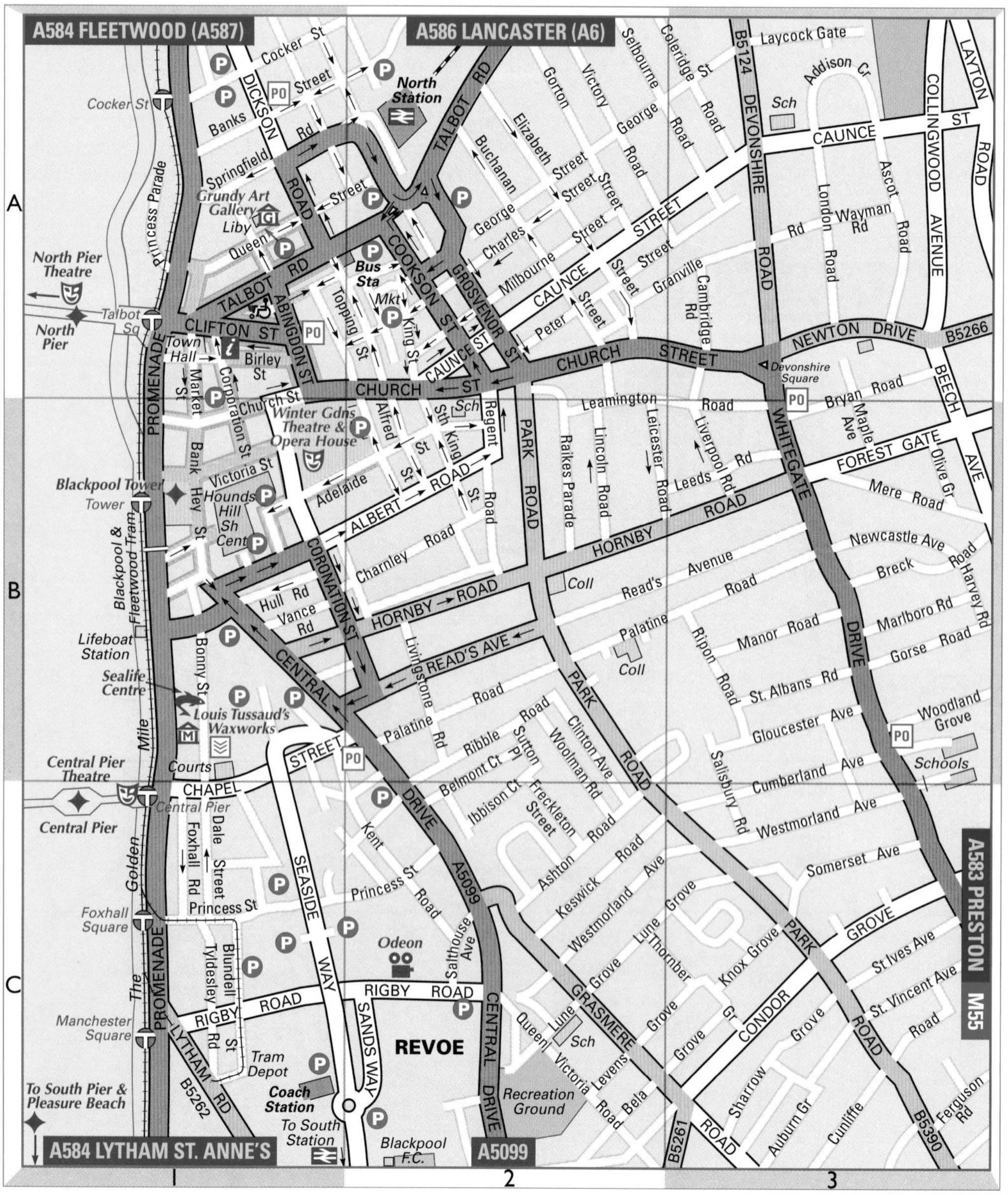

Blackpool

Abingdon St A1
Addison Cr A3
Adelaide St B1
Albert Rd B2
Alfred St B2
Ascot Rd A3
Ashton Rd C2
Auburn Gr C3
Bank Hey St B1
Banks St A1
Beech Ave B3
Bela Gr C2
Belmont Ct B2
Birley St A1
Blackpool & Fleetwood Tram .B1
Blackpool F.C. . . . C2
Blackpool Tower ✦ B1
Blundell St C1
Bonny St B1
Breck Rd B3
Bryan Rd A3
Buchanan St A2
Bus Station A2
Cambridge Rd . . . A3
Caunce St A2
Central Dr B1
Central Pier ✦ . . . C1
Central Pier (Tram stop) C1
Central Pier Theatre C1
Chapel St C1
Charles St A2
Charnley Rd B2
Church St A1
Clifton St A1
Clinton Ave B2
Coach Station . . . C1
Cocker St A1
Cocker St (Tram stop) A1
Coleridge Rd A3
Collingwood Ave. A3
Condor Gr C3
Cookson St A2
Coronation St B1
Corporation St . . A1
Courts B1
Cumberland Ave . .B3
Cunliffe Rd C3
Dale St C1
Devonshire Rd . . . A3
Devonshire Sq . . . A3
Dickson Rd A1
Elizabeth St A2
Ferguson Rd C3
Forest Gate B3
Foxhall Rd C1
Foxhall Sq (Tram stop) C1
Freckleton St C2
George St A2
Gloucester Ave . . .B3
Golden Mile, The. C1
Gorse Rd B3
Gorton St A2
Granville Rd A2
Grasmere Rd C2
Grosvenor St A2
Grundy Art Gallery A1
Harvey Rd B3
Hornby Rd B2
Hounds Hill Shopping Centre.B1
Hull Rd B1
Ibbison Ct C2
Information Ctr . A1
Kent Rd C2
Keswick Rd C2
King St A2
Knox Gr C3
Laycock Gate A3
Layton Rd A3
Leamington Rd . . .B2
Leeds Rd B3
Leicester Rd B2
Levens Gr C2
Library A1
Lifeboat Station . .B1
Lincoln Rd B2
Liverpool Rd B3
Livingstone Rd . . .B2
London Rd A3
Louis Tussaud's Waxworks B1
Lune Gr C2
Lytham Rd C1
Manchester Sq (Tram stop) C1
Manor Rd B3
Maple Ave B3
Market A2
Market St A1
Marlboro Rd B3
Mere Rd B3
Milbourne St A2
Newcastle Ave B3
Newton Dr A3
North Pier ✦ A1
North Pier Theatre A1
North Station A2
Odeon C2
Olive Gr B3
Palatine Rd B2
Park Rd B2
Peter St A2
Police Station . .B1
Post Office A1/B2/B3
Princess Pde A1
Princess St . . . C1/C2
Promenade . . A1/C1
Queen St A1
Queen Victoria Rd C2
Raikes Pde B2
Read's Ave B2
Regent Rd B2
Ribble Rd B2
Rigby Rd C1
Ripon Rd B3
St Albans Rd B3
St Ives Ave C3
St Vincent Ave . . . C3
Salisbury Rd B3
Salthouse Ave . . . C2
Sands Way C2
Sea Life Centre B1
Seaside Way C1
Selbourne Rd. A2/A3
Sharrow Gr C3
Somerset Ave . . . C3
Springfield Rd A1
South King St B2
Sutton Pl B2
Talbot Rd A1
Talbot Sq (Tram stop) A1
Thornber Gr C2
Topping St A1
Tower (Tram stop) B1
Town Hall A1
Tram Depot C1
Tyldesley Rd C1
Vance Rd B1
Victoria St B1
Victory Rd A2
Wayman Rd A3
Westmorland Ave C2
Whitegate Dr B3
Winter Gardens Theatre & Opera House B1
Woodland Gr B3
Woolman Rd B2

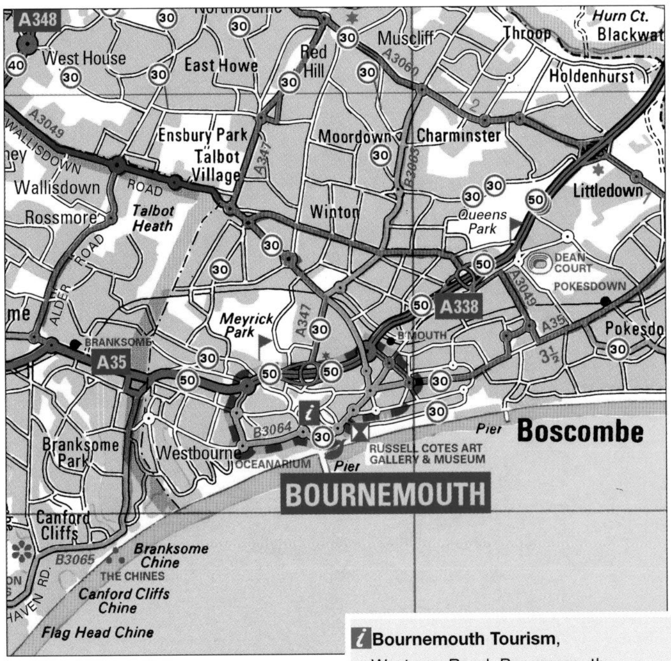

Bournemouth

Bournemouth is known primarily for its seven miles of beaches and also for its parks and gardens and has long been a destination for holidaymakers and people seeking the sea air. There are many diverse attractions available from the Russell-Cotes Art Gallery and Museum to the Bournemouth International Centre, the Oceanarium and the host of gardens. It has a vast array of shops from the high street chains to small independents and boutiques on Westover Road and Old Christchurch Road, plus The Avenue shopping centre on Commercial Road. North of the city are the Wild Things Play Centre and Alice in Wonderland Family Park. The wide range of restaurants, bars and clubs make it a great place for all ages.

▲View from Russell-Cotes

Bournemouth Tourism, Westover Road, Bournemouth BH1 2BU Tel 0845 051 1700

BBC Radio Solent 103.8 FM and 1359 AM • **Classic Gold** 828 AM **Fire** 107.6 FM • **2CR FM** 102.3 FM

www.bournemouth.gov.uk

★ Do not miss

★**Russell-Cotes Art Gallery & Museum**, Russell Cotes Road

★**Bournemouth Eye**, Lower Gardens – tethered balloon flight

★**Oceanarium**, Pier Approach – aquarium

Bournemouth

Ascham Rd. A3
Avenue Rd B1
Bath Rd. C2
Beacon Rd C1
Beach Office C2
Beechey Rd A3
Bodorgan Rd B1
Bourne Ave B1
Bournemouth Eye ✦. C2
Bournemouth International Ctr C1
Bournemouth Pier C2
Bournemouth Station A3
Bournemouth Station (r'about) .B3
Braidley Rd A1
Cavendish Place . A2
Cavendish Rd. . . . A2
Central Drive. . . . A1
Christchurch Rd . .B3
Cliff Lift C1/C3
Coach House La . A3
Coach Station . . . A3
College & Library .B3
Commercial Rd . . .B1
Cotlands Rd B3
Courts. B3
Cranborne Rd . . . C1
Cricket Ground . . A2
Cumnor Rd. B2
Dean Park A2
Dean Park Cr. B2
Dean Park Rd . . . A2
Durrant Rd B1
East Overcliff Dr . C3
Exeter Cr C1
Exeter La C2
Exeter Rd C1
Gervis Place. B1
Gervis Rd B3
Glen Fern Rd B2
Golf Club A1
Grove Rd B3
Hinton Rd. C2
Holdenhurst Rd. . .B3
Horseshoe Common. B2
Hospital (Private) H A2
IMAX C2
Information Ctr i .B2
Lansdowne (r'about). B3
Lansdowne Rd. . . A2
Lorne Park Rd B2
Lower Central Gdns B2
Madeira Rd B2
Methuen Rd. A3
Meyrick Park. . . . A1
Meyrick Rd. B3
Milton Rd A2
Oceanarium . . C2
Old Christchurch Rd B2
Ophir Rd. A3
Oxford Rd B3
Park Rd A3
Parsonage Rd B2
Pavilion C2
Pier Approach . . . C2
Pier Theatre . . C2
Police Station . . . A3/B3
Portchester Rd . . A3
Post Office PO .B1/B3
Priory Rd C1
Recreation Ground. A1
Richmond Hill Rd .B1
Russell Cotes Art Gallery & Mus C2
Russell Cotes Rd. C2
St Anthony's Rd . . A1
St Michael's Rd. . C1
St Paul's (r'about) B3
St Paul's La B3
St Paul's Rd. A3
St Peter's B2
St Peter's (r'about). B2
St Peter's Rd B2
St Stephen's Rd . .B1
St Swithun's (r'about). B3
St Swithun's Rd. . A3
St Swithun's Rd South B3
St Valerie Rd A2
St Winifred's Rd . A2
Stafford Rd B3
Terrace Rd B1
The Square B1
The Triangle. B1
Town Hall B1
Tregonwell Rd . . . C1
Trinity Rd B2
Undercliff Drive . C3
Upper Central Gdns B1
Upper Hinton Rd. .B2
Upper Terr Rd . . . C1
Wellington Rd . . . A3
Wessex Way B2
West Cliff Promenade C1
West Hill Rd. C1
West Undercliff Promenade C1
Westover Rd B2
Wimborne Rd . . . A2
Wootton Mount. . .B2
Wychwood Dr . . . A1
Yelverton Rd B2
York Rd. B3
Zig-Zag Walks C1/C3

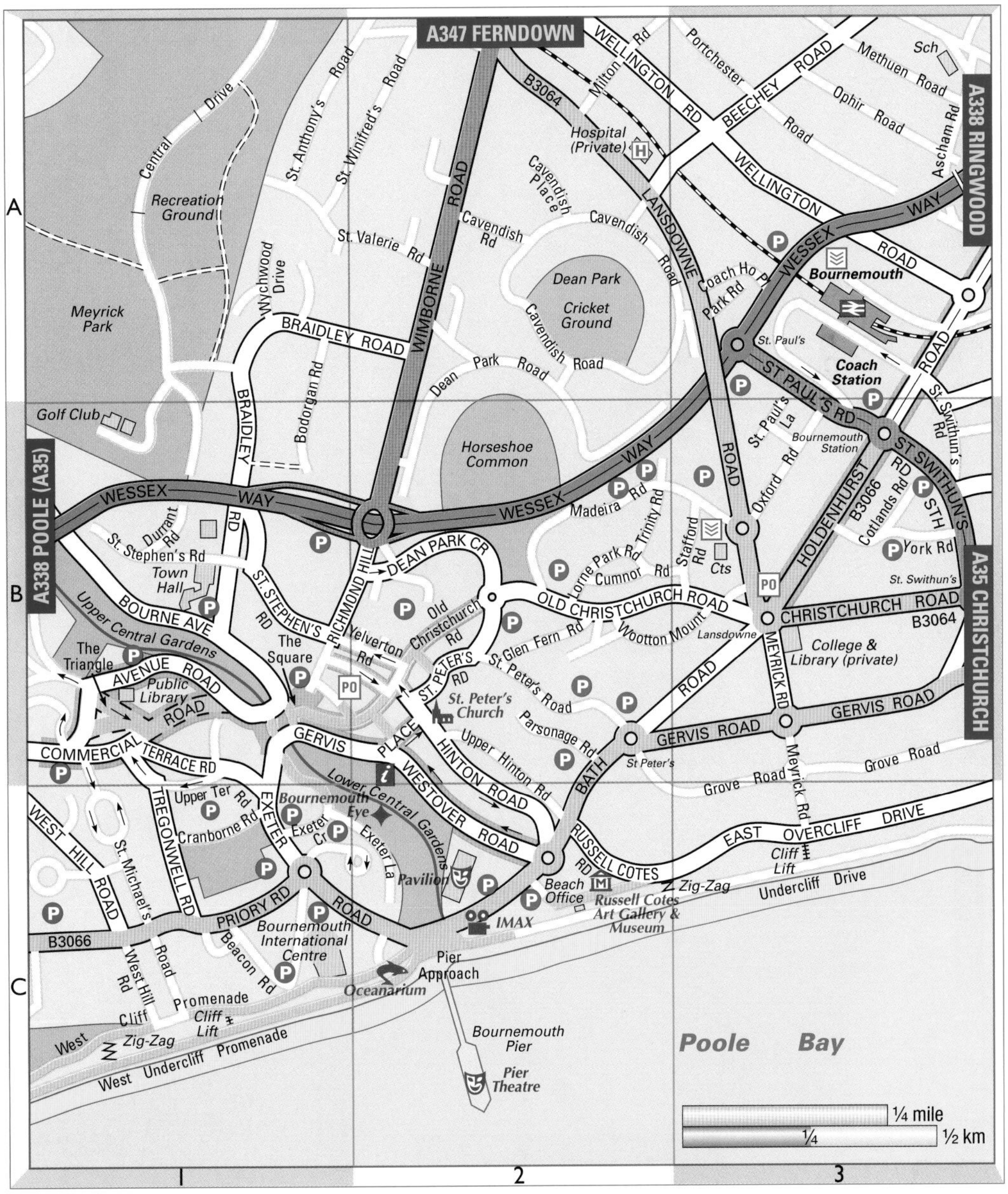

Bradford

An ethnically diverse city that grew from a 19th-century rural market town, with a rich industrial heritage as the world's one-time wool capital, still visible in Little Germany, the former merchants' quarter, the impressive Wool Exchange, and the many surrounding mills. The Bradford Industrial Museum & Working Horses re-creates 19th-century life here, while the Colour Museum is a unique venue charting the history, evolution and technology of colour, and the Peace Museum looks at peace history and conflict resolution. The Cartwright Hall Art Gallery and Museum specialises in 19th- and 20th-century British art, plus contemporary South Asian art. Historic buildings include the partly 15th-century cathedral with its William Morris windows, and the 17th-century Bolling Hall manor house. Shops range from high-street standards to Asian shops selling sumptuous fabrics and jewellery, and the newly created Mughal Gardens are based on 16th-19th-century Indian design. At Saltaire's Salt's Mill you'll find Europe's largest collection of works by David Hockney.

▲Bradford Town Hall

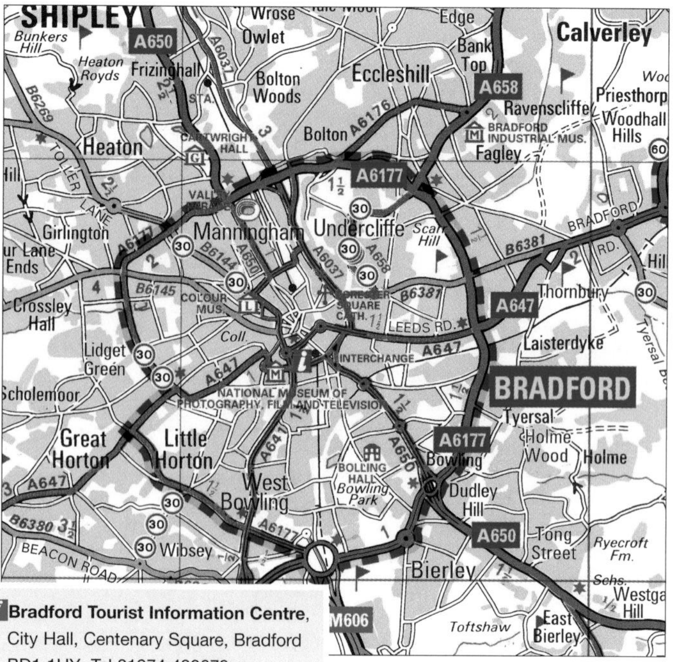

Bradford Tourist Information Centre, City Hall, Centenary Square, Bradford BD1 1HY Tel 01274 433678

BBC Radio Leeds 92.4, 95.3 FM and 774 AM • **Pulse Classic Gold** 1278 AM • **Sunrise Radio** 103.2 FM **The Pulse** 97.5 FM

www.visitbradford.com

★Do not miss

★**Brontë Birthplace**, Thornton

★**National Museum of Photography**, Film and Television, IMAX

★**Saltaire Victorian 'model' industrial village** (UNESCO World Heritage Site), Salt's Mill, Saltaire

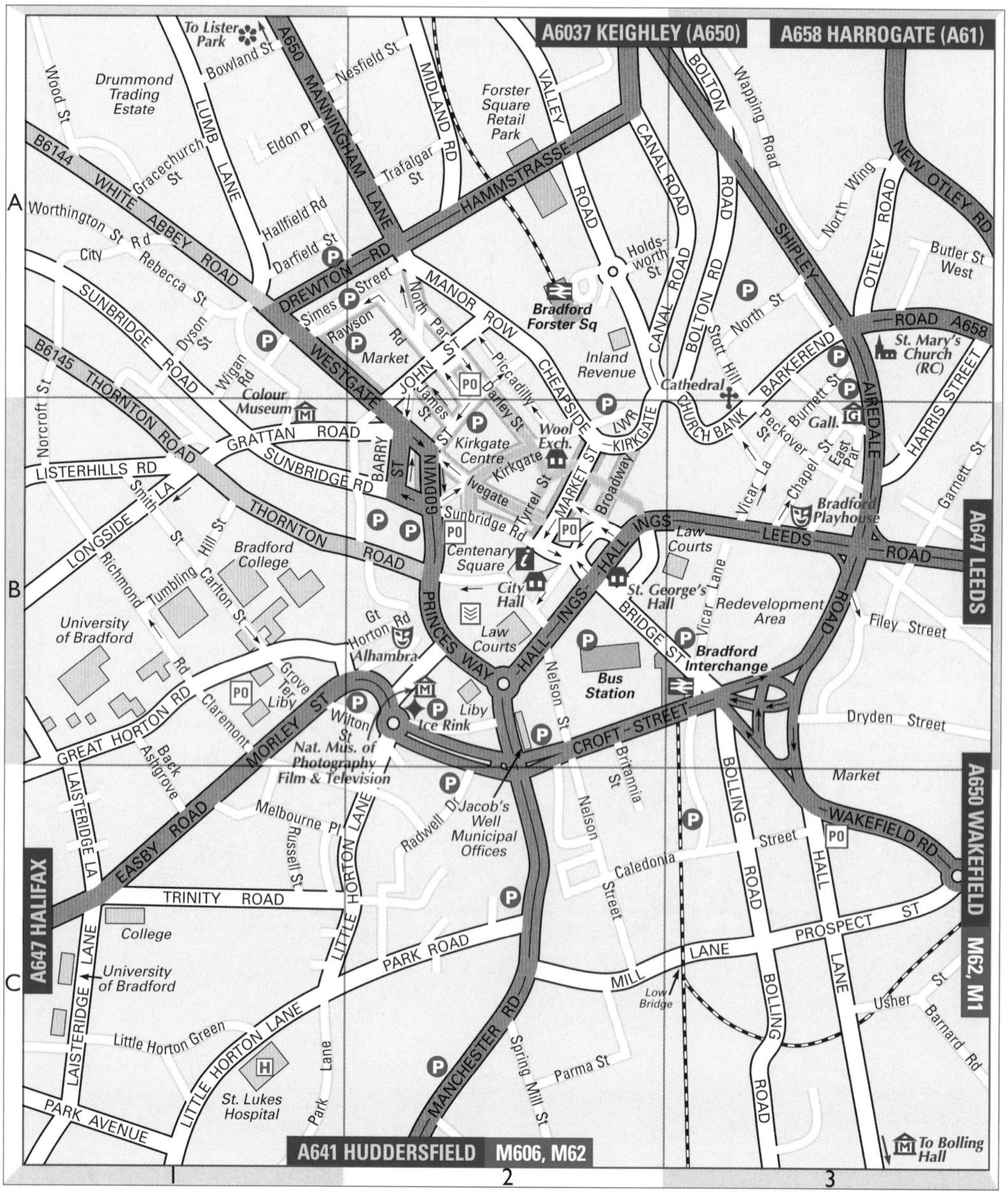

Bradford

Alhambra B2
Back Ashgrove . . . B1
Barkerend Rd. . . . A3
Barnard Rd. C3
Barry St B2
Bolling Rd C3
Bolton Rd. A3
Bowland St A1
Bradford College . B1
Bradford Forster Sq A2
Bradford Interchange . . . B3
Bradford Playhouse B3
Bridge St B2
Britannia St B2
Broadway B2
Burnett St B3
Bus Station B2
Butler St West . . . A3
Caledonia St C2
Canal Rd. A2
Carlton St. B1
Cathedral ✝. A3
Centenary Sq. B2
Chapel St B3
Cheapside A2
Church Bank B3
City Hall B2
City Rd A1
Claremont B1
Colour Mus B1
Croft St. B2
Darfield St A1
Darley St A2
Drewton Rd A1
Drummond Trading Estate A1
Dryden St. B3
Dyson St. A1
Easby Rd C1
East Parade B3
Eldon Pl A1
Filey St B3
Forster Square Retail Park A2
Gallery B3
Garnett St B3
Godwin St B2
Gracechurch St . . A1
Grattan Rd B1
Great Horton Rd . . B1
Grove Terr B1
Hall Ings B2
Hall La C3
Hallfield Rd A1
Hammstrasse. A2
Harris St. B3
Holdsworth St . . . A2
Ice Rink ✦. B2
Information Ctr . B2
Ivegate B2
James St A2
John St. A2
Kirkgate B2
Kirkgate Centre. . . B2
Laisteridge La C1
Law Courts. B3
Leeds Rd B3
Library B1/B2
Listerhills Rd B1
Little Horton La. . C1
Little Horton Gn . C1
Longside La B1
Lower Kirkgate . . . B2
Lumb La A1
Manchester Rd . . C2
Manningham La . A1
Manor Row A2
Market A2/C3
Market St B2
Melbourne Place C1
Midland Rd A2
Mill La. C2
Morley St B1
Nat. Museum of Photography, Film & Television . . B2
Nelson St B2
Nesfield St. A2
New Otley Rd. . . . A3
Norcroft St. B1
North Parade. . . . A2
North St A3
North Wing A3
Otley Rd A3
Park Ave. C1
Park La. C1
Park Rd C2
Parma St C2
Peckover St B3
Piccadilly A2
Police Station . . B2
Post Office A2/B1/B2/C3
Princes Way. B2
Prospect St C3
Radwell Drive . . . C2
Rawson Rd. A1
Rebecca St. A1
Richmond Rd. B1
Russell St. C1
St George's Hall B2
St Lukes Hospital C1
St Mary's A3
Shipley Airedale Rd A3/B3
Simes St. A1
Smith St B1
Spring Mill St . . . C2
Stott Hill. A3
Sunbridge Rd A1
Thornton Rd A1
Trafalgar St A2
Trinity Rd C1
Tumbling Hill St . . B1
Tyrrel St B2
University of Bradford. . . . B1/C1
Usher St C3
Valley Rd A2
Vicar La B3
Wakefield Rd C3
Wapping Rd A3
Westgate A1
White Abbey Rd . . A1
Wigan Rd A1
Wilton St B1
Wood St A1
Wool Exchange B2
Worthington St . . A1

¼ mile
¼ ½ km

Brighton

The Domesday Survey from 1086 shows a population of around 400 in Brighton and a well-established fishing industry. Brighton is now a fashionable, vibrant, cosmopolitan city. Massive investment has transformed the seafront and many of the town's landmarks. Brighton Dome is now a major venue. The Lanes are a network of alleyways with boutiques selling antiques, jewellery and interior design; the North Laine comprises a group of streets between the station and the Pavilion offering an eclectic range of independent clothes and shoe shops, music shops, bars and restaurants. The promenade running along the seafront is a great place for a stroll, or you can take Volks Electric Railway up to the revitalised Brighton Marina, now home to designer outlet shops, restaurants, bars, cinemas and a casino.

Tourist Information Centre, 10 Bartholomew Square, Brighton BN1 1JS Tel 0906 711 2255 (50p per minute)

BBC Radio Southern Counties 95.3 FM • **Capital Gold** 945 and 1323 AM • **Juice** 107.2 FM **Southern FM** 103.5 FM

www.visitbrighton.com

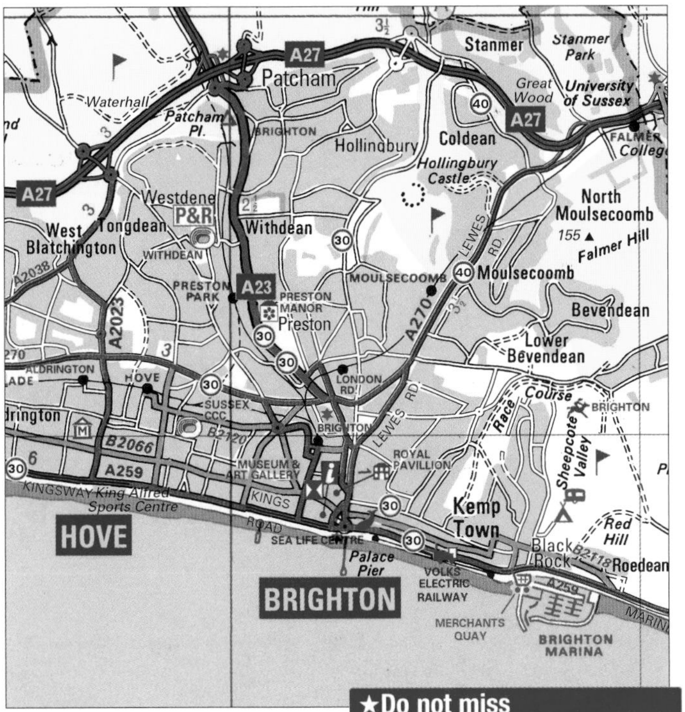

★Do not miss

★**Brighton Sea Life Centre**, Marine Parade – aquarium

★**Palace Pier** – arcades and rides

★**Royal Pavilion**, Pavilion Buildings

◀Royal Pavilion

Brighton

Addison Rd A1
Albert Rd B2
Albion Hill B3
Albion St B3
Ann St. A3
Art Gallery & Museum 🏛 B3
Baker St A3
Brighton ⇌ A2
Brighton Ctr 🏛 . . C2
Broad St C3
Buckingham Pl . . A2
Buckingham Rd. . B2
Cannon Pl C1
Carlton Hill B3
Chatham Pl A1
Cheapside A3
Church St. B2
Churchill Square Shopping Centre. B2
Clifton Hill B1
Clifton Pl B1
Clifton Rd. B1
Clifton Terr. B1
Clock Tower B2
Clyde Rd. A3
Coach Park C3
Compton Ave A2
Davigdor Rd. A1
Denmark Terr. . . . B1
Ditchling Rd. A3
Dome, The 🏛 B2
Duke St. B2
Duke's La C2
Dyke Rd A1
East St C2
Edward St. B3
Elmore Rd B3
Frederick St. B2
Fruit & Veg Market (Wholesale) B3
Gardner St B2
Gloucester Pl. . . . B3
Gloucester Rd . . . B2
Goldsmid Rd A1
Grand Junction Rd C2
Grand Pde B3
Hampton Pl B1
Hanover Terr A3
High St C3
Highdown Rd. . . . A1
Information Ctr ℹ C2
John St. B3
Kemp St B2
Kensington Pl B2
Kings Rd. C1
Law Courts. B3
Lewes Rd A3
Library (temp) . . . A2
London Rd A3
Madeira Dr. C3
Marine Pde C3
Middle St C2
Montpelier Pl B1
Montpelier Rd B1
Montpelier St B1
New England Rd . . A2
New England St . A2
New Rd. B2
Newhaven St A3
Nizells Ave A1
Norfolk Rd B1
Norfolk Terr B1
North Rd. B2
North St B2
Old Shoreham Rd A1
Old Steine C3
Osmond Rd A1
Over St B2
Oxford St A3
Paddling Pool . . . C1
Palace Pier ✦ . . . C3
Park Crescent Terr A3
Police Station ⊠ . . B3
Post Office PO . . A1/ A2/A3/B1/B2/B3/C3
Preston Rd A2
Preston St B1
Prestonville Rd . . A1
Queen's Rd B2
Regency Sq C1
Regent St B2
Richmond Pl. B3
Richmond St B3
Richmond Terr. . . A3
Rose Hill Terr. . . . A3
Royal Alexandra Hospital H B2
Royal Pavilion 🏛 . B2
St Bartholomew's ⛪ A2
St James' St. C3
St Nicholas' ⛪ . . . B2
St Peter's ⛪ A3
Sea Life Centre 🐟 C3
Shaftesbury Rd . . A3
Silwood Rd B1
Silwood St B1
Southover St A3
Spring Gdns. B2
Stanford Rd A1
Stanley Rd A3
Sussex St B3
Sussex Terr. B3
Swimming Pool. . . B3
Sydney St B3
Temple Gdns B1
Terminus Rd A2
The Lanes. C2
Theatre Royal 🎭 . . B2
Tidy St B2
Town Hall. C2
Toy & Model Museum 🏛 A1
Trafalgar St. B2
Union Rd A3
University of Brighton B3
Upper Lewes Rd . A3
Upper North St . . . B1
Vernon Terr A1
Viaduct Rd A3
Victoria Gdns. B3
Victoria Rd. B1
Volk's Electric Railway ✦ C3
West Pier (Closed to the Public) . . C1
West St. C2
Western Rd B1
Whitecross St B2
York Ave. B1
York Pl B3

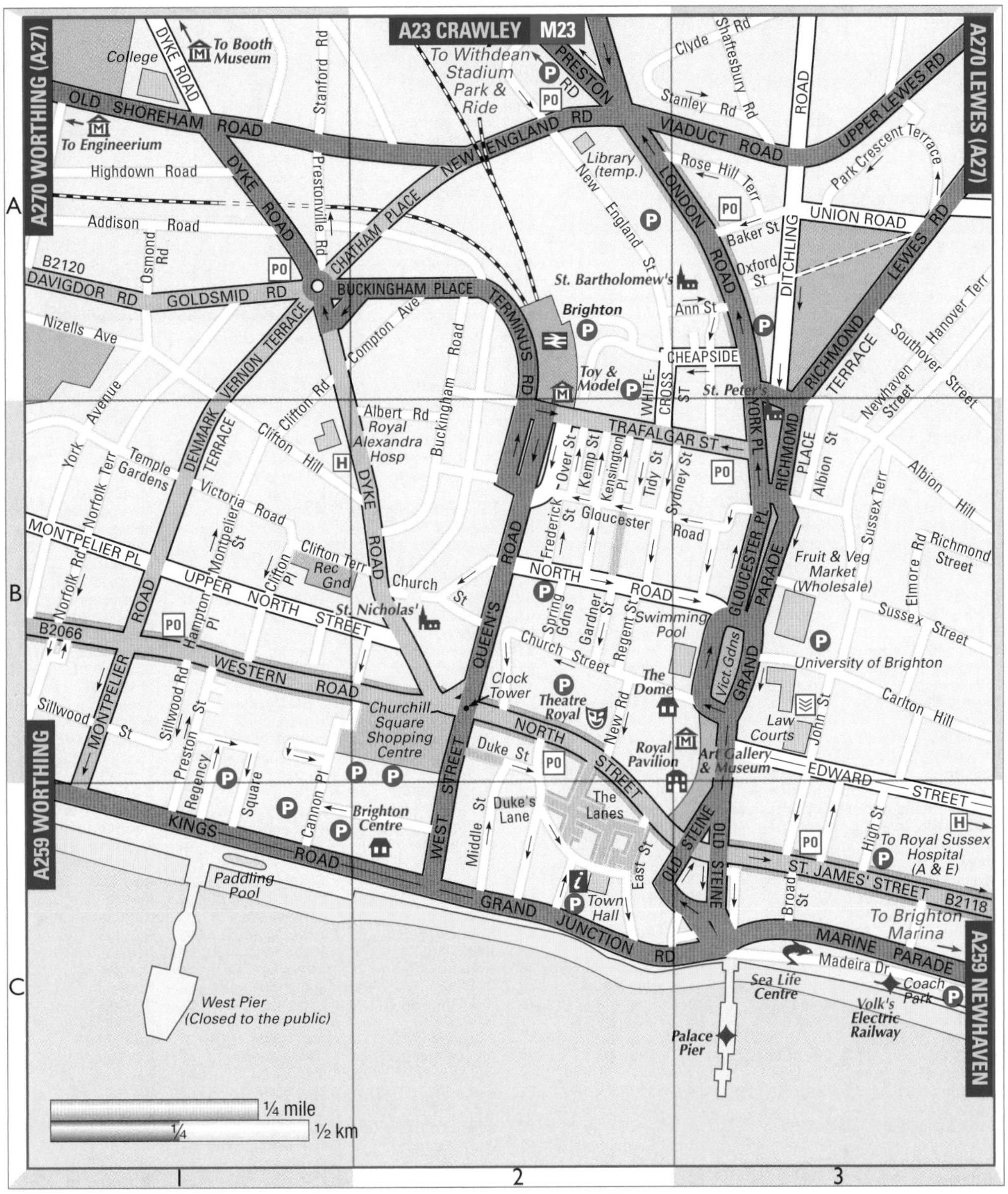

Bristol

▲Clifton Suspension Bridge

Historic city and seaport, manufacturing centre and university town. Places of interest include the Cathedral, Clifton Suspension Bridge, Maritime Heritage Centre, The Watershed Media Centre and the Bristol Industrial Museum. A major and diverse centre for shopping from Whiteladies Road and Clifton Village designer clothes, art and crafts, antiques, jewellery to St Nicholas Markets' hand-crafted goods and deli foods and the nearby Christmas Steps selling couture clothing, hand-made shoes and musical instruments. Big name shops can be found in Broadmead and the Galleries. There is a great variety of bars and restaurants in the centre of the city and the Clifton area.

★ Do not miss

★**Bristol Zoo Gardens**, Clifton
★**Bristol City Museum and Art Gallery**, Queen's Road
★**At-Bristol**, Anchor Road, Harbourside – Explore, Wildwalk, IMAX

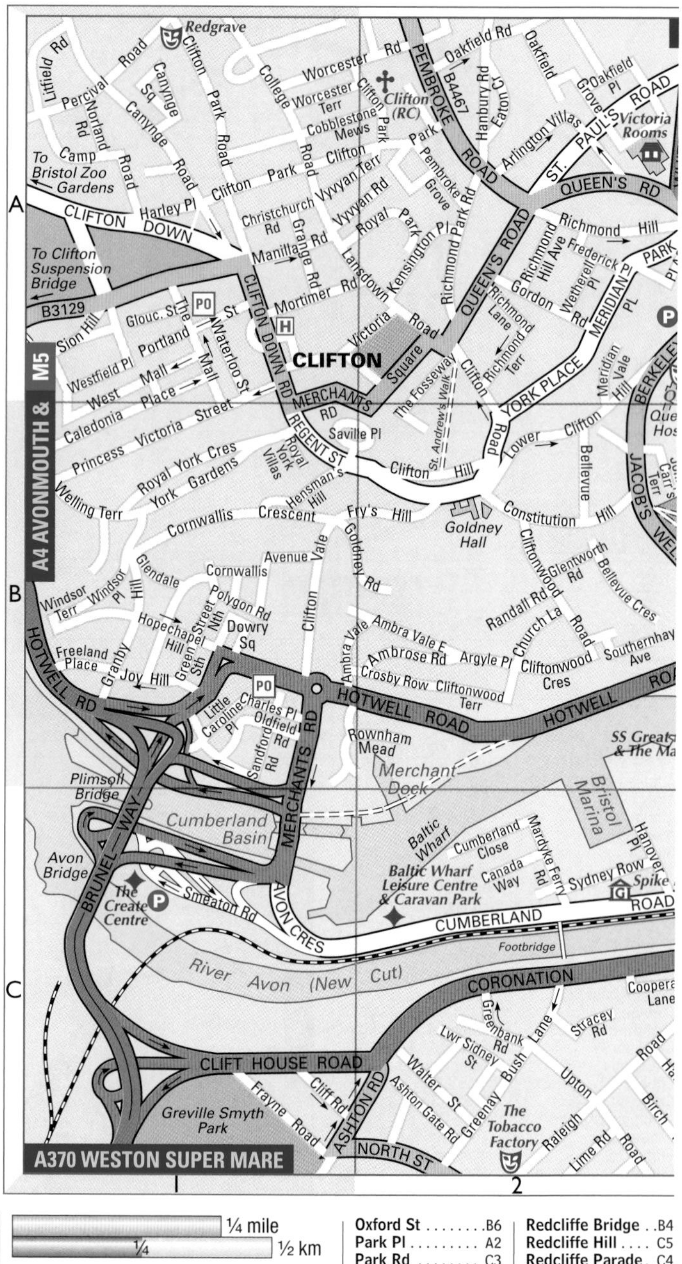

Bristol

Acramans Rd C4
Albert Rd C6
Alfred Hill. A4
All Saint's St A4
All Saints' ⛪ B4
Allington Rd. C3
Alpha Rd. C4
Ambra Vale. B1
Ambra Vale East . .B2
Ambrose Rd. B2
Amphitheatre. . . . C3
Anchor Rd B3
Anvil St. B6
Architecture Centre ✦ B4
Argyle Pl. B2
Arlington Villas . . A2
Arnolfini Arts Centre, The ✦ . . .B4
Art Gallery 🏛 . . . A3
Ashton Gate Rd . . C2
Ashton Rd C1
at-Bristol ✦. B3
Avon Bridge C1
Avon Cr. C1
Avon St. B6
Baldwin St B4
Baltic Wharf C2
Baltic Wharf Leisure Centre & Caravan Park ✦. C2
Barossa Pl C4
Barton Manor B6
Barton Rd. B6
Barton Vale B6
Bath Rd. C6
Bathurst Basin. . . C4
Bathurst Parade . C4
Beauley Rd. C3
Bedminster Bridge. C5
Bedminster Parade C4
Bellevue Cr B2
Bellevue B2
Bellevue Rd C6
Berkeley Pl. A2
Berkeley Sq A3
Birch Rd C2
Blackfriars A4
Bond St. A5
Braggs La. A6
Brandon Hill B3
Brandon Steep . . .B3
Bristol Bridge B5
Bristol Cathedral (CE) ✝ B3
Bristol Grammar School A3
Bristol Harbour Railway 🚂 C3
Bristol Marina . . . C2
Bristol Royal (A&E) Ⓗ. A4
Bristol Temple Meads Station ⇌. B6
Broad Plain B6
Broad Quay B4
Broad St. A4
Broad Weir. A5
Broadcasting House. A3
Broadmead A5
Brunel Way C1
Brunswick Sq . . . C5
Burton Cl C5
Bus Station A4
Butts Rd B3
Cabot Tower ✦ . . .B3
Caledonia Pl B1
Callowhill Ct A5
Cambridge St . . . C6
Camden Rd C3
Camp Rd. A1
Canada Way. C2
Cannon St A4
Canon's Rd. . . .B3/B4
Canon's Way B3
Cantock's Cl A3
Canynge Rd A1
Canynge Sq A1
Castle Park A5
Castle St. A5
Catherine Meade St. C4
Cattle Market Rd. C6
Charles Pl B1
Charlotte St B3
Charlotte St South B3
Chatterton House 🏛 B5
Chatterton Sq . . . C5
Chatterton St. . . . C5
Cheese La B5
Children's Hospital Ⓗ A4
Christchurch ⛪. . A4
Christchurch Rd . A1
Christmas Steps ✦ A4
Church La. B5
Church St. B5
City Museum 🏛 . . A3
City of Bristol College. B3
Clare St B4
Clarence Rd. C5
Cliff Rd. C1
Clift House Rd. . . C1
Clifton Cathedral (RC) ✝ A2
Clifton Down Rd . A1
Clifton Down A1
Clifton Hill B2
Clifton Park A2
Clifton Park Rd . . A1
Clifton Rd. A2
Cliftonwood Cr . . .B2
Cliftonwood Rd . . .B2
Cliftonwood Terr . .B2
Clifton Vale. B1
Cobblestone Mews A1
College Green B3
College Rd A1
College St B3
Colston Almshouses 🏛 . A4
Colston Ave B4
Colston Hall 🎭 . . .B4
Colston Parade . . C5
Colston St A4
Commercial Rd . . C4
Commonwealth Museum 🏛 B6
Constitution Hill . .B2
Cooperage La . . . C2
Corn St. B4
Cornwallis Ave . . .B1
Cornwallis Cr. B1
Coronation Rd. . . C3
Council House 🏛 .B3
Counterslip B5
Courts. A4
Create Centre, The ✦. B1
Crosby Row B2
Culver St B3
Cumberland Basin C1
Cumberland Cl . . C2
Cumberland Rd. . C2
Dale St A6
David St A6
Dean La C4
Deanery Rd B3
Denmark St B4
Dowry Sq B1
East St A5
Eaton Cr. A2
Elmdale Rd A3
Elton Rd A3
Eugene St. A6
Exchange, The & St Nicholas' Mkts 🏛 B4
Fairfax St A4
Fire Station B5
Floating Harbour C3
Foster Almshouses 🏛 . A4
Frayne Rd. C1
Frederick Pl. A2
Freeland Pl B1
Frogmore St B3
Fry's Hill. B2
Gas La. B6
Gasferry Rd C3
General Hospital Ⓗ. C4
Georgian House 🏛 B3
Glendale. B1
Glentworth Rd B2
Gloucester St. . . . A1
Goldney Hall B2
Goldney Rd B1
Gordon Rd A2
Granby Hill. B1
Grange Rd A1
Great Ann St A6
Great George St . A6
Great George St . .B3
Great Western Way. B6
Green St North . . .B1
Green St South . . .B1
Greenay Bush La. C2
Greenbank Rd . . . C2
Greville Smyth Park C1
Guildhall 🏛 A4
Guinea St. C4
Hamilton Rd. C3
Hanbury Rd A2
Hanover Pl C2
Harbour Way B3
Harley Pl A1
Haymarket A5
Hensman's Hill . . .B1
High St B4
Highbury Villas . . A3
Hill St B3
Hill St C6
Hippodrome 🎭 . . .B4
Hopechapel Hill . .B1
Horfield Rd A4
Horton St B6
Host St A4
Hotwell Rd B2
Houlton St A6
Howard Rd. C3
Ice Rink B3
IMAX Cinema 🎥 . .B4
Industrial Museum 🏛 C4
Information Ctr ℹ.B4
Islington Rd C3
Jacob St. A5/A6
Jacob's Wells Rd. .B2
John Carr's Terr . .B2
John Wesley's Chapel ⛪ A5
Joy Hill. B1
Jubilee St. B6
Kensington Pl . . . A2
Kilkenny St. B6
King St B4
Kingsland Rd B6
Kingston Rd C3
Lamb St A6
Lansdown Rd. . . . A2
Lawford St A6
Lawfords Gate . . . A6
Leighton Rd. C3
Lewins Mead A4
Lime Rd C2
Little Ann St. A6
Little Caroline Pl. .B1
Little George St. . A6
Little King St B4
Litfield Rd A1
Llandoger Trow 🏛 B4
Lloyds' Building, The C3
Lodge St. A4
Lord Mayor's Chapel ⛪ B4
Lower Castle St. . A5
Lower Church La. A4
Lower Clifton Hill .B2
Lower Guinea St. C4
Lower Lamb St . . .B3
Lower Maudlin St A4
Lower Park Rd . . . A4
Lower Sidney St . C2
Lucky La. C4
Lydstep Terr C3
Mall Galleries, The Shopping Ctr . . . A5
Manilla Rd A1
Mardyke Ferry Rd C2
Maritime Heritage Centre 🏛 B3
Marlborough Hill A4
Marlborough St. . A4
Marsh St. B4
Maternity Hospital Ⓗ. A4
Mead St C5
Meadow St. A5
Merchant Dock . . .B2
Merchant Seamen's Almshouses 🏛 . .B4
Merchant St. A5
Merchants Rd . . . A1
Merchants Rd . . . C1
Meridian Pl A2
Meridian Vale. . . . A2
Merrywood Rd. . . C3
Midland Rd A6
Milford St. C3
Millennium Sq. . . .B3
Mitchell La. B5
Mortimer Rd A1
Murray Rd C4
Myrtle Rd A3
Narrow Plain B5
Narrow Quay B4
Nelson St A4
New Charlotte St C4
New Kingsley Rd. .B6
New Queen St . . . C5
New St A6
Newfoundland St A5
Newgate A5
Newton St A6
Norland Rd. A1
North St C2
Oakfield Gr. A2
Oakfield Pl A2
Oakfield Rd A2
Old Bread St B6
Old Market St . . . A6
Old Park Hill A4
Oldfield Rd. B1
Orchard Ave. B4
Orchard La. B4
Orchard St B4
Osbourne Rd C3
Oxford St B6
Park Pl A2
Park Rd C3
Park Row A3
Park St A3
Passage St B5
Pembroke Gr A2
Pembroke Rd A2
Pembroke Rd. C3
Pembroke St A5
Penn St. A5
Pennywell Rd . . . A6
Percival Rd A1
Pero's Bridge B4
Perry Rd. A4
Pip & Jay ⛪. A5
Plimsoll Bridge . . .B1
Post Office PO. A1/A3/A4/A5/A6/B1/B4/C4/C5
Police Sta 🚓 . A4/A6
Polygon Rd B1
Portland St A1
Portwall La B5
Prewett St C5
Prince St B4
Prince St Bridge . C4
Princess St. C5
Princess Victoria St. B1
Priory Rd A3
Pump La. C5
QEH Theatre 🎭 . . A2
Queen Charlotte St. B4
Quakers Friars. . . A5
Quay St. A4
Queen Elizabeth Hospital School. A2
Queen Sq B4
Queen St A5
Queen's Ave. A3
Queen's Parade. . .B3
Queen's Rd A2
Raleigh Rd C2
Randall Rd B2
Redcliffe Backs . . .B5
Redcliffe Bridge . .B4
Redcliffe Hill C5
Redcliffe Parade. C4
Redcliffe St B5
Redcliffe Way B5
Redcross La A6
Redcross St A6
Redgrave Theatre 🎭 A1
Red Lodge 🏛 . . . A4
Regent St B1
Richmond Hill . . . A2
Richmond Hill Ave. A2
Richmond La A2
Richmond Park Rd. A2
Richmond St C6
Richmond Terr. . . A2
River St. A6
Rownham Mead . .B2
Royal Fort Rd. . . . A3
Royal Park A2
Royal West of England Academy 🏛 A3
Royal York Cr. B1
Royal York Villas . .B1
Rupert St A4
Russ St B6
St Andrew's Walk .B2
St George's 🎭. . . .B3
St George's Rd . . .B3
St James ⛪. A4
St John's ⛪. A4
St John's Rd C4
St Luke's Rd. C5
St Mary Redcliffe ⛪ C5
St Mary's Hospital Ⓗ. A3
St Matthias Park. A6
St Michael's Hill . A3
St Michael's Park A3
St Nicholas St B4
St Paul St A5
St Paul's Rd A2
St Peter's (Ruin) ⛪. A5

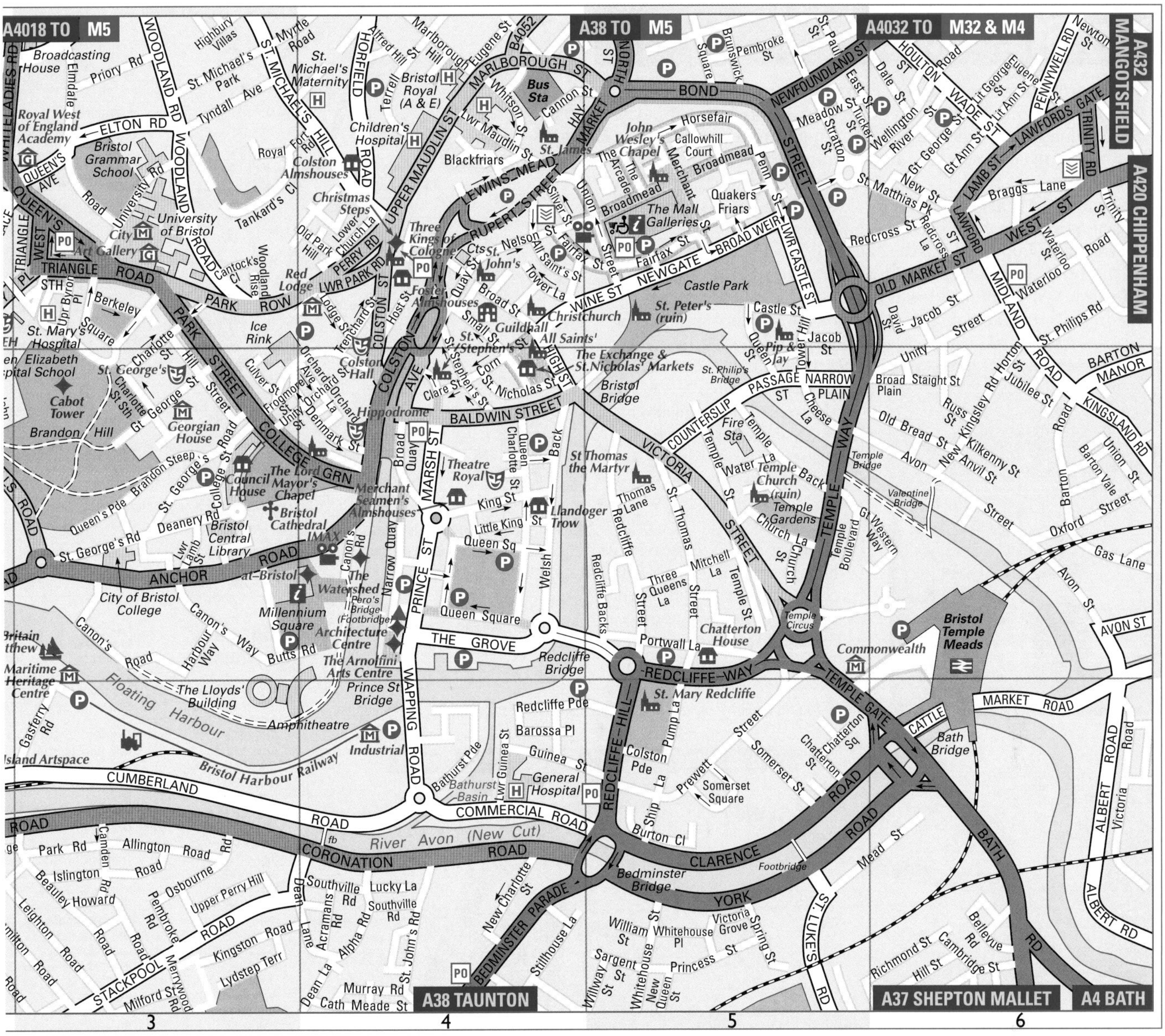

St Philip's Bridge .B5
St Philips Rd A6
St Stephen's Church B4
St Stephen's St...B4
St Thomas St.....B5
St Thomas the Martyr B5
Sandford Rd.......B1
Sargent St C5
Saville Pl B1
Ship La......... C5
Silver St A4
Sion Hill......... A1
Small St A4
Smeaton Rd..... C1
Somerset Sq C5
Somerset St..... C5
Southernhay Ave..B2
Southville Rd C4
Spike Island Artspace C2
Spring St C5
SS Great Britain & The Matthew C3
Stackpool Rd..... C3
Staight St........B6
Stillhouse La C4
Stracey Rd C2
Stratton St A5
Sydney Row C2
Tankard's Cl...... A3
Temple Back B5
Temple Blvd......B5
Temple Bridge....B5
Temple Church ...B5
Temple Gate C5
Temple St.........B5
Temple Way......B5
Terrell St A4
The Arcade A5
The Fosseway ... A2
The Grove B4
The Horsefair ... A5
The Mall......... A1
Theatre Royal ...B4
Thomas La.......B5

Bristol Tourist Information Centre, The Annexe, Wildscreen Walk, Harbourside, Bristol BS1 5DB
Tel 0906 711 2191

BBC Radio Bristol 95.5, 94.9 FM and 1548 AM • **Classic Gold** 1260 AM
GWR 96.3 FM • **Star** 107.3 FM

www.bristol-city.gov.uk

Three Kings of Cologne A4
Three Queens La. .B5
Tobacco Factory, The C2
Tower Hill........B5
Tower La........ A4
Trenchard St A4
Triangle South... A3
Triangle West ... A3
Trinity Rd A6
Trinity St........ A6
Tucker St A5
Tyndall Ave...... A3
Union St A5
Union St..........B6
Unity St......... A6
Unity St..........B3
Univ of Bristol ... A3
University Rd..... A3
Upper Maudlin St A4
Upper Perry Hill . C3
Upper Byron Pl .. A3
Upton Rd C2
Valentine Bridge ..B6
Victoria Gr C5
Victoria Rd...... C6
Victoria Rooms .. A2
Victoria Sq....... A2
Victoria St B5
Vyvyan Rd A1
Vyvyan Terr A1
Wade St A6
Walter St C2
Wapping Rd....... C4
Water La.........B5
Waterloo Rd...... A6
Waterloo St A1
Waterloo St A6
Watershed, The ✦.B4
Welling Terr B1
Wellington Rd ... A6
Welsh Back B4
West Mall........ A1
West St.......... A6
Westfield Pl...... A1
Wetherell Pl..... A2
Whitehouse Pl... C5
Whitehouse St... C5
Whiteladies Rd .. A2
Whitson St....... A4
William St C5
Willway St C5
Windsor Pl........B1
Windsor Terr B1
Wine St.......... A4
Woodland Rise ... A3
Woodland Rd..... A3
Worcester Rd..... A1
Worcester Terr.... A1
YHA B4
York Gdns.........B1
York Pl A2
York Rd.......... C5

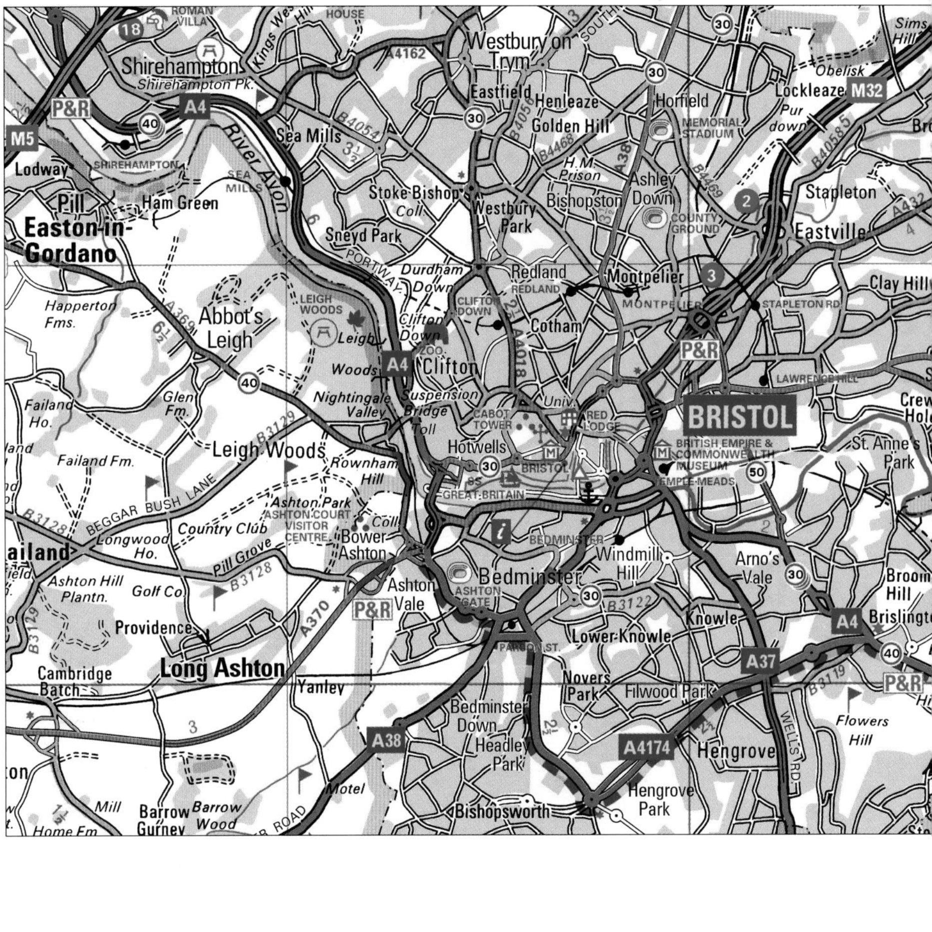

Bury St Edmunds

An attractive market town of Saxon origins that became home to one of medieval Europe's most powerful abbeys, which was founded in 1020 by King Canute and torn down in the mid 16th century: there are still ruins dotted about town. Mary Tudor, sister of Henry VIII, is buried in the sanctuary of the 14th-century St Mary's Church; the 1735 Manor House contains a museum of art, fashion and horology; there's an art gallery in a Robert Adams building; and the National Trust's Angel Corner is a Queen Anne house with the former mayor's parlour. The 16th-century St Edmundsbury is the country's only unfinished cathedral-church, lacking a spire but boasting a Norman tower as a belfry, and the 18th-century Theatre Royal is one of the UK's oldest and smallest working theatres. On Wednesdays and Saturdays the town hosts East Anglia's largest street market. Nearby are the Anglo-Saxon Village in nearby West Stow Country Park, Ickworth House (National Trust), with an 18th-century rotunda and fine art collection, Rede Hall Farm Park, the remains of Ixworth Abbey and the award-winning Lackford Wildfowl Reserve.

◀Bury St Edmunds Abbey Great Gate

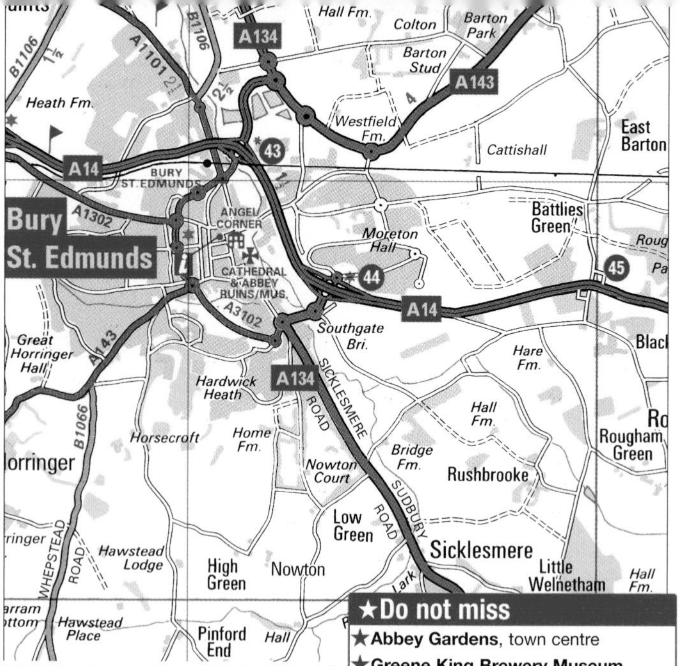

★Do not miss

★**Abbey Gardens**, town centre

★**Greene King Brewery Museum**, Westgate Street

★**Moyses Hall** (1180), Bronze Age to medieval archaeology and social history

Tourist Information Centre, 6 Angel Hill, Bury St Edmunds IP33 1UZ Tel 01284 764667

BBC Radio Suffolk 95.5, 95.9, 103.9, 104.6 FM • **Classic Gold Amber** 1170 AM • **SGR** 96.4 FM **Vibe FM** 105.0-108.0 FM

www.stedmundsbury.gov.uk

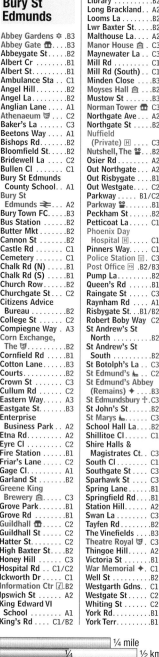

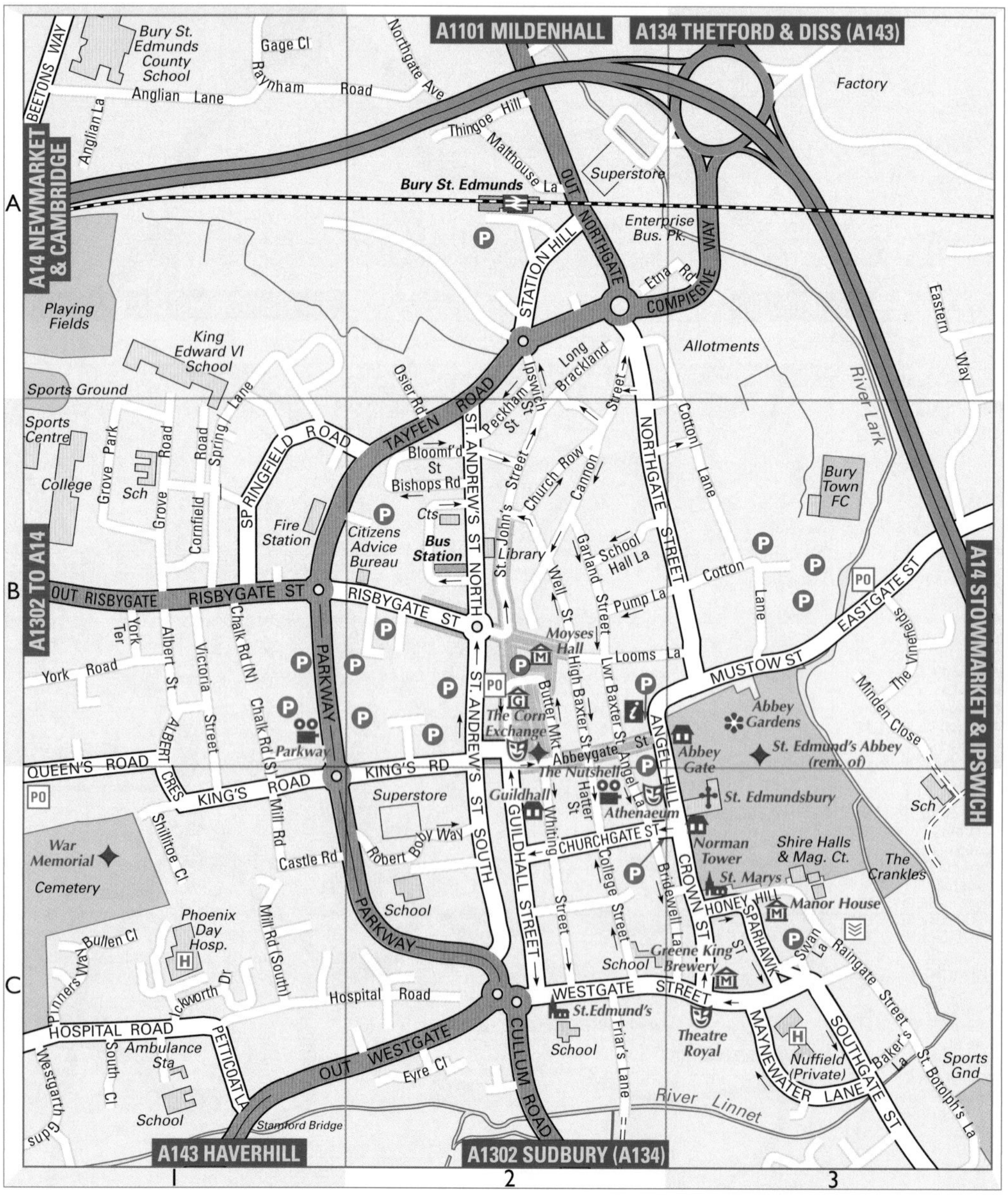

Bury St Edmunds

Abbey Gardens ✿ .B3
Abbey Gate B3
Abbeygate St B2
Albert Cr B1
Albert St. B1
Ambulance Sta . . C1
Angel Hill B2
Angel La B2
Anglian Lane A1
Athenaeum . . . C2
Baker's La C3
Beetons Way A1
Bishops Rd. B2
Bloomfield St. B2
Bridewell La C2
Bullen Cl C1
Bury St Edmunds County School. . A1
Bury St Edmunds . . . A2
Bury Town FC. B3
Bus Station B2
Butter Mkt B2
Cannon St B2
Castle Rd C1
Cemetery C1
Chalk Rd (N) B1
Chalk Rd (S) B1
Church Row B2
Churchgate St . . . C2
Citizens Advice Bureau B2
College St C2
Compiegne Way . A3
Corn Exchange, The B2
Cornfield Rd B1
Cotton Lane. B3
Courts. B2
Crown St C3
Cullum Rd C2
Eastern Way. A3
Eastgate St. B3
Enterprise Business Park . . A2
Etna Rd. A2
Eyre Cl C2
Fire Station B1
Friar's Lane C2
Gage Cl. A1
Garland St B2
Greene King Brewery C3
Grove Park. B1
Grove Rd B1
Guildhall C2
Guildhall St C2
Hatter St. C2
High Baxter St. . . .B2
Honey Hill C3
Hospital Rd . . C1/C2
Ickworth Dr C1
Information Ctr .B2
Ipswich St A2
King Edward VI School A1
King's Rd C1/B2
Library B2
Long Brackland. . A2
Looms La B2
Lwr Baxter St. B2
Malthouse La. . . . A2
Manor House . C3
Maynewater La . . C3
Mill Rd C1
Mill Rd (South) . . C1
Minden Close B3
Moyses Hall . . .B2
Mustow St B3
Norman Tower C3
Northgate Ave . . . A2
Northgate St B2
Nuffield (Private) C3
Nutshell, The . . .B2
Osier Rd A2
Out Northgate . . . A2
Out Risbygate B1
Out Westgate. . . . C2
Parkway B1/C2
Parkway B1
Peckham St B2
Petticoat La C1
Phoenix Day Hospital C1
Pinners Way. C1
Police Station . C3
Post Office .B2/B3
Pump La. B2
Queen's Rd B1
Raingate St C3
Raynham Rd A1
Risbygate St. . .B1/B2
Robert Boby Way C2
St Andrew's St North B2
St Andrew's St South B2
St Botolph's La . . C3
St Edmund's . . C2
St Edmund's Abbey (Remains) ✦ B3
St Edmundsbury ✝.C3
St John's St. B2
St Marys C3
School Hall La. . . .B2
Shillitoe Cl. C1
Shire Halls & Magistrates Ct. . C3
South Cl C1
Southgate St C3
Sparhawk St C3
Spring Lane B1
Springfield Rd B1
Station Hill. A2
Swan La C3
Tayfen Rd B2
The Vinefields B3
Theatre Royal . C3
Thingoe Hill. A2
Victoria St B1
War Memorial ✦. C1
Well St B2
Westgarth Gdns. . C1
Westgate St C2
Whiting St C2
York Rd. B1
York Terr. B1

¼ mile

¼ ½ km

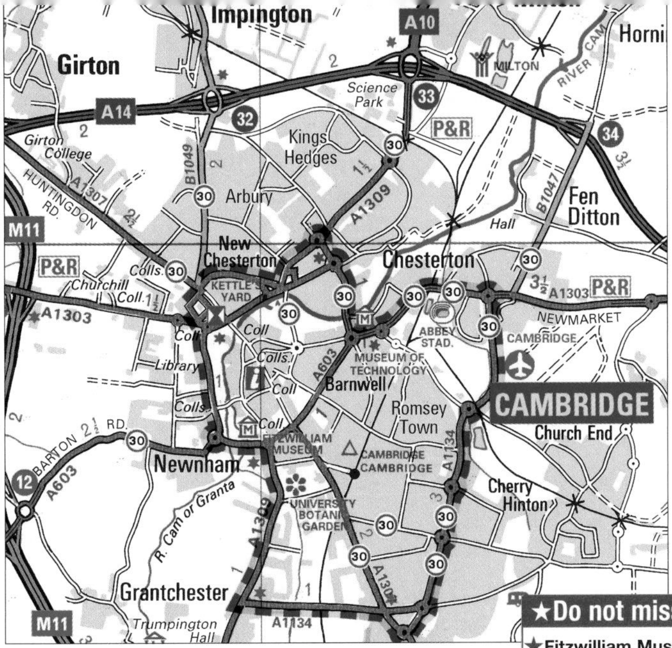

Cambridge

An ancient university town. Of its 31 colleges, the first was Peterhouse, founded in 1284. Other fine university buildings include the Old Schools (1350) and the Senate House (1722-30), and the University Botanic Garden is worth a visit. The town's museums and art galleries cover a wide range of subjects including polar exploration, technology, scientific instruments, folk, zoology and archaeology and it is also home to fine markets and a huge variety of bookshops. Pleasant activities include walking along the Backs (the banks of the Cam) and punting along the river, and there are many cultural activities. Close by are Milton and Wandlebury country parks and the National Trust's Anglesey Abbey.

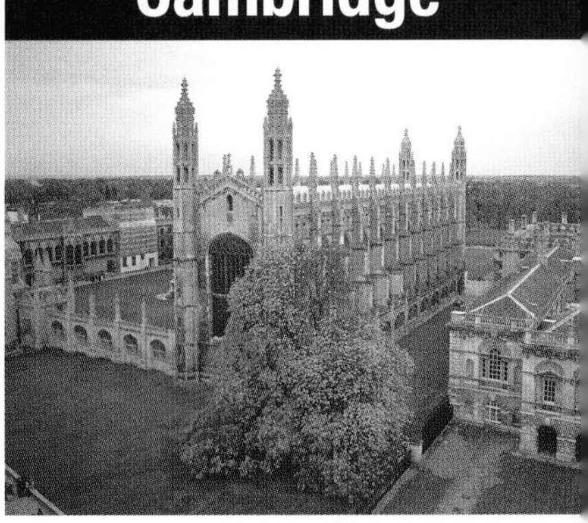

▲King's College Chapel

★Do not miss

- ★**Fitzwilliam Museum**, Trumpington Street – University art collection
- ★**Kettle's Yard**, Castle Street – gallery of 20th-century and contemporary art
- ★**King's College Chapel and Choir**, King's Parade

Tourist Information Centre, The Old Library, Wheeler Street, Cambridge CB2 3QB
Tel 0871 226 8006

BBC Radio Cambridgeshire 96.0 FM and 1026 AM
Q103 103.0 FM • **Star** 107.9 FM • **Vibe FM** 105.6 FM

www.cambridge.gov.uk

Cambridge

Abbey Rd A3
ADC A2
Anglia Polytechnic University B3
Archaeology & Anthropology .B2
Art Gallery ... A1
Arts Theatre ...B1
Auckland Rd A3
Bateman St C2
B.B.C. C3
Bene't St B1
Bradmore St B3
Bridge St A1
Broad St B3
Brookside....... C2
Brunswick Terr .. A3
Burleigh St.......B3
Bus Station B2
Butt Green A2
Cambridge Contemporary Art Gall B1
Castle Mound . A1
Castle St........ A1
Chesterton La ... A1
Christ's (Coll) ...B2
Christ's Pieces ...B2
City Rd B3
Clare (Coll) B1
Clarendon St B2
Coe Fen C2
Coronation St ... C2
Corpus Christi (Coll) B1
Council Offices .. C3
Cross St C3
Crusoe Bridge ... C1
Darwin (Coll)..... C1
Devonshire Rd... C3
Downing (Coll) ...B2
Downing St B2
Earl St...........B2
East Rd B3
Eden St B3
Elizabeth Way ... A3
Elm St...........B2
Emery St.........B3
Emmanuel (Coll). .B2
Emmanuel Rd B2
Emmanuel St.....B2
Fair St........... A3
Fenners (Cambridge Univ C.C.)........ C3
Fire Station B3
Fitzroy St A3
Fitzwilliam Mus C1
Fitzwilliam St.....B2
Folk Mus A1
Glisson Rd C3
Gonville & Caius (Coll) B1
Gonville Place....B3
Grafton Centre .. A3
Gresham Rd..... C3
Green St B1
Guest Rd.........B3
Guildhall B2
Harvey Rd....... C3
Hills Rd......... C3
Hobson St B2
Hughes Hall (Coll) .B3
Information Ctr .B2
James St A3
Jesus (Coll) A2
Jesus Green..... A2
Jesus La A2
Jesus Terr.........B3
John St..........B3
Kelsey Kerridge Sports Hall......B3
King St A2
King's (Coll) B1
King's College Chapel B1
King's Parade B1
Lensfield Rd..... C2
Lion Yard Centre . .B2
Little St Mary's La.B1
Lyndewod Rd.... C3
Magdalene (Coll) A1
Magdalene St ... A1
Maid's Causeway A3
Malcolm St...... A2
Market Hill.......B1
Market St B1
Mathematical Br ..B1
Mawson Rd C3
Midsummer Com A3
Mill La...........B1
Mill Rd B3
Napier St A3
New Square..... A2
Newmarket Rd... A3
Newnham Rd.... C1
Norfolk St........B3
Northampton St . A1
Norwich St...... C2
Orchard St B2
Panton St....... C2
Paradise Nature Reserve C1
Paradise St B3
Park Parade..... A1
Park St A2
Park Terr.........B2
Parker St B2
Parker's Piece.....B2
Parkside B3
Parkside Swimming Pool B3
Parsonage St.... A3
Pembroke (Coll) ..B2
Pembroke St B1
Perowne St B3
Peterhouse (Coll) C1
Petty Cury B2
Police Station ...B3
Post Office .. A1/A3/B2/B3/C1/C2/C3
Queens' (Coll) B1
Queen's La.......B1
Queen's Rd B1
Regent St B2
Regent Terr B2
Ridley Hall (Coll) C1
Riverside A3
Round Church, The A1
Russell St....... C2
St Andrew's St....B2
St Benet's B1
St Catharine's (Coll) B1
St Eligius St..... C2
St John's (Coll).. A1
St Mary's B1
St Paul's Rd..... C3
Saxon St........ C2
Scott Polar Research Inst & Mus .. C2
Sedgwick Mus .B2
Sheep's Green.... C1
Shelly Row...... A1
Shire Hall....... A1
Sidgwick Ave.... C1
Sidney St A1
Sidney Sussex (Coll) A2
Silver St B1
Station Rd C3
Tenison Ave..... C3
Tenison Rd...... C3
Tennis Court Rd ..B2
The Backs B1
The Fen Causeway C1
Thompson's La .. A1
Trinity (Coll) A1
Trinity Hall (Coll) .B1
Trinity St.........B1
Trumpington Rd . C2
Trumpington St .. C2
Union Rd C2
Univ Botanic Gardens C2
Victoria Ave..... A2
Victoria St B2
Warkworth St B3
Warkworth Terr...B3
Wesley Hse (Coll) A2
West Rd B1
Westcott Hse (Coll) A2
Westminster (Coll) A1
Whipple B2
Willis Rd.........B3
Willow Walk..... A2
Zoology B2

¼ mile
¼ ½ km

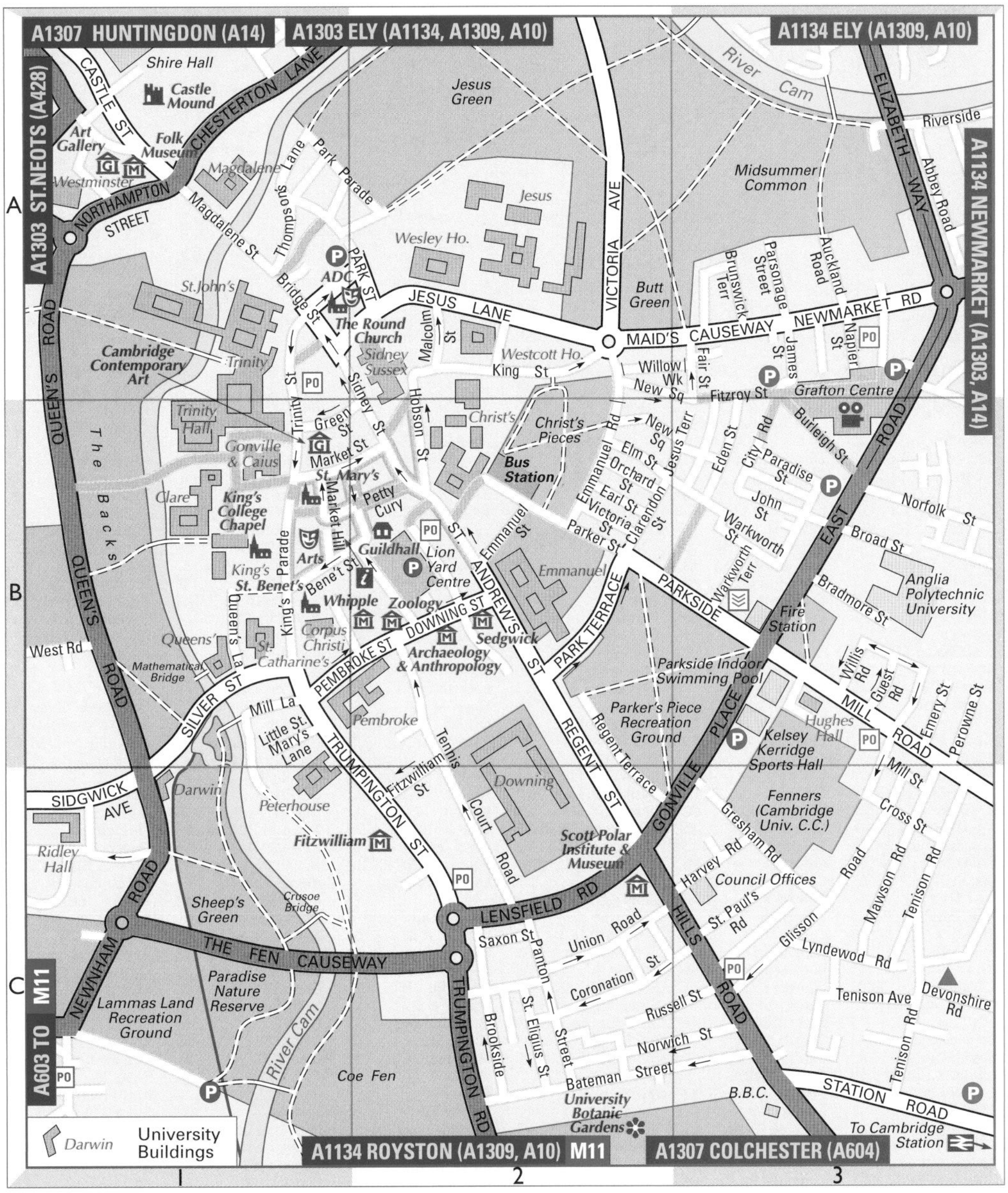

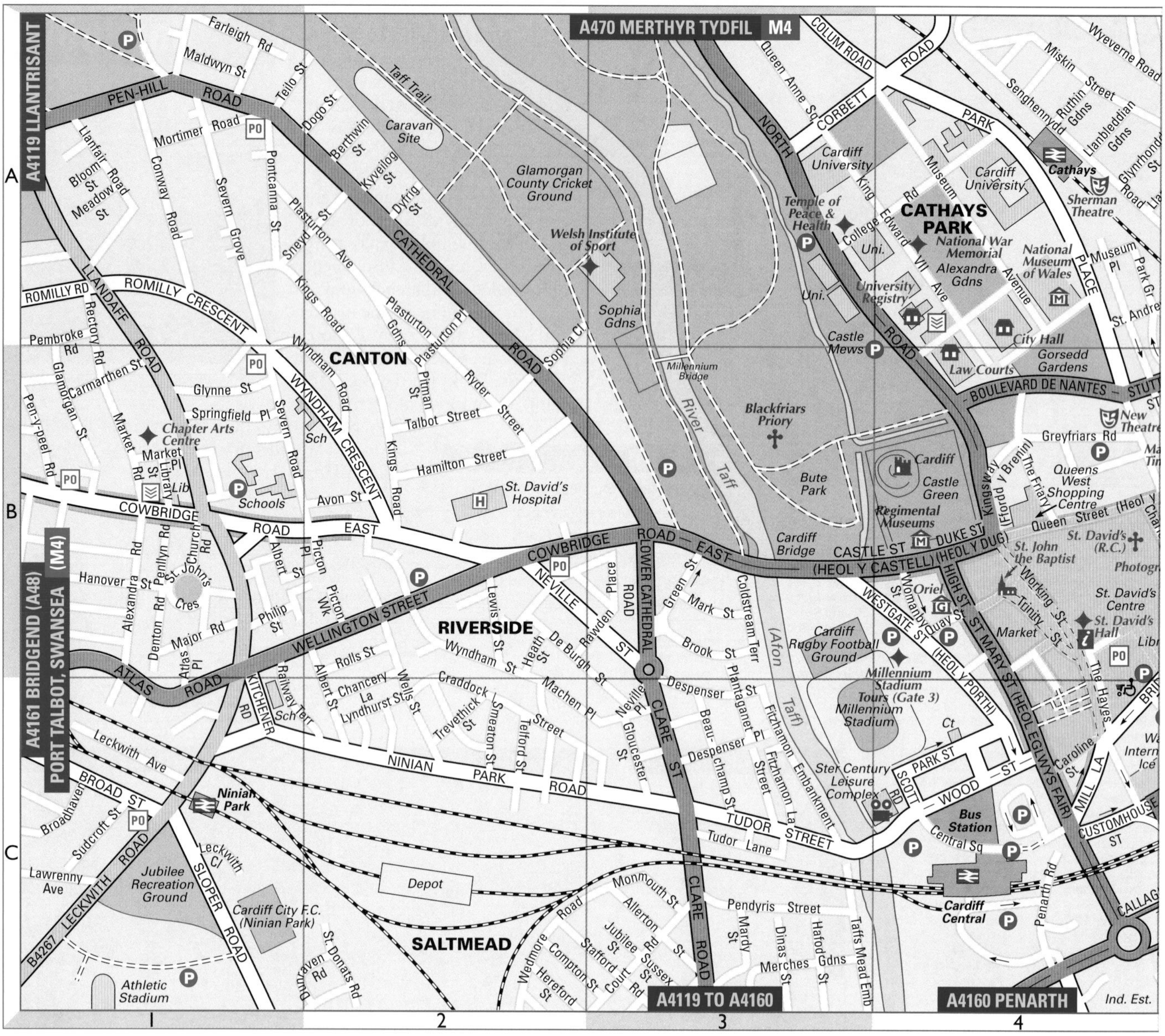

Cardiff/ Caerdydd

Adam St ... B5
Adamsdown La ... B6
Albert St ... B1
Alexandra Gdns .. A4
Alexandra Rd ... B1
Allerton St ... C3
Arran St ... A5
Athletic Stadium . C1
Atlas Pl ... B1
Atlas Rd ... C1
Augusta St ... B6
Avon St ... B2
Beauchamp St ... C3
Bedford St ... A5
Berthwin St ... A2
Blackfriars Priory ✝ ... B3
Bloom St ... A1
Boulevard De Nantes ... B4
Bridge St ... B5
Broad St ... C1
Broadhaven ... C1
Broadway ... A6
Brook St ... B3
Bus Station ... C4
Bute East Dock ... C6
Bute Park ... B3
Bute St ... C4
Bute Terr ... C5
Byron St ... A5
Callaghan Sq . C4/C5
Capitol Shopping Ctr, The ... B5
Caravan Site ... A2
Cardiff Bridge ... B3
Cardiff Castle ... B4
Cardiff Central Station ... C4
Cardiff Centre Trading Estate .. C5
Cardiff City F.C. (Ninian Park) ... C1
Cardiff International Arena ✦ ... C5
Cardiff Rugby Football Ground . B3
Cardiff Univ. A3/A4/B5
Carmarthen St ... B1
Caroline St ... C4
Castle Green ... B4
Castle Mews ... A3
Castle St (Heol y Castell) . B3
Cathays ... A4
Cathedral Rd ... A2
Celerity Drive ... C5
Central Link ... C6
Central Sq ... C4
Chancery La ... C2
Chapter Arts Ctr ✦ . B1
Charles St (Heol Siarl) ... B5
Church Rd ... B1
Churchill Way ... B5
City Hall ... A4
City Rd ... A5
Clare Rd ... C3
Clare St ... C3
Clifton St ... A6
Coburn St ... A5
Coldstream Terr .. B3
College of Cardiff A3
College Rd ... A3
Colum Rd ... A3
Comet St ... B6
Compton St ... C2
Constellation St . B6
Conway Rd ... A1
Copper St ... B6
Corbett Rd ... A3
Court ... C4
Court Rd ... C3
Cowbridge Rd East ... B1/B2
Craddock St ... C2
Craiglee Drive ... C5
Cranbrook St ... A5
Crofts St ... A6
Cumnock Pl ... B6
Customhouse St . C4
Cyfartha St ... A5
Davis St ... B5
De Burgh St ... B2
Denton Rd ... B1
Despenser Pl ... C3
Despenser St ... C3
Dinas St ... C3
Dogo St ... A2
Duke St (Heol y Dug) ... B4
Dumfries Pl ... B5
Dunraven Rd ... C1
Dyfrig St ... A2
East Grove ... A5
East Moors Rd ... C6
East Tyndall St ... C6
Eclipse St ... B6
Ellen St ... C5
Elm St ... A6
Farleigh Rd ... A1
Fire Station ... B5
Fitzalan Pl ... B5
Fitzhamon Emb .. C3
Fitzhamon La ... C3
Garesfield St ... B6
Glamorgan County Cricket Ground . A2
Glamorgan St ... B1
Glossop Rd ... B6
Gloucester St ... C3
Glynne St ... B1
Glynrhondda St .. A4
Gold St ... A6
Gordon Rd ... A5
Gorsedd Gdns ... B4
Green St ... B3
Greyfriars Rd ... B4
HM Prison ... B5
Hafod St ... C3
Hamilton St ... B2
Hanover St ... B1
Heath St ... B2
Herbert St ... C5
Hereford St ... C2
High St ... B4
Howard Pl ... B6
Industrial Estate . C5
Information Ctr ℹ . B4
John St ... C5
Jubilee Rec Gnd . C1
Jubilee St ... C3
King Edward VII Ave ... A3
Kings Rd ... A1/B2
Kingsway (Ffordd y Brenin) ... B4
Kitchener Rd ... C1
Knox Rd ... B5
Kyveilog St ... A2
Law Courts ... B4
Lawrenny Ave ... C1
Lead St ... B6
Leckwith Ave ... C1
Leckwith Close .. C1
Leckwith Rd ... C1
Lewis St ... B2
Library ... B1/B5
Library St ... B1
Lily St ... A6
Llanbleddian Gdns A4
Llandaff Rd ... A1
Llanfair Rd ... A1
Llantwit St ... A4
Lloyd George Ave C5
Longcross St ... B6
Lower Cathedral Rd ... B3
Lowther Rd ... A5
Lyndhurst St ... C2
Machen Pl ... C2
Magistrates Court . B5
Major Rd ... B1
Maldwyn St ... A1
Mansion House . A5
Mardy St ... C3
Mark St ... B3
Market ... B4
Market Pl ... B1
Market Rd ... B1
Martin Tinney ... B5
Mary Ann St ... C5
Meadow St ... A1
Merches Gdns ... C3
Metal St ... B6
Meteor St ... B6
Mill La ... C4
Millennium Bridge B3
Millennium Stadium ... C3
Millennium Stadium Tours (Gate 3) ✦ B4
Milton St ... A5
Miskin St ... A4
Moira Pl ... B6
Moira St ... B6
Moira Terr ... B6
Monmouth St ... C3
Mortimer Rd ... A1
Museum Ave ... A4
Museum Pl ... A4
National Museum of Wales ... A4
National Tennis Centre ... C6
National War Memorial ✦ ... A4
Neville Pl ... C3
Neville St ... B2
New Theatre ... B4
Newport Rd .. A6/B5
Newport Rd La .. B5
Ninian Park ... C1
Ninian Park Rd .. C2
North Rd ... A3
Northcote La ... A5
Northcote St ... A5
North Luton Pl ... B6
Oakfield St ... A6
Ocean Way ... C6
Orbit St ... A6
Oriel ... B4
Oxford La ... A6
Oxford St ... A6
Park Grove ... A4
Park Pl ... A4
Park St ... C4
Partridge La ... A6
Partridge Rd ... A6
Pembroke Rd ... A1
Pen-Hill Rd ... A1
Pen-y-Peel Rd .. B1
Penarth Rd ... C4
Pendyris St ... C3
Penllyn Rd ... B1
Philip St ... B1
Photographic Library ... B5
Picton Pl ... B2
Picton Walk ... B2
Piercefield Pl ... A6
Pitman St ... B2
Plat St ... B6
Plantaganet St .. C3
Plasnewydd Rd .. A5
Plasturton Ave ... A1
Plasturton Gdns . A2
Plasturton Pl ... A2
Police Station ... A4/A6/B1
Pontcanna St ... A1
Post Office ... A1/A5/A6/B1/B2/B4/B6/C1
Princes St ... A6
Quay St ... B4
Queen Anne Sq .. A3
Queen St (Heol y Frenhines) ... B4
Queen St ... B5
Queens West Shopping Ctr ... B4
Railway Terr ... C1
Rawden Pl ... B3
Rectory Rd ... A1
Regimental Museums ... B4
Rhymney St ... A5
Richmond Rd ... A5
Rolls St ... B2
Romilly Cr ... A1
Romilly Rd ... A1
Rose St ... A5
Royal Infirmary ... A6
Russell St ... A5
Ruthin Gdns ... A4
Ryder St ... B2
St Andrews Pl ... A4
St David's ✝ ... B4
St David's Centre . B4
St David's Hall ... B4
St David's Hospital ... B2
St Donats Rd ... C2
St John The Baptist ... B4
St John's Cr ... B1
St Mary St (Heol Eglwys Fair) ... B4
St Peter's St ... A5
Salisbury Rd ... A5
Sandon St ... B5
Sanquhar St ... B6
Scott Rd ... C4
Senghennydd Rd . A4
Severn Green ... A1
Severn Rd ... A1
Sherman Theatre ... A4
Silver St ... A6
Sloper Rd ... C1
Smeaton St ... C2
Sneyd St ... A1
Sophia Cl ... B2
Sophia Gdns ... A3
South Luton Pl .. B6
Southey St ... A6
Springfield Pl ... B1
Stafford Rd ... C3
Ster Century Leisure Complex ... C3
Star St ... B6
Station Terr ... B5
Stuttgarter Strasse ... B4
Sudcroft St ... C1
Sun St ... B6
Sussex St ... C3
System St ... B6
Taffs Mead Embankment ... C3
Taff Trail ... A2
Talbot St ... B2
Talworth St ... A5
Teal St ... A6
Teilo St ... A1
Telford St ... C2
Temple of Peace & Health ✦ ... A3
The Friary ... B4
The Hayes ... B4
The Parade ... A5
The Walk ... A5
Treharris St ... A5
Trevethick St ... C2
Trinity St ... B4
Tudor La ... C3
Tudor St ... C3
Tyndall St ... C5
UGC Leisure Complex ... C5
University Registry ... A4
Wales Int. Ice Rink C4
Wedmore Rd ... C2
Wellington St ... B2
Wells St ... C2
Welsh Institute of Sport ✦ ... A3
West Green ... A5
Westgate St (Heol y Porth) ... B4
Windsor Pl ... B5
Windsor Rd ... B5
Womanby St ... B4
Wood St ... C4
Wordsworth Ave . A6
Working St ... B4
Wyeverne Rd ... A4
Wyndham Cr ... A1
Wyndham Rd ... B2
Wyndham St ... B2

¼ mile
¼ ½ km

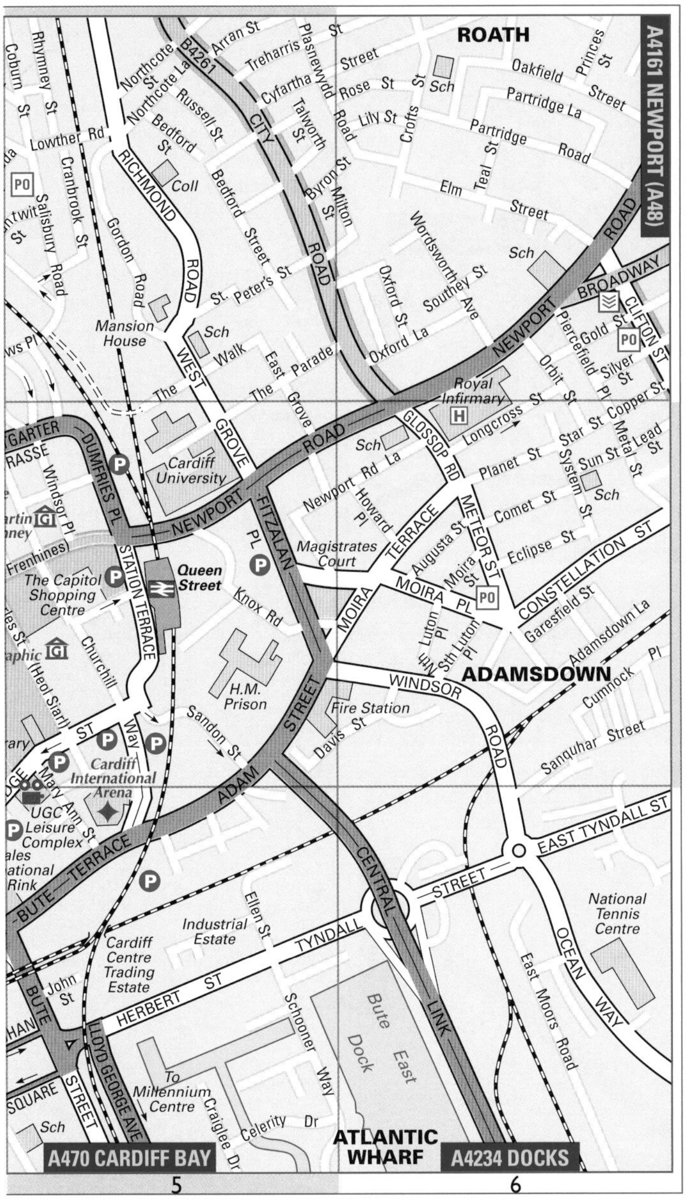

Cardiff

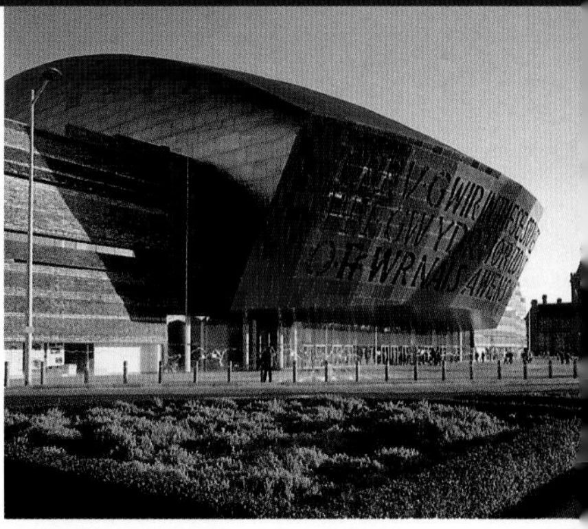

The Welsh capital since 1955, on the site of a fort established by the Romans in AD75, and the subject of large-scale regeneration over the past decade. Highlights include the Castle, with remains from Roman, Norman and medieval buildings and stunning 19th-century interiors and three military museums, the hi-tech Millennium Stadium (Europe's largest covered stadium), and the Techniquest science-discovery centre. The revitalised bay and docklands can be viewed by boat and road-train trips, at the Cardiff Bay Barrage, at the Tube (Cardiff Bay Visitor Centre), and at the Butetown History and Arts Centre. Lively, cosmopolitan and a designated Centre of Culture, the city has a thriving contemporary art scene (including the Wales Millennium Centre), good shops and department stores, and an array of glamorous restaurants and hotels.

▲The Wales Millennium Centre

▼The Millennium Stadium

Cardiff Gateway Visitor Centre, The Old Library, The Hayes, Cardiff CF10 1AH Tel 0870 121 1258

BBC Radio Wales 103.9 FM
Real Radio Wales 105.4 FM
Red Dragon FM 103.2 FM

www.visitcardiff.com

◀The Norwegian Church and Scott Memorial, Cardiff Bay

★Do not miss

★**Cardiff Castle**, Castle Street
★**Museum of Welsh Life**, St Fagans
★**National Museum and Gallery**, Cathays Park

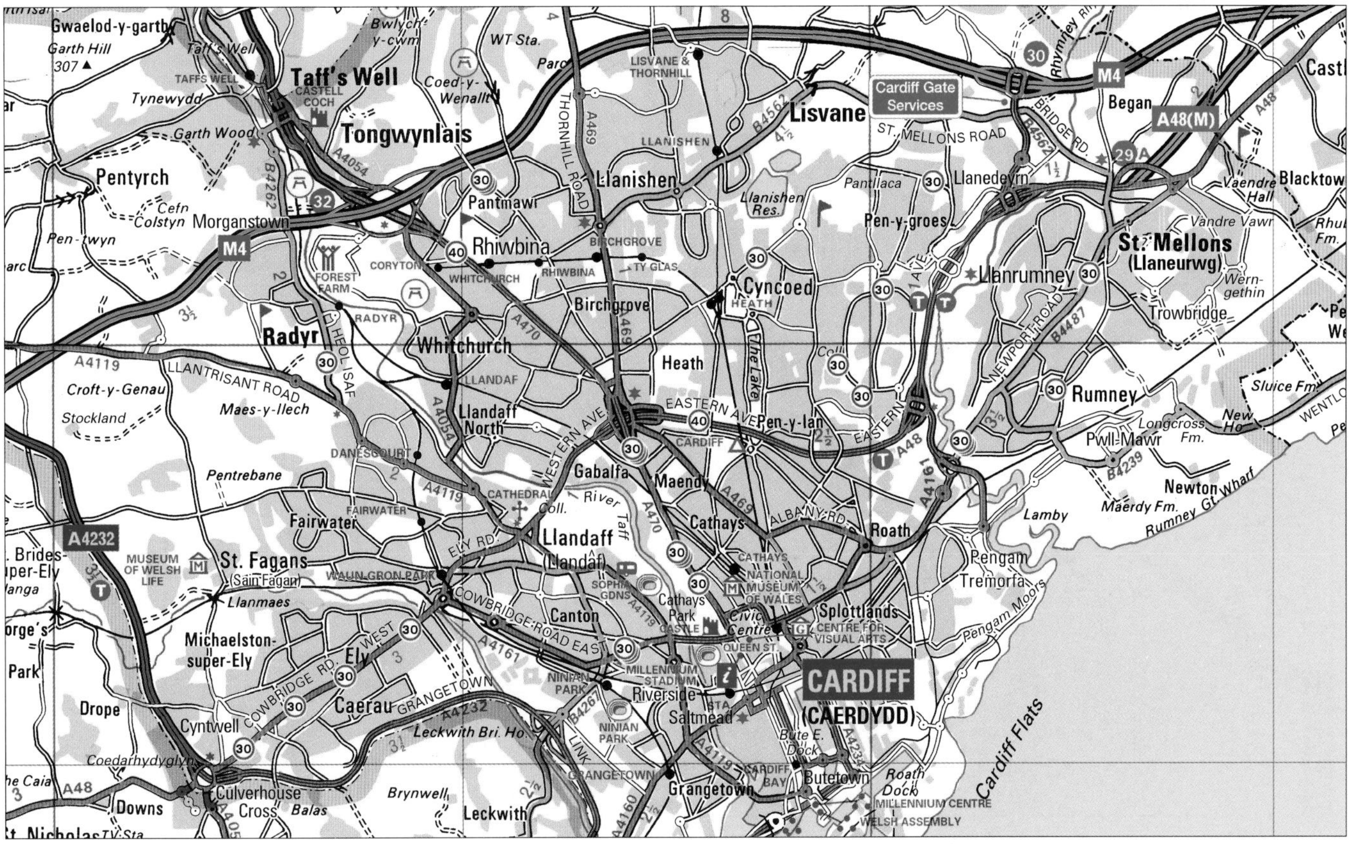

Canterbury

▲The Cathedral from King's School

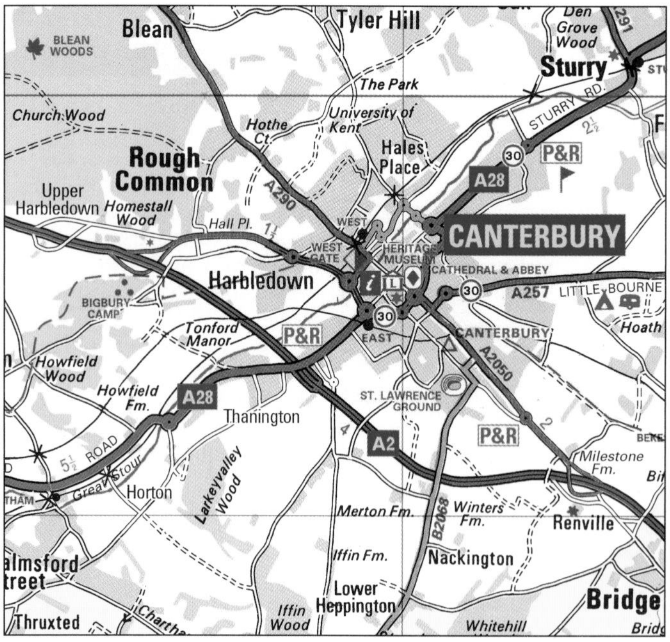

The Cathedral, St Martin's Church and St Augustine's Abbey form a UNESCO world heritage site. Places of interest include the Eastbridge Hospital of St Thomas the Martyr, founded in 1190; St Augustine's Abbey, founded in 598; the Norman Keep – also known as Canterbury Castle, West Gate Towers. Other attractions in the town centre include Planet Lazer on St George's Street, the Odeon Cinema and the Marlowe Theatre. Canterbury has a diverse selection of shops from the Marlowe arcade through to St Margaret's Street and Burgate, as well as a twice weekly street market, many of the city's restaurants, pubs and bars can also be found in this area.

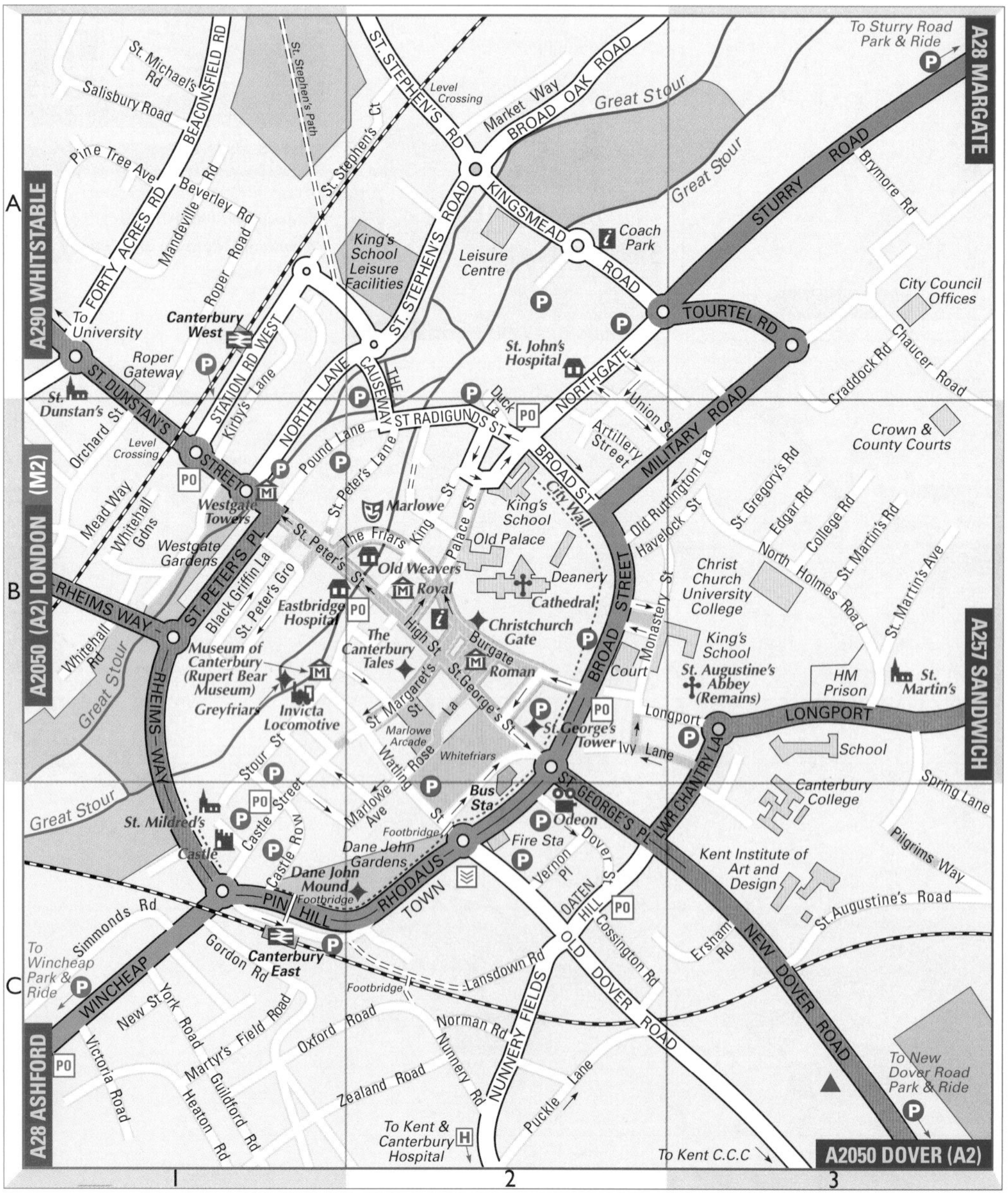

★Do not miss

★**Canterbury Cathedral**, The Precincts

★**Royal Museum and Art Gallery with Buffs Regimental Museum**, High Street

★**Canterbury Roman Museum**, Butchery Lane

Tourist Information Centre
12/13 Sun Street, The Buttermarket, Canterbury CT1 2HX
Tel 01227 378100

BBC Radio Kent 97.6 FM
KM-fm 106.0 FM

www.canterbury.co.uk

Canterbury

Artillery St B2
Beaconsfield Rd . A1
Beverley Rd A1
Black Griffin La . . . B1
Broad Oak Rd . . . A2
Broad St B2
Brymore Rd A3
Burgate B2
Bus Station C2
Canterbury Coll . . C3
Canterbury East ⇌ C1
Canterbury Tales, The ✦ B2
Canterbury West ⇌ A1
Castle C1
Castle Row C1
Castle St C1
Cathedral ✝ B2
Chaucer Rd A3
Christ Church University College B3
Christchurch Gate ✦ B2
City Council Offices A3
City Wall B2
Coach Park A2
College Rd B3
Cossington Rd . . . C2
Court B2
Craddock Rd A3
Crown & County Courts B3
Dane John Gardens C2
Dane John Mound ✦ C1
Deanery B2
Dover St C2
Duck La B2
Eastbridge Hospital B1
Edgar Rd B3
Ersham Rd C3
Fire Station C2
Forty Acres Rd . . A1
Gordon Rd C1
Greyfriars ✦ B1
Guildford Rd C1
Havelock St B2
Heaton Rd C1
High St B2
HM Prison B3
Information Ctr A2/B2
Invicta Locomotive . . . B1
Ivy La B2
Kent Institute of Art & Design . . . C3
King St B2
King's School B3
Kingsmead Rd . . . A2
Kirby's La B1
Lansdown Rd C2
Leisure Centre . . . A2
Longport B3
Lower Chantry La C3
Mandeville Rd . . . A1
Market Way A2
Marlowe Arcade . . B2
Marlowe Ave C2
Marlowe Theatre B2
Martyr's Field Rd C1
Mead Way B1
Military Rd B2
Monastery St B2
Mus of Canterbury (Rupert Bear Museum) B1
New Dover Rd C3
New St C1
Norman Rd C2
North Holmes Rd . B3
North La B1
Northgate A2
Nunnery Fields . . C2
Nunnery Rd C2
Oaten Hill C2
Odeon Cinema . C2
Old Dover Rd C2
Old Palace B2
Old Ruttington La . B2
Old Weavers . . . B2
Orchard St B1
Oxford Rd C1
Palace St B2
Pilgrims Way C3
Pin Hill C1
Pine Tree Ave A1
Police Station . C2
Post Office B1/B2/C1/C2
Pound La B1
Puckle La C2
Rheims Way B1
Rhodaus Town . . . C2
Roman Mus . . . B2
Roper Gateway . . . A1
Roper Rd A1
Rose La B2
Royal Mus B2
St Augustine's Abbey (Remains) ✝ . . . B3
St Augustine's Rd C3
St Dunstan's . . . A1
St Dunstan's St . . A1
St George's Pl . . . C2
St George's St . . . B2
St George's Tower ✦ B2
St Gregory's Rd . . B3
St John's Hospital A2
St Margaret's St . . B2
St Martin's B3
St Martin's Ave . . . B3
St Martin's Rd B3
St Michael's Rd . . A1
St Mildred's C1
St Peter's Gr B1
St Peter's La B2
St Peter's Pl B1
St Peter's St B1
St Radigunds St . . B2
St Stephen's Ct . . A1
St Stephen's Path A1
St Stephen's Rd . . A2
Salisbury Rd A1
Simmonds Rd . . . C1
Spring La C3
Station Rd West . . B1
Stour St B1
Sturry Rd A3
The Causeway . . . A2
The Friars B2
Tourtel Rd A3
Union St B2
Vernon Pl C2
Victoria Rd C1
Watling St B2
Westgate Towers B1
Westgate Gdns . . . B1
Whitefriars B2
Whitehall Gdns . . . B1
Whitehall Rd B1
Wincheap C1
York Rd C1
Zealand Rd C2

¼ mile
¼ ½ km

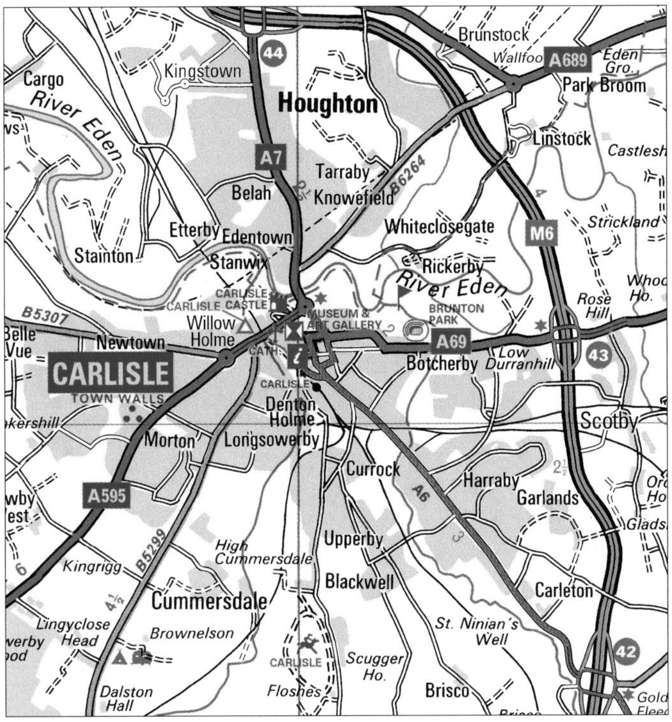

The city is surrounded by much of historical interest with a 900-year-old castle, a cathedral dating back to 1122 and the nearby Birdoswald Roman Fort on Hadrian's Wall. Tullie House Museum and Art Gallery portrays Carlisle's history as a border city as well as displaying traditional and modern artists and the Guildhall Museum, situated in a half-timbered late 14th-century building, features work from the various guildsmen of Carlisle dating to 18th century. A major shopping destination for Cumbria and south west Scotland it includes The Lanes and The Market Hall centres. There is a good range of sports and leisure facilities from golf and birdwatching to watersports and racing, and there are many bars, and restaurants of all cuisines.

Carlisle

▲The Citadel

★Do not miss

★**Tullie House Museum and Art Gallery**, Castle Street
★**Carlisle Cathedral**, Castle Street
★**Carlisle Castle**, Castle Way

Carlisle Visitor Centre, Old Town Hall, Greenmarket, Carlisle CA3 8JE
Tel 01228 625600

BBC Radio Cumbria 95.6, 96.1, 104.1 FM • **CFM Radio** 96.4 FM

www.carlisle.gov.uk

¼ mile
¼ ½ km

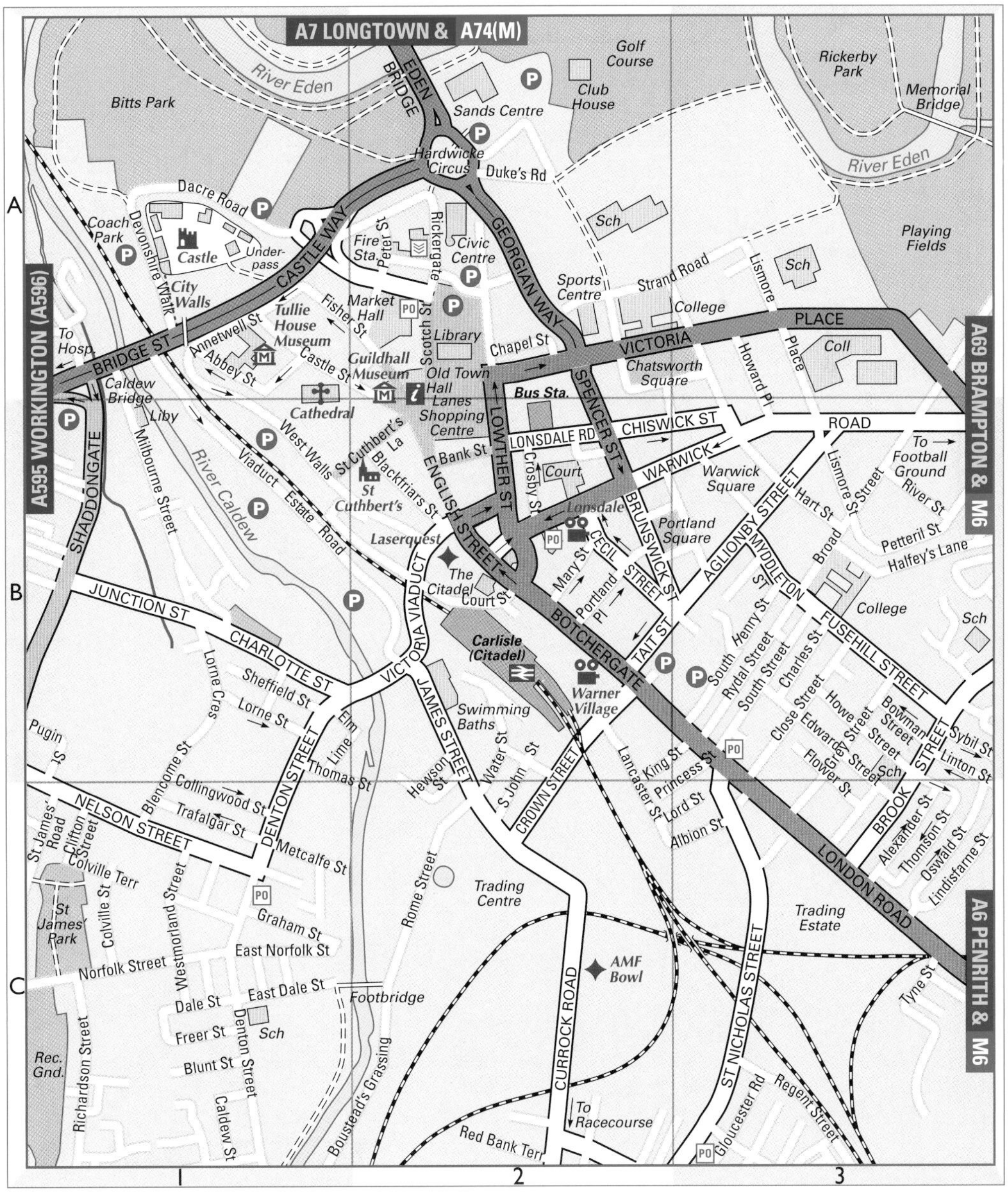

Carlisle

Abbey St . . . A1
Aglionby St . . . B3
Albion St . . . C3
Alexander St . . . C3
AMF Bowl ✦ . . . C2
Annetwell St . . . A1
Bank St . . . B2
Bitts Park . . . A1
Blackfriars St . . . B2
Blencome St . . . C1
Blunt St . . . C1
Botchergate . . . B2
Boustead's Grassing . . . C2
Bowman St . . . B3
Broad St . . . B3
Bridge St . . . A1
Brook St . . . C3
Brunswick St . . . B2
Bus Station . . . B2
Caldew Bridge . . . A1
Caldew St . . . C1
Carlisle (Citadel) Station . . . B2
Castle . . . A1
Castle St . . . A1
Castle Way . . . A1
Cathedral ✝ . . . A1
Cecil St . . . B2
Chapel St . . . A2
Charles St . . . B3
Charlotte St . . . B1
Chatsworth Square . . . A2
Chiswick St . . . B2
Citadel, The . . . B2
City Walls . . . A1
Civic Centre . . . A2
Clifton St . . . C1
Close St . . . B3
Collingwood St . . C1
Colville St . . . C1
Colville Terr . . . C1
Court . . . B2
Court St . . . B2
Crosby St . . . B2
Crown St . . . C2
Currock Rd . . . C2
Dacre Rd . . . A1
Dale St . . . C1
Denton St . . . C1
Devonshire Walk . A1
Duke's Rd . . . A2
East Dale St . . . C1
East Norfolk St . . C1
Eden Bridge . . . A2
Edward St . . . B3
Elm St . . . B1
English St . . . B2
Fire Station . . . A2
Fisher St . . . A1
Flower St . . . C3
Freer St . . . C1
Fusehill St . . . B3
Georgian Way . . . A2
Gloucester Rd . . . C3
Golf Course . . . A2
Graham St . . . C1
Grey St . . . B3
Guildhall Museum . . . A2
Halfey's La . . . B3
Hardwicke Circus A2
Hart St . . . B3
Hewson St . . . C2
Howard Pl . . . A3
Howe St . . . B3
Information Ctr . . . A2
James St . . . B2
Junction St . . . B1
King St . . . B2
Lancaster St . . . C2
Lanes Shopping Centre . . . A2/B2
Laserquest ✦ . . . B2
Library . . . A2/B1
Lime St . . . B1
Lindisfarne St . . . C3
Linton St . . . B3
Lismore Pl . . . A3
Lismore St . . . B3
London Rd . . . C3
Lonsdale . . . B2
Lonsdale Rd . . . B2
Lord St . . . C3
Lorne Cres . . . B1
Lorne St . . . B1
Lowther St . . . B2
Market Hall . . . A2
Mary St . . . B2
Memorial Bridge . A3
Metcalfe St . . . C1
Milbourne St . . . B1
Myddleton St . . . B3
Nelson St . . . C1
Norfolk St . . . C1
Old Town Hall . . . A2
Oswald St . . . C3
Peter St . . . A2
Petteril St . . . B3
Police Station . A2
Portland Pl . . . B2
Portland Sq . . . B2
Post Office . . . A2/B2/B3/C1/C3
Princess St . . . C3
Pugin St . . . B1
Red Bank Terr . . . C2
Regent St . . . C3
Richardson St . . . C1
Rickerby Park . . . A3
Rickergate . . . A2
River St . . . B3
Rome St . . . C2
Rydal St . . . B3
St Cuthbert's . . . B2
St Cuthbert's La . . B2
St James' Park . . C1
St James' Rd . . . C1
St Nicholas St . . . C3
Sands Centre . . . A2
Scotch St . . . A2
Shaddongate . . . B1
Sheffield St . . . B1
South Henry St . . B3
South John St . . . C2
South St . . . B3
Spencer St . . . B2
Sports Centre . . . A2
Strand Rd . . . A2
Swimming Baths . B2
Sybil St . . . B3
Tait St . . . B2
Thomas St . . . B1
Thomson St . . . C3
Trafalgar St . . . C1
Tullie House Museum . . . A1
Tyne St . . . C3
Viaduct Estate Rd . B1
Victoria Pl . . . A2/A3
Victoria Viaduct . . B2
Warner Village . B2
Warwick Rd . . . B3
Warwick Sq . . . B3
Water St . . . B2
West Walls . . . B1
Westmorland St . C1

Chelmsford

The county town of Essex, Chelmsford has Roman origins and has been home to its main market and assizes since the 12th century. Chelmsford Museum has local and natural history displays, a domestic life and costume gallery and art collections. The small cathedral is one of the country's newest (1914), as well as one of the few to also be a parish church. The town's pedestrianised high street and two large malls make it a prime shopping venue containing both national chain stores and independent shops, while Moulsham Mill is now a crafts and business centre with a number of retail outlets. There are extensive green spaces and riverside walks in the centre, Galleywood Common nature reserve lies to the south and Danbury Country Park is within easy reach.

Chelmsford Tourist Information Centre, County Hall, Market Road, Chelmsford CM1 1GG, Tel 01245 283400

BBC Essex 103.5 FM
Classic Gold Breeze 1359 AM
Essex FM 96.3, 102.6 FM

www.chelmsfordbc.gov.uk

▲Chelmsford Cathedral

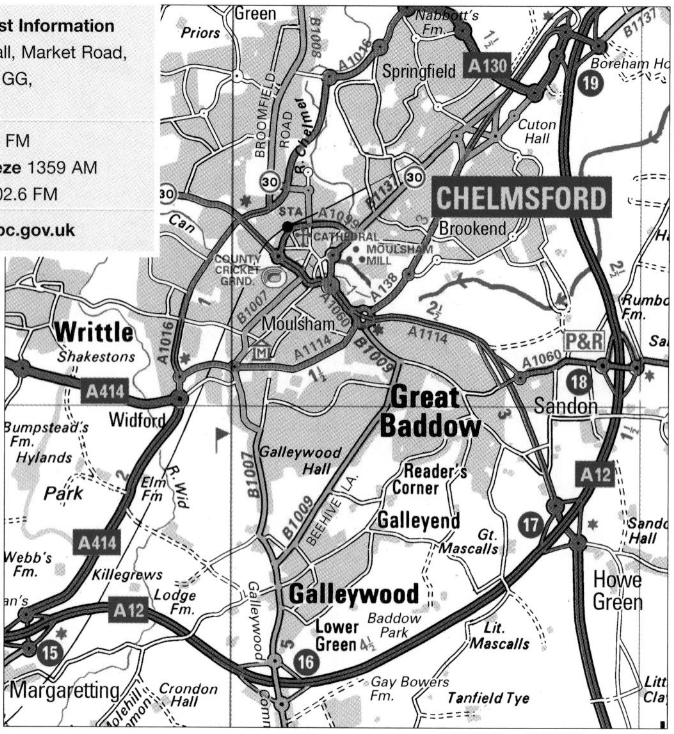

★Do not miss

★**Essex Regiment Museum**, Oaklands Park, Moulsham Street
★**Hylands House, Gardens and Parkland**, Writtle bypass
★**Royal Horticultural Society Gardens**, Hyde Hall

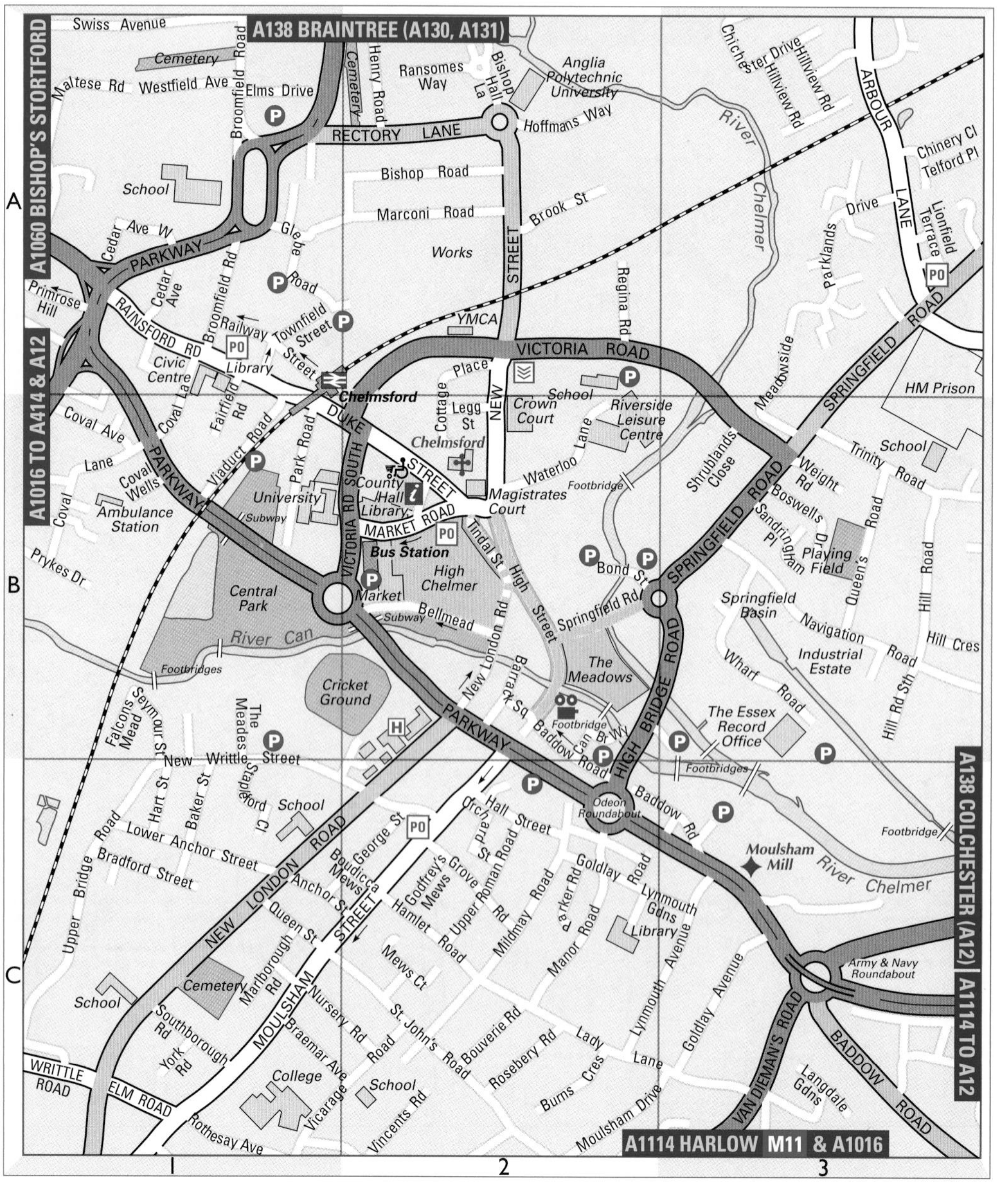

Chelmsford

Ambulance Station B1
Anchor St. C1
Anglia Polytechnic University. A2
Arbour La. A3
Baddow Rd. . . B2/C3
Baker St C1
Barrack Sq. B2
Bellmead B2
Bishop Hall La. . . A2
Bishop Rd. A2
Bond St. B2
Boswells Dr B3
Boudicca Mews. . C2
Bouverie Rd. C2
Bradford St C1
Braemar Ave C1
Brook St. A2
Broomfield Rd. . . A1
Burns Cres. C2
Bus Station B2
Can Bridge Way . .B2
Cedar Ave. A1
Cedar Ave W A1
Cemetery A1
Cemetery A2
Cemetery C1
Central Park B1
Chelmsford ✝ B2
Chelmsford ⇌. . A1
Chichester Dr . . . A3
Chinery Cl A3
Cinema B2
Civic Centre. A1
College. C1
Cottage Pl A2
County Hall B2
Coval Ave B1
Coval La B1
Coval Wells B1
Cricket Ground . . .B2
Crown Court B2
Duke St. B2
Elm Rd C1
Elms Dr. A1
Essex Record Office, The B3
Fairfield Rd B1
Falcons Mead B1
George St. C2
Glebe Rd A1
Godfrey's Mews . C2
Goldlay Ave C3
Goldlay Rd C2
Grove Rd C2
HM Prison A3
Hall St. C2
Hamlet Rd C2
Hart St C1
Henry Rd A2
High Bridge Rd . . .B2
High Chelmer Shopping Ctr. . . .B2
High St B2
Hill Cres B3
Hill Rd Sth B3
Hill Rd. B3
Hillview Rd. A3
Hoffmans Way . . . A2
Hospital Ⓗ B2
Information Ctr ℹ.B2
Lady La. C2
Langdale Gdns . . C3
Legg St. B2
Library A1
Library B2
Library C2
Lionfield Terr A3
Lower Anchor St. C1
Lynmouth Ave . . . C2
Lynmouth Gdns. . C3
Magistrates Court. B2
Maltese Rd. A1
Manor Rd C2
Marconi Rd A2
Market B2
Market Rd B2
Marlborough Rd . C1
Meadows Shopping Ctr, the B2
Meadowside A3
Mews Ct C2
Mildmay Rd C2
Moulsham Dr. . . . C2
Moulsham Mill ✦ C3
Moulsham St . C1/C2
Navigation Rd B3
New London Rd B2/C1
New St A2/B2
New Writtle St. . . C1
Nursery Rd. C2
Orchard St C2
Park Rd B1
Parker Rd. C2
Parklands Dr A3
Parkway . . A1/B1/B2
Police Station . A2
Post Office PO . . A1/A3/B2/C2
Primrose Hill A1
Prykes Dr B1
Queen St C1
Queen's Rd B3
Railway St A1
Rainsford Rd A1
Ransomes Way . . A2
Rectory La A2
Regina Rd A2
Riverside Leisure Ctr. B2
Rosebery Rd C2
Rothesay Ave. . . . C1
St John's Rd C2
Sandringham Pl . .B3
Seymour St B1
Shrublands Cl B3
Southborough Rd C1
Springfield Basin .B3
Springfield Rd A3/B2/B3
Stapleford Cl C1
Swiss Ave. A1
Telford Pl A3
The Meades B1
Tindal St. B2
Townfield St. A1
Trinity Rd B3
University. B1
Upper Bridge Rd. C1
Upper Roman Rd C2
Van Dieman's Rd. C3
Viaduct Rd B1
Vicarage Rd C1
Victoria Rd. A2
Victoria Rd South .B2
Vincents Rd C2
Waterloo La B2
Weight Rd B3
Westfield Ave. . . . A1
Wharf Rd B3
Writtle Rd C1
YMCA A2
York Rd. C1

¼ mile
¼ ½ km

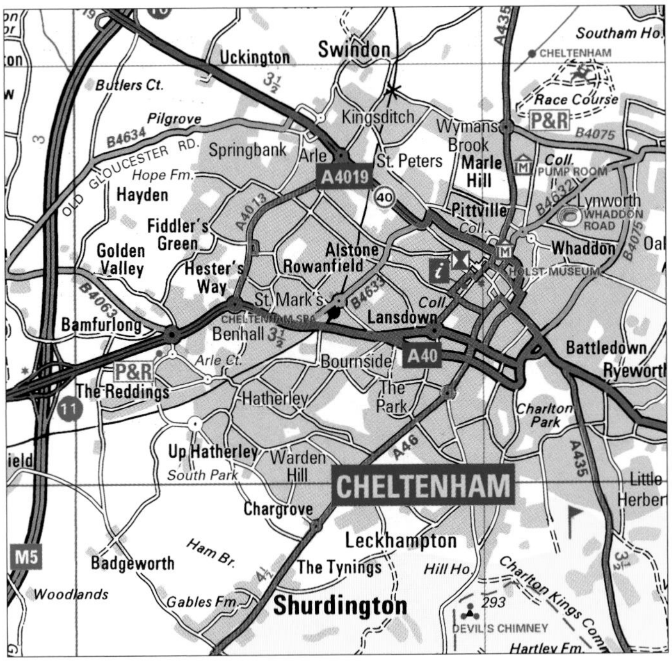

Cheltenham

An elegant town where medicinal waters were discovered in 1716, drawing King George III in 1788. A fashionable spa until 1840, attracting the likes of Byron, Jane Austen and Dickens, characterised by its wealth of Regency architecture; much of the centre is a Conservation Area. Notable buildings include the neo-Gothic Victorian Cheltenham College and Cheltenham Ladies' College, and the Holst Birthplace Museum. Additional attractions are the town's many parks and gardens, including the Promenade and Long Gardens, its upmarket shops, the nearby annual Badminton Horse Trials, and its proximity to the scenic Cotswolds. Add final sentence: Nearby attractions include Sudely Castle and Chedworth Roman Villa.

▲The Promenade

★Do not miss

★**Cheltenham Art Gallery and Museum**, Clarence Street

★**Cheltenham Racecourse**, Prestbury Park

★**Pump Room**, Pittville Park

Cheltenham Tourism, 77 Promenade, Cheltenham GL50 1PJ Tel 01242 522878

BBC Radio Gloucestershire 104.7 FM • **Classic Gold** 774 AM **Severn Sound** 102.4 FM **Star** 107.5 FM

www.visitcheltenham.gov.uk

Cheltenham

Albert Rd . . . A3
Albion St . . . B3
All Saints Rd . . . B3
Andover Rd . . . C1
Art Gallery & Museum . . . B2
Axiom Centre . . . B3
Bath Pde . . . B2
Bath Rd . . . C2
Bays Hill Rd . . . B1
Beechwood Shopping Ctr . . . B3
Bennington St . . . B2
Berkeley St . . . B3
Brewery Ctr . . . A2
Brunswick St South . . . A2
Bus Station . . . B2
Carlton St . . . B3
Cheltenham & Gloucester College . . . A2
Cheltenham College . . . C2
Cheltenham F.C. . . . A3
Cheltenham General (A&E) . . . C3
Christchurch Rd . . . B1
Cineworld . . . A2
Clarence Rd . . . A3
Clarence Sq . . . A2
Clarence St . . . B2
Cleeveland St . . . A1
Coach Park . . . A2
College Rd . . . C2
Colletts Dr . . . A1
Corpus St . . . C3
Devonshire St . . . A2
Douro Rd . . . B1
Duke St . . . B3
Dunalley Pde . . . A2
Dunalley St . . . A2
Everyman . . . B2
Evesham Rd . . . A3
Fairview Rd . . . B3
Fairview St . . . B3
Folly La . . . A2
Gloucester Rd . . . A1
Grosvenor St . . . B3
Grove St . . . A1
Gustav Holst . . . A3
Hanover St . . . A2
Hatherley St . . . C1
Henrietta St . . . A2
Hewlett Rd . . . B3
High St . . . B2/B3
Hudson St . . . A2
Imperial Gdns . . . C2
Imperial La . . . B2
Imperial Sq . . . C2
Information Ctr . . . B2
Keynsham Rd . . . C3
King St . . . A2
Knapp Rd . . . B2
Ladies College . . . B2
Lansdown Cr . . . C1
Lansdown Rd . . . C1
Leighton Rd . . . B3
London Rd . . . C3
Lypiatt Rd . . . C1
Malvern Rd . . . B1
Manser St . . . A2
Market St . . . A1
Marle Hill Pde . . . A2
Marle Hill Rd . . . A2
Millbrook St . . . A1
Milsom St . . . A2
Montpellier Gdns . . . C2
Montpellier Gr . . . C2
Montpellier Pde . . . C2
Montpellier Spa Rd . . . C2
Montpellier St . . . C1
Montpellier Terr . . . C2
Montpellier Walk . . . C2
New St . . . B2
North Pl . . . B2
Odeon . . . B3
Old Bath Rd . . . C3
Oriel Rd . . . B2
Overton Park Rd . . . B1
Overton Rd . . . B1
Oxford St . . . C3
Parabola Rd . . . B1
Park Pl . . . C1
Park St . . . A1
Pittville Circus . . . A3
Pittville Cr . . . A3
Pittville Lawn . . . A3
Pittville Pump Room & Racecourse ✦ A3
Playhouse . . . B2
Police Station . . . B1/C1
Portland St . . . B3
Post Office . . . B2/C1/C2
Prestbury Rd . . . A3
Prince's Rd . . . C1
Priory St . . . B3
Promenade . . . B2
Queen St . . . A1
Recreation Grnd . . . A2
Regent Arcade . . . B2
Regent St . . . B2
Rodney Rd . . . B2
Royal Cr . . . B2
Royal Wells Rd . . . B2
Sandford Lido . . . C3
Sandford Park . . . C3
Sandford Rd . . . C2
Selkirk St . . . A3
Sherborne Pl . . . B3
Sherborne St . . . B3
St George's Pl . . . B2
St George's Rd . . . B1
St Gregory's . . . B2
St James St . . . B3
St John's Ave . . . B3
St Luke's Rd . . . C2
St Margaret's Rd . . . A2
St Mary's . . . B2
St Matthew's . . . B2
St Paul's La . . . A2
St Paul's Rd . . . A2
St Paul's St . . . A2
St Stephen's Rd . . . C1
Suffolk Pde . . . C2
Suffolk Rd . . . C1
Suffolk Sq . . . C1
Sun St . . . A1
Swindon Rd . . . B2
Sydenham Villas Rd . . . C3
Tewkesbury Rd . . . A1
The Courtyard . . . B1
Thirlstaine Rd . . . C2
Tivoli Rd . . . C1
Tivoli St . . . C1
Town Hall & Theatre . . . B2
Townsend St . . . A1
Trafalgar St . . . C2
Victoria Pl . . . B3
Victoria St . . . A2
Vittoria Walk . . . C2
Wellesley Rd . . . A2
Wellington Rd . . . A3
Wellington Sq . . . A3
Wellington St . . . B2
West Drive . . . A3
Western Rd . . . B1
Winchcombe St . . . B3

¼ mile
½ km

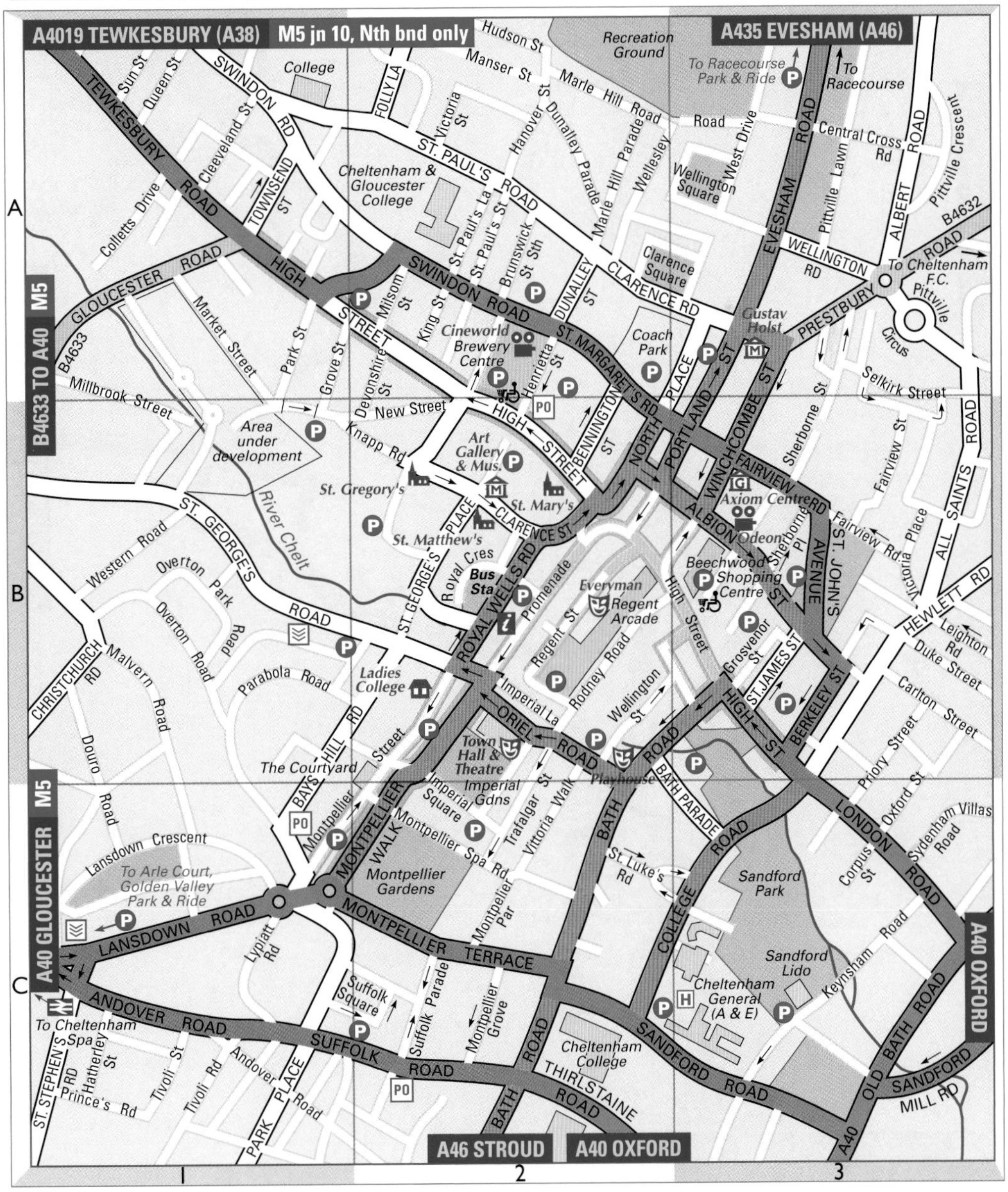

Chester

▲Half-timbered buildings in Chester

A town known to the Romans as Dewa, with an unparalleled range of Roman ruins, including a partially excavated amphitheatre (Britain's largest), and the country's most complete city walls, built in the 1st century AD and forming a 2-mile circular promenade with information plaques and views over the surrounding countryside. Among the countless sites of historical interest are the UK's oldest surviving mill dam, built by the Normans, the Roodee, Britain's oldest racecourse (constructed on the site of the Roman harbour), an 11th-century castle, a cathedral retaining parts of a Norman church (Handel rehearsed his Messiah here), the 1652 God's Providence House, the only one in the town spared the Plague, 17th-century Bishop Lloyd's House with its intricate carvings, the Rows, a set of unique half-timbered galleries forming a second row of shops above street level, and the Three Old Arches, the country's oldest shopfront. There is a wide variety of good shops.

★Do not miss

★**Chester Zoo**, Upton-by-Chester
★**Dewa Roman Experience**, Pierpoint Lane, Bridge Street
★**Roman Amphitheatre**, Little St John Street

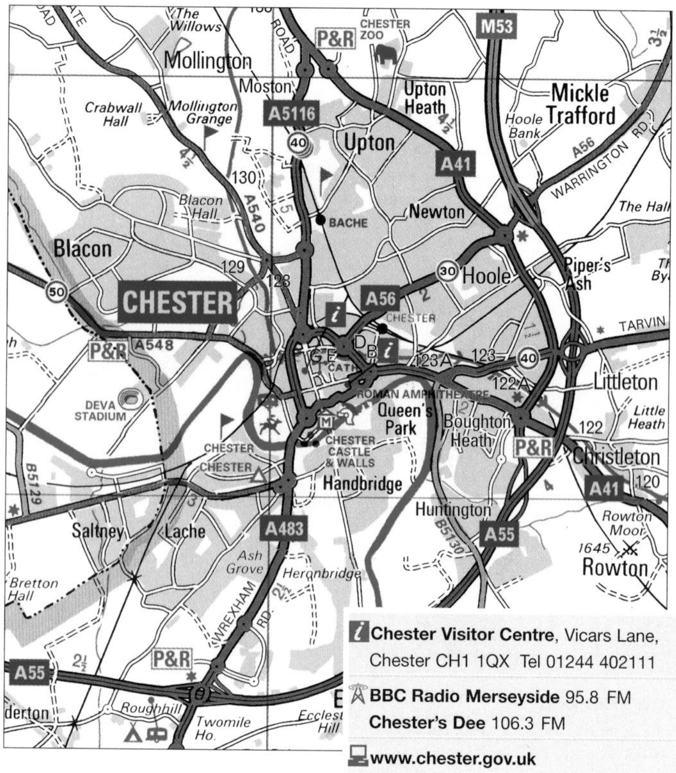

¼ mile
¼ ½ km

i **Chester Visitor Centre**, Vicars Lane, Chester CH1 1QX Tel 01244 402111
BBC Radio Merseyside 95.8 FM
Chester's Dee 106.3 FM
www.chester.gov.uk

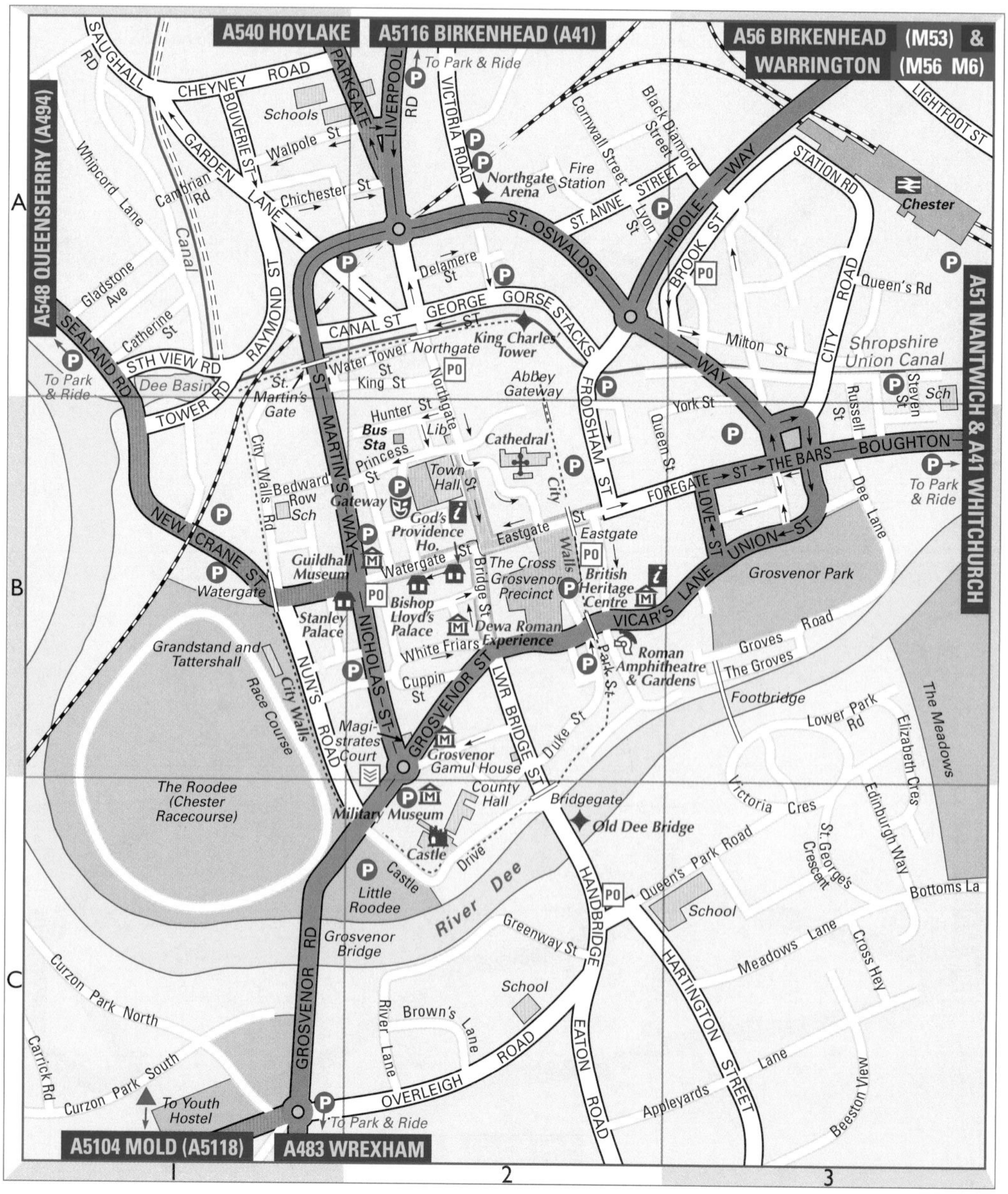

Chester

Abbey Gateway . . A2
Appleyards La . . . C3
Bedward Row B1
Beeston View. . . . C3
Bishop Lloyd's Palace B2
Black Diamond St A2
Bottoms La. C3
Boughton B3
Bouverie St A1
Bridge St B2
Bridgegate C2
British Heritage Centre B2
Brook St A3
Brown's La C2
Bus Station B2
Cambrian Rd A1
Canal St A2
Carrick Rd C1
Castle C2
Castle Dr C2
Cathedral B2
Catherine St A1
Chester A3
Cheyney Rd A1
Chichester St. . . . A1
City Rd A3
City Walls B1/B2
City Walls Rd B1
Cornwall St A2
County Hall C2
Cross Hey C3
Cuppin St B2
Curzon Park N C1
Curzon Park S C1
Dee Basin A1
Dee La B3
Delamere St. A2
Dewa Roman Experience . . B2
Duke St. B2
Eastgate B2
Eastgate St. B2
Eaton Rd. C2
Egerton St A3
Elizabeth Cr B3
Fire Station A2
Foregate St B2
Frodsham St B2
Gamul House B2
Garden La. A1
Gateway B2
George St. A2
Gladstone Ave . . . A1
God's Providence House B2
Gorse Stacks A2
Greenway St C2
Grosvenor Bridge C1
Grosvenor Mus .B2
Grosvenor Park. . .B3
Grosvenor Precinct B2
Grosvenor Rd. . . . C1
Grosvenor St B2
Groves Rd. B3
Guildhall Mus . .B1
Handbridge C2
Hartington St. . . . C3
Hoole Way A2
Hunter St B2
Information Ctr .B2
King Charles' Tower ✦. A2
King St A2
Library B2
Lightfoot St A3
Little Roodee. . . . C2
Liverpool Rd A2
Love St B3
Lower Bridge St . .B2
Lower Park Rd . . .B3
Lyon St A2
Magistrates Court.B2
Meadows La. C3
Military Mus . . C2
Milton St A3
New Crane St B1
Nicholas St B2
Northgate. A2
Northgate Arena ✦ A2
Northgate St A2
Nun's Rd. B1
Old Dee Bridge ✦ C2
Overleigh Rd C2
Park St B2
Police Station . .B2
Post Office A2/A3/B2/C2
Princess St. B2
Queen St B2
Queen's Park Rd. C3
Queen's Rd A3
Raymond St A1
River La C2
Roman Amphitheatre & Gardens B2
Roodee, The (Chester Racecourse) B1
Russell St A3
St Anne St A2
St George's Cr. . . C3
St Martin's Gate . A1
St Martin's Way. . .B1
St Oswalds Way. . A2
Saughall Rd A1
Sealand Rd. A1
South View Rd . . . A1
Stanley Palace .B1
Station Rd A3
Steven St A3
The Bars. B3
The Cross. B2
The Groves. B3
The Meadows B3
Tower Rd B1
Town Hall. B2
Union St. B3
Vicar's La B2
Victoria Cr C3
Victoria Rd. A2
Walpole St. A1
Water Tower St . . A1
Watergate B1
Watergate St B2
Whipcord La A1
White Friars. B2
York St B3

Chichester Tourist Information Centre, 29a South Street, Chichester PO19 1AH
Tel 01243 775888 / 539435

BBC Southern Counties 104.8 FM
Spirit 96.6, 102.3 FM

www.chichester.gov.uk

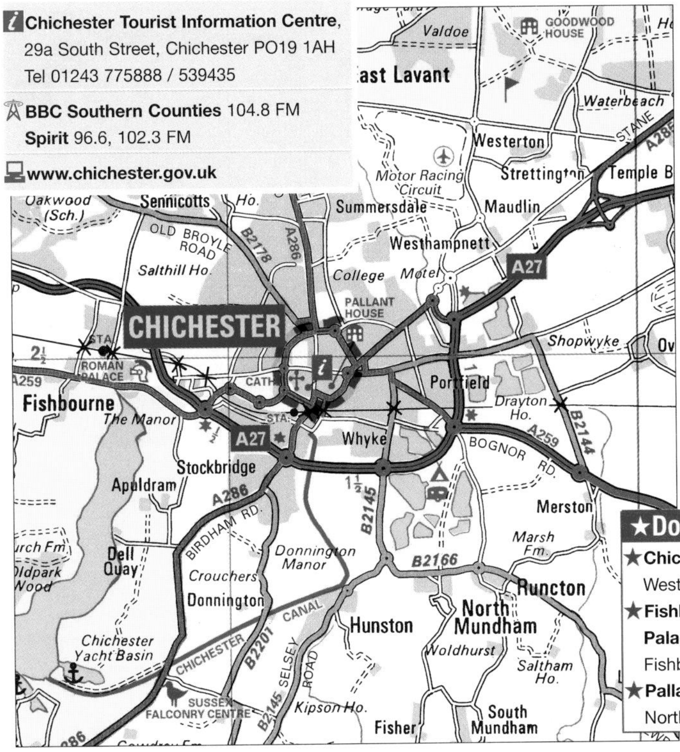

★Do not miss

★**Chichester Cathedral**, West Street

★**Fishbourne Roman Palace**, Salthill Road, Fishbourne

★**Pallant House Gallery**, North Pallant

West Sussex cathedral city retaining much of its Roman wall and Roman and medieval street plan, though it is predominantly Georgian in aspect. Sites of interest include the very fine 1501 market cross, the medieval St Mary's Hospital, and Pallant House, a 17th-century residence now housing a contemporary art gallery. The District Museum traces the city's history. The attractive harbour is popular with yachters, birdwatchers and walkers. Nearby are Goodwood House, an 18th-century mansion with a noteworthy art collection and outdoor sculpture exhibition, the Weald and Downland Open Air Museum of old buildings, West Dean Gardens and the Sussex Falconry Centre. The lovely South Downs are within easy reach.

Chichester

▲Chichester Cathedral

Chichester

Adelaide Rd A3
Alexandra Rd A3
Arts Centre B2
Ave de Chartres B1/B2
Barlow Rd A1
Basin Rd C2
Beech Ave B1
Bishops Palace Gdns B2
Bishopsgate Walk A3
Bramber Rd C3
Broyle Rd A2
Bus Station B2
Caledonian Rd....B3
Cambrai Ave B3
Canal Wharf....... C2
Canon La B2
Cathedral ✝ B2
Cavendish St A1
Cawley Rd B2
Cedar Dr........ A1
Chapel St A2
Cherry Orchard Rd C3
Chichester By-Pass C2/C3
Chichester Festival A2
Chichester B2
Churchside...... A2
Cinema ... B3/C1
City Walls........B2
Cleveland Rd.....B3
College La A2
College Of Science & Technology....B1
Cory Cl C2
Council Offices ...B2
County Hall B2
Courts...........B2
District B2
Duncan Rd...... A1
Durnford Cl A1
East Pallant B2
East Row B2
East St B2
East Walls B3
Eastland Rd C3
Ettrick Cl B3
Ettrick Rd........B3
Exton Rd........ C3
Fire Station A2
Football Ground . A2
Franklin Pl...... A2
Friary (Remains of) ... A2
Garland Cl C3
Green La....... A3
Grove Rd C3
Guilden Rd.......B3
Guildhall A2
Hawthorn Cl A1
Hay Rd C3
Henty Gdns B1
Herald Dr C3
Information Ctr .B2
John's St B2
Joys Croft....... A3
Jubilee Pk A3
Jubilee Rd A3
Juxon Cl.........B2
Kent Rd......... A3
King George Gdns A2
King's Ave C2
Kingsham Ave ... C3
Kingsham Rd C2
Laburnum Gr.....B2
Leigh Rd........ C1
Lennox Rd A3
Lewis Rd........ A3
Library B2
Lion St B2
Litten Terr....... A3
Little London.....B2
Lyndhurst Rd B3
Market B3
Market Ave.......B2
Market Cross B2
Market Rd B3
Martlet Cl....... C2
Melbourne Rd ... A3
Mount La B1
New Park Rd A3
Newlands La A1
North Pallant.....B2
North St A2
North Walls A2
Northgate....... A2
Oak Ave A1
Oak Cl.......... A1
Oaklands Park... A2
Oaklands Way ... A2
Orchard Ave..... A1
Orchard St A1
Ormonde Ave.....B3
Pallant House ..B2
Parchment St ... A1
Parklands Rd. A1/B1
Peter Weston Pl ..B3
Police Station .. C2
Post Office A1/B2/B3
Priory La A2
Priory Park A2
Priory Rd A2
Queen's Ave..... C1
Riverside A3
Roman Amphitheatre ...B3
St Cyriacs....... A2
St Pancras A3
St Paul's Rd..... A2
St Richard's Hospital (A&E) A3
Shamrock Cl A3
Sherbourne Rd .. A1
Somerstown..... A2
South Bank C2
South Pallant.....B2
South St B2
Southgate B2
Spitalfield La.... A3
Stirling Rd B3
Stockbridge Rd C1/C2
Swanfield Dr A3
Terminus Industrial Estate C1
Terminus Rd C1
The Hornet.......B3
The Litten....... A3
Tower St........ A2
Tozer Way A3
Turnbull Rd A3
Upton Rd C1
Velyn Ave B3
Via Ravenna......B1
Walnut Ave...... A1
West St B2
Westgate B1
Westgate Fields. .B1
Westgate Leisure Centre..........B1
Weston Ave C1
Whyke Cl C3
Whyke La B3
Whyke Rd........ C3
Winden Ave B3

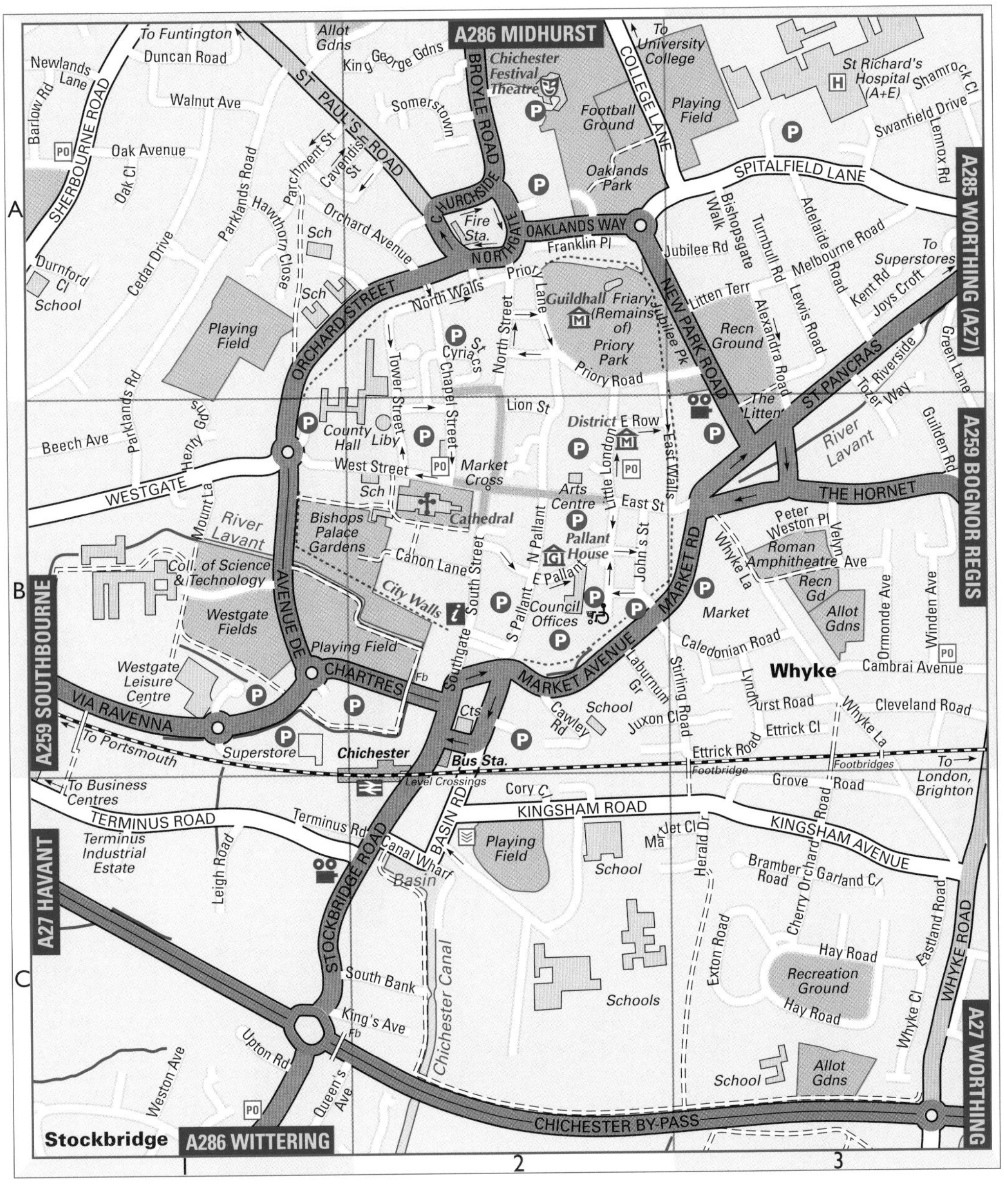

¼ mile

¼

½ km

Colchester

▲The Dutch Quarter

Colchester is Britain's oldest recorded town – documented since it was the Iron Age stronghold of Camulodunum. Archaeological evidence shows a settlement existed here 3,000 years ago. Today, most of Colchester town centre lies within the ancient boundaries of Camulodunum. Now home to the University of Essex, the town makes much of its heritage with places of interest such as Hollytrees Museum featuring local history, Colchester Castle Museum, and the Natural History Museum. The town centre offers a wide range of high street and a number of independent shops. Much of the main shopping can be found on the High Street and in the surrounding side streets as can the varied selection of pubs and restaurants. There are several activity centres to keep children amused whether it be bowling, karting or rollerskating.

Visitor Information Centre, 1 Queen Street, Colchester CO1 2PG
Tel 01206 282920

BBC Essex 103.5 FM
Essex FM 102.6 FM • **SGR** 96.1 FM

www.colchester.gov.uk

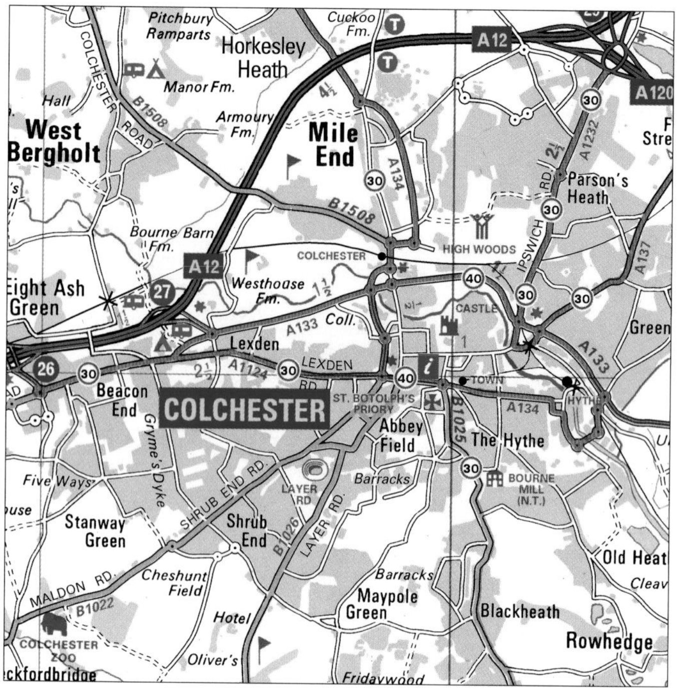

★Do not miss

★**Colchester Zoo**, Maldon Road

★**Colchester Arts Centre**, Church Street – music, film, theatre

Colchester

Abbey Gateway ✝ C2
Albert St. A1
Albion Grove C2
Alexandra Rd. C1
Artillery St C3
Arts Centre B1
Balkerne Hill B1
Barrack St C3
Barrington Rd C2
Beaconsfield Rd C1
Beche Rd C3
Bergholt Rd A1
Bourne Rd C3
Bristol Rd B2
Broadlands Way A3
Brook St B3
Bury Cl B2
Bus Station B2
Butt Rd C1
Camp Folley North C2
Camp Folley South C2
Campion Rd C2
Cannon St C3
Canterbury Rd C2
Castle B2
Castle Rd B2
Catchpool Rd A1
Causton Rd B1
Cavalry Barracks C1
Chandlers Row C3
Circular Rd East C2
Circular Rd North C1
Circular Rd West C1
Clarendon Way A1
Claudius Rd C2
Clock B1
Colchester Institute B1
Colchester ≉ A1
Colchester Town ≉ C2
Colne Bank Ave A1
Compton Rd A3
Cowdray Ave A1/A3
Cowdray Ctr, The A2
Crouch St B1
Crowhurst Rd B1
Culver Centre B1
Culver St East B2
Culver St West B1
Dilbridge Rd A3
East Hill B2
East St B3
East Stockwell St B1
Eld La B1
Essex Hall Rd A1
Exeter Dr B2
Fairfax Rd C2
Flagstaff Rd C1
George St B2
Gladstone Rd C2
Golden Noble Hill C2
Goring Rd A3
Granville Rd C3
Greenstead Rd B3
Guildford Rd B2
Harsnett Rd C3
Harwich Rd B3
Head St B1
High St B1
Hythe Hill C3
Information Ctr B2
Ipswich Rd A3
Kendall Rd C2
Kimberley Rd C3
King Stephen Rd C3
Le Cateau Barracks C1
Leisure World A2
Library B1
Lincoln Way B2
Lion Walk Shopping Centre B1
Lisle Rd C2
Lucas Rd C2
Magdalen St C2
Maidenburgh St B2
Maldon Rd C1
Manor Rd B1
Margaret Rd A1
Mason Rd A2
Mercers Way A1
Mercury B1
Mersea Rd C2
Meyrick Cr C2
Mile End Rd A1
Military Rd C2
Mill St C2
Minories B2
Moorside B3
Morant Rd C3
Napier Rd C2
Natural History B2
New Town Rd C2
Norfolk Cr A3
North Hill B1
North Station Rd A1
Northgate St B1
Nunns Rd B1
Odeon B1
Old Coach Rd B3
Old Heath Rd C3
Osborne St B2
Police Station C1
Popes La B1
Port La C3
Post Office B1/B2/C1
Priory St B2
Queen St B2
Rawstorn Rd B1
Rebon St C3
Recreation Rd C3
Ripple Way A3
Roman Rd B2
Roman Wall B2
Romford Cl A3
Rosebery Ave B2
St Andrew's Ave B3
St Botolph St B2
St Botolphs B2
St John's Abbey (Site of) ✝ C2
St John's St B1
St John's Walk Shopping Centre B1
St Leonards Rd C3
St Marys Fields B1
St Peters B1
St Peter's St B1
Salisbury Ave C1
Serpentine Walk A1
Sheepen Pl B1
Sheepen Rd B1
Simons La C3
Sir Isaac's Walk B1
Smythies Ave B2
South St C1
Sports Way A2
Station Way A1
Suffolk Cl A3
Town Hall B1
Turner Rd A1
Valentine Dr A3
Victor Rd C3
Wakefield Cl B2
Wellesley Rd C1
Wells Rd B2
West St C1
West Stockwell St B1
Weston Rd C3
Westway A1
Wickham Rd C1
Wimpole Rd C3
Winchester Rd C2
Winnock Rd C2
Wolfe Ave C2
Worcester Rd B2

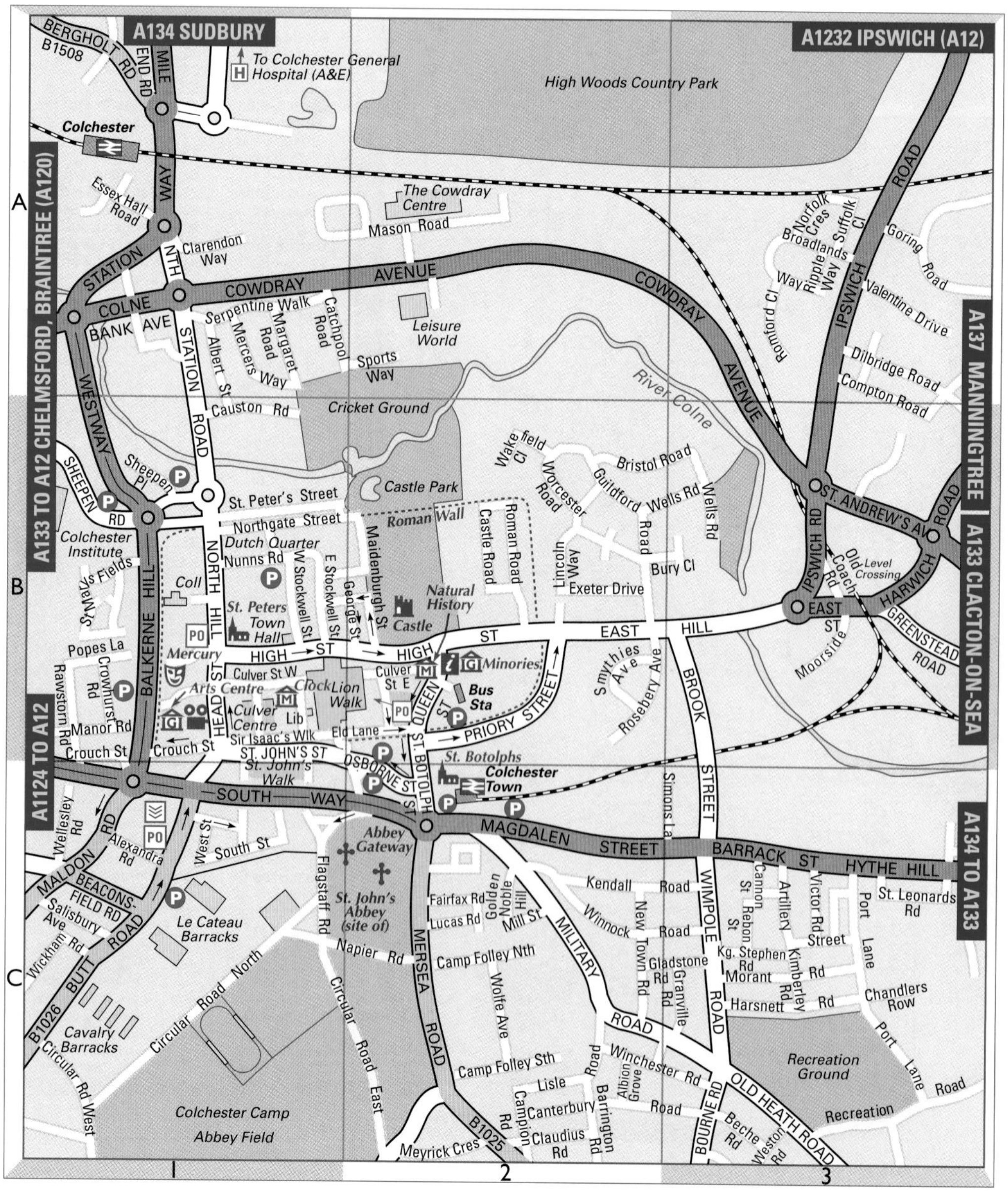

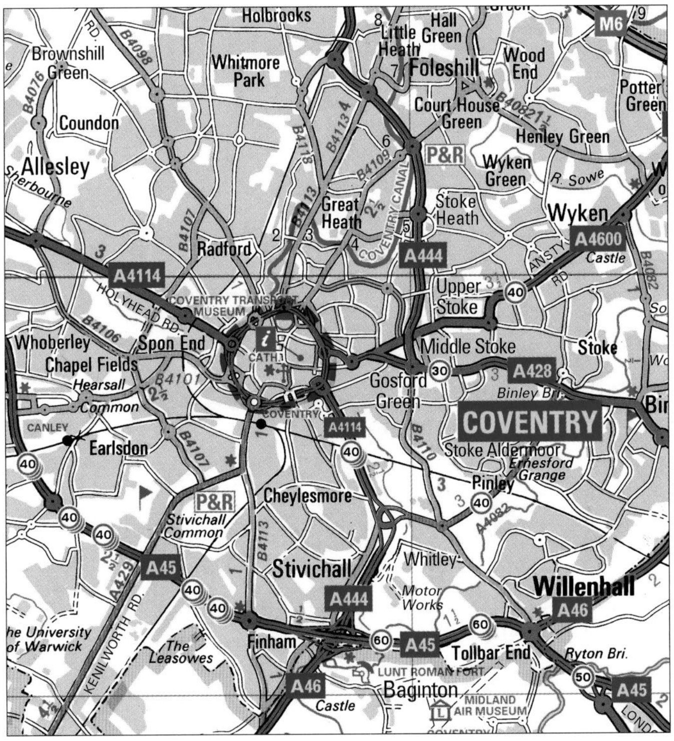

Coventry is known for the legend of Lady Godiva who rode through the streets in protest at the high taxes imposed by her husband Earl Leofric. Attractions include the remains of Lady Godiva's church; the extensive collections of the Coventry Road Transport Museum; the medieval St Mary's Guildhall and the world-renowned cathedral that combines the foundations of part of the 12th-century priory cathedral, the ruins of the 14th-century building destroyed in 1940 and the present cathedral. The city centre is pedestrianised and has three shopping centres, Lower Precinct, West Orchards and Cathedral Lanes. Other shops can be found on Spon Street and City Arcade, there is also an indoor market by the name of Retail Market. Coventry also has a great choice of entertainment from bars and restaurants to theatres and cinemas.

Coventry

▲Coventry Cathedral

★Do not miss

★**Coventry Cathedral**, Priory Row
★**Coventry Transport Museum**, Millennium Place, Hales Street
★**Herbert Art Gallery and Museum**, Jordan Well

Coventry Tourist Information Centre, 4 Priory Row, Coventry CV1 5EX Tel 024 7622 7264

BBC WM 94.8 FM
Classic Gold 1359 AM
Kix 96.2 FM • **Mercia** 97.0 FM

www.visitcoventry.co.uk

Coventry

Abbots La A1
Albany Rd B1
Alma St B3
Art Faculty B3
Asthill Grove C2
Bablake School A1
Barras La A1
Barrs Hill School A1
Belgrade B2
Bishop Burges St A2
Bond's Hospital B1
Broadgate B2
Broadway C1
Bus Station A3
Butts Radial B1
Canal Basin ✦ A2
Canterbury St A3
Cathedral ✝ B3
Chester St A1
Cheylesmore Manor House B2
Christ Church Spire ✦ B2
City Walls & Gates ✦ A2
Coach Park A3
Corporation St B2
Council House B2
Coundon Rd A1
Coventry & Warwickshire Hospital (A&E) A2
Coventry C2
Coventry Transport Museum A2
Cox St A3
Croft Rd B1
Deasy Rd C3
Earl St B2
Eaton Rd C2
Fairfax St B3
Foleshill Rd A2
Ford's Hospital B2
Fowler Rd A1
Friars Rd C2
Gordon St C1
Gosford St B3
Greyfriars Green B2
Greyfriars Rd B2
Gulson Rd B3
Hales St A2
Harnall Lane East A3
Harnall Lane West A2
Herbert Art Gallery & Museum B3
Hertford St B2
Hewitt Ave A1
High St B2
Hill St B1
Holy Trinity B2
Holyhead Rd A1
Howard St A3
Huntingdon Rd C1
Information Ctr B2
Jordan Well B3
King Henry VIII School C1
Lady Godiva Statue ✦ B2
Lamb St A2
Leicester Row A2
Library B2
Little Park St B2
London Rd C3
Lower Ford St B3
Magistrates & Crown Courts B2
Manor House Drive B2
Manor Rd C2
Market B2
Martyr's Mml ✦ C2
Meadow St B1
Meriden St A1
Michaelmas Rd C2
Middleborough Rd A1
Mile La C3
Millennium Place A2
Much Park St B3
Naul's Mill Park A1
New Union B2
Park Rd C2
Parkside C3
Police HQ B3
Primrose Hill St A3
Priory Gardens & Visitor Centre B2
Priory St B3
Puma Way C3
Quarryfield La C3
Queen's Rd B1
Quinton Rd C2
Radford Rd A2
Raglan St B3
Retail Park C1
Ringway (Hill Cross) A1
Ringway (Queens) B1
Ringway (Rudge) B1
Ringway (St Johns) B3
Ringway (St Nicholas) A2
Ringway (St Patricks) C2
Ringway (Swanswell) A2
Ringway (Whitefriars) B3
St John St B2
St John The Baptist B2
St Nicholas St A2
Skydome B1
Spencer Ave C1
Spencer Park C1
Spencer Rd C1
Spon St B1
Sports Centre B3
Stoney Rd C2
Stoney Stanton Rd A3
Swanswell Pool A3
Swanswell St A3
Sydney Stringer School A3
Technical College B1
Technology Park C3
The Precinct B2
Theatre B1
Thomas Landsdail St C2
Tomson Ave A1
Top Green C1
Toy Museum B3
Trinity St B2
University B3
Upper Hill St A1
Upper Well St A2
Victoria St A3
Vine St A3
Warwick Rd C2
Waveley Rd B1
Westminster Rd C1
White St A3
Windsor St B1

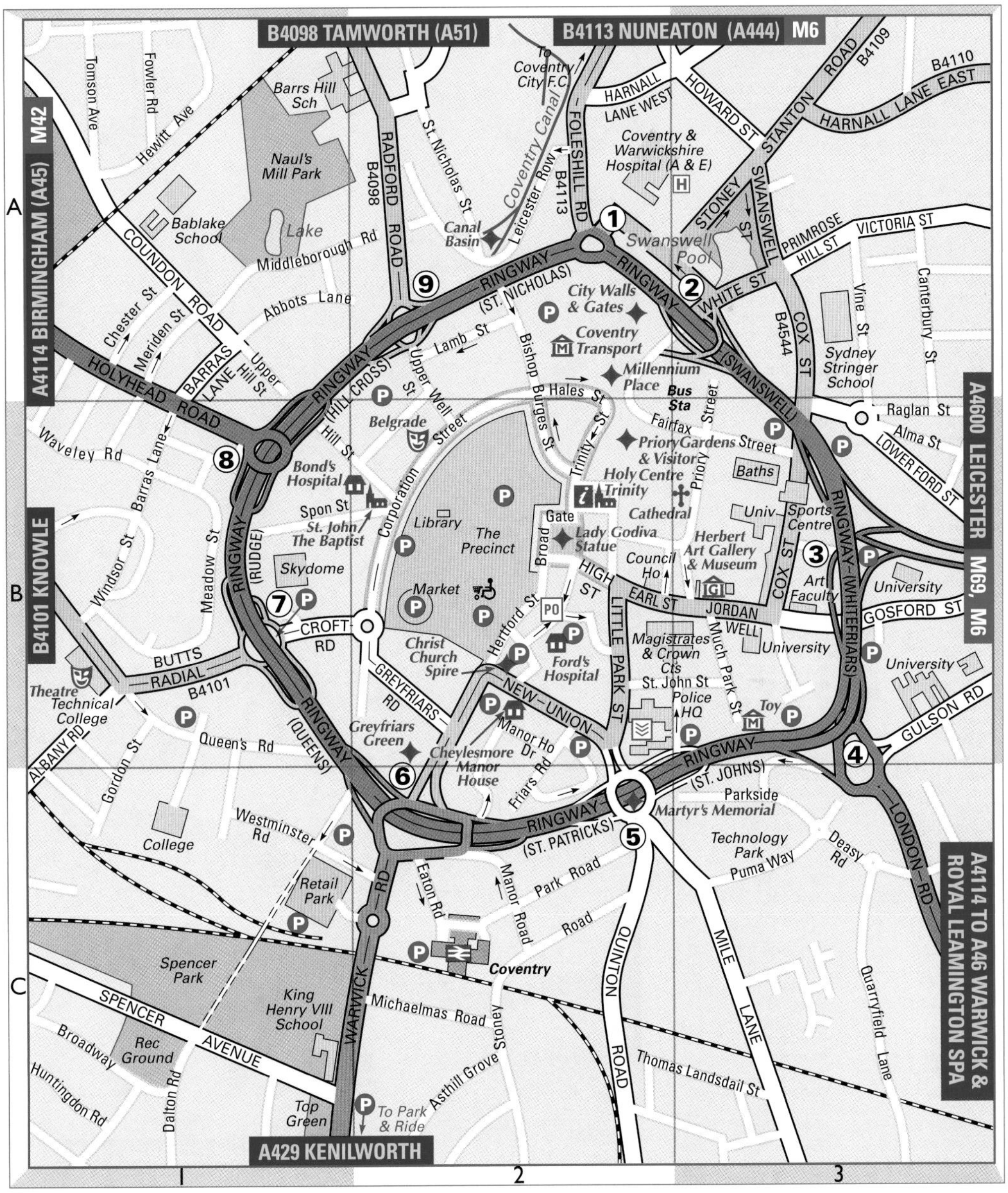

¼ mile
¼ ½ km

Croydon

▲ Croydon has an efficient tram network

One of the largest towns in southern England and still a London borough, it is a focal point for an extensive residential and industrial area to the south of London. Places to visit include Croydon Clocktower, an arts centre featuring photographic exhibitions, sculpture, local history and arthouse cinema; Croydon Palace, 1,000-year-old former home of Archbishops of Canterbury; Croydon Parish Church of St John the Baptist, a 15th-century church. There are two shopping centres, the Whitgift and the Drummond with a pedestrianised area between the two. Surrey Street Market is open every day except Sunday. There are many pubs and restaurants centred on the High Street and South End.

Tourist Information Centre, Croydon Clocktower, Katharine St, Croydon CR9 1ET Tel 020 8253 1009

BBC London 94.9 FM • **Capital FM** 95.8 FM • **Capital Gold** 1548 AM **Heart** 106.2 FM • **Kiss** 100.0 FM **LBC** 97.3 FM • **Magic** 105.4 FM **Virgin** 105.8 FM • **Xfm** 104.9 FM

www.croydononline.org

★Do not miss

- ★**Croydon Clocktower**, Katharine Street – multipurpose venue
- ★**Croydon Palace**, Old Palace Road
- ★**Croydon Parish Church of St John the Baptist**, Church Street

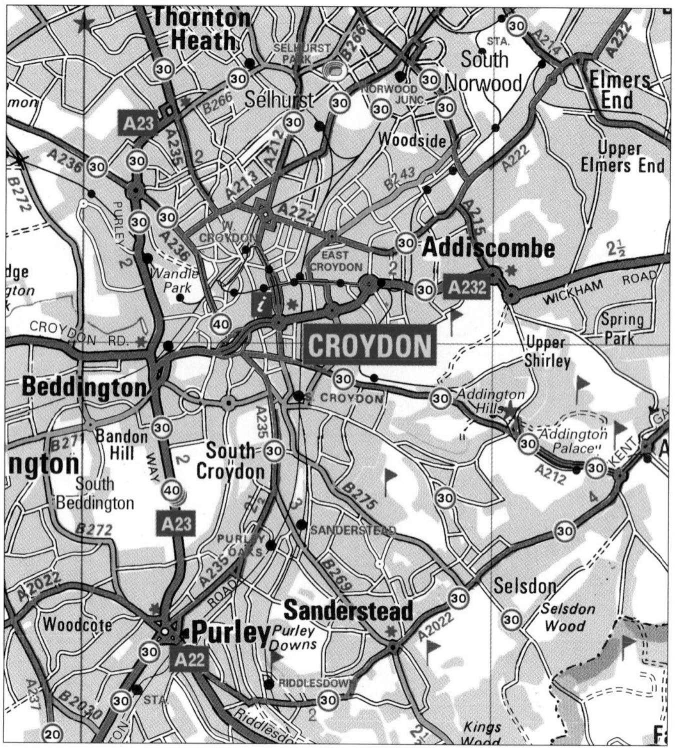

Croydon

Abbey Rd C1
Addiscombe Grove B3
Addiscombe Rd B3
Albion St A1
Alexandra Rd A3
Altyre Rd B3
Archbishop's Palace B1
Arnhem Gallery B2
Ashcroft B2
Barclay Rd B3
Bedford Park A2
Beech House Rd C2
Borough Hill C1
Brickwood Rd B3
Bus Interchange B3
Bus Station A2
Cedar Rd B3
Charles St C2
Chatfield Rd A1
Chatsworth Rd C3
Cherry Orchard Rd A3
Chichester Rd C3
Chisholm Rd B3
Church Rd C1
Church St B1
Church St (Tram Stop) B1
Clarendon Rd B1
College Rd B2
Colson Rd B3
Coombe Rd C3
Cranmer Rd C1
Cross Rd A3
Crown Hill B2
Croydon College B2
Croydon Flyover C1
Davidson Rd A3
Dennett Rd A1
Derby Rd B1
Dingwall Rd B2
Drummond Centre B2
Drummond Rd B2
Duppas Hill Rd C1
Duppas Hill Rec Ground C1
Duppas Hill Terr C1
East Croydon Station B3
East Croydon (Tram Stop) B3
Edridge Rd C2
Epsom Rd C1
Factory La B1
Fairfield Halls B2
Fairfield Rd B3
Farquharson Rd A2
Frith Rd B2
George St B2
George St (Tram Stop) B2
Gloucester Rd A3
Handcroft Rd A1
Harrison's Rise C1
Hathaway Rd A1
Hazledene Rd B3
Heathfield Rd C2
High St B2/C2
Hillside Rd C1
Howley Rd C1
Information Ctr B2
Katharine St B2
Kemble Rd B1
Kidderminster Rd A1
Lansdowne Rd A3/B2
Laud St C2
Leighton St East A1
Lennard Rd A1
Leslie Grove A3
Leslie Park A3
London Rd A1
Lower Addiscombe Rd A3
Lower Coombe St C2
Mead Place A1
Milton Rd A3
Mint Walk C2
Mitcham Rd A1
Montague Rd A1
Morland Ave A3
Mulgrave Rd C2
North End B2
Nova Rd A1
Oakfield Rd A2
Old Palace Rd B1
Old Town C1
Oval Rd B3
Park Hill Rd B3/C3
Park Hill Recreation Ground C3
Park La B2/C2
Park St B2
Parson's Mead A1
Police Station C2
Poplar Walk B2
Post Office B2/C2
Rectory Grove B1
Reeves Corner (Tram Stop) B1
Roman Way B1
Ruskin Rd B1
St James's Rd A1/A2
St John The Baptist B1
Salem Place C1
Scarbrook Rd C2
South End C2
Southbridge Rd C2
Stanhope Rd C3
Stanton Rd A2
Station Rd A2
Sumner Rd A1
Surrey St B2
Sydenham Rd A2/A3/B2
Tamworth Rd B1
Tanfield Rd C2
Tavistock Rd A2
Temple Rd C2
The Waldrons C1
Theobald Rd B1
Town Hall B2
Violet La C1
Waddon New Rd B1
Waddon Rd C1
Walpole Rd B2
Wandle Park B1
Wandle Park Trading Estate B1
Wandle Rd C2
Warrington Rd C1
Wellesley Rd A2/B2
Wellesley Rd (Tram Stop) B2
West Croydon Station A2
West Croydon (Tram Stop) A2
Whitehorse Rd A2
Whitgift Centre B2
Whitgift Hospital B2
Woodstock Rd C2

¼ mile
¼ ½ km

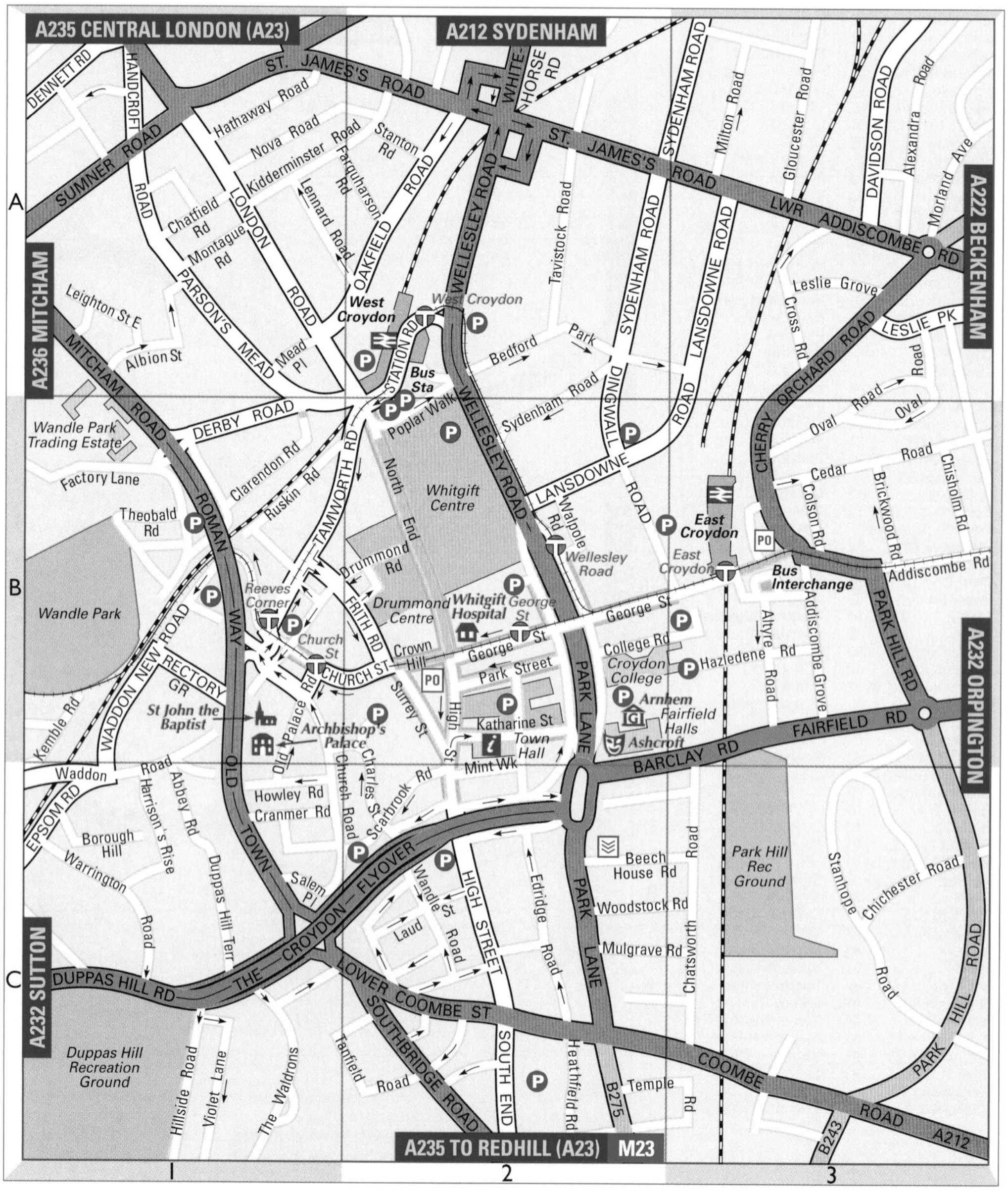

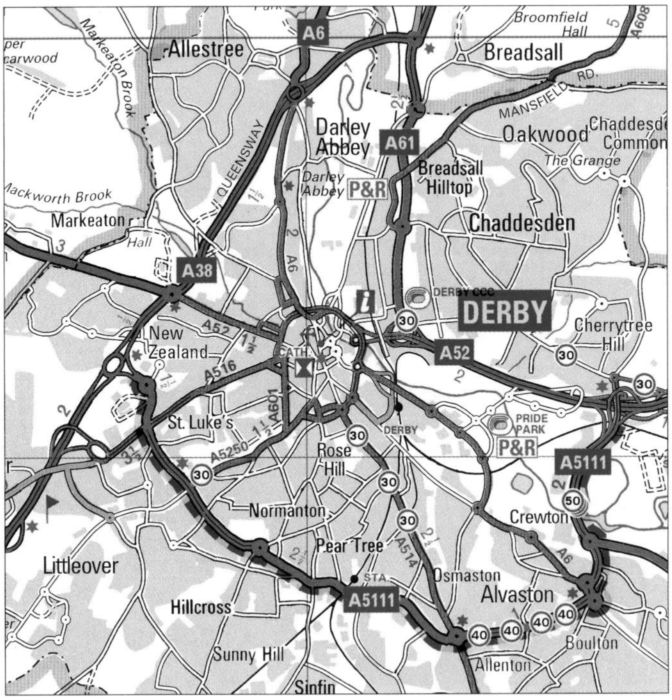

Derby

▲Interior of Derby Cathedral

A small city with a cathedral boasting Britain's second-highest church tower, and a proud industrial heritage (notably in silk manufacture, later in the making of Rolls-Royce engines) that can be explored along the Derwent Valley Mills World Heritage Site stretching 15 miles to Matlock Bath. Other attractions include the Central Museum and Art Gallery, which includes displays on local regiments and local porcelain, Pickford's House Museum of Georgian life, and a 1756 jailhouse. Nearby are the National Trust properties of Kedleston Hall, Calke Abbey, and Sudbury Hall and Museum of Childhood, and the award-winning CONKERS National Forest Discovery Centre. Green spaces include the Derby Arboretum, Markeaton Park and Craft Village, and Alveston Park with its riverside cycletrack to Elvaston Castle Country Park, while to the northwest lies the stunning Peak District National Park.

★Do not miss

★**Derby Cathedral**, Iron Gate
★**Royal Crown Derby Factory and Visitor Centre**, Osmaston Road
★**Silk Mill Museum of Industry and History**, Full Street

Derby Tourist Information Centre, The Assembly Rooms, Market Place, DE1 3AH Tel 01332 255802

BBC Radio Derby 104.5 FM and 1116 AM (weekdays only)
Ram FM 102.8 FM • **Saga** 106.6 FM
96 Trent FM 96.0 FM

www.visitderby.co.uk

Derby

Abbey St C1
Agard St B1
Albert St B2
Albion St B2
Ambulance Station B1
Arthur St A1
Ashlyn Rd B3
Assembly Rooms B2
Babington La C2
Becket St B1
Belper Rd A1
Bold La B1
Bradshaw Way C2
Bridge St B1
Brook St B1
Burrows Walk C2
Burton Rd C1
Bus Station B2
Caesar St A2
Canal St C3
Carrington St C3
Castle St C2
Cathedral ✝ B2
Cathedral Rd B1
Charnwood St C2
Chester Green Rd A2
City Rd A2
Clarke St A3
Cock Pitt B3
Council House B2
Cranmer Rd B3
Crompton St C1
Crown & County Courts B2
Crown Walk C2
Curzon St B1
Darley Grove A1
Derby C3
Derbyshire County Cricket Ground B3
Derbyshire Royal Infirmary (A&E) H C2
Derwent Business Centre A2
Derwent St B2
Devonshire Walk C2
Drewry La C1
Duffield Rd A1
Duke St A2
Dunton Cl B3
Eagle Market C2
Eastgate B3
East St B2
Exeter St B2
Farm St C1
Ford St B1
Forester St C1
Fox St A2
Friar Gate B1
Friary St B1
Full St B2
Gerard St C1
Gower St C2
Green La C2
Grey St C1
Guildhall B2
Highfield Rd A1
Hill La C2
Industrial B2
Information Ctr i B2
Iron Gate B2
John St C3
Kedleston Rd A1
Key St B2
King Alfred St C1
King St A1
Kingston St A1
Leopold St C2
Library B1
Liversage St C3
Lodge La B1
London Rd C2
Macklin St C1
Main Centre C2
Mansfield Rd A2
Market B2
Market Pl B2
May St C1
Meadow La B3
Melbourne St C2
Midland Rd C3
Monk St C1
Morledge B2
Mount St C1
Museum & Art Gallery B1
Noble St C3
North Parade A1
North St A1
Nottingham Rd B3
Osmaston Rd C2
Otter St A1
Park St C3
Parker St A1
Pickfords House B1
Playhouse C2
Police HQ A2
Police Station B1
Post Office A1/A2/B1/B2/C2/C3
Pride Parkway C3
Prime Parkway A2
Queens Leisure Centre B1
Racecourse A3
Railway Terr C3
Register Office C2
Sacheverel St C2
Sadler Gate B1
St Alkmund's Way B1/B2
St Helens House ✦ A1
St Mark's Bridge A2
St Mary's A1
St Mary's Bridge Chapel A2
St Mary's Gate B1
St Paul's Rd A2
St Peter's C2
St Peter's St C2
Siddals Rd C3
Sir Frank Whittle Rd A3
Spa La C1
Spring St C1
Station Approach C3
Stockbrook St C1
Stores Rd A3
Traffic St C2
Wardwick B1
Werburgh St C1
West Ave A1
West Meadows Industrial Est B3
Wharf Rd A2
Wilmot St C2
Wilson St C1
Wood's La C1

¼ mile
¼ ½ km

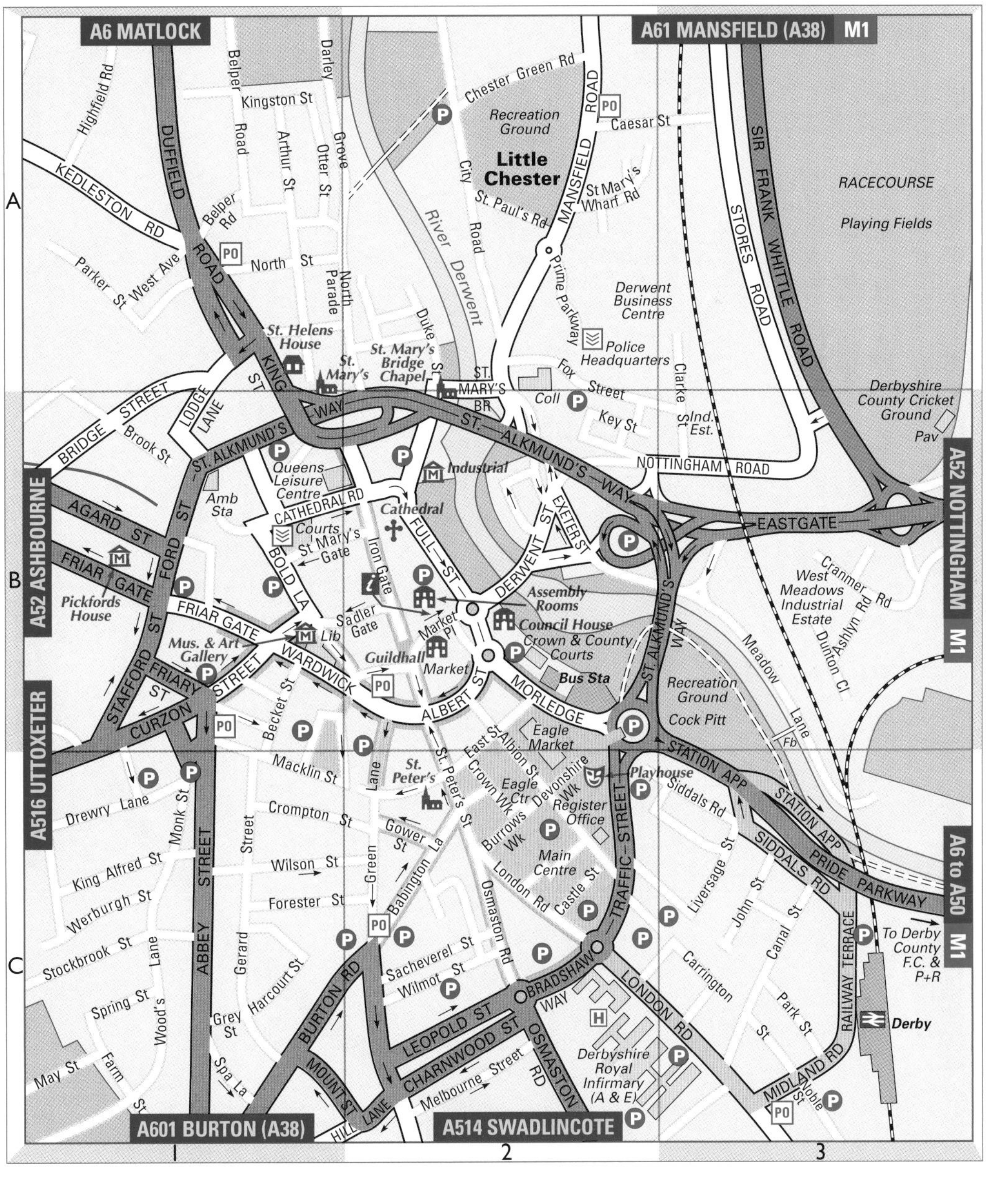

Dorchester

▲The Keep Military Museum

Dorset's historic county town, most famous for its association with novelist Thomas Hardy (of whom there is a statue) but with Roman origins: among relics are Maiden Castle, England's biggest hillfort, built *c.*3000 BC on the site of a Neolithic longbarrow; and the Maumbury Rings, which began as a Neolithic henge and was converted into a large Roman amphitheatre, and later, in the 17th century, into an artillery fort. The Gallows Tour traces the history of Judge George Jeffreys, known as the Hanging Judge for his severe treatment of local rebels, who lodged in the town, while the Shire Hall was the venue for the trial of the Tolpuddle Martyrs. Other sights include the Dinosaur Museum, the Tutankhamun Museum and the Keep Military Museum. The town centre, which has many tree-lined walks along the line of the old Roman wall, has a good range of speciality shops, and there's a large, long-established Wednesday market. Nearby are T.E. Lawrence's home, Clouds Hill, and Chesil Beach.

Dorchester Tourist Information Centre, Antelope Walk, Dorchester DT1 1BE Tel 01305 267992/252470

BBC Radio Solent 103.8 FM and 1359 AM • **Wessex FM** 97.2 FM

www.visit-dorchester.co.uk

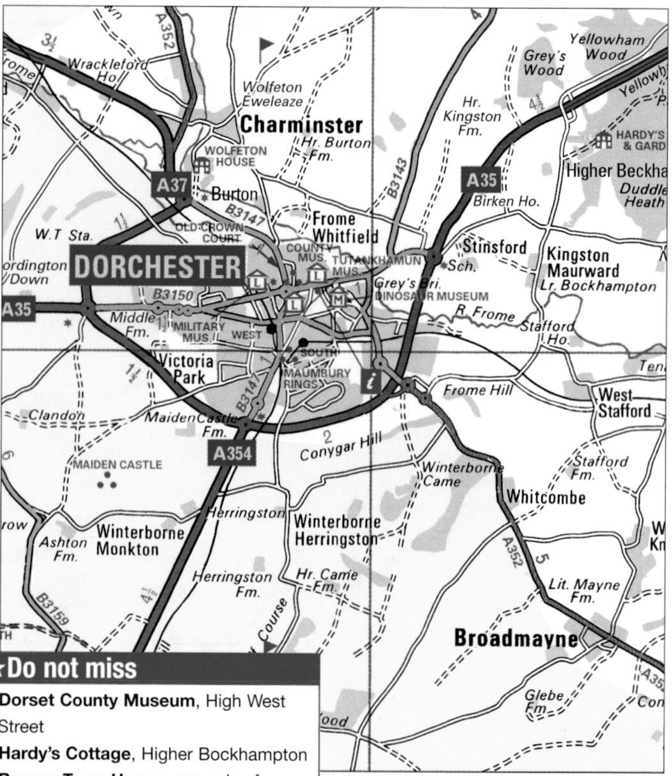

★Do not miss

★**Dorset County Museum**, High West Street

★**Hardy's Cottage**, Higher Bockhampton

★**Roman Town House**, grounds of County Hall

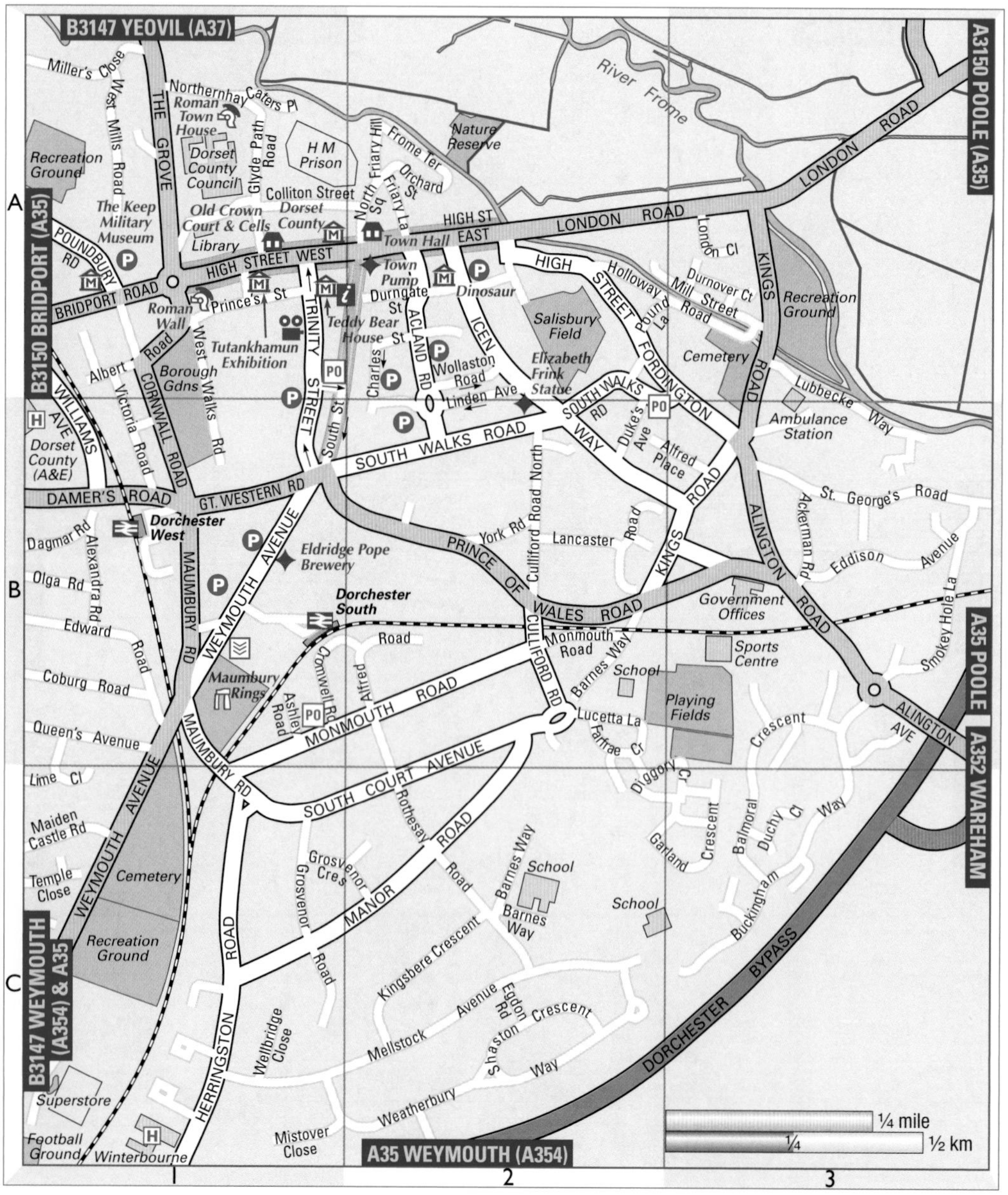

Dorchester

Ackerman Rd B3
Acland Rd. A2
Albert Rd A1
Alexandra Rd. B1
Alfred Place. B3
Alfred Rd B2
Alington Ave B3
Alington Rd B3
Ambulance Station B3
Ashley Rd. B1
Balmoral Cres . . . C3
Barnes Way . . B2/C2
Borough Gdns . . . A1
Bridport Rd A1
Buckingham Way C3
Caters Place A1
Charles St A2
Coburg Rd B1
Colliton St A1
Cornwall Rd. A1
Cromwell Rd B1
Culliford Rd B2
Culliford Rd North B2
Dagmar Rd. B1
Damer's Rd B1
Diggory Cres B2
Dinosaur Museum A2
Dorchester Bypass C3
Dorchester South Station B1
Dorchester West Station B1
Dorset County Council Offices . A1
Dorset County Hosp (A&E) B1
Dorset County Museum A1
Duchy Close. C3
Duke's Ave B2
Durngate St A2
Durnover Court. . A3
Eddison Ave. B3
Edward Rd B1
Egdon Rd C2
Eldridge Pope Brewery ✦ B1
Elizabeth Frink Statue ✦ B2
Farfrae Cres. B2
Friary Hill. A2
Friary Lane. A2
Frome Terr A2
Garland Cres C3
Glyde Path Rd A1
Gt. Western Rd . . . B1
Grosvenor Cres . . C1
Grosvenor Rd. . . . C1
HM Prison A1
Herringston Rd . . C1
High St East. A2
High Street Fordington. A2
High Street West. A1
Holloway Rd A2
Icen Way. A2
Kings Rd. A3/B3
Kingsbere Cres . . C2
Keep Military Museum, The . A1
Lancaster Rd B2
Library A1
Lime Cl B1
Linden Ave B2
London Cl. A3
London Rd A3
Lubbecke Way . . . A3
Lucetta La B2
Maiden Castle Rd C1
Manor Rd C2
Maumbury Rd B1
Maumbury Rings B1
Mellstock Ave . . . C2
Mill St. A3
Miller's Cl A1
Mistover Cl C1
Monmouth Rd B1
North Sq. A2
Northernhay A1
Old Crown Court & Cells A1
Olga Rd. B1
Orchard St A2
Police Station . . B1
Post Office . A1/B1/B2
Pound Lane A2
Poundbury Rd . . . A1
Prince of Wales Rd B2
Prince's St A1
Queen's Ave. B1
Roman Town House A1
Roman Wall . . . A1
Rothesay Rd. C2
St George's Rd . . B3
Salisbury Field . . A2
Shaston Cres C2
Smokey Hole La . . B3
South Court Ave . C1
South St B1
South Walks Rd. . . B2
Teddy Bear House A1
Temple Cl. C1
The Grove A1
Town Hall A2
Town Pump ✦ . . . A2
Trinity St. A1
Tutankhamun Exhibition . . . A1
Victoria Rd. B1
Weatherbury Way C2
Wellbridge Cl. . . . C1
West Mills Rd . . . A1
West Walks Rd . . . A1
Weymouth Ave. . . C1
Williams Ave B1
Winterbourne Hospital C1
Wollaston Rd. . . . A2
York Rd. B2

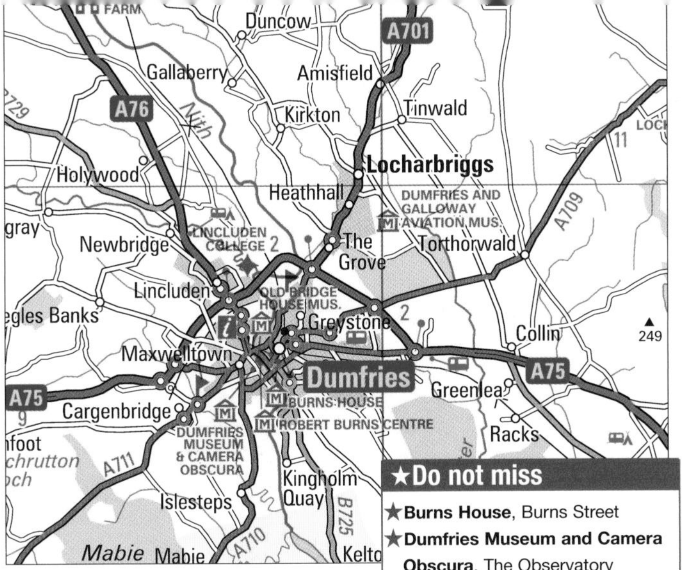

★Do not miss

★**Burns House**, Burns Street
★**Dumfries Museum and Camera Obscura**, The Observatory
★**Robert Burns Centre**, Mill Road

Dumfries

A former seaport, now southwest Scotland's largest town, best known for being the place where Robert Burns lived up until his death in 1796; visitors can view his house, containing some of his possessions, his mausoleum (St Michael's churchyard) and Ellisland Farm. Further sights of interest include the 15th-century Devorgilla Bridge across the Nith; Mid Steeple, an early-18th-century courthouse and prison; the remains of 15th-century Lincluden Collegiate Church; the Old Bridge House Museum of everyday life in the town and an award-winning aviation museum. Nearby attractions include Shambellie House Costume Museum, the ruined Sweetheart Abbey, the renovated New Abbey Corn Mill, Arbigland House and Gardens, the John Paul Jones Birthplace Museum about the father of the US navy and Mersehead RSPB Nature Reserve.

Dumfries Tourist Information Centre, Whitesands, Dumfries DG1 2RS Tel 01387 253862
BBC Radio Scotland 94.7 FM and 585 AM • **South Westsound** 97.0 FM
www.dumfriesandgalloway.co.uk

¼ mile
¼ ½ km

Dumfries

Academy St A2
Aldermanhill Rd . . B3
Ambulance Station C3
Annan Rd A3
Ardwall Rd A3
Ashfield Dr. A1
Atkinson Rd C1
Averill Cres C1
Balliol Ave C1
Bank St. B2
Bankend Rd C3
Barn Slaps B3
Barrie Ave B3
Beech Ave A1
Bowling Green . . A3
Brewery St. B2
Bridge House . . B1
Brodie Ave C2
Brooke St. B2
Broomlands Dr . . C1
Brooms Rd B3
Buccleuch St A2
Burns House . . . B2
Burns Mausoleum. B3
Burns St B2
Burns Statue ✦. . A2
Bus Station B1
Cardoness St A3
Castle St. A2
Catherine St A2
Cattle Market. . . . A3
Cemetery B3
Cemetery C2
Church Cres. A2
Church St. B2
College Rd A1
College St A1
Corbelly Hill. B1
Convent, The B1
Corberry Park B1
Cornwall Mt. A3
County Offices. . . A2
Court. A2
Craigs Rd C3
Cresswell Ave B3
Cresswell Hill . . . B3
Cumberland St . . B3
David Keswick Athletic Centre . A3
David St B1
Dock Park C3
Dockhead B2
Dumfries Academy A2
Dumfries Museum & Camera Obscura B2
Dumfries Royal Infirmary (A&E) C3
Dumfries ⇌ A3
E. Riverside Dr . . C3
Edinburgh Rd A2
English St. B2
Fire Station B3
Friar's Vennel . . . A2
Galloway St B1
George Douglas Dr C1
George St. A2
Gladstone Rd. . . . C2
Glasgow St. A1
Glebe St B3
Glencaple Rd. . . . C3
Goldie Ave A1
Goldie Cres A1
Golf Course C3
Greyfriars A2
Grierson Ave B3
HM Prison B1
Hamilton Ave. C1
Hamilton Starke Park C2
Hazelrigg Ave . . . C1
Henry St B3
Hermitage Dr. C1
High Cemetery . . C3
High St A2
Hill Ave. C2
Hill St B1
Holm Ave C2
Hoods Loaning . . A3
Howgate St B1
Huntingdon Rd . . A3
Information Ctr . B2
Irish St B2
Irving St A2
King St A1
Kingholm Rd C3
Kirkpatrick Ct . . . C2
Laurieknowe B1
Leafield Rd. B3
Library A2
Lochfield Rd A1
Loreburn Pk. A3
Loreburn St A2
Loreburne Shopping Centre. B2
Lover's Walk A2
Martin Ave B3
Maryholm Dr A1
Mausoleum B3
Maxwell St. B1
McKie Ave B3
Mews La A2
Mill Green B2
Mill Rd B1
Moat Rd C2
Moffat Rd. A3
Mountainhall Pk . C3
Nelson St B1
New Abbey Rd B1/C1
New Bridge B1
Newall Terr. A2
Nith Ave A2
Nith Bank. C3
Nithbank Hospital C3
Nithside Ave A1
Odeon B2
Old Bridge B1
Palmerston Park (Queen of the South F.C.) A1
Park Rd C1
Pleasance Ave. . . . C1
Police H.Q. A3
Police Station . . A2
Portland Dr A1
Post Office A2/B1/B2/B3/B3
Priestlands Dr . . . C1
Primrose St B1
Queen St B3
Queensberry St . . A2
Rae St. A2
Richmond Ave . . . C2
Robert Burns Ctr. B2
Roberts Cres C1
Robertson Ave. . . . C3
Robinson Dr. C1
Rosefield Rd C2
Rosemount St B1
Rotchell Park. . . . C1
Rotchell Rd B1
Rugby Football Ground C1
Ryedale Rd. C2
St Andrews B2
St John the Evangelist . . . A2
St Josephs Coll. . . B3
St Mary's Industrial Estate A3
St Mary's St. A3
St Michael St. B2
St Michael's Bridge. B2
St Michael's Bridge Rd. B2
St Michael's Cemetery B3
St Michael's. B2
Shakespeare St . . . B2
Solway Dr. C2
Stakeford St. A1
Stark Cres C2
Station Rd A3
Steel Ave A1
Sunderries Ave . . A1
Sunderries Rd . . . A1
Suspension Brae. . B2
Swimming Pool. . A1
Terregles St B1
Theatre Royal . . B2
Troqueer Rd. C2
Union St A1
West Riverside Dr C2
Wallace St B3
Welldale B2
White Sands B2

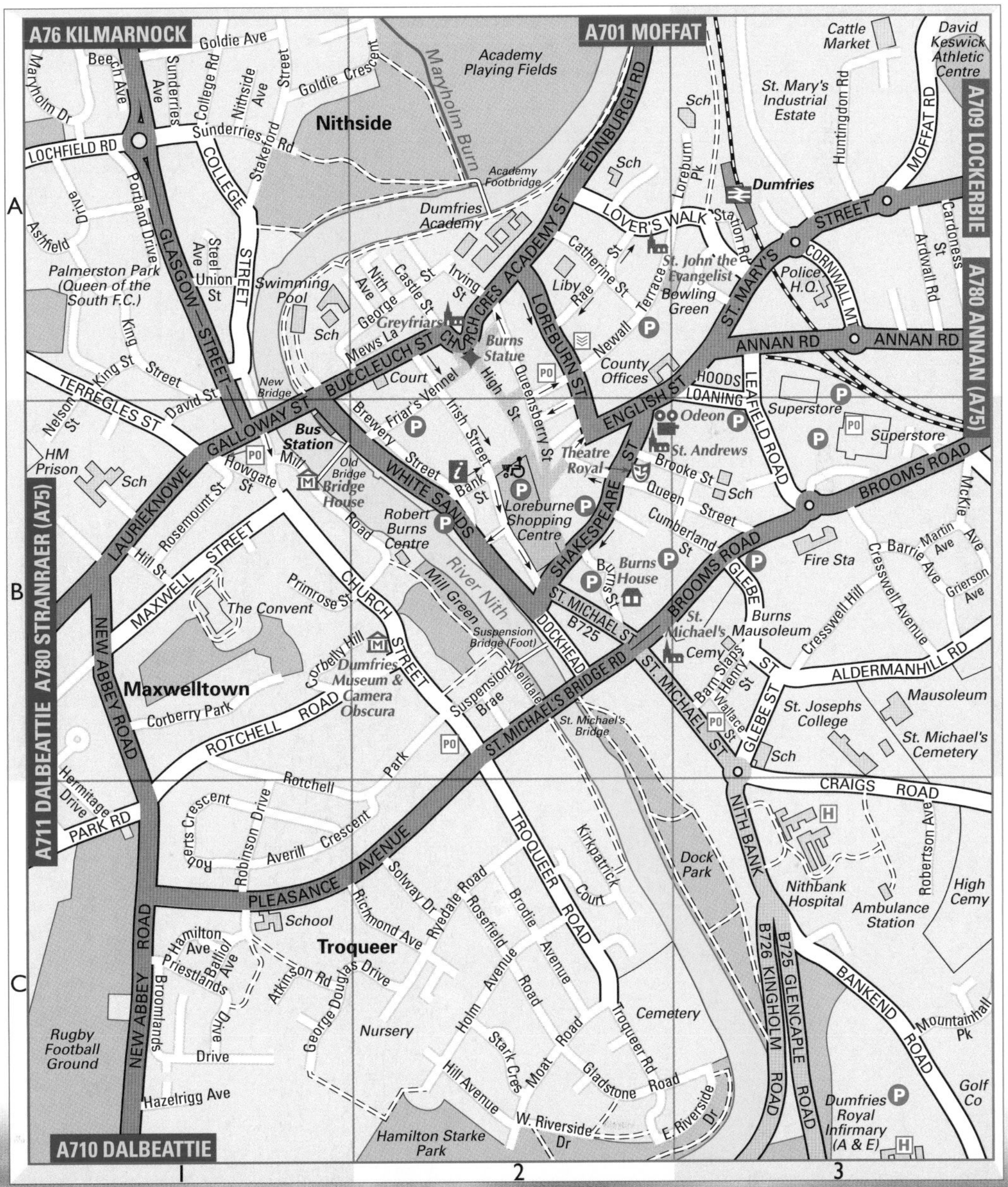

Dundee

▲ Claypotts Castle

The fourth-largest city in Scotland, with a rich seafaring and industrial history, a thriving cultural quarter including the Dundee Contemporary Arts Centre, and a wide range of department stores and specialist and high-street shops. Attractions include the RRS (Royal Research Ship) *Discovery*, the ship used during Captain Scott's Antarctic expedition; the HMS Frigate *Unicorn*, a former warship; Broughty Castle, a coastal fort with panoramic views, used as a museum about local history and wildlife, including whaling in the area; and Mills Observatory, with a planetarium. Among the parks and gardens are Camperdown Country Park with its award-winning wildlife centre, Templeton Woods and the University Botanic Gardens.

Dundee Information Centre, 21 Castle Street, Dundee DD1 3AA
Tel 0845 225 5121

BBC Radio Scotland 94.3 FM and 810 AM • **Tay AM** 1161 AM
Tay FM 102.8 FM • **Wave 102** 102.0 FM

www.angusanddundee.co.uk

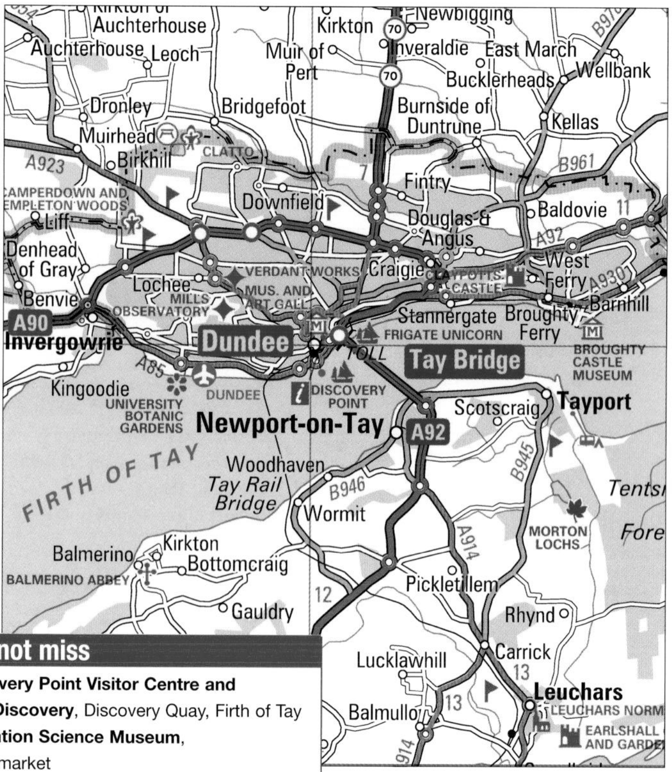

★Do not miss

- ★**Discovery Point Visitor Centre and RRS Discovery**, Discovery Quay, Firth of Tay
- ★**Sensation Science Museum**, Greenmarket
- ★**Verdant Works Textile Heritage Centre**, West Hendersons Wynd

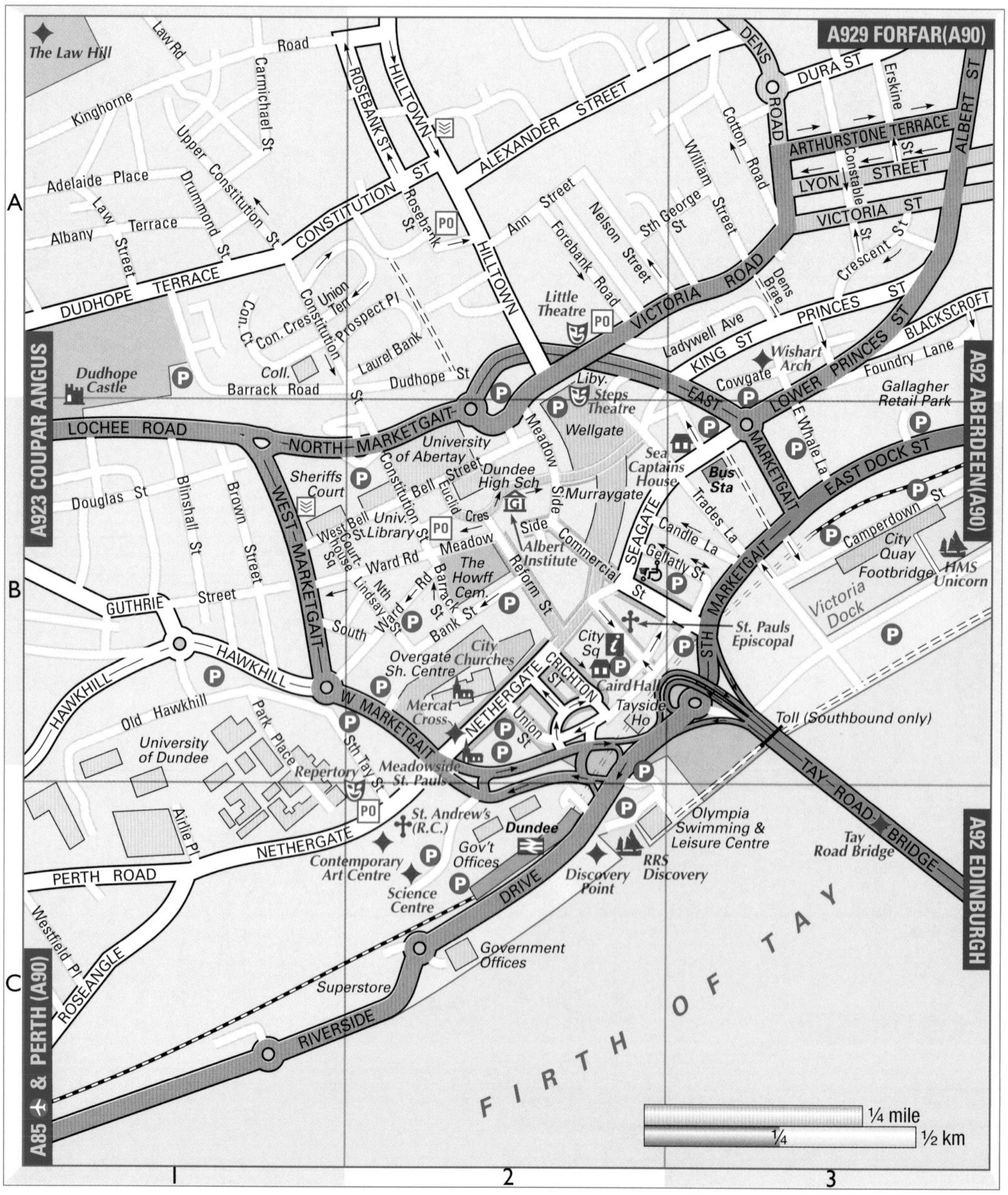

Dundee

Adelaide Pl A1
Airlie Pl C1
Albany Terr. A1
Albert B2
Albert St. A3
Alexander St A2
Ann St. A2
Arthurstone Terr . A3
Bank St. B2
Barrack Rd. A1
Barrack St B2
Bell St. B2
Blackscroft. A3
Blinshall St B1
Brown St B1
Bus Station B3
Caird Hall. B2
Camperdown St . . B3
Candle La. B3
Carmichael St . . . A1
Carnegie St A2
City Churches . . . B2
City Quay B3
City Sq B2
Commercial St . . . B2
Constable St A3
Constitution Ct . . . A1
Constitution Cres A1
Constitution St A1/B2
Contemporary Art Centre ✦ . . . C2
Cotton Rd. A3
Courthouse Sq . . . B1
Cowgate. A3
Crescent St A3
Crichton St. B2
Dens Brae A3
Dens Rd A3
Discovery Point ✦ C2
Douglas St. B1
Drummond St . . . A1
Dudhope Castle A1
Dudhope St A2
Dudhope Terr. A1
Dundee C2
Dundee High School B2
Dura St. A3
East Dock St B3
East Whale La B3
East Marketgait. . . B3
Erskine St. A3
Euclid Cr B2
Forebank Rd A2
Foundry La. A3
Gallagher Retail Park B3
Gellatly St B3
Government Offices C2
Guthrie St B1
Hawkhill. B1
Hilltown A2
HMS Unicorn . . . B3
Howff Cem, The. . . B2
Information Ctr . B2
King St A3
Kinghorne Rd . . . A1
Ladywell Ave A3
Laurel Bank A2
Law Hill, The ✦. . A1
Law Rd A1
Law St. A1
Library A2
Little Theatre . . A2
Lochee Rd B1
Lower Princes St A3
Lyon St A3
Meadow Side. B2
Meadowside St Pauls B2
Mercat Cross ✦. . . B2
Murraygate B2
Nelson St A2
Nethergate. . . B2/C1
North Marketgait . B2
North Lindsay St . B2
Old Hawkhill B1
Olympia Swimming & Leisure Ctr . . . C3
Overgate Shopping Centre. B2
Park Pl B1
Perth Rd. C1
Police Station . . . A2/B1
Post Office . A2/B2/C2
Princes St A3
Prospect Pl A2
Reform St. B2
Repertory C1
Riverside Dr. C2
Roseangle C1
Rosebank St. A2
RRS Discovery . . C2
St Andrew's ✝. . . C2
St Pauls Episcopal B3
Science Centre ✦ C2
Sea Captains House B3
Sheriffs Court B1
South Ward Rd . . . B2
South George St . A2
South Marketgait . B3
South Tay St. B2
Steps A2
Tay Road Bridge ✦ C3
Tayside House B2
Trades La B3
Union St B2
Union Terr A1
University Library . B2
Univ of Abertay . . . B2
Univ of Dundee . . . B1
Upper Constitution St . A1
Victoria Rd. A2
Victoria St A3
West Marketgait . . . B1/B2
Ward Rd B1
Wellgate. B2
West Bell St. B1
Westfield Pl C1
William St A3
Wishart Arch ✦. . A3

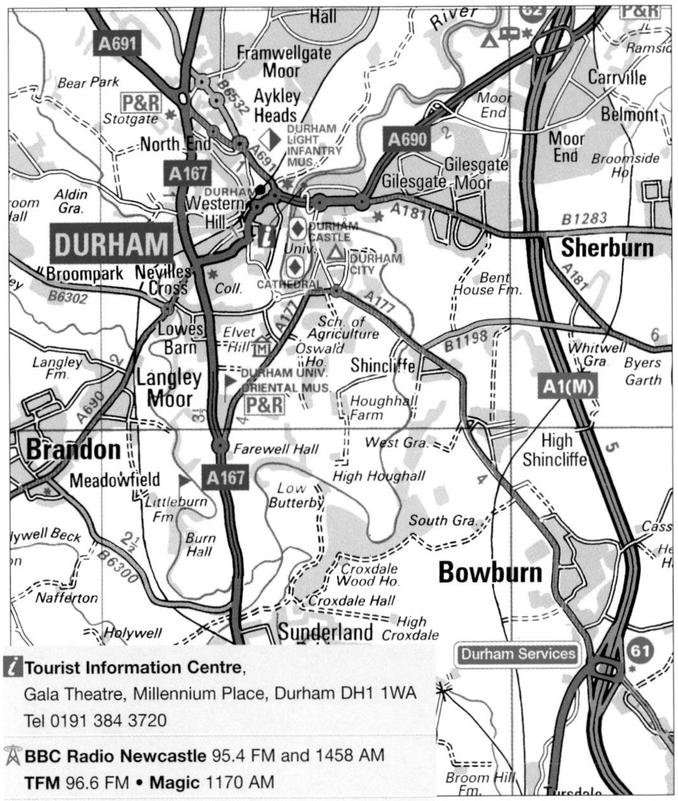

Tourist Information Centre,
Gala Theatre, Millennium Place, Durham DH1 1WA
Tel 0191 384 3720

BBC Radio Newcastle 95.4 FM and 1458 AM
TFM 96.6 FM • **Magic** 1170 AM

www.durhamtourism.co.uk

Durham

▲Durham Castle

A compact city founded 1000 years ago with the arrival of a religious community seeking a resting place for St Cuthbert of Lindisfarne. Later it was the base from which King William defended Northumbria from the Scots and it was during this period that the magnificent Norman cathedral and castle were constructed; the two are now a UNESCO World Heritage Site. In the 19th century the castle became the first college of the city's famous university. Other historic structures include the 12th-century Elvet and Framwellgate bridges, the Guildhall (1356), and the 1777 Prebends Bridge, from which Turner painted. Among sights of interest are Durham Heritage Centre and Museum, the university's Museum of Archaeology and the Durham Light Industry Museum. The main outdoor attractions are the university's Botanic Garden and the 17th-century riverside Old Durham Gardens. Shopping amenities include a Victorian indoor market.

★Do not miss

★**Durham Cathedral and Castle**, Palace Green
★**Crook Hall (14th-century manor) and Gardens**, Sidegate
★**Oriental Museum**, Elvet Hill

Durham

Alexander Cr B2
Allergate.........B2
Archery Rise C1
Assize Courts.....B3
Back Western Hill A1
Bakehouse La ... A3
Baths Bridge B3
Boat House B3
Boyd St.........C3
Bus Station B2
Castle B2
Castle Chare B2
Cathedral ✝......B2
Church St........C3
Clay La C1
Claypath B3
College of St Hild & St Bede..........B3
County Hall A1
County Hospital B1
Crook Hall ✦....A3
Crossgate.......B2
Crossgate Peth .. C1
Darlington Rd ... C1
Durham A2
Durham Light Infantry Mus & Arts Centre .. A2
Durham School .. C2
Ellam Ave....... C1
Elvet Bridge......B3
Elvet Court.......B3
Farnley Hey B1
Ferens Cl A3
Fieldhouse La ... A1
Flass St..........B1
Framwelgate A2
Framwelgate Bridge..........B2
Framwelgate Peth A2
Framwelgate Waterside...... A2
Frankland La A3
Freeman's Pl A3
Gala & Sacred Journey B3
Geoffrey Ave C1
Gilesgate B3
Grey College C3
Grove St C2
Hallgarth St C3
Hatfield College ..B3
Hawthorn Terr B1
Heritage Ctr ...B3
HM Prison B3
Information Ctr ..B2
John St..........B1
Kingsgate Bridge .B3
Laburnum Terr....B1
Lawson Terr B1
Leazes Rd.....B2/B3
Library B2
Margery La.......B2
Mavin St........ C3
Millburngate B2
Millburngate Bridge.........B2
Millburngate Ctr ..B2
Millennium Bridge (foot/cycle).... A2
Millennium Ctr ...B3
Museum of Archaeology ..B2
Neville's Cross College........ C1
Nevilledale Terr...B1
New Elvet........B3
New Elvet Bridge .B3
North Bailey......B3
North End....... A1
North Rd..... A1/B2
Observatory...... C1
Old Elvet.........B3
Oriental Mus . C2
Passport Office .. A2
Percy Terr........B1
Pimlico.......... C2
Police Station ..B3
Post Office A1/B2
Potters Bank . C1/C2
Prebends Bridge. C2
Prebends Walk .. C2
Princes St A1
Providence Row . A3
Quarryheads La .. C2
Redhills La.......B1
Redhills Terr......B1
Saddler St B3
St Chad's College C3
St Cuthbert's Society........ C2
St John's College C2
St Margaret's ..B2
St Mary The Less C2
St Mary's College C2
St Monica Grove ..B1
St Nicholas' B3
St Oswald's C3
Sidegate......... A2
Silver St B2
South Bailey C2
South Rd C3
South St.........B2
Springwell Ave ... A1
Stockton Rd..... C3
Students' Rec Ctr .B3
Sutton St B2
The Avenue B1
The Crescent..... A1
The Grove A1
The Sands A3
Town Hall........B2
Treasury Mus ..B2
University ✦ B2
Univ Arts Block ...B3
Univ Library..... C3
Univ Science Labs C3
Wearside Dr...... A3
Western Hill..... A1
Wharton Park ... A2
Whinney Hill C3

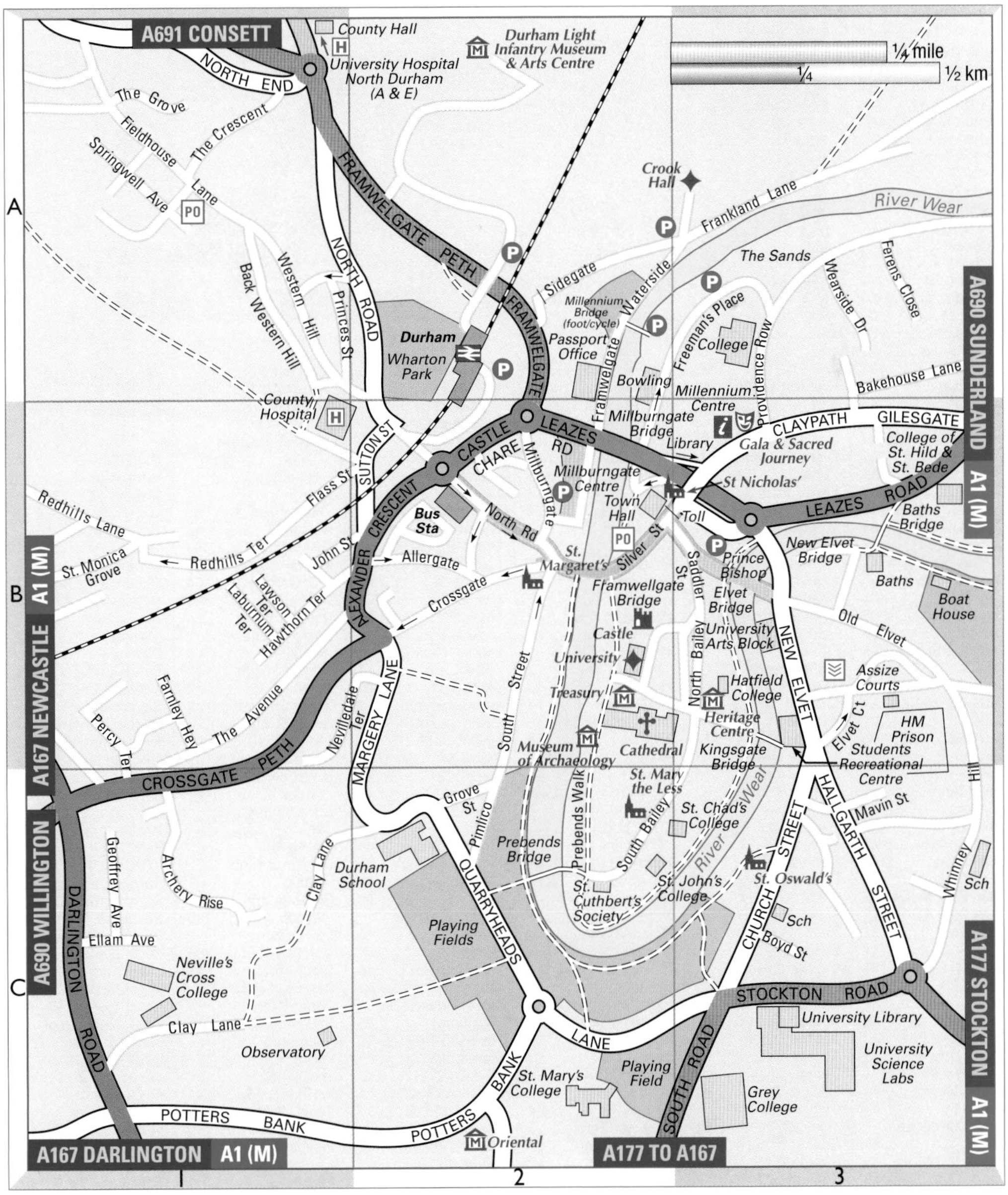

Edinburgh

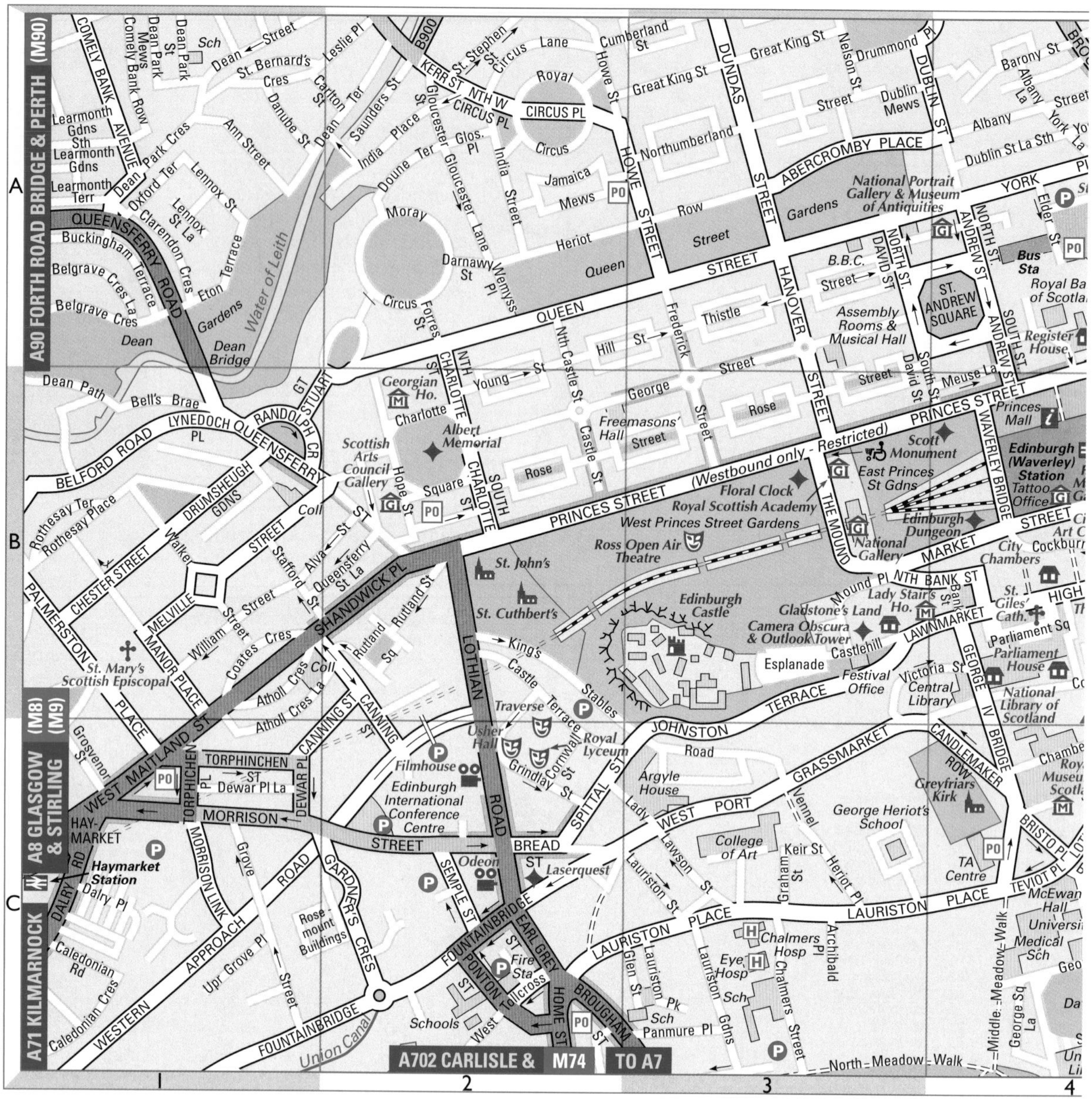

Abbey Strand B6
Abbeyhill A6
Abbeyhill Cr. B6
Abbeymount A6
Abercromby Pl . . A3
Adam St C5
Albany La A4
Albany St A4
Albert Memorial ✦ B2
Alva Pl A6
Alva St B1
Ann St. A1
Appleton Tower . . C4
Archibald Pl. C3
Argyle House C3
Assembly Rooms & Musical Hall . . . A3
Atholl Cr. B1
Atholl Crescent La C1
BBC A3
Bank St. B4
Barony St A4
Beaumont Pl C5
Belford Rd B1
Belgrave Cr A1
Belgrave Crescent La A1
Bell's Brae B1
Blackfriars St. B4
Blair St B4
Bread St C2
Bristo Pl C4
Bristo St C4
Brougham St C2
Broughton St A4
Brown St C5
Brunton Terr A6
Buckingham Terr. A1
Burial Ground . . . A6
Bus Station A4
Caledonian Cr . . . C1
Caledonian Rd. . . C1
Calton Hill A4
Calton Hill A5
Calton Rd B4
Camera Obscura & Outlook Tower ✦ B3
Candlemaker Row C4
Canning St B2
Canongate B5
Canongate ⛪ B5
Carlton St. A1
Carlton Terr A6
Carlton Terrace La A6
Castle St. B2
Castle Terr B2
Castlehill B3
Central Library . . . B4
Chalmers Hospital H C3
Chalmers St. C3
Chambers St C4
Chapel St C4
Charles St C4
Charlotte Sq B2
Chester St B1
Circus La A2
Circus Pl. A2
City Art Centre 🏛 . B4
City Chambers 🏛 . B4
City Observatory . A5
Clarendon Cr A1
Clerk St C5
Coates Cr B1
Cockburn St. B4
College of Art . . . C3
Comely Bank Ave A1
Comely Bank Row A1
Cornwall St C2
Cowans Cl C5
Cowgate B4
Cranston St B5
Crichton St. C4
Croft-An-Righ. . . . A6
Cumberland St . . A2
Dalry Pl C1
Dalry Rd C1
Danube St A1
Darnawy St A2
David Hume Tower C4
Davie St C5
Dean Bridge. A1
Dean Gdns A1
Dean Park Cr. . . . A1
Dean Park Mews. A1
Dean Park St. . . . A1
Dean Path B1
Dean St. A1
Dean Terr A1
Dewar Pl C1
Dewar Place La. . C1
Doune Terr A2
Drummond Pl . . . A3
Drummond St . . . C5
Drumsheugh Gdns B1
Dublin Mews A3
Dublin St A4
Dublin Street La South A4
Dumbiedykes Rd . B5
Dundas St A3
Earl Grey St C2
East Norton Pl. . . A6
East Crosscauseway . C5
East Market St. . . B4
East Princes St Gdns B3
Easter Rd A6
Edinburgh (Waverley) ⇌ . . B4
Edinburgh Castle 🏰 B3
Edinburgh Dungeon ✦ B4
Edinburgh Festival Theatre 🎭 C4
Edinburgh International Conference Ctr . C2
Elder St A4
Esplanade B3
Eton Terr. A1
Eye Hospital H . . C3
Festival Office . . . B3
Filmhouse 🎥 C2
Fire Station C2
Floral Clock ✦ . . . B3
Forres St A2
Forth St A4
Fountainbridge . . C2
Frederick St. A3
Freemasons' Hall . B3
Fruit Market 🏛 . . . B4
Gardner's Cr C2
George Heriot's School C3
George IV Bridge . B4
George Sq C4
George Sq La. . . . C4
George St. B2
Georgian House 🏛 B2
Gladstone's Land 🏛 B3
Glen St C3
Gloucester La . . . A2
Gloucester Pl. . . . A2
Gloucester St. . . . A2
Graham St C3
Grassmarket C3
Great King St. . . . A3
Great Stuart. B1
Greenside La A5
Greenside Row . . A5
Greyfriars Kirk ⛪ . C4
Grindlay St. C2
Grosvenor St C1
Grove St C1
Gullan's Cl B5
Guthrie St B4
Hanover St. A3
Hart St A4
Haymarket C1
Haymarket Station ⇌ C1
Heriot Pl. C3
Heriot Row. A2
High School Yard. . B5
High St B4
Hill Pl C5
Hill St A2
Hillside Cr A5
Holyrood Abbey (AD 1128) (Remains of) . . . A6
Holyrood Park . . . C6
Holyrood Rd. B5
Home St C2
Hope St B2
Horse Wynd B6
Howden St C5
Howe St A2
India Pl. A2
India St. A2
Infirmary St B4
Information Ctr i . B4
Jamaica Mews . . . A2
Jeffrey St B4
John Knox's House 🏛 B4
Johnston Terr . . . C3
Keir St. C3
Kerr St A2
King's Stables Rd . B2
Lady Lawson St. . C3
Lady Stair's House 🏛 B4
Laserquest ✦ C2
Lauriston Gdns . . C3
Lauriston Park. . . C3
Lauriston Pl C3
Lauriston St C3
Lawnmarket. B3
Learmonth Gdns . A1
Learmonth Terr . . A1
Leith St. A4
Lennox St. A1
Lennox St La A1
Leslie Pl A2
London Rd A5
Lothian Health Board C5
Lothian Rd B2
Lothian St C4
Lower Menz Pl . . A6
Lynedoch Pl. B1
Manor Pl B1
Market St B4
Marshall St C4
Maryfield A6
Maryfield Pl. A6
McEwan Hall C4
Medical School . . C4
Melville St B1
Meuse La B4
Middle Meadow Walk C4
Milton St A6
Montrose Terr . . . A6
Moray Circus A2
Moray House (College) B5
Morrison Link . . . C1
Morrison St C1
Mound Pl B3
Museum of Childhood 🏛 . . . B5
Museum of Edinburgh 🏛 . . . B5
National Gallery 🏛 B3
National Library of Scotland 🏛 B4
National Monument ✦ . . . A5
National Portrait Gallery & Museum of Antiquities 🏛 A3
Nelson Monument ✦ . . . A5
Nelson St A3
New St B5
Nicolson Sq C4
Nicolson St C4
Niddry St B4
North Bridge B4
North Meadow Walk C3
North Bank St . . . B3
North Castle St . . A2
North Charlotte St A2
North St Andrew St. A3
North St David St A3
North West Circus Pl. A2
Northumberland St. A3
Odeon 🎥 C2
Old Royal High School A5
Old Tolbooth Wynd. B5
Our Dynamic Earth ✦ B6
Oxford Terr. A1
Palace of Holyrood House 🏛 B6
Palmerston Pl. . . . B1
Panmure Pl C3
Parliament House 🏛 B4
Parliament Sq . . . B4
People's Story, The 🏛 B5
Playhouse Theatre 🎭 A4
Pleasance. C5
Police Station 🚓 . A4
Ponton St. C2
Post Office PO A2/A4/B2/B4/B5/C1/C2/C4/C5
Potterrow. C4
Princes Mall B4
Princes St B3
Queen St A2
Queen Street Gdns A3
Queen's Dr. . . . B6/C6
Queensferry Rd . . A1
Queensferry St . . . B1
Queensferry Street La B2
Radical Rd C6
Randolph Cr. B1
Regent Gdns A5
Regent Rd B5
Regent Rd Park. . . A6
Regent Terr A5
Register House 🏛 A4
Richmond La C5
Richmond Pl C5
Rose St. B2
Rosemount Bldgs C1
Ross Open Air Theatre 🎭 B3
Rothesay Pl B1
Rothesay Terr. . . . B1
Roxburgh Pl. C5
Roxburgh St. C5
Royal Bank of Scotland A4
Royal Circus. A2
Royal Lyceum 🎭 . C2
Royal Museum of Scotland 🏛 C4
Royal Scottish Academy 🏛 B3
Royal Terr A5
Royal Terrace Gdns A5
Rutland Sq B2
Rutland St B2
St Andrew Sq. . . . A3
St Andrew's House A4
St Bernard's Cr . . A1
St Cecilia's Hall. . . B4
St Cuthbert's ⛪ . . . B2
St Giles' ✝ B4
St James Centre . A4
St John St B5
St John's ⛪ B2
St John's Hill. B5
St Leonard's Hill . C5
St Leonard's La . . C5
St Leonard's St . . C5
St Mary's (R.C.) ✝ A4
St Mary's Scottish Episcopal ✝ B1
St Mary's St. B5
St Stephen St . . . A2
Salisbury Crags . . C6
Saunders St A2
Scott Monument ✦ . . . B4
Scottish Arts Council Gallery 🏛 B2
Scottish Parliament B6
Semple St. C2
Shandwick Pl. B2
South Bridge B4
South Charlotte St B2
South College St. C4
South Learmonth Gdns A1
South St Andrew St. A4
South St David St A3
Spittal St C2
Stafford St B1
Student Centre . . C4
TA Centre C4
Tattoo Office B4
Teviot Pl. C4
The Mall B5
The Mound B3
The Royal Mile . . . B5
Thistle St A3
Torphichen Pl . . . C1
Torphichen St . . . C1
Traverse Theatre 🎭 B2
Tron, The ✦ B4
Tron Sq. B4
Union St. A4
University C4
University Library C4
Upper Grove Pl . . C1
Usher Hall 🎭 C2
Vennel. C3
Victoria St B3
Viewcraig Gdns. . . B5
Viewcraig St B5
Walker St B1
Waterloo Pl A4
Waverley Bridge . . B4
Wemyss Pl A2
West Crosscauseway . C5
West Maitland St C1
West of Nicholson St. C4
West Port C3
West Princes Street Gdns B3
West Richmond St. C5
West Tollcross . . . C2
Western Approach Rd . . . C1
White Horse Cl . . . B5
William St B1
Windsor St. A5
York La A4
York Pl A4
Young St. B2

¼ mile
¼ ½ km

Edinburgh

▲The view from the Castle towards the National Gallery and Waverley Station

Scotland's lively, eclectic capital is perhaps best known for its architecture, which ranges from the cramped medieval tenements of the Old Town (including Gladstone's Land museum) to the elegant townhouses of the New Town (including the National Trust's Georgian House), from the Gothic Scott Monument to the new Scottish Parliament building. The Royal Mile runs down from the city's castle, built on a rock inhabited by Celts as early as 800BC and home to the 12th-century St Margaret's Chapel, to the Palace of Holyroodhouse, official Scottish residence of the royal family and the site of Mary Queen of Scots' Chambers. The world-class array of art venues and museums includes the Scottish National Gallery of Modern Art, National Gallery of Scotland, Royal Museum, Writers' Museum and Royal Yacht *Britannia*. Of interest to nature lovers are the Royal Botanic Garden, Holyrood Park & Arthur's Seat, the Water of Leith, and Our Dynamic Earth. The excellent shops, hotels and restaurants include plenty of budget options, and the year-round programme of special events includes the world-famous International Festival of theatre, and the Military Tattoo.

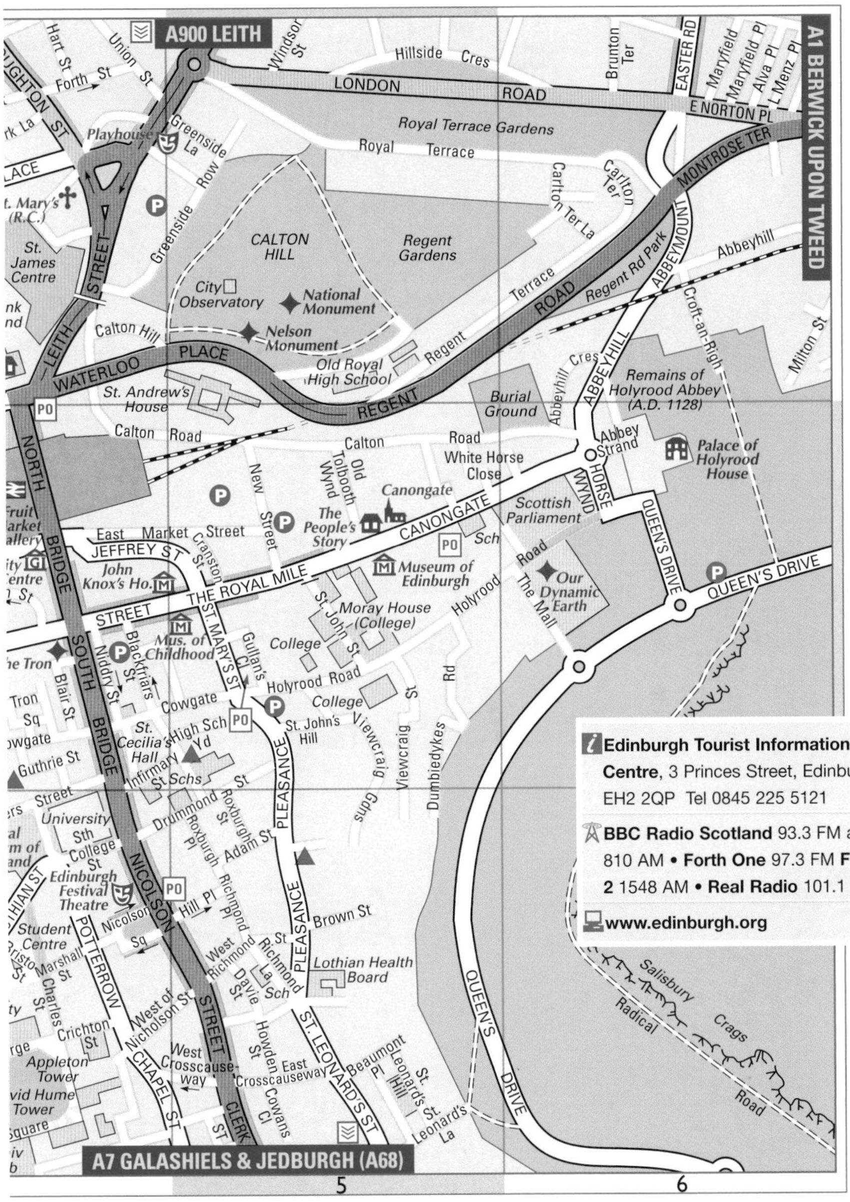

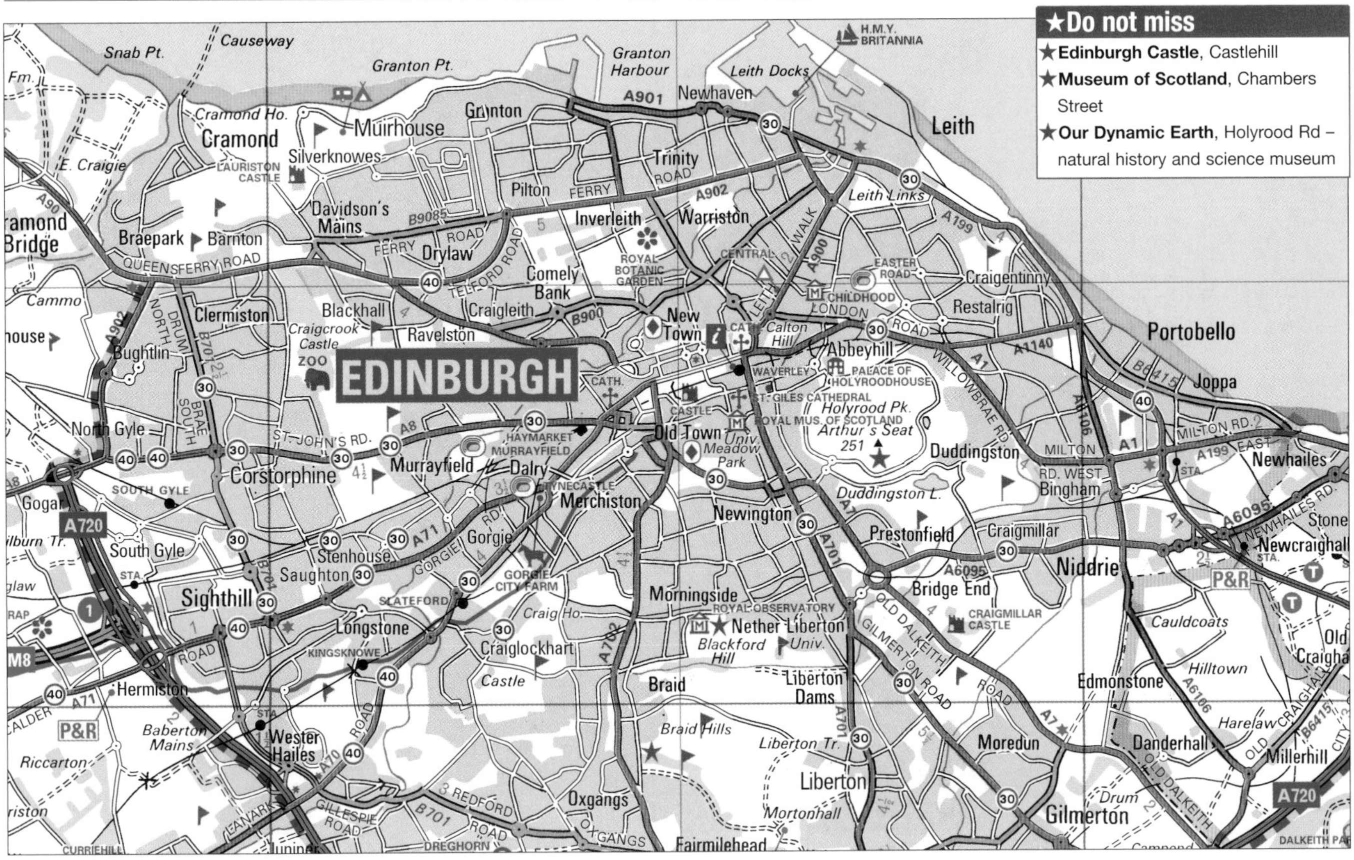

★Do not miss

- ★**Edinburgh Castle**, Castlehill
- ★**Museum of Scotland**, Chambers Street
- ★**Our Dynamic Earth**, Holyrood Rd – natural history and science museum

Edinburgh Tourist Information Centre, 3 Princes Street, Edinburgh EH2 2QP Tel 0845 225 5121

BBC Radio Scotland 93.3 FM and 810 AM • **Forth One** 97.3 FM **Forth 2** 1548 AM • **Real Radio** 101.1 FM

www.edinburgh.org

Exeter

Exeter is an historic cathedral and university city and the county town of Devon. It has grown from Roman origins with the historic centre now designated as an Area of Archaeological Importance. Exeter's Quayside was once a Roman waterway and 16th century port and now functions as a city centre riverside resort with shops, restaurants and outdoor activities. The Guildhall, dating from 1330, is reputed to be the oldest municipal building still in full civic use in England. The city is well served for all forms of entertainment from cinemas to theatres, pubs and restaurants. ▲The 17th-century Custom House on the Quayside

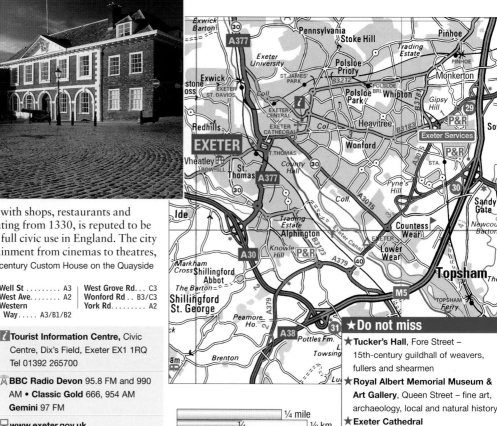

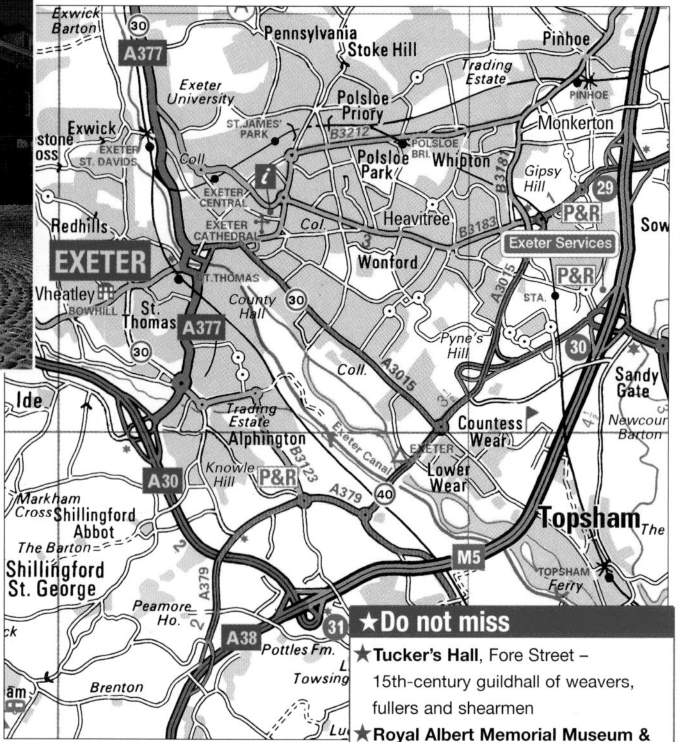

★Do not miss

★**Tucker's Hall**, Fore Street – 15th-century guildhall of weavers, fullers and shearmen

★**Royal Albert Memorial Museum & Art Gallery**, Queen Street – fine art, archaeology, local and natural history

★**Exeter Cathedral**

¼ mile
¼ ½ km

Exeter

Alphington St . . . C1
Athelstan Rd B3
Bampfylde St. B2
Barnardo Rd C3
Barnfield Hill. B3
Barnfield Rd. . .B2/B3
Barnfield ☊ B2
Bartholomew St East B1
Bartholomew St West. B1
Bear St B2
Beaufort Rd C1
Bedford St B2
Belgrave Rd A3
Belmont Rd A3
Blackall Rd. A2
Blackboy Rd. A3
Bonhay Rd B1
Bull Meadow Rd . C2
Bus & Coach Sta. .B3
Castle St. B2
Cecil Rd C1
Cheeke St. A3
Church Rd C1
Chute St. A3
City Industrial Est C2
City Wall. B1/B2
Civic Centre. B2
Clifton Rd. B3
Clifton St B3
Clock Tower. A1
College Rd. B3
Colleton Cr C2
Commercial Rd . . C1
Coombe St. B2
Cowick St. C1
Crown Courts B2
Custom House 🏛 C2
Danes' Rd. A2
Denmark Rd. B3
Devon Cty Hall . . C3
Devonshire Pl . . . A3
Dinham Rd. B1
East Grove Rd . . . C3
Edmund St. C1
Elmgrove Rd A1
Exe St B1
Exeter Central ⇌ A1
Exeter City Football Ground A3
Exeter College. . . A1
Exeter Picture House ☊. B1
Fire Station A1
Fore St B1
Friars Walk C2
Guildhall 🏛 B2
Guildhall Shopping Centre. B2
Harlequin's Shopping Centre.B1
Haven Rd C2
Heavitree Rd B3
Hele Rd. A1
High St. B2
HM Prison A2
Holloway St C2
Hoopern St A2
Horseguards A2
Howell Rd A1
Information Ctr ℹ .B3
Iron Bridge. B1
Isca Rd C1
Jesmond Rd. A3
King William St. . A2
King St B1
Larkbeare Rd. . . . C2
Leisure Centre. . . C1
Library B2
Longbrook St. . . . A2
Longbrook Terr . . A2
Lucky La. C2
Lower North St . . .B1
Lyndhurst Rd C3
Magdalen Rd B3
Magdalen St B2
Magistrates & Crown Courts A2
Market B2
Market St B2
Marlborough Rd . C3
Mary Arches St . . .B1
Matford Rd. C3
Matford Ave C3
Matford La. C3
May St A3
Mol's Coffee Ho 🏛 B2
New Bridge St. . . .B1
New North Rd A1/A2
North St B1
Northernhay St . . .B1
Norwood Ave. . . . C3
Odeon ☊ A3
Okehampton St . . C1
Old Mill Cl C2
Old Tiverton Rd . . A3
Oxford Rd. A3
Paris St. B2
Parr St A3
Paul St B1
Pennsylvania Rd . A2
Police H.Q. ▣ B3
Portland Street . . A3
Post Office PO. . . . A3/B1/B3/C1
Powderham Cr . . A3
Preston St B1
Princesshay development (2007) . .B2
Queen St A1
Queen's Rd C1
Queen's Terr A1
Radford Rd. C2
Richmond Rd. . . . A1
Roberts Rd. C2
Rougemont Castle ♜ A2
Rougemont Ho ✦ .B2
Royal Albert Memorial Mus 🏛B2
St David's Hill . . . A1
St James' Pk ⇌. . A3
St James' Rd A3
St Leonard's Rd. . C3
St Lukes College. .B3
St Mary Steps ⛪. . C1
St Nicholas Priory (AM) ✝ . . .B1
St Peter's Cathedral ✝. B2
St Thomas ⇌. . . C1
Sandford Walk. . . .B3
School for the Deaf C2
School Rd. C1
Sidwell St. A2
Smythen St B1
South St B2
Southernhay East .B2
Southernhay West B2
Spicer Rd B3
Spacex Gallery 🏛 .B1
Sports Centre . . . A3
Summerland St. . A3
Swimming Pool. . .B3
Sydney Rd C1
Tan La. C2
The Quay C2
Thornton Hill. . . . A2
Topsham Rd. C3
Tucker's Hall 🏛 . . .B1
Tudor St B1
Velwell Rd A1
Verney St A3
Water La. C1/C2
Weirfield Rd. C2
Well St A3
West Ave. A2
Western Way. A3/B1/B2
West Grove Rd. . . C3
Wonford Rd . . B3/C3
York Rd. A2

ℹ **Tourist Information Centre,** Civic Centre, Dix's Field, Exeter EX1 1RQ
Tel 01392 265700

BBC Radio Devon 95.8 FM and 990 AM • **Classic Gold** 666, 954 AM
Gemini 97 FM

www.exeter.gov.uk

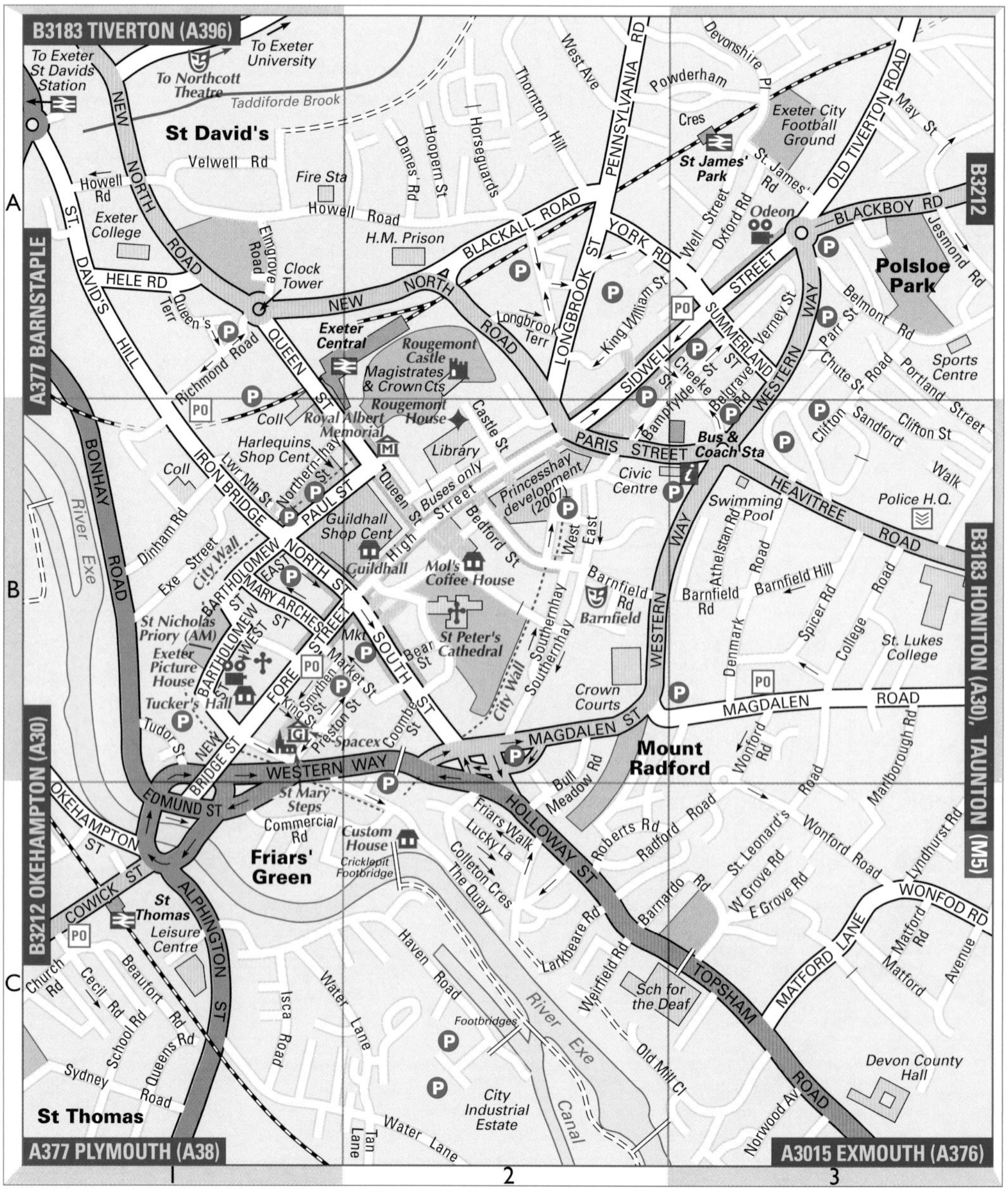

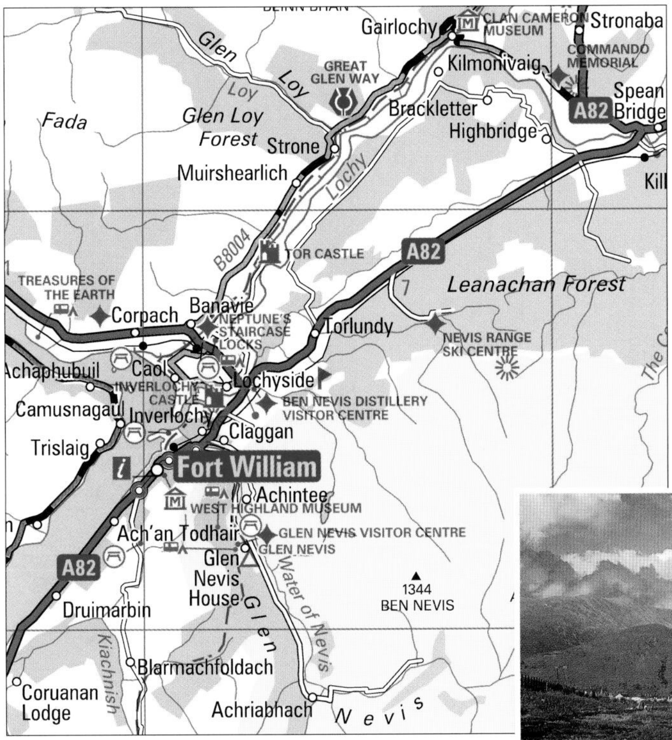

Fort William

A large town at the foot of Ben Nevis, Britain's highest mountain, in Scotland's scenic west Highlands, at the head of the Great Glen linking the Atlantic with the North Sea and accessible from London on a romantic sleeper train. Named after William of Orange's 18th-century military fort built for English Redcoat soldiers (of which the remains can be viewed), it is home to the West Highland Museum, Ben Nevis Distillery and two ruined castles, while nearby are Fort William Smelter & the Aluminium Story, the WWII Commando Memorial, the Clan Cameron Museum on the history of the Highlands and the Jacobite cause and Glen Roy National Nature Reserve, including the famous Parallel Roads glacial landform. There is reliable skiing and snowboarding in January, other outdoor sports year-round, and seal-spotting trips on Loch Linnhe.

►Ben Nevis from Corpach

Fort William Tourist Information Centre, Cameron Square, Fort William PH33 6AJ Tel 01397 703781

BBC Radio Scotland 93.7 FM and 810 AM • **Nevis Radio** 96.6 FM

www.visit-fortwilliam.co.uk

★Do not miss

- ★**Mountain Gondola**, Nevis Range
- ★**Treasures of the Earth**, Corpach – crystal, gemstone and fossil exhibition
- ★**West Highland Way** – long-distance footpath to Milngavie

Fort William

Abrach Rd A3
Achintore Rd C1
Alma Rd B2
Am Breun Chamas A2
Ambulance Station A3
An Aird A2
Argyll Rd C1
Argyll Terr C1
Bank St. B2
Belford Hospital B2
Belford Rd B2/B3
Black Parks A3
Braemore Pl C2
Bruce Pl C2
Bus Station B2
Camanachd Cr A3/B2
Cameron Rd. C1
Cameron Sq. B1
Carmichael Way . A2
Claggan Rd B3
Connochie Rd . . . C1
Cow Hill C3
Creag Dhubh A2
Croft Rd B3
Douglas Pl B2
Dudley Rd. B2
Dumbarton Rd. . . C1
Earl of Inverness Rd . . . A3
Fassifern Rd. B1
Fort William . . .B2
Fort William (Remains) ✦ B2
Glasdrum Rd C1
Glen Nevis Pl. B3
Gordon Sq B1
Grange Rd C1
Heather Croft Rd. C1
Henderson Row. . C2
High St B1
Highland Visitor Ctr B3
Hill Rd. B2
Hospital Belhaven Annexe B3
Information Ctr . A3
Inverlochy Ct A3
Kennedy Rd . . B2/C2
Library B2
Linnhe Rd. B1
Lochaber College A2
Lochaber Leisure Ctr. B3
Lochiel Rd A3
Lochy Rd A3
Lundavra Cres . . . C1
Lundavra Rd C1
Lundy Rd A3
Mamore Cr. B2
Mary St. B2
Middle St B1
Montrose Ave . . . A3
Moray Pl. C1
Morven Pl C2
Moss Rd B2
Nairn Cres C1
Nevis Bridge B3
Nevis Rd A3
Nevis Sports Ctr . A2
Nevis Terr. B2
North Rd. B3
Obelisk B2
Ocean Frontier Underwater Ctr. A2
Parade Rd B2
Police Station . . . A3/C1
Post Office . A3/B2
Ross Pl C1
St Andrews B2
Shaw Pl B2
Station Brae. B1
Studio B1
Treig Rd A3
Union Rd C1
Victoria Rd. B2
Wades Rd. A3
West Highland . .B2
Young Pl. B2

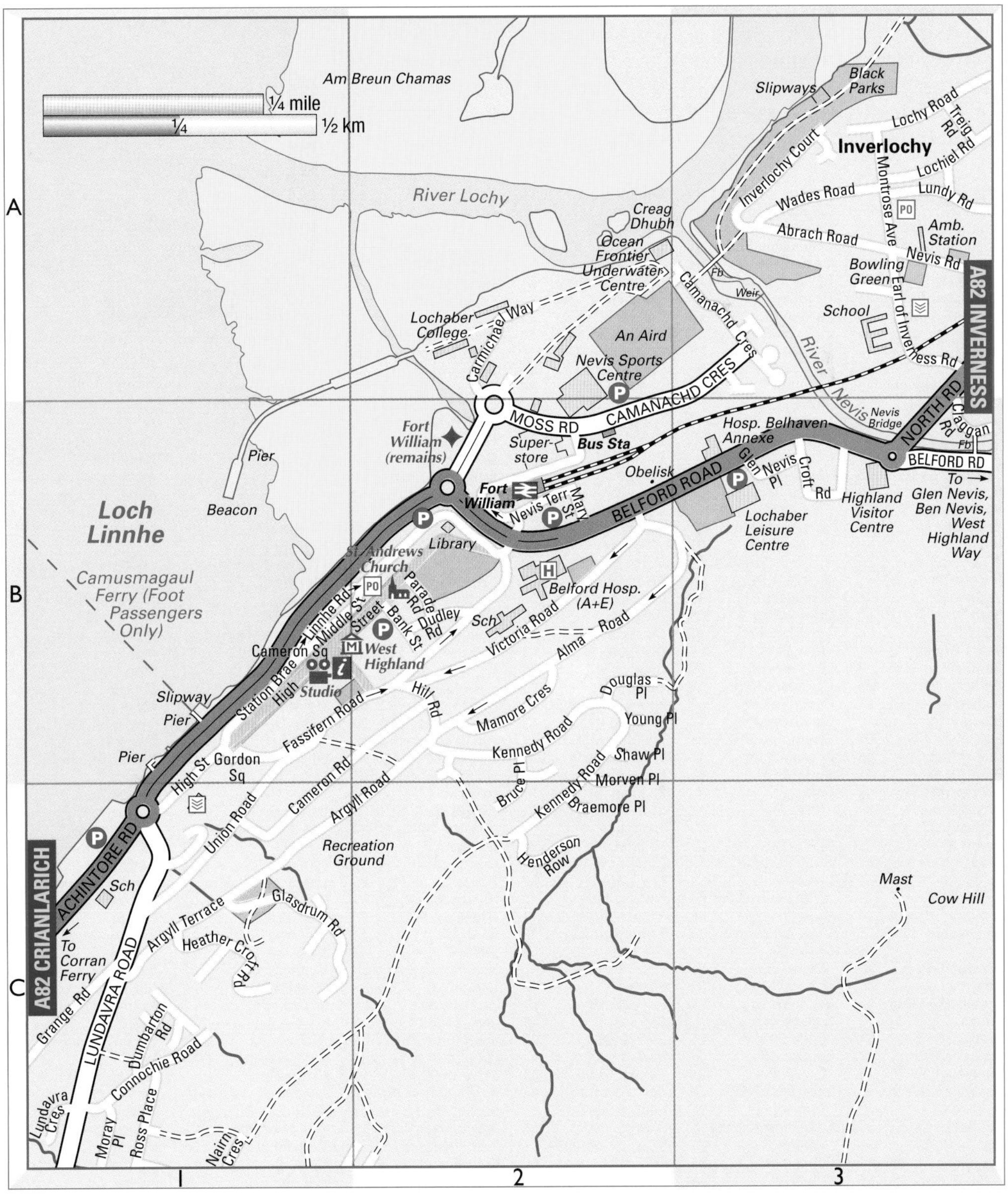

Glasgow

▲The River Clyde

★Do not miss

- ★**Burrell Collection**, Pollok Country Park (junction 1, M77 see approaches map) – art collection
- ★**Transport Museum**, Bunhouse Road, Kelvin Hall
- ★**Glasgow Gallery of Modern Art**, Royal Exchange Square
- ★**St Mungo's Museum of Religious Life and Art**, Castle Street

Scotland's largest city has a wealthy past and a great architectural and cultural heritage which is to be seen in the gold and red sandstone and the finest examples of Victorian architecture anywhere in the world. Glasgow is now a magnet for major investors, events, tourists and conference delegates worldwide. There is a wealth of choice for the visitor from museums and art galleries to great pubs and restaurants and a vibrant live music scene. The city is home to three universities, the Scottish Opera and Scottish Ballet. There are four centrally placed shopping centres Argyle Arcade, Princes Square, St Enoch Centre and Sauchiehall Street Centre and the famous Barras weekend market. Glasgow has 70 parks and gardens and is home to the two most successful Scottish football teams.

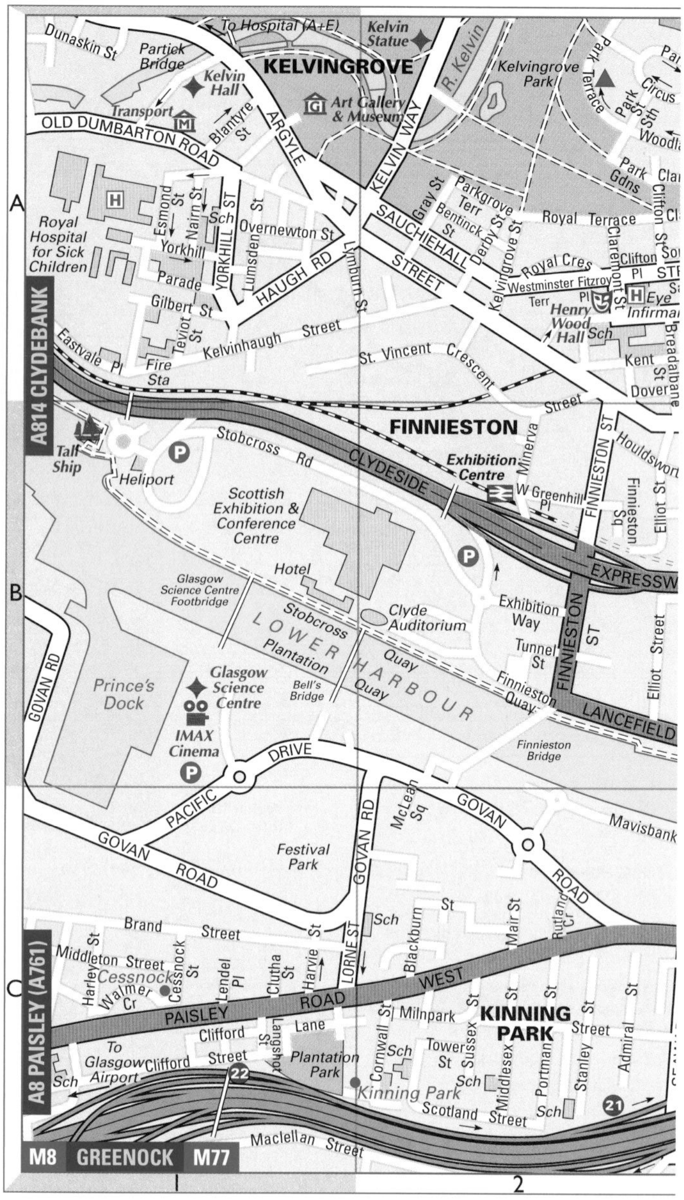

Glasgow

Admiral St C2
Albert Bridge C5
Albion St B5
Anderston Centre . B3
Anderston Quay . . B3
Anderston . . . B3
Arches B4
Argyle St A1/A2/B3/B4/B5
Argyle Street . . A3
Argyll Arcade B5
Arlington St A3
Art Gallery & Mus A1
Arts Centre B3
Ashley St A3
Bain St C6
Baird St A6
Baliol St A3
Ballater St C5
Barras, the (Market) C6
Bath St A3
Bell St C6
Bell's Bridge B1
Bentinck St A2
Berkeley St A3
Bishop La B3
Black St A6
Blackburn St C2
Blackfriars St B6
Blantyre St A1
Blythswood Sq . . A4
Blythswood St B4
Bothwell St B4
Brand St C1
Breadalbane St . . A2
Bridge St C4
Bridge St (Metro Station) . C4
Bridgegate C5
Briggait C5
Broomhill Park . . A6
Broomielaw B4
Broomielaw Quay Gdns B3
Brown St B4
Brunswick St B5
Buccleuch St A3
Buchanan Bus Stn A5
Buchanan Galleries A5
Buchanan St B5
Buchanan St (Metro Station) . . B5
Cadogan St B4
Caledonian Univ . A5
Calgary St A5
Cambridge St . . . A4
Campbell St B4
Canal St A5
Candleriggs B5
Carlton Pl C4
Carnarvon St A3
Carnoustie St C3
Carrick St B4
Castle St B6
Cathedral Sq B6
Cathedral St B5
Centre for Contemporary Arts A4
Centre St C4
Cessnock (Metro Station) . C1
Cessnock St C1
Charing Cross . A3
Charlotte St C6
Cheapside St B3
Citizens' C5
City Chambers Complex B5
City Halls B5
Clairmont Gdns . . A2
Claremont St A2
Claremont Terr . . A2
Claythorne St C6
Cleveland St A3
Clifford La C1
Clifford St C1
Clifton Pl A2
Clifton St A2
Clutha St C1
Clyde Auditorium . B2
Clyde Pl C4
Clyde Place Quay C4
Clyde St C5
Clyde Walkway . . C3
Clydeside Expressway B2
Coburg St C4
Cochrane St B5
College of Building C5
College of Commerce B5
College of Food Technology B5
College of Nautical Studies C5
College St B6
Collins St B6
Commerce St C4
Cook St C4
Cornwall St C2
Couper St A5
Cowcaddens (Metro Station) . A4
Cowcaddens Rd . A4
Crimea St B3
Custom House . C4
Custom House Quay Gdns C4
Dalhousie St A4
Dental Hospital A4
Derby St A2
Dobbie's Loan A4/A5
Dobbie's Loan Pl . A5
Dorset St A3
Douglas St B4
Doulton Fountain ✦ C6
Dover St A2
Drury St B4
Drygate B6
Duke St B6
Dunaskin St A1
Dunblane St A4
Dundas St B5
Dunlop St C5
East Campbell St C6
Eastvale Pl A1
Eglinton St C4
Elderslie St A3
Elliot St B2
Elmbank St A3
Esmond St A1
Exhibition Centre B2
Exhibition Way . . . B2
Eye Infirmary . . A2
Festival Park C1
Finnieston Bridge . B2
Finnieston Quay . . B2
Finnieston Sq B2
Finnieston St B2
Fitzroy Pl A2
Florence St C5
Fox St C5
Gallowgate C6
Garnet St A3
Garnethill St A4
Garscube Rd A4
George Sq B5
George St B5
George V Bridge . C4
Gilbert St A1
Glasgow Bridge . . C4
Cathedral † B6
Glasgow Central B4
Glasgow Film Theatre A4
Glasgow Green . . C6
Glasgow Science Ctr ✦ B1
Glasgow Science Ctr Footbridge B1
Glassford St B5
Glebe St A6
Gloucester St C3
Gorbals Cross . . . C5
Gorbals St C5
Gordon St B4
Govan Rd . B1/C1/C2
Grace St B3
Grafton Pl A5
Grant St A3
Granville St A3
Gray St A2
Greendyke St C6
Harley St C1
Harvie St C1
Haugh Rd A1
Heliport B1
Henry Wood Hall A2
High St B6
High Street . . . B6
Hill St A3
Holland St A3
Holm St B4
Hope St A5
Houldsworth St . . B2
Houston Pl C3
Houston St C3
Howard St C5
Hunter St B6
Hutcheson St B5
Hydepark St B3
IMAX B1
India St A3
Information Ctr . B5
Ingram St B5
Jamaica St B4
James Watt St B4
John Knox St B6
John St B5
Kelvin Hall ✦ A1
Kelvin Statue ✦ . . A2
Kelvin Way A2
Kelvingrove Park . A2
Kelvingrove St . . . A2
Kelvinhaugh St . . A1
Kennedy St A6
Kent Rd A2
Killermont St A5
King St B5
King's A3
Kingston Bridge . C3
Kingston St C4
Kinning Park (Metro Station) . C2
Kinning St C3
Kyle St A5
Laidlaw St C3
Lancefield Quay . . B2
Lancefield St B3
Langshot St C1
Lendel Pl C1
Lighthouse ✦ B4
Lister St A6
Little St B3
London Rd C6
Lorne St C1
Lower Harbour . . . B1
Lumsden St A1
Lymburn St A1
Lyndoch Cr A3
Lynedoch Pl A3
Lynedoch St A3
Maclellan St C1
Mair St C2
Maitland St A4
Mavisbank Gdns . C2
Mcalpine St B3
Mcaslin St A6
McLean Sq C2
McLellan Gallery A4
McPhater St A4
Merchants' House B5
Middlesex St C2
Middleton St C1
Midland St B4
Miller St B5
Millroad St C6
Milnpark St C2
Milton St A4
Minerva St A2
Mitchell Library . . A3
Mitchell St West . . B4
Mitchell A3
Modern Art Gallery B5
Moir St C6
Molendinar St . . . C6
Moncur St C6
Montieth Row . . . C6
Montrose St B5
Morrison St C3
Mosque C5
Museum of Religion B6
Nairn St A1
Nelson Mandela Sq B5
Nelson St C4
Nelson's Monument C6
New City Rd A4
Newton St A3
Newton Pl A3
Nicholson St C4
Nile St A5
Norfolk Court C4
Norfolk St C4
North Frederick St B5
North Hanover St . B5
North Portland St . B5
North St A3
North Wallace St . A5
Odeon C3
Old Dumbarton Rd A1
Osborne St . . . B5/C5
Oswald St B4
Overnewton St . . . A1
Oxford St C4
Pacific Dr B1
Paisley Rd C3
Paisley Rd West . C1
Park Circus A2
Park Gdns A2
Park St South . . . A2
Park Terr A2
Parkgrove Terr . . . A2
Parnie St C5
Parson St A6
Partick Bridge . . . A1
Passport Office . . A5
Paterson St C3
Pavilion A4
Pembroke St A3
People's Palace C6
Pinkston Rd A6
Piping Ctr, The ✦ . A5
Pitt St A4/B4
Plantation Park . . C1
Plantation Quay . . B1
Police Station . A4/A6/B5
Port Dundas Rd . . A5
Port St B2
Portman St C2
Prince's Dock B1
Princes Sq B5
Provand's Lordship B6
Queen St B5
Queen Street . . B5
Regimental Mus A3
Renfrew St . . . A3/A4
Renton St A5
Richmond St B5
Robertson St B4
Rose St A4
Rottenrow B5
Royal Concert Hall A5
Royal Cr A2
Royal Exchange Sq B5
Royal Hospital For Sick Children . A1
Royal Infirmary . B6
Royal Scottish Academy of Music & Drama . A4
Royal Terr A2
Rutland Cr C2
St Kent St C6
St Andrew's (R.C.) † C5
St Andrew's . . . C6
St Andrew's St . . . C5
St Enoch (Metro Station) . . B5
St Enoch Shopping Centre B5
St Enoch Sq B4
St George's Rd . . A3
St James Rd B6
St Mungo Ave A5/A6
St Mungo Pl A6
St Vincent Cr A2
St Vincent Pl B5
St Vincent St . . B3/B4
St Vincent Street Church B4
St Vincent Terr B3
Saltmarket C5
Sandyford Pl A3
Sauchiehall St A2/A4
School of Art A4
Scotland St . . C2/C3
Scott St A4
Scottish Exhibition & Conference Ctr . B1
Scottish Television A5
Seaward St C2
Shaftesbury St B3
Sheriff Court C5
Shields Rd C3
Shields Rd (Metro Station) . C3
Shuttle St B6
Somerset Pl A2
Springburn Rd . . . A6
Springfield Quay . C3
Stanley St C2
Stevenson St C6
Stewart St A4

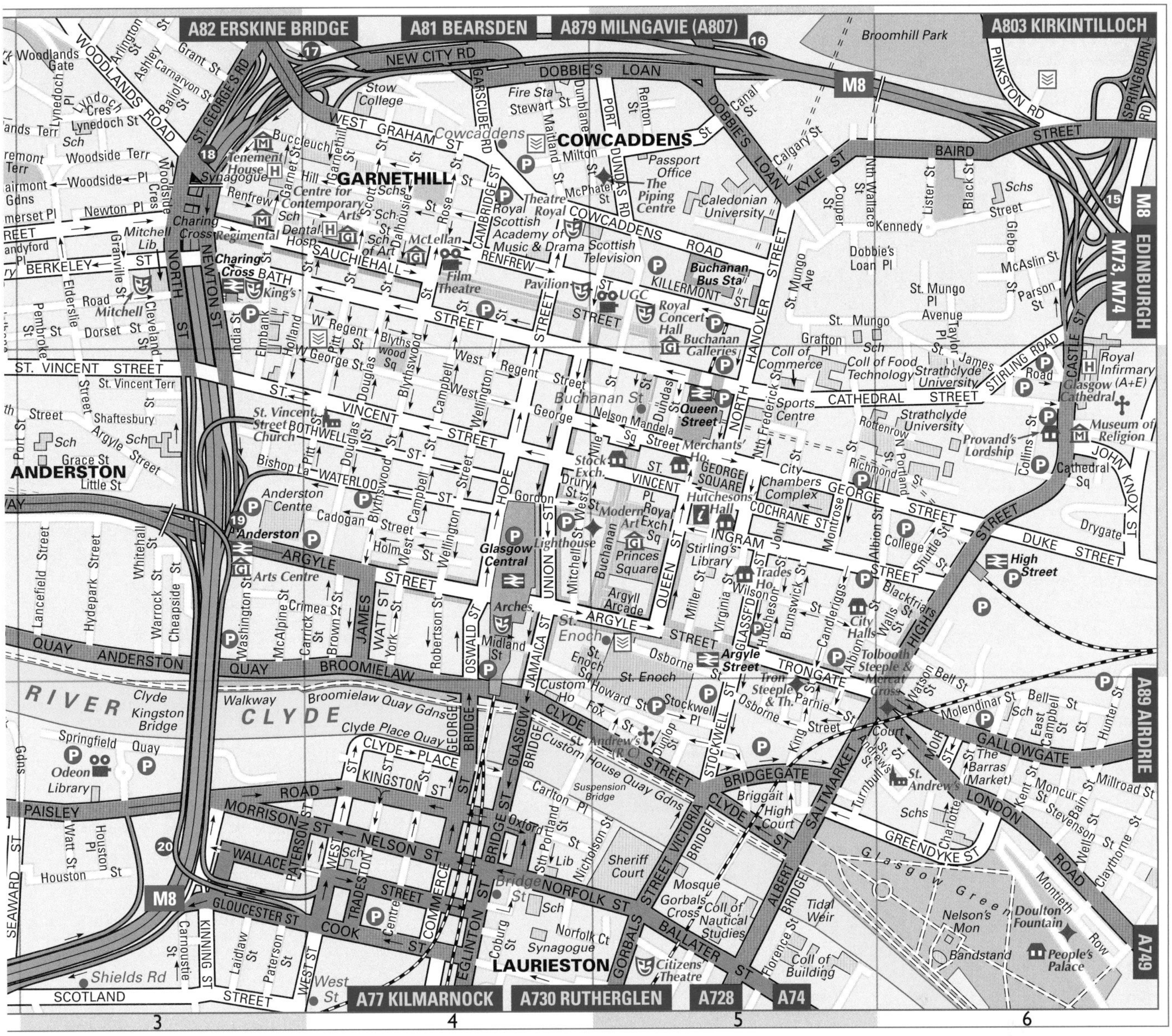

Sth Portland St . . C4	Victoria Bridge . . C5
Stirling Rd B6	Virginia St B5
Stirling's Library . . B5	West Greenhill Pl . B2
Stobcross Quay . . . B1	West Regent St . . A4
Stobcross Rd B1	Wallace St C3
Stock Exchange 🏛 B5	Walls St B6
Stockwell Pl. C5	Walmer Cr C1
Stockwell St. B5	Warrock St. B3
Stow College A4	Washington St. . . . B3
Strathclyde Univ . . B6	Waterloo St B4
Sussex St C2	Watson St. B6
Synagogues . . A3/C4	Watt St C3
Tall Ship B1	Well St C6
Taylor Pl. A6	Wellington St. B4
Tenement House 🏛 A3	West George St. . . B4
Teviot St. A1	West Graham St . A4
Theatre Royal . . A3	West Regent St . . . B4
Tolbooth Steeple & Mercat Cross ✦ . C6	West St. C4
Tower St. C2	West St (Metro Station). C4
Trades House 🏛 . . B5	Westminster Terr. A2
Tradeston St C4	Whitehall St. B3
Transport Mus 🏛 . A1	Wilson St B5
Tron Steeple & Theatre C5	Woodlands Gate . A3
Trongate. B5	Woodlands Rd . . . A3
Tunnel St B2	Woodlands Terr . . . A2
Turnbull St. C5	Woodside Cr A3
UGC A5	Woodside Pl A3
Union St. B4	Woodside Terr . . . A3
	York St West B4
	Yorkhill Pde A1
	Yorkhill St A1

Greater Glasgow and Clyde Valley Tourist Board, 11 George Square, Glasgow G2 1DY Tel 0141 204 4400

BBC Radio Scotland 93.1 FM and 810 AM • **Beat** 106.1 FM **Clyde 1** 102.5 FM • **Clyde 2** 1152 AM **Real Radio** 100.3 FM

www.seeglasgow.com

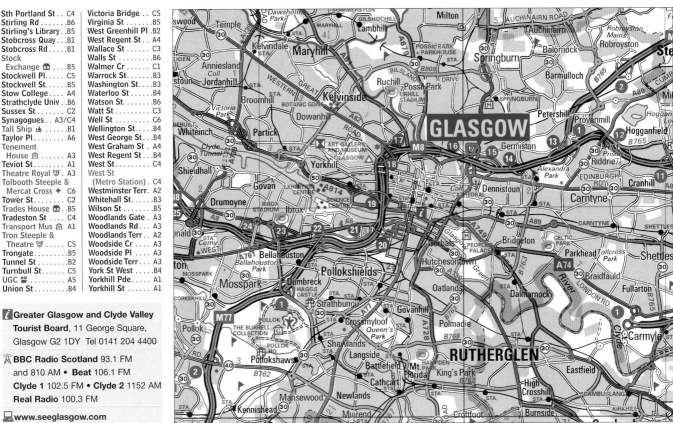

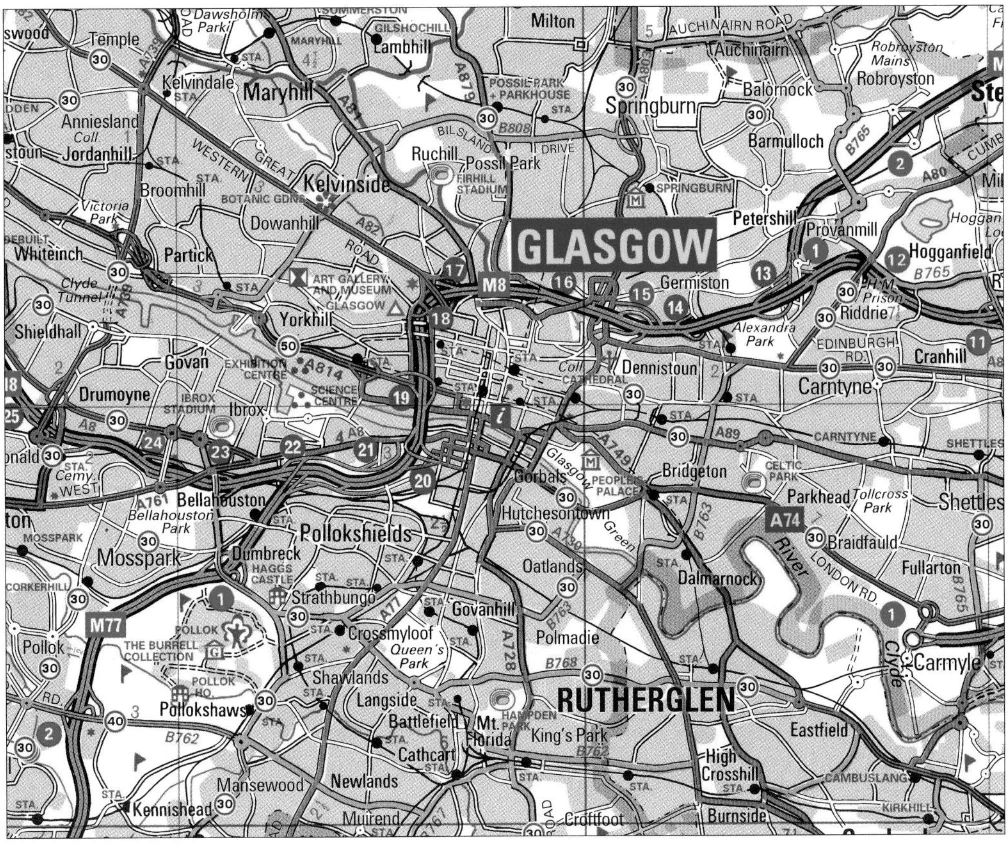

Gloucester

A city that grew on the site of an important Roman fortress; Edward the Confessor and William the Conqueror held Christmas parliaments here, and Elizabeth I made it Britain's most inland port in 1580. The docks now house various attractions amidst the Victorian warehouses, including the Soldiers of Gloucestershire Museum, the ruins of the Augustinian Llanthony Secunda medieval priory, boat trips, a 5-floor antiques centre, and bars, cafés and restaurants. The city's history is charted in the City Museum & Art Gallery, while the splendid cathedral, founded as an abbey church 1,300 years ago, has a Norman nave the country's most complete medieval cloisters, and the tomb of Edward II. Child-friendly attractions include St James City Farm and the Barn Owl Centre, and nearby are Robinswood Hill Country Park & Rare Breeds Centre on the edge of the Cotswolds, the working Prinknash Abbey, with a pottery, farm and bird park, English Heritage's Great Witcombe Roman Villa, and the Nature in Art museum.

▲Gloucester Cathedral

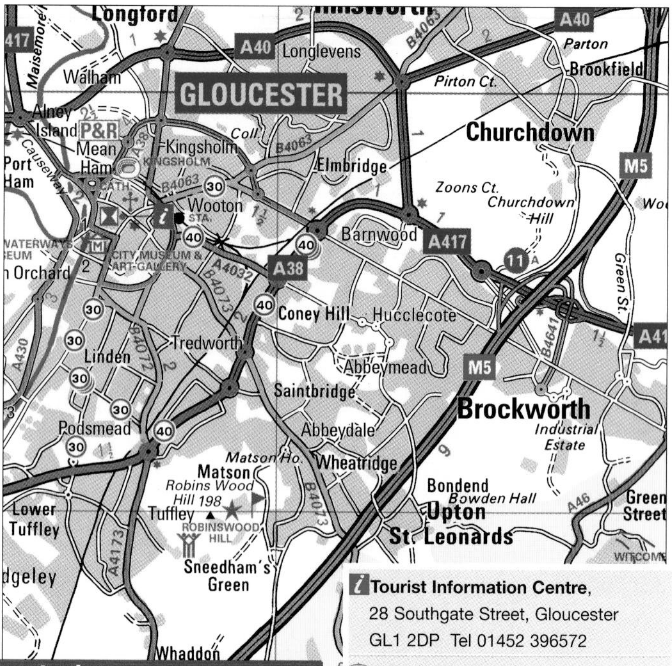

★Do not miss

★**Gloucester Folk Museum**, Westgate Street

★**Historic Gloucester Docks & National Waterways Museum**, the Docks

★**New Inn**, Northgate Street – Britain's finest surviving medieval galleried courtyard inn

Tourist Information Centre, 28 Southgate Street, Gloucester GL1 2DP Tel 01452 396572

BBC Radio Gloucestershire 104.7 FM • **Classic Gold** 774 AM, **Severn Sound** 102.4, 103.0 FM

www.glos-city.gov.uk

¼ mile
¼ ½ km

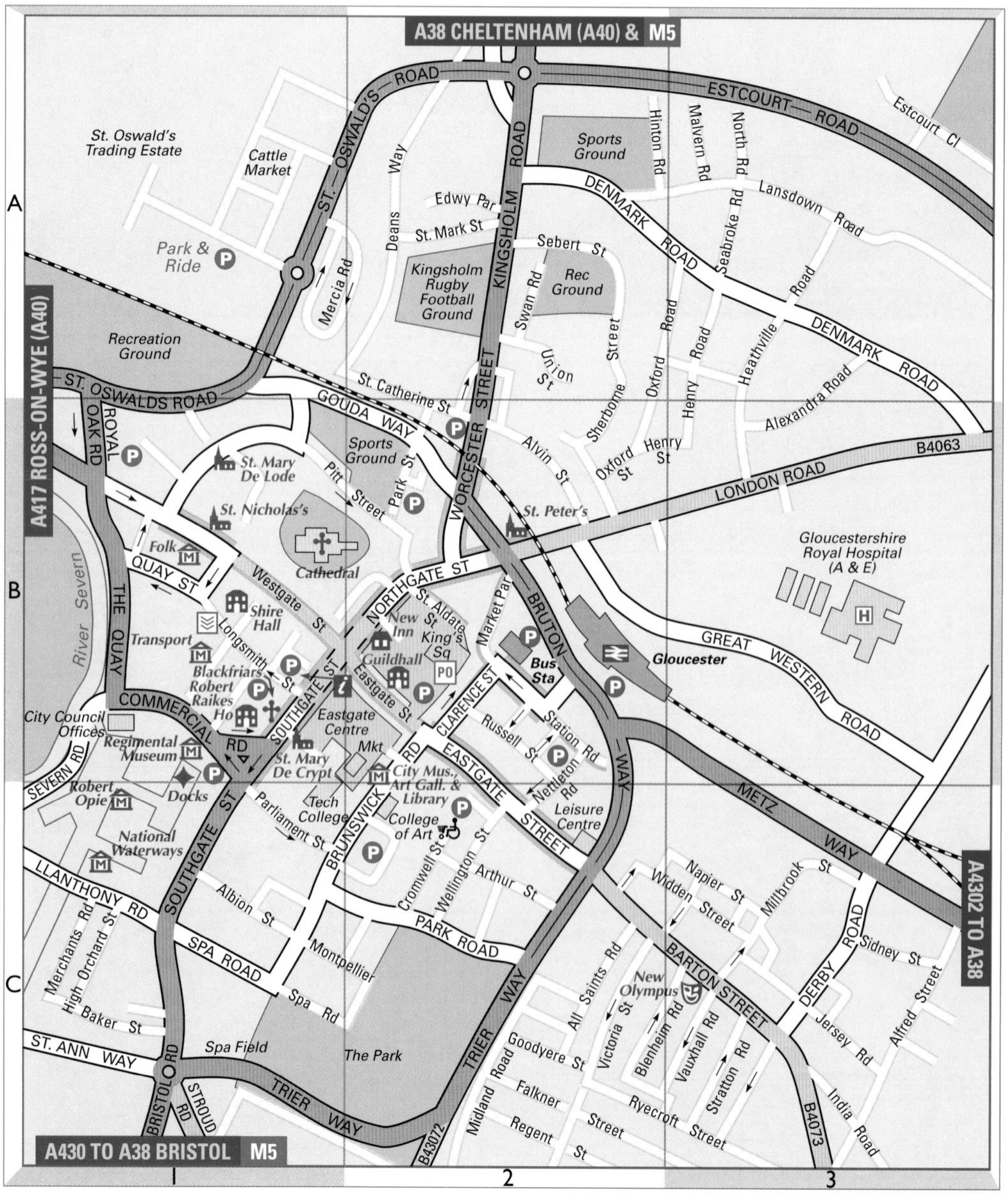

Gloucester

Albion St C1
Alexandra Rd B3
Alfred St C3
All Saints Rd C2
Alvin St B2
Arthur St C2
Baker St C1
Barton St C2
Blackfriars ✝ B1
Blenheim Rd C2
Bristol Rd C1
Brunswick Rd C2
Bruton Way B2
Bus Station B2
Cattle Market A1
City Council Offices B1
City Museum, Art Gallery & Library B2
Clarence St B2
College of Art C2
Commercial Rd B1
Cromwell St C2
Deans Way A2
Denmark Rd A3
Derby Rd C3
Docks ✦ C1
Eastgate Centre B1
Eastgate St B2
Edwy Pde A2
Estcourt Cl A3
Estcourt Rd A3
Falkner St C2
Folk Museum B1
Cathedral ✝ B1
Gloucester B2
Gloucestershire Royal Hospital (A&E) B3
Goodyere St C2
Gouda Way A1
Great Western Rd B3
Guildhall B2
Heathville Rd A3
Henry Rd B3
Henry St B2
High Orchard St C1
Hinton Rd A2
India Rd C3
Information Ctr B1
Jersey Rd C3
King's Sq B2
Kingsholm Rd A2
Kingsholm Rugby Football Ground A2
Lansdown Rd A3
Leisure Centre C2
Llanthony Rd C1
London Rd B3
Longsmith St B1
Malvern Rd A3
Market Pde B2
Merchants Rd C1
Mercia Rd A1
Metz Way C3
Midland Rd C2
Millbrook St C3
Market B2
Montpellier C1
Napier St C3
National Waterways C1
Nettleton Rd C2
New Inn B2
New Olympus C3
North Rd A3
Northgate St B2
Oxford Rd A2
Oxford St B2
Park & Ride Gloucester A1
Park Rd C2
Park St B2
Parliament St C1
Pitt St B1
Police Station B1
Post Office B2
Quay St B1
Recreation Ground A1/A2
Regent St C2
Regimental B1
Robert Opie C1
Robert Raikes House B1
Royal Oak Rd B1
Russell St B2
Ryecroft St C2
St Aldate St B2
St Ann Way C1
St Catherine St A2
St Mark St A2
St Mary De Crypt B1
St Mary De Lode B1
St Nicholas's B1
St Oswald's Rd A1
St Oswald's Trading Estate A1
St Peter's B2
Seabroke Rd A3
Sebert St A2
Severn Rd C1
Sherborne St B2
Shire Hall B1
Sidney St C3
Southgate St B1/C1
Spa Field C1
Spa Rd C1
Sports Ground A2/B2
Station Rd B2
Stratton Rd C3
Stroud Rd C1
Swan Rd A2
Technical College C1
The Park C2
The Quay B1
Transport B1
Trier Way C1/C2
Union St A1
Vauxhall Rd C3
Victoria St C2
Wellington St C2
Westgate St B1
Widden St C2
Worcester St B2

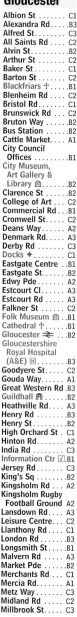

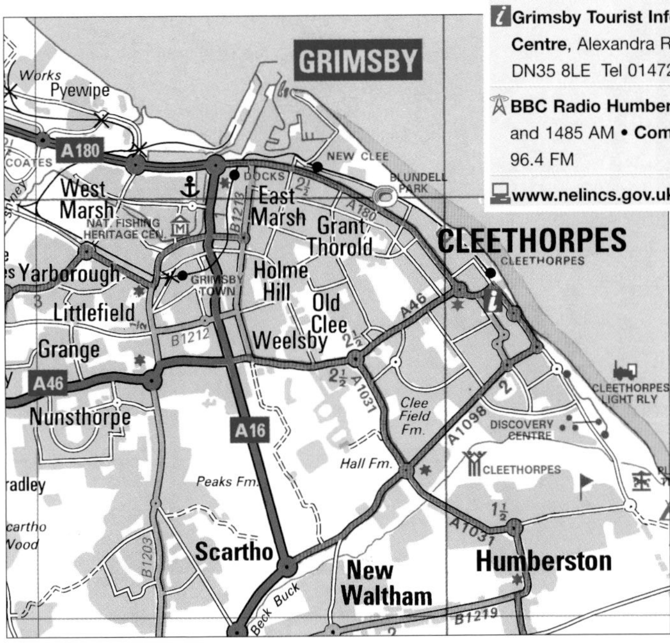

Grimsby Tourist Information Centre, Alexandra Rd, Cleethorpes DN35 8LE Tel 01472 323222

BBC Radio Humberside 95.9 FM and 1485 AM • **Compass FM** 96.4 FM

www.nelincs.gov.uk

▲The Docktower

Grimsby

A North East Lincolnshire coastal town that was the world's largest port during the 1950s. The impressive 19th-century buildings include the 350ft landmark Dock Tower, and resort attractions include the Cleethorpes Coast Light Railway; Cleethorpes Boating Lake; Cleethorpes Country Park; Pleasure Island Theme Park, with both traditional and hi-tech rides; the Deep Sea Experience aquarium; and the Time Trap museum of local history in the old jail cells beneath the town hall. Trips can be taken around the Humber Estuary on a full working trawler, beginning at the fish docks and taking in Spurn Head lighthouse and the Humber forts. Within easy reach are the working 19th-century 6-sailed Waltham Windmill and the Lincolnshire Wolds Area of Outstanding Natural Beauty.

★Do not miss

★**National Fishing Heritage Centre**, Alexandra Dock
★**Humber Estuary Discovery Centre**, Boating Lake, Kings Road, Cleethorpes
★**The Jungle** Lakeside, Kings Road, Cleethorpes – exotic animal and plant centre and animal rescue unit

Grimsby

Abbey Drive East. C2
Abbey Drive West C2
Abbey Park Rd... C2
Abbey Rd C2
Abbey Walk C2
Abbotsway C2
Adam Smith St A1/A2
Ainslie St C2
Albert St........ A3
Alexandra Rd. A2/B2
Annesley St A2
Armstrong St.... A1
Arthur St B1
Augusta St...... C1
Bargate......... C1
Beeson St....... A1
Bethlehem St.... C2
Bodiam Way......B3
Bradley St B3
Brighowgate . C1/C2
Bus Station C2
Canterbury Dr ... C1
Cartergate ... B1/C1
Catherine St C3
Caxton A3
Chantry La B1
Charlton St A1
Church La....... C2
Church St....... A3
Cleethorpe Rd... A3
College......... A3
College St C1
Compton Dr..... C1
Corporation Bridge......... A2
Corporation Rd .. A1
Court.............B3
Crescent St B1
Deansgate C1
Doughty Rd C2
Dover St.........B1
Duchess St...... C2
Dudley St C1
Duke of York Gdns B1
Duncombe St.....B3
Earl La B1
East Marsh St B3
East St B2
Eastgate B3
Eastside Rd A3
Eaton Ct C1
Eleanor St B3
Ellis Way.........B3
Fisherman's Chapel A3
Fisherman's Wharf B2
Fishing Heritage Centre B2
Flour Sq A3
Frederick St......B1
Frederick Ward Way............B2
Freeman St .. A3/B3
Freshney Dr......B1
Freshney Pl B2
Garden St....... C2
Garibaldi St A3
Garth La B2
Grime St.........B3
Grimsby Docks A3
Grimsby Town C2
Hainton Ave..... C3
Har Way B3
Hare St......... C3
Harrison St B1
Haven Ave B1
Hay Croft Ave B1
Hay Croft St......B1
Heneage Rd .. B3/C3
Henry St B1
Holme St B3
Hume St........ C1
James St B1
Joseph St........B1
Kent St A3
King Edward St.. A3
Lambert Rd C2
Library B2
Lime St..........B1
Lister St B1
Littlefield La C1
Lockhill......... A3
Lord St B1
Ludford St C3
Macaulay St......B1
Mallard Mews ... C3
Manor Ave C2
Market A3
Market Hall B2
Market St B3
Moss Rd C2
Nelson St A3
New St B2
Osbourne St......B2
Pasture St B3
Peaks Parkway .. C3
Pelham Rd C1
Police Station ... A3/B2
Post Office . B1/B2/B3/C2/C3
PS Lincoln Castle B2
Pyewipe Rd A1
Railway Pl A3
Railway St A3
Rendel St A2
Retail Park...... A2
Retail Park.......B3
Richard St B1
Ripon St B1
Robinson St East. .B3
Royal St A3
St Hilda's Ave ... C1
St James C2
Sheepfold St . B3/C3
Sixhills St....... C3
South Park.......B2
Spring St A3
Superstore.......B3
Tasburgh St C3
Tennyson St......B2
The Close....... C1
Thesiger St A3
Time Trap C2
Town Hall B2
Veal St B1
Victoria St North. A2
Victoria St South. .B2
Victoria St West ..B2
Watkin St A1
Welholme Ave ... C2
Welholme Museum & Gallery C3
Welholme Rd.... C3
Wellington St.....B3
Wellowgate C2
Werneth Rd B3
West Coates Rd.. A1
Westgate A2
Westminster Dr.. C1
Willingham St ... C3
Wintringham Rd . C2
Wood St B3
Yarborough Dr....B1
Yarborough Hotel C2

¼ mile
¼ ½ km

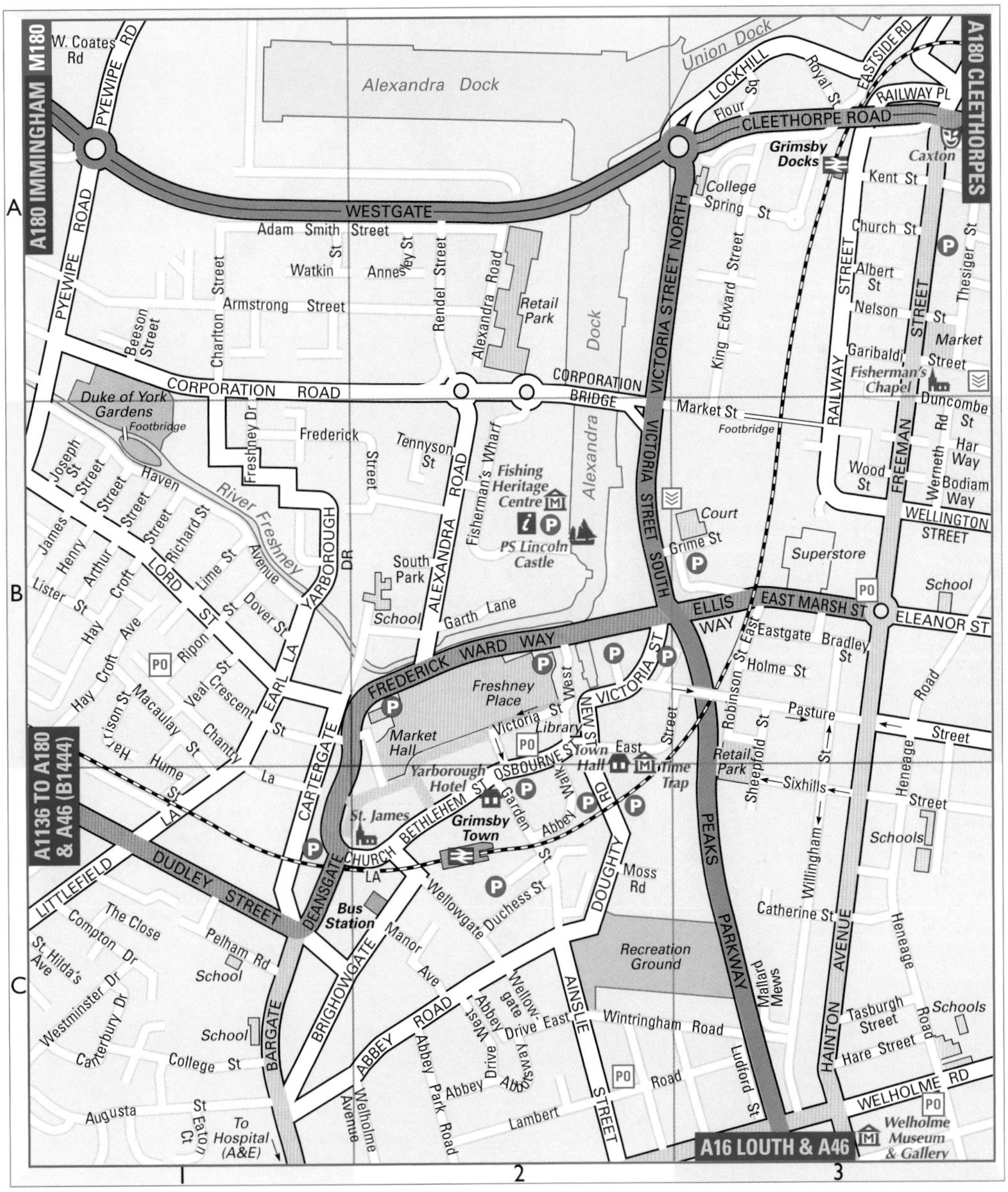

Hanley

▲Hanley town hall

Hanley is the city centre of Stoke-on-Trent, a city made up of six towns known collectively as The Potteries. The city is thus named as it is home to a host of world-renowned pottery manufacturers such as Aynsley, Portmeirion, Royal Doulton, Spode and Wedgwood. There are visitor centres, ceramic museums, and factory shops where you can buy direct from source. For your shopping requirements there is The Potteries Shopping Centre as well as two markets, one indoor and one outdoor. Hanley is very popular with the students of Staffordshire University who make good use of the theatres, pubs and restaurants in the Cultural Quarter, right in the centre of the town.

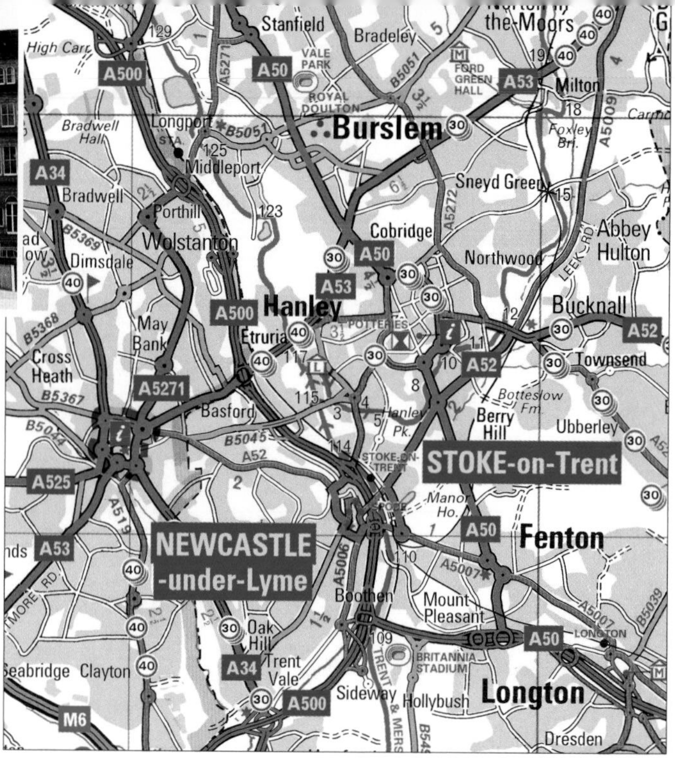

Stoke-on-Trent Tourist Information Centre, Victoria Hall, Cultural Quarter, Stoke-on-Trent City Centre ST1 3AD
Tel 01782 236000

BBC Radio Stoke 94.6 FM • **Signal 1** 102.6 FM • **Signal 2** 1170 AM

www.visitstoke.co.uk

★Do not miss

★**The Potteries Museum and Art Gallery**, Bethesda Street

★**The Dudson Museum**, Hope Street – 200 year old ceramics company museum housed in a Grade II listed bottle oven

Hanley

Acton St . . . A3
Albion St . . . B2
Argyle St . . . C1
Ashbourne Gr . . . A2
Avoca St . . . A3
Baskerville Rd . . . B3
Bedford Rd . . . C1
Bedford St . . . C1
Bethesda St . . . B2
Bexley St . . . A2
Birches Head Rd . A3
Botteslow St . . . C3
Boundary St . . . A2
Broad St . . . C2
Broom St . . . A3
Bryan St . . . A2
Bucknall New Rd . B3
Bucknall Old Rd . . B3
Bus Station . . . B3
Cannon St . . . C2
Castlefield St . . . C1
Hanley Park . . . C2
Cavendish St . . . B1
Central Forest Pk A2
Charles St . . . B3
Cheapside . . . B2
Chell St . . . A3
Clarke St . . . C1
Cleveland Rd . . . C2
Clifford St . . . C3
Clough St . . . B2
Clyde St . . . C1
College Rd . . . C2
Cooper St . . . C2
Corbridge Rd . . . A1
Cutts St . . . C2
Davis St . . . C1
Denbigh St . . . A1
Derby St . . . C3
Dilke St . . . A3
Dundas St . . . A3
Dundee Rd . . . C1
Dyke St . . . B3
Eastwood Rd . . . C3
Eaton St . . . A3
Etruria Park . . . B1
Etruria Rd . . . B1
Etruria Vale Rd . . C1
Festing St . . . A3
Fire Station . . . C2
Foundry St . . . B2
Franklyn St . . . C3
Garnet St . . . B1
Garth St . . . B3
George St . . . A3
Gilman St . . . B3
Glass St . . . B3
Goodson St . . . B3
Greyhound Way . . A1
Grove Pl . . . C1
Hampton St . . . C3
Hanley Park . . . C2
Harding Rd . . . C2
Hassall St . . . B3
Havelock Pl . . . C1
Hazlehurst St . . . C3
Hinde St . . . C2
Hope St . . . B2
Houghton St . . . C2
Hulton St . . . A3
Hypermarket . A1/B2
Information Ctr . B3
Jasper St . . . C2
Jervis St . . . A3
John Bright St . . A3
John St . . . B2
Keelings Rd . . . A3
Kimberley Rd . . . C1
Ladysmith Rd . . . C1
Lawrence St . . . C2
Leek Rd . . . C3
Library . . . C2
Lichfield St . . . C3
Linfield Rd . . . B3
Loftus St . . . A2
Lower Bedford St C1
Lower Bryan St . . A2
Lower Mayer St . . A3
Lowther St . . . A1
Magistrates Court . . . C2
Malham St . . . A2
Marsh St . . . B2
Matlock St . . . C3
Mayer St . . . A3
Milton St . . . C1
Mitchell Memorial Theatre . . . B2
Morley St . . . B2
Moston St . . . A3
Mount Pleasant . . C1
Mulgrave St . . . A1
Mynors St . . . B3
Nelson Pl . . . B3
New Century St . . B1
New Forest Industrial Estate A3
Octagon, The Shopping Park . . B1
Ogden Rd . . . C3
Old Hall St . . . B3
Old Town Rd . . . A3
Pall Mall . . . B2
Palmerston St . . . C3
Park and Ride . . . C2
Parker St . . . B2
Pavilion Dr . . . A1
Pelham St . . . C3
Percy St . . . B2
Piccadilly . . . B2
Picton St . . . B3
Plough St . . . A3
Police Station . . C2
Portland St . . . A1
Post Office . A3/B3/C3
Potteries Museum & Art Gallery . B2
Potteries Shopping Centre . . . B2
Potteries Way . . . C2
Powell St . . . A1
Pretoria Rd . . . C1
Quadrant Rd . . . B2
Ranelagh St . . . C2
Raymond St . . . C2
Rectory Rd . . . C1
Regent Rd . . . C2
Regent Theatre . . . B2
Richmond Terr . . . C2
Ridgehouse Dr . . A1
Robson St . . . C2
St Ann St . . . B3
St Luke St . . . B3
Sampson St . . . B2
Shaw St . . . A1
Sheaf St . . . C2
Shearer St . . . C1
Shelton New Rd . C1
Shirley Rd . . . C2
Slippery La . . . B2
Snow Hill . . . C2
Sports Stadium . . A1
Spur St . . . C3
Stafford St . . . B2
Statham St . . . B2
Stubbs La . . . C3
Sun St . . . C1
Talbot St . . . C3
The Parkway . . . C2
Town Hall . . . B2
Town Rd . . . A3
Trinity St . . . B2
Union St . . . A2
Upper Hillchurch St . . A3
Upper Huntbach St . . . B3
Victoria Hall Theatre . . . B3
Warner St . . . C2
Warwick St . . . C1
Waterloo Rd . . . A1
Waterloo St . . . B3
Well St . . . B3
Wellesley St . . . C2
Wellington Rd . . . B3
Wellington St . . . B3
Whitehaven Dr . . A2
Whitmore St . . . C1
Windermere St . . A1
Woodall St . . . A1
Yates St . . . C2
York St . . . A2

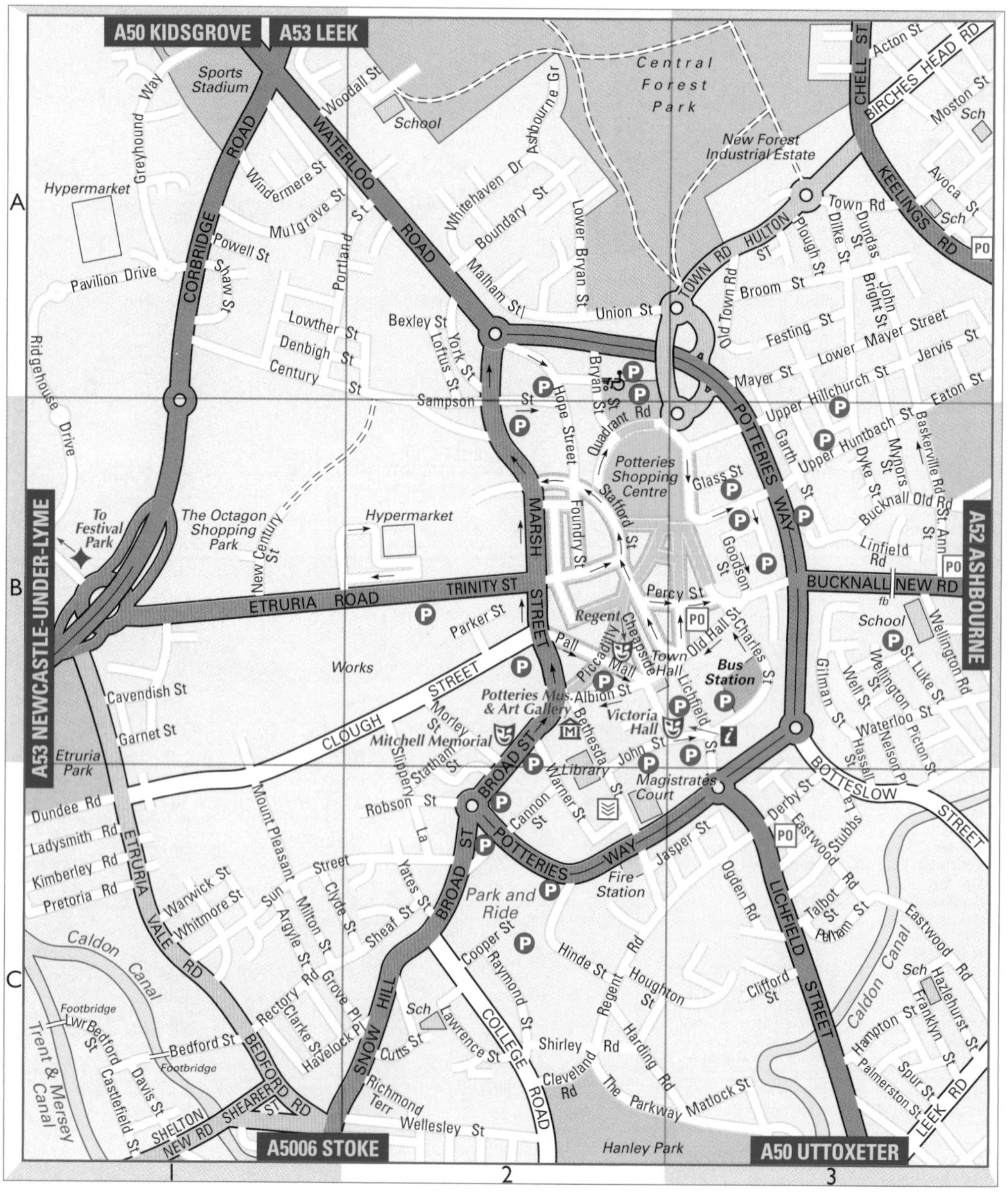

¼ mile
¼ ½ km

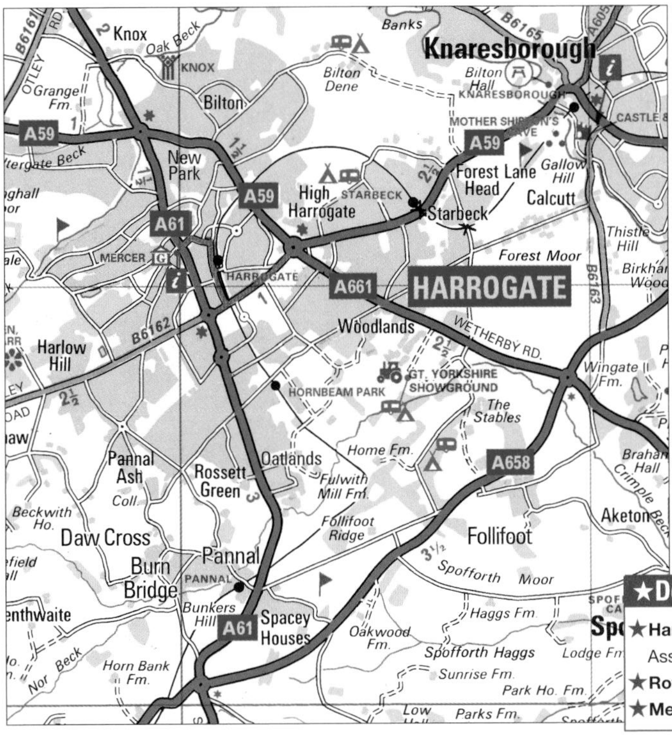

Harrogate

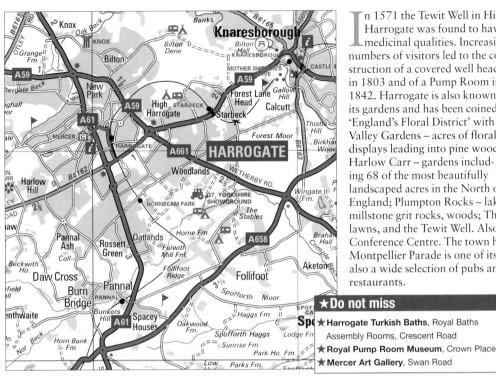

In 1571 the Tewit Well in High Harrogate was found to have medicinal qualities. Increasing numbers of visitors led to the construction of a covered well head in 1803 and of a Pump Room in 1842. Harrogate is also known for its gardens and has been coined 'England's Floral District' with Valley Gardens – acres of floral displays leading into pine woods; Harlow Carr – gardens including 68 of the most beautifully landscaped acres in the North of England; Plumpton Rocks – lake, millstone grit rocks, woods; The Stray – over 200 acres of resplendent lawns, and the Tewit Well. Also home to the Harrogate International Conference Centre. The town has a reputation for affluence and Montpellier Parade is one of its exclusive shopping streets, there is also a wide selection of pubs and restaurants.

▲ The Royal Pump Room

★Do not miss

- ★**Harrogate Turkish Baths**, Royal Baths Assembly Rooms, Crescent Road
- ★**Royal Pump Room Museum**, Crown Place
- ★**Mercer Art Gallery**, Swan Road

Tourist Information Centre, Royal Baths, Crescent Road, Harrogate HG1 2RR Tel 01423 537300

BBC Radio York 104.3 FM
Stray FM 97.2 FM

www.harrogate.gov.uk

Harrogate

Albert St C2
Alexandra Rd B2
Arthington Ave . . .B2
Ashfield Rd A2
Back Cheltenham Mount B2
Beech Grove C1
Belmont Rd C1
Bilton Dr. A2
Bower Rd B2
Bower St B2
Bus Station B2
Cambridge Rd B2
Cambridge St B2
Chatsworth Pl . . . A2
Chatsworth Grove A2
Chatsworth Rd. . . A2
Chelmsford Rd . . .B3
Cheltenham Cr . . .B2
Cheltenham Mt . . .B2
Cheltenham Pde . .B2
Christ Church . . .B3
Christ Church Oval. B3
Chudleigh Rd. B3
Clarence Dr B1
Claro Rd A3
Claro Way. A3
Coach Park B2
Coach Rd B3
Cold Bath Rd C1
Commercial St . . .B2
Coppice Ave A1
Coppice Dr A1
Coppice Gate . . . A1
Cornwall Rd B1
Crescent Gdns . . .B1
Crescent Rd B1
Dawson Terr A2
Devonshire Pl B3
Diamond Mews. . C1
Dixon Rd A2
Dixon Terr A2
Dragon Ave B3
Dragon Parade . . .B2
Dragon Rd. B2
Duchy Rd. B1
East Parade. B2
East Park Rd C3
Esplanade B1
Fire Station A2
Franklin Mount. . . A2
Franklin Rd B2
Franklin Square . . A2
Glebe Rd C1
Grove Park Ct . . . A3
Grove Park Terr . . A3
Grove Rd A2
Hampswaite Rd . . A1
Harcourt Dr. B3
Harcourt Rd B3
Harrogate International Ctr .B1
Harrogate Ladies College. B1
Harrogate ⇌ B2
Harrogate B2
Heywood Rd C1
Hollins Cr A1
Hollins Mews . . . A1
Hollins Rd A1
Homestead Rd . . C3
Hydro Leisure Centre, The A1
Information Ctr B1
James St B2
Jenny Field Dr . . A1
John St B2
Kent Dr A1
Kent Rd A1
Kings Rd A2
Kingsway. B3
Kingsway Dr B3
Lancaster Rd. . . . C1
Leeds Rd C2
Library C2
Lime Grove B3
Lime St A3
Mayfield Grove . . .B2
Mayfield Pl A2
Mercer B1
Montpellier Hill . .B1
Mornington Cr . . A3
Mornington Terr . .B3
Mowbray Sq B3
North Park Rd. . . .B3
Nydd Vale Rd B2
Oakdale Ave. A1
Oatlands Dr C3
Odeon B2
Osborne Rd A2
Otley Rd C2
Oxford St B2
Park Chase. B3
Park Parade. B3
Park View B2
Parliament St B1
Police Station . .B3
Post Office A2/B2/B3/C1
Providence Terr. . A2
Queen Parade . . . C3
Queen's Rd C1
Raglan St C2
Regent Ave. A3
Regent Grove. . . . A3
Regent Parade . . A3
Regent St A3
Regent Terr A3
Rippon Rd A1
Robert St C2
Royal Baths & Turkish Baths .B1
Royal Pump Room B1
St Luke's Mount . A2
St Mary's Ave. . . . C1
St Mary's Walk . . C1
Scargill Rd A1
Skipton Rd A3
Skipton St A2
Slingsby Walk . . . C3
South Park Rd. . . C2
Spring Grove A1
Springfield Ave . . .B1
Station Ave B2
Station Parade . . .B2
Strawberry Dale . .B2
Stray Rein C3
Studley Rd A2
Swan Rd. B1
The Parade B2
The Stray or Two Hundred Acre . . C3
Tower St. C2
Trinity Rd C2
Union St. B2
Valley Dr. C1
Valley Gdns C1
Valley Mount C1
Victoria Ave C2
Victoria Rd. C1
Victoria Shopping Centre. B2
Waterloo St A2
West Park. C2
West Park St C2
Wood View A1
Woodfield Ave . . . A3
Woodfield Dr A3
Woodfield Grove . A3
Woodfield Rd. . . . A3
Woodside B3
York Pl C3
York Rd. B1

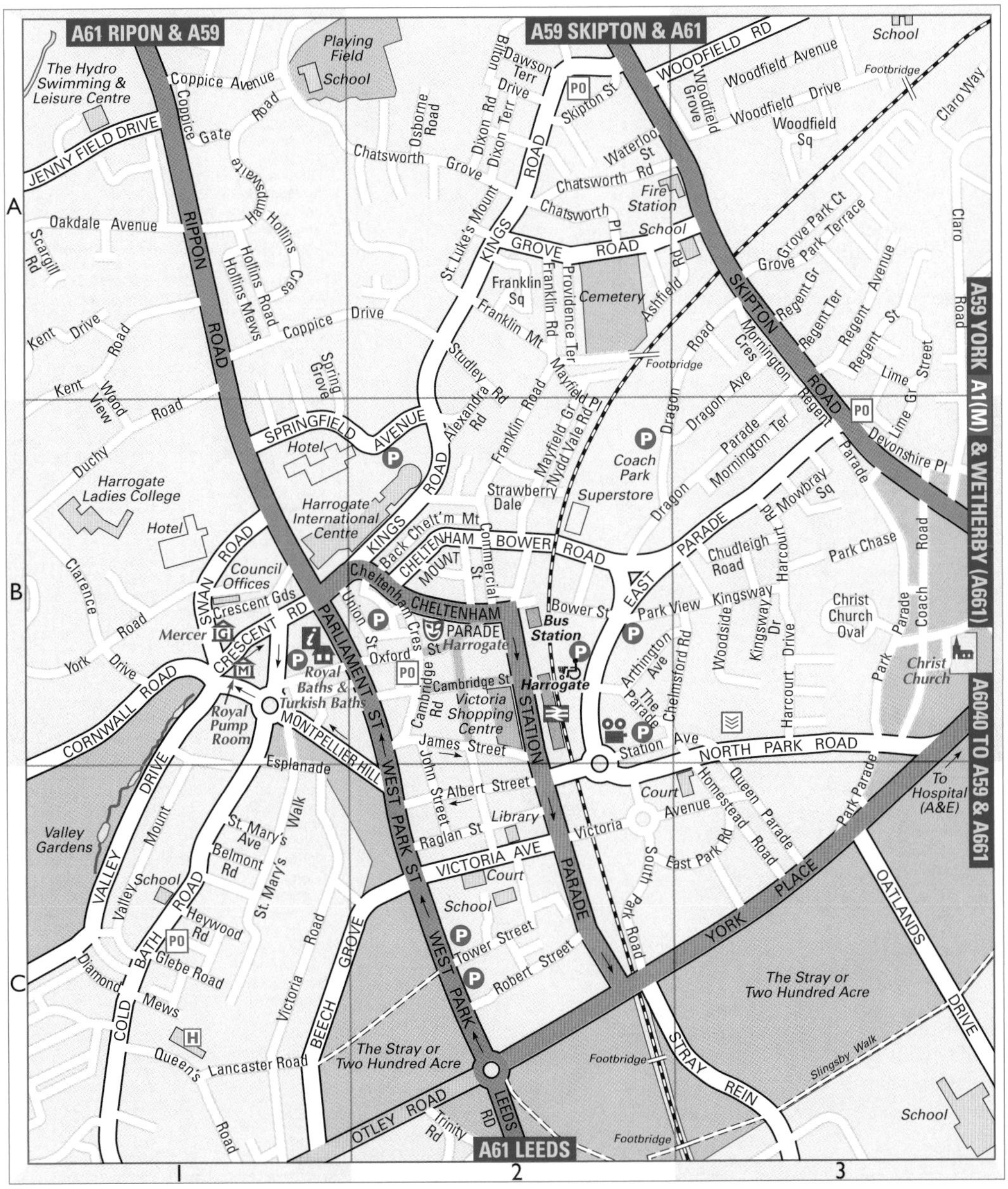

¼ mile
¼ ½ km

Haywards Heath

Mid Sussex's admininstrative centre, which flourished with the arrival of a railway link with London in 1841 and boasts nearly 50 listed buildings, including St Wilfrid's parish church. At its entrance is the Muster Green conservation area, consisting of a lovely green with a war memorial, surrounded by Victorian and Edwardian houses and the 16th-century Dolphin pub. Green spaces include Beech Hurst Gardens with its views of the South Downs, and nearby are Heaven Farm & Museum, Ditchling Common Country Park, Bookers Vineyard at Bolney, High Beeches Gardens and Nyman's Garden (National Trust) at Handcross, Leonardslee Gardens near Horsham and the wonderful Wakehurst Place Gardens, managed by the Royal Botanic Garden at Kew (in association with the National Trust).

Mid Sussex District Council, Oaklands, Oaklands Road, Haywards Heath RH16 1SS Tel 01444 458166

BBC Southern Counties 104.5 FM **Bright** 106.4 FM

www.midsussex.gov.uk

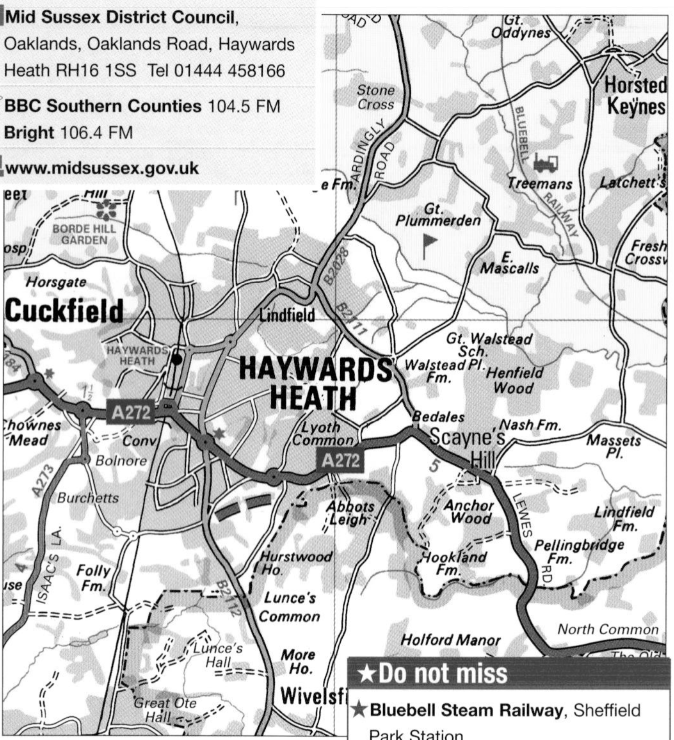

◄The restored station at Horsted Keynes on the Bluebell Steam Railway

¼ mile
¼ ½ km

★Do not miss

★**Bluebell Steam Railway**, Sheffield Park Station

★**Borde Hill Garden**, Balcombe Road

★**Sheffield Park Garden (National Trust)**, Sheffield Green

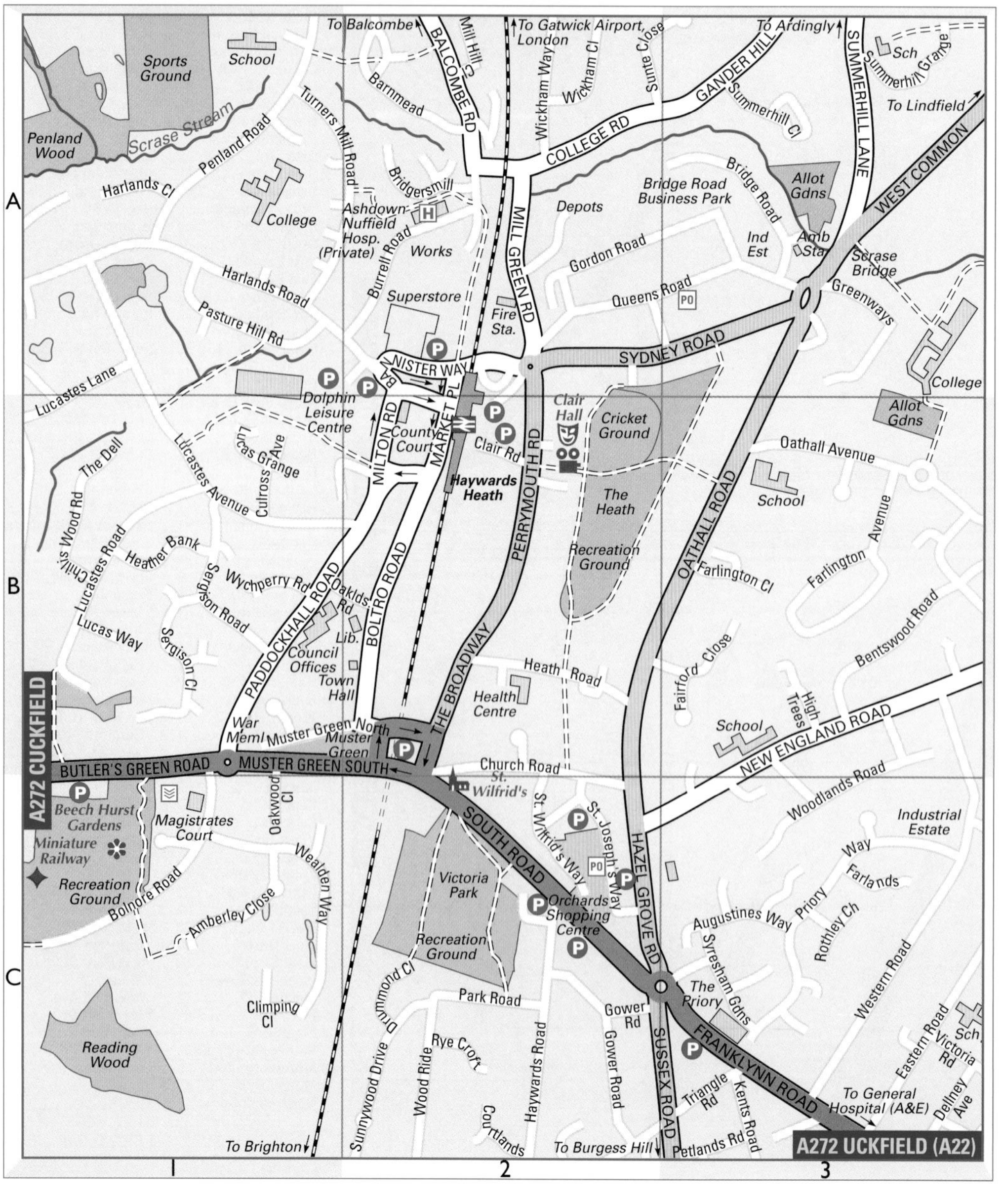

Haywards Heath

Amberley Cl C1
Ambulance Station A3
Ashdown Nuffield Hospital (Private) 🄷 A2
Augustines Way . . C3
Balcombe Rd A2
Bannister Way . . . A2
Barnmead A2
Beech Hurst Gardens ✽ C1
Bentswood Rd B3
Bolnore Rd C1
Boltro Rd B2
Bridge Rd A3
Bridge Road Business Park . . A3
Bridgersmill A2
Burrell Rd A2
Butler's Green Rd . B1
Chillis Wood Rd . . B1
Church Rd B2
Clair Hall B2
Clair Rd B2
Climping Cl C1
College Rd A2
Council Offices . . . B1
County Court B2
Courtlands C2
Cricket Ground . . . B2
Culross Ave B1
Dellney Ave C3
Dolphin Leisure Centre A1
Drummond Cl C2
Eastern Rd C3
Fairford Cl B3
Farlands B3
Farlington Ave B3
Farlington Cl B3
Fire Station A2
Franklynn Rd C3
Gander Hill A3
Gordon Rd A2
Gower Rd C2
Greenways A3
Harlands Cl A1
Harlands Rd A1
Haywards Heath Station ⇌ B2
Haywards Rd C2
Hazel Grove Rd . . C2
Health Centre B2
Heath Rd B2
Heather Bank B1
High Trees B3
Kents Rd C3
Library B2
Lucas Grange B1
Lucas Way B1
Lucastes Ave B1
Lucastes La A1
Lucastes Rd B1
Magistrates Court C1
Market Pl B2
Mill Green Rd . . . A2
Mill Hill Cl A2
Milton Rd B2
Miniature Railway ✦ C1
Muster Green B2
Muster Green North B1
Muster Green South B1
New England Rd . . B3
Oaklands Rd B2
Oakwood Cl C1
Oathall Ave B3
Oathall Rd B3
Orchards Shopping Centre C2
Paddockhall Rd . . . B1
Park Rd C2
Pasture Hill Rd . . . A1
Penland Rd A1
Penland Wood . . . A1
Perrymouth Rd . . . B2
Petlands Rd C3
Police Station 🅂 . . C1
Post Office 🄿🄾 A3/C2
Priory Way C3
Queens Rd A2
Reading Wood . . . C1
Rothley Chase . . . C3
Rye Croft C2
St Joseph's Way . C2
St Wilfrid's ⛪ . . . C2
St Wilfrid's Way . C2
Scrase Bridge . . . A3
Sergison Cl B1
Sergison Rd B1
South Rd C2
Summerhill Cl . . . A3
Summerhill Grange A3
Summerhill La . . . A3
Sunnywood Dr . . . C2
Sunte Cl A2
Sussex Rd C3
Sydney Rd A2/A3
Syresham Gdns . . C3
The Broadway B2
The Dell B1
The Heath B2
The Priory C3
Town Hall B2
Triangle Rd C3
Turners Mill Rd . . A1
Victoria Park C2
Victoria Rd C3
War Memorial B1
Wealden Way C1
West Common . . . A3
Wickham Cl A2
Wickham Way . . . A2
Wood Ride C2
Woodlands Rd . . . C3
Wychperry Rd B1

Hull

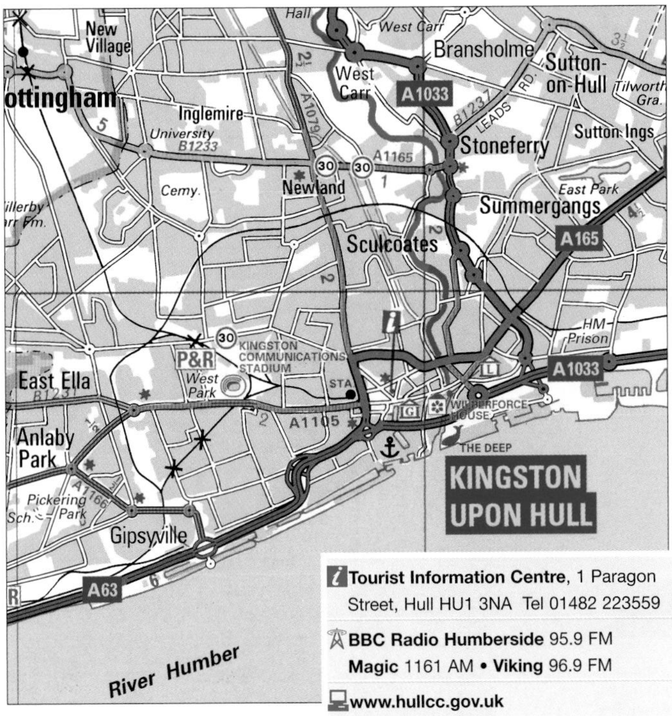

Tourist Information Centre, 1 Paragon Street, Hull HU1 3NA Tel 01482 223559

BBC Radio Humberside 95.9 FM
Magic 1161 AM • **Viking** 96.9 FM

www.hullcc.gov.uk

▲Hull marina

Kingston-upon-Hull (known as Hull) is situated at the point where the River Hull flows into the River Humber and has long been an important port for the fish trade, though this has reduced significantly. Many places of interest dedicated to this heritage such as the Spurn Lightship and the Arctic Corsair – the last remaining side-fishing trawler of the Hull distant-water fishing fleet and now a tribute to the men of the Deep Sea Fisheries. There is also a fishing trail that takes you through the old town and an ale trail which takes you to various watering holes – from pubs to stylish bars – in the old town. The old docks are now home to the Marina, Princes Quay Shopping Centre and Queens Gardens. The centre offers the full range of shopping from high street names and department stores to boutiques and a covered market.

★Do not miss

★**The Deep**, Old Harbour – the story of the world's oceans
★**Ferens Art Gallery**, Queen Victoria Square – painting and sculpture
★**Hull Maritime Museum**, Queen Victoria Square

Hull

Adelaide St C1
Albion St B2
Alfred Gelder St . .B2
Anlaby Rd. B1
Beverley Rd A1
Blanket Row. C2
Bond St. B2
Bridlington Ave . . A2
Brook St B1
Brunswick Ave. . . A1
Bus Station B1
Camilla Cl C3
Canning St B1
Cannon St A2
Cannon's C1
Caroline St A2
Carr La B2
Castle St. B2
Central Library . . .B1
Charles St A2
Citadel Way B3
City Hall B2
Clarence St B3
Cleveland St A3
Clifton St A1
Collier St B1
Colonial St. B1
Court. B2
Deep, The C3
Dock Office Row. . B3
Dock St. B2
Drypool Bridge . . . B3
Egton St A3
English St. C1
Ferens Gallery . B2
Ferensway B1
Francis St. A2
Francis St West. . A2
Freehold St A1
Freetown Way . . . A2
Garrison Rd B3
George St. B2
Gibson St. A2
Great Union St . . A3
Green La. A2
Grey St A1
Grimston St B2
Grosvenor St A1
Gt Thornton St. . . .B1
Guildhall B2
Guildhall Rd. B2
Hands-on History B2
Harley St A1
Hessle Rd. C1
High St B3
Holy Trinity B2
Hull & East Riding Mus . . .B3
Hull Arena C1
Hull College. B3
Hull (Paragon) B1
Hull Truck B1
Humber Dock Marina C2
Humber Dock St . C2
Humber St C2
Hyperion St A3
Information Ctr . B2
Jameson St B1
Jarratt St B2
Jenning St A3
King Billy Statue ✦ C2
King Edward St . . B2
King St A2
Kingston Retail Park C1
Kingston St C2
Library Theatre . B1
Liddell St A1
Lime St. A3
Lister St C1
Lockwood St A2
Maister House B3
Maritime Mus . . B2
Market B2
Market Place B2
Minerva Pier C2
Mulgrave St. A3
Myton Bridge. . . . C3
Myton St. B1
Nelson St C2
New Cleveland St A3
New George St . . A2
New Theatre . . A2
Norfolk St. A1
North Bridge A3
North St B1
Odeon C1
Osborne St. B1
Paragon St. B2
Park St B1
Percy St A2
Pier St C2
Police Station . . B2
Post Office . A3/B1/B2
Porter St C1
Portland St B1
Posterngate B2
Prince's Quay B2
Prospect Centre . . B1
Prospect St B1
Queen's Gdns B2
Railway Dock Marina C2
Railway St C2
Reform St. A2
Riverside Quay . . C2
Roper St. B2
St James St C1
St Luke's St B1
St Mark St A3
St Mary the Virgin B3
Scott St. A2
South Bridge Rd . . B3
Spring Bank. A1
Spring St B1
Spurn Lightship C2
Spyvee St. A3
Streetlife Transport Mus B3
Sykes St A2
Tidal Surge Barrier ✦ C3
Tower St. B3
Trinity House. B2
University. B3
Vane St. A1
Victoria Pier C2
Waterhouse La . . .B2
Waterloo St A1
Waverley St C1
Wellington St. . . . C2
Wellington St W . C2
West St B1
Whitefriargate. . . .B2
Wilberforce Dr . . .B2
Wilberforce Ho . B3
Wilberforce Monument ✦. . . .B3
William St C1
Wincolmlee A3
Witham. A3
Wright St A1

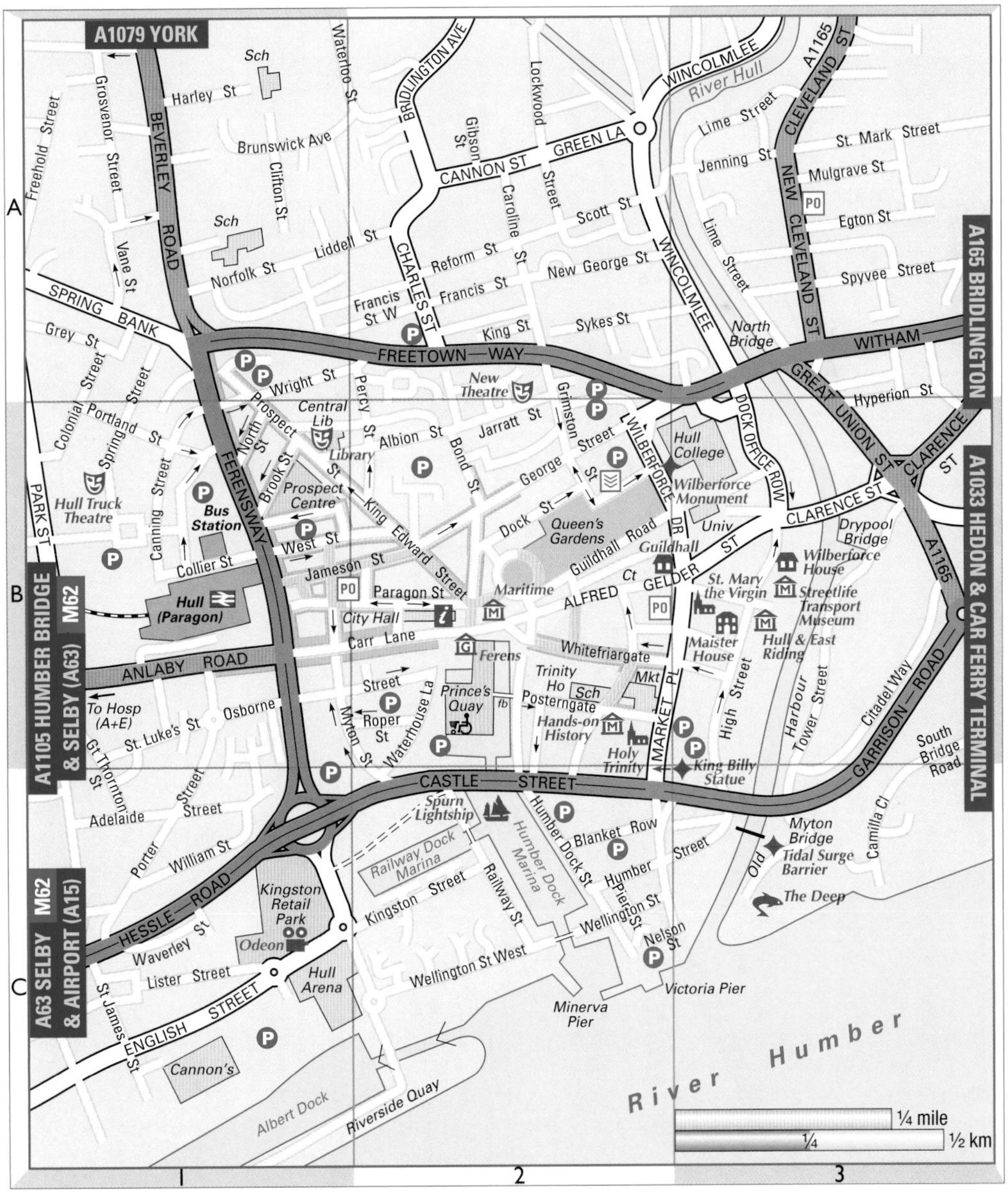

Inverness

The Highlands capital, awarded city status in 2001, situated on the Caledonian Canal linking Loch Ness and the Moray Firth. Inverness Castle (1834), on the site of a 12th-century castle built by King David I and destroyed by Robert the Bruce, contains courthouses and the Castle Garrison Encounter re-creating the life of an 18th-century soldier. Other buildings of historic interest include Abertarff House (1590s), with one of the last surviving turnpike stairs, St Andrew's Cathedral (1860s), and the Old High Church, in the graveyard of which prisoners taken at Culloden were executed. The city's history is traced in the Museum & Art Gallery, while nature-based attractions include the awardwinning Bught Floral Hall, Dolphins & Seals of the Moray Firth, and Black Isle Wildlife & Country Park. On the outskirts of the city is the Clava Cairns Bronze Age burial ground, and on the shore of Loch Ness is the dramatic ruined Urquhart Castle (mostly 14th century), one of Scotland's biggest.

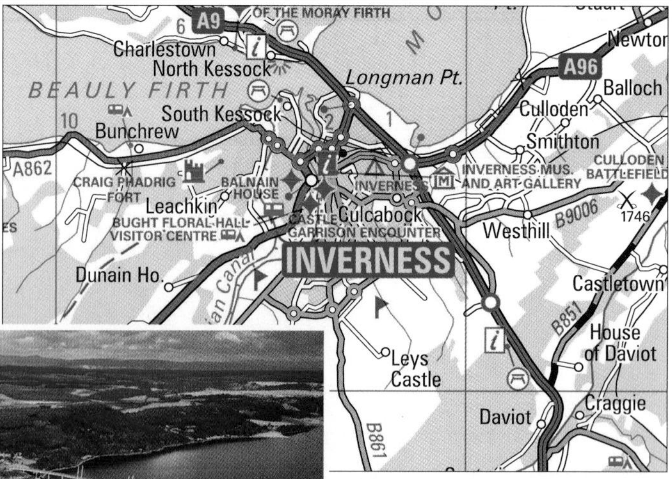

►Inverness from the air

★Do not miss

★**Culloden Battlefield & Visitor Centre (1745-6)**, east of city

★**Loch Ness & Ness Islands**, south of city

Inverness Tourist Information Centre, Castle Wynd, Inverness IV2 3BJ Tel 01463 234353

BBC Radio Scotland 92.4-94.7 FM and 810 AM • **Moray Firth Radio** 97.4 FM and 1107 AM

www.inverness-scotland.com

Inverness

Abban St A1
Academy St B2
Alexander Pl B2
Anderson St A2
Annfield Rd C3
Ardconnel St B3
Ardconnel Terr . . . B3
Ardross Pl B2
Ardross St B2
Argyle St B3
Argyle Terr B3
Attadale Rd B1
Ballifeary La. C2
Ballifeary Rd . C1/C2
Balnacraig La . . . A1
Balnain St B2
Bank St. B2
Bellfield Park. . . . C2
Bellfield Terr C3
Benula Rd A1
Birnie Terr A1
Bishop's Rd C2
Bowling Green . . A2
Bowling Green . . . B2
Bowling Green . . C2
Bridge St B2
Brown St A2
Bruce Ave. C1
Bruce Gdns C1
Bruce Pk C1
Burial Ground . . . A2
Burnett Rd A3
Bus Station B3
Caledonian Rd. . . . B1
Cameron Rd. A1
Cameron Sq. A1
Carse Rd. A1
Carsegate Rd S . . A1
Castle (Courts) . . . B3
Castle Rd B2
Castle St. B3
Celt St. B2
Chapel St A2
Charles St B3
Church St B2
Clachnacuddin Football Ground A1
College A3
Columba Rd. . B1/C1
Crown Ave B3
Crown Circus B3
Crown Dr B3
Crown Rd B3
Crown St B3
Culduthel Rd C3
Dalneigh Cres . . . C1
Dalneigh Rd. C1
Denny St. B3
Dochfour Dr. . B1/C1
Douglas Row B2
Duffy Dr C3
Dunabran Rd A1
Dunain Rd B1
Duncraig St B2
Eastgate Shopping Centre. B3
Eden Court . . . C2
Fairfield Rd B1
Falcon Sq. B3
Fire Station A3
Fraser St B2
Fraser St C2
Friars' Bridge . . . A2
Friars' La B2
Friars' St A2
George St. A2
Gilbert St A2
Glebe St A2
Glendoe Terr A1
Glenurquhart Rd . C1
Gordon Terr B3
Gordonville Rd . . C2
Grant St A2
Greig St B2
HM Prison B3
Harbour Rd A3
Harrowden Rd B1
Haugh Rd C2
Heatherley Cres . C3
High St B3
Highland Council H.Q. C2
Hill Park C3
Hill St B3
Huntly Pl A2
Huntly St B2
India St. A2
Industrial Estate . A3
Information Ctr . B2
Innes St A2
Inverness High School B1
Inverness B3
Jamaica St. A2
Kenneth St B2
Kilmuir Rd A1
King St B2
Kingsmills Rd B3
Laurel Ave . . . B1/C1
Library A3
Lilac Gr. B1
Lindsay Ave C1
Lochalsh Rd. . A1/B1
Longman Rd A3
Lotland Pl. A2
Lower Kessock St A1
Madras St. A2
Market Hall B3
Maxwell Dr. C1
Mayfield Rd C3
Midmills College. . B3
Millburn Rd B3
Mitchell's La C3
Montague Row . . . B2
Muirfield Rd. C3
Muirtown St. B1
Museum B2
Nelson St A2
Ness Bank C2
Ness Bridge B2
Ness Walk . . . B2/C2
Old Edinburgh Rd C3
Old High B2
Park Rd C1
Paton St C2
Perceval Rd B1
Planefield Rd. B2
Police Station . . A3
Porterfield Bank . C3
Porterfield Rd . . . C3
Portland Pl. A2
Post Office A2/B1/B2/B3
Queen St B2
Queensgate B2
Railway Terr. A3
Rangemore Rd . . . B1
Reay St B3
Riverside St A2
Rose St. A2
Ross Ave. B1
Rowan Rd. B1
Royal Northern Infirmary C2
St Andrew's . . . C2
St Columba B2
St John's Ave. . . . C1
St Mary's Ave. . . . C1
Shore St A2
Smith Ave. C1
Southside Pl C3
Southside Rd. . . . C3
Spectrum Centre. . B2
Strothers La. B3
TA Centre C2
Telford Gdns B1
Telford Rd A1
Telford St A1
Tomnahurich Cem C1
Tomnahurich St. . . B2
Town Hall B3
Union Rd B3
Union St B3
Walker Pl A2
Walker Rd A3
War Memorial . C2
Waterloo Bridge . A2
Wells St B1
Young St. B2

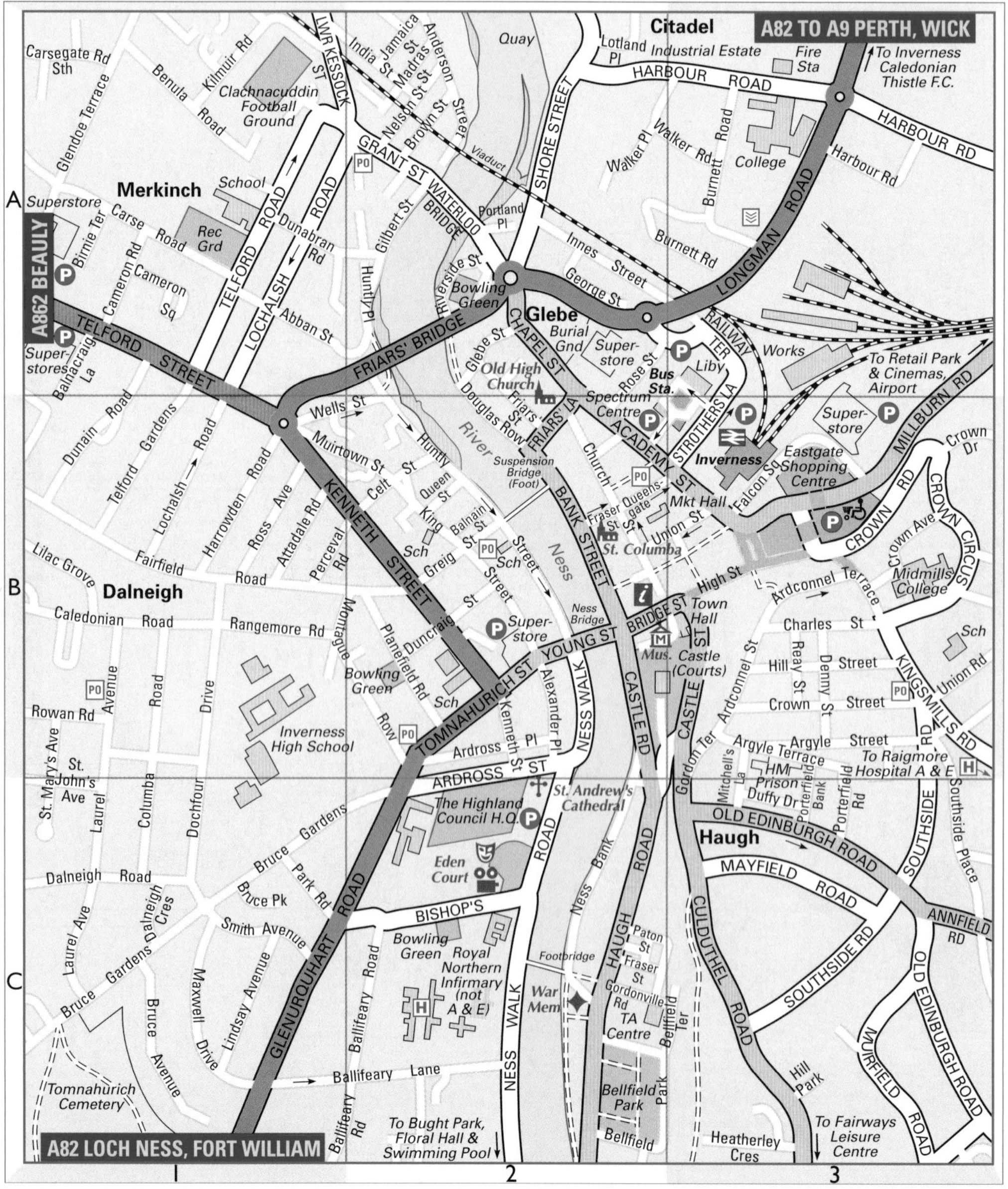

¼ mile

¼ ½ km

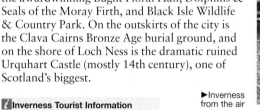

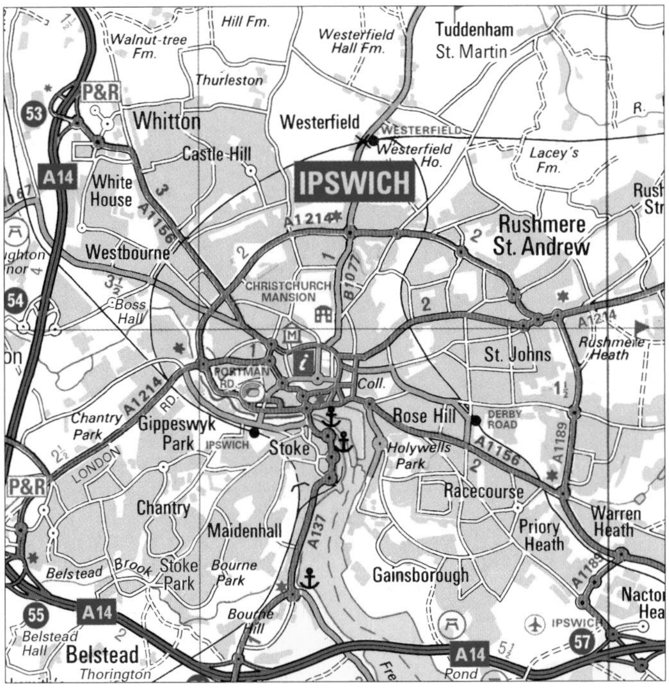

Ipswich

Ipswich was founded in the 6th/7th century as a port trading with continental Europe. It is now an important regional centre and county town. Places of interest include Christchurch Mansion a 16th-century house in historic park with a collection of paintings by Gainsborough and Constable; The Ancient House – an unusual timber-framed building (now a shop) with beautiful plasterwork 'pargeting' (a Suffolk speciality). There is a variety of trails taking you to some of the best churches, and the historic waterfront. There are three shopping centres featuring all the high street names and the centre is also well served with restaurants and pubs to suit all tastes. Nearby attractions include the royal Anglo-Saxon cemetery at Sutton Hoo near Woodbridge (National Trust).

★Do not miss

★**Christchurch Mansion, Christchurch Park** – Tudor house

★**Unitarian Meeting House**, Friars St – 1699 grade I listed Meeting House

★**Ipswich Transport Museum**, Old Trolleybus Depot, Cobham Road

Tourist Information Centre, St Stephen's Church, St Stephen's Lane, Ipswich IP1 1DP Tel 01473 258070

BBC Radio Suffolk 103.9 FM
Classic Gold Amber 1251 AM
SGR 97.1 FM • **Vibe FM** 106.4 FM

www.ipswich.gov.uk

Ipswich

Alderman Rd B2
All Saints' Rd A1
Alpe St B2
Ancaster Rd C1
Ancient House . . B3
Anglesea Rd B2
Ann St B2
Austin St C2
Belstead Rd C2
Berners St B2
Bibb Way B1
Birkfield Dr C1
Black Horse La . . .B2
Bolton La B3
Bond St C3
Bowthorpe Cl B2
Bramford La A1
Bramford Rd A1
Bridge St C2
Brookfield Rd . . . A1
Brooks Hall Rd . . A1
Broomhill Rd A1
Broughton Rd . . . A2
Bulwer Rd B1
Burrell Rd C2
Bus Station . . B2/C3
Butter Market B2
Butter Market Ctr .B3
Carr St B3
Cecil Rd B2
Cecilia St C2
Chancery Rd C2
Charles St B2
Chevallier St A1
Christchurch Mans & Wolsey Art Gal B3
Christchurch Park A3
Christchurch St . . .B3
Civic Centre B2
Civic Dr B2
Clarkson St B1
Cobbold St B3
Commercial Rd . . C2
Constable Rd A3
Constantine Rd . . C1
Constitution Hill . A2
Corder Rd A3
Corn Exchange . . .B2
Cotswold Ave A2
Council Offices . . C2
County Hall B3
Crown Court C2
Crown St B2
Cullingham Rd B1
Cumberland St . . .B2
Curriers La B2
Dale Hall La A2
Dales View Rd . . . A1
Dalton Rd B2
Dillwyn St B1
Elliot St B1
Elm St B2
Elsmere Rd A3
End Quay C3
Falcon St C2
Felaw St C3
Flint Wharf C3
Fonnereau Rd B2
Fore St C3
Foundation St . . . C3
Franciscan Way . . C2
Friars St C2
Gainsborough Rd A3
Gatacre Rd B1
Geneva Rd B2
Gippeswyk Ave . . C1
Gippeswyk Park . C1
Grafton Way C2
Graham Rd A1
Grimwade St C3
Great Whip St . . . C3
Handford Cut B1
Handford Rd B1
Henley Rd A2
Hervey St B3
High St B2
Holly Rd A2
Information Ctr .B3
Ipswich School . . A2
Ipswich C2
Ipswich Town F.C. (Portman Road) C2
Ivry St A2
Kensington Rd . . . A1
Kesteven Rd C1
Key St C3
Kingsfield Ave . . . A3
Kitchener Rd A1
Magistrates Court .B2
Little's Cr C2
London Rd B1
Low Brook St C3
Lower Orwell St . C3
Luther Rd C2
Manor Rd A3
Mornington Ave . A1
Mus & Art Gal .B2
Museum St B2
Neale St B3
New Cardinal St . C2
New Cut East C3
New Cut West . . . C3
Newson St B2
Norwich Rd . . A1/B1
Oban St B2
Old Customs House C3
Old Foundry Rd . . .B3
Old Merchant's House C3
Orford St B2
Paget Rd A2
Park Rd A3
Park View Rd A2
Peter's St C2
Philip Rd C2
Pine Ave A2
Pine View Rd A2
Police Station . .B2
Portman Rd B2
Portman Walk . . . C1
Post Office .B2/B3
Princes St C2
Prospect St B1
Queen St B2
Ranelagh Rd C1
Rectory Rd C2
Regent Theatre .B3
Richmond Rd A1
Rope Walk C3
Rose La C2
Russell Rd C1
St Edmund's Rd . A2
St George's St B2
St Helen's St B3
Samuel Rd B3
Sherrington Rd . . A1
Silent St C2
Sir Alf Ramsey Wy C1
Sirdar Rd B1
Soane St B3
Springfield La . . . A1
Star La C3
Stevenson Rd B1
Suffolk College . . C3
Suffolk Retail Pk . .B1
Superstore B1
Surrey Rd B1
Swimming Pool . . A1
Tacket St C3
Tavern St B3
The Avenue A3
Tolly Cobbold Museum C3
Tower Ramparts . .B2
Tower St B3
Town Hall B2
Tuddenham Rd . . A3
UGC C2
Upper Brook St . . .B3
Upper Orwell St . .B3
Valley Rd A2
Vermont Cr B3
Vermont Rd B3
Vernon St C3
Warrington Rd . . . A2
Waterloo Rd A1
Waterworks St . . . C3
Wellington St B1
West End Rd B1
Westerfield Rd . . . A3
Westgate St B2
Westholme Rd . . . A1
Westwood Ave . . . A1
Willoughby Rd . . . C2
Withipoll St B3
Wolsey Theatre .B2
Woodbridge Rd . . .B3
Woodstone Ave . . A3
Yarmouth Rd B1

¼ mile
¼ ½ km

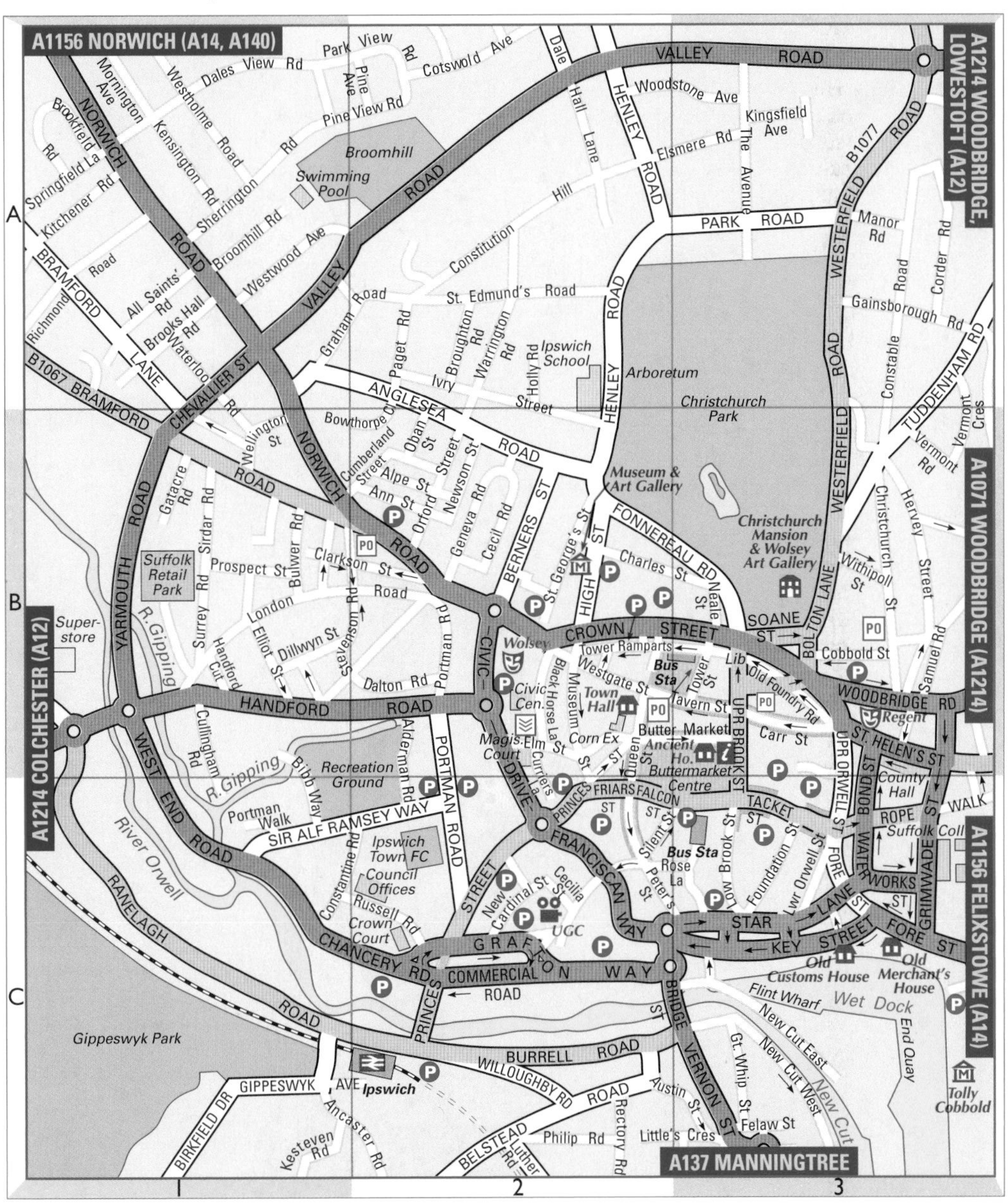

Kendal

The town of Kendal is just outside the Lake District National Park. The 12th-century stone ruins of Kendal Castle sit on a hill on the western edge of the town, offering views over the town and the surrounding hills. Holy Trinity is the largest parish church in Cumbria. Set beside the River Kent, Kendal has much in the way of historic buildings, galleries, museums, shopping and restaurants. The town's old cobbled lanes off the attractive main street feature many antique and speciality shops. There are also a number of high street shops in the main pedestrianised shopping area. The Brewery Arts Centre has a cinema, theatre, live music venue, bars and restaurant. The Westmorland Shopping Centre has both high-street shops and local independents. South of the town are Sizergh Castle and Gardens (National Trust) and Levens Hall with is spectacular topiary gardens.

Kendal Tourist Information Centre, Town Hall, Highgate, Kendal LA9 4DL
Tel 01539 725758

BBC Radio Cumbria 95.2 FM
Lakeland Radio 100.8 FM
The Bay 96.9 FM, 103.2 FM

www.cumbria-the-lake-district.co.uk

▲Branthwaite Brow, Kendal

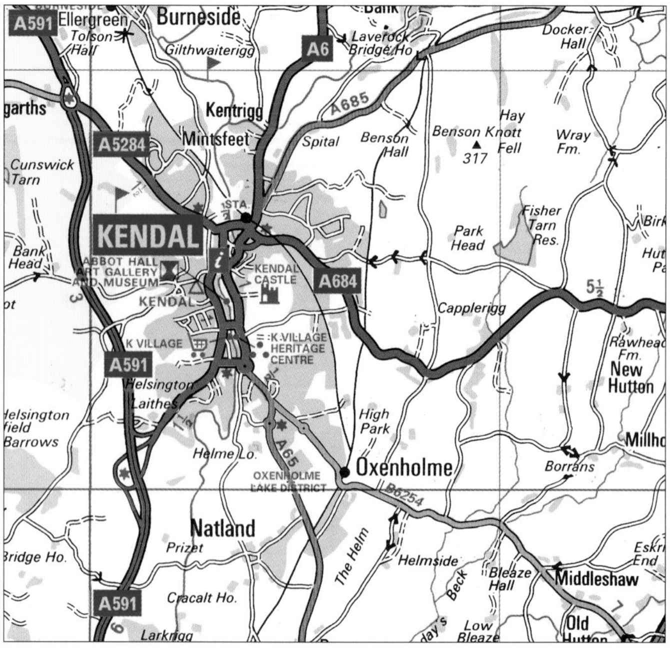

★Do not miss

★**Abbot Hall Art Gallery**, Kirkland
★**Museum of Lakeland Life**, Kirkland
★**The Quaker Tapestry**, Friends Meeting House, Stramongate

Kendal

Abbot Hall Art Gallery C2
Ambulance Station A2
Anchorite Fields . C2
Anchorite Rd C2
Ann St. A3
Appleby Rd A3
Archers Meadow. C3
Ashleigh Rd A2
Aynam Rd. B2
Bankfield Rd B1
Beast Banks. B2
Beezon Fields . . . A2
Beezon Rd A2
Beezon Trad Est. . A3
Belmont B2
Birchwood Cl. . . . C1
Blackhall Rd B2
Brewery Arts Centre B2
Bridge St B2
Brigsteer Rd C1
Burneside Rd. . . . A2
Bus Station B2
Buttery Well La . . C2
Canal Head North .B3
Captain French La C2
Caroline St. A2
Castle Hill B3
Castle Howe. B2
Castle Rd B3
Castle St. A3/B3
Cedar Gr. C1
Council Offices . . .B2
County Council Offices A2
Cricket Ground . . A3
Cricket Ground . . C3
Cross La C2
Dockray Hall Industrial Estate A2
Dowker's La. B2
Dry Ski Slope ✦ . .B3
East View B1
Echo Barn Hill . . . C1
Elephant Yard Shopping Ctr. . . .B2
Fairfield La. A1
Finkle St. B2
Fire Station A2
Fletcher Square . . C3
Football Ground . C3
Fowling La. A3
Gillinggate. C2
Glebe Rd C2
Golf Course B1
Goose Holme. B3
Gooseholme Br . . .B3
Green St. A1
Greengate C2
Greengate La. C1/C2
Greenside. B1
Greenwood C1
Gulfs Rd B2
High Tenterfell. . . .B1
Highgate. B2
Hillswood Ave . . . C1
Horncop La A2
Information Ctr . .B2
K Village and Heritage Ctr ✦ . C2
Kendal Business Park A3
Kendal Castle (Remains Of). . . .B3
Kendal Fell. B1
Kendal Green. . . . A1
Kendal A3
Kendal Station . . A3
Kent Pl B2
Kirkbarrow. C2
Kirkland C2
Library B2
Library Rd B2
Little Aynam B3
Little Wood B1
Long Cl. C1
Longpool A3
Lound Rd C3
Lound St. C3
Low Fellside B2
Lowther St. B2
Maple Dr C1
Market Pl B2
Maude St B2
Miller Bridge B2
Milnthorpe Rd . . . C2
Mint St A3
Mintsfeet Rd A3
Mintsfeet Rd South A2
New Rd. B2
Noble's Rest B2
Parish Church . . C2
Park Side Rd C3
Parkside Business Park C3
Parr St B3
Police Station . . A2
Post Office . A2/A3/B1/B2/C2
Quaker Tapestry ✦B2
Queen's Rd B1
Riverside Walk . . C2
Rydal Mount A2
Sandes Ave A2
Sandgate A3
Sandylands Rd. . . A3
Serpentine Rd B1
Serpentine Wood .B1
Shap Rd A3
South Rd C2
Stainbank Rd. . . . C1
Station Rd A3
Stramongate B2
Stramongate Br. . .B2
Stricklandgate A2/B2
Sunnyside C3
Thorny Hills. B3
Town Hall. B2
Undercliff Rd. B1
Underwood C1
Union St. A2
Vicar's Fields. . . . C2
Vicarage Dr . . C1/C2
Wasdale Cl. C3
Well Ings C2
Westmorland Shopping Ctr & Market Hall . . .B2
Westwood Ave. . . C1
Wildman St A3
Windermere Rd. . . A1
YHA. B2
YWCA B2

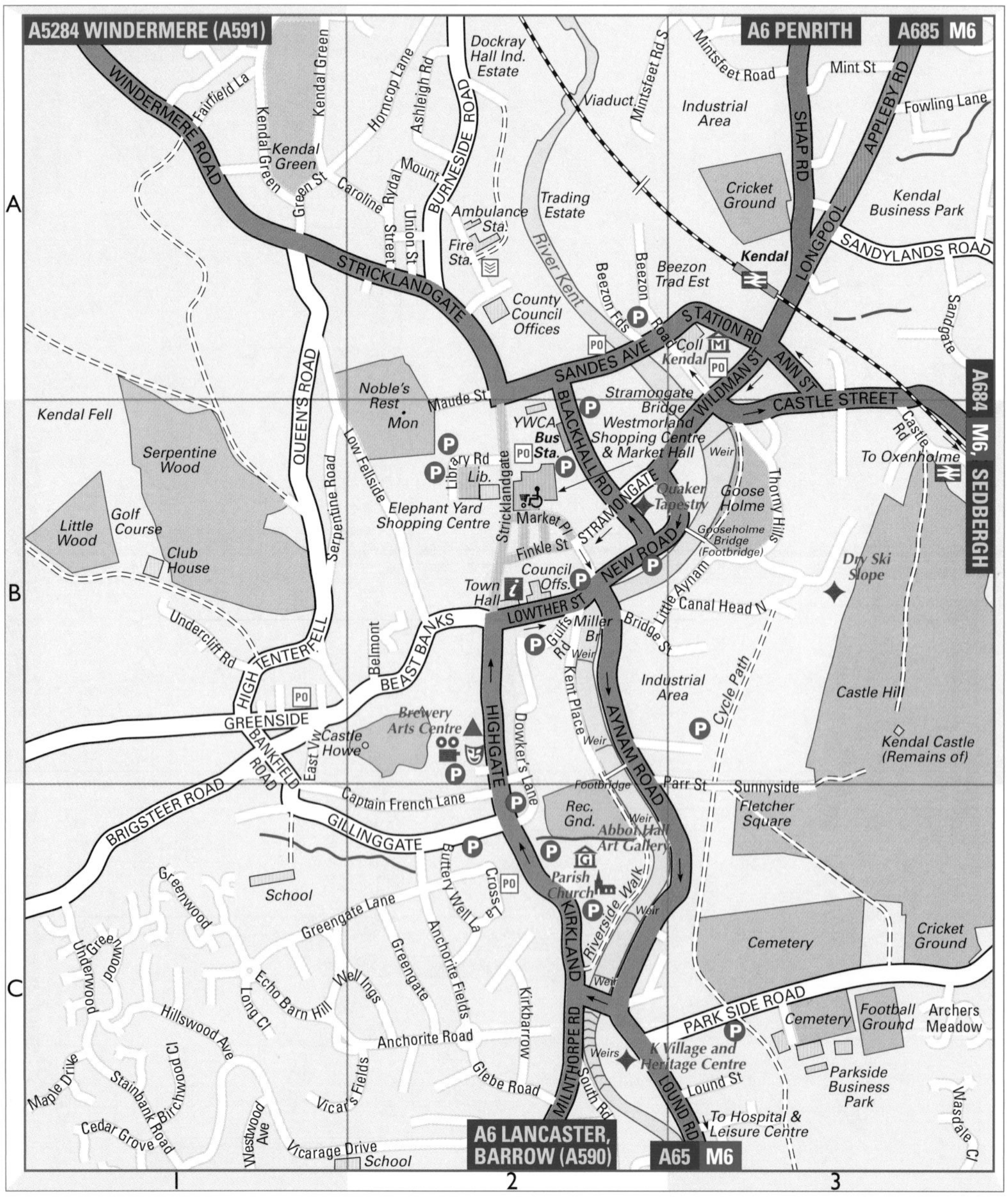

¼ mile
¼ ½ km

★ Do not miss

- ★ **Green Quay wildlife discovery centre**, Marriott's Warehouse
- ★ **St George's Guildhall (National Trust)**, King Street
- ★ **True's Yard Fishing Heritage Museum**, North Street

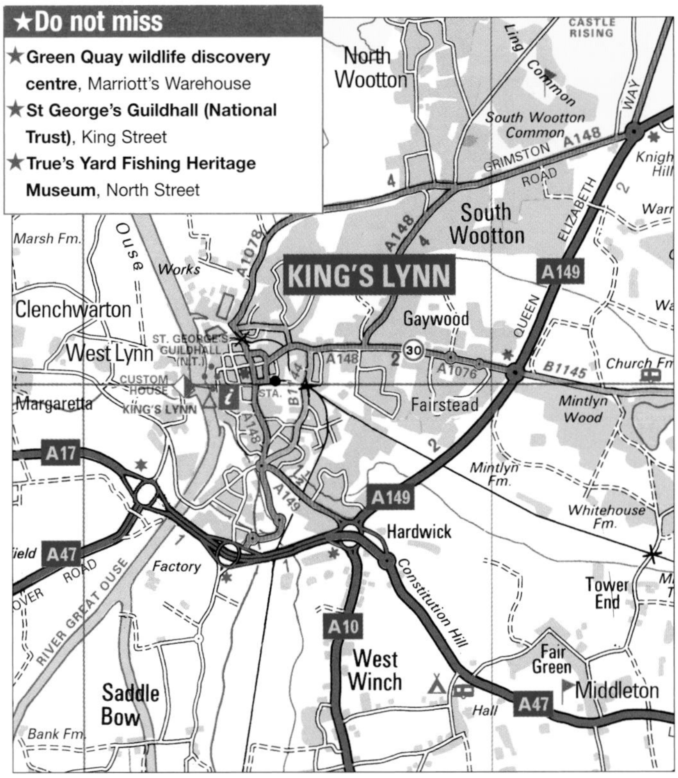

▲The Custom House

i **King's Lynn Tourist Information Centre**, The Custom House, Purfleet Quay, King's Lynn PE30 1HP
Tel 01553 763044

BBC Radio Norfolk 104.4 FM and 873 AM • **KLFM** 96.7 FM
North Norfolk Radio 96.2 FM

□ www.west-norfolk.gov.uk

King's Lynn

A West Norfolk market town and port dating back to the 12th century, with a rich maritime heritage. Attractions in the historic centre include Tales of the Old Gaol House, tracing the town's criminal past and housing its civic treasures, the Town House Museum charting local life from medieval times, the Lynn Museum of archaeology and history, and the country's largest surviving medieval guildhall, now housing an arts centre and Georgian theatre. Shopping amenities range from 3 weekly markets to specialist craft and antiques shops and high-street chains. Nearby sights include the ruined 12th-century Castle Rising Castle, Norfolk Lavender in Heacham, Castle Acre Priory, Sandringham House, Congham Hall Herb Garden and Peckover House and Garden (National Trust) in Wisbech.

77

King's Lynn

Albert St A2
Albion St B2
All Saints ⌂ B2
All Saints St B2
Austin Fields A2
Austin St A2
Avenue Rd B3
Bank Side B1
Beech Rd C2
Birch Tree Cl B2
Birchwood St A2
Blackfriars Rd . . . B2
Blackfriars St B2
Boal St B1
Bridge St B2
Broad St A2
Broad Walk B3
Burkitt St A2
Bus Station B2
Carmelite Terr . . . C2
Chapel St A2
Chase Ave C3
Checker St C2
Church St B2
Clough La. B2
Coburg St B2
College of
   West Anglia A3
Columbia Way . . . A3
Corn Exchange ⌂ . A1
County Court Rd . . B2
Cresswell St A2
Custom House ⌂ . . A1
Eastgate St A2
Edma St A2
Exton's Rd C3
Ferry La B1
Ferry St B1
Framingham's
   Almshouses ⌂ . . B2
Friars St C2
Gaywood Rd A3
George St A2
Gladstone Rd C2
Goodwin's Rd . . . C3
Green Quay ✦ . . . B1
Greyfriars'
   Tower ✦ B2
Guanock Terr C2
Guildhall ⌂ A1
Hansa Rd C3
Hardwick Rd C2
Hextable Rd A2
High St B2
Holcombe Ave . . . C3
Hospital Walk . . . B2
Information Ctr ⌂ . B1
John Kennedy Rd . A2
Kettlewell Lane . . A2
King George V
   Ave B3
King's Lynn
   Art Centre ⌂ . . . A1
King's Lynn
   Station ⇄ B2
King St A2
Library B2
Littleport St A2
Loke Rd A2

London Rd B2
Lynn Museum B2
Majestic ▣ B2
Magistrates
   Court B1
Market La A1
Millfleet B2
Milton Ave A3
Nar Valley Walk . . C2
Nelson St B1
New Conduit St. . . B2
Norfolk St A2
North St A2
Oldsunway B2
Ouse Ave B2
Page Stair Lane . . A1
Park Ave B3
Police Station ▣ . . B2
Portland Pl. C1
Portland St B2
Post Office
   ▣ A3/B2/C2
Purfleet B1
Queen St B1
Raby Ave A3
Railway Rd A2
Red Mount
   Chapel ⌂ B3
Regent Way B2
River Walk A1
Robert St C2
Saddlebow Rd . . . C2
St Ann's St A1
St James' Rd B2
St James St B2
St John's Walk . . . B3
St Margaret's ⌂ . . B1
St Nicholas ⌂ . . . A2
St Nicholas St . . . A1
St Peter's Rd B1
S Everard St C2
Sir Lewis St A2
Smith Ave A3
South Gate ✦ C2
Southgate St C2
South Quay B1
South St B2
Stonegate St B2
Surrey St A1
Sydney St C3
Tennyson Ave. . . . B3
Tennyson Rd B3
The Friars C2
Tower St B2
Town Hall B1
Town House & Tales
   of The Old Gaol
   House ⌂ B1
Town Wall
   (Remains) ✦ . . . B3
True's Yard
   Museum ⌂ A2
Valingers Rd C2
Vancouver Ave. . . C2
Waterloo St B2
Wellesley St B2
White Friars Rd. . . C2
Windsor Rd C2
Winfarthing St. . . C2
Wyatt St A2
York Rd C3

¼ mile
¼
½ km

A1078 TO A148 & HUNSTANTON (A149)

A148 FAKENHAM & A149 (A1076)

Lynnsport and Leisure Park

North End

Highgate

King's Lynn

West Lynn

South Lynn

A148 WISBECH (A47) & SPALDING (A17)

A149 SWAFFHAM (A47) & DOWNHAM MKT (A10)

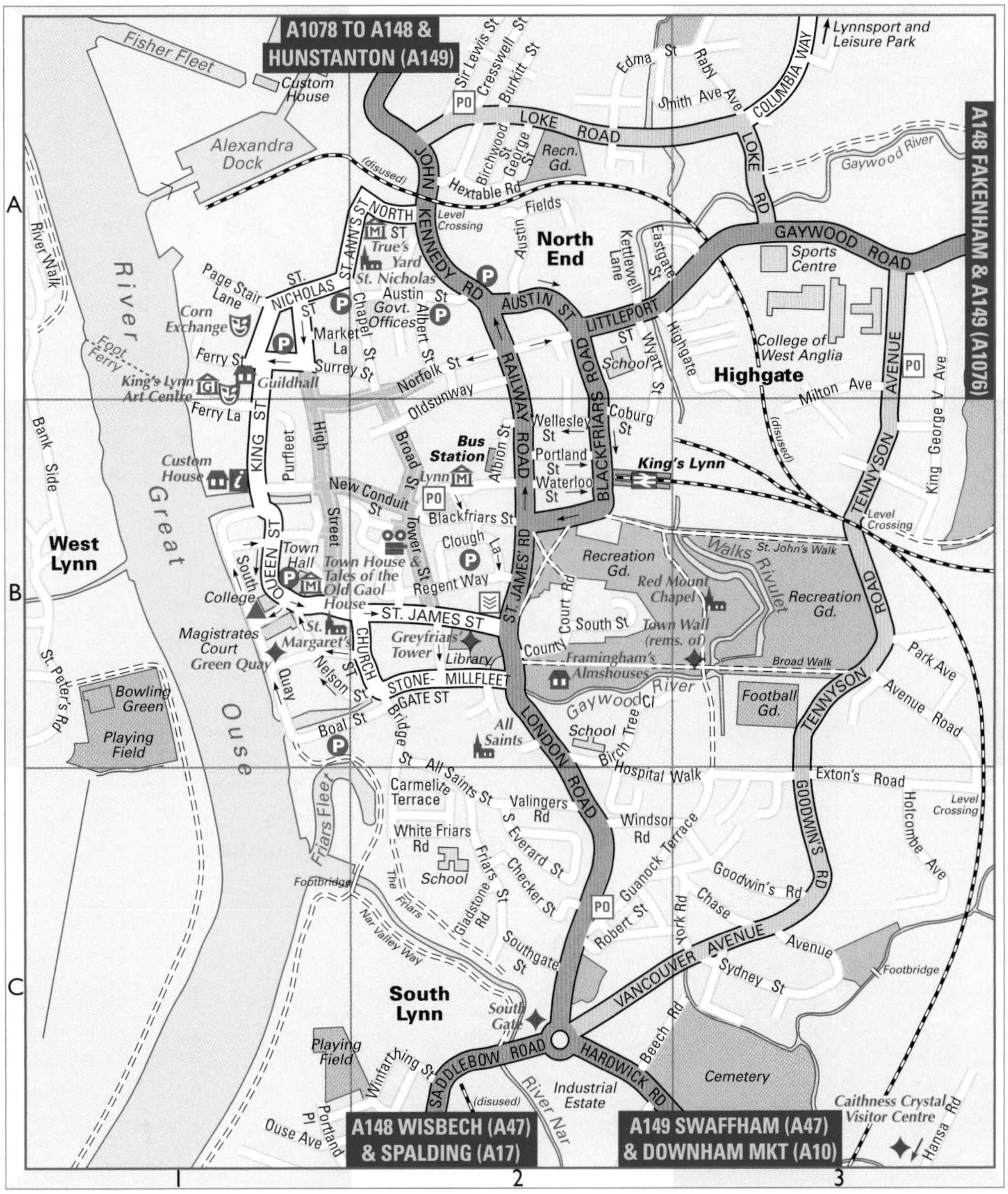

Lancaster

▲Lancaster Castle

The Romans established a settlement nearly 2,000 years ago and remains of one of their buildings are still visible on Castle Hill close to the Priory. The Norman castle is still a working court and prison. The town was an important maritime centre in the 19th century and many notable buildings still exist from this time, for example the former Town Hall in Market Square, now the City Museum, and the Custom House of 1764, which now serves as the Maritime Museum. Lancaster is now an important educational centre. As well as St Nicholas Arcades shopping centre and the Leisure Park and GB Antiques Centre, there is an indoor market, a twice-weekly outdoor charter market and twice-monthly farmers' market, while antiques, pop memorabilia and vintage, retro and alternative clothing can be found in the Assembly Rooms market.

Lancaster Tourist Information Centre, 29 Castle Hill, Lancaster LA1 1YN Tel 01524 32878

BBC Radio Lancashire 104.5 FM • **105.4 Century** 105.4 FM

www.lancaster.gov.uk

★Do not miss

★**Lancaster Castle**, Castle Parade

★**Ashton Memorial**, Williamson Park – art gallery and park with butterfly house and exotic birds

★**Judge's Lodgings**, Church Street – Gillow & Town House Museum; Museum of Childhood

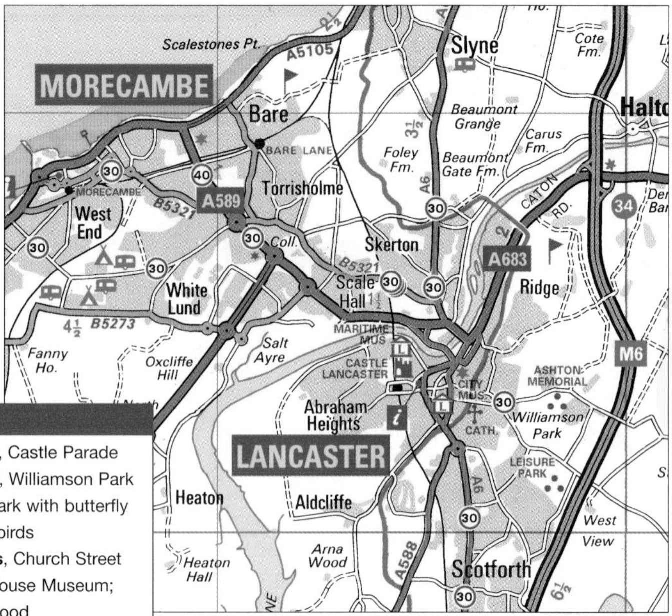

Lancaster

Aberdeen Rd C3
Adult College, The C3
Aldcliffe Rd C2
Alfred St B3
Ambleside Rd . . . A3
Ambulance Sta . . A3
Ashfield Ave B1
Ashton Rd C2
Assembly Rooms, The B2
Balmoral Rd B3
Bath House B2
Bath Mill La B3
Bath St B3
Blades St B1
Borrowdale Rd . . B3
Bowerham Rd . . . C3
Brewery La B2
Bridge La B2
Brook St C1
Bulk Rd A3
Bulk St B2
Bus Station B2
Cable St B2
Carlisle Bridge . . A1
Carr House La . . . C2
Castle B1
Castle Park B1
Caton Rd A3
China St B2
Church St B2
City Museum . . B2
Clarence St C3
Common Gdn St . B2
Coniston Rd A3
Cottage Mus . . . B2
Council Offices . . . B2
Court B2
Cromwell Rd C1
Dale St C3
Dallas Rd B1/C1
Dalton Rd B3
Dalton Sq B2
Damside St B2
De Vitre St B3
Dee Rd A1
Denny Ave A1
Derby Rd A2
Dukes B2
Earl St A2
East Rd B3
Eastham St C3
Edward St B3
Fairfield Rd B1
Fenton St B2
Firbank Rd A3
Fire Station B2
Folly Gallery . . . B2
Friend's Meeting House B1
Garnet St B3
George St B2
Giant Axe Field . . . B1
Gov. Offices B2
Grand, The B2
Grasmere Rd B3
Greaves Rd C2
Green St A3
Gregson Ctr, The . . B3
Gregson Rd C3
Greyhound Br Rd . A2
Greyhound Br A2
High St B2
Hill Side B1
Hope St C3
Hubert Pl B1
Information Ctr . B2
Judges Lodgings B2
Kelsy St B1
Kentmere Rd B3
King St B2
Kingsway A3
Kirkes Rd C3
Lancaster & Lakeland C3
Lancaster City Football Club B1
Lancaster B1
Langdale Rd A3
Ley Ct B1
Library B2
Lincoln Rd B1
Lindow St C2
Lodge St B2
Long Marsh La . . . B1
Lune Rd A1
Lune St A2
Lune Valley Ramble A3
Mainway A2
Maritime Mus . . A1
Market St B2
Marketgate Shopping Ctr B2
Meadowside C2
Meeting House La . B1
Millennium Br . . . A2
Moorgate B3
Moor La B2
Morecambe Rd A1/A2
Nelson St B2
North Rd B2
Orchard La C1
Owen Rd A2
Park Rd B3
Parliament St . . . A3
Patterdale Rd . . . A3
Penny St B2
Police Station . . B2
Portland St C2
Post Office . . A2/A3/B1/B2/B3/C3
Primrose St C3
Priory B1
Prospect St C3
Quarry Rd B3
Queen St C2
Regal B2
Regent St C2
Ridge La A3
Ridge St A3
Royal Lancaster Infirmary (A&E) C2
Rydal Rd B3
Ryelands Park . . . A1
St John's B2
St Nicholas Arcades Shopping Ctr B2
St Peter's Rd B3
St Georges Quay . A1
St Leonard's Gate . B2
St Martin's Coll . . . C3
St Martin's Rd C3
St Oswald St C3
St Peter's B3
Salisbury Rd B1
Scotch Quarry Urban Park C3
Shire Hall/ HM Prison B1
Sibsey St B1
Skerton Bridge . . A2
South Rd C2
Station Rd B1
Stirling Rd C3
Storey Ave B1
Storey Gallery . . B2
Sunnyside La C1
Sylvester St C1
Tarnsyke Rd A1
Thurnham St C2
Town Hall B2
Troutbeck Rd B3
Ulleswater Rd B3
Vicarage Field B1
West Rd B1
Westbourne Dr . . . C1
Westbourne Rd . . . B1
Westham St C3
Wheatfield St B1
White Cross Education Ctr . . C2
Williamson Rd B3
Willow La B1
Windermere Rd . . . B3
Wingate-Saul Rd . B1
Wolseley St B3
Woodville St B3
Wyresdale Rd C3

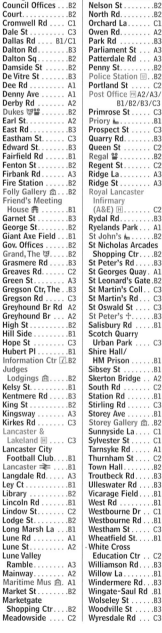

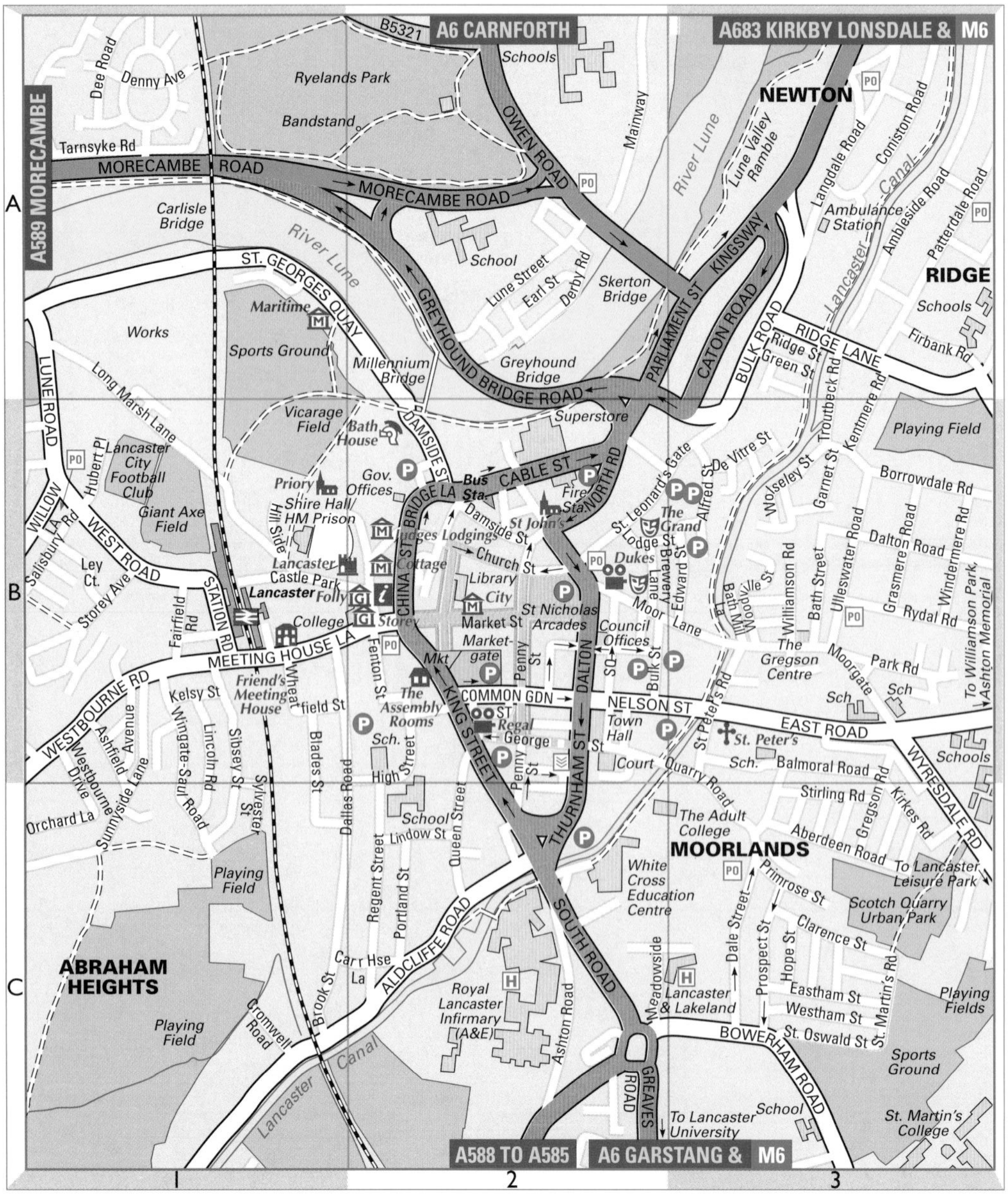

¼ mile

½ km

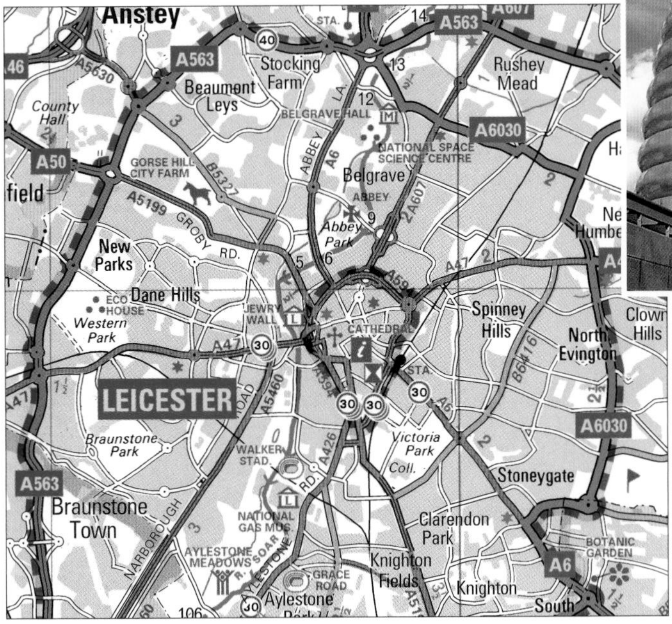

Leicester

A multi-ethnic city on the site of an important Roman settlement. Castle Park contains the timber-framed Guildhall, the Cathedral and St Mary de Castro church. The Newarke Houses Museum details the city's social history; the New Walk Museum & Art Gallery takes in Egyptology, natural history and German Expressionism; Belgrave Hall and Gardens has Georgian and Victorian period rooms and Wygston's House houses the museum of costume. Other sights include the Abbey Pumping Station science and technology museum; Ecohouse, an environmentally friendly showhouse and the National Gas Museum. Among green spaces are the award-winning Abbey Park, with the ruins of Leicester Abbey; the university's Botanic Garden; Gorse Hill City Farm; Stoughton Farm Park; and Aylestone Meadows and Water-mead country parks. There is a wide range of shops, and a 700-year-old produce market. Outside the city centre, the 'Golden Mile' on Belgrave Road is the place to go for Indian food and jewellery.

▲The National Space Centre

Leicester Tourist Information Centre, 7-9 Every Street, Town Hall Square, Leicester LE1 6AG, Tel 0906 294 1113 (25p per minute)

BBC Radio Leicester 104.9 FM
Leicester Sound 105.4 FM
Sabras Radio 1260 AM

www.leicester.gov.uk

★Do not miss

★**Guru Nanak Sikh Museum**, 9 Holy Bones

★**Jewry Wall History Museum**, St Nicholas Circle

★**National Space Centre**, Exploration Drive

Leicester

Abbey St A2
All Saints' A1
Aylestone Rd C2
Bath La A1
Bede Park C1
Bedford St A3
Bedford St South A3
Belgrave Gate A2
Belle Vue A2
Belvoir St B2
Braunstone Gate B1
Burleys Way A2
Burnmoor St C2
Bus Station A2
Canning St A2
Castle B1
Castle Gardens B1
Cathedral B2
Causeway La A2
Charles St B3
Chatham St B2
Christow St A3
Church Gate A2
City Gallery B3
Civic Centre B2
Clock Tower B2
Clyde St A3
Colton St B3
Conduit St B3
Corn Exchange B2
Crafton St A3
Craven St A1
Crown Courts B3
Deacon St C2
De Montfort Hall C3
De Montfort St C3
De Montfort Univ C1
Dover St B3
Duns La B1
Dunton St A1
East St B3
Eastern Boulevard C1
Edmonton Rd A3
Erskine St A3
Filbert St C1
Filbert St East C2
Fire Station C3
Fleet St A3
Friar La B2
Friday St A2
Gateway St C2
Glebe St B3
Granby St B3
Grange La C2
Grasmere St C1
Great Central St A1
Guildhall B2
Guru Nanak Sikh Museum B1
Halford St B2
Havelock St C2
Haymarket A2
Haymarket Shopping Ctr A2
High St A2
Highcross St A1
HM Prison C2
Horsefair St B2
Humberstone Gate B2
Humberstone Rd A3
Information Ctr B2
Jarrom St C2
Jewry Wall B1
Kamloops Cr A3
King Richards Rd B1
King St B2
Lancaster Rd C3
Lee St A3
Leicester B3
Leicester R.F.C. C2
Leicester Royal Infirmary (A&E) C2
Library B2
Little Theatre B3
London Rd C3
Lower Brown St B2
Magistrates Court B2
Manitoba Rd A3
Mansfield St A2
Market B2
Market St B2
Mill La C2
Montreal Rd A3
Museum & Art Gallery C3
Narborough Rd N B1
Nelson Mandela Park C2
New St B2
New Walk C3
New Park St B1
Newarke Houses B2
Newarke St B2
Northgate St A1
Orchard St A2
Ottawa Rd A3
Oxford St C2
Phoenix B2
Police Station B3
Post Office A1/B2/C2/C3
Prebend St C3
Princess Rd East C3
Princess Rd West C3
Queen St B3
Rally Community Park, The A2
Regent College C3
Regent Rd C2/C3
Repton St A1
Rutland St B3
St George St B3
St Georges Way B3
St John St A2
St Margaret's A2
St Margaret's Way A2
St Martins B2
St Mary de Castro B1
St Matthew's Way A3
St Nicholas B1
St Nicholas Circle B1
St Peter's La A2
Sanvey Gate A2
Shires Shopping Centre A2
Silver St B2
Slater St A1
Soar La A1
South Albion St B3
Southampton St B3
Swain St B3
Swan St A1
The Gateway C2
The Newarke B1
Tigers Way C3
Tower St C3
Town Hall B2
Tudor Rd B1
Univ of Leicester C3
University Rd C3
Upperton Rd C1
Vaughan Way A2
Walnut St C2
Watling St A2
Welford Rd B2
Wellington St B2
West Bridge B1
West St C3
West Walk C3
Western Blvd C1
Western Rd C1
Wharf St North A3
Wharf St South A3
'Y' Theatre B3
Yeoman St A3
York Rd B2

¼ mile
¼ ½ km

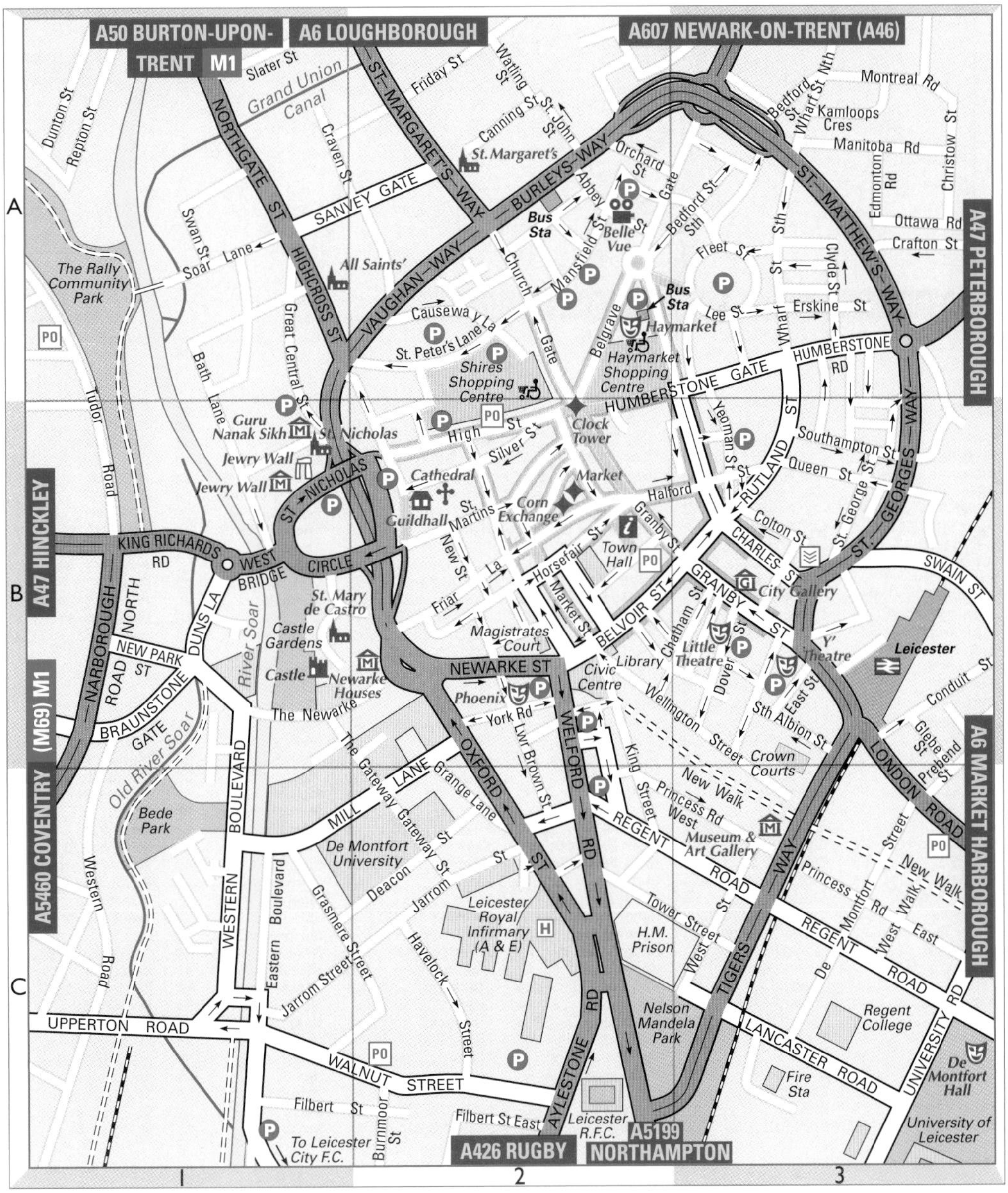

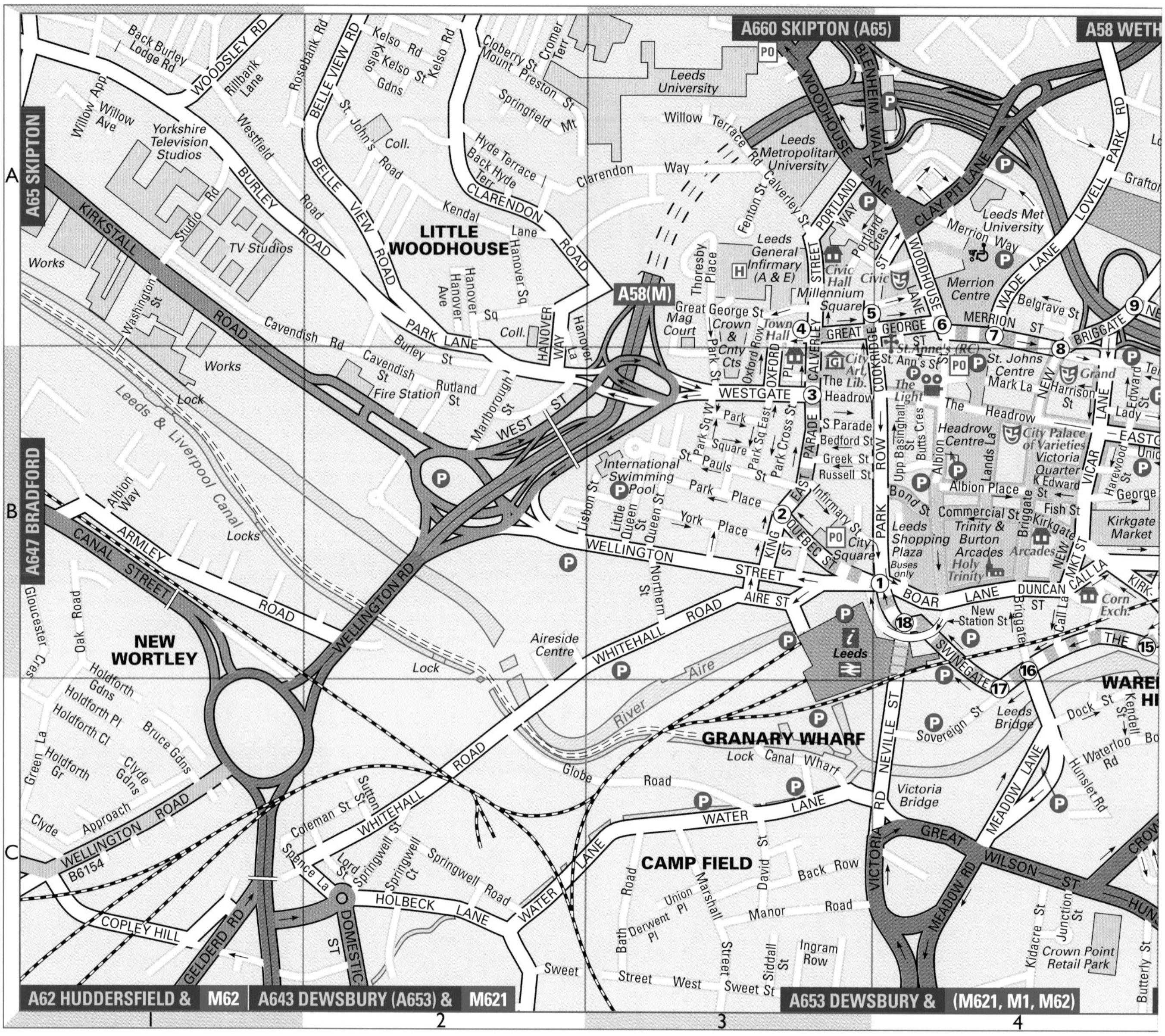

¼ mile
¼
½ km

Leeds

Aire St B3
Aireside Centre B2
Albion Pl B4
Albion St A4
Albion Way B1
Alma St A6
Arcades B4
Armley Rd B1
Back Burley Lodge Rd A1
Back Hyde Terr A2
Back Row C3
Bath Rd C3
Beckett St A6
Bedford St B3
Belgrave St A4
Belle View Rd A2
Benson St A5
Black Bull St C5
Blenheim Walk A3
Boar La B4
Bond St B4
Bow St C5
Bowman La C4
Bridge St A5/B5
Briggate B4
Bruce Gdns C1
Burley Rd A1
Burley St B1
Burmantofs St B6
Bus & Coach Station B5
Butterly St C4
Butts Cr B4
Byron St A5
Call La B4
Calverley St A3/B3
Canal St B1
Canal Wharf C3
Carlisle Rd C5
Cavendish Rd A1
Cavendish St A2
Chadwick St C5
Cherry Pl A6
Cherry Row A5
City Art Gallery & Library B3
City Palace of Varieties B4
City Sq B3
Civic Theatre A4
Civic Hall A3
Clarendon Rd A2
Clarendon Way A3
Clark La C6
Clay Pit La A4
Cloberry St A2
Clyde Approach C1
Clyde Gdns C1
Coleman St C2
Commercial St B4
Concord St A5
Cookridge St A4
Corn Exchange B4
Cromer Terr A2
Cromwell St A5
Cross Catherine St B6
Cross Green La C6
Cross Stamford St A5
Crown & County Courts A3
Crown Point Bridge C5
Crown Point Retail Park C4
Crown Point Rd C4
David St C3
Dent St C6
Derwent Pl C3
Dial St C6
Dock St C4
Dolly La A6
Domestic St C2
Duke St B5
Duncan St B4
Dyer St B5
East Field St B6
East Pde B3
East St C5
Eastgate B5
Easy Rd C6
Edward St B4
Ellerby La C6
Ellerby Rd C6
Fenton St A3
Fire Station B2
Fish St B4
Flax Pl B5
Gelderd Rd C1
George St B4
Globe Rd C2
Gloucester Cr B1
Gower St A5
Grafton St A4
Grand Theatre B4
Granville Rd A6
Great George St A3
Great Wilson St C4
Greek St B3
Green La C1
Hanover Ave A2
Hanover La A2
Hanover Sq A2
Hanover Way A2
Harewood St B4
Harrison St B4
Haslewood Cl B6
Haslewood Drive B6
Headrow Centre B4
High Court B5
Hill St A6
Holbeck La C2
Holdforth Cl C1
Holdforth Gdns B1
Holdforth Gr C1
Holdforth Pl C1
Holy Trinity B4
Hope Rd A5
Hunslet La C4
Hunslet Rd C4
Hyde Terr A2
Infirmary St B4
Information Ctr B3
Ingram Row C3
International Swimming Pool B3
Junction St C4
King Edward St B4
Kelso Gdns A2
Kelso Rd A2
Kelso St A2
Kendal La A2
Kendell St C4
Kidacre St C4
King St B3
Kippax Pl C6
Kirkgate B4
Kirkgate Market B4
Kirkstall Rd A1
Kitson St C6
Lady La B4
Lands La B4
Lavender Walk B6
Leeds Bridge C4
Leeds General Infirmary (A&E) A3
Leeds Metropolitan University A3/A4
Leeds Shopping Plaza B4
Leeds Station B3
Leeds University A3
Light, The B4
Lincoln Green Rd A6
Lincoln Rd A5
Lindsey Gdns A6
Lindsey Rd A6
Lisbon St B3
Little Queen St B3
Long Close La C6
Lord St C2
Lovell Park Rd A4
Lovell Rd A5
Lower Brunswick St A5
Mabgate A5
Macauly St A5
Magistrates Court A3
Manor Rd C3
Mark La B4
Marlborough St B1
Marsh La B6
Marshall St C3
Meadow La C4
Meadow Rd C4
Melbourne St A5
Merrion Centre A4
Merrion St A4
Merrion Way A4
Mill St B5
Millennium Sq A3
Mount Preston St A2
Mushroom St A5
Neville St C4
New Briggate A4/B4
New Market St B4
New Station St B4
New Wade La A4
New York Rd A5
New York St B5
Nile St A5
Nippet La A6
North St A4
Northern St B3
Oak Rd B1
Oxford Pl B3
Oxford Row A3
Park Cross St B3
Park La A2
Park Pl B3
Park Row B4
Park Sq B3
Park Sq East B3
Park Sq West B3
Park St B3
Police Station B5
Pontefract La B6
Portland Cr A3
Portland Way A3
Post Office PO A3/B3/B5
Quarry House (NHS/DSS Headquarters) B5
Quebec St B3
Queen St B3
Railway St B5
Rectory St A6
Regent St A5
Richmond St C5
Rigton Approach B6
Rigton Dr B6
Rillbank La A1
Rosebank Rd A1
Royal Armouries C5
Russell St B3
Rutland St B1
St Ann's St B4
St Anne's Cathedral (RC) ✝ A4
St James' Hospital A6
St Johns Centre B4
St John's Rd A2
St Mary's St B5
St Pauls St B3
St Peter's B5
Saxton La B5
Sayner La C5
Shakespeare Ave A6
Shannon St B6
Sheepscar St South A5
Siddall St C3
Skinner La A5
South Pde B3
Sovereign St C4
Spence La C2
Springfield Mt A2
Springwell Ct C2
Springwell Rd C2
Springwell St C2
Stoney Rock La A6
Studio Rd A1
Sutton St C2
Sweet St C3
Sweet St West C3
Swinegate B4
Templar St B5
The Calls B5
The Close B6
The Drive B6
The Garth B5
The Headrow B3/B4
The Lane B5
The Parade B6
Thoresby Pl A3
Torre Rd A6
Town Hall A3
Trinity & Burton Arcades B4
Union Pl C3
Union St B5
Upper Basinghall St B4
Upper Accomodation Rd B6
Vicar La B4
Victoria Bridge C4
Victoria Quarter B4
Victoria Rd C4
Washington St A1
Water La C3
Waterloo Rd C3
Wellington Rd B2/C1
Wellington St B3
West St B1
West Yorkshire Playhouse B5
Westfield Rd A1
Westgate B3
Whitehall Rd B3/C2
Whitelock St A5
Willis St C6
Willow Approach A1
Willow Ave A1
Willow Terrace Rd A3
Wintoun St A5
Woodhouse La A3/A4
Woodsley Rd A1
York Pl B3
York Rd B6
Yorkshire Television Studios A1

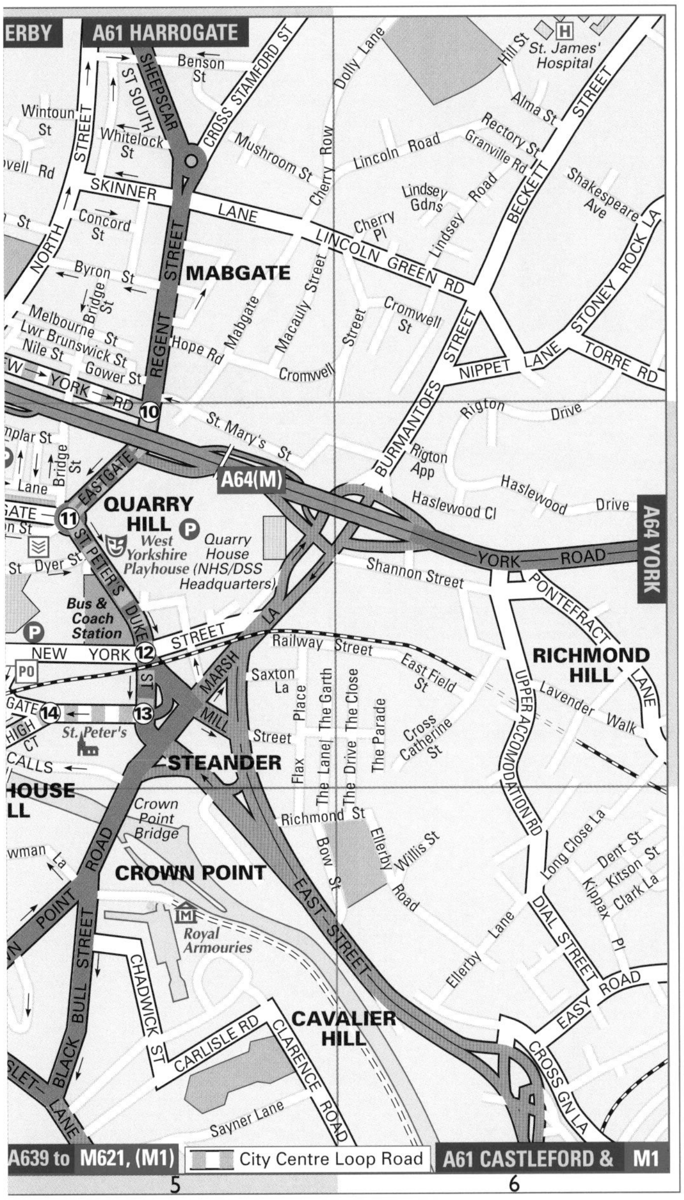

The history of Leeds is in the engineering and textiles industries, in the manufacture of machinery for spinning, machine tools, steam engines and gears as well as other industries based on textiles, chemicals and leather and pottery. In recent years Leeds has been rejuvenated and has become a major shopping centre for northern England, attracting names such as Harvey Nichols, Vivienne Westwood and Joseph in the Victoria Quarter, whilst Briggate boasts a selection of independents, Corngate Exchange and surrounds features all manner of styles. There is also Granary Wharf featuring more alternative style, and gift shops. Kirkgate Market is the largest of its kind in Europe and sells everything from groceries to underwear. Several important theatres have made their home in Leeds and there's no shortage of clubs, bars and restaurants.

Gateway Yorkshire, Regional Travel & Tourism Centre, The Arcade, Leeds City Station, Leeds LS1 1PL
Tel 0113 242 5242

BBC Radio Leeds 92.4 FM and 774 AM • **Radio Aire** 96.3 FM
Galaxy 105 105 FM

www.leeds.gov.uk

★Do not miss

- ★**Leeds Art Gallery**, The Headrow
- ★**Henry Moore Institute**, The Headrow
- ★**Royal Armouries Museum**, Armouries Drive

▲Leeds Corn Exchange

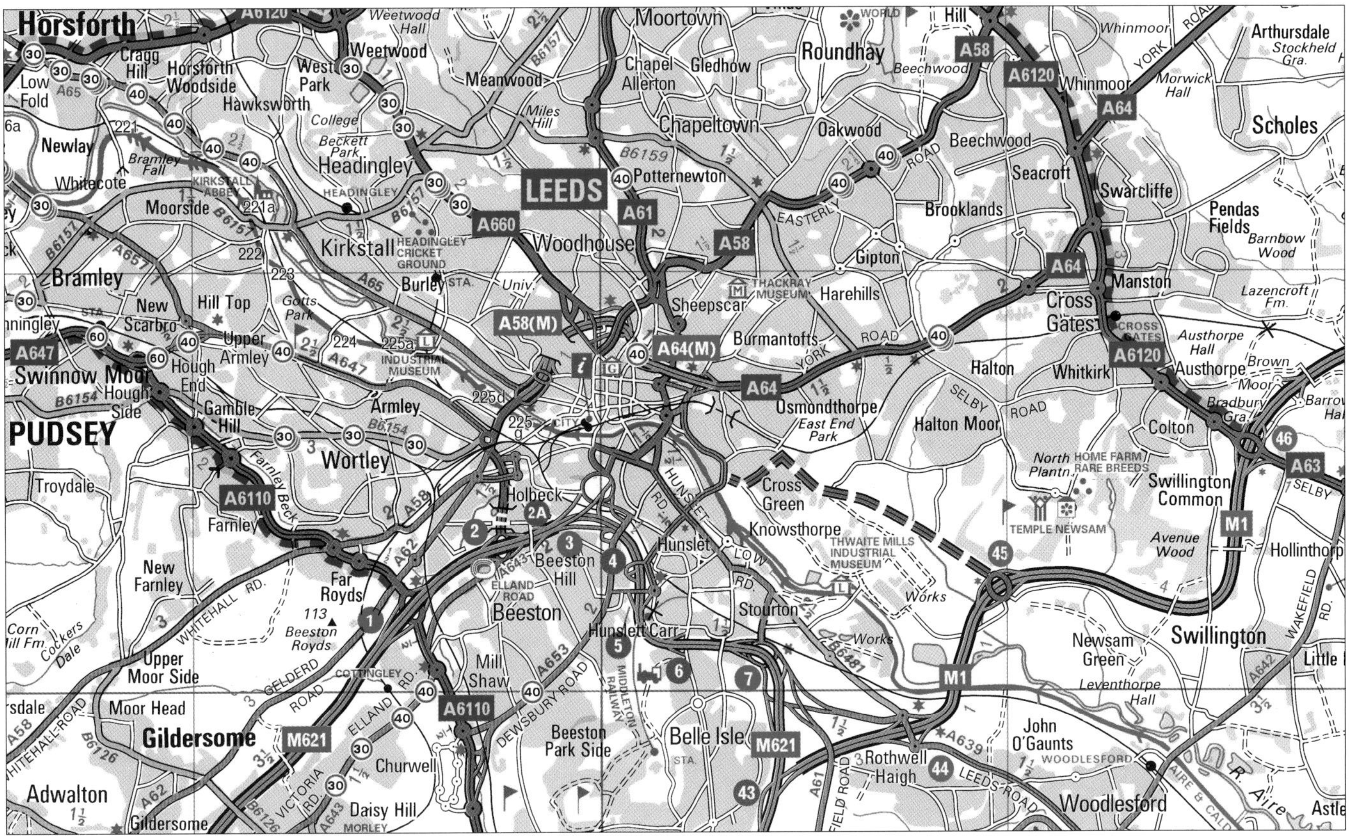

Lewes

▲Anne of Cleves House

A Saxon-origin county town on the edge of the rolling South Downs, where William de Warenne, a favourite of William the Conqueror, built an impressive castle and priory (now ruined). Characterised by its narrow medieval 'twittens' (twisting lanes), it also has some impressive Georgian townhouses. Other buildings of interest are the Victorian-Gothic Harvey's Brewery, the restored late-16th-century Southover Grange, the town hall with its Renaissance staircase and mayor's parlour displaying local treasures. The many speciality and antiques shops include the The Old Needlemakers' Factory crafts centre. Nearby attractions include the South Downs; Firle Place and Glynde Place country houses and parks; Charleston Farmhouse and Monks House, both owned by members of the Bloomsbury set; Berwick Church, which has murals they painted; Michelham Priory; Glyndebourne Opera House; the Long Man of Wilmington and Bentley Wildfowl & Motor Museum.

Lewes Tourist Information Centre, 187 High Street, Lewes BN7 2DE
Tel 01273 483448

BBC Southern Counties 104.5 FM and 1161 AM • **Southern FM** 103.5 FM

www.lewes.gov.uk

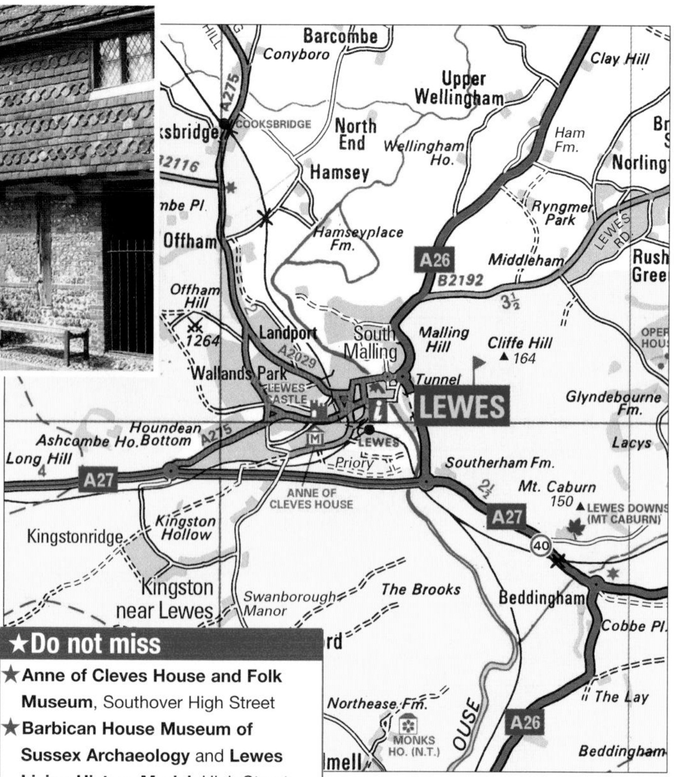

★Do not miss

★**Anne of Cleves House and Folk Museum**, Southover High Street

★**Barbican House Museum of Sussex Archaeology** and **Lewes Living History Model**, High Street

★**Lewes Castle**, Castle Hill

★**St Pancras Priory**, Southover

¼ mile
¼ ½ km

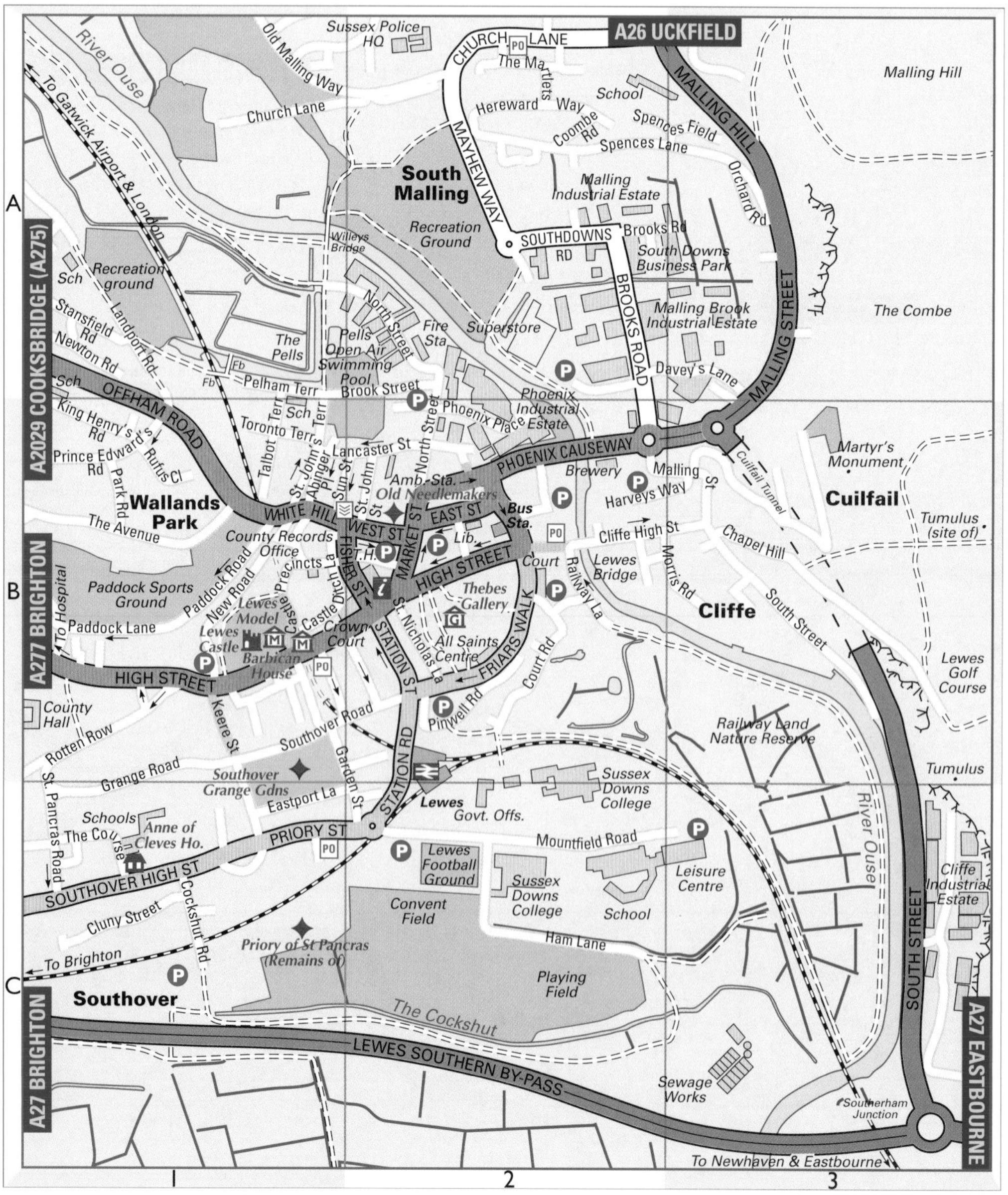

Lewes

Abinger Pl B1
All Saints Centre. .B2
Ambulance Station B2
Anne of Cleves House C1
Barbican House Museum B1
Brewery B2
Brook St......... A2
Brooks Rd A2
Bus Station B2
Castle Ditch La ...B1
Castle Precincts ..B1
Chapel Hill.......B3
Church La.... A1/A2
Cliffe High St.....B2
Cliffe Industrial Estate.......... C3
Cluny St C1
Cockshut Rd C1
Convent Field ... C2
Coombe Rd A2
County Hall B1
County Records Office..........B1
Court............B2
Court Rd.........B2
Crown Court B2
Cuilfail Tunnel B3
Davey's La A3
East St B2
Eastport La C1
Fire Station A2
Fisher St.........B2
Friars Walk B2
Garden St........B1
Government Offices C2
Grange Rd B1
Ham La.......... C2
Harveys Way B2
Hereward Way... A2
High St B1/B2
Information Ctr .B2
Keere St B1
King Henry's Rd ..B1
Lancaster St.......B2
Landport Rd...... A1
Leisure Centre... C3
Lewes Bridge.....B2
Lewes Castle ...B1
Lewes Football Ground C2
Lewes Golf CourseB3
Lewes Living History Model B2
Lewes Southern By-Pass C2
Lewes Station .B2
Library B2
Malling Ind Est .. A2
Malling Brook Ind Est A3
Malling Hill A3
Malling St ... A3/B3
Market St.........B2
Martyr's Monument......B3
Mayhew Way A2
Morris Rd.........B3
Mountfield Rd ... C2
New Rd...........B1
Newton Rd....... A1
North St A2/B2
Offham Rd B1
Old Malling Way . A1
Old Needlemakers Craft Centre ✦ ..B2
Orchard Rd A3
Paddock La B1
Paddock Rd B1
Paddock Sports Ground..........B1
Park Rd B1
Pelham Terr A1
Pells Open Air Swimming Pool. A1
Phoenix CausewayB2
Phoenix Ind Est...B2
Phoenix Pl B2
Pinwell Rd B2
Police Station ..B1
Post Office A2/B1/B2/C1
Prince Edward's Rd..............B1
Priory St......... C1
Priory of St Pancras (remains of) ✦ . C1
Railway La B2
Railway Land Nature Reserve..B3
Rotten Row B1
Rufus Cl B1
St Pancras Rd ... C1
St John St B2
St John's Terr B1
St Nicholas La....B2
Sewage Works... C3
South Downs Business Park .. A3
South St B3/C3
Southdowns Rd.. A2
Southerham Junction....... C3
Southover Grange Gdns ✦..B1
Southover High St C1
Southover Rd.....B1
Spences Field ... A3
Spences La A2
Stansfield Rd.... A1
Station Rd B2
Station St.........B2
Sun St............B1
Sussex Downs College........ C2
Sussex Police HQ A2
Talbot Terr B1
The Avenue B1
The Course C1
The Martlets A2
The Pells A1
Thebes Gallery .B2
Toronto Terr......B1
Town Hall.........B2
West St...........B2
White Hill.........B1
Willeys Bridge... A1

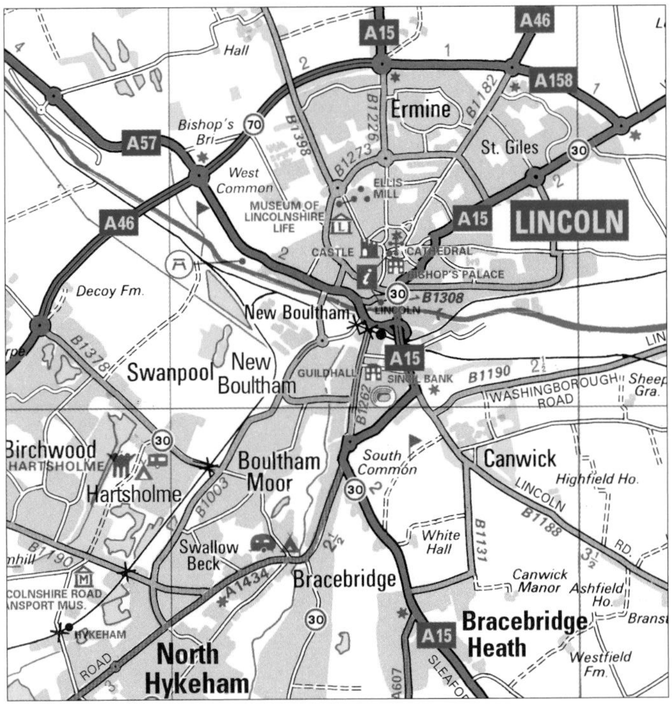

Lincoln

▲Lincoln Cathedral

The city of Lincoln has had many incarnations – a prehistoric fort, a Roman settlement, captured by the Angles, then the Danes, and one of the largest cities in the country. William the Conqueror commissioned the magnificent castle in 1068 and the Cathedral in 1072. One of only four copies of the Magna Carta, sealed by King John, is to be found at the castle. Newport Arch in the town is the only Roman arch still used by traffic. The narrow hilly cobbled streets are lined with interesting shops of all types. There's a regular Farmer's Market and a host of restaurants and pubs for every taste.

Lincoln Tourist Information Centre, 21 Cornhill, Lincoln LN5 7HB Tel 01522 873256

BBC Radio Lincolnshire 94.9 FM • **Lincs FM** 102.2 FM

www.visitlincolnshire.com

★Do not miss

★**Lincoln Cathedral**
★**Lincoln Castle**
★**Bishop's Palace**, Minster Yard

Lincoln

Alexandra Terr . . . B1
Anchor St . . . C1
Arboretum . . . B3
Arboretum Ave . . . B3
Baggholme Rd . . . B3
Bailgate . . . A2
Beaumont Fee . . . B1
Bishop's Palace . . . B2
Brayford Way . . . C1
Brayford Wharf East . . . C1
Brayford Wharf North . . . B1
Bruce Rd . . . A2
Burton Rd . . . A1
Bus Station (City) C2
Canwick Rd . . . C2
Cardinal's Hat ✦ . . B2
Carline Rd . . . B1
Castle . . . B1
Castle St . . . A1
Cathedral & Treasury ✝ . . . B2
Cathedral St . . . B2
Cecil St . . . A2
Chapel La . . . A2
Cheviot St . . . B3
Church La . . . A2
City Hall . . . B1
Clasketgate . . . B2
Clayton Sports Ground . . . A3
Collection, The . . B2
County Hospital (A&E) H . . . B3
County Office . . . B1
Courts . . . C1
Croft St . . . B2
Cross St . . . C2
Crown Courts . . . B1
Curle Ave . . . A3
Danesgate . . . B2
Drury La . . . B1
East Bight . . . A2
East Gate . . . A2
Eastcliff Rd . . . B3
Eastgate . . . B2
Egerton Rd . . . A3
Ellis Mill . . . A1
Environment Agency . . . C2
Exchequer Gate ✦ B2
Firth Rd . . . C1
Flaxengate . . . B2
Florence St . . . B3
George St . . . C3
Good La . . . A2
Gray St . . . A1
Great Northern Terr . . . C3
Great Northern Terrace Industrial Estate . . . C3
Greetwell Rd . . . B3
Greetwellgate . . . B3
Haffenden Rd . . . A2
High St . . . B2/C1
Hospital (Private) H . . . A2
Hungate . . . B2
Information Ctr i . B2
James St . . . A2
Jews House & Court . . . B2
Kesteven St . . . C2
Langworthgate . . . A2
Lawn Visitor Centre, The . . . B1
Lee Rd . . . A3
Library . . . B2
Lincoln . . . C2
Lincolnshire Life/ Royal Lincolnshire Regiment Mus A1
Lindum Rd . . . B2
Lindum Sports Ground . . . A3
Lindum Terr . . . B3
Mainwaring Rd . . . A3
Manor Rd . . . A2
Massey Rd . . . A3
Mildmay St . . . A1
Mill Rd . . . A1
Millman Rd . . . B3
Minster Yard . . . B2
Market . . . C2
Monks Rd . . . B3
Montague St . . . B2
Mount St . . . A1
Nettleham Rd . . . A2
Newland . . . B1
Newport . . . A2
Newport Arch . . . A2
Newport Cemetery . . . A2
North Lincs College . . . B2
Northgate . . . A2
Odeon . . . C1
Orchard St . . . B1
Oxford St . . . C2
Pelham Bridge . . . C2
Pelham St . . . C2
Police Station . . . B1
Portland St . . . C2
Post Office PO . A1/A2/B1/B3/C2
Potter Gate . . . B2
Priory Gate . . . B2
Queensway . . . A3
Rasen La . . . A1
Ropewalk . . . C1
Rosemary La . . . B2
St Anne's Rd . . . B3
St Benedict's . . . C1
St Giles Ave . . . A3
St John's Rd . . . A2
St Mark St . . . C1
St Mark's Retail Park . . . C1
St Mark's Shopping Centre C1
St Mary-Le-Wigford . . . C1
St Mary's St . . . C2
St Nicholas St . . . A2
St Swithin's . . . B2
Saltergate . . . C1
Saxon St . . . A1
Sewell Rd . . . B3
Silver St . . . B2
Sincil St . . . C2
Spital St . . . A2
Spring Hill . . . B1
Stamp End . . . C3
Steep Hill . . . B2
Stonefield Ave . . . A2
Tentercroft St . . . C1
The Avenue . . . B1
The Grove . . . A3
Theatre Royal . . B2
Tritton Retail Pk . C1
Tritton Rd . . . C1
Union Rd . . . B1
Univ of Lincoln . . C1
Upper Lindum St . . B3
Upper Long Leys Rd . . . A1
Vere St . . . A2
Victoria St . . . B1
Victoria Terr . . . B1
Vine St . . . B3
Wake St . . . A1
Waldeck St . . . A1
Waterside Ctr . . . C2
Waterside North . C2
Waterside South . C2
West Pde . . . B1
Westgate . . . A2
Wigford Way . . . C1
Williamson St . . . A2
Wilson St . . . A1
Winn St . . . B3
Wragby Rd . . . A3
Yarborough Rd . . A1

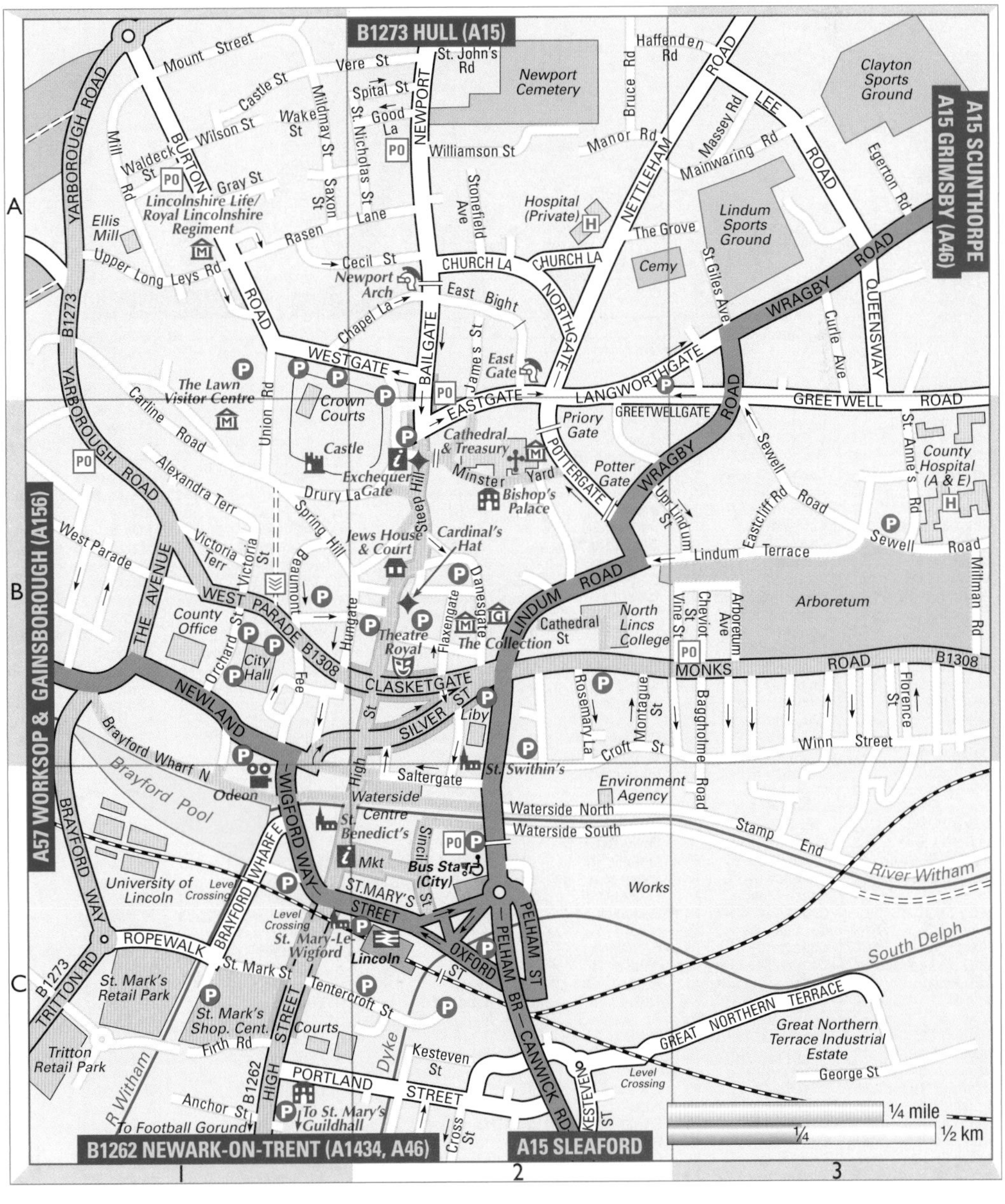

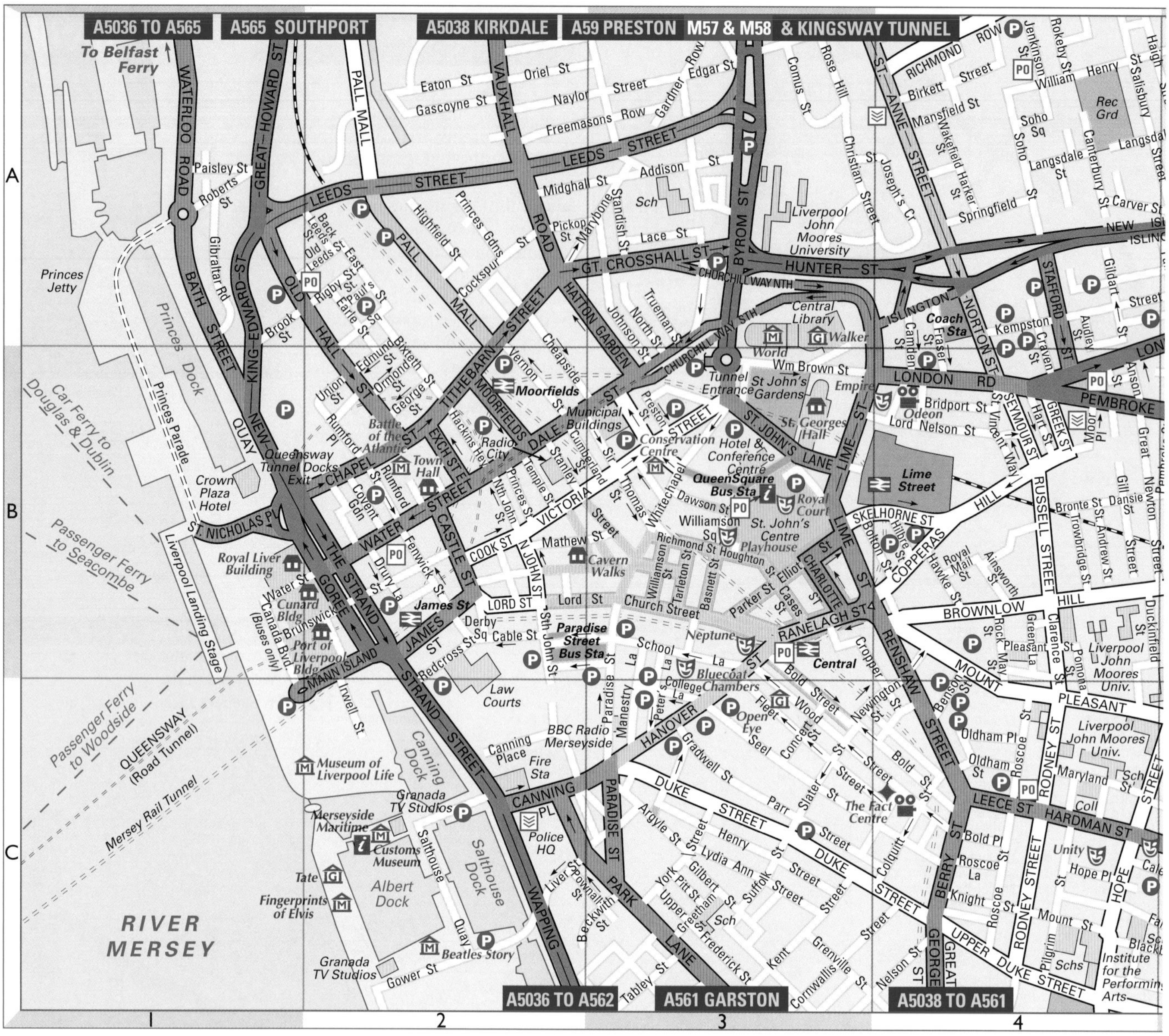

Liverpool

Abercromby Sq C5
Addison St A3
Adelaide Rd B6
Ainsworth St B4
Albany Rd B6
Albert Dock C2
Albert Edward Rd B6
Angela St C6
Anson St B4
Archbishop Blanche High School B6
Argyle St C2
Arrad St C4
Ashton St B5
Audley St A4
Back Leeds St A2
Basnett St B3
Bath St A1
Battle of the Atlantic B2
BBC Radio Merseyside C2
Beatles Story C2
Beckwith St C3
Bedford Close C5
Bedford St North C5
Bedford St South C5
Benson St C4
Berry St C4
Birkett St A4
Bixteth St B2
Blackburne Place C4
Bold Place C4
Bold St C4
Bolton St B3
Bridport St B4
Bronte St B4
Brook St A1
Brownlow Hill B4/B5
Brownlow St B5
Brunswick Rd A5
Brunswick St B1
Butler Cr A6
Byrom St A3
Cable St B2
Caledonia St C4
Cambridge St C5
Camden St A4
Canada Blvd B1
Canning Dock C2
Canning Place C2
Canterbury St A4
Cardwell St C6
Carver St A4
Cases St B3
Castle St B2
Cavern Walks B3
Central Library A3
Central Station B3
Chapel St B2
Charlotte St B3
Chatham Place C6
Chatham St C5
Cheapside B2
Chestnut St C5
Christian St A3
Church St B3
Churchill Way North A3
Churchill Way South B3
Clarence St B4
Coach Station A4
Cobden St A5
Cockspur St A2
College La C3
College St North A5
College St South A5
Colquitt St C4
Comus St A3
Concert St C3
Connaught Rd B6
Conservation Centre B3
Cook St B2
Copperas Hill B3
Cornwallis St C3
Covent Garden B2
Craven St A4
Cropper St B3
Crown St B5/C6
Cumberland St B2
Cunard Building B1
Dale St B2
Dansie St B4
Daulby St B5
Dawson St B3
Dental Hospital Museum B5
Derby Sq B2
Drury La B2
Duckinfield St B4
Duke St C3
Earle St A2
East St A2
Eaton St A2
Edgar St A3
Edge La B6
Edinburgh Rd A6
Edmund St B2
Elizabeth St B5
Elliot St B3
Empire Theatre B4
Empress Rd B6
Epworth St A5
Erskine St A5
Everyman Theatre C5
Exchange St East B2
Fact Centre, The C4
Falkland St A5
Falkner St C5/C6
Farnworth St A6
Fenwick St B2
Fielding St A6
Fingerprints of Elvis C2
Fleet St C3
Fraser St A4
Freemasons Row A2
Gardner Row A3
Gascoyne St A2
George St B2
Gibraltar Row A1
Gilbert St C3
Gildart St A4
Gill St B4
Goree B2
Gower St C2
Gradwell St C3
Granada TV Studios C2
Great Crosshall St A3
Great George St C4
Great Howard St A1
Great Newton St B4
Greek St B4
Green La B4
Greenside A5
Greetham St C3
Gregson St A5
Grenville St C3
Grinfield St C6
Grove St C5
Guelph St A6
Hackins Hey B2
Haigh St A4
Hall La B6
Hanover St B3
Harbord St C6
Hardman St C4
Harker St A4
Hart St B4
Hatton Garden A2
Hawke St B4
Helsby St B6
Henry St C3
Highfield St A2
Highgate St B6
Hilbre St B4
HM Customs & Excise National Museum C2
Hope Place C4
Hope St C4
Houghton St B3
Hunter St A3
Hutchinson St A6
Information Ctr B3/C2
Institute For The Performing Arts C4
Irvine St B6
Irwell St B2
Islington A4
James St B2
James St Station B2
Jenkinson St A4
Johnson St A3
Jubilee Drive B6
Kempston St A4
Kensington A6
Kensington Gdns B6
Kensington St A6
Kent St C3
King Edward St A1
Kinglake St B6
Knight St C4
Lace St A3
Langsdale St A4
Law Courts C2
Leece St C4
Leeds St A2
Leopold Rd B6
Lime St B3
Lime St Station B4
Little Woolton St B5
Liver St C2
Liverpool John Moores University A3/B4/C4
Liverpool Landing Stage B1
London Rd A4/B4
Lord Nelson St B4
Lord St B2
Lovat St C6
Low Hill A5
Low Wood St A6
Lydia Ann St C3
Manestry La C3
Mann Island B2
Mansfield St A4
Marmaduke St B6
Marsden St A6
Martensen St B6
Marybone A3
Maryland St C4
Mason St B6
Mathew St B2
May St B4
Melville Place C6
Merseyside Maritime Museum C2
Metropolitan Cathedral (RC) B5
Midghall St A2
Molyneux Rd A6
Moor Place B4
Moorfields B2
Moorfields Station B2
Moss St A5
Mount Pleasant B4/B5
Mount St C4
Mount Vernon View B6
Mulberry St C5
Municipal Buildings B2
Museum of Liverpool Life C2
Myrtle Gdns C6
Myrtle St C5
Naylor St A2
Nelson St C4
Neptune Theatre B3
New Islington A4
New Quay B1
Newington St C3
North John St B2
North St A3
North View B6
Norton St A4
Oakes St B5
Odeon B4
Old Hall St A1
Old Leeds St A2
Oldham Place C4
Oldham St C4
Olive St C5
Open Eye Gallery C3
Oriel St A2
Ormond St B2
Orphan St C6
Overbury St C6
Overton St B6
Oxford St C5
Paisley St A1
Pall Mall A2
Paradise St C3
Paradise St Bus Station B2
Park La C3
Parker St B3
Parr St C3
Peach St B5
Pembroke Place B4
Pembroke St B5
Peter's La C3
Philharmonic Hall C5
Pickop St A2
Pilgrim St C4
Pitt St C3
Playhouse Theatre B3
Pleasant St B4
Police Headquarters C2
Police Station A4/B4
Pomona St B4
Port of Liverpool Building B2
Post Office A2/A4
Pownall St C2
Prescot St A5
Preston St B3
Princes Dock A1
Princes Gdns A2
Princes Jetty A1
Princes Pde B1
Princes St B2
Pythian St A6
Queen Square Bus Station B3
Queensland St C6
Queensway Tunnel (Docks exit) B1
Queensway Tunnel (Entrance) B3
Radio City B2
Ranelagh St B3
Redcross St B2
Renfrew St B6
Renshaw St B4
Richmond Row A4
Richmond St B3
Rigby St A2
Roberts St A1
Rock St B4
Rodney St C4
Rokeby St A4
Romily St A6
Roney St C4
Roscoe La C4
Roscoe St C4
Rose Hill A3
Royal Court Theatre B3
Royal Liver Building B1
Royal Liverpool Hospital (A&E) B5
Royal Mail St B4
Rumford Place B2

¼ mile
½ km

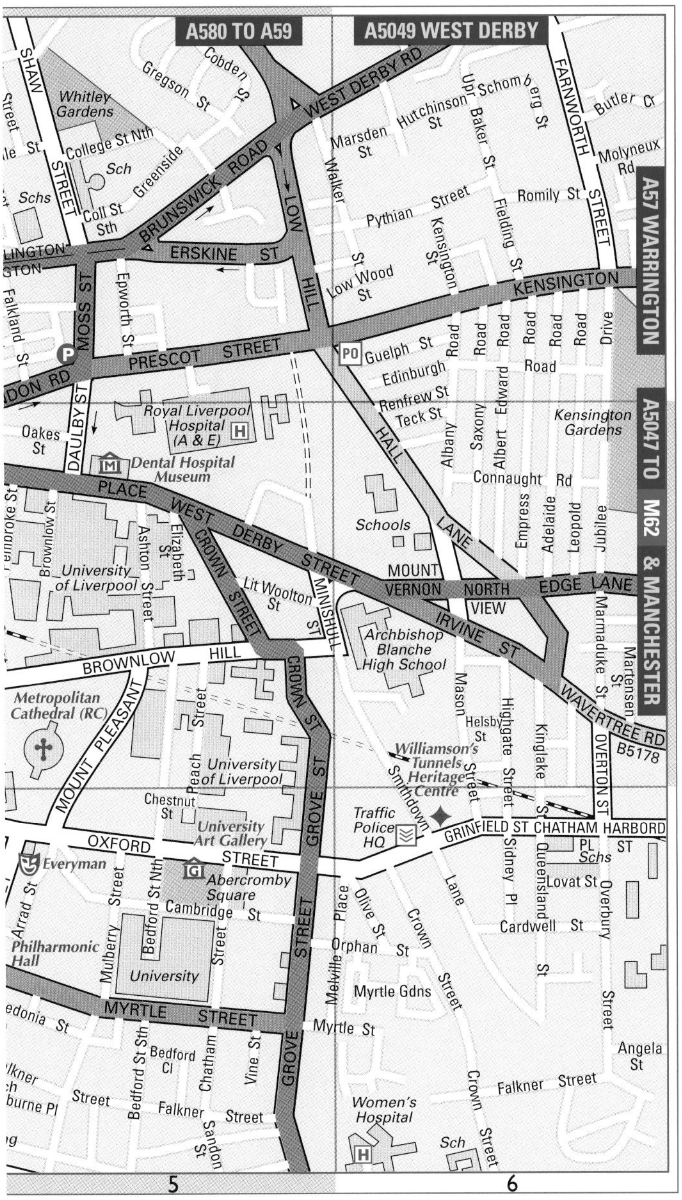

Liverpool

A city on the site of a port founded by King John in 1207 and focused around the 1846 Albert Dock, now a heritage attraction including the Merseyside Maritime Museum, the Pier Master's House & Offices; and the HM Customs & Excise National Museum. Other historic houses and buildings include Croxteth Hall & Country Park (Edwardian); the half-timbered Speke Hall; Sudley House, home to a Victorian shipping magnate and art collector; the Royal Liver Building; and Liverpool Cathedral, off Upper Duke Street, the UK's largest Anglican cathedral, designed in 1901 by Giles Gilbert Scott (there's also a Roman Catholic Metropolitan Cathedral, built 1967). Important art venues include the Walker Art Gallery, The Lady Lever Art Gallery at Port Sunlight and the University of Liverpool Art Gallery. There are many Beatles-related attractions. For sports fans there are tours of Everton Football Club and the Liverpool Football Club Museum, and tours of the Aintree racecourse.

▲The waterfront

★Do not miss

★**The Beatles Story**, Britannia Vaults, Albert Dock

★**Mersey Ferries**, Pier Head

★**Tate Liverpool**, Albert Dock – modern art gallery

Tourist Information Centre, Queens Square, Liverpool L1 1RG
Tel 0906 680 6886 (calls cost 25p per minute)

BBC Radio Merseyside 95.8 FM and 1485 AM • **Radio City** 96.7 FM **Juice** 107.6 FM • **Magic** 1548 AM

www.visitliverpool.com

Rumford St B2
Russell St. B4
St Andrew St B4
St Anne St A4
St Georges Hall B3
St John's Centre . . B3
St John's Gdns . . . B3
St John's La. B3
St Joseph's Cr. . . A4
St Minishull St. . . . B5
St Nicholas Place . B1
St Paul's Sq A2
St Vincent Way . . . B4
Salisbury St A4
Salthouse Dock . . C2
Salthouse Quay . . C2
Sandon St C5
Saxony Rd B6
Schomberg St . . . A6
School La. B2
Seel St C3
Seymour St B4
Shaw St A4
Sidney Place C6
Sir Thomas St B3
Skelhorne St B4
Slater St. C3
Smithdown La B5
Soho Sq A4
Soho St. A4
Springfield. A4
Stafford St A4
Standish St A3
Stanley St. B2
South John St B2
Strand St C2
Suffolk St. C3
Tabley St. C2
Tarleton St. B3
Tate Liverpool . . . C2
Teck St B6
Temple St. B2
The Strand. B2
Tithebarn St. B2
Town Hall B2
Traffic Police Headquarters . C6
Trowbridge St B4
Trueman St A3
Union St. B1
Unity Theatre . C4
University Art Gallery C5
University. C5
University of Liverpool B5
Upper Duke St. . . C4
Upper Frederick St. C3
Upper Baker St . . A6
Vauxhall Rd A2
Vernon St. B2
Victoria St B2
Vine St C5
Wakefield St A4
Walker Art Gallery A3
Walker St A6
Wapping. C2
Water St. B1/B2
Waterloo Rd. A1
Wavertree Rd. B6
West Derby Rd . . A6
West Derby St B5
Whitechapel B3
Whitley Gdns A5
Williamson Sq B3
Williamson St B3
Williamson's Tunnels Heritage Centre ✦ C6
William Brown St . B3
Willian Henry St . A4
Women's Hospital C6
Wood St B3
World Museum, Liverpool A3
York St C3

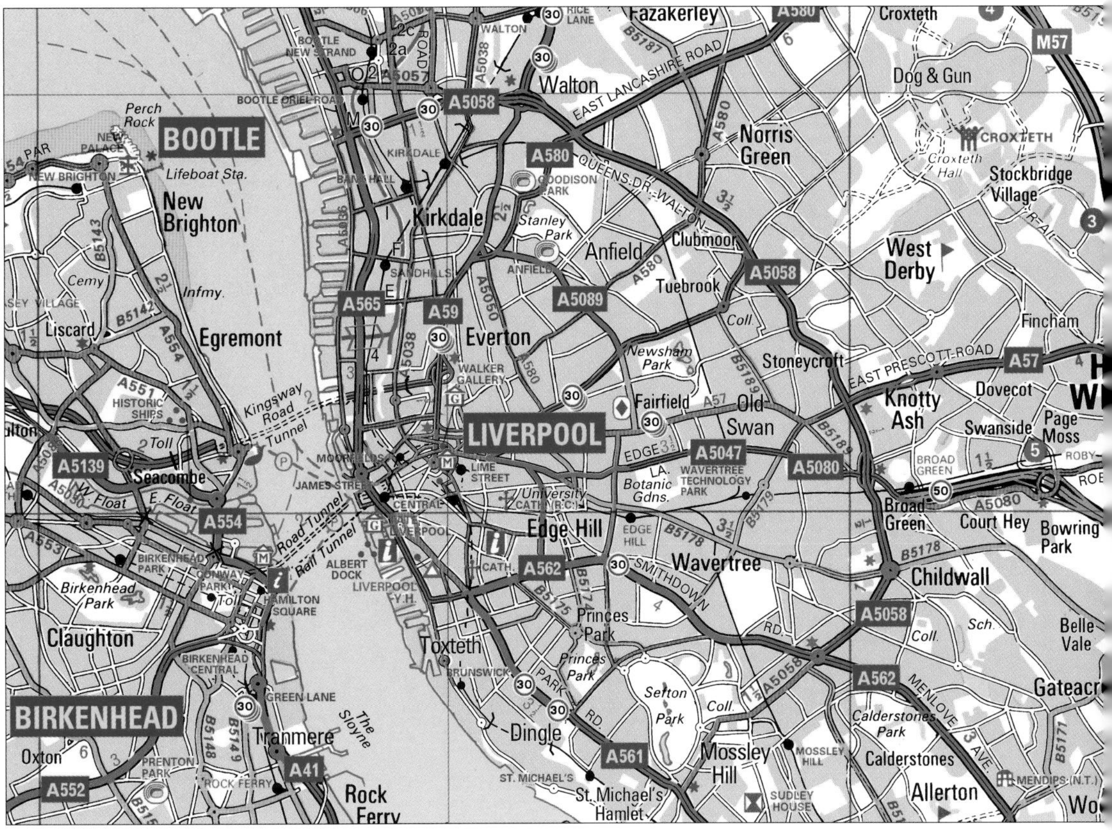

Llandudno

A North Wales Victorian seaside resort with a promenade; a 120-year-old Indian-Gothic-style pier (Wales' longest); two beaches; a cablecar and tramway to the summit of the Great Orme headland, where there is a country park with a Bronze Age copper mine and a visitor centre offering a live video link to a seabird colony; Happy Valley Park with its restored 1890 camera obscura, toboggan run and more; and St Tudno's 12th-century church on the site of the cave-cell of a 6th-century Celtic monk. Llandudno Museum shows the town's history from prehistoric times, The Llandudno Story charts how the town developed as a resort and the Oriel Mostyn contemporary art gallery has a programme of exhibitions. Nature/animal attractions include Bodafon Farm Park and RSPB Conwy Nature Reserve, and nearby are Bodnant Gardens with their views across to Snowdonia.

▲Great Orme Tramway

★Do not miss

★**Alice in Wonderland Centre**, Trinity Square

★**Great Orme Country Park**, Great Orme headland

★**Conwy Castle**, Conwy

Llandudno Tourist Information Centre, 1-2 Chapel Street, Llandudno LL30 2YU Tel 01492 876413

BBC Radio Wales 94.8 FM
Champion 103.0 FM • **Coast** 96.3 FM

www.llandudno-tourism.co.uk

¼ mile
¼ ½ km

Llandudno

Abbey Pl B1
Abbey Rd B1
Adelphi St B3
Alexandra Rd C2
Alice in Wonderland Centre ✦ B3
Anglesey Rd A1
Argyll Rd B3
Arvon Ave A2
Atlee Cl C3
Augusta St B3
Back Madoc St . . . B2
Bodafon St B3
Bodhyfryd Rd A2
Bodnant Cr C3
Bodnant Rd C3
Bridge Rd C2
Bryniau Rd C1
Builder St B3
Builder St West . . C2
Cabin Lift A2
Camera Obscura ✦ A3
Caroline Rd B2
Chapel St A2
Charlton St B3
Church Cr C1
Church Walks A2
Claremont Rd B2
Clement Ave A2
Clifton Rd B2
Clonmel St B3
Conway Rd B3
Council St West . . C3
Cricket and Recreation Grnd . B2
Cwlach Rd A2
Cwlach St A1
Cwm Howard La . C3
Cwm Pl C3
Cwm Rd C3
Dale Rd C1
Deganwy Ave B2
Denness Pl C2
Dinas Rd C2
Dolydd B1
Erol Pl B2
Ewloe Dr C3
Fairways C2
Ffordd Dewi C3
Ffordd Dulyn C2
Ffordd Dwyfor . . . C3
Ffordd Elisabeth . C3
Ffordd Gwynedd . C3
Ffordd Las C3
Ffordd Morfa C3
Ffordd Penrhyn . . C3
Ffordd Tudno C3
Ffordd yr Orsedd . C3
Ffordd Ysbyty C2
Garage St B3
George St A2
Gloddaeth Ave B1
Gloddaeth St B2
Gogarth Rd B1
Great Orme Mines ✦ A1
Great Ormes Rd . . B1
Happy Valley A2
Happy Valley Rd . . A3
Haulfre Gdns ✿ . . A1
Herkomer Cr C1
Hill Terr A2
Hospice B1
Howard Rd B3
Information Ctr ℹ . B2
Invalids' Walk B1
James St B2
Jubilee St B3
King's Ave C2
King's Rd C2
Knowles Rd C2
Lees Rd C2
Library B2
Lifeboat Station . . B2
Llandudno 🏛 A2
Llandudno (A&E) 🅷 C2
Llandudno ⇌ . . . B3
Llandudno Story ✦ B2
Llandudno Town Football Ground C2
Llewelyn Ave A2
Lloyd St West B1
Lloyd St B2
Llwynon Rd A1
Llys Maelgwn B1
Madoc St B2
Maelgwn Rd B2
Maesdu Bridge . . C2
Maesdu Rd . . . C2/C3
Maes-y-Cwm C3
Maes-y-Orsedd . . C3
Marian Pl C2
Marian Rd C2
Marine Dr (Toll) . A3
Market Hall A2
Market St A2
Miniature Golf Course A1
Morfa Rd B1
Mostyn 🏛 B3
Mostyn Broadway B3
Mostyn St B3
Mowbray Rd C2
New St A2
Norman Rd B3
North Parade A2
North Wales Golf Links C1
North Wales 🎭 . . A3
Old Rd A2
Oxford Rd B3
Pier ✦ A2
Plas Rd A2
Police Station 🏢 . . B3
Post Office 🅿🅾 B3/C2
Promenade A3
Pyllau Rd A1
Rectory La A2
Retail Park B3
Rhuddlan Ave . . . C3
St Andrew's Ave . B2
St Andrew's Pl . . . B2
St Beuno's Rd . . . A1
St David's Pl B2
St David's Rd B2
St George's Pl . . . A3
St Mary's Rd B2
St Seriol's Rd B2
Salisbury Pass . . . B1
Salisbury Rd B2
Somerset St B3
South Parade A2
Stephen St B3
TA Centre B3
Tabor Hill A2
The Oval B1
The Parade B3
Town Hall B2
Trinity Ave B1
Trinity Cres C1
Trinity Sq B3
Tudno St A2
Ty-Coch Rd A2
Ty-Gwyn Rd A1
Ty-Gwyn Rd A2
Ty'n-y-Coed Rd . . A1
Vaughan St B3
Victoria Shopping Centre B3
Victoria Tram Station A2
War Memorial ✦ . A2
Werny Wylan C3
West Parade B1
Whiston Pass A2
Winllan Ave C2
Wyddfyd Rd A2
York Rd A2

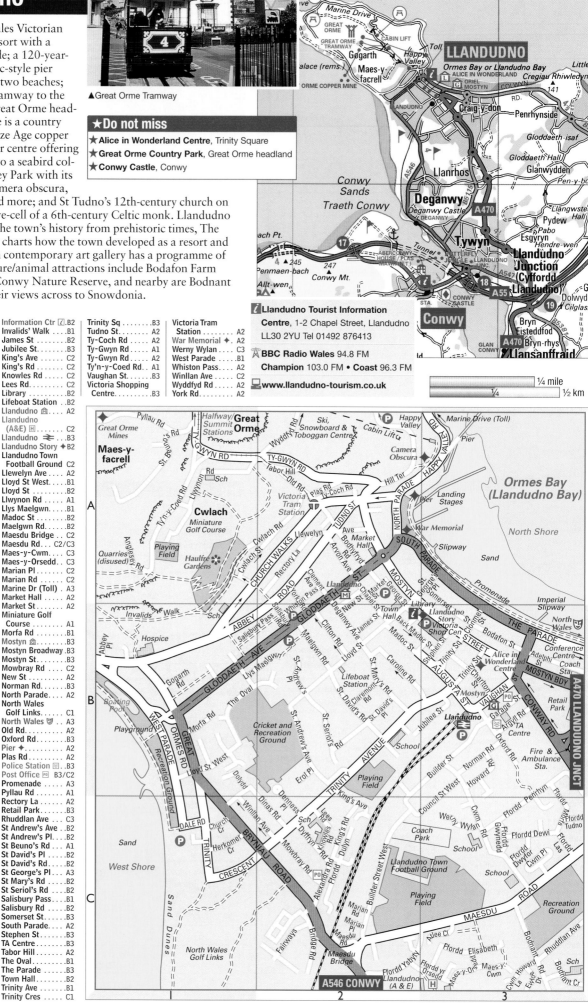

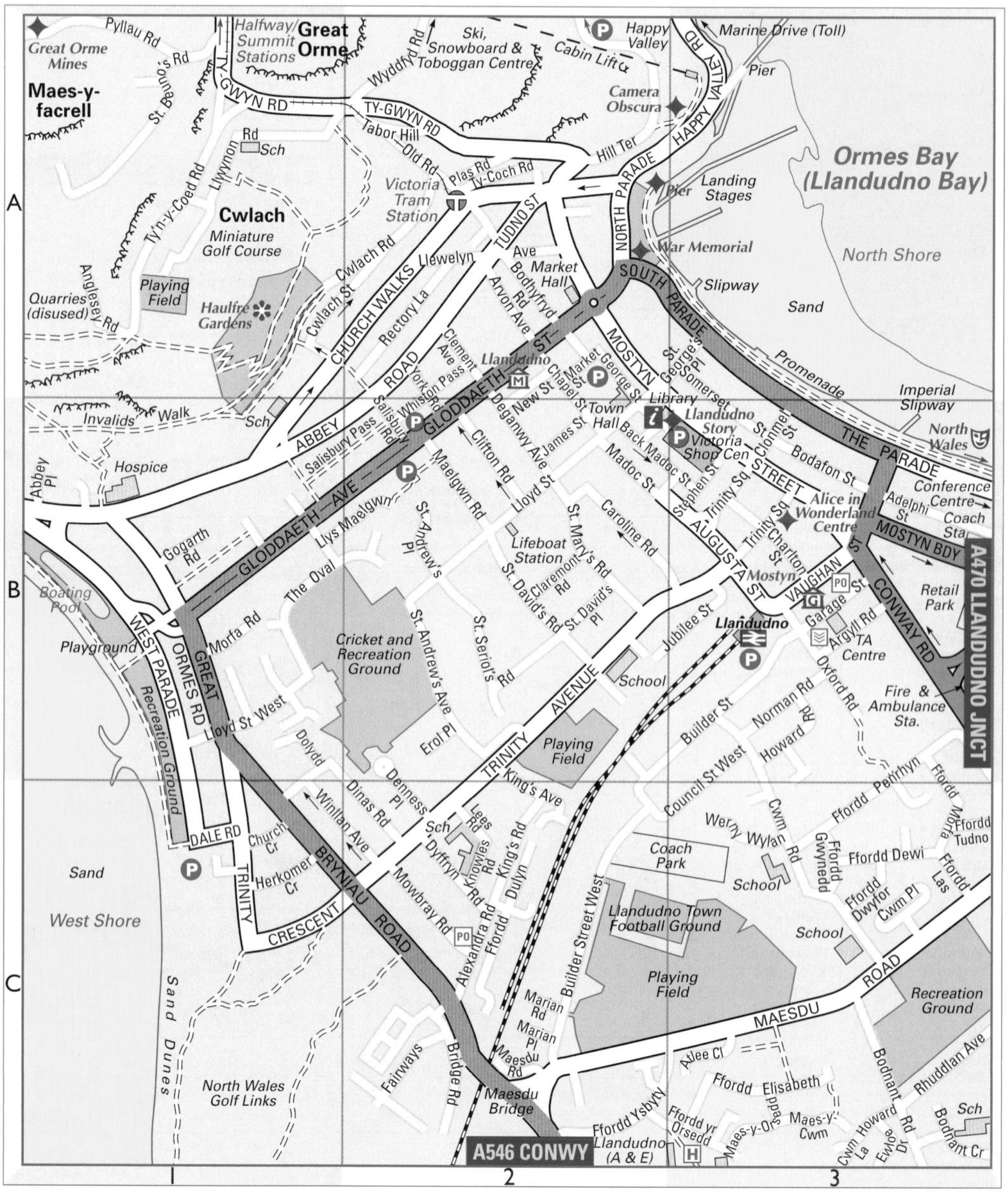

Llanelli

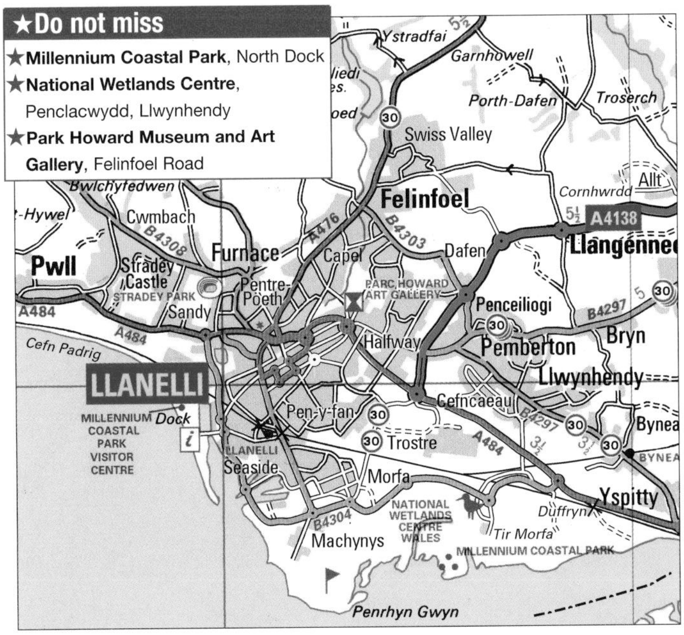

★Do not miss

★**Millennium Coastal Park**, North Dock
★**National Wetlands Centre**, Penclacwydd, Llwynhendy
★**Park Howard Museum and Art Gallery**, Felinfoel Road

▲St Elli's Church

A Carmarthenshire town that grew prosperous in the late 18th century through its metal manufacture and role as a coal port, now a popular venue for watersports, with a 12-mile coastal park with a promenade, a cyclepath (part of the Celtic Trail or Lon Geltaidd), 250 acres of wetland habitat, a golf course, and views over the Gower Peninsula. Nearby are Kidwelly with its well-preserved half-moon-shaped castle, Industrial Museum and award-winning 7-mile sandy beach; Pembrey Country Park with its outstanding beach, children's attractions and picnic sites; and the mainly 13th-century remains of Loughor Castle across the River Loughor.

Llanelli Tourist Information Centre, Public Library, Vaughan Street, Llanelli SA15 3AS Tel 01554 772020

BBC Radio Wales 93.9 FM • **Real Radio** 106 FM • **The Wave** 96.4 FM **Swansea Sound** 1170 AM

www.carmarthenshire.gov.uk

Llanelli

Alban Rd B3
Albert St B1
Als St B3
Amos St C1
Andrew St A3
Ann St C2
Annesley St B2
Arfryn Ave A3
Arthur St B2
Belvedere Rd A1
Bigyn La B3
Bigyn Park Terr C3
Bigyn Rd C3
Bond Ave C3
Brettenham St A1
Bridge St B2
Brintirion Hospital A3
Bryn Pl C1
Bryn Rd C1
Bryn Terr C1
Brynhyfryd Rd A2
Brynmelyn Ave A3
Brynmor Rd B1
Bryn-More Rd C1
Burry St C1
Bus Station B2
Caersalem Terr C2
Cambrian St C1
Caswell St C3
Cedric St B3
Cemetery A2
Chapman St A1
Charles Terr C2
Church St B2
Clos Caer Elms A1
Clos Sant Paul C2
Coastal Link Rd B1/C1
Coldstream St B2
Coleshill Terr B1
College Hill B3
College Sq B3
Copperworks Rd C2
Coronation Rd C3
Corporation Ave A3
Council Offices B2
Court B2
Cowell St B2
Cradock St C2
Craig Ave C3
Cricket Ground A1
Derwent St A1
Dillwyn St C2
Druce St C1
Elizabeth St B2
Emma St C2
Erw Rd B1
Felinfoel Rd A2
Fire Station A3
Firth Rd C3
Fron Terr C3
Furnace Rugby Football Ground A1
Gelli-On B2
George St C2
Gilbert Cres A2
Gilbert Rd A2
Glanmor Rd C2
Glanmor Terr C2
Glasfryn Terr A3
Glenalla Rd B3
Glevering St B3
Goring Rd A2
Gorsedd Circle A2
Grant St C3
Graveyard C2
Great Western Cl C2
Greenway St B1
Hall St B2
Harries Ave A2
Hedley Terr A2
Heol Elli B3
Heol Goffa A3
Heol Nant-y-Felin A3
Heol Siloh B2
Hick St C2
High St C1
Indoor Bowls Centre B1
Inkerman St B2
Island Pl B2
James St B3
John St B2
King George Ave B3
Lake View Cl A2
Lakefield Pl C1
Lakefield Rd C1
Langland Rd C3
Leisure Centre B1
Library B2
Llanelli House B2
Llanelli Parish Church B2
Llanelli R.U.F.C. (Stradey Park) A1
Llanelli Station C2
Llewellyn St C2
Lliedi Cres A3
Lloyd St B2
Llys Alys B3
Llys Fran A3
Llysnewedd C1
Long Row A3
Maes Gors C2
Maesyrhaf A3
Mansel St C3
Marblehall Rd B3
Marborough Rd A2
Margam St C3
Marged St C2
Marine St C1
Market B2
Market St B2
Marsh St C2
Martin Rd C3
Miles St A1
Mill La A3/B2
Mincing La B2
Murray St B2
Myn y Mor B1
Nathan St C1
Nelson Terr C1
Nevill St C2
New Dock Rd C2
New Rd A1
New Zealand St A1
Old Lodge C2
Old Rd A2
Paddock St C2
Palace Ave B3
Park Howard A2
Park Howard Museum & Art Gallery A2
Park Cres B1
Park St B2
Parkview Terr B1
Pemberton St C2
Pembrey Rd A1
Peoples Park B1
Police Station B2
Post Office A1/A2/B2/C1/C2
Pottery Pl B3
Pottery St B3
Princess St B1
Prospect Pl A2
Pryce St A1
Queen Mary's Walk C3
Queen Victoria Rd C1
Raby St B1
Railway Terr C2
Ralph St B2
Ralph Terr C1
Regalia Terr B3
Rhydyrafon A3
Richard St B2
Robinson St B2
Roland Ave A1
Russell St C3
St David's Cl C1
St Elli Shopping Centre B2
St Margaret's Dr A1
Spowart Ave A1
Station Rd B2/C2
Stepney Pl B2
Stepney St B2
Stewart St A1
Stradey Park Ave A1
Sunny Hill A2
Swansea Rd A3
TA Centre B2
Talbot St C3
Temple St B3
The Avenue Cilfig A2
The Mariners C1
Theatr Elli B2
Thomas St A2
Toft Pl A3
Town Hall B2
Traeth Ffordd C1
Trinity Rd C3
Trinity Terr C2
Tunnel Rd B3
Tyisha Rd C3
Union Blgs A2
Upper Robinson St B2
Vauxhall Rd B2
Walter's Rd B3
Waun Lanyrafon B2
Waun Rd A3
Wern Rd B3
West End A2
Y Bwthyn C3
Zion Row B3

¼ mile
¼ ½ km

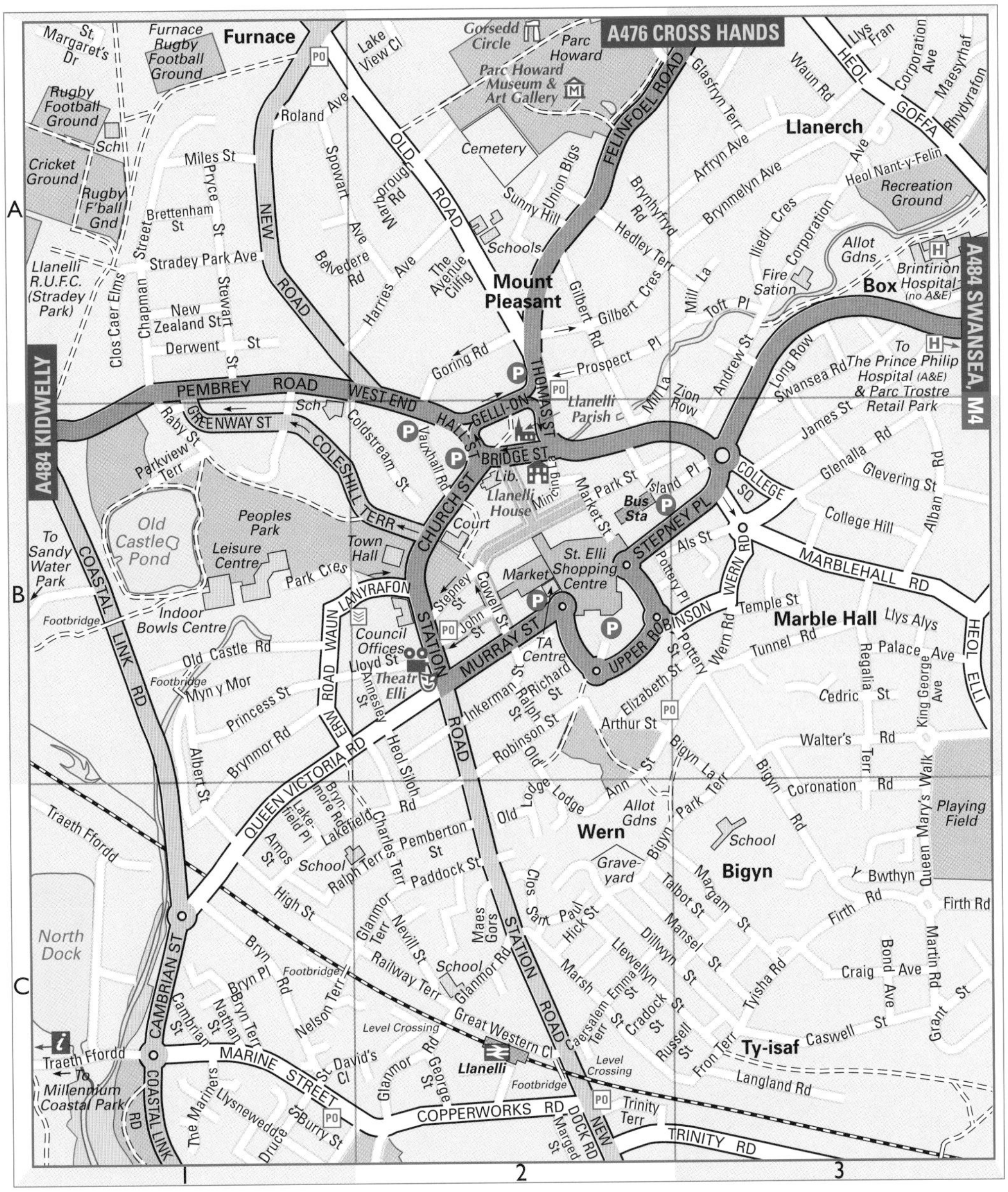

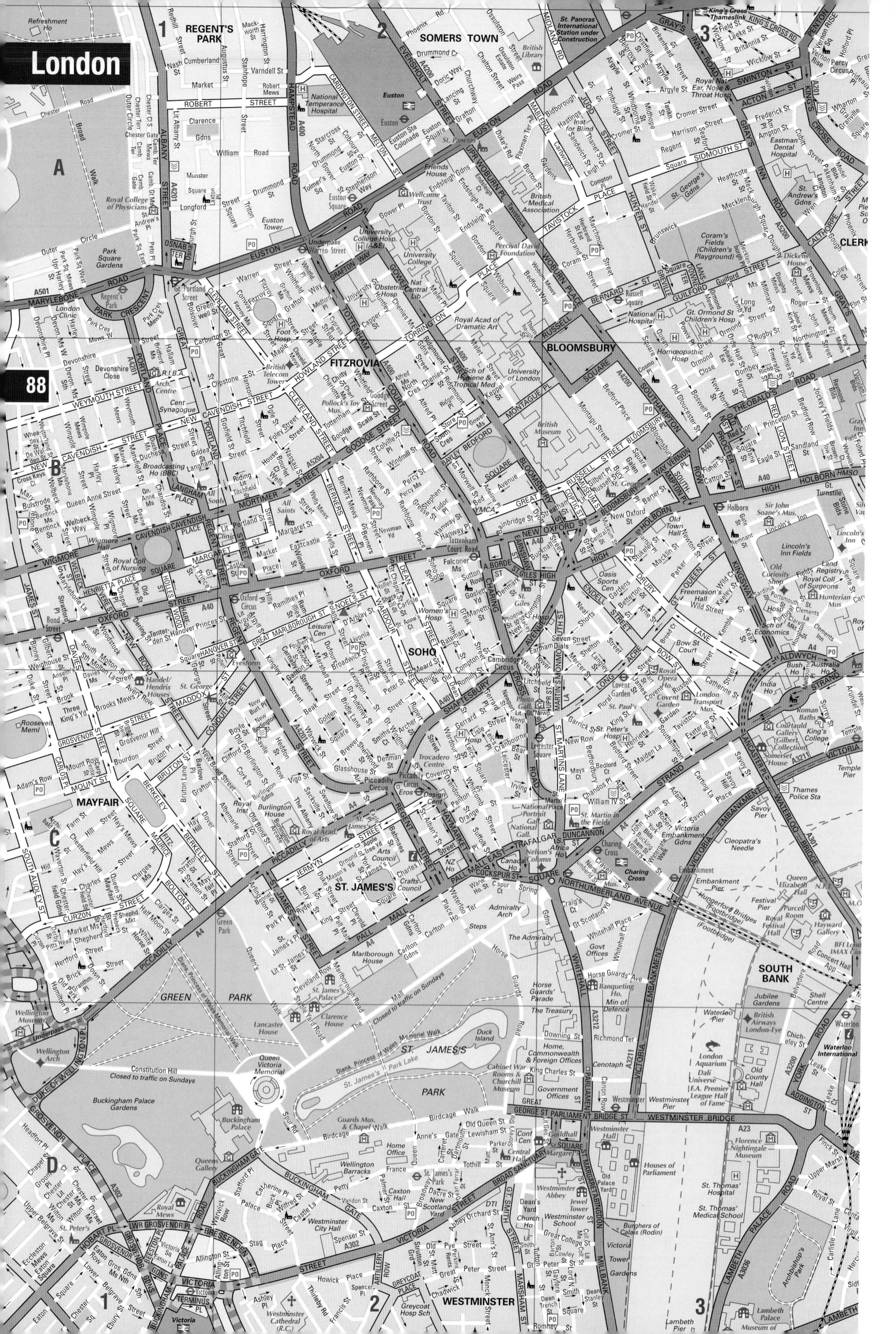

London
88
1
2
3
A
B
C
D
REGENT'S PARK
SOMERS TOWN
St. Pancras International Station under Construction
King's Cross Thameslink
British Library
Euston
National Temperance Hospital
Euston Sta Colonade
Royal College of Physicians
Park Square Gardens
Euston Tower
MARYLEBONE
ROAD
EUSTON
Regent's Park
PARK CRESCENT
University College Hosp. (A&E)
University College
Wellcome Trust
Percival David Foundation
British Medical Association
Inst for Blind
Friends House
Coram's Fields (Children's Playground)
Royal Nat Ear, Nose & Throat Hosp
Eastman Dental Hospital
Russell Square
National Hospital
Gt. Ormond St Children's Hosp
Homoeopathic Hosp
BLOOMSBURY
FITZROVIA
British Telecom Tower
R.I.B.A.
Royal Acad of Dramatic Art
Sch of Hygiene & Tropical Med
University of London
British Museum
Pollock's Toy Mus.
Broadcasting Ho (BBC)
All Souls
Cent Synagogue
WEYMOUTH STREET
NEW CAVENDISH STREET
CAVENDISH SQUARE
WIGMORE STREET
Wigmore Hall
Royal Coll of Nursing
OXFORD STREET
Oxford Circus
Tottenham Court Road
NEW OXFORD ST
HIGH HOLBORN
Holborn
Sir John Soane's Mus.
Lincoln's Inn Fields
Lincoln's Inn
Old Curiosity Shop
Royal Coll of Surgeons
Hunterian Mus
London Sch of Economics
KINGSWAY
ALDWYCH
Bush Ho
Australia Ho
India Ho
STRAND
SOHO
Soho Square
Women's Hosp
Leisure Cen
GREAT MARLBOROUGH ST
Handel/Hendrix Houses
HANOVER ST
Oasis Sports Cen
Seven Dials
Cambridge Circus
Royal Opera Ho
Covent Garden
London Transport Mus.
St. Paul's
Photo Gall.
Leicester Square
Trocadero Centre
Piccadilly Circus
Eros
National Portrait Gall.
National Gall.
St. Martin in the Fields
Nelson's Column
TRAFALGAR SQUARE
Charing Cross
Courtauld Gallery (Gilbert Collection)
Somerset House
King's College
Roman Baths
Temple Pier
Thames Police Sta
Savoy Pier
Cleopatra's Needle
Embankment Pier
Victoria Embankment Gdns
Hungerford Bridges (Footbridge)
Festival Pier
Queen Elizabeth Hall
Purcell Room
Royal Festival Hall
Hayward Gallery
BFI London IMAX Cinema
Concert Hall App
SOUTH BANK
Jubilee Gardens
Shell Centre
British Airways London Eye
Waterloo Pier
London Aquarium
Dali Universe
F.A. Premier League Hall of Fame
Old County Hall
Waterloo
Waterloo International
MAYFAIR
GROSVENOR SQUARE
BERKELEY SQUARE
Roosevelt Meml
Royal Inst
Burlington House
Royal Acad. of Arts
The Albany
PICCADILLY
Green Park
GREEN PARK
ST. JAMES'S
JERMYN ST
PALL MALL
Marlborough House
St. James's Palace
Clarence House
Lancaster House
Admiralty Arch
The Admiralty
Horse Guards' Parade
Banqueting Ho.
Min of Defence
The Treasury
Downing St
Home, Commonwealth & Foreign Offices
Cabinet War Rooms & Churchill Museum
Government Offices
Cenotaph
WHITEHALL
Wellington Museum
Wellington Arch
Constitution Hill Closed to traffic on Sundays
Queen Victoria Memorial
Buckingham Palace
Buckingham Palace Gardens
ST. JAMES'S PARK
St. James's Park Lake
Duck Island
Guards Mus. & Chapel
Wellington Barracks
Home Office
Queens Gallery
Royal Mews
WESTMINSTER BRIDGE
Westminster Pier
Westminster Hall
Houses of Parliament
Old Palace Yard
Westminster Abbey
Central Hall
Jewel Tower
Westminster School
Burghers of Calais (Rodin)
Victoria Tower Gardens
Florence Nightingale Museum
St. Thomas' Hospital
St. Thomas' Medical School
Archbishop's Park
Lambeth Palace
New Scotland Yard
Caxton Hall
Westminster City Hall
Westminster Cathedral (R.C.)
Greycoat Hosp Sch
WESTMINSTER
VICTORIA STREET
Victoria
BUCKINGHAM PALACE RD
GROSVENOR PLACE

FINSBURY
SHOREDITCH
CLERKENWELL
HOLBORN
THE CITY
SOUTHWARK
NEWINGTON
RIVER THAMES
The Barbican Centre For Arts
Bunhill Fields
Honourable Artillery Co HQ
Museum of London
St. Paul's Cathedral
Liverpool Street
Broadgate Arena
Farringdon
Moorgate
Old Street
City Thameslink
Blackfriars
Cannon Street
Fenchurch Street
London Bridge
Waterloo
Waterloo East
Southwark
Borough
Elephant & Castle
Tower Hill
Aldgate
Monument
Bank
Mansion House
Barbican
Tate Modern
Shakespeare's Globe Theatre
Imperial War Museum
Guy's Hospital
Southwark Cathedral
The Temple
Temple Church
The Millennium Bridge (Footbridge)
London Bridge
Blackfriars Bridge
Southwark Bridge
River Bus Route
King's Reach
Queenhithe Dock
Tower Pier
H.M.S. Belfast
London City Hall
Newington Garden
Tabard Garden
CITY ROAD
OLD STREET
GOSWELL ROAD
ALDERSGATE STREET
LONDON WALL
HOLBORN VIADUCT
FLEET STREET
CHEAPSIDE
QUEEN VICTORIA STREET
CANNON STREET
UPPER THAMES STREET
LOWER THAMES STREET
BISHOPSGATE
EMBANKMENT
SOUTHWARK STREET
STAMFORD STREET
BOROUGH HIGH STREET
GREAT DOVER STREET
LONG LANE
TOOLEY STREET
BLACKFRIARS ROAD
WATERLOO ROAD
ST. GEORGE'S ROAD
KENNINGTON ROAD
0 Miles 1/4
4
5
6
A
B
C
D

London

Canary Wharf

A vibrant modern capital that grew from the nucleus of the one-square-mile Roman city, which is now an international finance centre but retains, among the office blocks, some of the old Roman wall, much of its medieval street plan, many of the churches constructed after the Great Fire of 1666 and a variety of ceremonial buildings. Areas range from 'villagey' Marylebone to the regenerated riverside South Bank area, home to some of the city's foremost art venues and theatres (many in the vast complex of the South Bank Centre), as well as historic inns and fashionable restaurants.

London's heritage comes to life in historic buildings and attractions such as the Monument, commemorating the Great Fire; the Mansion House, the Lord Mayor's official residence; the Guildhall, seat of the Corporation of London; the Museum of London, which is particularly informative on London's Roman heritage; the Jewish Museum; the National Maritime Museum and the Museum of Docklands, which charts the history of London's river and historic port. In addition, there are many past and present royal residences that can be visited: Buckingham Palace and the Royal Mews, Hampton Court Palace, Kensington Palace, Kew Palace and the Queen's House at Greenwich. Religious buildings of particular note are Hawksmoor's Christ Church Spitalfields, London Central Mosque, the Brompton Oratory, Wren's St Stephen Walbrook, Southwark Cathedral, St Bartholomew the Great and the Shri Swaminarayan Mandir Hindu temple in Neasden.

Among the historic houses and buildings owned or administered by the conservation-oriented National Trust and English Heritage are the George Inn, Chiswick House, Osterley, Eltham Palace, Ham House and the landmark Wellington Arch (1925). Modern structures of note include City Hall, headquarters of the Mayor of London; the stations of the Jubilee Line underground extension; Lloyd's of London; the Millennium Bridge; the Swiss-Re building (the Gherkin); and 1 Canada Square (Canary Wharf tower), London's tallest building.

The array of world-class art venues includes the National Portrait Gallery, the Royal Academy of Arts, Somerset House (comprising the Courtauld Institute Galleries, the Gilbert Collection of Decorative Arts and the Hermitage Rooms) and Tate Britain. For modern and contemporary art, there is the Dali Universe, the Estorick Collection of Modern Italian Art, the Photographers' Gallery and the Saatchi Collection. Exhibitions are also held at the Serpentine and Hayward Galleries and the ICA. Smaller-scale art galleries/museums include Sir John Soane's Museum, Dulwich Picture Gallery, the Museum of Garden History and the Wallace Collection, while the Design Museum traces the evolution of everyday objects and the Geffrye Museum deals with interior design from Tudor times on. Much cutting-edge artistic activity can be found in the rapidly gentrifying areas of the East End (Hoxton, Shoreditch, Spitalfields and Whitechapel) with their artists' studios and small commercial galleries.

The city's rich literary history can be explored in, for example, the former houses of Dickens, Dr Johnson, Keats, Freud and Carlyle, as well as the British Library Exhibition Galleries while those interested in legal London should visit the Inns of Court, the Old Bailey and the Royal Courts of Justice. Various aspects of medical history can be traced at the Florence Nightingale Museum; the Old Operating Theatre, Museum & Herb Garret, the Welcome Trust Gallery; the Royal London Hospital Museum and the Hunterian Museum (Royal College of Surgeons). Military museums include the Imperial War Museum, the Cabinet War Rooms, the RAF Museum at Hendon and HMS *Belfast*.

Venues that will appeal to children include Madame Tussaud's, the London Aquarium, the Diana Princess of Wales Memorial Playground and Fountain, the London Transport Museum, the Thames Barrier Visitor Centre, Pollock's Toy Museum and the Tower Bridge exhibition.

Tourist Information Centre, 1 Regent Street, SW1Y 4XT (personal callers only)

BBC London 94.9 FM **Capital FM** 94.8 FM

www.london.gov.uk

Green spaces amidst the urban sprawl include Hyde Park and Kensington Gardens, Regent's Park, Green Park, St James' Park, Holland Park, Greenwich Park, Richmond Park, Wimbledon Common, Chelsea Physic Garden, Highgate Wood, the London Wetland Centre, many squares and the Victorian cemetaries including Highgate and Kensal Green.

The unparalleled range of shopping facilities takes in everything from the high-street chains of Oxford Street to the boutiques of Covent Garden; the designer shops of Regent Street, Bond Street and Knightsbridge and landmark stores such as Liberty, Fortnum & Mason and Harrods. Charing Cross Road is home to secondhand bookshops and Tottenham Court Road to computer stores. There is a wide range of markets, which tend to have their own specialities: Portobello Road for jewellery and clothes; Columbia Road for flowers; Petticoat Lane for bargain clothing and bags; and Brick Lane and Whitechapel for food, clothing and bric-a-brac. The six markets in Camden sell just about anything, but specialise in second-hand clothing and music. There is a growing number of weekly farmers' markets, the best known of which, if by far most expensive, is Borough Market.

Seasonal attractions include events such as Wimbledon Lawn Tennis Championships; the Chelsea Flower Show; Shakespeare's Globe Theatre Season, the Regents Park Open-Air season and the Proms season of classical concerts at the Royal Albert Hall. More frequent events include the Ceremony of the Keys at the Tower of London (daily) and the Changing of the Guard at Buckingham Palace (daily or every other day).

Popular entertainment is clustered around Leicester Square and Shaftsbury Avenue, but there is a vast choice of superb venues elsewhere, including the National Theatre, the National Film Theatre and the Barbican.

The eclectic range of restaurants, bars and clubs has something to suit everyone's taste and wallet. Many of the best are to be found in Soho, Covent Garden or Mayfair, while Chinatown is great for far-eastern food and Brick Lane is the place to head for a curry.

★Do not miss

- ★**British Museum**, Great Russell St, WC1
- ★**Hampstead Heath & Kenwood House**, NW3
- ★**Houses of Parliament**, St Margaret St, SW1
- ★**Royal Botanic Gardens, Kew**, Kew Rd, TW9
- ★**London Eye**, Jubilee Gardens, SE1
- ★**London Zoo**, Regent's Park, NW1
- ★**National Gallery**, Trafalgar Square, WC2
- ★**Natural History Museum**, Cromwell Rd, SW7
- ★**St Paul's Cathedral**, EC4
- ★**Science Museum**, Exhibition Rd, SW7
- ★**Tate Modern**, Queen's Walk, SE1
- ★**Tower of London**, Tower Hill, EC3
- ★**Victoria & Albert Museum**, Cromwell Rd, SW7
- ★**Westminster Abbey**, SW1

▲The Queen Elizabeth II Great Court at the British Museum

London

Abingdon St D3
Acton St A3
Addington St D3
Air St C2
Albany St A1
Albemarle St C2
Aldersgate St B5
Aldgate B6
Aldgate ⊖ B6
Aldwych B3
Amwell St A4
Andrew Borde St B2
Appold St B6
Argyle Sq A3
Argyle St A3
Argyll St B2
Arnold Circus A6
Artillery La B6
Artillery Row D2
Association of Photographers Gallery A5
Baldwin's Gdns B4
Baltic St A5
Bank ⊖ B5
Bank Museum B5
Bank of England B5
Bankside C4
Bankside Gallery C4
Banner St A5
Barbican ⊖ B5
The Barbican Centre for Arts B5
Barbican Gallery B5
Basinghall St B5
Bastwick St A5
Bateman's Row A6
Bath St A5
Bath Terr D5
Bayley St B2
Baylis Rd D4
Beak St C2
Becket St D5
Bedford Row B3
Bedford Sq B2
Bedford St C3
Bedford Way A2
Beech St B5
Bell La B6
Belvedere Rd D3
Berkeley Sq C1
Berkeley St C1
Bermondsey St D6
Bernard St A3
Berners Pl B2
Berners St B2
Berwick St B2
Bethnal Green Rd A6
Bevenden St A5
Bevis Marks B6
BFI London IMAX Cinema C4
Bidborough St A3
Binney St B1
Birdcage Walk D2
Bishopsgate B6
Blackfriars Bridge C4
Blackfriars ⊖ C4
Blackfriars Rd D4
Blomfield St B5
Bloomsbury St B2
Bloomsbury Way B3
Bolton St C1
Bond Street ⊖ B1
Borough ⊖ D5
Borough High St C5
Borough Rd D4
Boswell St B3
Bowling Green La A4
Bow St B3
Brad St C4
Bressenden Pl D2
Brewer St C2
Brick St C1
Bridge St D3
Britain at War C6
Britannia Walk A5
British Library A2
British Museum B3
Britton St A4
Broad Sanctuary D2
Broadway D2
Brook St C1
Brunswick Pl A5
Brunswick Sq A3
Brushfield St B6
Bruton St C1
Buckingham Gate D2
Buckingham Palace D2
Buckingham Palace Rd D1
Bunhill Row A5
Byward St C6
Cabinet War Rooms D2
Calthorpe St A3
Calvert Ave A6
Cambridge Circus B2
Camomile St B6
Cannon St ⊖ C5
Carey St B3
Carlisle La D3
Carlton House Terr C2
Carmelite St C4
Carnaby St B2
Carter La B4
Carthusian St B5
Cartwright Gdns A3
Castle Baynard St C4
Cavendish Pl B1
Cavendish Sq B1
Caxton Hall D2
Caxton St D2
Central St A5
Chalton St A2
Chancery La ⊖ B4
Chapel St D1
Charing Cross ⊖ C3
Charing Cross Rd B2
Charles II St C2
Charles Sq A5
Charles St C1
Charlotte Rd A6
Charlotte St B2
Charterhouse Sq B4
Charterhouse St B4
Chart St A5
Cheapside B5
Chenies St B2
Chesterfield Hill C1
Chiltern St B1
Chiswell St B5
City Rd A5
City Thameslink B4
The City Univ A4
Clarges St C1
Clerkenwell Cl A4
Clerkenwell Green A4
Clerkenwell Rd A4
Cleveland St B2
Clifford St C2
Clink Prison Museum C5
Clock Museum B5
Cockspur St C2
Coleman St B5
Commercial St B6
Compton St A4
Conduit St C1
Constitution Hill D1
Copperfield St D4
Coptic St B3
Cornhill B5
Cornwall Rd C4
Coronet St A6
Courtauld Gallery C3
Covent Garden ✦ C3
Covent Garden ⊖ C3
Cowcross St B4
Cowper St A5
Cranbourne St C2
Craven St C2
Creechurch La B6
Cromer St A3
Crucifix La D6
Curtain Rd A6
Curzon St C1
The Cut D4
Dalí Universe D3
Davies St B1
Dean St B2
Deluxe Gallery A6
Denmark St B2
Dering St B1
Devonshire St B1
Diana, Princess of Wales Memorial Walk D2
Dingley Rd A5
D'arblay St B2
Doughty St A3
Dover St C1
Downing St D3
Druid St D6
Drummond St A2
Drury La B3
Drysdale St A6
Duchess St B1
Dufferin St A5
Duke of Wellington Pl D1
Duke's Pl B6
Duke St C2
Duke St Hill C5
Duncannon St C3
Eastcastle St B2
Eastcheap C6
Eastman Dental Hospital A3
East Rd A5
Eaton Sq D1
Ebury St D1
Eldon St B5
Elephant and Castle ⊖ D4
Embankment ⊖ C3
Endell St B3
Endsleigh Pl A2
Euston ⊖ A2
Euston Rd A2
Euston Square ⊖ A2
Eversholt St A2
Exmouth Market A4
Eyestorm B2
Fair St D6
Falmouth Rd D5
Fann St A5
Farringdon ⊖ B4
Farringdon Rd B4
Farringdon St B4
Featherstone St A5
Fenchurch St C6
Fenchurch St C6
Fetter La B4
Finsbury Circus B5
Finsbury Pavement B5
Finsbury Sq A5
Fitzmaurice Pl C1
Fleet St B4
Floral St C3
Florence Nightingale Museum D3
Folgate St B6
Foot Hospital A2
Fore St B5
Foster La B5
Frazier St D4
Freemason's Hall B3
Friday St B5
Garden Row D4
Gee St A5
Gerrard St C2
Giltspur St B4
Glasshouse St C2
Golden Hinde C5
Golden La A5
Golden Sq C2
Goodge St B2
Goodge Street ⊖ B2
Gordon Sq A2
Goswell Rd A4
Gough St A3
Gower St A2
Gracechurch St C5
Grafton Way A2
The Grange D6
Grange Rd D6
Grange Walk D6
Gray's Inn Rd A3
Great College St D3
Great Dover St D5
Great Eastern St A6
Great Guildford St C5
Great Marlborough St B2
Great Ormond St A3
Great Ormond St Children's Hospital A3
Great Percy St A3
Great Peter St D2
Great Portland St B1
Great Portland Street ⊖ A1
Great Queen St B3
Great Russell St B3
Great Scotland Yd C3
Great Smith St D2
Great Suffolk St D4
Great Titchfield St B2
Great Tower St C6
Great Windmill St C2
Greek St B2
Green Park ⊖ C2
Gresham St B5
Greville St A3
Greycoat Hospital School D2
Greycoat Pl D2
Grosvenor Gdns D1
Grosvenor Pl D1
Grosvenor St C1
Guards Museum & Chapel D2
Guildhall Art Gallery B5
Guilford St A3
Guy's Hospital C5
Haberdasher St A5
Hackney Rd A6
Half Moon St C1
Hallam St B1
Hall St A4
Hampstead Rd A2
Hanover Sq B1
Hanway St B2
Hardwick St A4
Harley St B1
Harper Rd D5
Harrison St A3
Hastings St A3
Hatfields C4
Haymarket C2
Hayne St B4
Hay's Galleria C6
Hay's Mews C1
Hayward Gallery C3
Helmet Row A5
Herbrand St A3
Hercules Rd D3
Hertford St C1
High Holborn B3
Hill St C1
HMS Belfast C6
Hobart Pl D1
Holborn B4
Holborn ⊖ B3
Holborn Viaduct B4
Holland St C4
Holywell La A6
Horse Guards' Rd C2
Houndsditch B6
Houses of Parliament D3
Howland St B2
Hoxton Sq A6
Hoxton St A6
Hunter St A3
Hunterian Museum B3
Hyde Park Corner ⊖ D3
Imperial War Museum D4
Ironmonger Row A5
James St B1/C3
Jermyn St C2
Jockey's Fields B3
John Carpenter St C4
John St A3
Judd St A3
Kennington Rd D4
Keyworth St D4
King Charles St D3
King James St D4
Kingley St B2
King's Cross Rd A3
King's Cross Thameslink A3
Kingsland Rd A6
King St C2/C3
Kingsway B3
King William St B5
Kipling St D5
Lambeth North ⊖ D4
Lambeth Palace D3
Lambeth Palace Rd D3
Lambeth Rd D3/D4
Lamb's Conduit St B3
Lancaster Pl C3
Lancaster St D4
Langham Pl B1
Lant St D5
Leadenhall St B6
Leake St D3
Leather La B4
Leathermarket St D6
Leicester Sq ⊖ C2
Leicester St C2
Leonard St A5
Lever St A5
Lexington St C2
Lime St C6
Lincoln's Inn Fields B3
Lindsey St B4
Lisle St C2
Liverpool St B6
Liverpool Str ⊖ B6
Lloyd Baker St A4
Lloyd Sq A4
Lombard St B5
London Aquarium D3
London Bridge C5
London Bridge Hospital C5
London Bridge ⊖ C5
London City Hall C6
London Dungeon C5
London-Eye ✦ D3
London Guildhall University B5
London Rd D4
London Transport Museum C3
London Wall B5
Long Acre C3
Longford St A1
Long La B4/D5
Lower Belgrave St D1
Lower Grosvenor Pl D1
Lower Marsh D4
Lower Thames St C5
Ludgate Circus B4
Ludgate Hill B4
Macclesfield Rd A5
Maddox St C1
Malet St B2
The Mall D2
Mancipie St D5
Mansion House ⊖ C5
Mansion House B5/C5
Maple St B2
Marchmont St A3
Margaret St B2
Margery St A4
Mark La C6
Marlborough Rd C2
Marshall St B2
Marshalsea Rd D5
Marsham St D2
Martin's La C3
Marylebone La B1
Marylebone Rd A1
Marylebone St B1
Mecklenburgh Sq A3
Middlesex St (Petticoat La) B6
Middle Temple La B4
Midland Rd A2/A3
Mildmay Mission Hospital A6
Millbank D3
Monck St D2
Monmouth St B3
Montague Pl B2
Montagu St B3
The Monument ✦ C5
Monument ⊖ C5
Monument St C5
Moorfields B5
Moorfields Eye Hospital A5
Moorgate B5
Moorgate ⊖ B5
Moor La B5
Moreland St A4
Morley St D4
Mortimer St B2
Mount Pleasant A4
Museum of Garden History D3
Museum of London B5
Museum St B3
Myddelton Sq A4
Myddelton St A4
National Film Theatre C3
National Gallery C2
National Hospital A3
National Portrait Gallery C2
Neal St B3
Nelson's Column ✦ C3
New Bond St B1/C1
New Bridge St B4
New Cavendish St B1
New Change B5
Newcomen St D5
New Fetter La B4
Newgate St B4
Newington Causeway D5
New Inn Yard A6
New Kent Rd D5
New Oxford St B2
New Scotland Yd D2
New Sq B3
Newton St B3
Nile St A5
Noble St B5
Noel St B2
Northampton Sq A4
North Cr B2
Northington St A3
Northumberland Ave C3
Norton Folgate B6
Obstetric Hospital A2
Old Bailey B4
Old Broad St B5
Old Compton St B2
Old County Hall D3
Old Gloucester St B3
Old King Edward St B5
Old Street ⊖ A5
Old St A5
Old Town Hall B3
Ontario St D4
Operating Theatre Museum C5
Orange St C2
Outer Circle A1
Oxford Circus ⊖ B2
Oxford St B1/B2
Palace St D2
Pall Mall C2
Pall Mall East C2
Panton St C2
Paris Gdns C4
Park Cr A1
Parker St B3
Park St C5
Parliament Sq D3
Parliament St D3
Paternoster Sq B4
Paul St A5
Pear Tree St A4
Penton Rise A3
Percival St A4
Petticoat La (Middlesex St) B6
Petty France D2
Phoenix Pl A3
Photo Gallery C2
Piccadilly C1/C2
Piccadilly Circus ⊖ C2
Pilgrimage St D5
Pitfield St A6
Pocock St D4
Pollock's Toy Museum B2
Portland Pl B1
Portugal St B3
Poultry B5
Primrose St B6
Princes St B5
Procter St B3
Provost St A5
Queen Anne St B1
Queen Elizabeth Hall C3
Queens Gallery D2
Queen Sq A3
Queen St C5
Queen St Pl C5
Queen Victoria St C4
Radnor St A5
Rathbone Pl B2
Rawstorne St A4
Redchurch St A6
Redcross Way C5
Red Lion Sq B3
Red Lion St B3
Regent's Park ⊖ A1
Regent Sq A3
Regent St B2
Richmond Terr D3
Ridgmount St B2
Riley Rd D6
Rivington St A6
Robert St A1
Rockingham St D5
Ropemaker St B5
Rosebery Ave A4
Rothsay St D6
Roupell St C4
Royal Academy of Arts C2
Royal Academy of Dramatic Art A2
Royal College of Nursing B1
Royal College of Surgeons B3
Royal Festival Hall C3
Royal National Theatre C4
Royal National Throat, Nose & Ear Hospital A3
Royal Opera House C3
Rushworth St D4
Russell Sq ⊖ A3
Russell Sq A2/A3
Sackville St C2
Sadlers Wells A4
Saffron Hill B4
St Alban's St C2
St Andrew St B4
St Bartholomew's Hospital B4
St Bride St B4
St George's Rd D4
St Giles High St B2
St James's Palace C2
St James's Park ⊖ D2
St James's St C2
St John St A4
St Margaret St D3
St Mark's Hosp A4
St Martin's le Grand B5
St Mary Axe B6
St Paul's ⊖ B5
St Paul's Cathedral B5
St Paul's Churchyard B4
St Peter's Hospital C3
St Thomas' Hospital D3
St Thomas St C5
Savile Row C2
Savoy Pl C3
Savoy St C3
School of Hygiene & Tropical Medicine B2
Scrutton St A6
Sekforde St A4
Seven Dials B3
Seward St A4
Shaftesbury Ave C2
Shakespeare's Globe Theatre C5
Shepherdess Walk A5
Shepherd Market C1
Sherwood St C2
Shoe La B4
Shoreditch High St A6
Shorts Gardens B3
Sidmouth St A3
Silk St B5
Sir John Soane's Museum B3
Skinner St A4
Snow Hill B4
Snows Fields D5
Soho Sq B2
Somerset House C3
Southampton Row B3
Southampton St C3
South Audley St C1
South Bank Univ D4
South Molton St B1
South Pl B5
Southwark Bridge C5
Southwark Bridge Rd C5
Southwark ⊖ C4
Southwark Cathedral C5
Southwark St C5
Spencer St A4
Spital Sq B6
Stamford St C4
Stanhope St A2
Stephenson Way A2
Stoney St C5
Strand B4/C3
Stratton St C1
Sumner St C4
Swan St D5
Swinton St A3
Tabard St D5
Tabernacle St A5
Tanner St D6
Tate Modern C5
Tavistock Pl A3
Tavistock Sq A2
Temple Ave C4
Temple ⊖ C4
Temple Pl C3
Terminus Pl D1
Theobald's Rd B3
Threadneedle St B5
Throgmorton St B5
Tonbridge St A3
Tooley St C5/C6
Torrington Pl A2
Tothill St D2
Tottenham Court Road ⊖ B2
Tottenham Court Rd A2/B2
Tottenham St B2
Tower Bridge Rd D6
Tower Hill C6
Tower Hill ⊖ C6
The Tower of London C6
Trafalgar Sq C2
Trinity Sq C6
Trinity St D5
Trocadero Centre C2
Tudor St C4
Turnmill St B4
Ufford St D4
Union St C4
Univ College A2
Univ College Hospital (A&E) A2
Univ of London B2
University St A2
Upper Belgrave St D1
Upper Ground C4
Upper St Martin's La C3
Upper Thames St C5
Upper Wimpole St B1
Upper Woburn Pl A2
Vere St B1
Vernon Pl B3
Vestry St A5
Victoria ⊖ D1
Victoria Embankment C3
Victoria St D2
Villiers St C3
Vinopolis City of Wine C5
Virginia Rd A6
Wakley St A4
Walbrook B5
Wardour St B2/C2
Warner St A4
Warren St A2
Warren Street ⊖ A2
Waterloo Bridge C3
Waterloo ⊖ D3
Waterloo East C4
Waterloo International D3
Waterloo Rd D4
Watling St B5
Webber St D4
Welbeck St B1
Wellington Arch ✦ D1
Wellington Museum D1
Wells St B2
Westminster Abbey D3
Westminster Bridge D3
Westminster Bridge Rd D4
Westminster Cathedral (RC) D2
Westminster City Hall D2
Westminster ⊖ D3
Westminster Hall D3
Weston St D5
West Smithfield B4
Weymouth St B1
Wharf Rd A5
Wharton St A3
Whitcomb St C2
Whitecross St A5
Whitefriars St B4
Whitehall C3
Whitehall Pl C3
White Lion Hill C4
Whites Grounds D6
Wigmore Hall B1
Wigmore St B1
William IV St C3
Wilmington Sq A4
Wilson St B5
Wimpole St B1
Windmill Walk C4
Woburn Pl A3
Woburn Sq A2
Women's Hospital B2
Woodbridge St A4
Wood St B5
Wootton St C4
Wormwood St B6
Worship St A5
Wren St A3
Wynyatt St A4
York Rd D3

92
RICKMANSWORTH
Mill End
Oxhey
Watford Heath
South Oxhey
Northwood
Harefield
Ruislip Common
RUISLIP
Denham
New Denham
Ickenham
UXBRIDGE
Hillingdon
Cowley
Yiewsley
HAYES
West Drayton
Harlington
Heston
Southall
Hanwell
EALING
Greenford
NORTHOLT
Pinner
HARROW
Wealdstone
KENTON
WEMBLEY
Stanmore
Edgware
HENDON
Finchley
Friern Barnet
East Barnet
Mill Hill
Hampstead
WILLESDEN
Harlesden
Acton
HAMMERSMITH
Chiswick
Kew Bridge
Paddington
Kensington
Chelsea
Westminster
Highgate
Golders Green
London Gateway Services
Heston Services

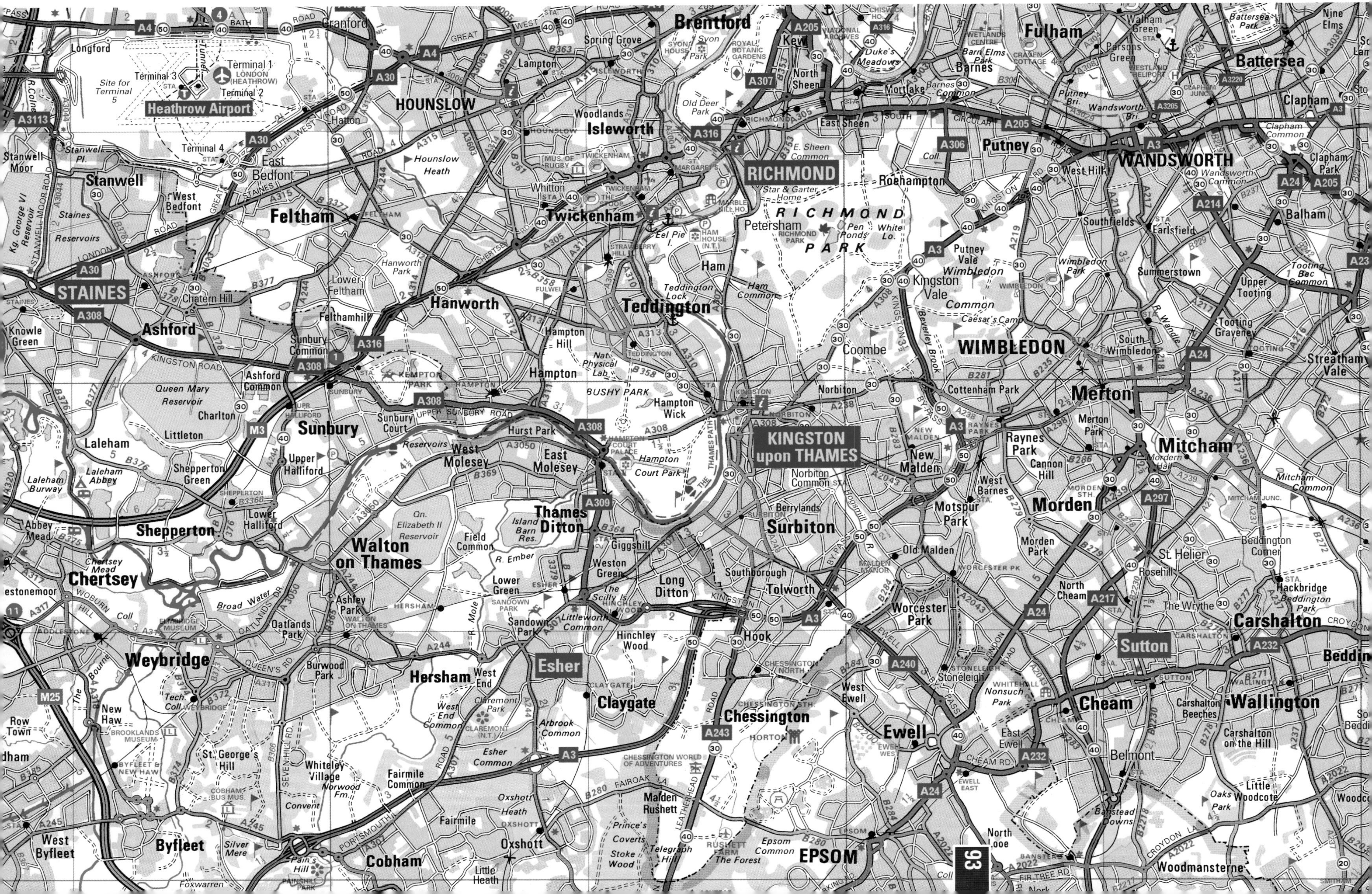
Heathrow Airport
Terminal 1
Terminal 2
Terminal 3
Terminal 4
Site for Terminal 5
Longford
Cranford
Stanwell
Stanwell Moor
West Bedfont
East Bedfont
Hatton
HOUNSLOW
Hounslow Heath
Lampton
Spring Grove
Brentford
Isleworth
Woodlands
Twickenham
Whitton
Feltham
Lower Feltham
Hanworth
Hanworth Park
STAINES
Staines Reservoirs
Ashford
Chattern Hill
Knowle Green
Sunbury Common
Felthamhill
Queen Mary Reservoir
Charlton
Littleton
Laleham
Laleham Abbey
Laleham Burway
Sunbury
Upper Halliford
Lower Halliford
Shepperton
Shepperton Green
Chertsey
Chertsey Mead
Abbey Mead
Addlestone
Weybridge
New Haw
Row Town
West Byfleet
Byfleet
St. George's Hill
Whiteley Village
Burwood Park
Oatlands Park
Walton on Thames
Qn. Elizabeth II Reservoir
West Molesey
East Molesey
Hurst Park
Hampton
Hampton Hill
Hampton Wick
BUSHY PARK
Teddington
Teddington Lock
Ham
Ham Common
Petersham
RICHMOND
RICHMOND PARK
Kew
North Sheen
East Sheen
Old Deer Park
Mortlake
Barnes
Fulham
Putney
Roehampton
WANDSWORTH
Battersea
Clapham
Balham
Earlsfield
Southfields
Summerstown
Upper Tooting
Tooting Graveney
Streatham Vale
WIMBLEDON
South Wimbledon
Wimbledon Common
Kingston Vale
Coombe
Norbiton
KINGSTON upon THAMES
New Malden
Merton
Mitcham
Morden
Raynes Park
Cannon Hill
Motspur Park
West Barnes
Old Malden
Worcester Park
Surbiton
Berrylands
Tolworth
Hook
Southborough
Long Ditton
Thames Ditton
Weston Green
Hinchley Wood
Esher
Claygate
Hersham
West End
Esher Common
Oxshott
Fairmile
Cobham
Little Heath
Chessington
Malden Rushett
Epsom Common
EPSOM
Ewell
West Ewell
Stoneleigh
Nonsuch Park
Cheam
North Cheam
Sutton
Belmont
Banstead Downs
Carshalton
Wallington
Carshalton Beeches
Carshalton on the Hill
Little Woodcote
Woodmansterne
St. Helier
Rosehill
Beddington Corner
Hackbridge
Mitcham Common
93

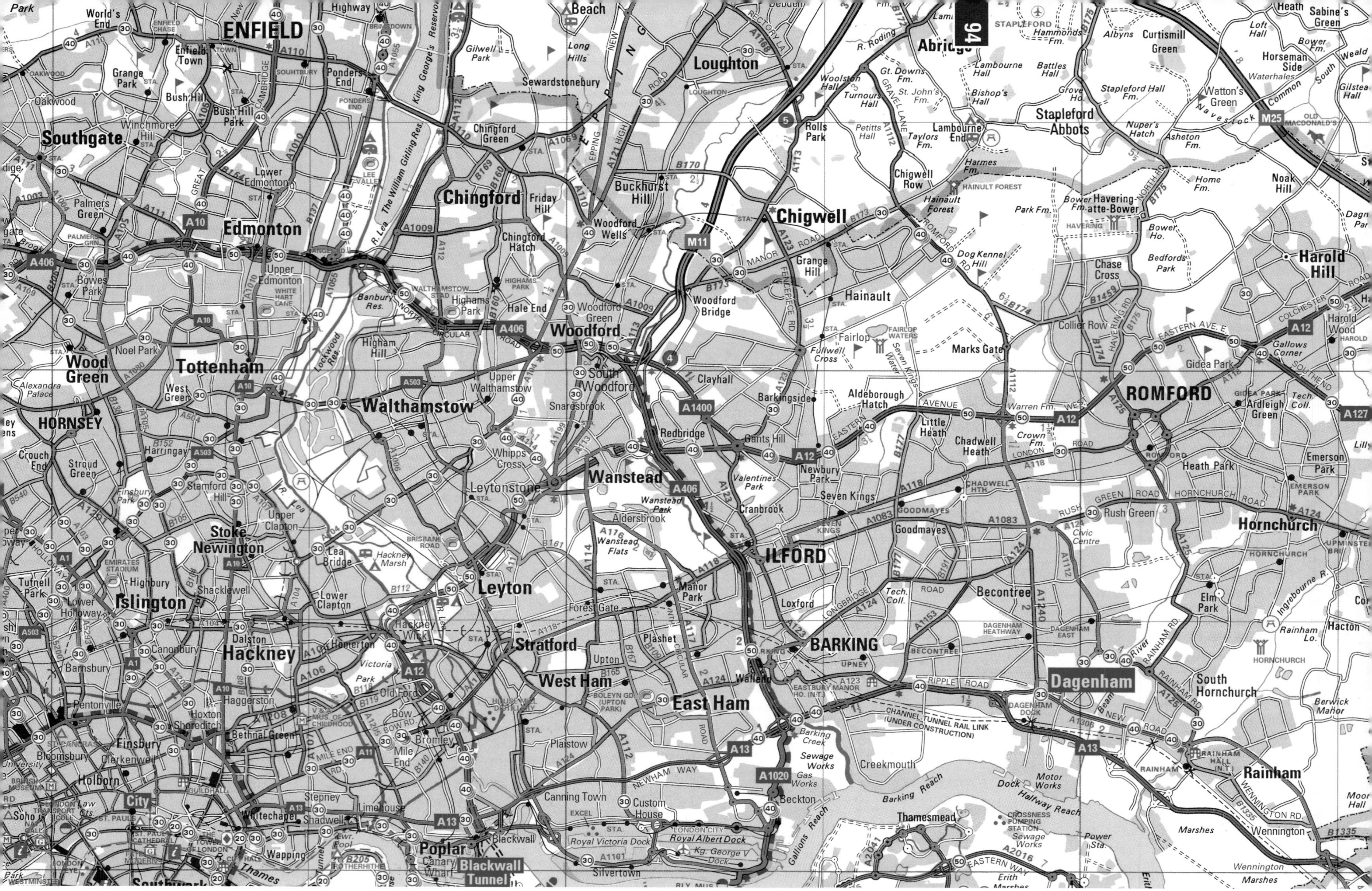
94
ENFIELD
Enfield Town
Southgate
Edmonton
Wood Green
Tottenham
HORNSEY
Walthamstow
Chingford
Loughton
Chigwell
Abridge
Stapleford Abbots
Harold Hill
Woodford
Wanstead
Leytonstone
Leyton
Stratford
West Ham
East Ham
ILFORD
BARKING
ROMFORD
Hornchurch
Dagenham
Rainham
Hackney
Islington
Stoke Newington
City
Poplar
Blackwall Tunnel
Holborn
Finsbury
Bloomsbury
Clerkenwell
Whitechapel
Shadwell
Wapping
Stepney
Limehouse
Canning Town
Custom House
Silvertown
Beckton
Thamesmead
Becontree
Goodmayes
Seven Kings
Chadwell Heath
Hainault
Barkingside
Redbridge
Gants Hill
South Woodford
Buckhurst Hill
Gidea Park
Harold Wood
Elm Park
South Hornchurch
Upminster
Creekmouth
Barking Reach
Gallions Reach
Halfway Reach
Royal Albert Dock
Royal Victoria Dock
Channel Tunnel Rail Link (Under Construction)
R. Thames

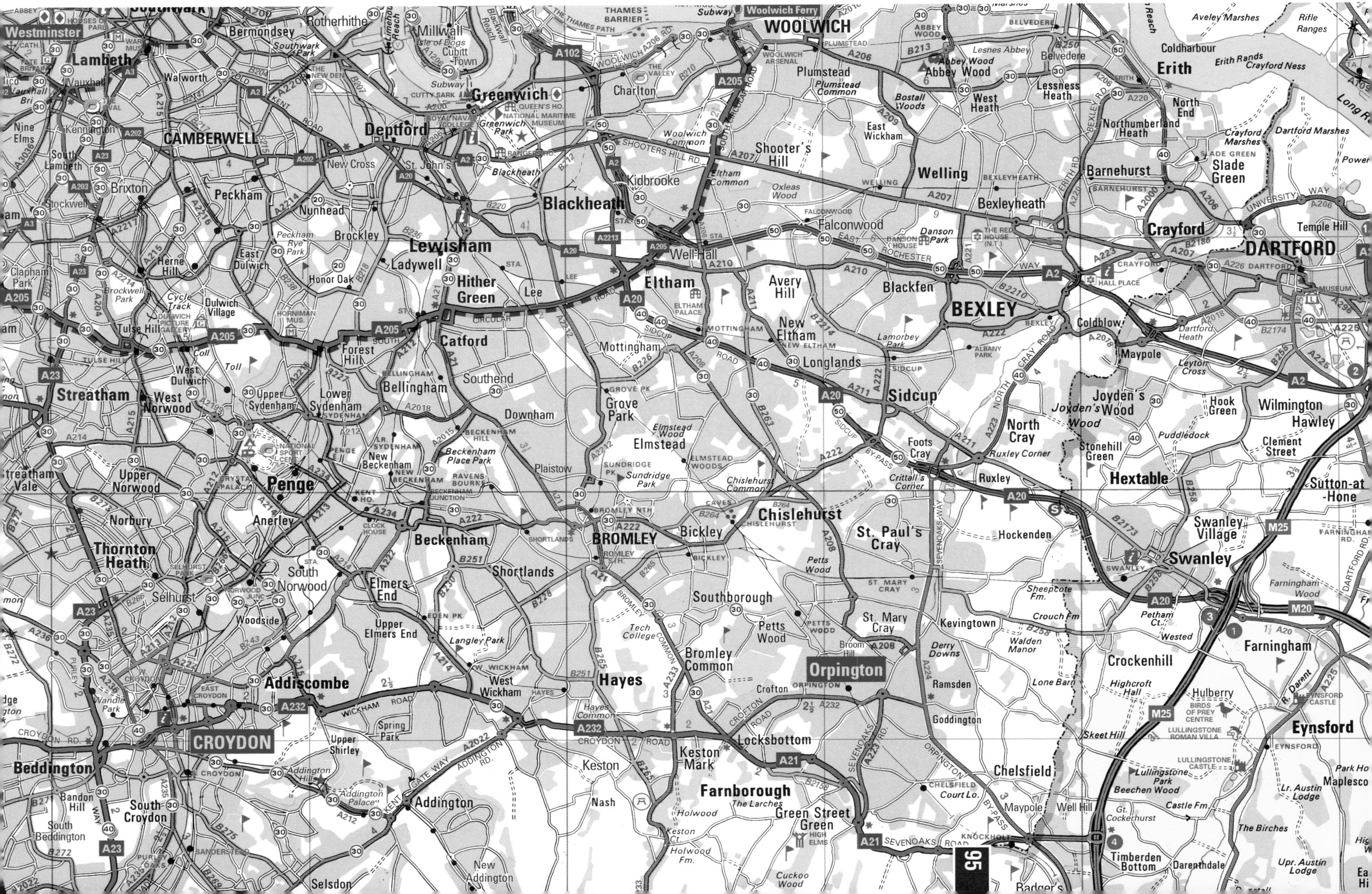
Westminster
Lambeth
Vauxhall
Southwark
Bermondsey
Rotherhithe
Millwall
Isle of Dogs
Cubitt Town
Greenwich
Deptford
CAMBERWELL
Walworth
Kennington
Nine Elms
South Lambeth
Stockwell
Brixton
Peckham
Nunhead
New Cross
St. John's
Brockley
Lewisham
Ladywell
Hither Green
Lee
Blackheath
Charlton
WOOLWICH
Woolwich Ferry
Plumstead
Plumstead Common
Shooter's Hill
Kidbrooke
Eltham
Well Hall
Falconwood
Welling
East Wickham
Abbey Wood
West Heath
Lessness Heath
Belvedere
Erith
Coldharbour
North End
Northumberland Heath
Barnehurst
Bexleyheath
Slade Green
Crayford
DARTFORD
Temple Hill
Wilmington
Hawley
BEXLEY
Blackfen
Sidcup
Avery Hill
New Eltham
Longlands
Mottingham
Catford
Forest Hill
Bellingham
Southend
Downham
Grove Park
Elmstead
Plaistow
BROMLEY
Bickley
Chislehurst
St. Paul's Cray
St. Mary Cray
Foots Cray
North Cray
Ruxley
Coldblow
Maypole
Joyden's Wood
Hextable
Swanley
Swanley Village
Sutton-at-Hone
Farningham
Eynsford
Crockenhill
Hockenden
Kevingtown
Orpington
Petts Wood
Southborough
Bromley Common
Hayes
West Wickham
Shortlands
Beckenham
New Beckenham
Lower Sydenham
Upper Sydenham
Dulwich Village
East Dulwich
Herne Hill
West Dulwich
Streatham
West Norwood
Upper Norwood
Penge
Anerley
South Norwood
Elmers End
Upper Elmers End
Norbury
Thornton Heath
Selhurst
Woodside
Addiscombe
CROYDON
Beddington
South Croydon
Upper Shirley
Addington
New Addington
Selsdon
Keston
Keston Mark
Locksbottom
Farnborough
Green Street Green
Chelsfield
Goddington
Ramsden
Timberden Bottom
Darenthdale
Maplesco
Crittall's Corner
Ruxley Corner
Stonehill Green
Puddledock
Hook Green
Clement Street
Dartford Heath
Leyton Cross
Crayford Marshes
Dartford Marshes
Aveley Marshes
Erith Rands
Crayford Ness
Rifle Ranges
95

Luton

▲ An airliner approaching Luton Airport

Luton lies at the northern end of a river gap in the Chiltern Hills and spans about 12 square miles. Early in the 19th century, the straw hat industry changed Luton into a factory town. The 20th century decline of the hat industry brought new industries, primarily in the engineering fields. The Luton Arndale Centre is a focal point for shopping in the town and the recently opened Hat Factory is now a major centre for art exhibitions, theatre, cinema and music. There are also many pubs, restaurants and clubs. Attractions nearby include Dunstable Downs and Shaw's Corner (both National Trust) and Whipsnade Wild Animal Park.

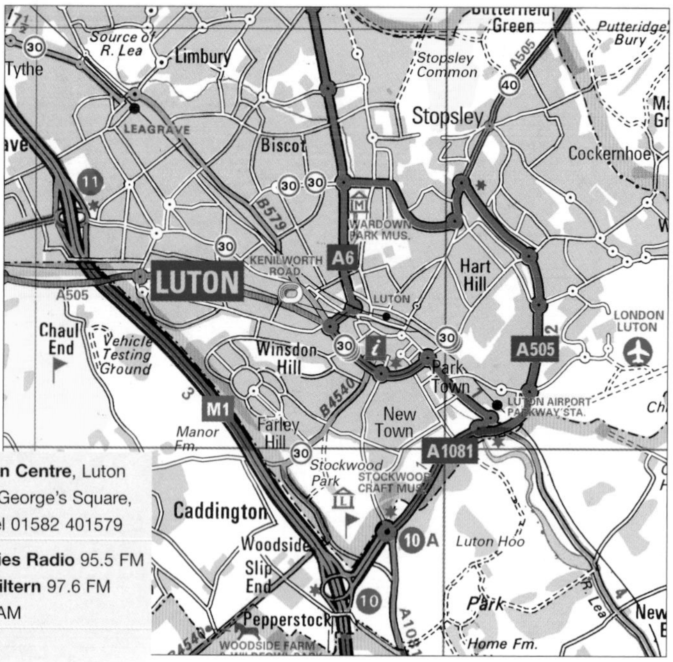

Tourist Information Centre, Luton Central Library, St George's Square, Luton LU1 2NG Tel 01582 401579

BBC Three Counties Radio 95.5 FM and 1161 AM • **Chiltern** 97.6 FM **Classic Gold** 828 AM

www.luton.gov.uk

★Do not miss

★**The Hat Factory**, Bute Street – Arts centre

★**Luton Museum and Art Gallery**, Wardown Park, Old Bedford Road – local history

★**Stockwood Park Museum**, Farley Hill

Luton

Adelaide St B1
Albert Rd C2
Alma St. B2
Alton Rd C3
Anthony Gdns . . . C1
Arndale Centre . . . B2
Arthur St C2
Ashburnham Rd . . B1
Ashton Rd C2
Avondale Rd. A1
Back St A2
Bailey St C3
Baker St C2
Biscot Rd A1
Bolton Rd B3
Boyle Cl A2
Brantwood Rd B1
Bretts Mead C1
Bridge St B2
Brook St A1
Brunswick St A3
Burr St A3
Bury Park Rd A1
Bus Station B2
Bute St B2
Buxton Rd B2
Cambridge St . . . C3
Cardiff Grove B1
Cardiff Rd. B1
Cardigan St A2
Castle St. B2/C2
Chapel St C2
Charles St A3
Chase St C2
Cheapside B2
Chequer St. C3
Church St. B2/B3
Cinema A2
Cobden St A3
Collingdon St. . . . A1
Concorde Ave . . . A3
Corncastle Rd . . . C1
Cowper St C2
Crawley Green Rd . B3
Crawley Rd. A1
Crescent Rise . . . A3
Crescent Rd A3
Cromwell Rd A1
Cross St A2
Crown Court B2
Cumberland St . . . B2
Cutenhoe Rd C3
Dallow Rd. B1
Downs Rd. B1
Dudley St A2
Duke St. A2
Dumfries St B1
Dunstable Place . . B2
Dunstable Rd. A1/B1
Edward St. A3
Elizabeth St C2
Essex Cl C3
Farley Hill. C1
Flowers Way B2
Francis St. A1
Frederick St. A2
Galaxy Leisure Complex. A2
George St West . . . B2
George St. B2
Gillam St A3
Gordon St. B2
Grove Rd B1
Guildford St A2
Haddon Rd. A3
Harcourt St C2
Hart Hill Drive . . . A3
Hart Hill Lane . . . A3
Hartley Rd A3
Hastings St. B2
Hat Factory, The B2
Hatters Way A1
Havelock Rd. A2
Hibbert St C2
High Town Rd . . . A3
Highbury Rd. A1
Hillary Cres C1
Hillborough Rd . . C1
Hitchin Rd A3
Holly St. C2
Holm C1
Hucklesby Way . . A2
Hunts Cl C1
Information Ctr . B2
Inkerman St A2
John St. B2
Jubilee St. A3
Kelvin Cl. C2
King St B2
Kingsland Rd C3
Latimer Rd C2
Lawn Gdns C2
Lea Rd B3
Library B2
Library Rd B2
Liverpool Rd B1
London Rd C2
Luton Station A2
Lyndhurst Rd B1
Magistrates Court. B2
Manchester St. . . . B2
Manor Rd B3
May St C3
Meyrick Ave C1
Midland Rd A2
Mill St. A2
Milton Rd B1
Moor, The A1
Moor St A1
Moorland Gdns . . A2
Moulton Rise A3
Museum & Art Gallery A2
Napier Rd. B1
New Bedford Rd . A1
New Town St C2
North St A3
Old Bedford Rd . . A2
Old Orchard C2
Osbourne Rd C3
Oxen Rd A3
Park Sq. B2
Park St B3/C3
Park St West B2
Park Viaduct B3
Parkland Dr C1
Police Station . . B1
Pomfret Ave. A3
Pondwicks Rd B3
Post Office A1/A2/B2/C3
Power Court B3
Princess St. B1
Red Rails C1
Regent St. B2
Reginald St A2
Rothesay Rd. B1
Russell Rise C1
Russell St. C1
Ruthin Cl C1
St Ann's Rd B3
St George's B2
St Mary's B3
St Mary's Rd B3
St Paul's Rd. C2
St Saviour's Cres C1
Salisbury Rd B1
Seymour Ave C3
Seymour Rd. C3
Silver St B2
South Rd C2
Stanley St. B1
Station Rd A2
Stockwood Cres . C2
Stockwood Park . C1
Strathmore Ave. . C2
Stuart St. B2
Studley Rd A1
Surrey St C3
Sutherland Place C1
Tavistock St C2
Taylor St. A3
Telford Way A1
Tennyson Rd C2
Tenzing Grove . . . C1
The Cross Way. . . C1
The Larches. A2
Thistle Rd. B3
Town Hall. B2
Townsley Cl C2
Union St B2
University of Bedfordshire B3
Upper George St. . B2
Vicarage St B3
Villa Rd. A2
Waldeck Rd A1
Wellington St. . B1/B2
Wenlock St. A2
Whitby Rd A1
Whitehill Ave. . . . C1
William St A2
Wilsden Ave. C1
Windmill Rd. B3
Windsor St. C2
Winsdon Rd B1
York St A3

¼ mile

¼ ½ km

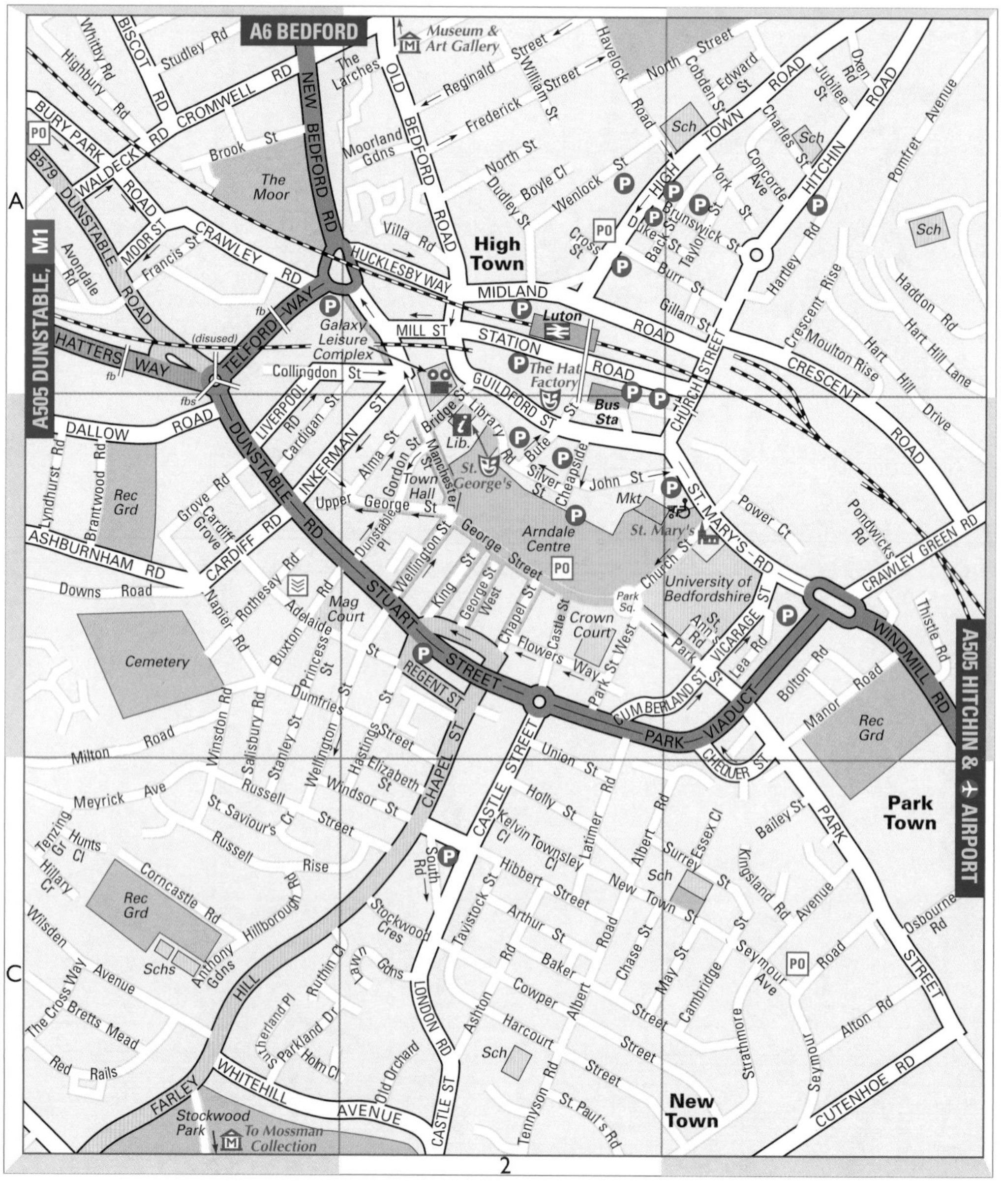

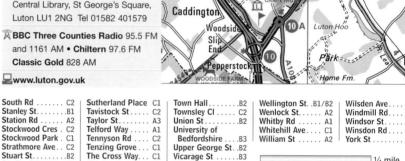

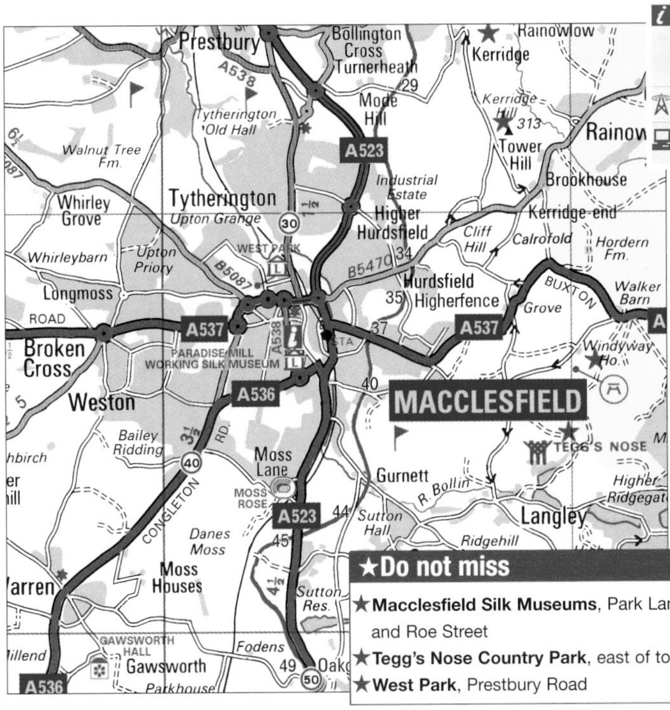

★Do not miss

★**Macclesfield Silk Museums**, Park Lane and Roe Street

★**Tegg's Nose Country Park**, east of town

★**West Park**, Prestbury Road

Macclesfield Tourist Information Centre, Town Hall, Macclesfield SK10 1DX Tel 01625 504114

BBC GMR 95.1 FM • **Silk FM** 106.9 FM

www.macclesfield.gov.uk

Macclesfield

▲ Outdoor market and Town Hall

A medieval town long associated with the silk industry, with cobbled streets and many quaint old buildings, including the former Hovis Mill. The 1854 West Park has a museum and art gallery, a woodland walk, an aviary and three pre-Norman cross-shafts. Good walks include the 10-mile Middlewood Way (also a cycle and riding path) along an old railway line to Marple near the border of the Peak District National Park, and the Macclesfield Canal (part of the Cheshire Ring Canal Walk). Close by are Gawsworth Hall; Capesthorne Hall; Alderley Edge, a dramatic red sandstone escarpment with old copper mines and a historic beacon (National Trust); the restored 15th-century Nether Alderley watermill (National Trust); Hare Hill Garden (National Trust), Adlington Hall and Jodrell Bank Visitor Centre.

Macclesfield

108 Steps B2
Abbey Rd A1
Alton Dr A3
Armett St C1
Athey St B1
Bank St C3
Barber St C3
Barton St C1
Beech La A2
Beswick St B1
Black La A2
Black Rd C3
Blakelow Gdns C3
Blakelow Rd C3
Boden St B2
Bond St B1/C1
Bread St C1
Bridge St B1
Brock St A2
Brocklehurst Ave A3
Brook St B3
Brookfield La B3
Brough St West C1
Brown St C1
Brynton Rd A2
Buckley St C2
Bus Station B2
Buxton Rd B3
Byrons St C2
Canal St B3
Carlsbrook Ave A3
Castle St B2
Catherine St B1
Chadwick Terr A3
Chapel St C2
Charlotte St B2
Chester Rd B1
Chestergate B1
Churchill Way B2
Coare St A1
Commercial Rd B2
Conway Cres A3
Copper St C3
Cottage St B1
Court A2
Court B2
Crematorium A1
Crew Ave A3
Crompton Rd B1/C1
Cross St C2
Crossall St C1
Cumberland St A1/B1
Dale St B3
Duke St B2
Eastgate B3
Exchange St B2
Fence Ave B3
Fence Avenue Industrial Estate A3
Flint St B3
Foden St A2
Fountain St B3
Garden St A3
Gas Rd B2
George St B2
Glegg St B3
Golf Course C3
Goodall St B3
Grange Rd C1
Great King St B1
Green St B3
Grosvenor Shopping Centre B2
Gunco La C3
Half St C2
Hallefield Rd B3
Hatton St C1
Hawthorn Way A3
Heapy St C3
Henderson St B1
Heritage Centre & Silk Museum B2
Hibel Rd A2
High St C2
Hobson St C2
Hollins Rd C3
Hope St West B1
Horseshoe Dr B1
Hurdsfield Rd A3
Information Ctr B2
James St C2
Jodrell St B3
John St C2
Jordangate A2
King Edward St B2
King George's Field C3
King St B2
King's School A1
Knight St C3
Lansdowne St A3
Library B2
Lime Gr B3
Little Theatre C2
Loney St B1
Longacre St B1
Lord St C2
Lowe St C2
Lowerfield Rd A3
Lyon St B1
Macclesfield ⇌ B2
Marina B3
Market B2
Market Pl B2
Masons La A3
Mill La C2
Mill Rd C2
Mill St B2
Moran Rd C1
New Hall St A2
Newton St C1
Nicholson Ave A3
Nicholson Cl A3
Northgate Ave A2
Old Mill La C2
Paradise Mill C2
Paradise St B1
Park Green B2
Park La C1
Park Rd C1
Park St C2
Park Vale Rd C1
Parr St B1
Peel St C2
Percyvale St A3
Peter St C1
Pickford St B2
Pierce St B1
Pinfold St B1
Pitt St C2
Police Station B2
Pool St C2
Poplar Rd C2
Post Office B1/B2/B3
Pownall St A2
Prestbury Rd A1/B1
Queen Victoria St B2
Queen's Ave A3
Registrar B2
Richmond Hill C3
Riseley St B1
Roan Ct B3
Roe St B2
Rowan Way A3
Ryle St C2
Ryle's Park Rd C1
St Michael's B2
St George's St C2
Samuel St B2
Saville St C3
Shaw St B1
Slater St C1
Snow Hill C3
South Park C1
Spring Gdns A2
Statham St C2
Station St A2
Steeple St A3
Sunderland St B2
Swettenham St B3
The Silk Rd A2/B2
Thistleton Cl C2
Thorp St B2
Town Hall B2
Townley St B2
Turnock St C3
Union Rd B3
Union St B2
Victoria Park B3
Vincent St C2
Waterside C2
West Bond St B1
West Park A1
Westbrook Dr A1
Westminster Rd A1
Whalley Hayes B1
Windmill St C3
Withyfold Dr A2
York St B3

¼ mile
¼ ½ km

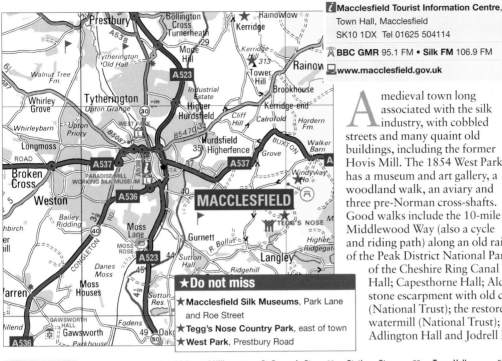

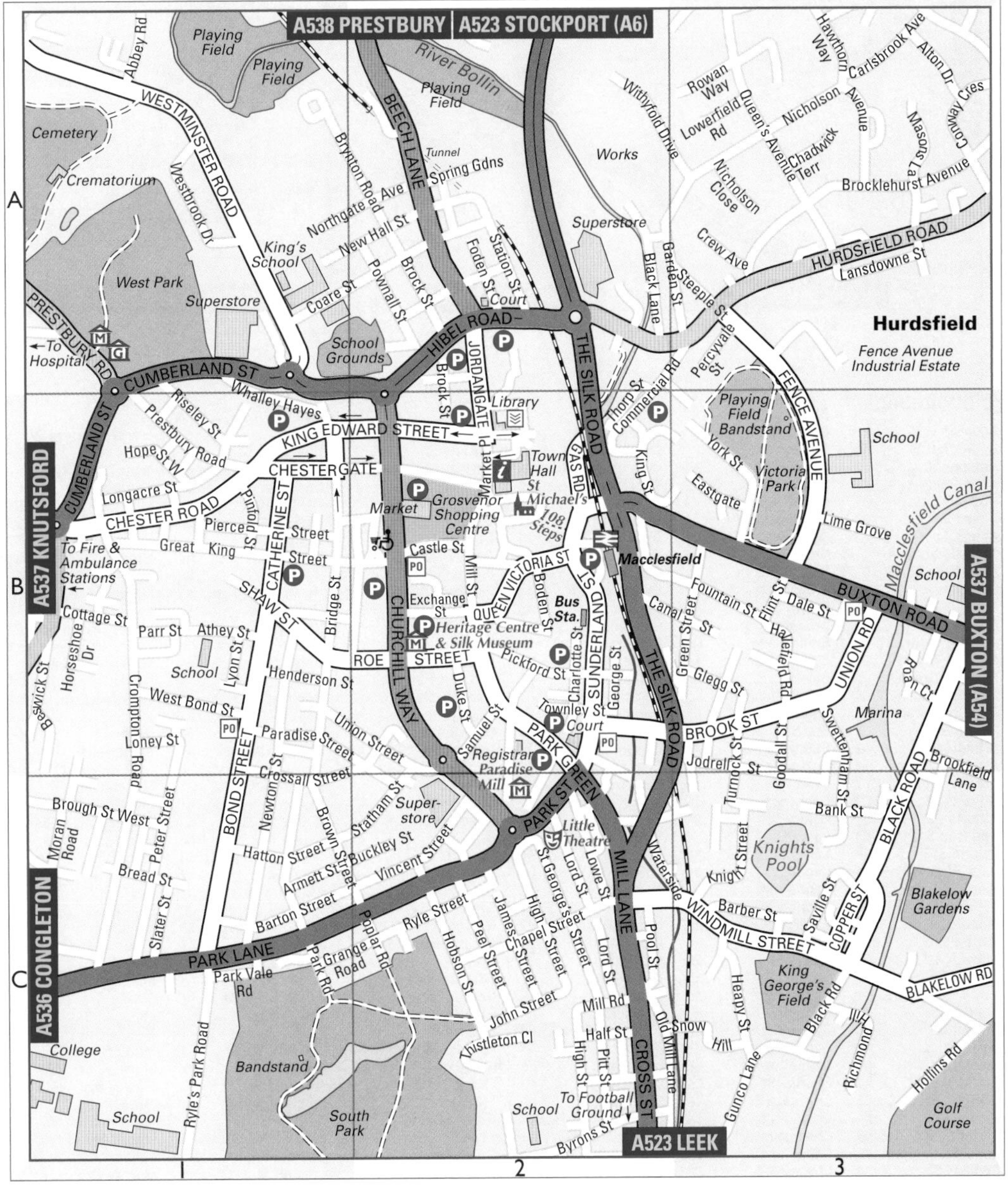

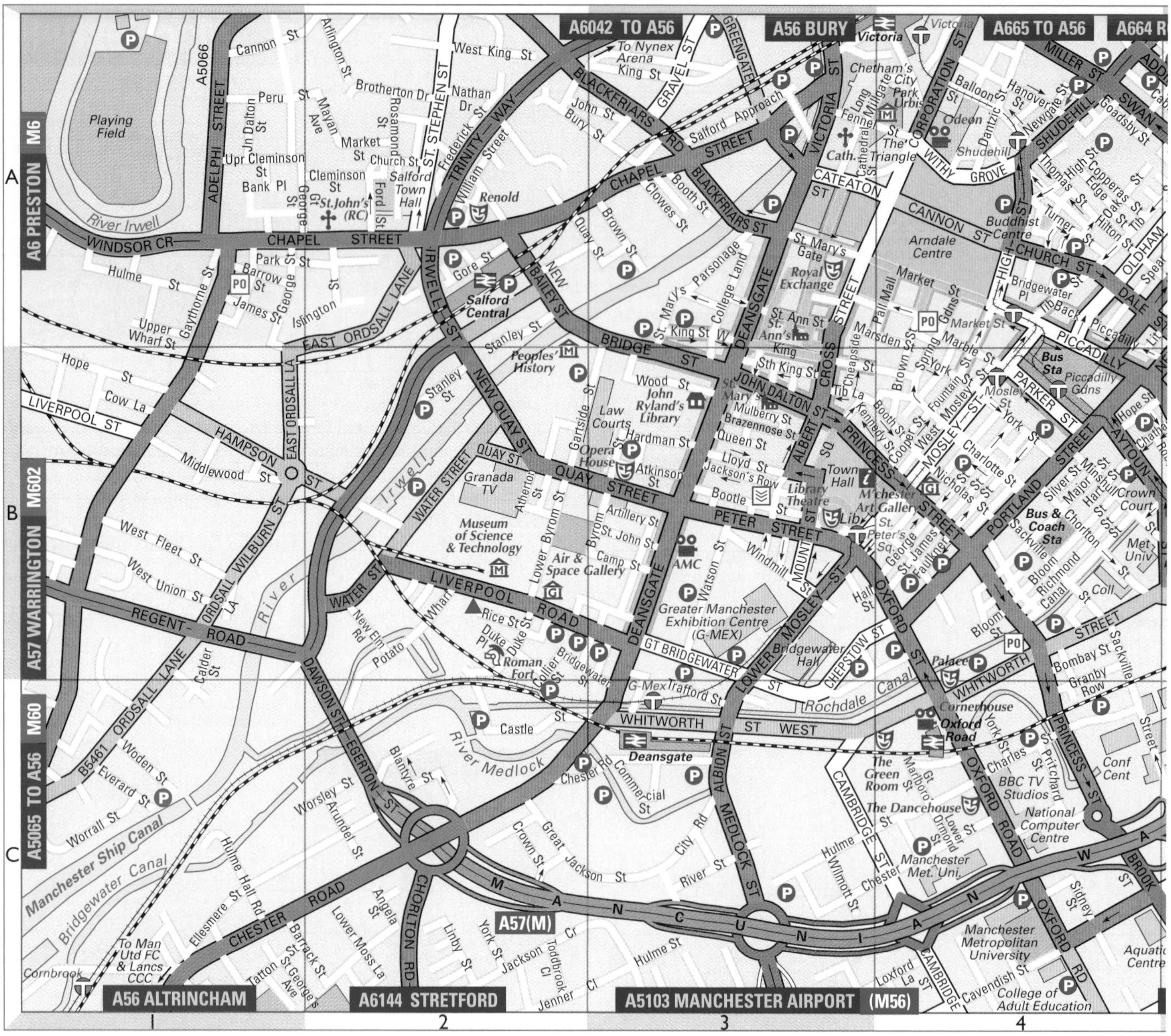

Manchester

Adair St B6
Addington St A5
Adelphi St A1
Air & Space Gallery B2
Albert Sq B3
Albion St C3
AMC Great Northern 16 . . B3
Ancoats Gr B6
Ancoats Gr North . B6
Angela St C2
Aquatic Centre . . C4
Ardwick Green . . C5
Ardwick Green North C5
Ardwick Green South C5
Arlington St A2
Arndale Centre . . . A4
Artillery St B3
Arundel St C2
Atherton St B2
Atkinson St B3
Aytoun St B4
Back Piccadilly . . A4
Baird St B5
Balloon St A4
Bank Pl A1
Baring St B5
Barrack St C1
Barrow St A1
BBC TV Studios . . C4
Bendix St A5
Bengal St A5
Berry St C5
Blackfriars Rd . . . A3
Blackfriars St A3
Blantyre St C2
Bloom St B4
Blossom St A5
Boad St B5
Bombay St B4
Booth St A3
Booth St B4
Bootle St B3
Brazennose St B3
Brewer St A5
Bridge St A3
Bridgewater Hall . B3
Bridgewater Pl . . A4
Bridgewater St . . B2
Brook St C4
Brotherton Dr . . . A2
Brown St A3
Brown St B4
Brunswick St C6
Brydon Ave C6
Buddhist Centre . A4
Bury St A2
Bus & Coach Station B4
Bus Station B4
Butler St A6
Buxton St C5
Byrom St B3
Cable St A5
Calder St B1
Cambridge St C3/C4
Camp St B3
Canal St B4
Cannon St A1
Cannon St A4
Cardroom Rd A6
Carruthers St A6
Castle St C2
Cateaton St A3
Cathedral ✝ A3
Cathedral St A3
Cavendish St C4
Chapel St A1/A3
Chapeltown St B5
Charles St C4
Charlotte St B4
Chatham St B4
Cheapside A3
Chepstow St B3
Chester Rd . . . C1/C2
Chester St C4
Chetham's (Dept Store) . . . A3
China La B5
Chippenham Rd . A6
Chorlton Rd C2
Chorlton St B4
Church St A2
Church St A4
City Park A4
City Rd C3
Cleminson St A2
Clowes St A3
College Land A3
College of Adult Education C4
Collier St B2
Commercial St . . C3
Conference Centre C4
Cooper St B4
Copperas St A4
Cornbrook (Metro Station) . C1
Cornell St A5
Cornerhouse . . C4
Corporation St . . A4
Cotter St C6
Cotton St A5
Cow La B1
Cross St B3
Crown Court B4
Crown St C2
Dalberg St C6
Dale St A4/B5
Dancehouse Theatre C4
Dantzic St A4
Dark La C6
Dawson St C2
Dean St A5
Deansgate A3/B3
Deansgate ⇌ C3
Dolphin St C6
Downing St C5
Ducie St B5
Duke Pl B2
Duke St B2
Durling St C6
East Ordsall La A2/B1
Edge St A4
Egerton St C2
Ellesmere St C1
Everard St C1
Every St B6
Fairfield St B5
Faulkner St B4
Fennel St A3
Ford St A2
Ford St C6
Fountain St B4
Frederick St A2
Gartside St B2
Gaythorne St A1
George Leigh St . A5
George St A1
George St B4
G-Mex (Metro Station) . C3
Goadsby St A4
Gore St A2
Goulden St A4
Granada TV Studios B2
Granby Row B4
Gravel St A3
Great Ancoats St . A5
Great Bridgewater St . . B3
Great George St . A1
Great Jackson St C2
Great Marlborough St . C4
Greater Manchester Exhibition Centre (G-Mex) B3
Green Room, The C4
Greengate A3
Grosvenor St C5
Gun St A5
Hadrian Ave B6
Hall St B3
Hampson St B1
Hanover St A4
Hanworth Cl C5
Hardman St B3
Harkness St C6
Harrison St B6
Hart St B4
Helmet St B6
Henry St A5
Heyrod St B6
High St A4
Higher Ardwick . . C6
Hilton St A4/A5
Holland St A6
Hood St A5
Hope St B1
Hope St B4
Houldsworth St . . A5
Hoyle St C6
Hulme Hall Rd . . . C1
Hulme St A1
Hulme St C3
Hyde Rd C6
Information Ctr . B3
Irwell St A2
Islington St A2
Jackson Cr C2
Jackson's Row . . . B3
James St A1
Jenner Cl C2
Jersey St A5
John Dalton St . . A1
John Dalton St . . . B3
John Ryland's Library B3
John St A2
Kennedy St B3
Kincardine Rd . . . C4
King St A3
King St West A3
Law Courts B3
Laystall St B5
Lever St A5
Library B3
Library Theatre . B3
Linby St C2
Little Lever St . . . A4
Liverpool Rd B2
Liverpool St B1
Lloyd St B3
Lockton Cl C5
London Rd B5
Long Millgate . . . A3
Longacre St B6
Loom St A5
Lower Byrom St . . B2
Lower Mosley St . B3
Lower Moss La . . C2
Lower Ormond St C4
Loxford La C4
Luna St A5
Major St B4
Manchester Art Gallery . . . B4
Manchester Metropolitan University . . . B4/C4
Mancunian Way . . C3
Manor St C5
Marble St A4
Market St A2
Market St A4
Market St (Metro Station) . A4
Marsden St A3
Marshall St A5
Mayan Ave A2
Medlock St C3
Middlewood St . . . B1
Miller St A4
Minshull St B4
Mosley St A4
Mosley St (Metro Station) . . B4
Mount St B3
Mulberry St B3
Murray St A5
Museum of Science & Technology . B2
Nathan Dr A2
National Computer Centre C4
Naval St A5
New Bailey St . . . A2
New Elm Rd B2
New Islington A6
New Quay St B2
New Union St A6
Newgate St A4
Newton St A5
Nicholas St B4
North George St . A1
North Western St C6
Oak St A4
Odeon A4
Old Mill St A6
Oldfield Rd . . . A1/C1
Oldham Rd A5
Oldham St A4
Opera House . . . B3
Ordsall La C1
Oxford Rd C4
Oxford Rd ⇌ C4
Oxford St B4
Paddock St C6
Palace Theatre . B4
Pall Mall A3
Palmerston St B6
Park St A1
Parker St B4
Peak St B5
Penfield Cl C5
Peoples' History Museum B2
Peru St A1
Peter St B3
Piccadilly A4
Piccadilly (Metro Station) B5
Piccadilly Gdns (Metro Station) . B4
Piccadilly ⇌ B5
Piercy St A6
Poland St A5
Police Station B3/B5
Pollard St B6
Port St A5
Portland St B4
Portugal St East . B5
Post Office . A1/A4/A5/B4/B6
Potato Wharf B2
Princess St . . . B3/C4
Pritchard St C4
Quay St A2
Quay St B2
Queen St B3
Radium St A5
Redhill St A5
Regent Rd B1
Renold Theatre A2
Retail Park A5
Rice St B2
Richmond St B4
River St C3
Roby St B5
Rodney St A6
Roman Fort B2
Rosamond St A2
Royal Exchange A3
Sackville St B4
St Andrew's St . . . B6
St Ann St A3
St Ann's A3
St George's Ave . . C1
St James St B4
St John St B3

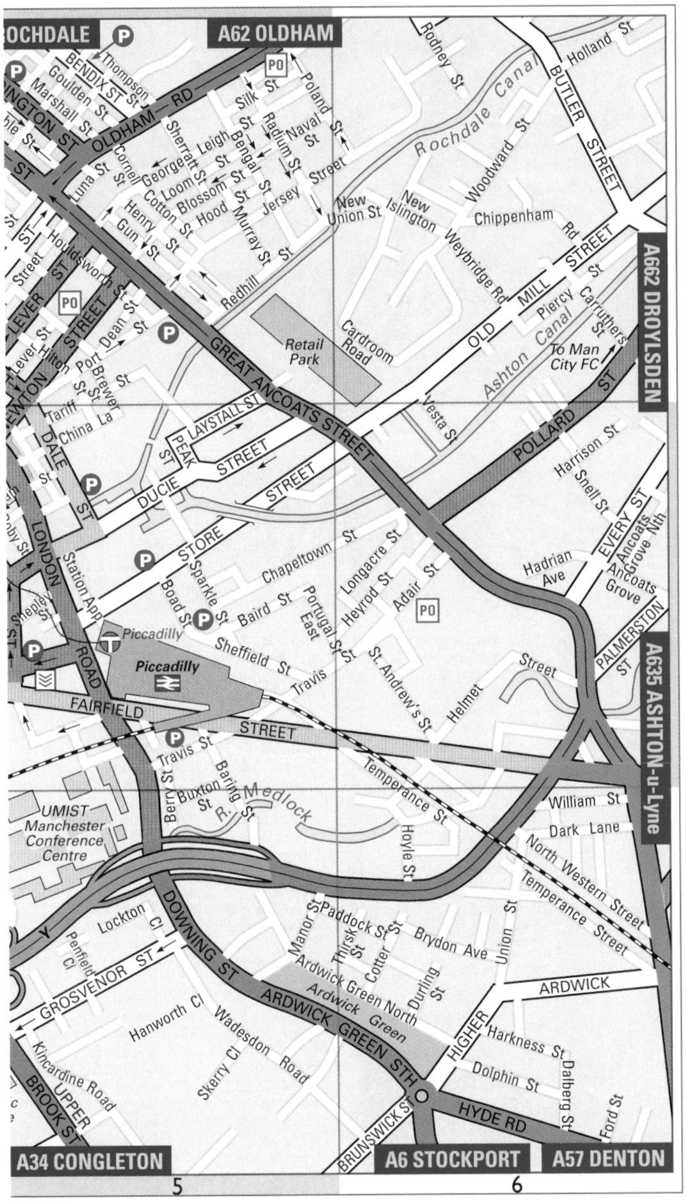

Manchester

A city founded on a Roman settlement of AD79 (with a re-created fort on the original Castlefields site) and a main player in the Industrial Revolution. Historic buildings include the Victorian Gothic Town Hall, the Royal Exchange, the Cathedral and local artist JS Lowry's House in Salford. Much activity is focused around the revitalised Salford Quays at the head of the Manchester Ship Canal, linked to the centre by the flamboyant curving Calatrava Bridge (1995) and also crossed by the £5 million Lowry Footbridge. Among museums and art venues are the Manchester Jewish Museum; the Pankhurst Centre, where the suffragette movement was formed; the Pumphouse People's History Museum; the Museum of Science and Technology; the Museum of Transport; the Imperial War Museum North; the Chinese Arts Centre; Manchester Art Gallery; and the outstanding Whitworth Art Gallery. Manchester has been regenerated with a wealth of smart new shops, restaurants and hotels from the high street chains in the Arndale Centre to the more bohemian individual shops and markets of the Northern Quarter. It is also home to a large gay community and this is reflected in the some of the more flamboyant bars and restaurants in the centre of town.

▲Canal Street

★Do not miss

★**The Lowry art museum**, Pier 8, The Quays, Salford
★**Steam, Coal and Canal: the Bridgewater Canal Linear Industrial Heritage Park**, Salford
★**Urbis – Museum of the Modern City**, Cathedral Gardens

Tourist Information Centre, Town Hall Extension (off St Peter's Square), Lloyd Street, Manchester M60 2LA
Tel 0871 222 8223

BBC GMR 95.1 FM • **Capital Gold** 1458 AM • **Century** 105.4 FM **Galaxy** 102 FM • **Key** 103 FM **Magic** 1152 AM

www.manchester.gov.uk

St John's Cathedral (RC) ✝ A2
St Mary's ⛪ B3
St Mary's Gate... A3
St Mary's Parsonage A3
St Peter's Sq (Metro Station) .. B3
St Stephen St ... A2
Salford Approach A3
Salford Central ⇌ A2
Sheffield St B5
Shepley St B5
Sherratt St...... A5
Shudehill A4
Shudehill (Metro Station). A4
Sidney St C4
Silk St A5
Silver St B4
Skerry Cl C5
Snell St.......... B6
South King St ... B3
Sparkle St B5
Spear St A4
Spring Gdns..... A4
Stanley St.... A2/B2
Station Approach .B5
Store St B5
Swan St A4
Tariff St B5
Tatton St........ C1
Temperance St.......... B6/C6
The Triangle..... A4
Thirsk St........ C6
Thomas St A4
Thompson St.... A5
Tib La B3
Tib St A4
Toddbrook Cl.... C2
Town Hall (Manchester)... B3
Town Hall (Salford)....... A2
Trafford St C3
Travis St B5
Trinity Way...... A2
Turner St A4
UMIST Manchester Conference Centre......... C5
Union St......... C6
Upper Brook St .. C5
Upper Cleminson St... A1
Upper Wharf St.. A1
Urbis Museum 🏛 A4
Vesta St B6
Victoria (Metro Station). A4
Victoria Station ⇌.... A4
Victoria St A3
Wadesdon Rd C5
Water St......... B2
Watson St........ B3
Wellington St.... A2
West Fleet St..... B1
West King St A2
West Mosley St .. B4
West Union St B1
Weybridge Rd A6
Whitworth St..... B4
Whitworth St West C3
Wilburn St B1
William St A2
William St C6
Wilmott St C3
Windmill St B3
Windsor Cr....... A1
Withy Gr A4
Woden St C1
Wood St B3
Woodward St.... A6
Worrall St....... C1
Worsley St C2

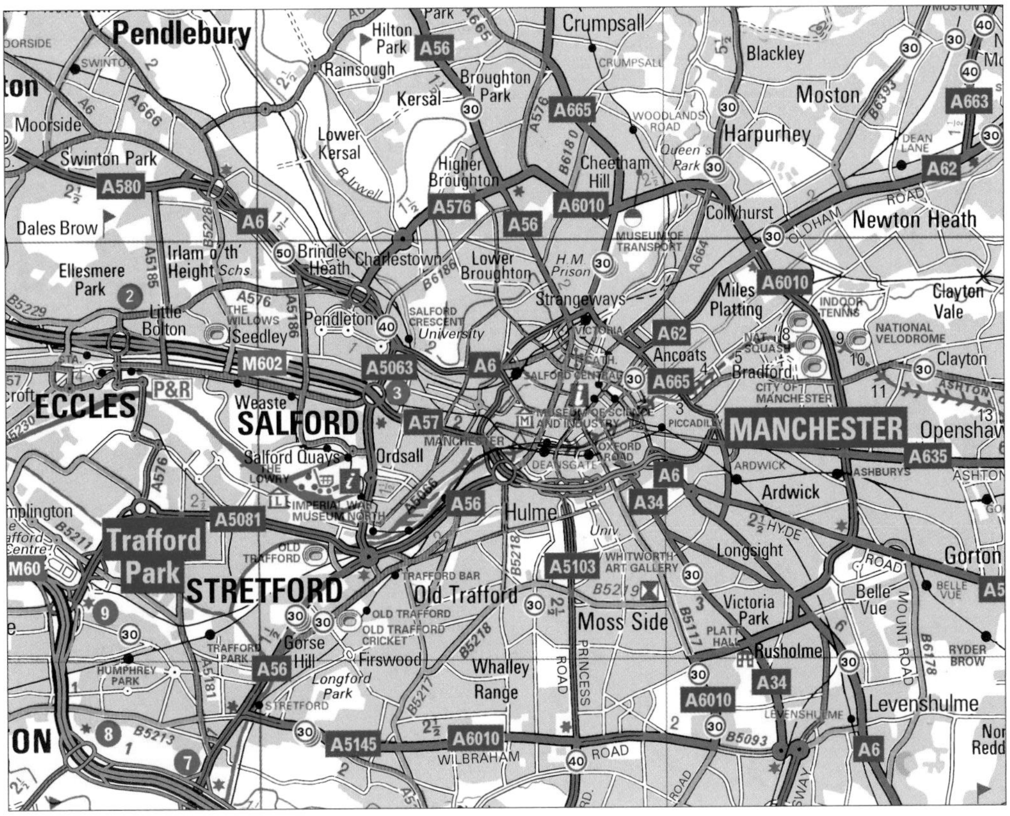

Maidstone

The Town Hall Information Centre, Town Hall, High Street, Maidstone, Kent ME14 1TF Tel 01622 602169

BBC Radio Kent 69.7 FM and 1602 AM • Capital Gold 1242 AM CTR 105.6 FM • Invicta 102.8 FM

www.maidstone.gov.uk

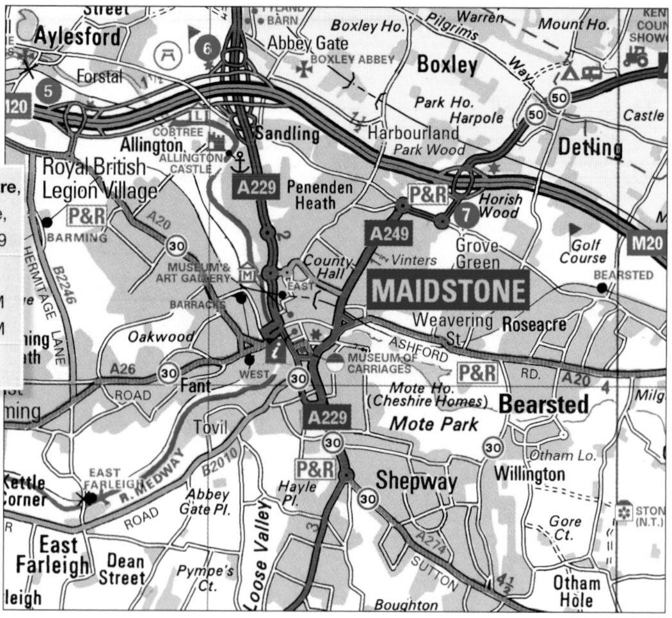

A town of Roman origins that lay on the pilgrimage route between London and Dover, became a medieval market centre and was awarded a royal charter in 1549. Buildings of interest include the 14th-century visitors lodgings of the Archbishop's Palace (containing the Tyrwhitt-Drake Carriage Museum) and All Saints parish church (1395). The Maidstone Museum and Bentlif Art Gallery includes an Earth Heritage gallery. After the decline of the papermakingand brewing industries in the 20th century, tourism and retail expanded. Close by are the prehistoric burial chambers of Kits Coty House; The Friars, a working medieval priory; Yalding Organic Gardens; the ruins of 12th-century Boxley Abbey; Stoneacre (National Trust), and Boughton Monchelsea Place, a 16th-century manor.

★Do not miss

★**Leeds Castle**, Hollingbourne
★**Maidstone Millennium River Park** and **Whatman Recreational Park**, banks of the Medway
★**Museum of Kent Life**, Lock Lane, Sandling

Maidstone

Albion Pl B3
All Saints B2
Allen St. A3
Amphitheatre ✦ . C2
Archbishop's Palace. B2
Bank St. B2
Barker Rd C2
Barton Rd. C3
Beaconsfield Rd . C1
Bedford Pl B1
Bishops Way B2
Bluett St. A3
Bower La C1
Bower Mount Rd. . B1
Bower Pl C1
Bower St B1
Bowling Alley B3
Boxley Rd A3
Brenchley Gdns. . A2
Brewer St A3
Broadway B2
Brunswick St C3
Buckland Hill. . . . A1
Buckland Rd B1
Bus Station B3
Campbell Rd C3
Carriage Mus . . B2
Chequers Shopping Ctr. . . . B3
Church Rd C1
Church St. B3
Cinema C2
College Ave C2
College Rd C2
Collis Memorial Gdn C3
Cornwallis Rd B1
Corpus Christi Hall B2
County Rd A3
Crompton Gdns. . C3
Crown & County Courts. B2
Curzon Rd A3
Dixon Cl C2
Douglas Rd C1
Earl St. B2
Eccleston Rd C2
Fairmeadow. B2
Fisher St. A2
Florence Rd C1
Foley St A3
Foster St. C3
Fremlin Walk Shopping Ctr B2
Gabriel's Hill B3
George St. C3
Grecian St A3
Hardy St A3
Hart St C2
Hastings Rd C3
Hayle Rd. C3
Hazlitt Theatre . B2
Heathorn St. A3
Hedley St A3
High St. B2
HM Prison A3
Holland Rd. A3
Hope St A2
Information Ctr . B2
James St A3
James Whatman Way. A2
Jeffrey St A3
Kent County Council Offices . A2
King Edward Rd . C2
King St B3
Kingsley Rd C3
Knightrider St B3
Launder Way C1
Lesley Pl. A1
Library B2
Little Buckland Ave A1
Lockmeadow Leisure Complex C2
London Rd B1
Lower Boxley Rd. A2
Lower Fant Rd. . . C1
Magistrates Court. B3
Maidstone Barracks Station A1
Maidstone Borough Council Offices . . B1
Maidstone East Station A2
Maidstone West Station B2
Market C2
Market Buildings. . B2
Marsham St B3
Medway St B2
Medway Trading Estate C2
Melville Rd. C3
Mill St. B2
Millennium Br . . . C2
Mote Rd B3
Muir Rd C3
Old Tovil Rd C2
Palace Ave B3
Perryfield St A2
Police Station . . B2
Post Office . A2/A3/B2/B3/C1
Priory Rd C3
Prospect Pl C1
Pudding La. B2
Queen Anne Rd. . . B3
Queens Rd A1
Randall St A2
Rawdon Rd C3
Reginald Rd C1
Rock Pl. B1
Rocky Hill. B1
Romney Pl B3
Rose Yard B2
Rowland Cl. C1
Royal Engineers' Rd A2
Royal Star Arcade. B2
St Annes Ct B1
St Faith's St. B2
St Luke's Rd. A3
St Peter's Br B2
St Peter St B2
St Philip's Ave C3
Salisbury Rd A3
Sandling Rd. A2
Scott St. A2
Scrubs La. B1
Sheal's Cres. C3
Somerfield, The A1
Somerfield La B1
Somerfield Rd B1
Staceys St A2
Station Rd A2
Terrace Rd B1
Tonbridge Rd. . . . C1
Tovil Rd C2
Town Hall. B2
Trinity Park B3
Tufton St B3
Union St. B3
Upper Fant Rd. . . C1
Upper Stone St . . C3
Victoria St B1
Visitor Centre . . . A1
Warwick Pl. B1
Wat Tyler Way B3
Waterloo St C3
Waterlow Rd A3
Week St B2
Well Rd. A3
Westree Rd C1
Wharf Rd C1
Whatman Park . . A1
Wheeler St. A3
Whitchurch Cl B1
Woodville Rd C3
Wyatt St B3
Wyke Manor Rd. . . B3

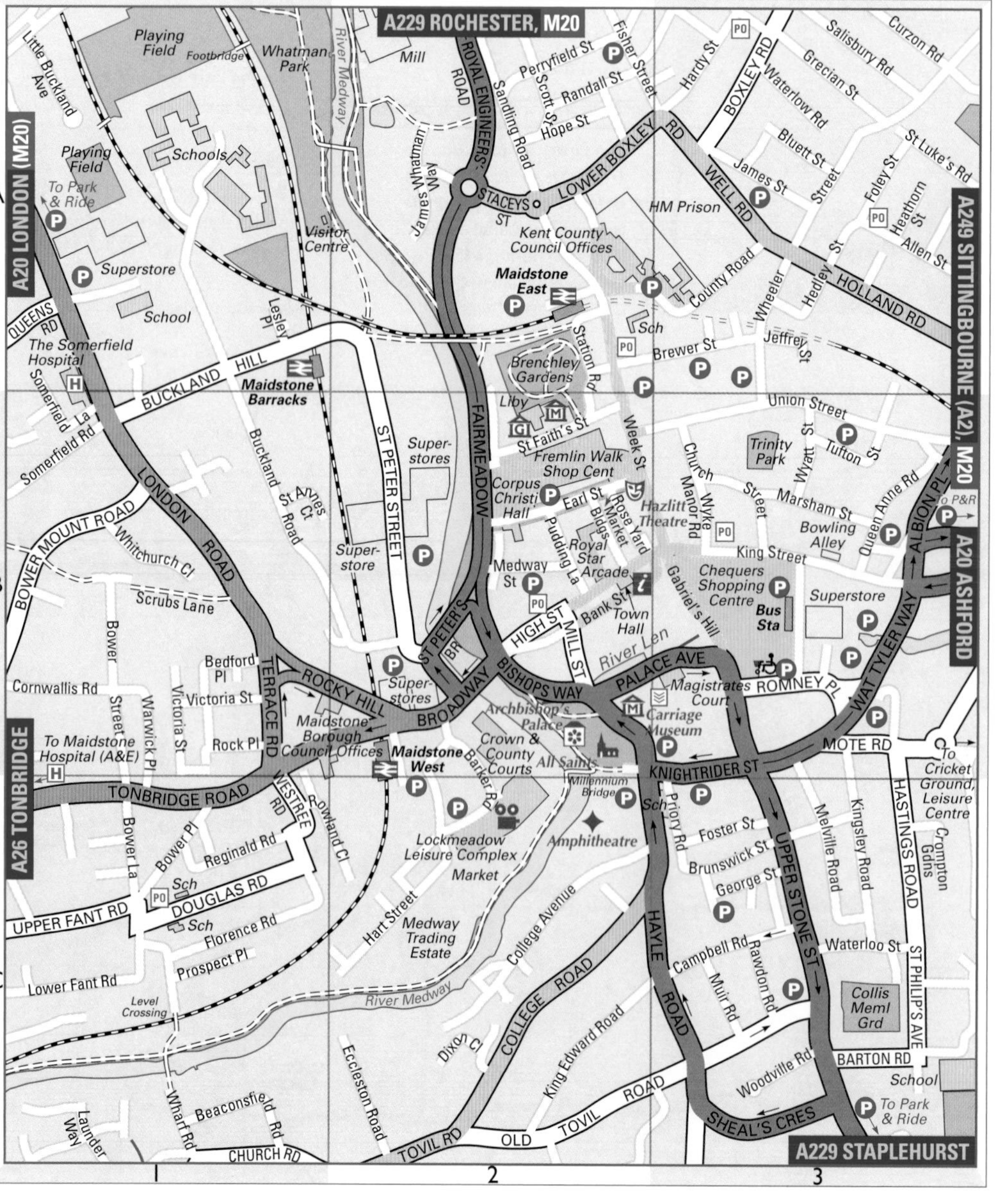

¼ mile
¼ ½ km

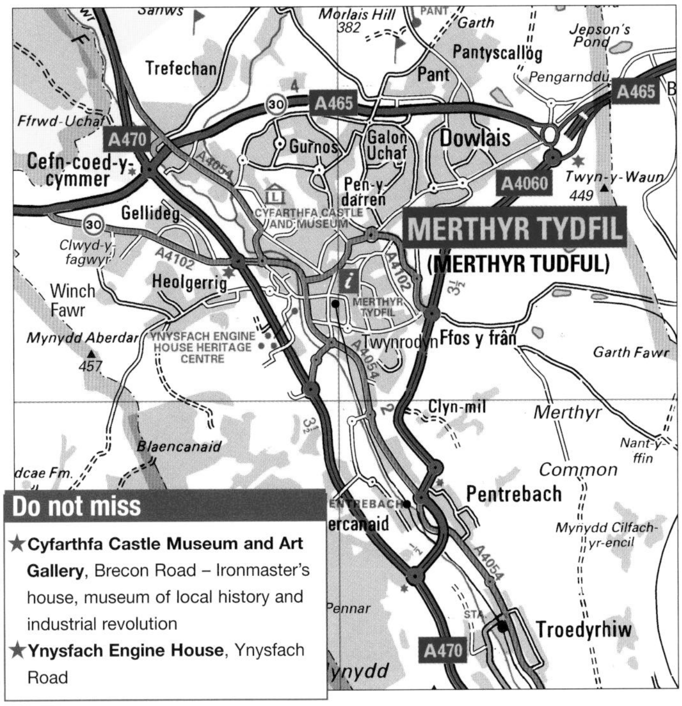

Do not miss

★**Cyfarthfa Castle Museum and Art Gallery**, Brecon Road – Ironmaster's house, museum of local history and industrial revolution

★**Ynysfach Engine House**, Ynysfach Road

Merthyr Tydfil

Merthyr Tydfil was the largest iron-making town in the world in the early to mid-nineteeth century and the most significant Welsh town of the Industrial Revolution. The primarily late-eighteenth to nineteenth centuries landscape is still evident. Dr Joseph Parry's house, built by the Cyfarthfa Iron Company is a restored example of a period ironworker's cottage in Chapel Row and also the birthplace of the renowned composer. Adjoining the Cyfarthfa Ironworks lies the Pontycafnau bridge, built in 1793, the first ever iron railway bridge to be built. Other local sites of interest include St Tydfil's Church and the Robert and Lucy Thomas Cast Iron Fountain Canopy, situated adjacent to each other at the lower end of the town centre. The town is the commercial and shopping destination for the Heads of the Valleys region, in addition to which there are several night clubs and many restaurants and pubs.

▲Cyfarthfa Castle

Tourist Information Centre, 14a Glebeland Street, Merthyr Tydfil CF47 8AU Tel 01685 379884

BBC Radio Wales 103.7 FM
Real Radio 105-106 FM
Valleys 999, 1116 AM

www.merthyr.gov.uk

Merthyr Tydfil

Aberdare Rd B2
Abermorlais Terr . . B2
Alexandra Rd A3
Alma St C3
Arfryn Pl C3
Argyle St C3
Avenue De Clichy C2
Bethesda St B2
Bishops Gr A3
Brecon Rd . . . A1/B2
Briarmead A3
Bryn St C3
Bryntirion Rd. B3/C3
Bus Station B2
Cae Mari Dwn . . . B3
Caedraw Rd C2
Castle Sq A1
Castle St B2
Chapel C2
Chapel Bank B1
Church St B3
Civic Centre B2
Coedcae'r Ct C3
Court B3
Court St C3
Courts B2
Cromwell St B2
Cyfarthfa Castle School and Museum A1
Cyfarthfa Ind Est . A1
Cyfarthfa Park . . . A1
Cyfarthfa Rd A1
Dane St A2
Dane Terr A2
Danyparc B3
Darren View A3
Dixon St B2
Dyke St C3
Dynevor St B2
Elwyn Dr C3
Fire Station B2
Fothergill St B3
Galonuchaf Rd . . . A3
Garth St B2
Georgetown B2
Grawen Terr A2
Grove Pk A2
Gurnos Rd A2
Gwaelodygarth Rd A2/A3
Gwaunfarren Gr . A3
Gwaunfarren Rd . A3
Gwendoline St . . . A3
Hampton St C3
Hanover St A2
Heol S O Davies . . B1
Heol-Gerrig B1
High St A3/B2/B3/C2
Highland View . . . C3
Howell Cl B1
Information Ctr . B2
Jackson's Bridge . B2
James St C3
John St B3
Joseph Parry's Cottage B2
Lancaster St A2
Llewellyn St A2
Llwyfen St B2
Llwyn Berry B1
Llwyn Dic Penderyn B1
Llwyn-y-Gelynen C1
Lower Thomas St . B3
Market C2
Mary St C3
Masonic St C2
Merthyr College . . B2
Merthyr Tydfil FC . B3
Merthyr Tydfil R.U.F.C. C2
Merthyr Tydfil ⇌ C3
Meyrick Villas . . . A2
Miniature Railway ✦ A1
Mount St A2
Nantygwenith St . . B1
Norman Terr B2
Oak Rd A2
Old Cemetery B3
Pandy Cl A1
Pantycelynen B1
Park Terr B2
Penlan View C2
Penry St B2
Pentwyn Villas . . . A2
Penyard Rd B3
Penydarren Park . A3
Penydarren Rd . . . B3
Plymouth St C3
Police Station . C2
Pont Marlais West B2
Post Office . A3/B2/C3
Quarry Row B2
Queen's Rd B3
Rees St C3
Rhydycar Leisure Centre C3
Rhydycar Link C2
Riverside Park . . . A1
St David's B3
St Tydfil's C2
St Tydfil's Ave . . . C3
St Tydfil's Hospital (No A&E) H B3
St Tydfil's Square Shopping Centre C2
Saxon St A2
School of Nursing A2
Seward St A3
Shiloh La B3
Stone Circles . . B3
Stuart St A2
Summerhill Pl B3
Superstore B3
Swan St C2
Swansea Rd B1
Taff Glen View . . . C3
Taff Vale Ct B3
The Grove A2
The Parade B3
The Walk B2
Thomastown Park . B3
Tramroad La A3
Tramroad Side . . . B2
Tramroad Side North B3
Tramroad Side South C3
Trevithick Gdns . . C3
Trevithick St A3
Tudor Terr B2
Twynyrodyn Rd . . C3
Union St B3
Upper Colliers Row B1
Upper Thomas St . B3
Victoria St B2
Vulcan Rd B2
Warlow St C3
Well St A2
Wern La C1
West Gr A2
William St C3
Yew St C3
Ynysfach Engine House ✦ C2
Ynysfach Rd C2

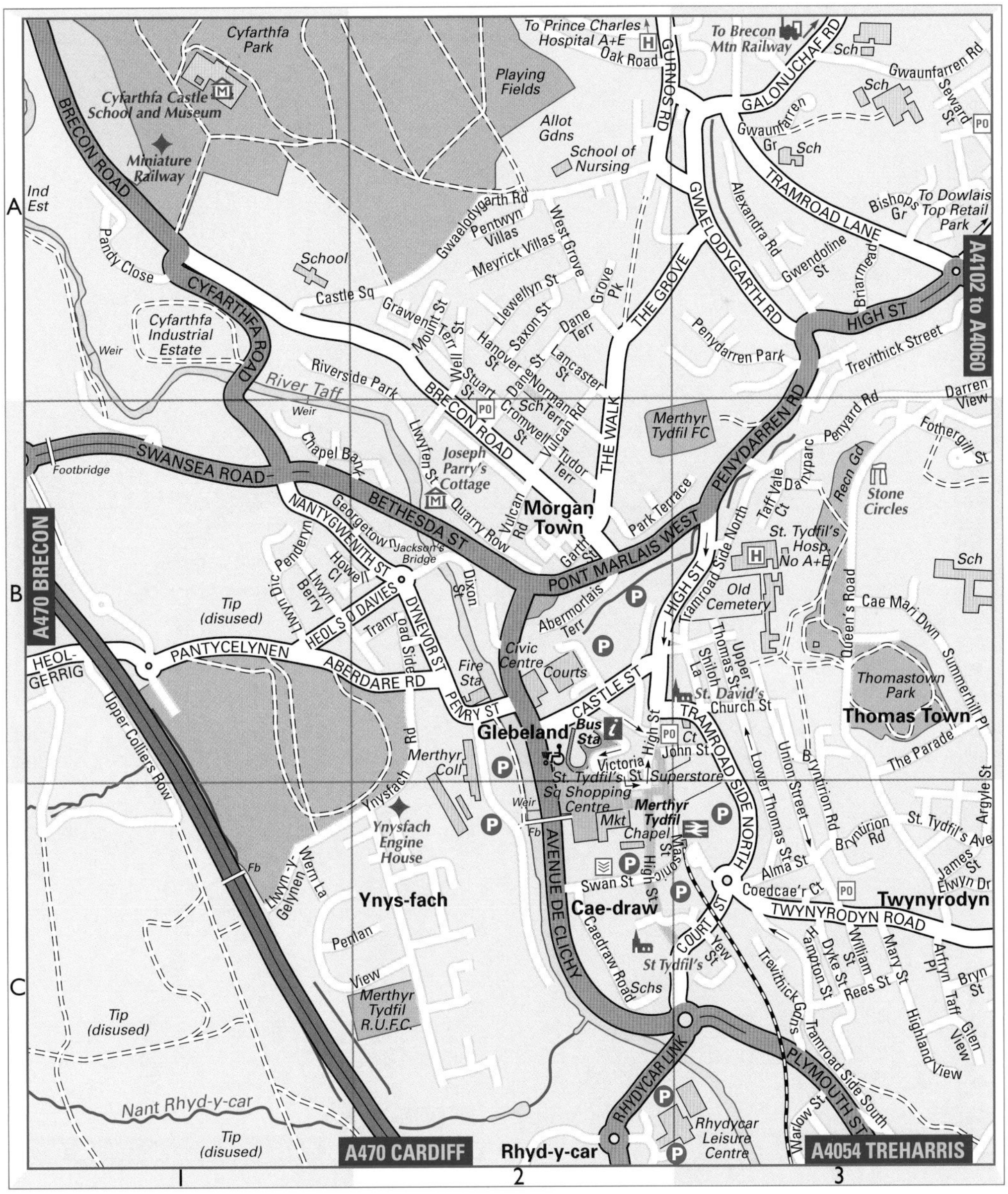

Middlesbrough

An agricultural hamlet until 1829, when Quaker businessmen founded the town to supply labour to a nearby coal port. The 18th-century maritime explorer was baptised in St Cuthbert's church, Marton, and educated at what is now the Captain Cook Schoolroom Museum. Notable structures in the town include the Victorian Gothic town hall, the Transporter Bridge and Visitor Centre, and Newport Bridge, Britain's first vertical-lift bridge. Outdoor attractions include Stewart Park; Newham Grange Farm and Rare Breeds Centre; and Nature's World explores sustainable technologies. There are four shopping centres. A new contemporary arts gallery – MIMA – opened in January 2007.

▲Middlesbrough Transporter Bridge

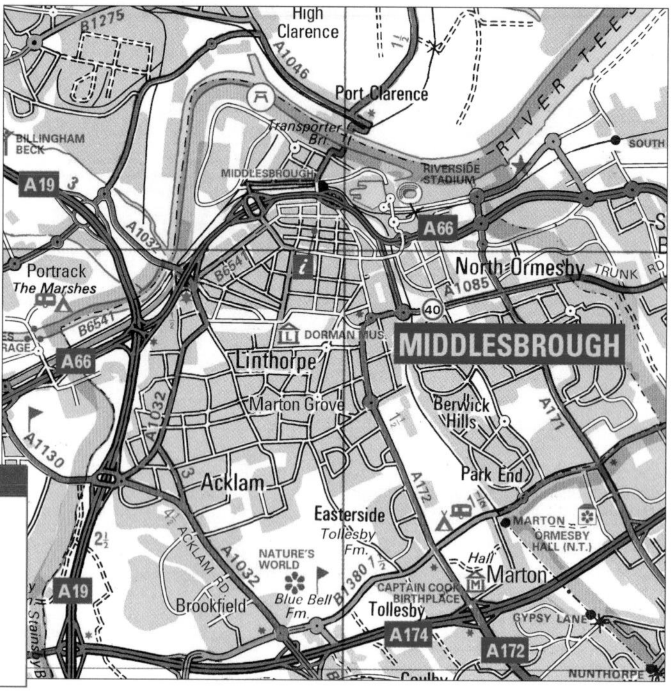

★ Do not miss

★**Captain Cook Birthplace Museum**, Stewart Park
★**Middlesbrough Institute of Modern Art (MIMA)**, Middlesbrough Centre Square
★**Dorman Museum of local history and Linthorpe pottery**, Linthorpe Rd
★**Ormesby Hall**, Church Lane

Tourist Information Centre, The Town Hall, Albert Rd, Middlesbrough TS1 2QQ Tel 01642 729700

BBC Radio Cleveland 95 FM
Magic 1170 AM • **96.6TFM** 96.6 FM

www.middlesbrough.gov.uk

Middlesbrough

Abingdon Rd C3
Acklam Rd C1
Albert Park C2
Albert Rd B2
Albert Terr C2
Aubrey St C3
Ayresome Gdns . . C2
Ayresome Green La C1
Ayresome St C2
Barton Rd. A1
Bilsdale Rd. C3
Bishopton Rd. . . . C2
Borough Rd . . .B2/B3
Bowes Rd. A2
Breckon Hill Rd. . .B3
Bridge St East B3
Bridge St West . . .B2
Brighouse Rd. A1
Burlam Rd C1
Bus Station B2
Cannon Park B1
Cannon Park Way .B2
Cannon St B1
Captain Cook Sq . .B2
Carlow St B1
Castle Way C3
Chipchase Rd C2
Clairville Sports Stadium C3
Cleveland Centre .B2
Clive Rd C2
Commercial St . . A2
Corporation Rd . . .B2
Costa St C2
Council Offices . . .B3
Crescent Rd C1
Cumberland Rd . . C2
Depot Rd A2
Derwent St. B1
Devonshire Rd. . . . C2
Diamond Rd. B2
Disabled Driver Test Circuit B1
Dorman Mus . . C2
Douglas St B3
Eastbourne Rd. . . C2
Eden Rd C3
Enterprise Centre A2
Forty Foot Rd . . . A2
Gilkes St. B2
Gosford St A2
Grange Rd B2
Gresham Rd. B2
Harehills Rd. C1
Harford St C2
Hartington Rd B2
Haverton Hill Rd . A1
Hey Wood St B1
Highfield Rd. C3
Hill St Centre. B2
Holwick Rd B1
Hutton Rd. C3
I.C.I. Works A1
Information Ctr .B2
Lambton Rd C3
Lancaster Rd C2
Lansdowne Rd. . . . C3
Latham Rd C2
Law Courts. . . .B2/B3
Lees Rd. B2
Leeway B3
Linthorpe Cem . . C1
Linthorpe Rd B2
Little Theatre, The C2
Longford St C2
Longlands Rd. . . . C3
Lower East St . . . A3
Lower Lake C3
Macmillan Coll . . C1
Maldon Rd C1
Manor St B2
Marsh St. B1
Marton Rd B3
Middlehaven B3
Middlesbrough By-Pass B2/C1
Middlesbrough F.C. B3
Middlesbrough General (A&E) C2
Middlesbrough Leisure Park B3
Middlesbrough Station B2
Middletown Park C2
MIMA B3
Mosque ✦ B2
Mosque ✦ C3
Mulgrave Rd C2
North Ormesby Rd B3
Newport Bridge. . . .B1
Newport Bridge Approach Rd B1
Newport Rd B2
North Rd. B2
Northern Rd. C1
Outram St. B2
Oxford Rd C2
Park La C2
Park Rd North . . . C2
Park Rd South. . . . C2
Park Vale Rd C3
Parliament Rd B1
Police Station . .B3
Port Clarence Rd A3
Portman St. B2
Post Office . B2/B3/C1/C2/C3
Princes Rd B2
Riverside Business Park . . A2
Riverside Park Rd A1
Rockliffe Rd C2
Romaldkirk Rd . . .B1
Roman Rd C2
Roseberry Rd. . . . C3
St Paul's Rd. B2
St Barnabas' Rd . C2
Saltwells Rd. B3
Scott's Rd. A3
Seaton Carew Rd A3
Shepherdson Way.B3
Sikh Temple ✦. . . .B2
Snowdon Rd A2
South West Ironmasters Pk . .B1
Southfield Rd. B3
Southwell Rd. C2
Springfield Rd . . . C1
Startforth Rd A2
Stockton Rd. C1
Stockton St A2
Surrey St C2
Sycamore Rd C2
Synagogue ✦ B2
Tax Offices B3
Tees Viaduct. C1
Teessaurus Park . A2
Teesside Tertiary Coll C3
The Avenue C2
The Crescent C2
Thornfield Rd . . . C1
Town Hall B2
Transporter Bridge (Toll) . . . A3
UGC B3
Union St B2
Univ of Teesside . .B2
Upper Lake C2
Valley Rd C3
Ventnor Rd. C2
Victoria Rd. B2
Vulcan St A2
Warwick St. C2
Wellesley Rd B3
West Lane C1
Westminster Rd. . C2
Wilson St B2
Windward Way . . .B3
Woodlands Rd. . . .B2
York Rd. C3

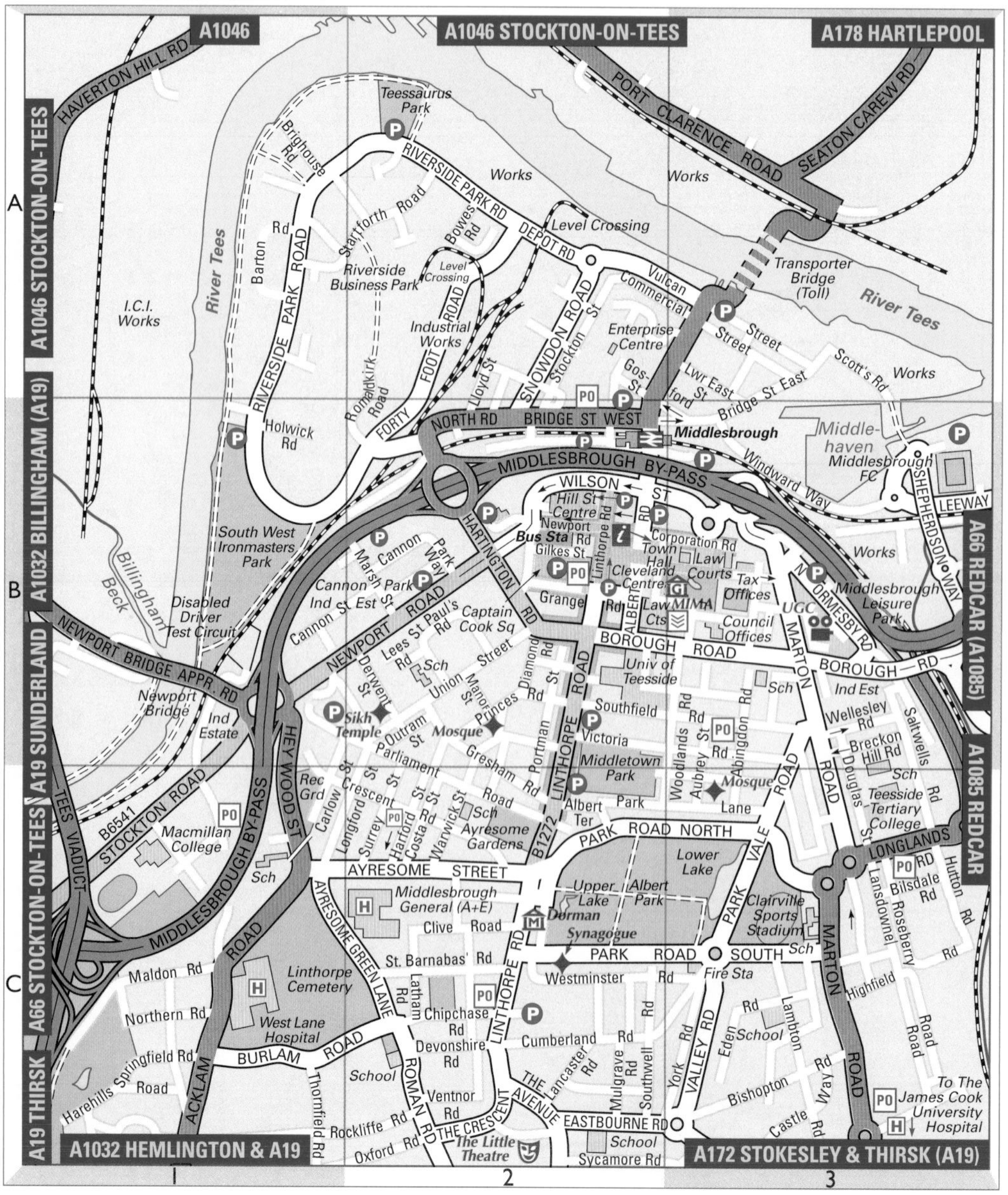

¼ mile
¼ ½ km

▲Xscape

Milton Keynes

The famous Buckinghamshire 'new town', built in the 1970s on a site that had been settled as early as 2000BC. A major Roman villa with mosaic floors was uncovered at Bancroft and the remains can still be seen. The city boasts the country's biggest collection of publicly sited artworks (more than 200, including Elisabeth Frink's Black Horse). It is also home to the vast National Bowl concert venue and the more intimate Stables live music venue. Trips can be taken on the Grand Union Canal through the city, along which there are a number of traditional pubs, and Linford Manor Park is a good place for walks. Family entertainment is provided at Xscape, with an indoor ski slope, rock-climbing wall and more, Gulliver's Land, and Willen Lakeside Park. There is a very wide selection of shops centred on The Centre: MK and Midsummer Place shopping centres, plus plenty of bars and restaurants for the evening's entertainment.

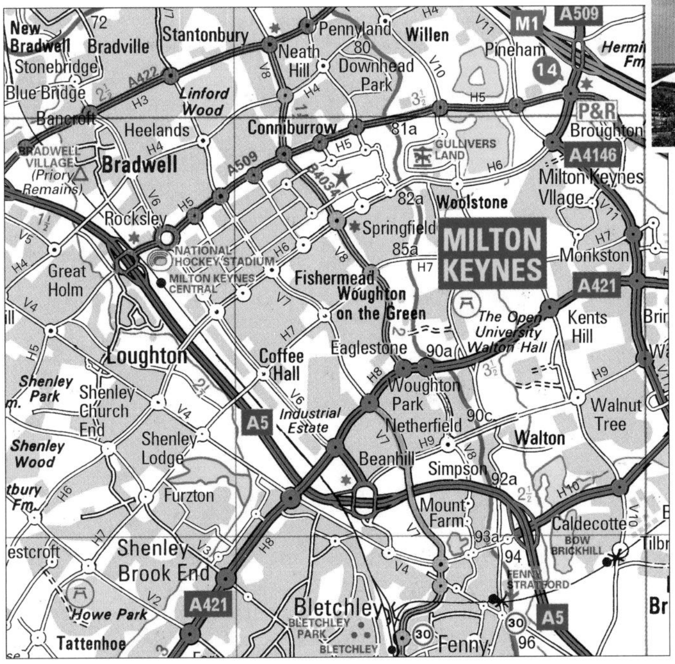

★Do not miss

★**'Artwalks'**, various locations

★**Bletchley Park (home to WWII codebreakers)**, off Wilton Avenue, Bletchley

★**Milton Keynes Gallery**, Midsummer Boulevard – contemporary art

Milton Keynes Visitor Information Centre, 890 Midsummer Boulevard, Milton Keynes MK9 3QA
Tel 01908 558300

BBC Three Counties Radio 104.5 FM • **Horizon** 103.3 FM
Classic Gold AM 828, 792 AM

www.mkweb.co.uk

Milton Keynes

Abbey Way A1
Arbrook Ave. B1
Armourer Dr A3
Arncliffe Dr A1
Avebury (r'about) C2
Avebury Blvd C2
Bankfield (r'about). B3
Bayard Ave. A2
Belvedere (r'about) A2
Bishopstone. A1
Blundells Rd A1
Boycott Ave C2
Bradwell Common Blvd . . .B1
Bradwell Rd. C1
Bramble Ave A2
Brearley Ave C2
Breckland. A1
Brill Place B1
Burnham Dr. B1
Bus Station C1
Campbell Park (r'about). B3
Cantle Ave A3
Central Milton Keynes Shopping Area B2
Century Ave C2
Chaffron Way. . . . C3
Childs Way C1
Christ the Cornerstone ⛪ . .B2
Cineworld 🎥 B3
Civic Offices. B2
Cleavers Ave B2
Colesbourne Dr. . A3
Conniburrow Blvd .B2
County Court B2
Currier Dr A2
Dansteed Way. A2/A3/B1
Deltic Ave B1
Downs Barn (r'about). A2
Downs Barn Blvd A3
Eaglestone (r'about). C3
Eelbrook Ave B1
Elder Gate B1
Evans Gate. C2
Fairford Cr A3
Falcon Ave B3
Fennel Dr. A2
Fishermead Blvd. C3
Food Centre. B3
Fulwoods Dr C3
Glazier Dr. A2
Glovers La A1
Grafton Gate C1
Grafton St . . . A1/C2
Gurnards Ave. B3
Harrier Dr C3
Ibstone Ave B1
Langcliffe Dr A1
Leisure Plaza. . . . C1
Leys Rd. C1
Library B2
Linford Wood. . . . A2
Marlborough Gate B3
Marlborough St. A2/B3
Mercers Dr. A1
Midsummer (r'about). C2
Midsummer Blvd. .B2
Milton Keynes Central ⇌ C1
Monks Way A1
Mullen Ave. A3
Mullion Pl C3
National Hockey Stadium B1
Neath Hill (r'about). A3
North Elder (r'about). C1
North Grafton (r'about). B1
North Overgate (r'about). A3
North Row B2
North Saxon (r'about). B2
North Secklow (r'about). B2
North Skeldon (r'about). A3
North Witan (r'about). B1
Oakley Gdns. A3
Oldbrook Blvd . . . C2
Open-Air Theatre 🎭 B3
Overgate. A3
Overstreet A3
Patriot Dr. B1
Pencarrow Pl. B3
Penryn Ave. B3
Perran Ave. C3
Pitcher La C1
Place Retail Park, The C1
Point Centre, The .B2
Police Station ▣ . .B2
Portway (r'about) .B2
Post Office 📮. A2/B2/C3
Precedent Dr. B1
Quinton Dr B1
Ramsons Ave B2
Rockingham Dr . . A2
Rooksley (r'about) B1
Rooksley Retail Park C1
Saxon Gate. B2
Saxon St. A1/C3
Secklow Gate B2
Shackleton Pl . . . C2
Silbury (r'about) . C1
Silbury Blvd B2
Skeldon (r'about) A3
South Grafton (r'about). C2
South Row C2
South Saxon (r'about). C2
South Secklow (r'about). B3
South Witan (r'about). C2
Springfield (r'about). B3
Stanton Wood (r'about). A1
Stantonbury (r'about). A1
Stantonbury Leisure Ctr ✦ . . A1
Strudwick Dr C2
Sunrise Parkway. A2
Telephone Exchange C3
The Boundary . . . C3
Theatre & Art Gallery 🎭 B3
Tolcarne Ave C3
Towan Ave C3
Trueman Pl C2
Vauxhall A1
Winterhill Retail Park C2
Witan Gate. B2
Xscape B3

¼ mile
¼ ½ km

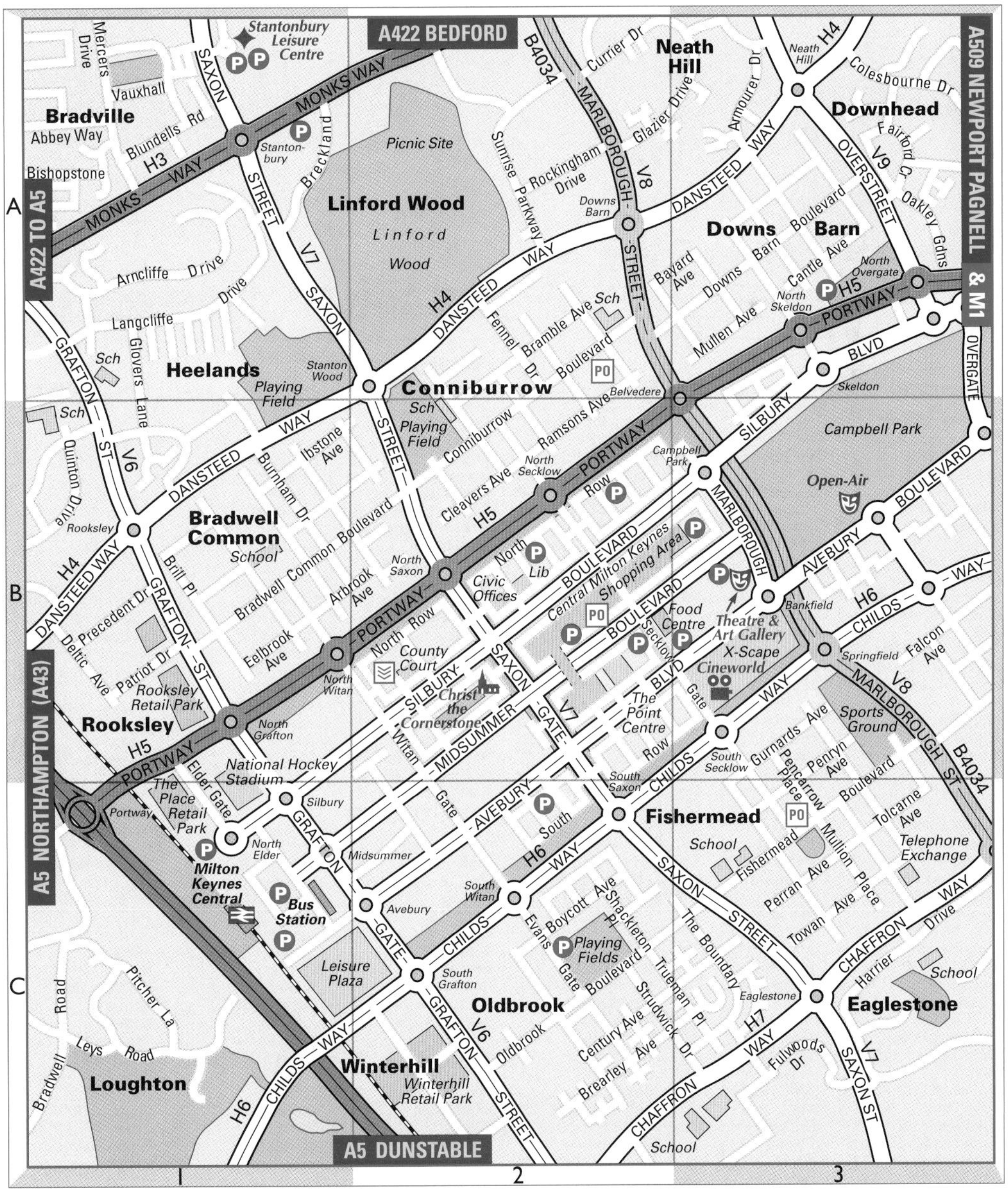

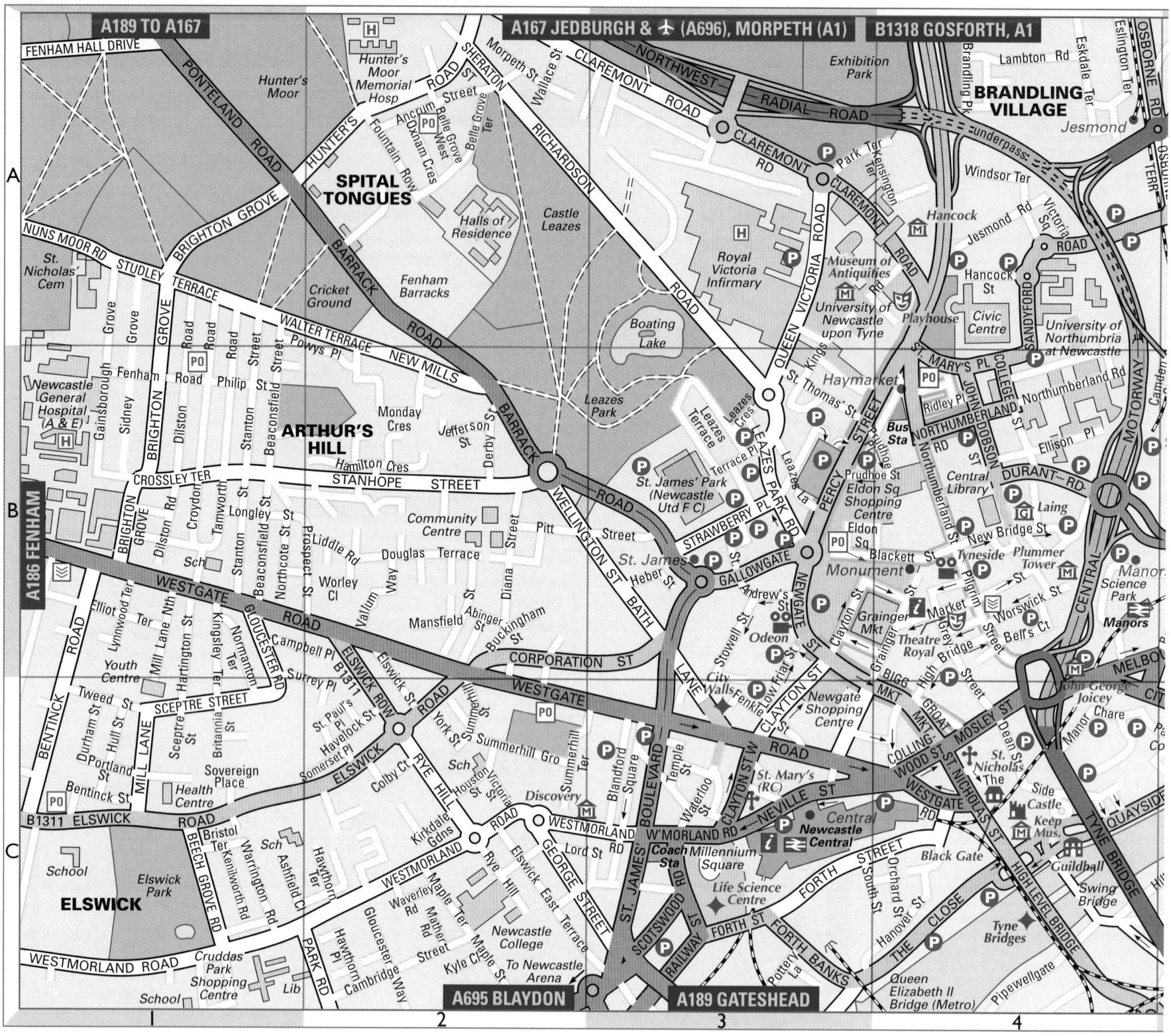

¼ mile
¼
½ km

Newcastle upon Tyne

Abinger St B2
Albany Rd....... C6
Albert St.........B5
Albion Row B6
Ancrum St A2
Argyle St B5
Arthur's Hill......B1
Ashfield Cl C1
Athletics Stadium C6
Back New Bridge St..............B5
Ballast Hills Park .B6
BALTIC The Centre for Contemporary Art 🏛 C5
Bank Rd C5
Barker St A5
Barrack Rd... A2/B2
Bath La..........B3
Beaconsfield St...B1
Beckett St C6
Beech Grove Rd . C1
Belle Grove Terr . A2
Belle Grove West A2
Bell's Court B4
Bentinck Rd...... C1
Bentinck St C1
Bigg Market..... C4
Biscuit Factory 🏛 .B5
Black Gate 🏛 ... C4
Blackett St.......B4
Blandford Sq C3
Boating Lake A3
Bolingbroke St .. A6
Boyd St..........B5
Brandling Park .. A4
Breamish St......B5
Brighton Gr .. A1/B1
Bristol Terr...... C1
Britannia St C1
Buckingham St ...B2
Bus Station B4
Buxton St........B5
Byker Bank.......B6
Byker Bridge B6
Byron St.........A5
Cambridge St ... C2
Camden St........B4
Campbell Pl.......B1
Cardigan Terr..... A6
Castle 🏰......... C4
Castle Leazes.... A2
Central (Metro Station). C3
Central Library ...B4
Central Motorway.B4
Chelmsford Gr... A5
Chester St A5
City Rd B5/C5
City Walls ✦ C3
Civic Centre...... A4
Claremont Rd A3
Clarence St B5
Clarence Walk....B5
Clayton St B3
Clayton St West.. C3
Coach Station C3
Colby Court C2
College St B4
Collingwood St .. C4
Community Ctr ...B2
Copland Terr B5
Coppice Way B5
Coquet St.........B5
Corporation St ...B2
Coulthards La ... C5
Coulthards Pl..... C6
Courts.......... C5
Crawhall Rd......B5
Cricket Ground .. A2
Criddle St....... C6
Crossley Terr B1
Croydon Rd B1
Cruddas Park Shopping Ctr.... C1
Cut Bank B6
Dean St......... C4
Deptford Rd..... C6
Derby St.........B2
Diana St.........B2
Dilston Rd B1
Dinsdale Pl A5
Dinsdale Rd...... A5
Discovery Mus 🏛 C2
Doncaster Rd..... A5
Dorset Rd........ C6
Douglas Terr B2
Durant Rd........B4
Durham St C1
Eldon Sq.........B3
Eldon Sq Shopping Ctr....B3
Elizabeth St B6
Elliot Terr B1
Ellison Pl B4
Elswick East Terr. C2
Elswick Park C1
Elswick Rd ... C1/C2
Elswick Row B2
Elswick St B2
Eskdale Terr...... A4
Eslington Terr ... A4
Exhibition Park .. A3
Falconar St B5
Falmouth Rd A6
Fenham Barracks A2
Fenham Hall Dr.. A1
Fenham Rd B1
Fenkle St C3
Ford St B6
Forth Banks..... C3
Forth St C3
Foundry La.......B6
Fountain Row ... A2
Gainsborough Gr..B1
Gallowgate.......B3
Gateshead Millennium Bridge.......... C5
George St........ C2
Gibson St B5
Gloucester Rd B1
Gloucester Way.. C2
Goldspink La A5
Grainger Market ..B4
Grainger St B4
Grantham Rd A5
Granville Rd..... A5
Grey St B4
Greystoke Ave ... A5
Groat Market..... C4
Guildhall 🏛 C4
Halls of Residence A2
Hamilton Cr.......B2
Hanover St...... C4
Hartington St.....B1
Havelock St C2
Hawks Rd....... C5
Hawthorn Pl C2
Hawthorn Terr ... C2
Haymarket (Metro Station) ...B4
Health Centre ... C1
Heaton Park..... A6
Heaton Park Rd.. A6
Heaton Park View A6
Heaton Rd A6
Heaton Terr B6
Heber St.........B3
Helmsley Rd..... A5
High Bridge.......B4
High Level Bridge C4
Hillgate......... C5
Horatio St B6
Hotspur St A6
Houston St...... C2
Howard St B5
Hull St.......... C1
Hunter's Moor... A1
Hunter's Moor Memorial Hospital 🏥 A2
Hunter's Rd A2
Hutton Terr...... A5
Information Ctr ℹ ... B3/B4/C3
Jefferson St......B2
Jesmond (Metro Station) A4
Jesmond Rd.. A4/A5
John Dobson St ..B4
John George Joicey Mus 🏛 .. C4
Jubilee Rd B5
Keep Mus 🏛 C4
Kelvin Gr A5
Kenilworth Rd ... C1
Kensington Terr.. A4
Kings Rd.........B3
Kingsley Terr B1
Kirkdale Gdns C2
Kyle Cl C2
Laing Gallery 🏛 ..B4
Lambton Rd A4
Leazes Cr B3
Leazes La B3
Leazes Park B3
Leazes Park Rd ...B3
Leazes Terr.......B3
Library A6/C1
Liddle Rd B2
Life Science Centre ✦ C3
Lime St..........B6
Longley St B1
Lord St C2
Low Friar St..... C3
Lynnwood Terr....B1
Malcolm St...... A6
Manor Chare C4
Manors (Metro Station) B4
Manors Station ⇌......B4
Mansfield St B2
Maple St........ C2
Maple Terr C2
Market St B4
Mather Rd C2
Melbourne St......B4
Mill La......... C1
Mill La North......B1
Mill Rd C5
Millennium Sq... C3
Monday Cr.......B2
Monument (Metro Station) B4
Morpeth St...... A2
Mosley St C4
Mowbray St A6
Museum of Antiquities 🏛 .. A3
Napier St A5
Nazareth House.. A5
Neville St C3
New Bridge St.B4/B5
New Mills........B2
Newcastle Central Station ⇌ C3
Newcastle College C2
Newcastle General Hospital (A&E) 🏥........B1
Newgate Shopping Centre......... C3
Newgate St B3
Newington Rd A5/A6
Nixon St C6
Norfolk Rd C6
Normanton Terr...B1
North View A6
Northcote St B1
Northumberland Rd B4
Northumberland St...............B4
Northwest Radial Rd A3
Nuns Moor Rd.... A1
Oakwellgate...... C5
Odeon 🎥 B3
Orchard St C4
Osborne Rd A4
Osborne Terr A5
Ouse Burn A6
Ouse St..........B6
Ouseburn Rd A6
Oxnam Cr....... A2
Pandon Bank......B4
Pandon.......... C5
Park Rd C2
Park Terr........ A3
Percy St B3
Philip St.........B1
Pilgrim St.........B4
Pipewellgate C4
Pitt St B2
Playhouse Theatre 🎭 A4
Plummer Tower 🏛 B4
Police Station 🏛 B1/B4/C4
Ponteland Rd.... A1
Portland Rd .. A5/B5
Portland St C1
Portland Terr A5
Post Office PO ... A2/A5/A6/B1/B3/B4/B5/C1/C2
Pottery La C3
Powys Pl......... A1
Prospect St B2
Prudhoe Pl........B3
Prudhoe St........B3
Quality Row B6
Quayside C4/C6
Queen Elizabeth II Bridge......... C4
Queen Victoria Rd A3
Railway St C3
Richardson Rd... A3
Ridley Pl.........B4
Rock Terr B5
Roger St..........B6
Rosedale Terr.... A5
Royal Victoria Infirmary 🏥 A3
Rye Hill......... C2
St Andrew's St....B3
St James (Metro Station) B3
St James' Blvd... C3
St James' Park (Newcastle Utd F.C.) B3
St Lawrence Rd.. C6
St Mary's (RC) ✝. C3
St Mary's Place...B4
St Nicholas ✝ C4
St Nicholas' Cem A1
St Nicholas St ... C4
St Paul's Pl C2
St Thomas' St.....B3
Saltmeadows Rd. C6
Sandyford Rd. A4/A5
Sceptre St C1
Science Park......B4
Scotswood Rd ... C3
Sheraton St A2
Shield St.........B5
Shieldfield B5
Shields Rd B6
Shields Rd By-Pass B6
Sidney Gr.........B1
Simpson Terr B5
Somerset Pl...... C2
South Shore Rd.. C5
South St C3
South View West..B6
Sovereign Pl C1
Springbank Rd .. A6
Stanhope St.......B2
Stanton St B1
Starbeck Ave..... A5
Stepney Bank B5
Stepney Rd........B5
Stoddart St B5
Stowell St.........B3
Stratford Gr West A6
Stratford Rd..... A6
Strawberry Pl B3
Studley Terr A1
Suffolk Pl....... C6
Summerhill Gr... C2

A1058 TYNEMOUTH
JESMOND VALE
Heaton Park
HEATON PARK VIEW
WARWICK STREET
SHIELDFIELD
BYKER BRIDGE
NEW BRIDGE STREET
A193 WALLSEND (A187)
BATTLE FIELD
CITY ROAD
WALKER ROAD
QUAYSIDE
ST. LAWRENCE
RIVER TYNE
BALTIC The Centre for Contemporary Art
Gateshead Millennium Bridge
The Sage Music Centre
GATESHEAD
SALT MEADOWS
To Athletics Stadium
A167 DURHAM & A1(M)
5
6

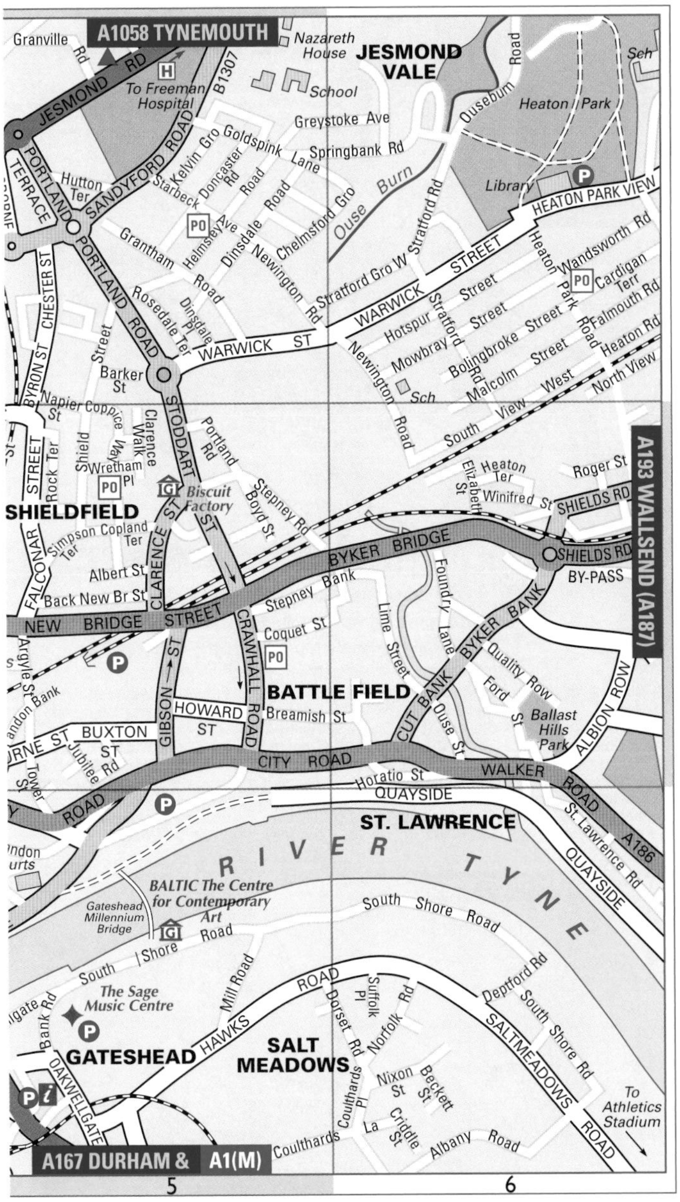

Newcastle-upon-Tyne

A large city that grew from a Roman fort, over which a castle was built in 1080 by William the Conqueror's son; the fine keep added by Henry II now houses a museum of local history. A key player in the Industrial Revolution (chiefly as a coal supplier), Newcastle is now undergoing large-scale regeneration, especially around its Quayside area with its public artworks, new hotels and restaurants, and the dramatic Millennium Bridge across to Gateshead. Other attractions include the 12th-century cathedral, Hancock Museum of Natural History, Life Science interactive centre with its motion rides, John George Joicey Museum of Natural History, and Military Vehicle Museum. The best green space is the Tyne Riverside Country Park, while the story of the railways is traced at the nearby George Stephenson's Birthplace (National Trust) and Stephenson Railway Museum and Steam Railway. Newcastle is the main city in the northeast with the centre made up of seven distinct quarters between them offering a wealth of choice in shopping, drinking and eating, plus theatre, cinema, music venues and St James' Park for Newcastle Football Club.

▲ The Millennium Bridge and The Baltic Arts Centre

Tourist Information Centre, 132 Grainger Street, Newcastle-upon-Tyne NE1 5AF Tel 0191 277 8000

BBC Radio Newcastle 95.4 FM and 1458 AM • **Century** 101.8 FM
Galaxy 105.3 FM • **Magic** 1152 AM
Metro Radio 97.1 FM

www.newcastle.gov.uk

★Do not miss

- ★**Baltic Centre for Contemporary Art**, Gateshead
- ★**Castle Keep Museum**, Castle Garth
- ★**Discovery Museum**, Blandford Square – history of the Tyne

Summerhill St . . . C2
Summerhill Terr . C2
Surrey Pl B1
Swing Bridge. . . . C4
Tamworth Rd B1
Temple St. C3
Terrace Pl B3
The Close C4
The Sage Music Centre ✦ C5
The Side C4
Theatre Royal . . .B4
Tower St. B5
Tweed St C1
Tyne Bridge C4
Tyne Bridges ✦. . C4
Tyneside B4
University of Newcastle upon Tyne. A3
University of Northumbria at Newcastle A4
Vallum Way B2
Victoria Sq A4
Victoria St C2
Walker Rd B6
Wallace St A2
Walter Terr A1
Wandsworth Rd. . A6
Warrington Rd. . . C1
Warwick St. . . A5/A6
Waterloo St C3
Waverley Rd. C2
Wellington St. B2
Westgate Rd B1/C2/C4
Westmorland Rd C1/C2/C3
Windsor Terr A4
Winifred St. B6
Worley Cl B2
Worswick St. B4
Wretham Pl B5
York St C2
Youth Centre C1

Longbenton
NEWCASTLE upon Tyne
WALLSEND
Gosforth
Kenton
Westerhope
Fenham
Jesmond
Heaton
Benwell
Scotswood
Elswick
Byker
Walker
Hebburn
Blaydon
Dunston
Whickham
GATESHEAD
Felling
Saltwell
A1
A167
A184
A194(M)

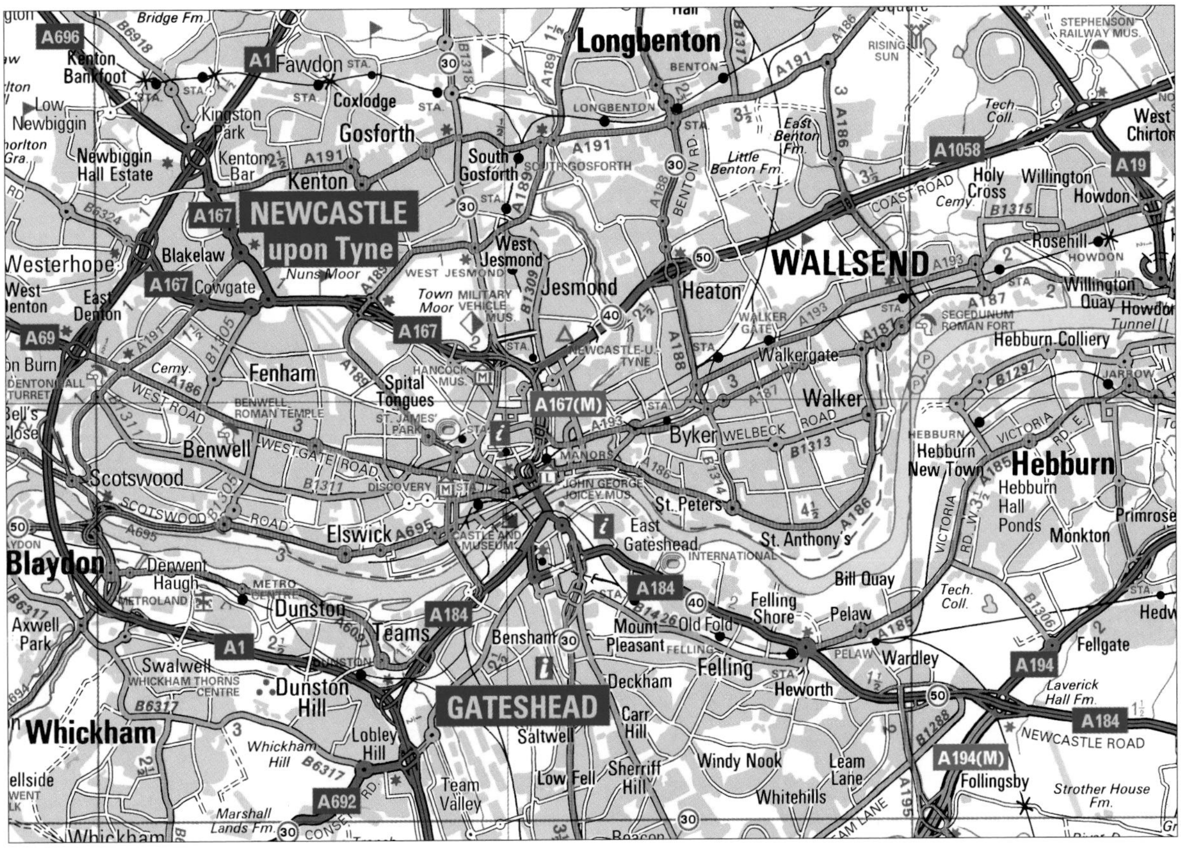

Newport

A South Wales cathedral and university city on the western bank of the Severn Estuary, with a rich Roman heritage concentrated in Caerleon, with its excellent museum and the remains of a fortress baths, amphitheatre and barracks. Other attractions include the remains of an early 14th-century castle; the 12th-century St Woolos Cathedral; the 17th-century Tredegar House; and Newport Museum and Art Gallery. The Riverfront Arts Centre will eventually display the remains of the Newport Medieval Ship, and Newport is home to the Newport International Sports Village. The Newport Wetlands nature reserve is near Uskmouth. Nearby Penhow Castle is the oldest inhabited castle in Wales, and there's a 30-mile walk along the Brecon and Monmouthshire Canal through the Brecon Beacons National Park to Brecon.

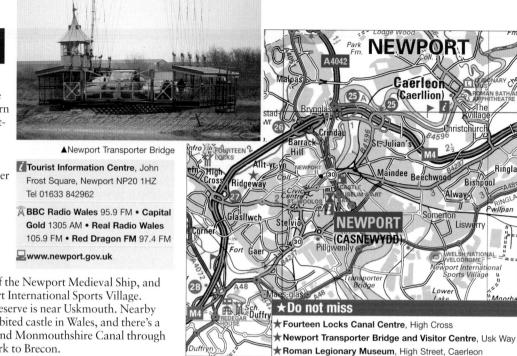

▲Newport Transporter Bridge

Tourist Information Centre, John Frost Square, Newport NP20 1HZ
Tel 01633 842962

BBC Radio Wales 95.9 FM • **Capital Gold** 1305 AM • **Real Radio Wales** 105.9 FM • **Red Dragon FM** 97.4 FM

www.newport.gov.uk

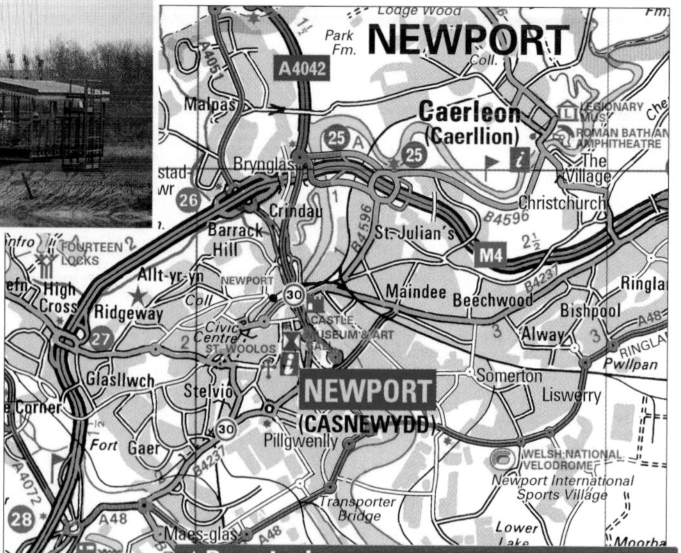

★Do not miss

★**Fourteen Locks Canal Centre**, High Cross

★**Newport Transporter Bridge and Visitor Centre**, Usk Way

★**Roman Legionary Museum**, High Street, Caerleon

Newport/ Casnewydd

Albert Terr B1
Allt-yr-Yn Ave . . . A1
Alma St. C2
Ambulance Station C3
Bailey St. B2
Barrack Hill A2
Bath St A3
Bedford Rd. B3
Belle Vue La. C1
Belle Vue Park . . . C1
Bishop St A3
Blewitt St B1
Bolt Cl. C3
Bolt St. C3
Bond St. A2
Bosworth Dr A1
Bridge St B1
Bristol St A3
Bryngwyn Rd B1
Brynhyfryd Ave . . C1
Brynhyfryd Rd . . . C1
Bus Station B2
Caerau Cres C1
Caerau Rd B1
Caerleon Rd. A3
Cambrian Retail Centre B2
Capel Cres C2
Cardiff Rd. C2
Caroline St. B3
Castle (Remains) A2
Cattle Market and Saturday General Market C3
Cedar Rd B3
Charles St B2
Charlotte Dr. C2
Chepstow Rd A3
Church Rd A3
City Cinema . . . B1
Civic Centre B1
Clarence Pl A2
Clifton Pl B1
Clifton Rd. C1
Clyffard Cres B1
Clytha Park Rd . . . B1
Clytha Sq C2
Coldra Rd. C1
Collier St A3
Colne St B3
Comfrey Cl. A1
Commercial Rd . . C3
Commercial St . . . B2
Corelli St A3
Corn St. B2
Corporation Rd . . . B3
Coulson Cl C2
County Court A2
Courts. A1
Courts. B1
Crawford St A3
Cyril St B3
Dean St. A3
Devon Pl. B1
Dewsland Park Rd C2
Dolman B2
Dolphin St C3
East Dock Rd C3
East St B1
East Usk Rd A3
Ebbw Vale Wharf. . B3
Emlyn St. B2
Enterprise Way . . C3
Eton Rd. B3
Evans St A2
Factory Rd A2
Fields Rd B1
Francis Dr C2
Frederick St. C3
Friars Rd C1
Gaer La. C1
George St. C3
George Street Bridge. C3
Godfrey Rd. B1
Gold Tops B1
Gore St. A3
Gorsedd Circle . . . C1
Grafton Rd. A3
Graham St B1
Granville St C3
Harlequin Dr A1
Harrow Rd B3
Herbert Rd. A3
Herbert Walk. . . . C2
Hereford St A3
High St B2
Hill St B2
Hoskins St A2
Information Ctr . B2
Ivor Sq B2
John Frost Sq B2
Jones St B1
Junction Rd A3
Keynshaw Ave . . . C2
King St C2
Kingsway B2
Kingsway Shopping Centre. B2
Ledbury Dr. A2
Library A3
Library, Museum & Art Gallery . . . B2
Liverpool Wharf . . B3
Llanthewy Rd. . . . B1
Llanvair Rd. A3
Locke St A2
Lower Dock St. . . C3
Lucas St A2
Manchester St. . . A3
Market B2
Marlborough Rd . . B3
Mellon St C3
Mill St. A2
Morgan St A3
Mountjoy Rd C2
Newport Athletic Club Grounds . . . B3
Newport Bridge. . A2
Newport Leisure & Conference Ctr . . B2
Newport B2
North St B2
Oakfield Rd B1
Park Sq. C2
Police Station . . . A3/C2
Post Office B1/B2/C1/C3
Power St A1
Prince St A3
Pugsley St A2
Queen St C2
Queen's Cl A1
Queen's Hill A1
Queen's Hill Cres A1
Queensway. B2
Railway St B2
Riverfront Arts Centre B2
Riverside A3
Rodney Rd B2
Royal Gwent (A&E) C2
Rudry St A3
Rugby Rd B3
Ruperra La C3
Ruperra St C3
St Edmund St B1
St Mark's Cres. . . A1
St Mary St B1
St Vincent Rd. . . . A3
St Woolos ✝ C2
St Woolos General (no A&E) C1
St Woolos Rd. B1
School La. B2
Serpentine Rd B1
Shaftesbury Park A2
Sheaf La. A3
Skinner St B2
Sorrel Dr A1
South Market St . C3
Spencer Rd B1
Stow Hill. . B2/C1/C2
Stow Park Ave. . . C1
Stow Park Dr. . . . C1
TA Centre. A1
Talbot St. B2
Tennis Club A1
Tregare St A3
Trostrey St A3
Tunnel Terr. B1
Turner St A3
Usk St. A3
Usk Way B3/C3
Victoria Cr B1
War Memorial . . . A3
Waterloo Rd. C1
West St. B1
Wharves B2
Wheeler St. A2
Whitby Pl A3
Windsor Terr B1
York Pl C1

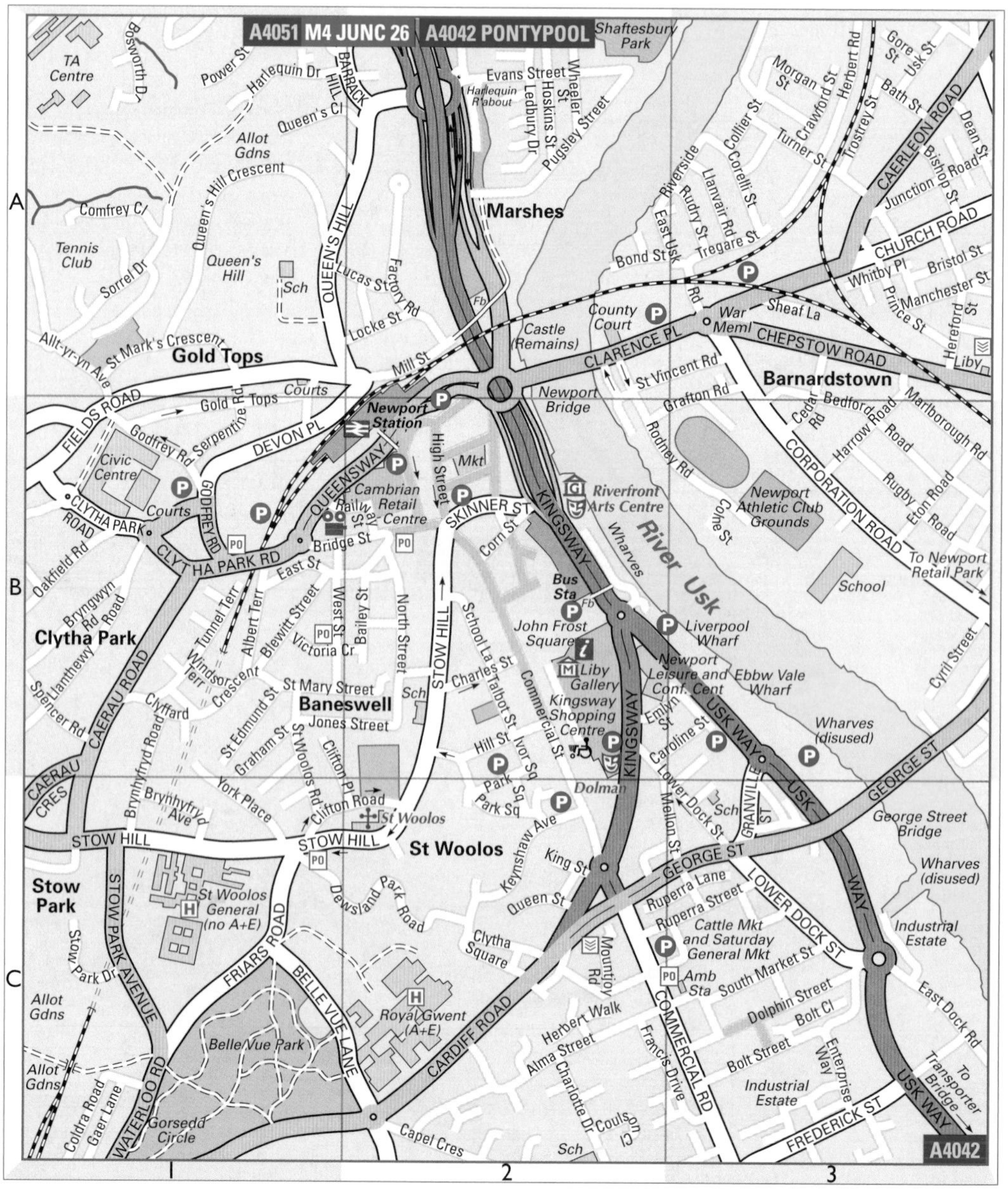

¼ mile
¼ ½ km

Newquay

▲Gig racing

A popular 11-beach resort that began life as a fortified Iron Age cliff settlement (the history of which is explored in Tunnels Through Time), and became an important fishing port; the whitewashed Huer's Hut is one of few surviving buildings recalling its pilchard fishing industry. The best family beach is sheltered Lusty Glaze with its creche, bar and restaurant. Attractions include the Blue Reef Aquarium, Trenance Leisure Park and Gardens with its waterworld, and nearby Holywell Bay Fun Park, World in Miniature Theme Park, Dairyland Farm World and Lappa Valley Steam Railway. To the south, Perranporth is the site of an early Celtic monastery and pilgrimage site excavated in the 19th century but reburied for preservation purposes in 1981; the location is marked by a memorial stone. Some nearby Norman walls remain from the parish church of St Piran's, also abandoned to the sand, and beside them is the Perran Cross, possibly an ancient boundary point. Just to the north, Carnewas and the Bedruthan Steps is a dramatic National Trust owned stretch of coastline with spectacular clifftop views over rock stacks.

Tourist Information Centre, Marcus Hill, Newquay TR7 1BD
Tel 01637 854020

BBC Radio Cornwall 103.9 FM
Pirate FM 102.8 FM

www.newquay.co.uk

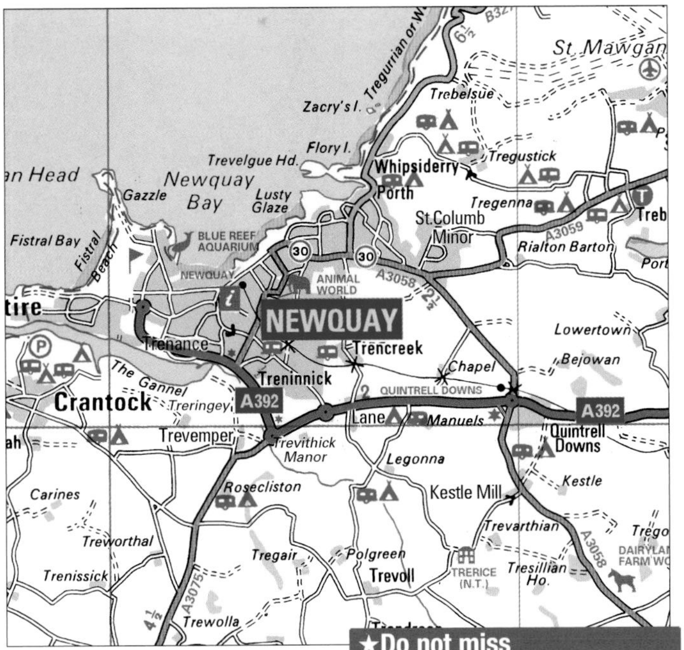

★Do not miss

★**Fistral Beach** (famous for its surfing), west of Towan Head

★**Newquay Zoo and Conservation Centre**, Trenance Gardens

★**Trerice** (Elizabethan manor; National Trust), Kestle Mill

Newquay

Agar Rd B2
Alma Pl. B1
Ambulance Station B2
Anthony Rd C1
Atlantic Hotel . . . A1
Bank St. B1
Barrowfields A3
Bay View Terr B2
Beach St. B1
Beachfield Ave . . . B1
Beacon Rd A1
Belmont Pl A1
Berry Rd B2
Blue Reef Aquarium B1
Boating Lake C2
Bus Station B2
Chapel Hill B1
Chester Rd A3
Cheviot Rd . . . C1/C2
Chichester Cres. . C2
Chynance Drive Rd C1
Chyverton Cl C1
Cliff Rd B2
Colvreath Rd A3
Crantock St B1
Criggar Rocks . . . A3
Dale Cl C3
Dale Rd. C3
Dane Rd A1
East St B2
Edgcumbe Ave . . . B3
Edgcumbe Gdns . . B3
Eliot Gdns B3
Elm Cl. C3
Ennor's Rd B1
Fernhill Rd. B1
Fire Station B1
Fore St B1
Gannel Rd C2
Golf Driving Range B3
Gover La. B1
Great Western Beach A2
Grosvenor Ave. . . . B2
Harbour A1
Hawkins Rd C2
Headleigh Rd. B2
Hillgrove Rd. . A3/B3
Holywell Rd B3
Hope Terr B1
Huer's House, The A1
Information Ctr . B1
Island Cres. B2
Jubilee St. B1
Kew Cl C3
Killacourt Cove . . A2
King Edward Cres A1
Lanhenvor Ave. . . . B2
Library B1
Lifeboat Station . A1
Linden Ave C2
Listry Rd C2
Lusty Glaze Beach A3
Lusty Glaze Rd. . . . A3
Manor Rd B1
Marcus Hill B2
Mayfield Rd B2
Meadowside C3
Mellanvrane La . . C2
Michell Ave B2
Miniature Golf Course C3
Miniature Railway ✦ B3
Mount Wise B1
Mowhay Cl C3
Narrowcliff. A3
Newquay B2
Newquay & District Hospital (No A&E) B2
Newquay Town Football Ground . B1
Newquay Zoo . . . B3
North Pier A1
Northquay Hill. . . A1
Oakleigh Terr B2
Pargolla Rd B2
Pendragon Cres . C3
Penganel Cl. . . . C1
Penina Ave. C3
Police Station & Courts B2
Post Office . B1/B2
Quarry Park Rd . . B3
Rawley La. C2
Reeds Way. B1
Robartes Rd. B2
St Anne's Rd A3
St Aubyn Cres . . . B3
St George's Rd . . . B1
St John's Rd B1
St Mary's Rd B1
St Michael's . . . B1
St Michael's Rd. . . B1
St Thomas' Rd B2
Seymour Ave B2
South Pier A1
Southquay Hill. . . A1
Sweet Briar Cres. C3
Sydney Rd A1
The Crescent. B1
Tolcarne Beach . . A2
Tolcarne Point. . . A2
Tolcarne Rd B2
Tor Rd. B2
Towan Beach. . . . A1
Towan Blystra Rd . B3
Tower Rd A1
Trebarwith Cres. . . B2
Tredour Rd. C2
Treforda Rd C3
Tregoss Rd B3
Tregunnel Hill B1/C1
Tregunnel Saltings C1
Trelawney Rd. B2
Treloggan La C3
Treloggan Rd. . . . C3
Trembath Cres. . . C1
Trenance Ave. B2
Trenance Gardens.B2
Trenance La. C2
Trenance Leisure Park B3
Trenance Rd. B2
Trenarth Rd B2
Treninnick Hill. . . C3
Tretherras Rd. . . . B3
Tretheway Way . . C1
Trevemper Rd . . . C2
Tunnels Through Time B1
Ulalia Rd. B3
Vivian Cl. B2
Waterworld B3
Whitegate Rd. B3
Wych Hazel Way . C3

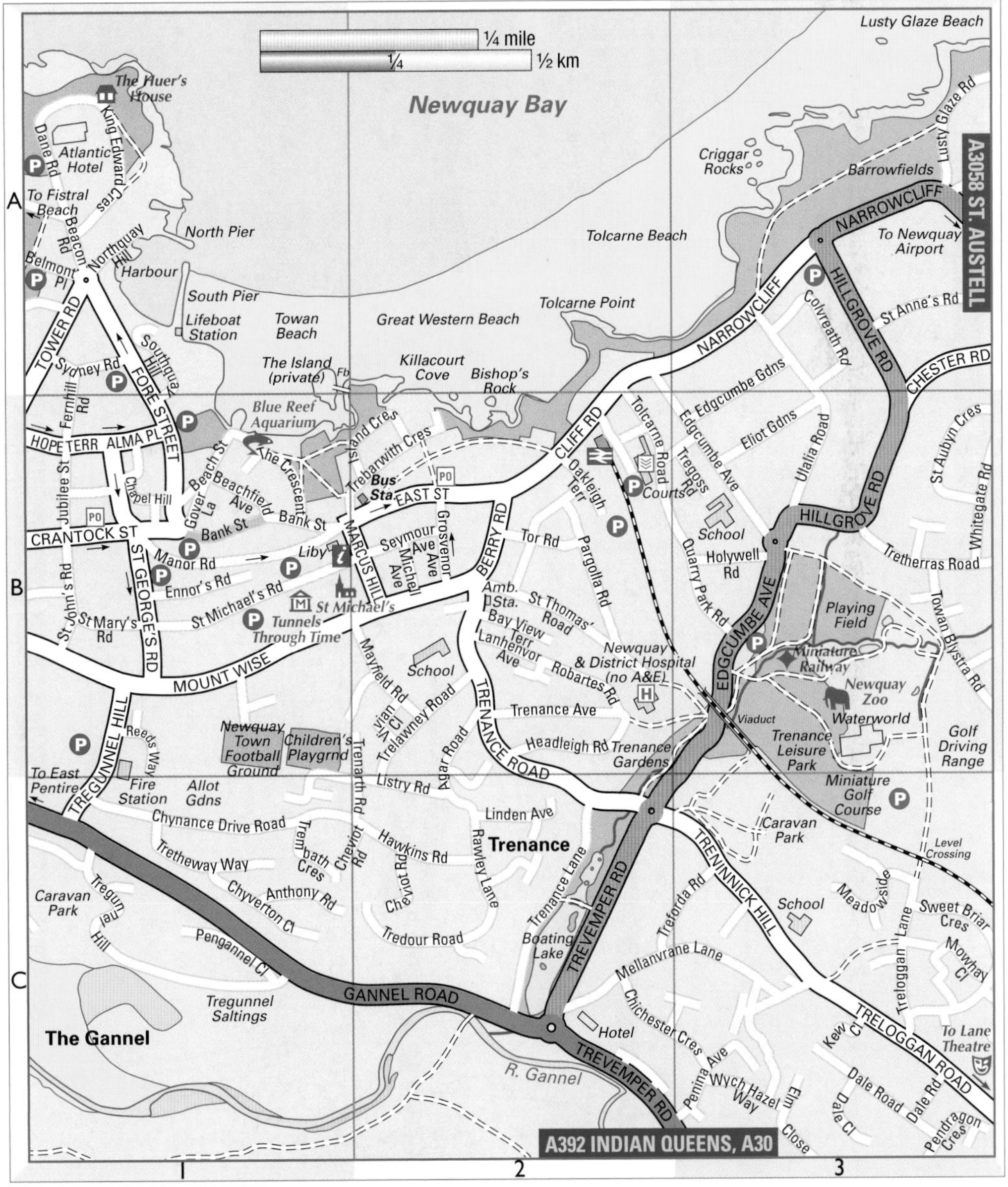

Northampton

▲The Guildhall

Northampton is a town with its origins before the Domesday book of 1086, which has built itself into an important town at the centre of the shoe manufacturing industry. The town is fortunate to retain several buildings of historic interest such as the Church of the Holy Sepulchre, which was built in 1100 to commemorate the return of the 1st Earl of Northampton from the Crusades. Shopping opportunities include Market Square and Market Hall outdoor and indoor markets, and the Grosvenor shopping centre. The River Nene, parks and gardens are all pleasant characteristics of the town. The railway station now occupies the site of the old castle. Both the cathedral and the Guildhall date from 1864.

Visitor Information Centre, The Guildhall, St Giles Square, Northampton NN1 1DE
Tel 01604 838800

BBC Radio Northampton 104.2 FM
Classic Gold 1557AM
Northants 96.6 FM

www.northampton.gov.uk

★Do not miss

★**Northampton Musuem and Art Gallery**, Guildhall Road – includes world's largest collection of footwear

★**Abington Museum**, Abington Park – local history

★**Church of the Holy Sepulchre**, Sheep Street

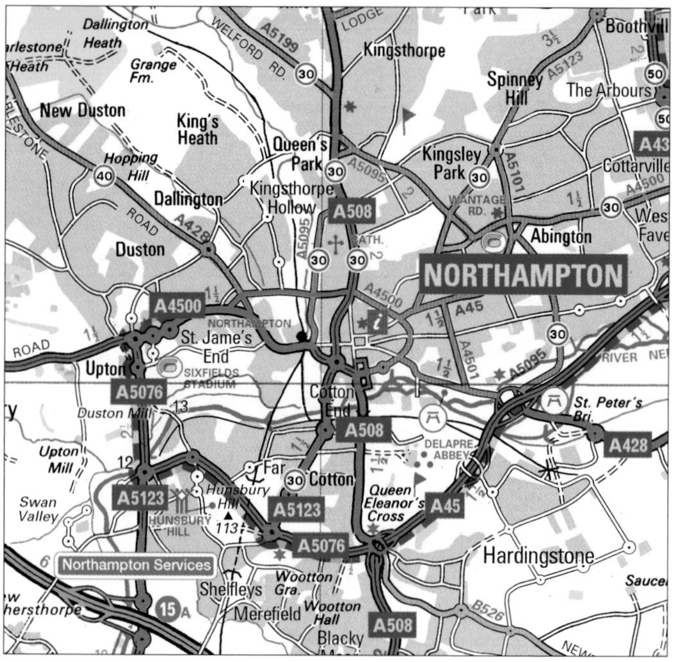

Northampton

78 Derngate ...B3
Abington Sq ...B3
Abington St ...B3
All Saints' ...B2
Ambush St ...B1
Angel St ...B2
Arundel St ... A2
Ash St ... A2
Auctioneers Way. C2
Bailiff St ... A2
Barrack Rd ... A2
Bath St ...B2
Beaconsfield Terr A3
Becketts Park ... C3
Bedford Rd ...B3
Billing Rd ...B3
Brecon St ... A1
Brewery ... C2
Bridge St ... C2
Bridge St Depot . C3
Broad St ...B2
Burns St ... A3
Bus Station ...B2
Campbell St ... A2
Castle (Site of) ...B2
Castle St ...B2
Cattle Market Rd. C2
Central Museum & Art Gallery ...B2
Charles St ... A3
Cheyne Walk ...B3
Church La ... A2
Clare St ... A3
Cloutsham St ... A3
College St ...B2
Colwyn Rd ... A3
Cotton End ... C2
Countess Rd ... A1
County Hall ...B2
Craven St ... A3
Crown & County Courts ...B3
Denmark Rd ...B3
Derngate ...B3
Derngate & Royal Theatres ...B3
Doddridge ...B2
Duke St ... A3
Earl St ... A3
Euston Rd ... C2
Foot Meadow ...B2
Gladstone Rd ... A1
Gold St ...B2
Grafton St ... A2
Gray St ... A3
Greenwood Rd ...B1
Grey Friars ...B2
Grosvenor Centre .B2
Grove Rd ... A3
Guildhall ...B2
Hampton St ... A2
Harding Terr ... A2
Hazelwood Rd ...B3
Herbert St ...B2
Hervey St ... A3
Hester St ... A2
Holy Sepulchre A2
Hood St ... A3
Horse Market ...B2
Hunter St ... A3
Industrial Estate . C1
Information Ctr .B2
Kettering Rd ... A3
Kingswell St ...B2
Lady's La ...B2
Leicester St ... A2
Leslie Rd ... A2
Library ...B3
Lorne Rd ... A2
Lorry Park ... A1
Louise Rd ... A2
Lower Harding St A2
Lower Mounts ...B3
Lower Priory St .. A2
Main Rd ... C1
Marefair ...B2
Market Sq ...B2
Marlboro Rd ...B1
Marriott St ... A2
Military Rd ... A3
Nene Valley Retail Park ... C1
New South Bridge Rd ... C2
Northampton General Hospital (A&E) ...B3
Northampton Station ...B1
Northcote St ... A2
Old Towcester Rd C2
Overstone Rd ... A3
Peacock Pl ...B2
Pembroke Rd ... A1
Penn Court ... C2
Police Station ..B3
Post Office ...B3
Quorn Way ... A2
Ransome Rd ... C3
Regent Sq ... A2
Retail Park ... C2
Robert St ... A2
St Andrew's Rd ...B1
St Andrew's St ... A2
St Edmund's Rd ..B3
St George's St ... A2
St Giles ...B3
St Giles St ...B3
St Giles' Terr ...B3
St James' Mill Rd .B1
St James' Mill Rd East ... C1
St James Park Rd .B1
St James Retail & Leisure Park ... C1
St James Rd ...B1
St Leonard's Rd .. C2
St Mary's St ...B2
St Michael's Rd .. A3
St Peter's ...B2
St Peter's Square Shopping Precinct ...B2
St Peter's Way ...B2
Salisbury St ... A2
Scarletwell St ...B2
Semilong Rd ... A2
Sheep St ...B2
Sol Central (Leisure Centre) .B2
South Bridge ... C2
Southfield Ave ... C2
Spencer Bridge Rd ... A1
Spencer Rd ... A3
Spring Gdns ...B3
Spring La ...B2
Swan St ...B3
The Drapery ...B2
The Riding ...B3
Tintern Ave ... A1
Towcester Rd ... C2
Upper Mounts ... A2
Victoria Park ... A1
Victoria Promenade ...B2
Victoria Rd ...B3
Victoria St ... A2
Wellingborough Rd ...B3
West Bridge ...B1
York Rd ...B3

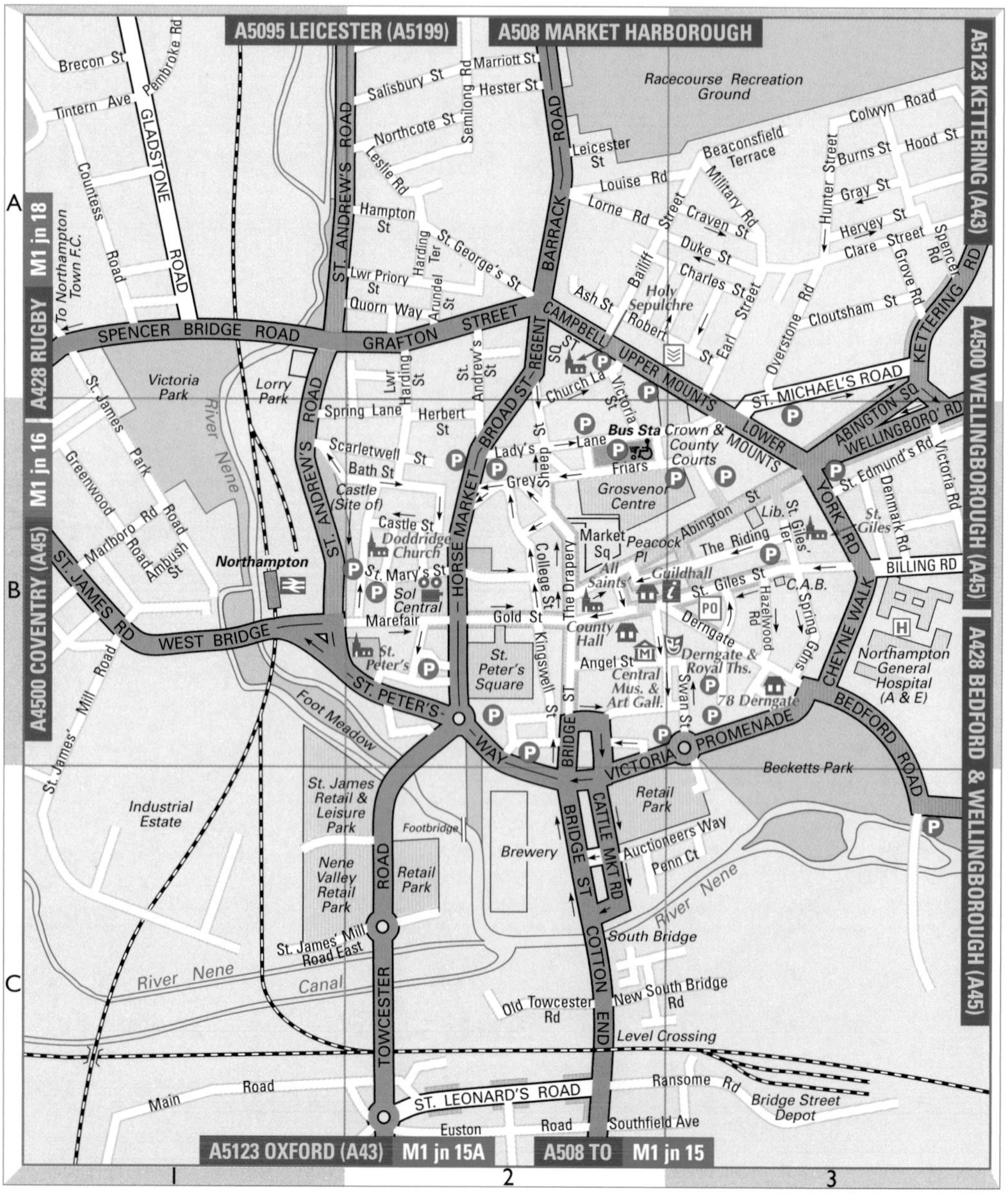

¼ mile
¼ ½ km

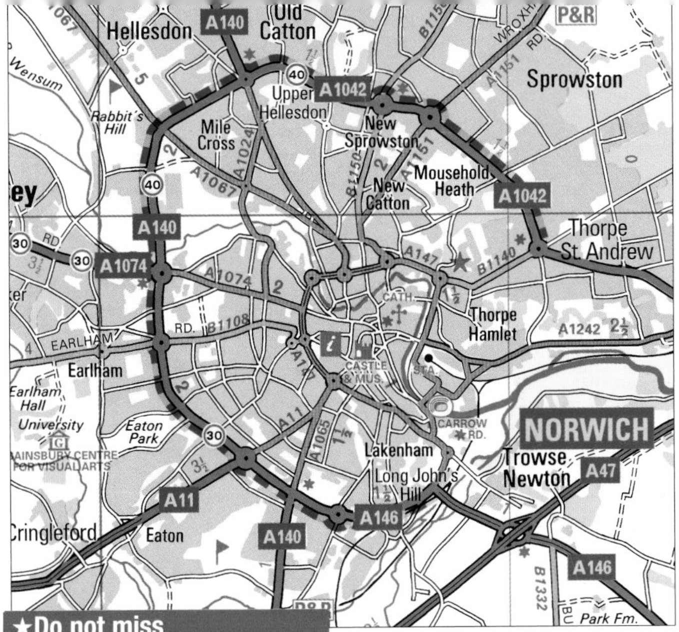

Norwich

A bustling, prosperous East Anglian city, originally an Anglo-Saxon settlement, with more than 1,500 historic buildings, including a magnificent Norman cathedral, a Catholic cathedral, more than 30 pre-Reformation churches (more than any other Western European city), a fine medieval guildhall, a Norman castle, England's most complete medieval street plan, and remnants of the ancient city walls. Outdoor attractions include riverside walks and the 4-acre Castle Green Park on top of Castle Mall. The city centre with its cobbled lanes and alleys has both familiar high-street outlets and a good range of traditional independent shops, and a local speciality can be sampled at Colman's Mustard Shop. The nearby University of East Anglia is home to the Sainsbury Centre for Visual Arts and between Norwich and the east coast lie the Norfolk Broads, popular for boating, walking, birdwatching and cycling.

▲St Ethelbert's Gate

★Do not miss

★**Norwich Castle Museum and Art Gallery**, Castle Meadow
★**Norwich Cathedral** (1096-1278), Cathedral Close
★**Origins**, The Forum – history discovery centre

Norwich Tourist Information Centre, The Forum, Norwich NR2 1TF
Tel 01603 727927

BBC Radio Norfolk 95.1, 104.4FM
Broadland 102.4 FM • **Classic Gold** 1152 AM • **Vibe FM** 106.1 FM

www.norwich.gov.uk

Norwich

Albion Way C3
All Saints Green . C2
Anchor Cl A3
Anchor St A3
Anglia Sq B2
Argyle St C3
Ashby St C2
Assembly House B1
Bank Plain B2
Barker St A1
Barn Rd A1
Barrack St A3
Ber St C2
Bethel St B1
Bishop Bridge . . . A3
Bishopbridge Rd . A3
Bishopgate A3
Blackfriars St A2
Botolph St A2
Bracondale C3
Brazen Gate C2
Bridewell B2
Brunswick Rd . . . C1
Bull Close Rd A2
Bus Station C2
Calvert St A2
Cannell Green . . . A3
Carrow Rd C3
Castle Mall B2
Castle Meadow . . .B2
Castle & Mus . .B1
Cathedral ✝ B2
Cattlemarket St . . .B2
Chantry Rd B1
Chapel Loke C2
Chapelfield East . .B1
Chapelfield Gdns .B1
Chapelfield North .B1
Chapelfield Rd B1
Chapelfield Shopping Ctr . . . C1
City Hall ✦ B1
City Rd C2
City Wall C1/C3
Colegate A2
Coslany St B1
Cow Hill B1
Cow Tower A3
Cowgate A2
Crown & Magistrates Courts B2
Dragon Hall Heritage Ctr . C3
Duke St A1
Edward St A2
Elm Hill B2
Erpingham Gate ✦ B2
Fire Station B1
Fishergate A2
Foundry Bridge . . .B3
Fye Bridge A2
Garden St C2
Gas Hill B3
Grapes Hill B1
Great Hospital Halls, The A3
Grove Ave C1
Grove Rd C1
Guildhall ✦ B1
Gurney Rd A3
Hall Rd C2
Heathgate A3
Heigham St A1
Horn's La C2
Information Ctr .B1
Inspire (Science Centre) ✦ A1
Ipswich Rd C1
James Stewart Gdns B3
King Edward VI School ✦ B2
King St B2
King St C3
Koblenz Ave C3
Library B1
London St B2
Lower Clarence Rd B3
Lower Cl B3
Maddermarket .B1
Magdalen St A2
Mariners La C2
Market B2
Market Ave B2
Mountergate B3
Mousehold St . . . A3
Newmarket Rd . . . C1
Norfolk Gallery .B2
Norfolk St C1
Norwich City FC . C3
Norwich B3
Oak St A1
Palace St A2
Pitt St A1
Police Station . .B1
Post Office A2/B1/B2/C2
Pottergate B1
Prince of Wales Rd B2
Princes St B2
Pull's Ferry ✦ B3
Puppet Theatre A2
Quebec Rd B3
Queen St B2
Queens Rd C2
Recorder Rd B3
Retail Park C3
Riverside Leisure Complex C3
Riverside Rd B3
Rosary Rd B3
Rose La B2
Rouen Rd C2
Royal Norfolk Regiment Mus B2
St Andrew's & Blackfriars Hall ✦ B2
St Andrews St B2
St Augustines St . A1
St Benedicts St . . .B1
St Crispins Rd . . . A1
St Ethelbert's Gate ✦ B2
St Faiths La B3
St Georges St . . . A2
St Giles St B1
St James Cl A3
St Julians C2
St Martin's La . . . A1
St Peter Mancroft B2
St Peters St B1
St Stephens Rd . . C1
St Stephens St . . C1
Silver Rd A2
Silver St A2
Southwell Rd C2
Strangers Hall .B1
Superstore C2
Surrey St C2
Sussex St A1
Swimming Pool . . .B3
The Close B3
The Forum B1
The Walk B2
Theatre Royal . .B1
Theatre St B1
Thorn La C2
Thorpe Rd B3
Tombland B2
Union St C1
Vauxhall St B1
Victoria St C1
Walpole St B1
Wensum St A2
Wessex St C1
Westwick St A1
Wherry Rd C3
Whitefriars A2
Willow La B1
Yacht Station B3

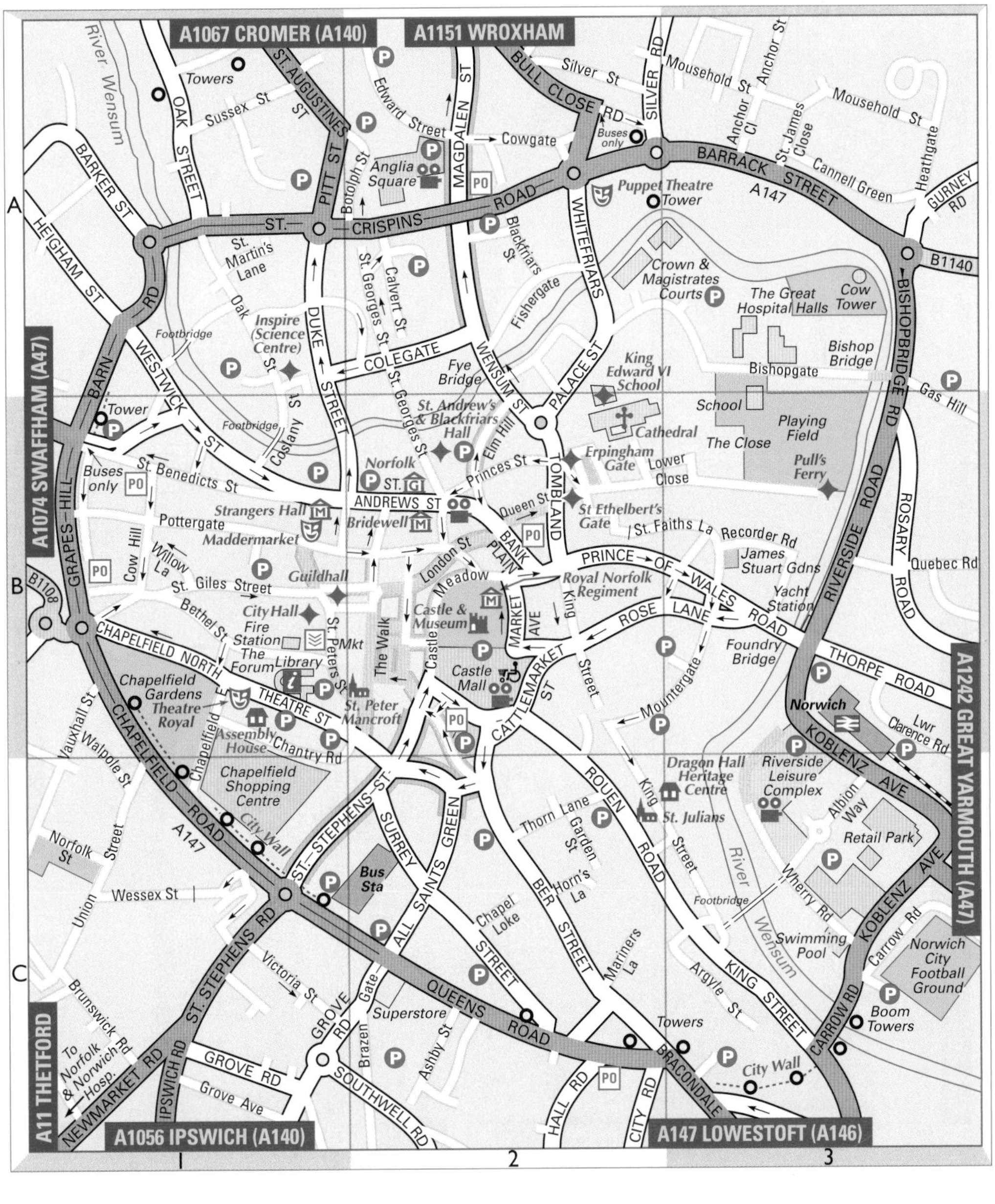

Nottingham

▲Robin Hood Statue

A vibrant Midlands city with a host of new bars, restaurants, hotels and designer shops, many around the cobbled Lace Market area, once the focus of the local lace-making industry. The city is considered one of the top three centres for shopping in the country. Henry II replaced William the Conqueror's original castle with a stone structure in the 12th century. Other sights include the Brewhouse Yard Museum of local history; Green's Mill, a functioning windmill with a science centre; Britain's biggest market square; medieval St Mary's Church; Ye Olde Trip to Jerusalem, said to be Britain's oldest pub; Tales of Robin Hood recounting exploits of the famous outlaw; and the Tudor Wollaton Hall with its industrial and natural history museums. Contemporary art is strong at the Angel Row Gallery and the university's Bonington Gallery, and sports amenities include the new National Ice Centre and the National Water-sports Centre. The annual Goose Fair is the country's biggest, oldest travelling fair.

★Do not miss

★**City of Caves**, Broadmarsh Centre – 13th century man-made dwellings

★**Galleries of Justice**, Old Gaol, Shire Hall, High Pavement – museum of law, crime and punishment

★**Nottingham Castle, Museum and Art Gallery**, off Friar Lane

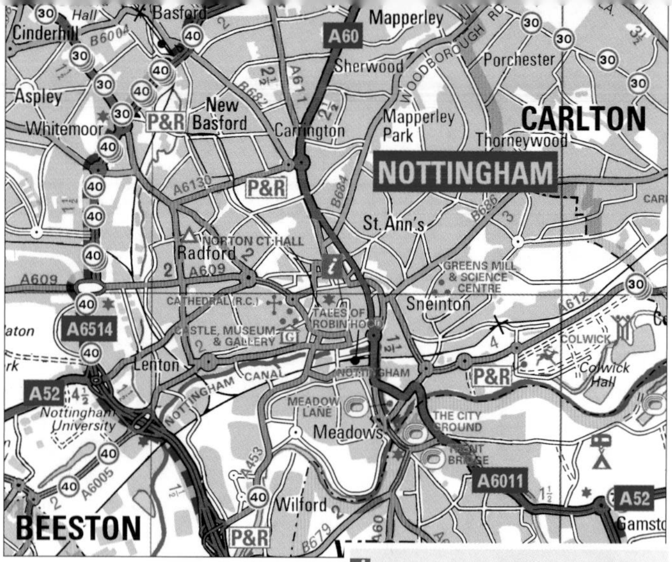

City Information Centre, 1-4 Smithy Row, Nottingham NG1 2BY Tel 0115 915 5330

BBC Radio Nottingham 103.8 FM
Classic Gold GEM 999 AM
Saga 106.6 FM • **Trent** 96.2 FM

www.nottinghamcity.gov.uk

Nottingham

Abbotsford Dr . . . A3
Addison St A1
Albert Hall ✦ B1
Alfred St South . . A3
Alfreton Rd B1
All Saints Rd A1
Annesley Gr A2
Arboretum ✽ A1
Arboretum St. . . . A1
Arthur St A1
Arts Theatre . . .B3
Ashforth St. A3
Balmoral Rd. A1
Barker Gate B3
Bath St B3
Belgrave Centre . .B1
Bellar Gate. B3
Belward St B3
Blue Bell Hill Rd . .B3
Brewhouse Yd C2
Broad Marsh Bus Station C2
Broadmarsh Ctr. . C2
Broad St B3
Brook St B3
Burns St A1
Burton St B2
Bus Station A2
Canal St C2
Carlton St. B3
Carrington St. . . . C2
Castle Blvd C1
Castle C2
Castle Gate C2
Castle Meadow Retail Park. C1
Castle Meadow Rd C2
Castle Museum & Gallery C2
Castle Rd C2
Castle Wharf C2
Cavendish Rd East C1
Cemetery B1
Chaucer St. B1
Cheapside B2
Church Rd A3
City Link C3
City of Caves ✦. . C2
Clarendon St B1
Cliff Rd C3
Clumber Rd East. C1
Clumber St. B2
College St B1
Collin St C2
Conway Cl A2
Council House .B2
Court. B2
Cranbrook St B3
Cranmer St A2
Cromwell St. B1
Curzon St B3
Derby Rd B1
Dryden St. A2
Fishpond Dr. C1
Fletcher Gate. B3
Forest Rd East. . . A1
Forest Rd West . . A1
Friar La. C2
Galleries of Justice C3
Gedling Gr A1
Gedling St B3
George St. B3
Gill St A2
Glasshouse St B2
Goldsmith St B2
Goose Gate B3
Great Freeman St A2
Guildhall B2
Hamilton Dr. C1
Hampden St. A1
Heathcote St B3
High Pavement . . C3
High School (Tram stop) A1
Holles Cr C1
Hope Dr C1
Hungerhill Rd . . . A3
Huntingdon Dr . . C1
Huntingdon St. . . A2
Ice Centre C3
Information Ctr .B2
Instow Rise A3
Int Community Ctr A2
Kent St B3
King St B2
Lace Market (Tram stop) B3
Lamartine St B3
Lenton Rd C1
Lewis Cl A3
Lincoln St. B2
London Rd C3
Long Row. B2
Low Pavement. . . C2
Lower Parliament St. B3
Magistrates Court C2
Maid Marian Way .B2
Mansfield Rd . A2/B2
Middle Hill C2
Milton St B2
Mount St B2
Newcastle Dr. B1
Newdigate House C2
Newstead Gr A2
North Sherwood St. A2
Nottingham ⇌. . C3
Old Market Square (Tram stop) B2
Oliver St A1
Park Dr. C1
Park Row C1
Park Terr. B1
Park Valley C1
Peas Hill Rd. A3
Peel St A1
Pelham St B2
Peveril Dr. C1
Plantagenet St . . A3
Playhouse B1
Plumptre St C3
Police Station . .B2
Poplar St C3
Portland Rd B1
Post Office B2/C1
Queen's Rd C3
Raleigh St A1
Regent St B1
Rick St B3
Robin Hood Statue ✦ C2
Robin Hood St. . . .B3
Royal Centre (Tram stop) B2
Royal Children Inn C2
Royal Concert Hall B2
St Ann's Hill Rd. . A2
St Ann's Way A2
St Ann's Well Rd. A3
St Barnabas ✝. . . .B1
St James' St. B2
St Mark's St. B3
St Mary's Garden of Rest B3
St Mary's Gate. . . .B3
St Nicholas . . . C2
St Peter's C2
St Peter's Gate . . .B2
Salutation Inn C2
Shakespeare St . . .B2
Shelton St A2
South Pde B2
South Rd C1
South Sherwood St B2
Station St. C3
Station Street (Tram stop) C3
Stoney St B3
Talbot St. B1
Tales of Robin Hood ✦ C2
Tattershall Dr. . . . C1
Tennis Dr B1
Tennyson St. A1
The Park. C1
The Ropewalk B1
Theatre Royal . .B2
Trent St. C3
Trent Univ . . . A2/B2
Trent University (Tram stop) B2
Trip To Jerusalem Inn ✦ C2
Union Rd B3
Upper Parliament St. B2
Victoria Centre . . .B2
Victoria Leisure Centre. B3
Victoria Park B3
Victoria St B2
Walter St A1
Warser Gate. B3
Watkin St A2
Waverley St A1
Wheeler Gate B2
Wilford Rd C2
Wilford St. C2
Willoughby House C2
Wollaton St B1
Woodborough Rd A2
Woolpack La B3
York St A2

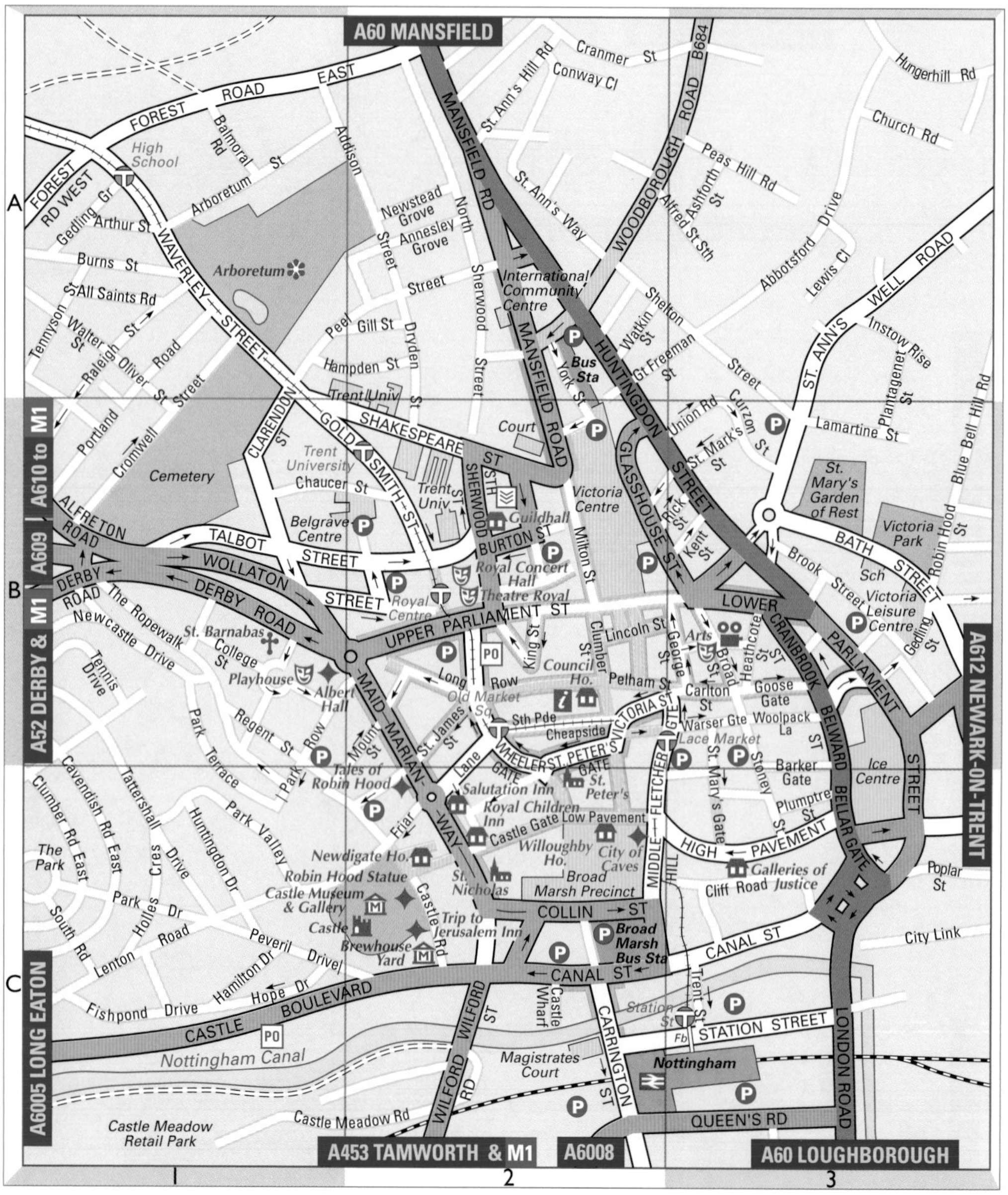

¼ mile
¼ ½ km

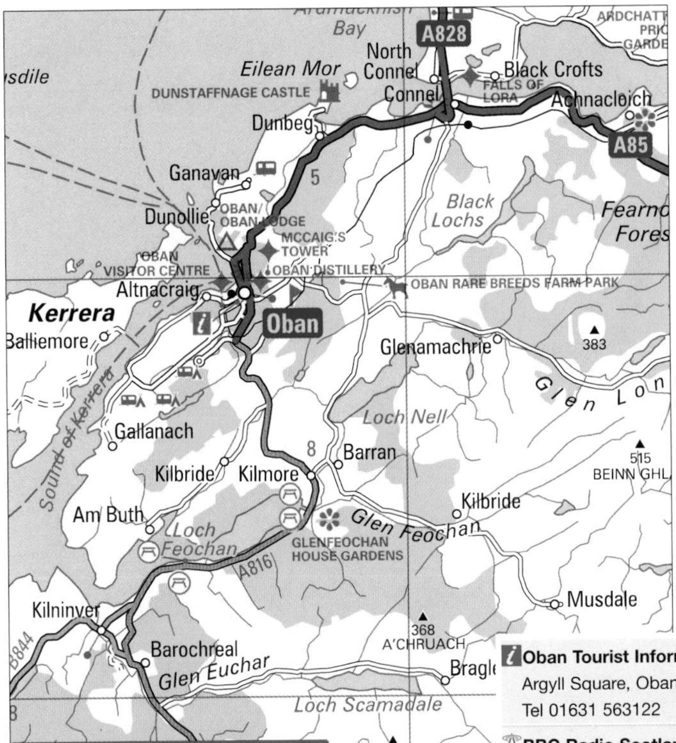

Oban

A busy port, resort and ferry terminal on Scotland's west coast, with panoramic views towards the Hebrides islands to which it forms the gateway. Historic buildings include 13th-century Dunstaffnage Castle, on what is said to be the site of the capital of Dalriada (the original Kingdom of the Scots) at the mouth of one of Scotland's loveliest lochs, which forms rapids at the Falls of Lora, the only seawater falls in Europe. Other sights include McCaig's Tower, a 1902 folly in the form of the Coliseum overlooking the town, the Distillery Visitor Centre on Stafford Street, the Rare Breeds Farm Park, and the Zoological World. The surrounding waters attract watersports enthusiasts, and there are several local marinas from which boat trips are run. Nearby attractions include the gardens of Barguillean, Achnacloich and Ardchattan Priory.

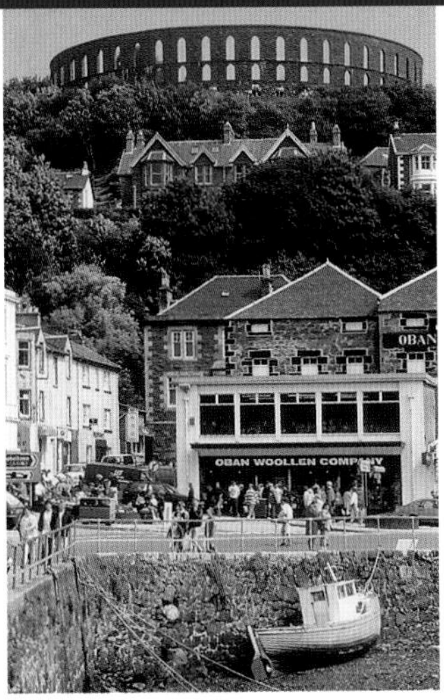

▲Oban harbour and McCaig's Tower

Oban Tourist Information Centre, Argyll Square, Oban PA34 4AR
Tel 01631 563122

BBC Radio Scotland 94.3 FM and 810 AM • **Oban FM** 103.3 FM

www.oban.org.uk

★Do not miss

- ★**Loch Etive Cruises**, Loch Etive
- ★**Oban War and Peace Museum**, Corran Esplanade
- ★**Scottish Sealife Sanctuary**, Barcaldine

Oban

Aird's Cres B2
Albany St B2
Albert La A2
Albert Rd A2
Alma Cres. B1
Ambulance Station C2
Angus Terr C3
Ardconnel Rd. . . . A2
Ardconnel Terr. . . . B2
Argyll Sq. B2
Argyll St B2
Atlantis Leisure Centre. A2
Bayview Rd A1
Benvoulin Rd A2
Bowling Green . . A2
Breadalbane St . . A2
Bus Station B2
Campbell St. B2
College. B2
Colonsay Terr. . . . C3
Columbia Building B2
Combie St B2
Corran Brae. A1
Corran Esplanade . . A1/A2
Corran Halls & Library A2
Court. B2
Crannaig-a-Mhinisteir B1
Crannog La C2
Croft Ave A2
Dalintart Dr C3
Dalriach Rd A2
Drummore Rd . . . C2
Duncraggan Rd . . A2
Dunollie Rd A2
Dunuaran Rd B1
Feochan Gr C3
Ferry Terminal . . . B1
Gallanach Rd B1
George St. A2
Glencruitten Dr . . C3
Glencruitten Rd . . B3
Glenmore Rd C1
Glenshellach Rd . C1
Glenshellach Terr . B2
Harbour Bowl B2
Hazeldean Cres . . A3
High St B2
Highland Discovery Centre. A2
Highland Theatre Cinema A2
Hill St B2
Industrial Estate . C2
Information Ctr . B2
Islay Rd. C3
Jacob's Ladder ✦ . B2
Jura Rd. C3
Knipoch Pl C3
Laurel Cres A2
Laurel Rd A2/A3
Lifeboat Station . . B1
Lighthouse Pier. . . B1
Lismore Cres A2
Lochavullin Dr . . . B2
Lochavullin Rd . . . C2
Lochside St B2
Longsdale Cres . . A3
Longsdale Rd. A2/A3
Longsdale Terr. . . A3
Lunga Rd C3
Lynn Rd C2
Market St B2
McCaig Rd C3
McCaig's Tower ✦ A2
Mill La. C2
Miller Rd C2
Millpark Ave C2
Millpark Rd C2
Mossfield Ave . . . B3
Mossfield Dr B3
Mossfield Stadium B3
Nant Dr. C3
Nelson Rd C2
North Pier B2
Nursery La A2
Oban Station . B2
Police Station . . B2
Polvinister Rd . . . B3
Post Office A2/B2
Pulpit Dr. C1
Pulpit Hill. C1
Pulpit Hill Viewpoint ✦ B1
Quarry Rd. C2
Queen's Park Pl . . B2
Railway Quay. B1
Rockfield Rd B2
St Columba's ✝ . . . A1
St John's ✝ A2
Scalpay Terr. C3
Shore St B1
Shuna Terr C3
Sinclair Dr C2
Soroba Rd . . . B2/C2
South Pier B1
Stevenson St B2
Tweedale St B2
Ulva Rd. C2
Villa Rd. B1
War & Peace . A2

¼ mile
¼ ½ km

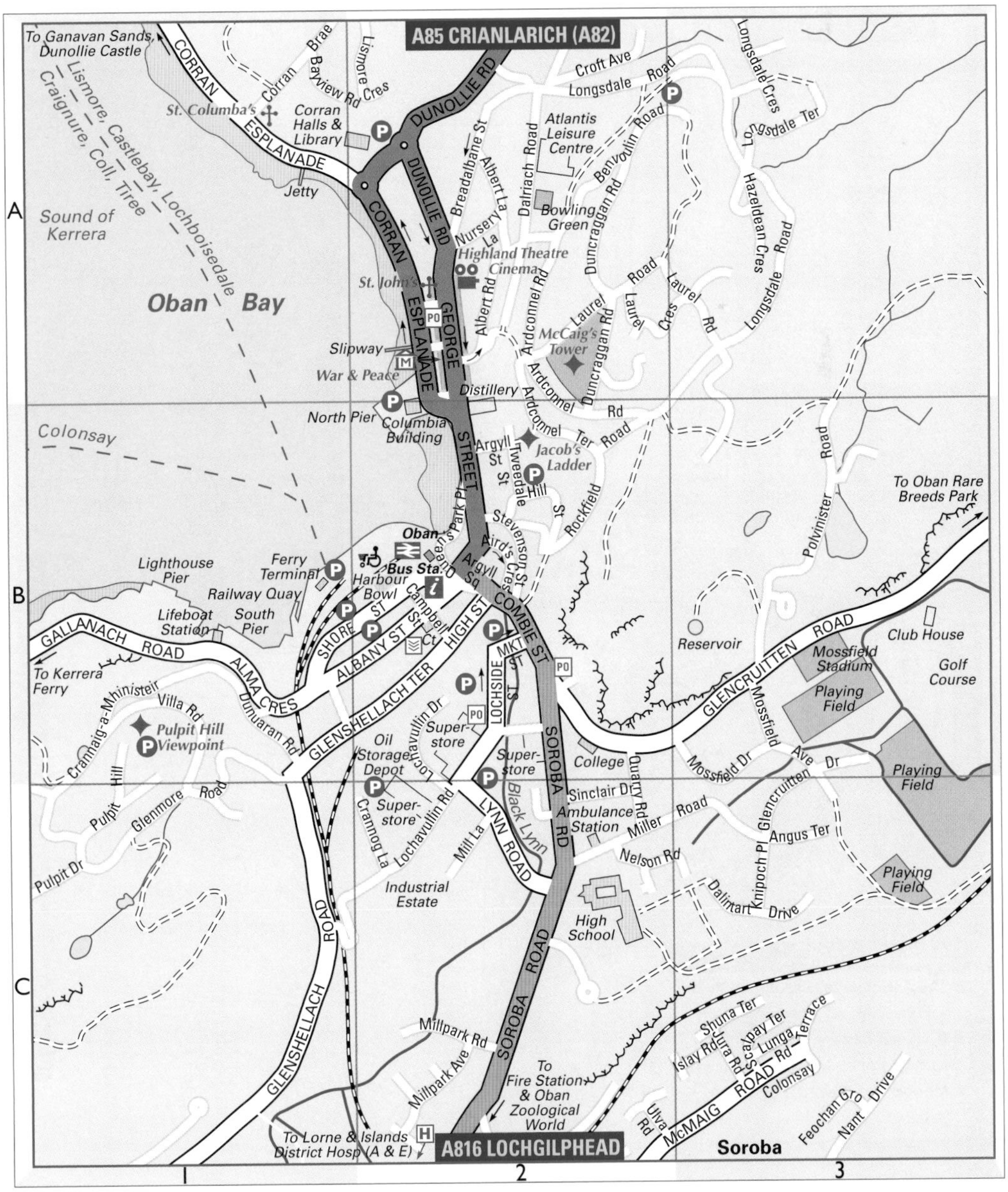

Oxford

A world-famous university city, founded by Alfred the Great and centre of learning since the 12th century. Christ Church Cathedral is among the city's oldest buildings. Museums and galleries include the Museum of Oxford, about the city and University; The Oxford Story, about the University; Handson, an interactive science exhibition; the Pitt Rivers Museum of anthropology and world archaeology; and Christ Church Gallery. The University also owns the lovely Botanic Garden and Harcourt Arboretum. Oxford has a wide selection of shops, with the Covered Market offering an eclectic range from butchers to boot shops via cakes and candles. There are countless alehouses, and restaurants of all nations.

▲Radcliffe Camera

The Oxford Information Centre, 15-16 Broad Street, Oxford OX1 3AS
Tel 01865 726871

BBC Radio Oxford 95.2 FM
Fox 102.6 FM • **Passion** 107.9 FM

www.oxford.gov.uk

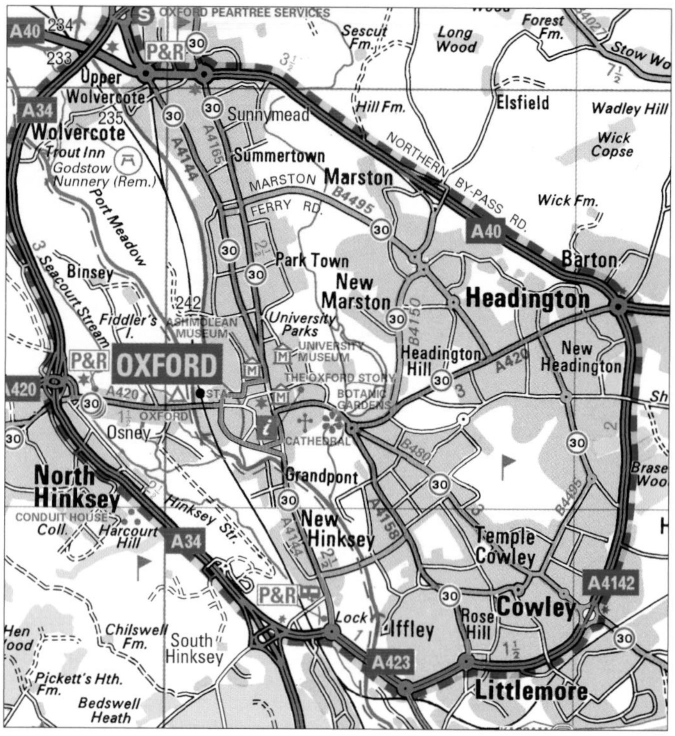

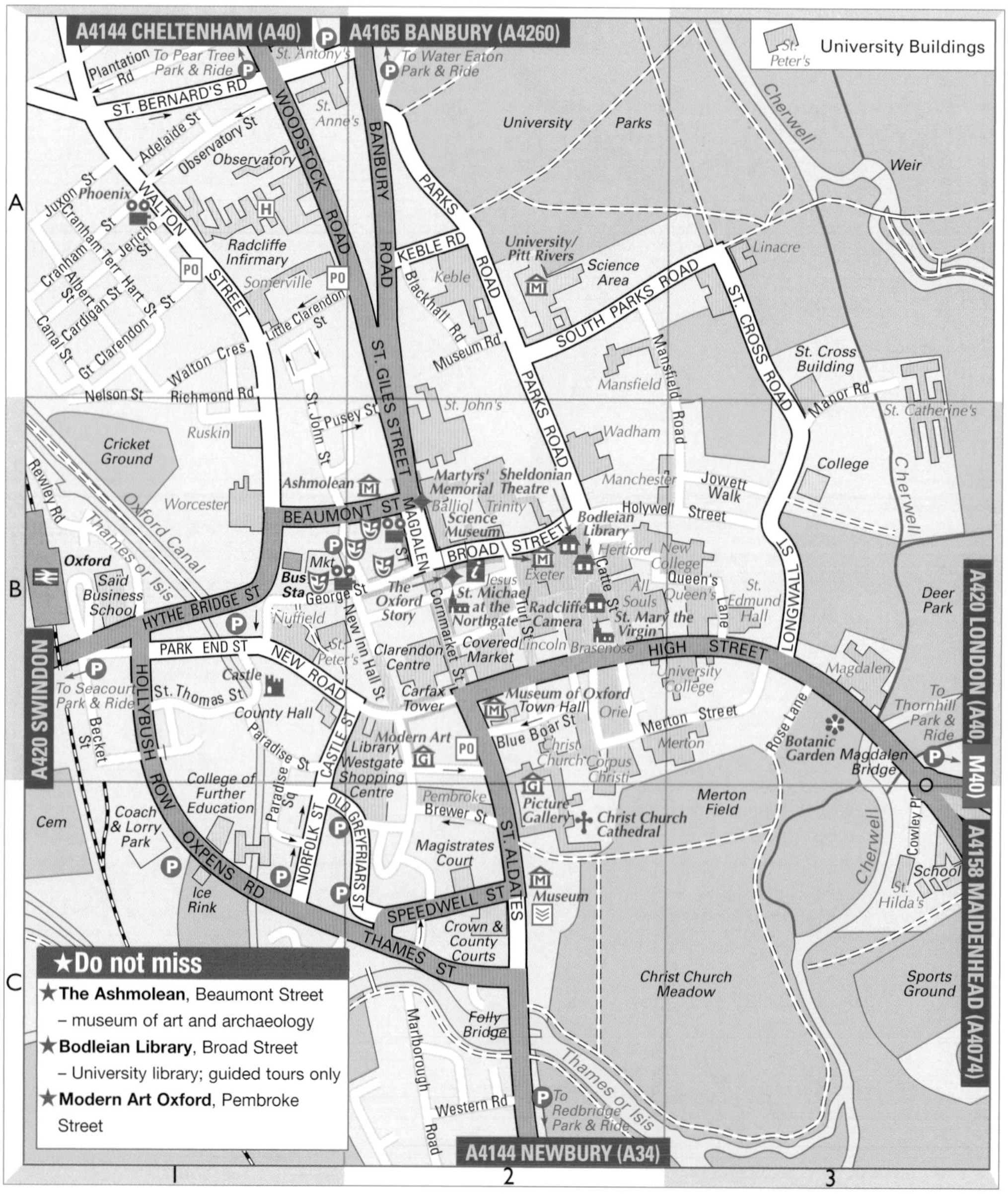

★Do not miss

★**The Ashmolean**, Beaumont Street – museum of art and archaeology
★**Bodleian Library**, Broad Street – University library; guided tours only
★**Modern Art Oxford**, Pembroke Street

Oxford

Adelaide St A1
All Souls (Coll) . . .B2
Ashmolean Mus B2
Balliol (Coll) B2
Banbury Rd A2
Beaumont St B1
Becket St B1
Blackhall Rd A2
Blue Boar St B2
Bodleian Library B2
Botanic Garden . .B3
Brasenose (Coll) . .B2
Brewer St. C2
Broad St. B2
Burton-Taylor Theatre B2
Bus Station B1
Cardigan St A1
Carfax Tower B2
Castle B1
Castle St. B1
Catte St B2
Cemetery C1
Christ Church (Coll) B2
Christ Church . C2
Christ Church Meadow C2
Clarendon Centre .B2
Coach & Lorry Park C1
College of Further Education. C1
Cornmarket St. . . .B2
Corpus Christi (Coll) B2
County Hall B1
Covered Market. . .B2
Cowley Pl C3
Cranham St A1
Cranham Terr. . . . A1
Cricket Ground . . .B1
Crown & County Courts. C2
Deer Park. B3
Exeter (Coll) B2
Folly Bridge C2
George St. B1
Great Clarendon St. A1
Hart St A1
Hertford (Coll). . . .B2
High St B3
Hollybush Row . . .B1
Holywell St. B2
Hythe Bridge St. . .B1
Ice Rink C1
Information Ctr .B2
Jericho St A1
Jesus (Coll) B2
Jowett Walk. B3
Juxon St. A1
Keble (Coll) A2
Keble Rd. A2
Library B2
Linacre (Coll) . . . A3
Lincoln (Coll) B2
Little Clarendon St. A1
Longwall St B3
Magdalen (Coll) . .B3
Magdalen Bridge .B2
Magdalen St B2
Magistrate's Court C2
Manchester (Coll).B2
Manor Rd B3
Mansfield (Coll) . A2
Mansfield Rd A3
Market B1
Marlborough Rd . C2
Martyrs' Memorial B2
Merton Field B3
Merton (Coll). B3
Merton St. B2
Museum of Modern Art . . .B2
Museum of Oxford B2
Museum Rd A2
New College (Coll) B3
New Inn Hall St. . .B2
New Rd. B1
New Theatre . . .B2
Norfolk St. C1
Nuffield (Coll) B1
Observatory A1
Observatory St. . . A1
Odeon B1/B2
Old Fire Station B1
Old Greyfriars St. C2
Oriel (Coll). B2
Oxford Station B1
Oxpens Rd C1
Oxford Story, The B2
Paradise Sq C1
Paradise St B1
Park End St B1
Parks Rd. A2/B2
Pembroke (Coll) . C2
Phoenix A1
Picture Gallery C2
Plantation Rd . . . A1
Playhouse B2
Police Station . C2
Post Office B2
Pusey St B1
Queen's La. B3
Queen's (Coll) B3
Radcliffe Camera B2
Radcliffe Infirmary A1
Rewley Rd B1
Richmond Rd. A1
Rose La. B3
Ruskin (Coll) B1
Saïd Business School B1
St Aldates. C2
St Anne's (Coll). . A1
St Antony's (Coll) A1
St Bernard's Rd . . A1
St Catherine's (Coll) B3
St Cross Rd A3
St Edmund Hall (Coll) B3
St Giles St A2
St Hilda's (Coll) . . C3
St John St B2
St John's (Coll) . . .B2
St Mary the Virgin B2
St Michael at the Northgate B2
St Peter's (Coll) . . .B1
St Thomas St B1
Science Area A2
Science Mus . . .B2
Sheldonian Theatre B2
Somerville (Coll). A1
South Parks Rd . . A2
Speedwell St C2
Sports Ground . . . C3
Thames St C2
Town Hall B2
Trinity (Coll) B2
Turl St. B2
University College (Coll) B3
University Mus & Pitt Rivers Mus . . A2
University Parks . A2
Wadham (Coll) . . .B2
Walton Cr. A1
Walton St A1
Western Rd C2
Westgate Shopping Centre. B2
Woodstock Rd . . . A1
Worcester (Coll) . .B1

¼ mile
¼ ½ km

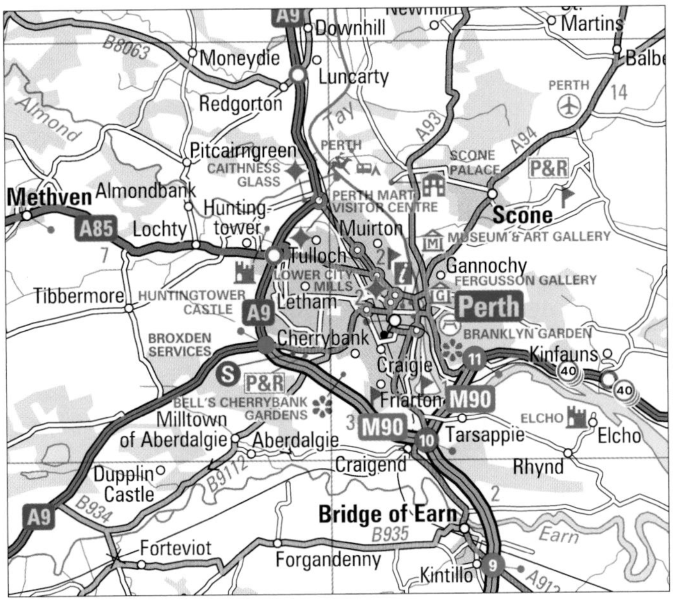

A market town known to the Romans as Bertha and dubbed 'the ancient capital of Scotland' for its role as a medieval royal residence; nearby Scone was the traditional coronation site of Scottish kings. In the town centre visitors can explore the striking medieval St John's Kirk, the Perth Mart Visitor Centre tracing the area's agricultural history, the Museum and Art Gallery, the JD Fergusson Collection of art in the historic Round House, and the Caithness Glass Visitor Centre, and relax in Branklyn Gardens and the public parks of the North and South Inches. Houses to visit within easy reach include Elcho, Huntingtower Castle and Megginch Castle, while at nearby Abernethy is an 11th-century Round Tower and local-history museum. Perth Racecourse is just on the outskirts of the town, and just to the east is the Fairways Heavy Horse Centre with its Clydesdale horses.

Perth

▲The River Tay at Perth

Perth

A K Bell Library . . . B2
Abbot Cres C1
Abbot St C1
Albany Terr A1
Albert Monument A3
Alexandra St B2
Art Gallery B3
Atholl St A2
Balhousie Ave . . . A2
Balhousie Castle Black Watch Museum A2
Balhousie St A2
Ballantine Pl A1
Barossa Pl A2
Barossa St A2
Barrack St A2
Bell's Sports Ctr . A2
Bellwood B3
Blair St B1
Burn Park C1
Bus Station B2
Caledonian Rd . . . B2
Canal Cres B2
Canal St B3
Cavendish Ave . . . C1
Charles St B2
Charlotte Pl A2
Charlotte St A3
Church St A1
City Hall B3
Club House C3
Clyde Pl C1
Commercial St . . A3
Concert Hall ✦ . . . B3
Council Chambers B3
County Pl B2
Court B3
Craigie Pl C2
Crieff Rd A1
Croft Park C2
Cross St B2
Darnhall Cres . . . C1
Darnhall Dr C1
Dundee Rd B3
Dunkeld Rd A1
Earl's Dykes B1
Edinburgh Rd . . . C3
Elibank St B1
Fair Maid's House ✦ A3
Fergusson B3
Feus Rd A1
Fire Station A1
Fitness Centre . . . B3
Foundary La A2
Friar St C1
George St B3
Glamis Pl C1
Glasgow Rd B1
Glenearn Rd C2
Glover St B1/C1
Golf Course A2
Gowrie St A3
Gray St B1
Graybank Rd B1
Greyfriars Burial Ground B3
Hay St A2
High St B2/B3
Hospital H B2
Hotel B2
Ice Rinks B1
Inchaffray St A1
Industrial/Retail Park B1
Information Ctr i . B2
Isla Rd A3
James St B2
Keir St A3
King Edward St . . . B3
King James VI Golf Course C3
King St B2
Kings Pl C2
Kinnoull Causeway B2
Kinnoull Church (Remains of) ✦ . . B3
Kinnoull St B2
Knowelea Pl C1
Knowelea Terr . . . C1
Ladeside Business Centre A1
Leisure Pool B1
Leonard St B2
Lickley St B2
Lochie Brae A3
Long Causeway . . . A1
Low St A2
Main St A3
Marshall Pl C3
Melville St A2
Mill St B3
Milne St B2
Murray Cres C1
Murray St B2
Needless Rd C1
New Rd B2
North Inch A3
North Methven St A2
Park Pl C1
Perth B2
Perth Bridge A3
Perth Business Park B1
Perth Station . . C2
Pickletulllum Rd . B1
Pitheavlis Cres . . C1
Playhouse B2
Police Station . . A2
Pomarium St B2
Post Office PO A3/B2/C2
Princes St B3
Priory Pl C2
Queen St C1
Queen's Bridge . . . B3
Riggs Rd B1
Riverside B3
Riverside Park . . . B3
Rodney Park B3
Rose Terr A2
St Catherines Retail Park A1
St Catherine's Rd A1/A2
St John St B3
St John's Kirk . . . B3
St John's Shopping Ctr . . . B2
St Leonards Br . . C2
St Ninians ✝ A2
Scott Monument . C2
Scott St B2
Sheriff Court B3
Shore Rd C3
Skate Park C3
South Inch C2
South Inch Business Centre C3
South Inch Park . C2
South Inch View . C2
South Methven St . B2
South St B3
South William St . . B2
Stormont St A2
Strathmore St . . . A3
Stuart Ave C1
Tay St B3
The Stables A1
The Stanners B3
Union La A2
Victoria St B2
Watergate B3
Wellshill Cem . . . A1
West Bridge St . . A3
West Mill St B2
Whitefriers Cres . . B1
Whitefriers St . . . B1
Wilson St C1
Windsor Terr C1
Woodside Cres . . C1
York Pl B2
Young St C1

¼ mile
¼ ½ km

Perth Tourist Information Centre, Lower City Mills, West Mill Street, Perth PH1 5QP Tel 01738 450600

BBC Radio Scotland 93.5 FM and 810 AM • **Tay FM** 96.4 **Tay AM** 1584 AM • **Wave** 102.0 FM

www.perthshire.co.uk

★Do not miss

★**Balhousie Castle and Black Watch Regimental Museum**, Hay Street
★**Cherrybank Gardens and Bells National Heather Collection**, Cherrybank
★**Scone Place (early 1800s)**, Scone

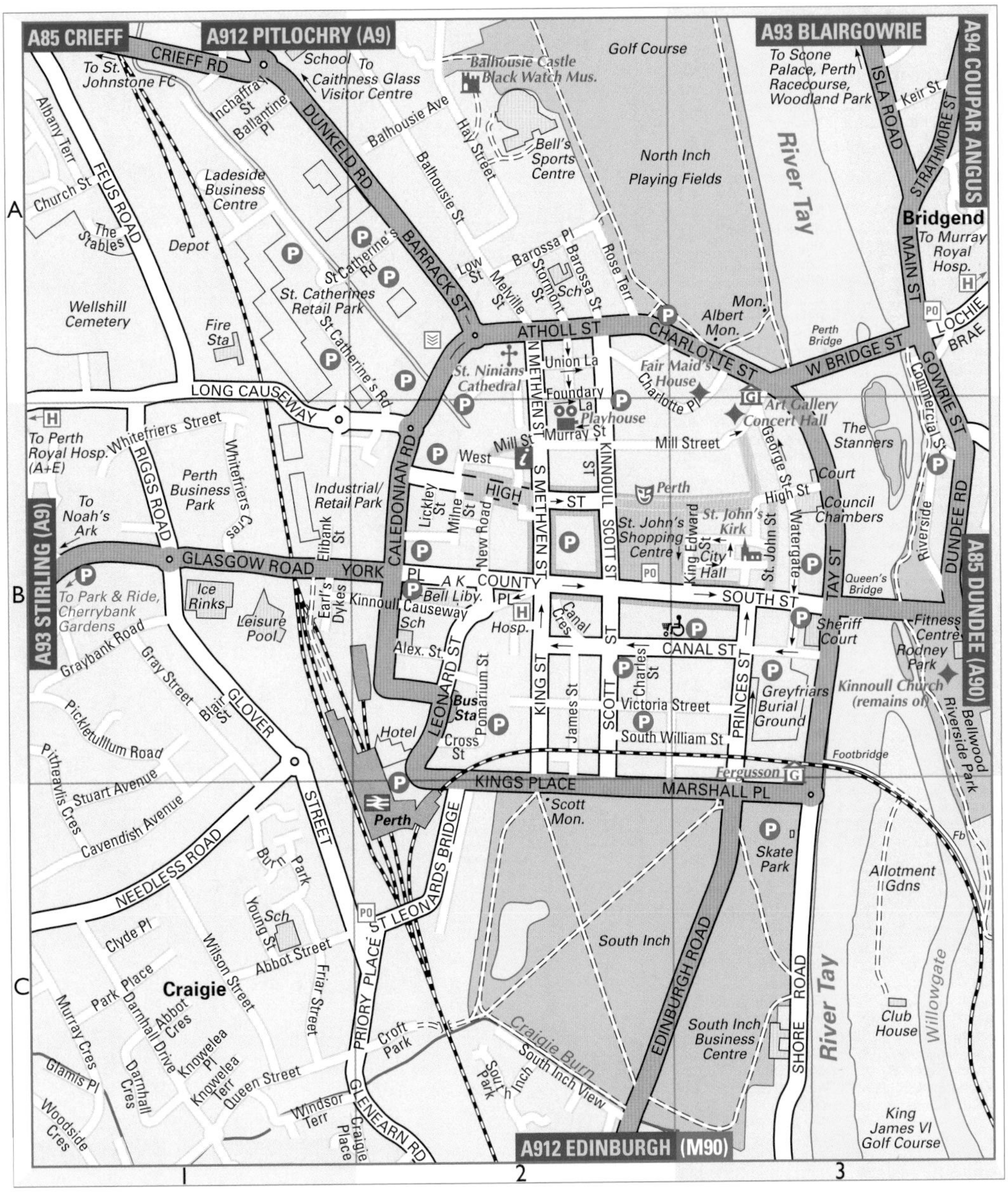

Peterborough

★Do not miss

★**Flag Fen Excavations and Museum**, East of city

★**Nene Valley Railway**, half a mile from Peterborough station

★**Peterborough Cathedral and Tomb of Katherine of Aragon**, Cathedral Square

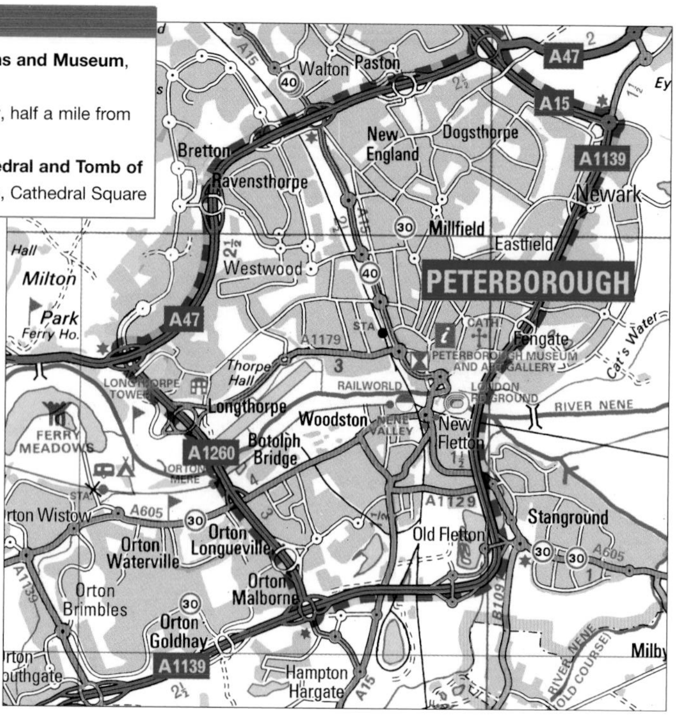

An ancient cathedral city and thriving modern business centre on the site of a Roman fortified town established *c.*AD 43, with an important Bronze Age archaeological site at nearby Flag Fen. Later a major pottery production centre, it was also the site of a Saxon monastery built by Paeda, King of Mercia, in AD 654, over which the splendid Norman cathedral was constructed. Other buildings of historical interest include Longthorpe Tower (1300) with its medieval wall paintings, and Thorpe Hall, a mansion built under Cromwell with gardens open to the public, and there's a Museum and Art Gallery. The best green space is Ferry Meadows, focal point of Nene Park, with 50 acres of riverside meadows, woods and lakes and a host of sports activities.

▲Peterborough Cathedral

Peterborough Tourist Information Centre, 3-5 Minster Precincts, Peterborough PE1 1XS
Tel 01733 452336

BBC Radio Cambridgeshire 95.7 FM • **Classic Gold** 1332 AM
Hereward 102.7 FM • **Lite** 106.8 FM

www.peterborough.gov.uk

Peterborough

Bishop's Palace B2
Bishop's Rd . . . B2/B3
Boongate A3
Bourges Blvd A1
Bread St C1
Bourges Retail Park B1/B2
Bridge House (Council Offices) C2
Bridge St B2
Bright St A1
Broadway A2
Broadway A2
Brook St A2
Burghley Rd A2
Bus Station B2
Cavendish St A3
Charles St A3
Church St B2
Church Walk A2
Cobden Ave A1
Cobden St A1
Cowgate B2
Craig St A2
Crawthorne Rd . . A2
Cripple Sidings La C2
Cromwell Rd A1
Dickens St A3
Eastfield Rd A3
Eastgate B3
Fire Station A1
Fletton Ave. C2
Frank Perkins Parkway C3
Geneva St. A2
George St. C1
Gladstone St A1
Glebe Rd C2
Gloucester Rd . . . C3
Granby St. B3
Grove St C1
Guildhall B2
Hadrians Ct C3
Henry St A2
Hereward Rd B3
Information Ctr . B2
Jubilee St. C1
Key Theatre . . . C2
Kent Rd. B1
Kirkwood Cl B1
Lea Gdns B1
Library A2
Lincoln Rd A2
London Rd C2
Long Causeway . . . B2
Lower Bridge St . C2
Magistrates Court. B2
Manor House St . A2
Mayor's Walk. . . . A1
Midland Rd A1
Monument St. . . . A2
Museum & Art Gallery B2
Nene Valley Railway C1
New Rd. A2
New Rd. C1
North Minster . . . A2
Old Customs House C2
Oundle Rd C1
Padholme Rd. . . . A3
Palmerston Rd . . C1
Park Rd A2
Passport Office . . . B2
Peterborough District Hospital (A&E) B1
Peterborough . B1
Peterborough Nene Valley Station C1
Peterborough United FC. C2
Police Station . . B2
Post Office A3/B1/B2/B3/C1
Priestgate B2
Queen's Walk . . . C2
Queensgate Ctr . . . B2
Railworld C1
River La B1
Rivergate Shopping Centre. B2
Riverside Mead . . C3
Russell St. A1
St John's B2
St John's St. A3
St Mark's St. A2
St Peter's B2
St Peter's Rd B2
Saxon Rd A3
Spital Bridge A1
Stagshaw Dr C3
Star Rd B3
Thorpe Lea Rd. . . . B1
Thorpe Rd B1
Thorpe's Lea Rd . . B1
Town Hall B2
Viersen Platz B2
Vineyard Rd B3
Wake Rd B3
Wellington St. . . . A3
Wentworth St B2
Westgate B2
Whalley St A3
Wharf Rd C1
Whitsed St A3
YMCA A3

¼ mile
¼ ½ km

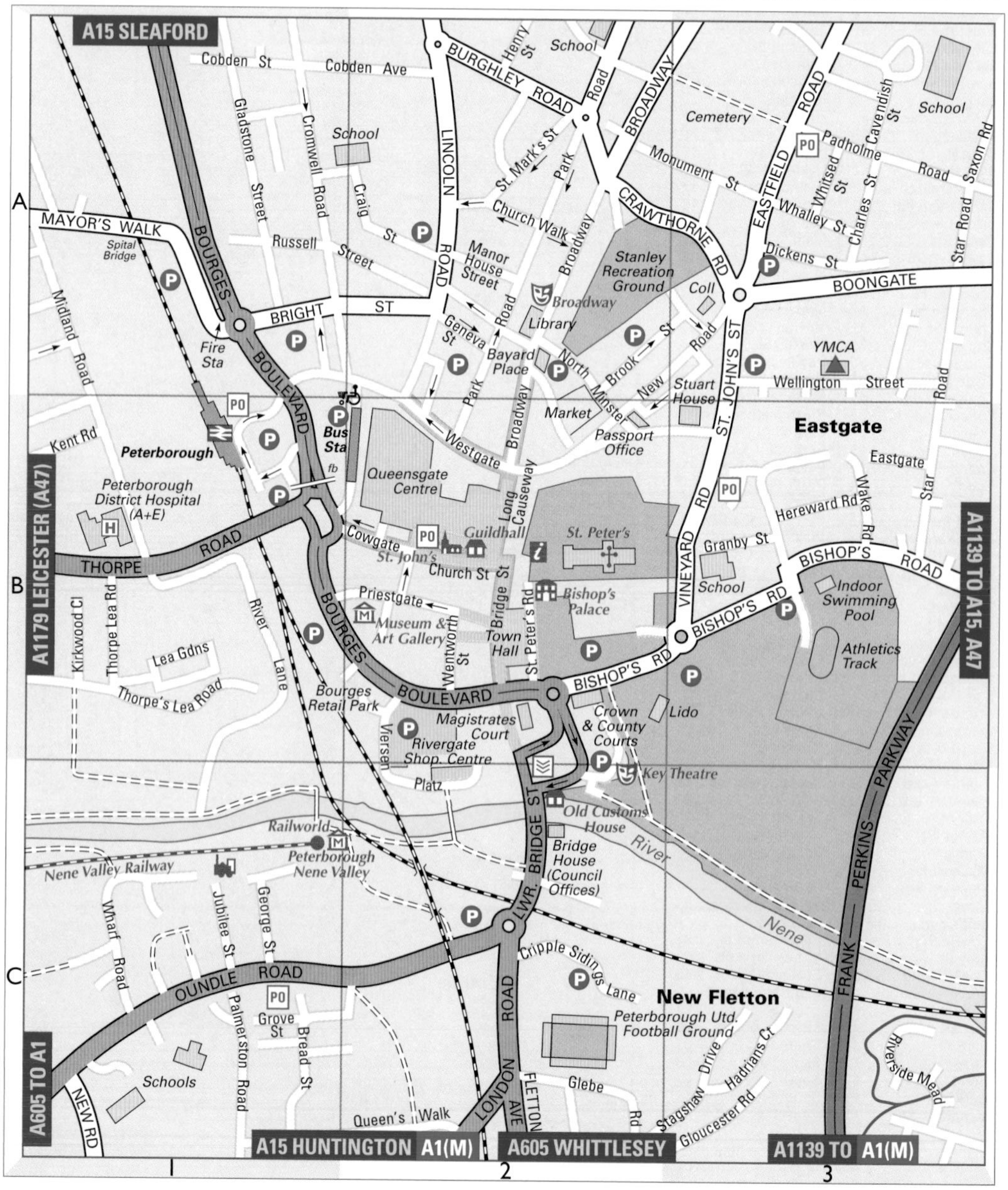

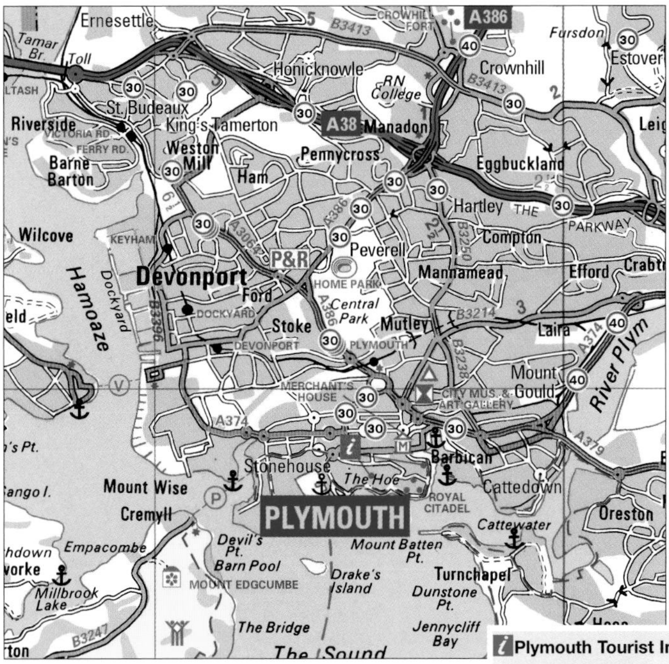

The regional capital of Devon and Cornwall, most famous as the city from which Sir Francis Drake, the Pilgrim Fathers, Charles Darwin, Captain Cook and others set sail, with magnificent views from the 18th-century Smeaton's Tower Lighthouse and from the Waterfront Walkway (part of the South West Coast Path). Other sights are the mid-18th-century Crownhill Fort with its artillery collection; the Black Friars gin distillery; the Elizabethan House, a Tudor sea captain's home; the City Museum and Art Gallery; and the Royal Citadel, built in the 17th century to defend the coastline from the Dutch. There are excellent shopping facilities in the pedestrianised centre and the narrow streets of The Barbican, with its specialist shops, craft workshops, art galleries, restaurants and cafes. The city is handy for Dartmoor National Park and Wildlife Park, the Tamar Valley Area of Outstanding Natural Beauty, the National Trust properties Saltram House and Antony House, Mount Edgcumbe House and Country Park and Mary Newman's Cottage, the family home of Drake's first wife.

Plymouth

▲ Smeaton's Tower and The Hoe

Plymouth Tourist Information Centre, The Barbican, Plymouth PL1 2LR
Tel 01752 306330

BBC Radio Devon 103.4 FM and 855 AM • **Classic Gold** 1152 AM
Plymouth Sound 97 FM

www.visitplymouth.co.uk

★Do not miss

★**The Merchants House**, St Andrew's Street – features reconstructed Elizabethan chemist's shop
★**National Marine Aquarium**, The Barbican
★**Plymouth City Museum & Art Gallery**, Drake Circus

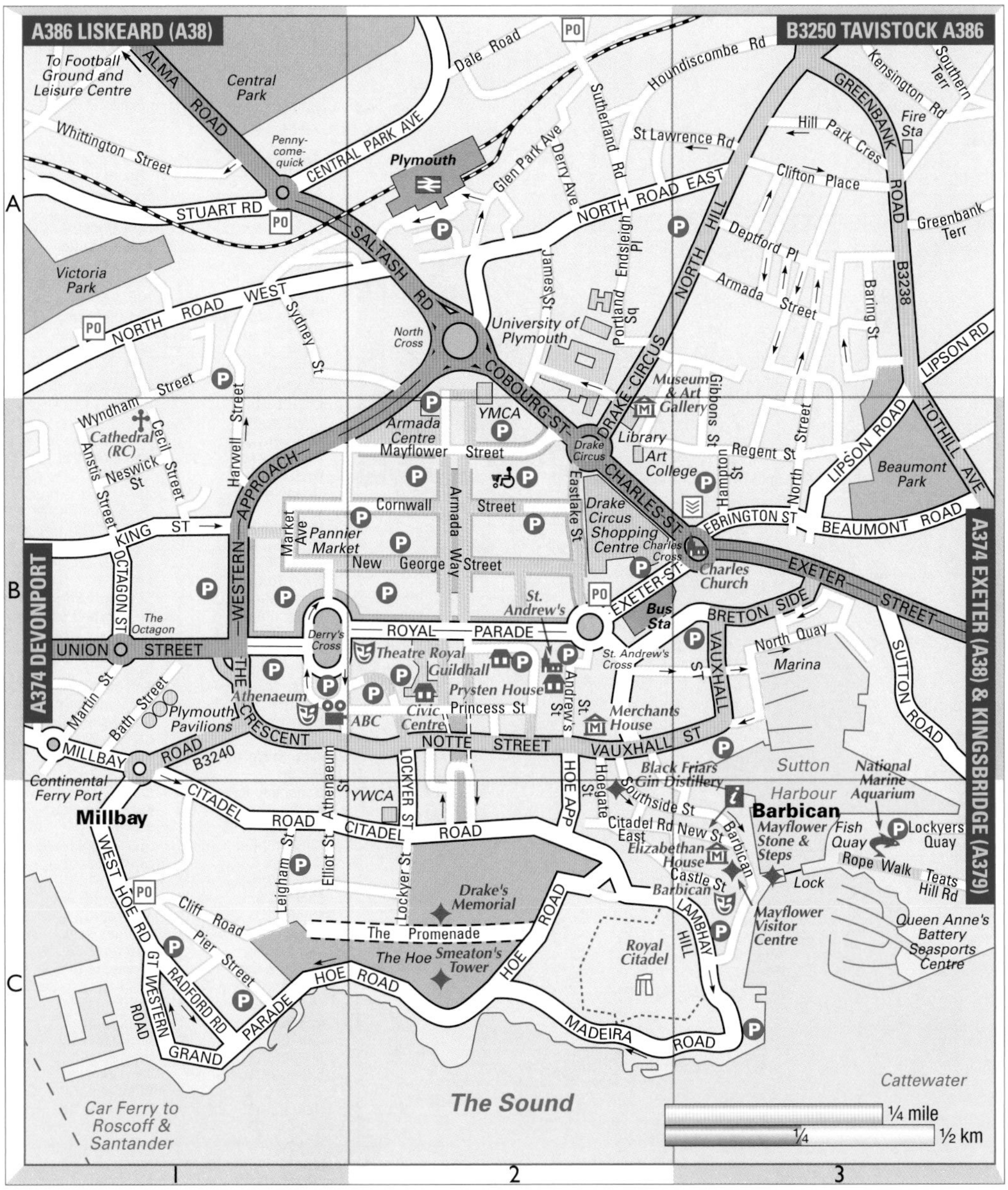

Plymouth

ABC B2
Alma Rd A1
Anstis St B1
Armada Centre . . . B2
Armada St A3
Armada Way B2
Art College B2
Athenaeum St . . . C1
Athenaeum B1
Barbican C3
Barbican C3
Baring St A3
Bath St B1
Beaumont Park . . . B3
Beaumont Rd B3
Black Friars Gin Distillery ✦ C2
Breton Side B3
Bus Station B2
Castle St C3
Cathedral (RC) . . B1
Cecil St B1
Central Park A1
Central Park Ave . . A2
Charles Church . . B3
Charles Cross (r'about) B3
Charles St B2
Citadel Rd C2
Citadel Rd East . . . C2
Civic Centre . . . B2
Cliff Rd C1
Clifton Pl A3
Cobourg St A2
Continental Ferry Port B1
Cornwall St B2
Dale Rd A2
Deptford Pl A3
Derry Ave A2
Derry's Cross (r'about) B1
Drake Circus B2
Drake Circus Shopping Ctr . . . B2
Drake's Memorial ✦ C2
Eastlake St B2
Ebrington St B3
Elizabethan House C3
Elliot St C1
Endsleigh Pl A2
Exeter St B3
Fire Station A3
Fish Quay C3
Gibbons St A3
Glen Park Ave A2
Grand Pde C1
Great Western Rd C1
Greenbank Rd A3
Greenbank Terr . . . A3
Guildhall B2
Hampton St B3
Harwell St B1
Hill Park Cr A3
Hoe Approach B2
Hoe Rd C2
Hoegate St C2
Houndiscombe Rd A2
Information Ctr C3
James St A2
Kensington Rd . . . A3
King St B1
Lambhay Hill C3
Leigham St C1
Library B2
Lipson Rd A3/B3
Lockyer St C2
Lockyers Quay . . . C3
Madeira Rd C2
Marina B3
Market Ave B1
Martin St B1
Mayflower St B2
Mayflower Stone & Steps ✦ C3
Mayflower Visitor Ctr ✦ C3
Merchants House B2
Millbay Rd B1
Museum & Art Gallery B2
National Marine Aquarium . . . C3
Neswick St B1
New George St . . . B2
New St C3
North Cross (r'about) A2
North Hill A3
North Quay B2
North Rd East A2
North Rd West A1
North St B3
Notte St B2
Octagon St B1
Pannier Market . . . B1
Pennycomequick (r'about) A1
Pier St C1
Plymouth City Mus & Art Gal B2
Plymouth Pavilions B1
Plymouth A2
Police Station . . B3
Portland Sq A2
Post Office A1/A2/B2/C1
Princess St B2
Prysten House . . B2
Queen Anne's Battery Seasports Centre C3
Radford Rd C1
Regent St B3
Rope Walk C3
Royal Citadel . . C2
Royal Pde B2
St Andrew's B2
St Andrew's Cross (r'about) B2
St Andrew's St B2
St Lawrence Rd . . A2
Saltash Rd A2
Smeaton's Tower ✦ C2
Southern Terr A3
Southside St C2
Stuart Rd A1
Sutherland Rd A2
Sutton Rd B3
Sydney St A1
Teats Hill Rd C3
The Crescent B1
The Hoe C2
The Octagon (r'about) B1
The Promenade . . C2
Theatre Royal . . B2
Tothill Ave B3
Union St B1
Univ of Plymouth A2
Vauxhall St B2/3
Victoria Park A1
West Hoe Rd C1
Western Approach B1
Whittington St . . . A1
Wyndham St B1

Poole

▲Poole Harbour

An important Middle Ages port and modern Channel ferry terminus on Europe's largest natural harbour, in the middle of which lies the National Trust's wildlife-rich Brownsea Island, visitable by boat trip. The lively Quayside area with its cobbled streets and 18th-century architecture is home to the Poole Pottery factory shop and a wide range of shops, pubs, cafes and restaurants. Scalpens Court Museum, in Poole's most complete medieval domestic building, is open to the general public in August, and there's a small lifeboat museum. There are also 3 miles of sandy beaches popular with watersports enthusiasts, including the award-winning Sandbanks, the 100-acre Upton Country Park, and Compton Acres Gardens, and within close proximity are the National Trust's Corfe Castle and Kingston Lacy Italian Renaissance palazzo, Farmer Palmer's Farm Park, and some outstanding areas of natural beauty, including the New Forest National Park and the Isle of Purbeck. Poole and adjoining Bournemouth are also home to the famous Chines (dry wooded ravines).

★Do not miss

★**Cockle Trail** – around the Quayside and Old Town

★**Upton Country Park**, A35

★**Waterfront Museum**, Lower High Street – Poole's social, domestic and maritime history

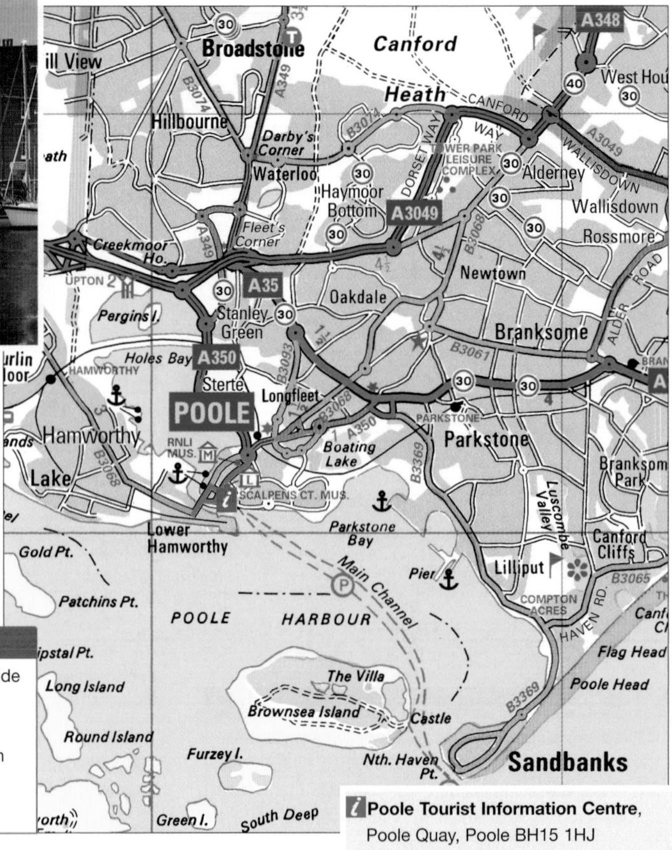

Poole Tourist Information Centre, Poole Quay, Poole BH15 1HJ
Tel 01202 253253

BBC Radio Solent 103.8 FM 1359 AM
Fire 107.6 FM • **Classic Gold** 828 AM

www.pooletourism.com

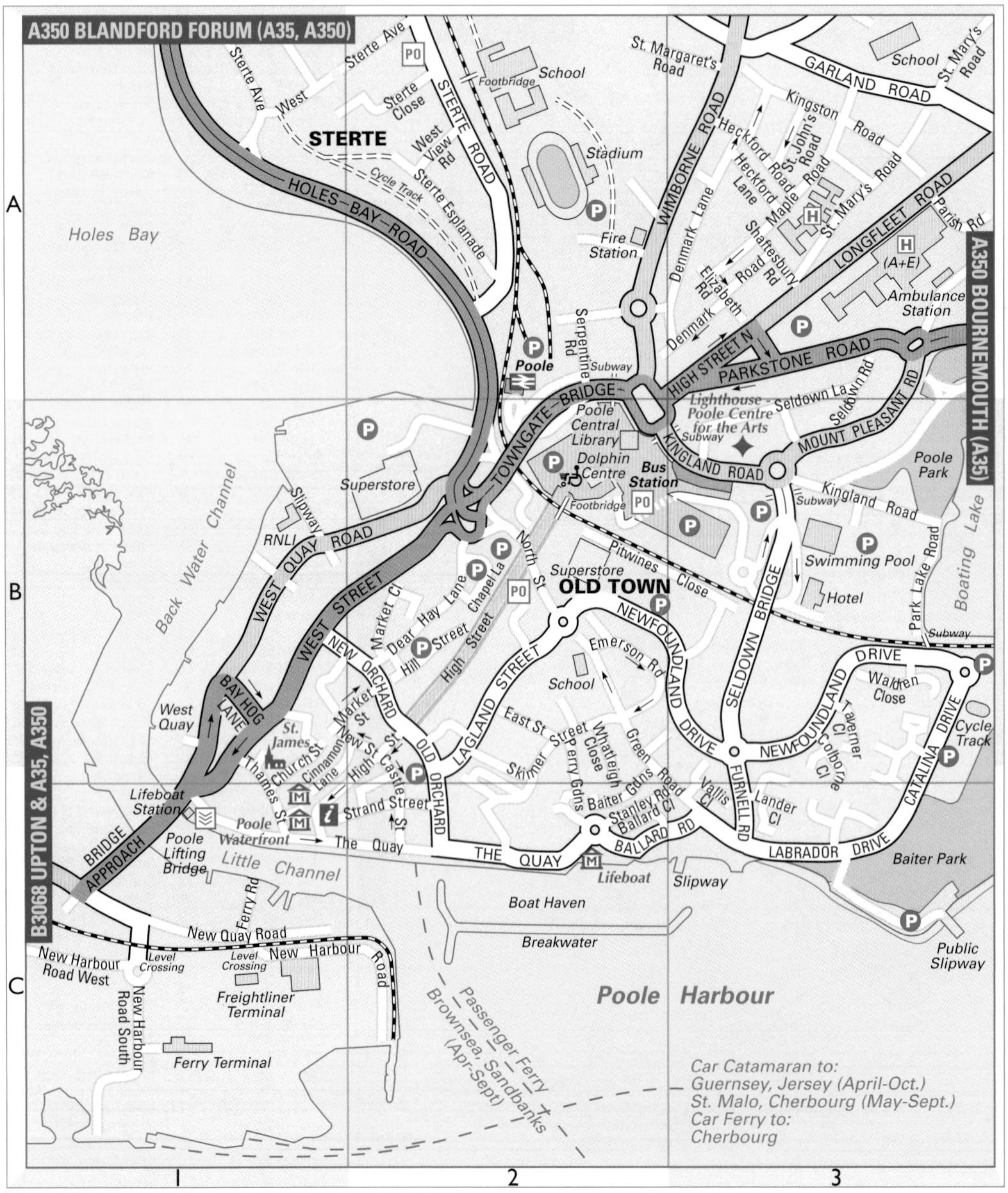

Poole

Street	Grid
Ambulance Station	A3
Baiter Gdns	C2
Baiter Park	C3
Ballard Cl	C2
Ballard Rd	C2
Bay Hog La	B1
Bridge Approach	C1
Bus Station	B2
Castle St	B2
Catalina Dr	B3
Chapel La	B2
Church St	B1
Cinnamon La	B1
Colborne Cl	B3
Dear Hay La	B2
Denmark La	A3
Denmark Rd	A3
East St	B2
Elizabeth Rd	A3
Emerson Rd	B2
Ferry Rd	C1
Ferry Terminal	C1
Fire Station	A2
Freightliner Terminal	C1
Furnell Rd	B3
Garland Rd	A3
Green Rd	B2
Heckford La	A3
Heckford Rd	A3
High St	B2
High St North	A3
Hill St	B2
Holes Bay Rd	A1
Hospital (A&E)	A3
Information Ctr	C1
Kingland Rd	B3
Kingston Rd	A3
Labrador Dr	C3
Lagland St	B2
Lander Cl	C3
Lifeboat	C2
Lighthouse – Poole Centre for the Arts ✦	B3
Longfleet Rd	A3
Maple Rd	A3
Market Cl	B2
Market St	B2
Mount Pleasant Rd	B3
New Harbour Rd	C1
New Harbour Rd South	C1
New Harbour Rd West	C1
New Orchard	B1
New Quay Rd	C1
New St	B2
Newfoundland Dr	B2
North St	B2
Old Orchard	B2
Parish Rd	A3
Park Lake Rd	B3
Parkstone Rd	A3
Perry Gdns	B2
Pitwines Cl	B2
Police Station	C1
Poole Lifting Br.	C1
Poole Central Library	B2
Poole Park	B2
Poole Station	A2
Poole Waterfront Museum	C1
Post Office	A2/B2
RNLI	B2
St John's Rd	A3
St Margaret's Rd	A2
St Mary's Rd	A3
Seldown Bridge	B3
Seldown La	B3
Seldown Rd	B3
Serpentine Rd	A2
Shaftesbury Rd	A3
Skinner St	B2
Slipway	B1
Stanley Rd	C2
Sterte Ave	A2
Sterte Ave West	A1
Sterte Cl	A2
Sterte Esplanade	A2
Sterte Rd	A2
Strand St	C2
Swimming Pool	B3
Taverner Cl	B3
Thames St	B1
The Quay	C2
Towngate Bridge	B2
Vallis Cl	C3
Waldren Cl	B3
West Quay	B1
West Quay Rd	B1
West St	B1
West View Rd	A2
Whatleigh Cl	B2
Wimborne Rd	A3

¼ mile
¼ ½ km

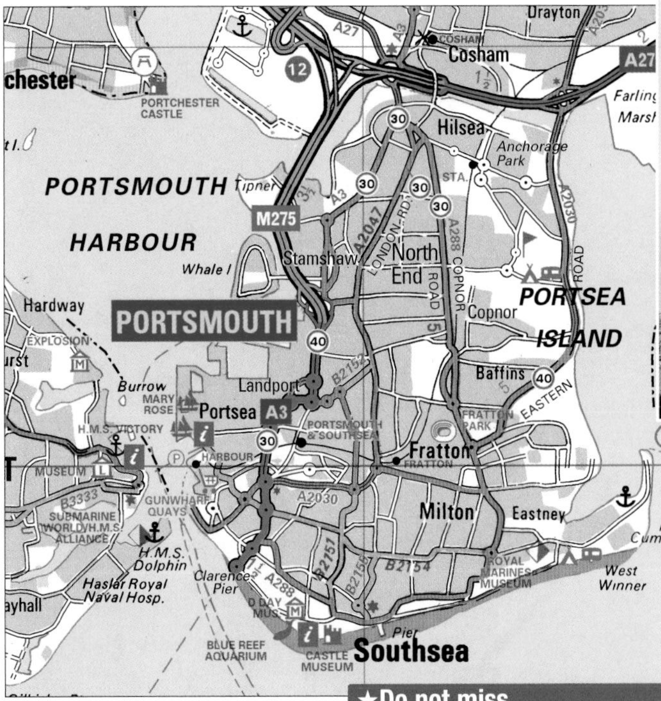

▼HMS *Warrior*

Portsmouth

The city of Portsmouth dates back to medieval times and has been home to the British Royal Navy for more than 500 years. The historic dockyard houses Nelson's flagship HMS *Victory*, HMS *Warrior*, 1860, Britain's first iron-clad battleship, the Royal Naval Museum and the remains of Henry VIII's 16th century warship, the *Mary Rose*. There is also a new interactive naval attraction – Action Stations. Other attractions include Charles Dickens' Birthplace Museum, the City Museum and the D-Day Museum. The Continental Ferry Port links the city with north-west France, northern Spain and the Channel Islands. St Thomas' Cathedral has maritime links as does the Garrison Church. Two major shopping centres serve the city – Cascades and Gunwharf Quays. The 170-m Spinnaker Tower's three viewing platforms allow views of up to 23 miles.

Tourist Information Centre,
The Hard, Portsmouth PO1 3QJ
Tel 023 9282 6722

BBC Radio Solent 96.1 FM, 999 AM • **The Quay** 107.4 FM • **Capital Gold** 1170 AM • **Ocean** 97.5 FM **Power** 103.2 FM • **Wave** 105.2 FM

www.visitportsmouth.co.uk

★Do not miss

★**HMS Victory**, HM Naval Base
★**Royal Naval Museum**, HM Naval Base
★**The Mary Rose**, HM Naval Base

Portsmouth

Action Stations ✦ A1
Admiralty Rd A1
Alfred Rd A2
Anglesea Rd B2
Arundel St B3
Bishop St A2
Broad St C1
Buckingham House C2
Burnaby Rd B2
Bus Station B1
Camber Dock C1
Cambridge Rd B2
Car Ferry to Isle of Wight B1
Cascades Shopping Centre A3
Castle Rd C3
Cathedral ✝ C1
Cathedral (RC) ✝ A3
City Museum & Art Gallery B2
Civic Offices B3
Clarence Pier C2
College of Art B3
College St B1
Commercial Rd A3
Cottage Gr B3
Cross St A1
Cumberland St A2
Duisburg Way C2
Durham St A3
East St B1
Edinburgh Rd A2
Elm Gr C3
Great Southsea St C3
Green Rd B3
Greetham St B3
Grosvenor St B3
Grove Rd North C3
Grove Rd South C3
Guildhall B3
Guildhall Walk B3
Gunwharf Quays Retail Park B1
Gunwharf Rd B1
Hambrook St C2
Hampshire Terr B2
Hanover St A1
High St C2
HM Naval Base A1
HMS Nelson (Royal Naval Barracks) A2
HMS Victory A1
HMS Warrior A1
Hovercraft Terminal C2
Hyde Park Rd B3
Information Ctr A1/B3
Isambard Brunel Rd B3
Isle of Wight Car Ferry Terminal B1
Kent Rd C3
Kent St A2
King St B3
King's Rd C3
King's Terr C2
Lake Rd A3
Law Courts B3
Library B3
Long Curtain Rd C2
Market Way A3
Marmion Rd C3
Mary Rose Exhibition A1
Mary Rose Ship Hall A1
Middle St B3
Millennium Blvd B2
Millennium Promenade A1/C1
Museum Rd B2
Naval Recreation Ground C2
Nightingale Rd C3
Norfolk St B3
North St A2
Osborne Rd C3
Park Rd B2
Passenger Catamaran to Isle of Wight B1
Passenger Ferry to Gosport B1
Pelham Rd C3
Pembroke Gdns C2
Pembroke Rd C2
Pier Rd C2
Point Battery C1
Police Station B3
Portsmouth & Southsea A3
Portsmouth Harbour B1
Post Office A1/A3/B3/C1/C3
Queen St A1
Queen's Cr C3
Round Tower ✦ C1
Royal Garrison Church C1
Royal Naval Museum A1
St Edward's Rd C3
St George's Rd B2
St George's Sq B1
St George's Way B2
St James's Rd B3
St James's St A2
St Thomas's St B2
Somers Rd B3
Southsea Com C2
Southsea Terr C2
Station St B3
Spinnaker Tower ✦ B1
Square Tower ✦ C1
Swimming Pool A2
The Hard B1
Town Fortifications ✦ C1
Unicorn Rd A2
United Services Recreation Ground B2
University of Portsmouth A2/B2
Upper Arundel St A3
Victoria Park A2
Victory Gate A1
Vue B1
Warblington St B1
Western Pde C2
White Hart Rd C1
Winston Churchill Ave B3

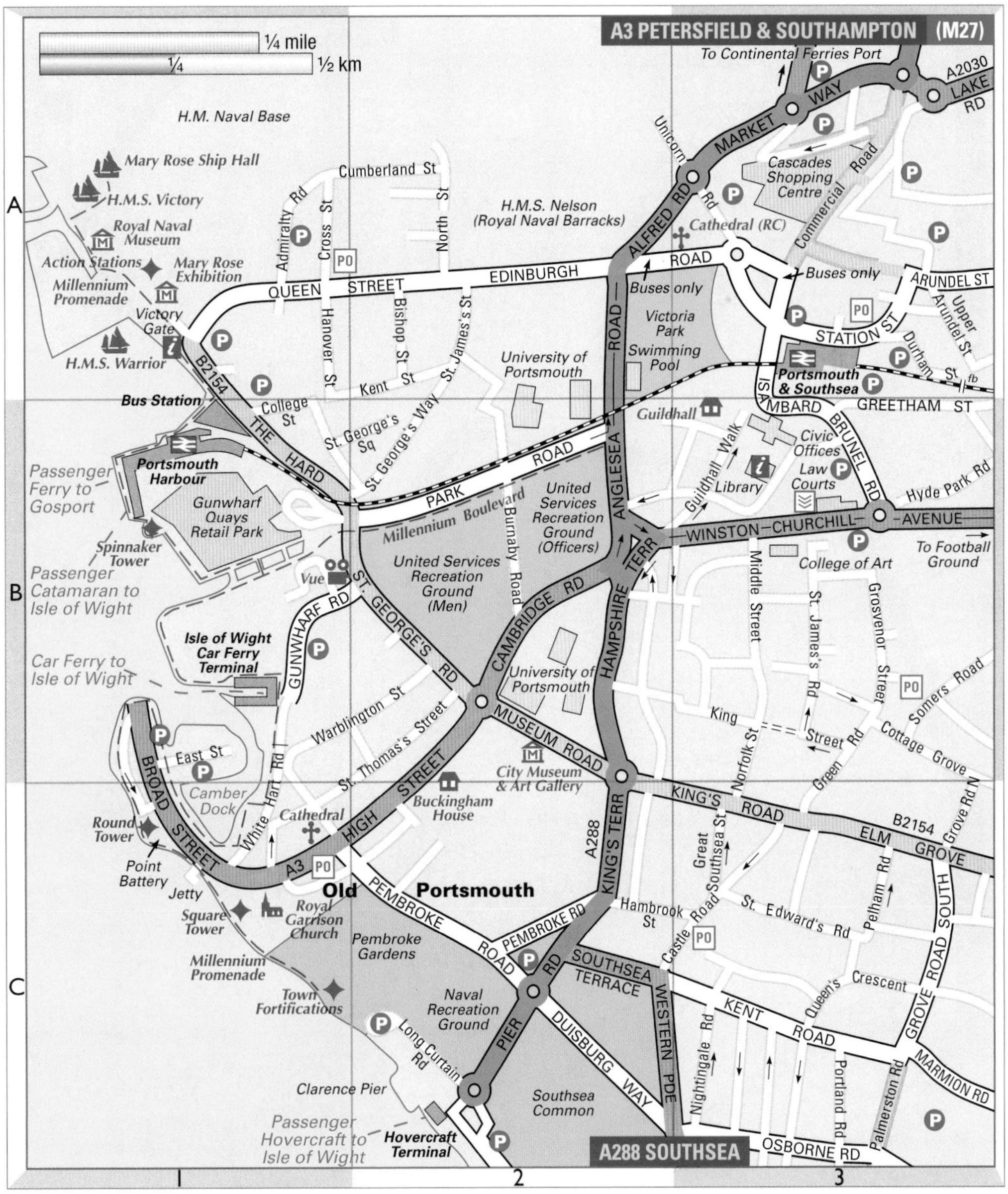

Preston

▲Preston marina

One of England's oldest boroughs, dating back to 670 AD, Preston was a wealthy market town by the 17th century and became an important cotton and textile finishing centre in the 19th century. It boasts the largest single dock basin in Europe, Riversway, containing a marina, leisure complex and shops. Interesting structures are Giles Gilbert Scott's classical Cenotaph; the 1903 neo-Baroque Sessions house; the Harris Museum and Art Gallery; Winckley Square, a Georgian development. Outdoor attractions include Avenham Park with its Japanese rock gardens. The Forest of Bowland Area of Outstanding Natural Beauty, home to a Wild Boar Park and the Beacon Fell moorland with its sculptures and visitor centre, is within easy reach. Nearby is Samlesbury Hall Tudor manor and Hoghton Tower, a 16th-century Renaissance house and the Ribble Steam Railway.

Tourist Information Centre, The Guildhall, Lancaster Road, Preston PR1 1HT Tel 01772 253731

BBC Radio Lancashire 103.9 FM
Magic 999 AM • **Rock** 97.4 FM

www.visitpreston.com

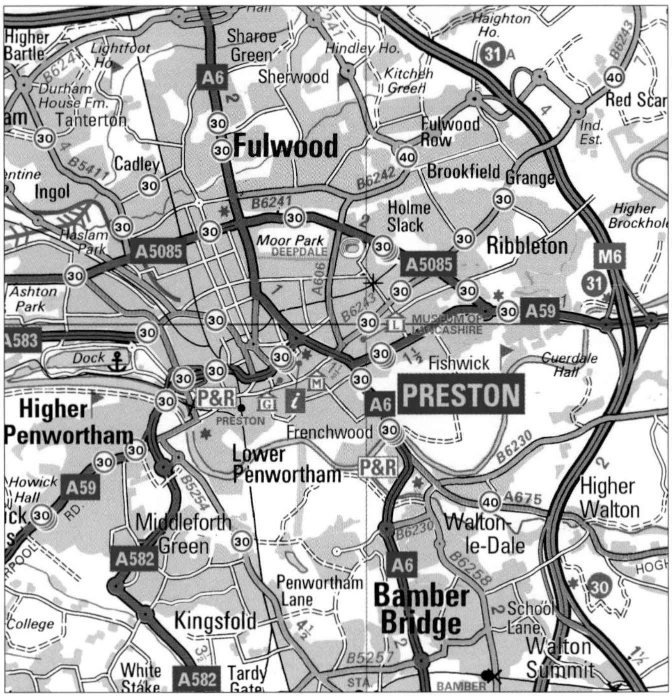

★Do not miss

★**Museum of Lancashire and Museum of the Queen's Lancashire Regiment**, Stanley Street
★**National Football Museum**, Sir Tom Finney Way, Deepdale
★**Ribble Way** – footpath from Preston estuary to Ribblehead

Preston

Adelphi St A2
Anchor Ct. B3
Aqueduct St. A1
Ardee Rd C1
Arthur St B2
Ashton St A1
Avenham La B3
Avenham Park . . . C3
Avenham Rd. B3
Avenham St B3
Bairstow St B3
Balderstone Rd . . C1
Beamont Dr A1
Beech St South . . C2
Bird St C1
Bow La B2
Brieryfield Rd . . . A1
Broadgate C1
Brook St A2
Bus Station A3
Butler St. B2
Cannon St B3
Carlton St. A1
Chaddock St B3
Channel Way B1
Chapel St B3
Christ Church St . .B2
Christian Rd. B2
Cold Bath St A2
Coleman Ct C1
Connaught Rd . . . C2
Corn Exchange B3
Corporation St. A2/B2
County Hall B2
County Records Office B2
Court. A3
Court. B3
Cricket Ground . . C2
Croft St. A1
Cross St A3
Crown Court A3
Crown St A3
East Cliff. C3
East Cliff Rd. B3
Edward St. A2
Elizabeth St A3
Euston St B1
Fishergate B2/B3
Fishergate Hill. . . .B2
Fishergate Shopping Ctr. . . .B2
Fitzroy St B1
Fleetwood St. . . . A1
Friargate A3
Fylde Rd. A1/A2
Gerrard St B2
Glover's Ct. B3
Good St B2
Grafton St B2
Great George St . A3
Great Shaw St . . . A3
Greenbank St. . . . A2
Guild Way. B1
Guildhall & Charter B3
Guildhall St B3
Harrington St . . . A2
Harris Mus B3
Hartington Rd B1
Hasset Cl C2
Heatley St. B2
Hind St. C2
Information Ctr . .B3
Kilruddery Rd . . . C1
Lancaster Rd . . A3/B3
Latham St. B3
Lauderdale St . . . C2
Lawson St A3
Leighton St A2
Leyland Rd. C1
Library A1
Library B3
Liverpool Rd C1
Lodge St. B2
Lune St. B3
Main Sprit West . .B3
Maresfield Rd . . . C1
Market St West . . A3
Marsh La B1/B2
Maudland Bank. . A2
Maudland Rd A2
Meadow Ct. C2
Meath Rd C1
Mill Hill. A2
Miller Arcade ✦ . .B3
Miller Park. C3
Moor La A3
Mount St B3
North Rd. A3
North St A3
Northcote Rd. B1
Old Milestones . . .B1
Old Tram Rd. C3
Pedder St. A1/A2
Peel St A2
Penwortham Br. . C2
Penwortham New Br C1
Pitt St B2
Playhouse A3
Police Station . . A3
Port Way B1
Post Office A1/B3//C1
Preston ⇌ B2
Ribble Bank St . . .B2
Ribble Viaduct . . . C2
Ribblesdale Pl B3
Ringway B3
River Parade C1
Riverside C2
St Georges B3
St Georges Shopping Ctr. . . .B3
St Johns B3
St Johns Shopping Ctr. . . A3
St Mark's Rd A1
St Walburges . . . A1
Salisbury Rd B1
Sessions House B3
Snow Hill A3
South End C2
South Meadow La C2
Spa Rd B1
Sports Ground. . . . C2
Strand Rd. B1
Syke St B3
Talbot Rd B1
Taylor St. C1
Tithebarn St. A3
Town Hall B3
Tulketh Brow A1
Univ of Central Lancashire A2
Valley Rd C1
Victoria St A2
Walker St A3
Walton's Parade . .B2
Warwick St. A3
Wellfield Business Park . . A1
Wellfield Rd. A1
Wellington St. . . . A1
West Cliff C2
West Strand. A1
Winckley Rd. C1
Winckley Square. .B3
Wolseley Rd. C2

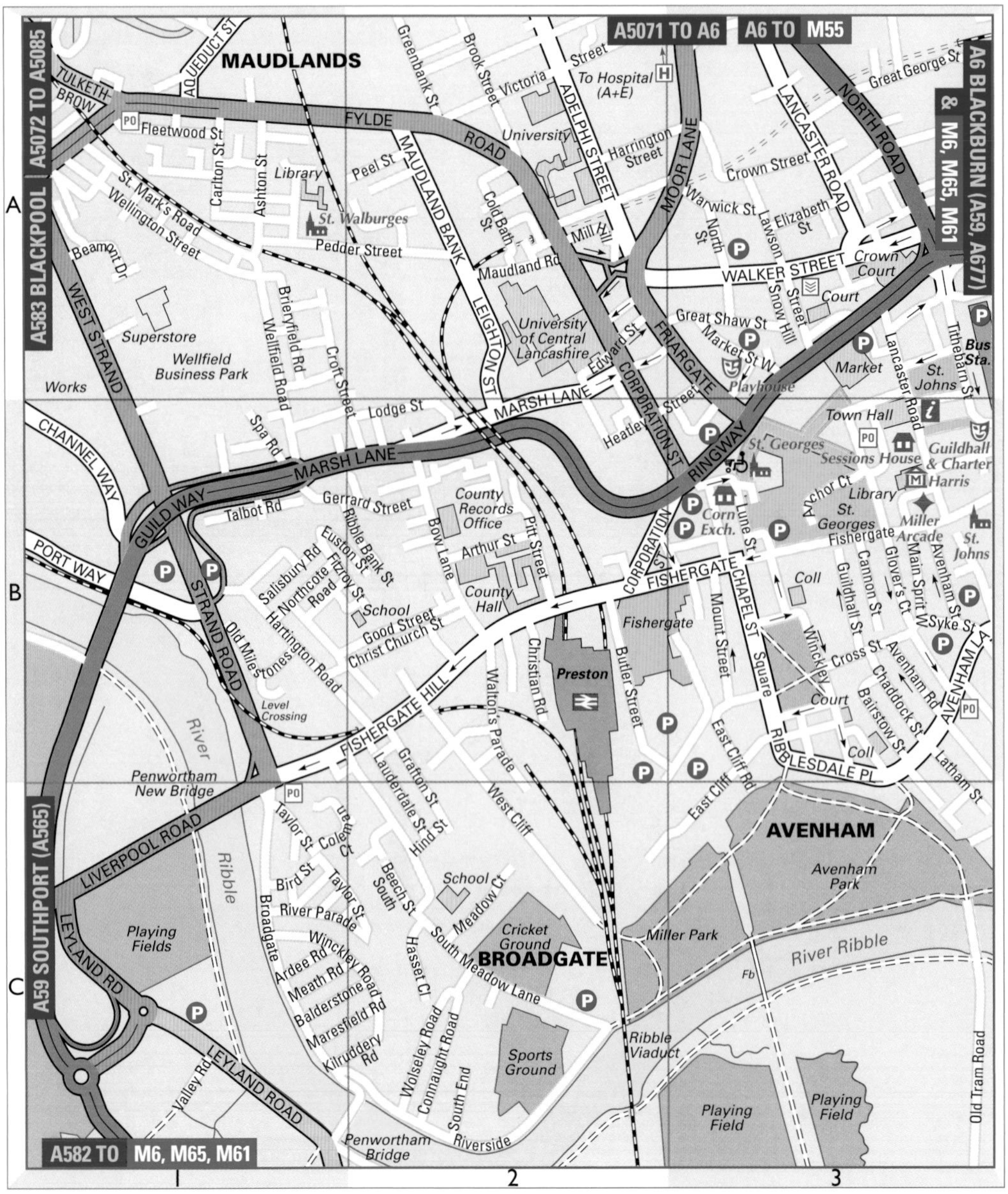

Reading

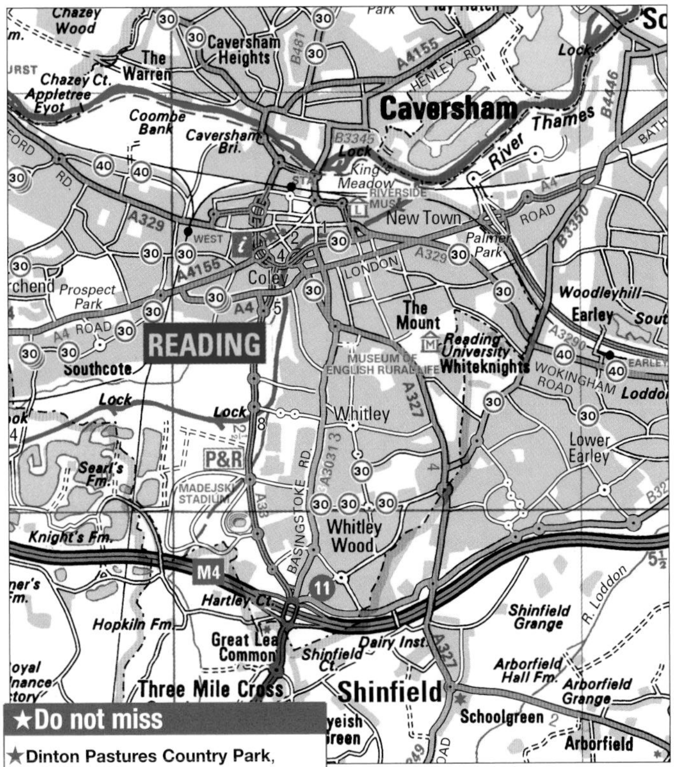

¼ mile
½ km

★Do not miss

★**Dinton Pastures Country Park**, Davis Street

★**Museum of English Rural Life**, University of Reading, Shinfield Road

★**Riverside Museum at Blake's Lock**, New Town – about the Kennet and Thames rivers

The Saxon-origin county town of Royal Berkshire, burial place of Henry I, has a wealth of medieval churches, old coaching inns and red-brick Victorian buildings, though today it's best known as a retail centre, transport hub and focus of hi-tech industry. Landmarks in its historic centre include the Gothic town hall, also home to the Museum and Art Gallery (including Roman items and a copy of the Bayeux Tapestry); Forbury Gardens, once part of Reading Abbey, the ruins of which can still be seen; and Reading Gaol, the most famous inmate of which was Oscar Wilde. The University has a museum of Greek archaeology and a museum of zoology. The nearby Herb Farm at Sonning has one of the UK's biggest collections of herbal plants and a Saxon maze, Stratfield Saye has memorabilia of the Duke of Wellington, and Mapledurham House is an Elizabethan mansion with one of the country's last working watermills.

▲The water mill at Mapledurham House

Reading Visitor Centre and Travel Shop, Church House, Chain Street, Reading RG1 2HX Tel 0118 956 6226

BBC Radio Berkshire 104.4 FM
Classic Gold 1431 AM
Reading 107 FM • **2-Ten** 97.0 FM

www.readingtourism.org.uk

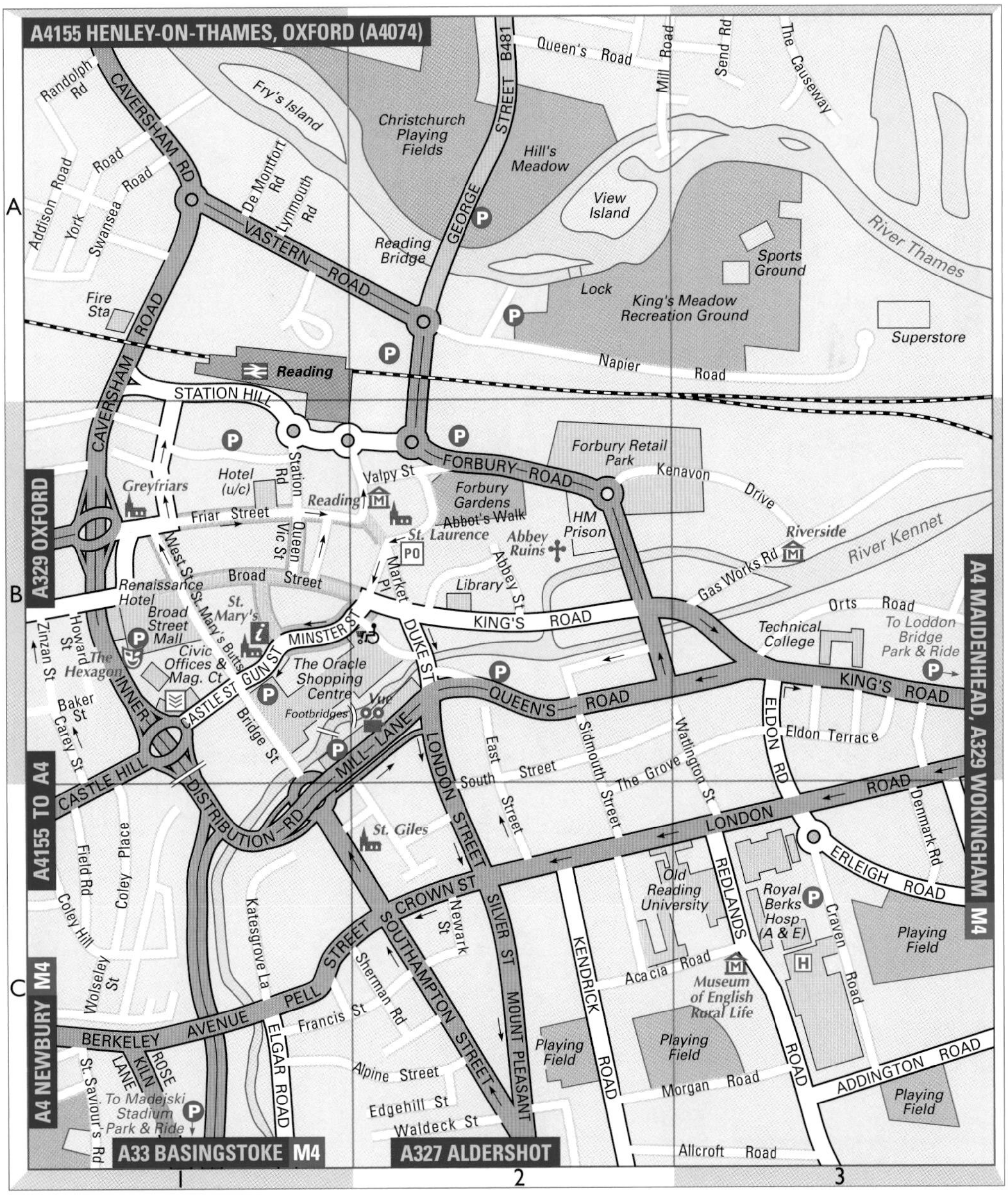

Reading

Abbey Ruins ✝ . . . B2
Abbey St. B2
Abbot's Walk B2
Acacia Rd. C2
Addington Rd . . . C3
Addison Rd A1
Allcroft Rd C3
Alpine St C2
Baker St B1
Berkeley Ave C1
Bridge St B1
Broad St. B1
Broad Street Mall . B1
Carey St B1
Castle Hill C1
Castle St. B1
Caversham Rd . . . A1
Christchurch Playing Fields . . A2
Civic Offices & Magistrate's Court. B1
Coley Hill C1
Coley Pl C1
Craven Rd C3
Crown St C2
De Montfort Rd. . . A1
Denmark Rd. C3
Duke St. B2
East St B2
Edgehill St C2
Eldon Rd. B3
Eldon Terr. B3
Elgar Rd C1
Erleigh Rd C3
Field Rd C1
Fire Station A1
Forbury Gdns. B2
Forbury Retail Pk . B2
Forbury Rd. B2
Francis St. C1
Friar St. B1
Gas Works Rd B3
George St. A2
Greyfriars ⛪ B1
Gun St. B1
Hexagon, The 🎭 . . B1
Hill's Meadow . . . A2
HM Prison B2
Howard St B1
Information Ctr ℹ . B1
Inner Distribution Rd B1
Katesgrove La . . . C1
Kenavon Dr B2
Kendrick Rd. C2
King's Meadow Rec Ground A2
King's Rd B2
Library B2
London Rd C3
London St. B2
Lynmouth Rd A1
Market Pl B2
Mill La. B2
Mill Rd A2
Minster St B1
Morgan Rd. C3
Mount Pleasant . . C2
Museum of English Rural Life 🏛 C3
Napier Rd. A2
Newark St C2
Old Reading Univ C3
Oracle Shopping Centre, The B1
Orts Rd B3
Pell St. C1
Queen Victoria St . B1
Queen's Rd A2
Queen's Rd B2
Police Station 🚓 . . B1
Post Office PO B2
Randolph Rd A1
Reading Bridge . . . A2
Reading ⇌. A1
Redlands Rd C3
Renaissance Hotel. B1
Riverside Mus 🏛 . B3
Rose Kiln La. C1
Royal Berks Hospital (A&E) H C3
St Giles ⛪ C2
St Laurence ⛪ B2
St Mary's ⛪ B1
St Mary's Butts . . B1
St Saviour's Rd . . C1
Send Rd A3
Sherman Rd. C2
Sidmouth St. B2
Silver St C2
South St B2
Southampton St . C2
Station Hill. A1
Station Rd B1
Superstore A3
Swansea Rd. A1
Technical College . B3
The Causeway A3
The Grove B2
Valpy St B2
Vastern Rd A1
Vue 🎥. B2
Waldeck St. C2
Watlington St B3
West St. B1
Wolseley St C1
York Rd. A1
Zinzan St B1

St Andrews

▲St Andrews Cathedral ruins

A picturesque royal burgh best known as the home of golf (it is the seat of the sport's main authority and home to the famous Old Course) but also the site of Scotland's oldest university, dating back to 1412. Especially noteworthy are the ruined Middle Ages archbishops' castle, and the remains of what was Scotland's largest cathedral, with a collection of Celtic and medieval carved stones and wonderful views over the town from its St Rule's tower. For nature lovers there's a Botanic Garden and Craigtoun Country Park, and local history is explored at St Andrews Museum and St Andrews Preservation Trust Museum and Garden. The wealth of attractions around the Fife coast south of St Andrews include Scotland's Secret Bunker, a remnant of the Cold War, while to the north at Guardbridge is the Eden Centre birdwatching observatory.

Kingdom of Fife Tourist Information Centre, 70 Market Street, St Andrews KY16 9NU
Tel 01334 472021

BBC Radio Scotland 94.3 FM and 810 AM • **Tay FM** 96.4, 102.8 FM
Tay AM 1161, 1584 AM

www.standrews.co.uk

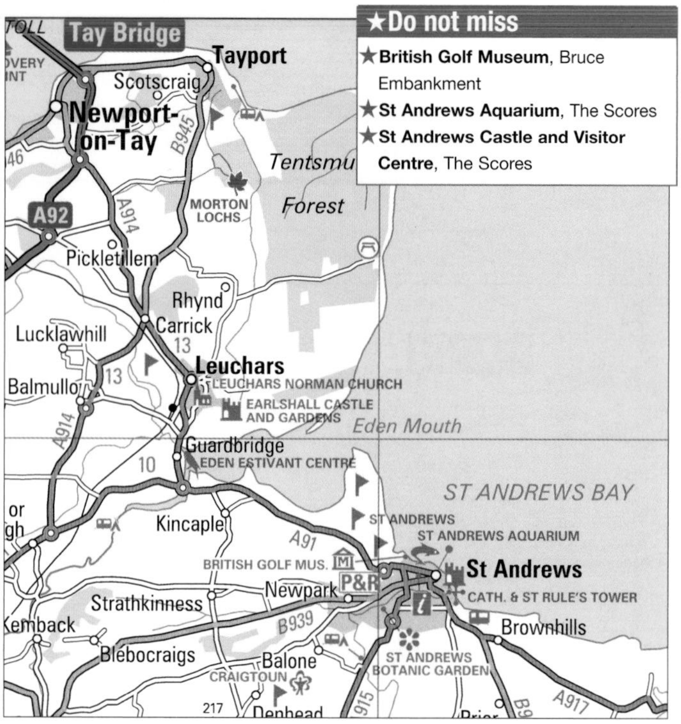

★Do not miss

★**British Golf Museum**, Bruce Embankment
★**St Andrews Aquarium**, The Scores
★**St Andrews Castle and Visitor Centre**, The Scores

St Andrews

Abbey St B2
Abbey Walk B3
Abbotsford Cres . A1
Albany Pk C3
Allan Robertson Dr C2
Ambulance Station C1
Anstruther Rd . . . C3
Argyle St B1
Argyll Business Park C1
Auld Burn Rd B2
Bassaguard Industrial Estate . B1
Bell St B2
Blackfriars Chapel (Ruins) . . B2
Boase Ave B2
Braid Cres C3
Brewster Pl C3
Bridge St B1
British Golf Museum A1
Broomfaulds Ave. C1
Bruce Embankment . . . A1
Bruce St C2
Bus Station A1
Byre B2
Canongate C1
Cathedral and Priory (Ruins) . B3
Cemetery B3
Chamberlain St . . C1
Church St B2
Churchill Cres . . . C2
City Rd A1
Claybraes C1
Cockshaugh Public Park B1
Cosmos Community Ctr . . B3
Council Office . . . A2
Crawford Arts Ctr A2
Crawford Gdns . . C1
Doubledykes Rd . . B1
Drumcarrow Rd. . C1
East Sands B3
East Scores A3
Fire Station C1
Forrest St C1
Fraser Ave C1
Freddie Tait St . . . C2
Gateway Centre. . A1
Glebe Rd B2
Golf Pl A1
Grange Rd C3
Greenside Pl B2
Greyfriars Gdns . . A2
Hamilton Ave C2
Hepburn Gdns B1
Horseleys Park . . C1
Information Ctr . B2
Irvine Cres C3
James Robb Ave . C1
James St B1
John Knox Rd . . . C1
Kennedy Gdns B1
Kilrymont Cl. C3
Kilrymont Pl. C3
Kilrymont Rd C3
Kinburn Park B1
Kinkell Terr. C3
Kinnesburn Rd . . . B2
Ladebraes Walk . . B2
Lady Buchan's Cave A3
Lamberton Pl. . . . C1
Lamond Dr C2
Langlands Rd B2
Largo Rd C1
Learmonth Pl C1
Library B2
Links Clubhouse . A1
Livingstone Cres . B2
Long Rocks A2
Madras College . . B2
Market St A2
Martyr's Monument A1
Memorial Hospital (No A&E) B3
Murray Pk A2
Murray Pl A2
Nelson St B2
New Picture House A2
North Castle St . . A3
North St A2
Old Station Rd A1
Park & Ride A1
Pilmour Links . . . A1
Pipeland Rd . . B2/C2
Police Station . A2
Post Office B2
Preservation . . . B3
Priestden Pk C3
Priestden Pl. C3
Priestden Rd C3
Queen's Gdns B2
Queen's Terr B2
Roundhill Rd C2
Royal & Ancient Golf Club A1
St Andrews B1
St Andrews Aquarium A2
St Andrews Botanic Gardens B1
St Andrews Castle (Ruins) & Visitor Centre A2
St Mary St B3
St Mary's College . B2
St Nicholas St . . . C3
St Rules Tower. . . . B3
St Salvator's Coll A2
Sandyhill Cres . . . C2
Sandyhill Rd C2
Scooniehill Rd. . . C2
Shields Ave C3
Shoolbraids C2
Sloan St B1
South St B2
Spottiswoode Gdns C1
Station Rd A1
Swilken Bridge . . A1
The Links A1
The New Course . . A1
The Old Course . . A1
The Pends B3
The Scores. A2
The Shore B3
Tom Morris Dr . . . C2
Tom Stewart La . . C1
Town Church . . . B2
Town Hall B2
Union St A2
University Chapel A2
University of St Andrews A1
University Library A2
Viaduct Walk B1
War Memorial . . . A3
Wardlaw Gdns B1
Warrack St C3
Watson Ave B2
West Port B2
West Sands A1
Westview B2
Windmill Rd A1
Winram Pl C1
Wishart Gdns C2
Woodburn Pk B3
Woodburn Pl B3
Woodburn Terr . . . B3
Younger Hall . A2

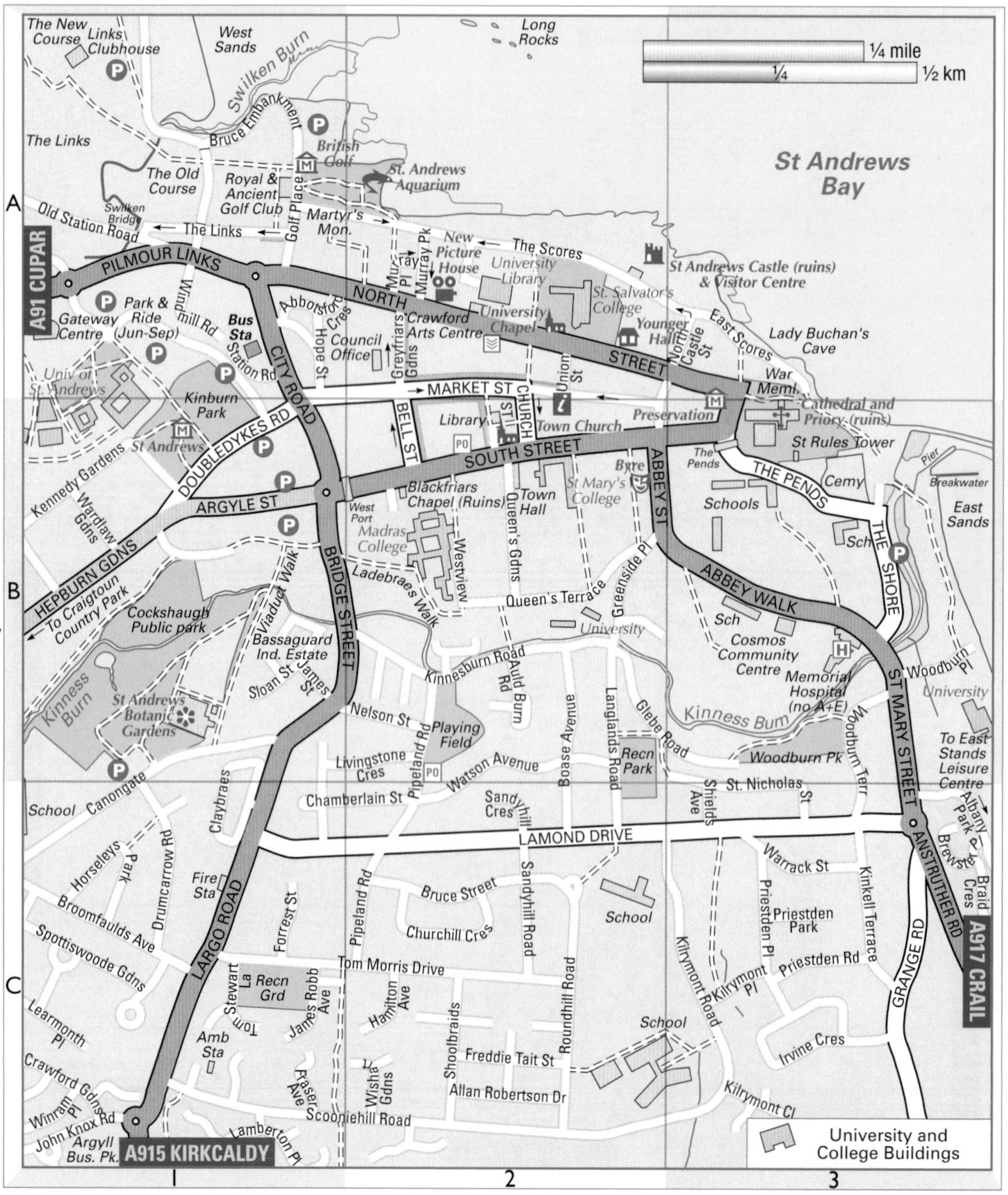

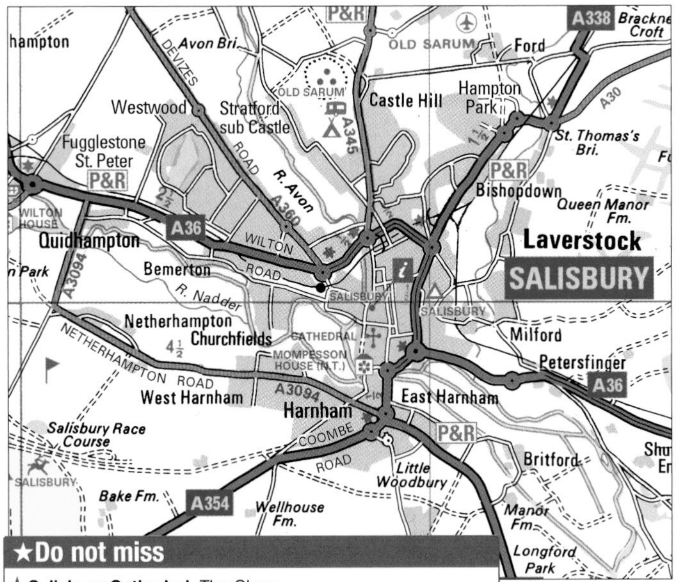

★Do not miss

★**Salisbury Cathedral**, The Close

★**Salisbury and South Wiltshire Museum**, The King's House, The Close – archaeology, costume, art

★**The Medieval Hall**, Cathedral Close – 13th-century banqueting hall including Discover Salisbury

A market town, Salisbury was founded in 1220 when the bishopric was moved there from Old Sarum. The cathedral has the tallest spire in England: at 404 feet it dominates the city. The cathedral clock's mechanism dates from 1386 and is said to be the oldest piece of machinery still at work in Britain. The city boasts many diverse places of interest such as Salisbury Arts Centre featuring music, dance, theatre and exhibitions; Mompesson House, an 18th-century period house; and The Wardrobe, the museum of the local regiment. For shopping there is the Maltings Shopping Centre, Wilton Shopping Village and Salisbury Charter Market (outdoor), plus many small independent shops. There are many pubs and bars, and the varied international cuisine on offer in the city's restaurants reflects its popularity as a tourist destination. Nearby attractions include the Wilton Carpet Factory and Wilton House.

Salisbury

▲Salisbury Cathedral

Tourist Information Centre, Fish Row, Salisbury SP1 1EJ
Tel 01722 334956

BBC Radio Wiltshire 103.5 FM
Spire 102 FM

www.visitsalisburyuk.com

Salisbury

Albany Rd A2
Arts Centre A3
Ashley Rd A1
Avon Approach A2
Ayleswade Rd C2
Bedwin St A2
Belle Vue A2
Bishop's Palace C2
Bishops Walk B2
Blue Boar Row B2
Bourne Ave A3
Bourne Hill A3
Britford La C2
Broad Walk C2
Brown St B2
Bus Station B2
Castle St A2
Catherine St B2
Chapter House B2
Church House B2
Churchfields Rd B1
Churchill Way East B3
Churchill Way North A3
Churchill Way South C2
Churchill Way West A1
City Hall B2
Close Wall B2
Coldharbour La A1
College of Further Education B3
College St A3
Council House A3
Court A1
Crane Bridge Rd B2
Crane St B2
Cricket Ground C1
Culver St South B3
De Vaux Pl C2
Devizes Rd A1
Dews Rd B1
Elm Grove B3
Elm Grove Rd A3
Endless St A2
Estcourt Rd A3
Exeter St C2
Fairview Rd A3
Fire Station A1
Fisherton St A1
Folkestone Rd C1
Fowlers Hill B3
Fowlers Rd B3
Friary Estate C3
Friary La B2
Gas La A1
Gigant St B3
Greencroft B3
Greencroft St A3
Guildhall B2
Hall of John Halle B2
Hamilton Rd A2
Harnham Mill B1
Harnham Rd C1/C2
High St B2
Hospital A1
House of John A'Port B2
Information Ctr B2
Kelsey Rd A3
King's Rd A2
Laverstock Rd B3
Library B2
London Rd A3
Lower St C1
Manor Rd A3
Marsh La A1
Medieval Hall & Discover Salisbury B2
Milford Hill B3
Milford St B3
Mill Rd B1
Millstream Approach A2
Mompesson House (N.T.) B2
New Bridge Rd C2
New Canal B2
New Harnham Rd C2
New St B2
North Canonry B2
North Gate B2
North Walk B2
Old Blandford Rd C1
Old Deanery B2
Park St A3
Parsonage Green C1
Playhouse Theatre A2
Post Office A2/B2/C2
Poultry Cross B2
Precinct B2
Queen Elizabeth Gdns B1
Queen's Rd A3
Rampart Rd B3
St Ann's Gate B2
St Ann St B2
St Marks Rd A3
St Martins B3
St Mary's Cathedral B2
St Nicholas Hospital C2
St Paul's A1
St Thomas B2
Salisbury & South Wiltshire Museum B2
Salisbury General Hospital (A&E) C2
Salisbury Station A1
Salt La A3
Saxon Rd C1
Scots La A2
Shady Bower B3
South Canonry C2
South Gate C2
Southampton Rd B2
Sports Ground C3
The Friary B3
The Maltings B2
Tollgate Rd B3
Town Path B1
Wain-a-Long Rd A3
Wardrobe, The B2
Wessex Rd A3
West Walk C2
Wilton Rd A1
Winchester St B3
Windsor Rd A1
Winston Churchill Gdns C3
Wyndham Rd A2
YHA B3
York Rd A1

¼ mile
¼ ½ km

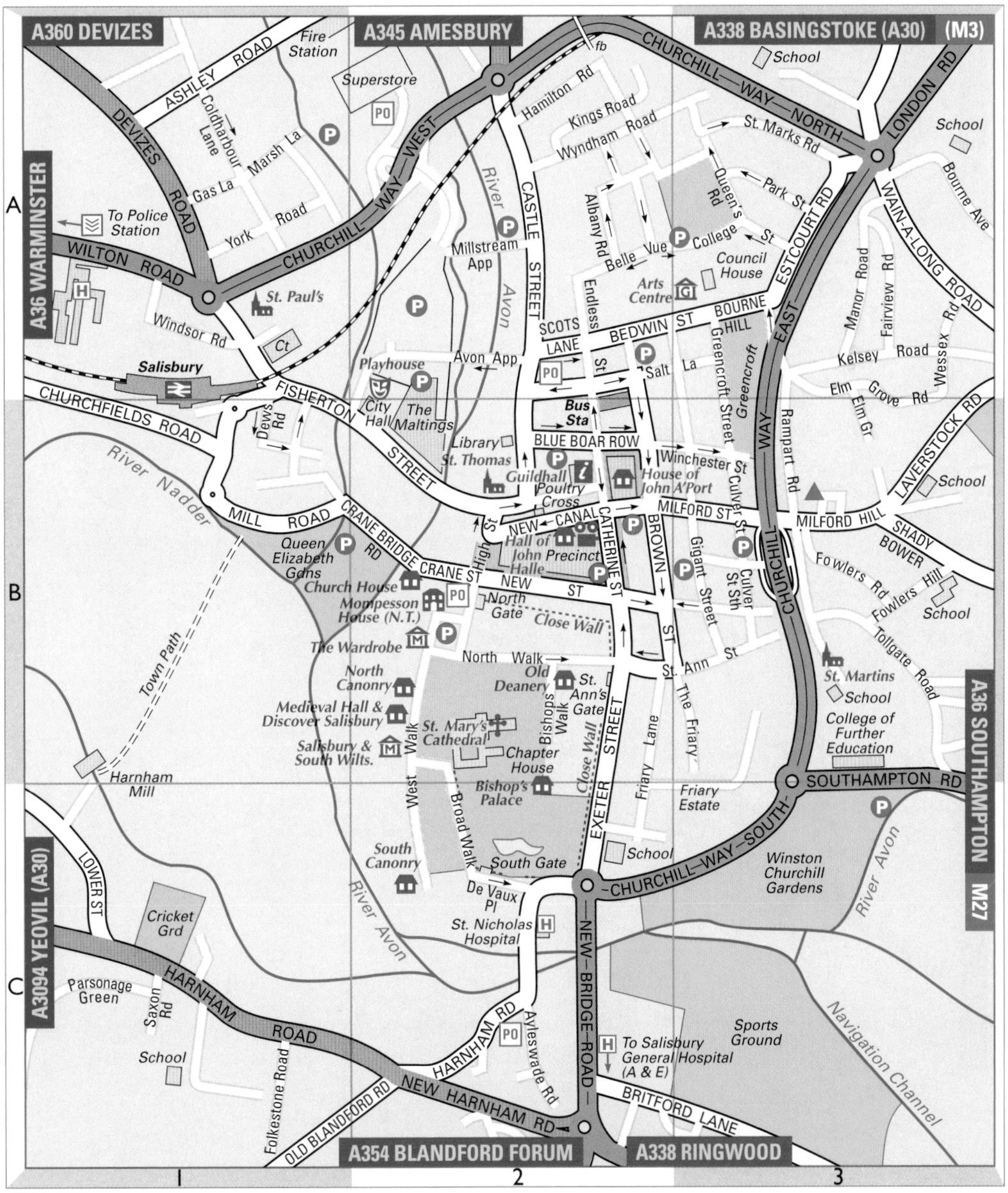

Scarborough

▲Scarborough Harbour

A busy Victorian family resort with a still-active harbour, safe, sandy beaches accessed by famous cliff-lifts, a fine esplanade, some elegant parks and gardens (including Northstead Manor Gardens with its miniature railway), a spa complex and a popular shopping centre. It is overlooked by the ruins of its 12th-century Norman castle, now the setting for mock battles, and has a magnificent church in the form of St-Martin-on-the-Hill, with superb pre-Raphaelite stained glass. Museums include the Wood End Museum of natural history (in the house where Edith Sitwell was born), the Rotunda Museum and Art Gallery, and a contemporary toy museum in the Windmill Hotel. Typical seaside attractions include Watersplash World, with 2 of the world's longest waterslides, while nearby are the Betton Visitor Centre and Animal Farm (including a honey farm and bird of prey centre) and the North York Moors National Park with its moorland, dales, woodland and spectacular coastline.

Scarborough Tourist Information Centre, Brunswick Shopping Centre, Westborough, Scarborough YO11 1UE Tel 01723 383636

BBC Radio York 95.5 FM and 1260 AM • **Yorkshire Coast Radio** 96.2, 103.1 FM • **Galaxy** 105.0 FM

www.scarborough.gov.uk

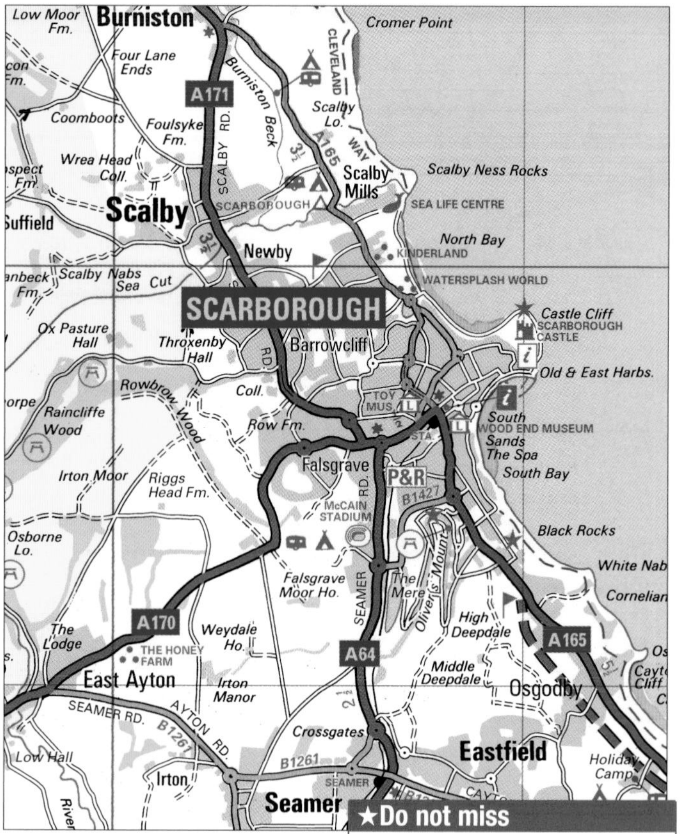

★Do not miss

★**Cleveland Way**, Scarborough to Filey

★**Kinderland**, Burniston Road – play and activity park

★**Sea Life Centre and Marine Sanctuary**, Scalby Mills Road

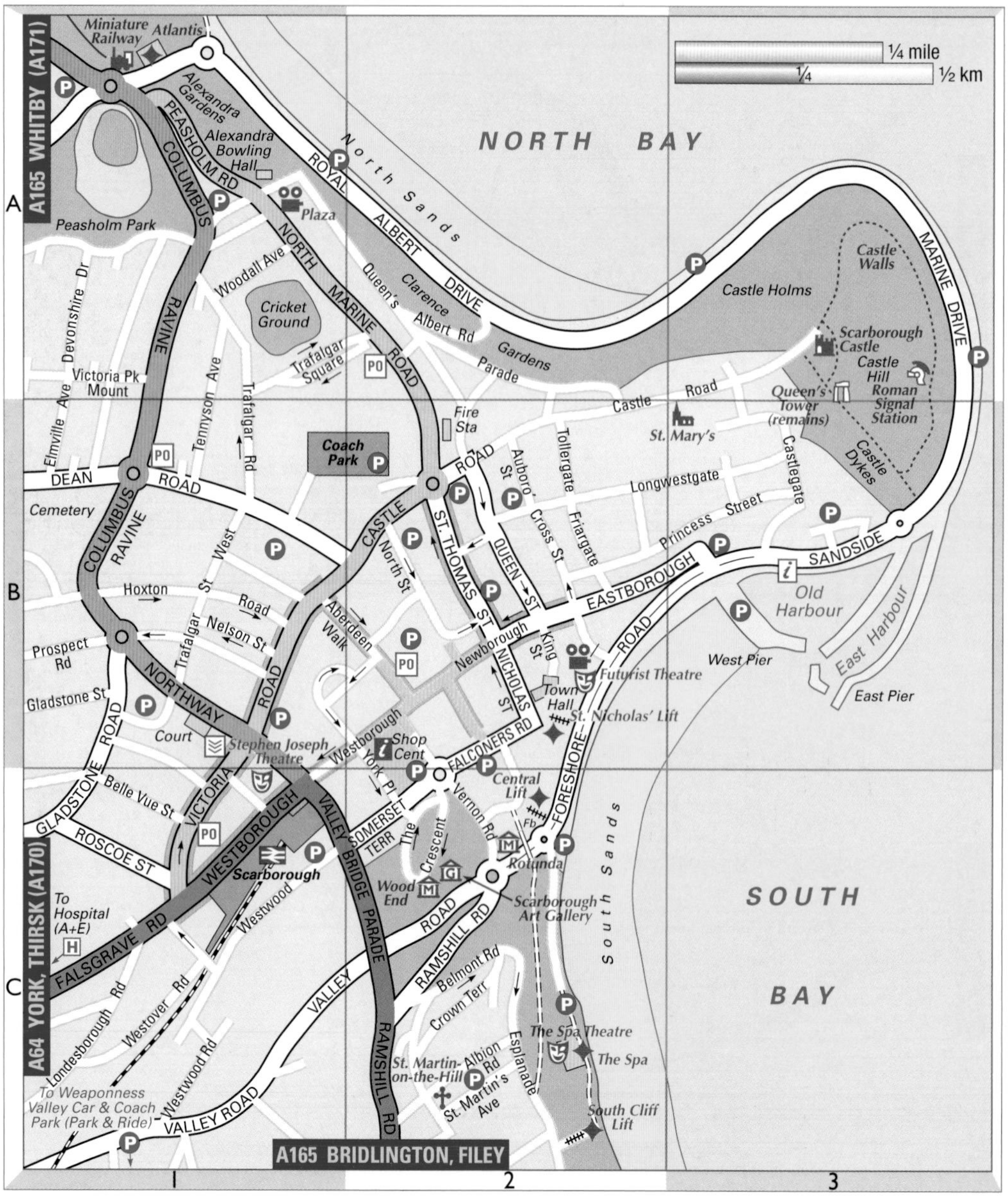

Scarborough

Aberdeen Walk . . .B2
Albert Rd A2
Albion Rd C2
Alexandra Bowling Hall . . . A1
Alexandra Gdns . . A1
Atlantis ✦ A1
Auborough St B2
Belle Vue St C1
Belmont Rd C2
Brunswick Shopping Ctr B2
Castle Dykes B3
Castlegate B3
Castle Holms A3
Castle Hill A3
Castle Rd B2
Castle Walls A3
Cemetery B1
Central Lift ✦ . . . C2
Clarence Gardens A2
Coach Park B1
Columbus Ravine A1
Court. B1
Cricket Ground . . A1
Cross St B2
Crown Terr C2
Dean Rd B1
Devonshire Dr . . . A1
East Harbour B3
East Pier. B3
Eastborough B2
Elmville Ave B1
Esplanade C2
Falconers Rd B2
Falsgrave Rd C1
Fire Station B2
Foreshore Rd. B2
Friargate B2
Futurist B2
Gladstone Rd. B1
Gladstone St B1
Hoxton Rd B1
Information Ctr B2/B3
King St B2
Londesborough Rd C1
Longwestgate B3
Marine Dr. A3
Miniature Railway A1
Nelson St B1
Newborough B2
Nicolas St. B2
North Marine Rd . A1
North St B2
Northway B1
Old Harbour. B3
Peasholm Park . . A1
Peasholm Rd A1
Plaza A1
Police Station . .B1
Post Office A2/B1/B2/C1
Princess St. B3
Prospect Rd. B1
Queen St B2
Queen's Parade. . A2
Queen's Tower (Remains) . . . A3
Ramshill Rd C2
Roman Signal Station A3
Roscoe St. C1
Rotunda C2
Royal Albert Dr . . A2
St Martin-on-the-Hill C2
St Martin's Ave . . C2
St Mary's B3
St Nicholas' Lift ✦ B2
St Thomas St B2
Sandside B3
Scarborough Art Gallery C2
Scarborough Castle A3
Scarborough . C1
Somerset Terr . . . C2
South Cliff Lift ✦ C2
Spa, The ✦ C2
Spa Theatre . . . C2
Stephen Joseph Theatre B1
Tennyson Ave. B1
The Crescent C2
Tollergate. B2
Town Hall B2
Trafalgar Rd. B1
Trafalgar Square . A1
Trafalgar St West .B1
Valley Bridge Pde C2
Valley Rd C1
Vernon Rd C2
Victoria Park Mt . A1
Victoria Rd. B1
West Pier B3
Westborough C1
Westover Rd C1
Westwood C1
Woodall Ave. A1
Wood End C2
York Pl B2

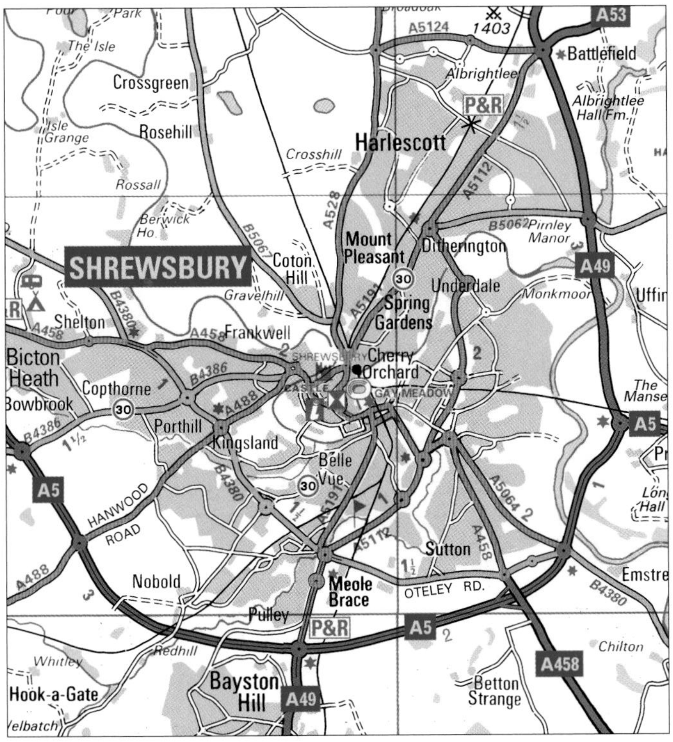

Shrewsbury

Shrewsbury is situated within a great loop of the River Severn with the sole land approach guarded by the castle. The original castle was built under the order of William the Conqueror and was rebuilt and enlarged by Edward II. The town is an important centre for artists and is home to many galleries from contemporary art to photography. There is a wealth of timber-framed and Georgian houses, steep narrow streets and little alleys with many independent shops as well as high street names, and an indoor market four days a week. The Music Hall incorporates a theatre and restaurant, and there are many other restaurants and pubs based in the centre of the town.

▲Shrewsbury from Coleham Head

★Do not miss

★**Shrewsbury Castle** (including Museum of Shropshire Regiments)
★**Shrewsbury Museum and Art Gallery**, Barker Street
★**Coleham Pumping Station**, Longden Road

Shrewsbury Tourist Information Centre, The Music Hall, The Square, Shrewsbury SY1 1LH
Tel 01743 281200

BBC Radio Shropshire 96.0 FM
Classic Gold 1017 AM
Beacon 97.2 and 103.1 FM

www.shrewsbury.gov.uk

¼ mile
¼ ½ km

Shrewsbury

Abbey Church B3
Abbey Foregate B3
Abbey Lawn Business Park B3
Abbots House B2
Agricultural Show Ground A1
Albert St. A2
Alma St. B1
Ashley St A3
Ashton Rd C1
Avondale Dr. A3
Bage Way C3
Barker St B1
Beacall's La A2
Beeches La C2
Belle Vue Gdns C2
Belle Vue Rd C2
Belmont Bank C1
Berwick Ave. A1
Berwick Rd A1
Betton St C2
Bishop St B3
Bradford St B3
Bridge St B1
Bus Station B2
Butcher Row B2
Burton St A3
Butler Rd C1
Bynner St C2
Canon St B3
Canonbury C1
Castle Business Park, The A2
Castle Foregate A2
Castle Gates B2
Castle Museum B2
Castle St. B2
Cathedral (RC) C1
Chester St A2
Cineworld C3
Claremont Bank B1
Claremont Hill B1
Cleveland St B3
Coleham Head B2
Coleham Pumping Station C2
College Hill B1
Corporation La A1
Coton Cres. A1
Coton Hill A2
Coton Mount A1
Crescent La C1
Crewe St. A2
Cross Hill B1
Darwin Centre B2
Dingle, The B1
Dogpole B2
Draper's Hall B2
English Bridge B2
Fish St B2
Frankwell B1
Gateway Ctr A2
Gravel Hill La. A1
Greyfriars Rd C2
Guildhall B1
Hampton Rd. A3
Haycock Way C3
HM Prison B2
Hereford Rd C3
High St B1
Hills La B1
Holywell St. B3
Hunter St A1
Information Ctr B1
Ireland's Mansion & Bear Steps B1
John St. A3
Kennedy Rd C1
King St B3
Kingsland Br C1
Kingsland Br (toll) C1
Kingsland Rd C1
Library B2
Lime St. C2
Longden Coleham C2
Longden Rd C1
Longner St. B1
Luciefelde Rd C1
Mardol B1
Market B1
Monkmoor Rd B3
Moreton Cr C2
Mount St A1
Music Hall B1
New Park Cl. A3
New Park Rd A2
New Park St. A3
North St A2
Oakley St C1
Old Coleham C2
Old Market Hall B1
Old Potts Way C3
Parade Centre B2
Police Station B1
Post Office A2/B1/B2/B3
Pride Hill B1
Pride Hill Centre B1
Priory Rd B1
Queen St A3
Raby Cr. C2
Rad Brook C1
Rea Brook C3
Riverside B1
Roundhill La A1
Rowley's House B1
St Alkmund's B2
St Chad's B1
St Chad's Terr B1
St John's Hill B1
St Julians Friars C2
St Mary's B2
St Mary's St B2
Scott St. C3
Severn Bank A3
Severn St A2
Shrewsbury B2
Shrewsbury High School for Girls C1
Shrewsbury Sch C1
Shrewsbury Town F.C. B2
Shropshire Wildlife Trust B3
Smithfield Rd. B1
South Hermitage C1
Swan Hill B1
Sydney Ave. A3
Tankerville St. B3
The Dana B2
The Quarry B1
The Square B1
Tilbrook Dr A3
Town Walls C1
Trinity St. C2
Underdale Rd B3
Victoria Ave B1
Victoria Quay B1
Victoria St B2
Welsh Bridge B1
Whitehall St. B3
Wood St A2
Wyle Cop B2

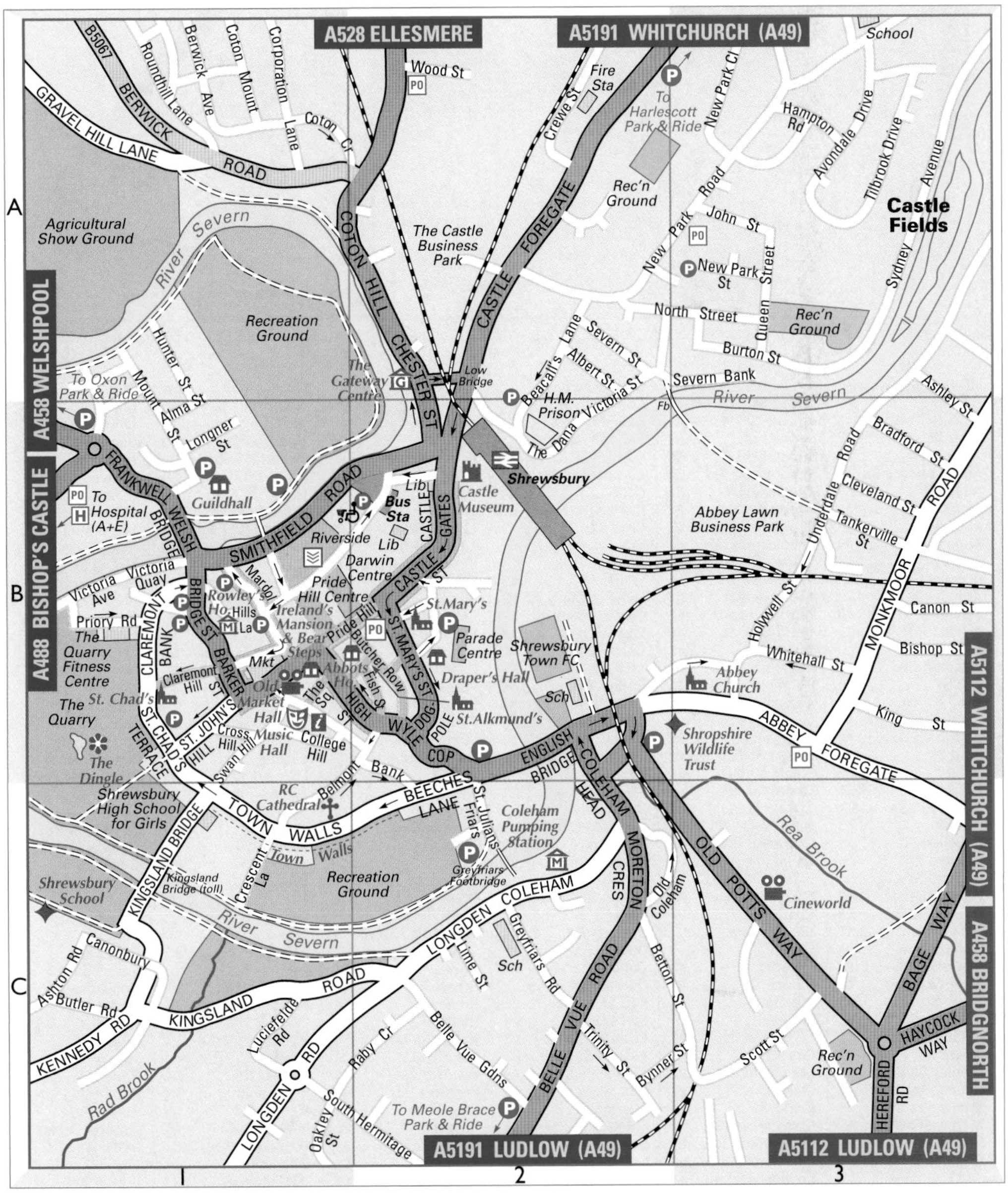

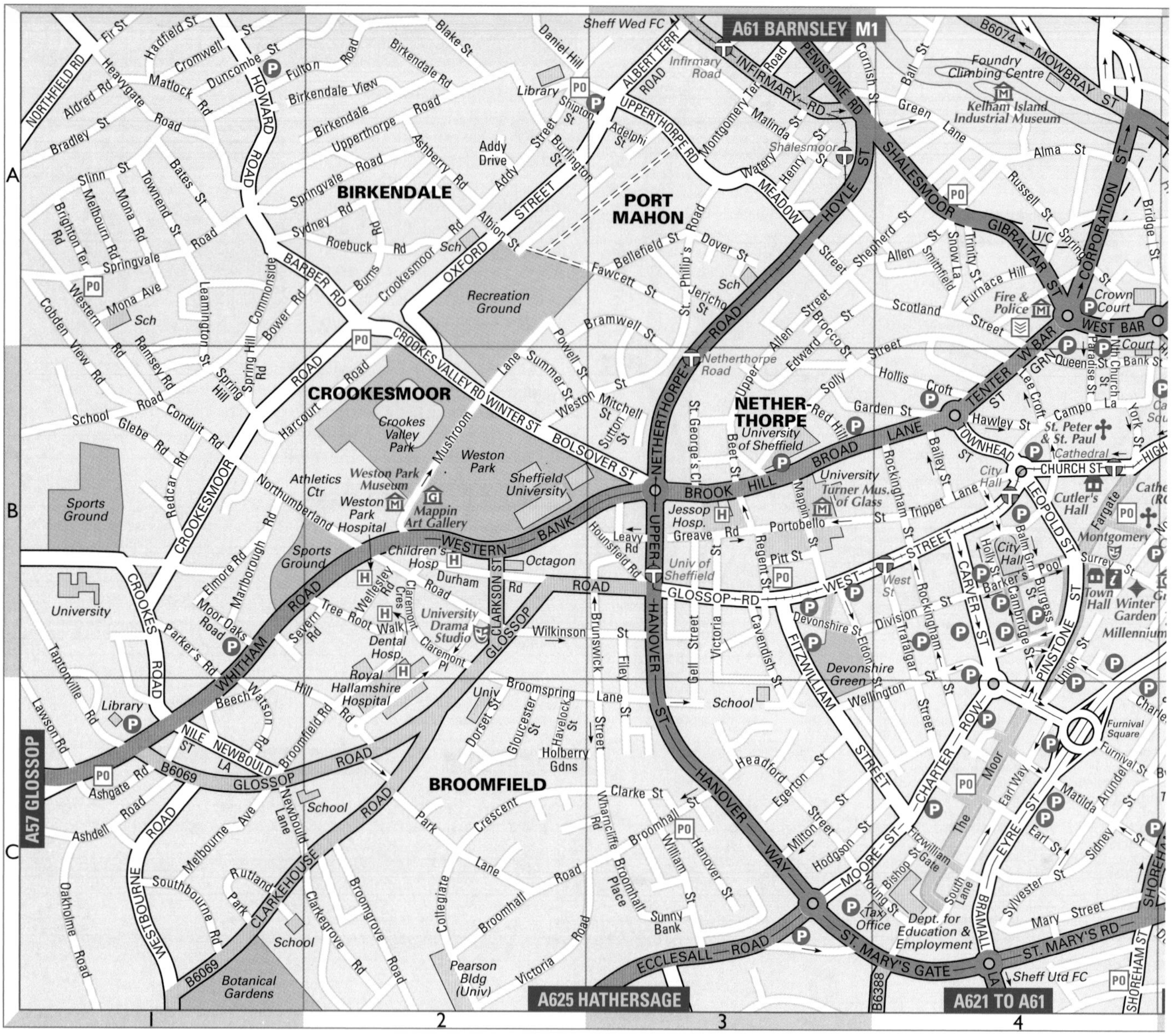

Sheffield

Addy Dr A2
Addy St A2
Adelphi St A3
Albert Terrace Rd A3
Albion St A2
Aldred Rd A1
Allen St A4
Alma St A4
Angel St B5
Arundel Gate B5
Arundel St C4
Ashberry Rd A2
Ashdell Rd C1
Ashgate Rd C1
Attercliffe Rd A6
Ball St A4
Balm Green B4
Bank St B4
Barber Rd A2
Bard St B5
Barker's Pool B4
Bates St A1
Beech Hill Rd C1
Beet St B3
Bellefield St A3
Bernard Rd A6
Bernard St B6
Birkendale A2
Birkendale Rd A2
Birkendale View A1
Bishop St C4
Blackwell Pl B6
Blake St A2
Blonk St A5
Bolsover St B2
Botanical Gdns C1
Bower Rd A1
Bradley St A1
Bramall La C4
Bramwell Gdns B3
Bramwell St A3
Bridge St A4/A5
Brighton Terrace Rd A1
Broad La B3
Broad St B6
Brocco St A3
Brook Hill B3
Broomfield Rd C1
Broomgrove Rd C2
Broomhall Pl C3
Broomhall Rd C2
Broomhall St C3
Broomspring La C2
Brown St C5
Brunswick Rd A5
Brunswick St B3
Burgess St B4
Burlington St A2
Burns Rd A2
Bus/Coach Station B5
Cadman St A6
Cambridge St B4
Campo La B4
Carver St B4
Castle Market B5
Castle Square (Tram Station) B5
Castlegate A5
Cathedral (RC) ✝ B4
Cathedral (Tram Station) B4
Cavendish St B3
Charles St C4
Charter Row C4
Children's Hospital 🏥 B2
Church St B4
City Hall B4
City Hall (Tram Station) B4
City Rd C6
Claremont Cr B2
Claremont Pl B2
Clarke St C3
Clarkegrove Rd C2
Clarkehouse Rd C1
Clarkson St B2
Cobden View Rd A1
Collegiate Cr C2
Commercial St B5
Commonside A1
Conduit Rd B1
Cornish St A3
Corporation St A4
Court B4
Cricket Inn Rd B6
Cromwell St A1
Crookes Rd B1
Crookes Valley Park B2
Crookes Valley Rd B2
Crookesmoor Rd A2
Crown Court A4
Crucible Theatre B5
Cutlers Gate A6
Cutler's Hall B4
Daniel Hill A2
Dental Hospital 🏥 B2
Dept for Education & Employment C4
Destination Sheffield B5
Devonshire Green B3
Devonshire St B3
Division St B4
Dorset St C2
Dover St A3
Duchess Rd C5
Duke St B5
Duncombe St A1
Durham Rd B2
Earl St C4
Earl Way C4
Ecclesall Rd C3
Edward St B3
Effingham Rd A6
Effingham St A6
Egerton St C3
Eldon St B3
Elmore Rd B1
Exchange St B5
Eyre St C4
Fargate B4
Farm Rd C5
Fawcett St A3
Filey St B3
Fire & Police Museum A4
Fitzalan Sq/Ponds Forge (Tram Station) B5
Fitzwater Rd C6
Fitzwilliam Gate C4
Fitzwilliam St B3
Flat St B5
Foley St A6
Foundry Climbing Centre A4
Fulton Rd A1
Furnace Hill A4
Furnival Rd A5
Furnival Sq C4
Furnival St C4
Garden St B3
Gell St B3
Gibraltar St A4
Glebe Rd B1
Glencoe Rd C6
Glossop Rd B2/B3/C1
Gloucester St C2
Granville Rd C6
Granville Rd/Sheffield College (Tram Station) C5
Graves Gallery B5
Greave Rd B3
Green La A4
Hadfield St A1
Hallam University B5
Hanover St C3
Hanover Way C3
Harcourt Rd B1
Harmer La B5
Havelock St C2
Hawley St B4
Haymarket B5
Headford St C3
Heavygate Rd A1
Henry St A3
High St B4
Holberry Gdns C2
Hollis Croft B4
Holly St B4
Hounsfield Rd B3
Howard Rd A1
Hoyle St A3
Hyde Park (Tram Station) A6
Infirmary Rd A3
Infirmary Rd (Tram Station) A3
Jericho St A3
Jessop Hospital 🏥 B3
Johnson St A5
Kelham Island Industrial Museum A4
Leadmill Rd C5
Leadmill St C5
Leamington St A1
Leavy Rd B3
Lee Croft B4
Leopold St B4
Leveson St A6
Library A2
Library B5
Library C1
Lyceum Theatre B5
Malinda St A3
Maltravers St A5
Manor Oaks Rd B6
Mappin St B3
Marlborough Rd B1
Mary St C4
Matilda St C4
Matlock Rd A1
Meadow St A3
Melbourn Rd A1
Melbourne Ave C1
Millennium Galleries B5
Milton St C3
Mitchell St B3
Mona Ave A1
Mona Rd A1
Montgomery Terrace Rd A3
Montgomery Theatre B4
Monument Gdns C6
Moor Oaks Rd B1
Moore St C3
Mowbray St A4
Mushroom La B2
Netherthorpe Rd B3
Netherthorpe Rd (Tram Station) B3
Newbould La C1
Nile St C1
Norfolk Park Rd C6
Norfolk Rd C6
Norfolk St B4
North Church St B4
Northumberland Rd B1
Nursery St A5
Oakholme Rd C1
Octagon B2
Odeon B5
Old St B6
Oxford St A2
Paradise St B4
Park La C2
Park Sq B5
Parker's Rd B1
Penistone Rd A3
Pinstone St B4
Pitt St B3
Police Station A4/B5
Pond Hill B5
Pond St B5
Ponds Forge Sports Centre B5
Portobello St B3
Post Office B5/C4
Powell St A2

¼ mile
¼ ½ km

Queen St B4
Queen's Rd C5
Ramsey Rd B1
Red Hill B3
Redcar Rd B1
Regent St B3
Rockingham St B4
Roebuck Rd A2
Royal Hallamshire Hospital 🏥 C2
Russell St A4
Rutland Park C1
St George's Cl B3
St Mary's Gate C3
St Mary's Rd C4/C5
St Peter & St Paul Cathedral ✝ B4
St Philip's Rd A3
Savile St A5
School Rd B1
Scotland St A4
Severn Rd B1
Shalesmoor A4
Shalesmoor (Tram Station) A3
Sheaf Sq C5
Sheffield Ice Sports Centre C5
Sheffield Parkway A6
Sheffield Station C5
Sheffield Station/Sheffield Hallam University (Tram Station) B5
Sheffield University B2
Shepherd St A3
Shipton St A2
Shoreham St C4
Showroom, The C5
Shrewsbury Rd C5
Sidney St C4
Slinn St A1
Smithfield A4
Snig Hill A5
Snow La A4
Solly St B3
South La C4
South St B5
Southbourne Rd C1
Spital Hill A5
Spital St A5
Spring Hill B1
Spring Hill Rd B1
Spring St A4
Springvale Rd A1
Stafford Rd C6
Stafford St B6
Stanley St A5
Stone Gr B2
Suffolk Rd C5
Summer St B2
Sunny Bank C3
Surrey St B4
Sussex St A6
Sutton St B3
Sydney Rd A2
Sylvester St C4
Talbot St B5
Taptonville Rd B1
Tax Office C4
Tenter St B4
The Leadmill C5
The Moor C4
Town Hall B4
Townend St A1
Townhead St B4
Trafalgar St B4
Tree Root Walk B2
Trinity St A4
Trippet La B4

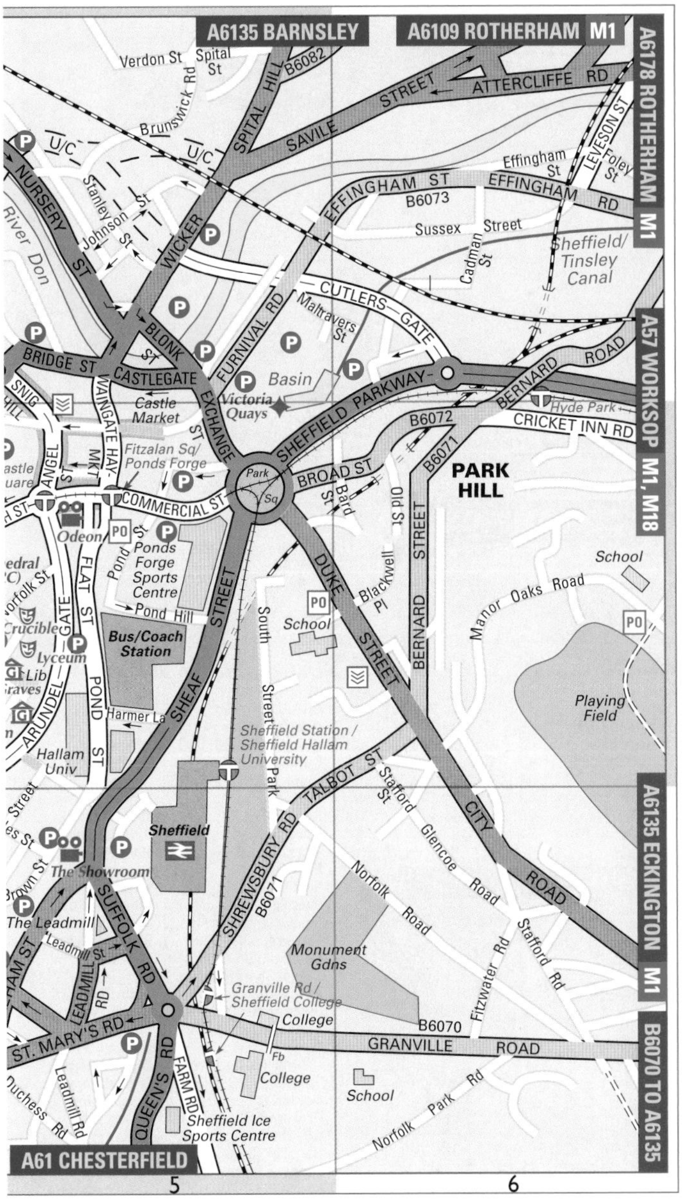

Sheffield

A former steel-producing and coal-mining city where industrial heritage rubs shoulders with a surprising array of green spaces, from Ecclesall Woods to the Botanical Gardens, Graves Park, with its bird and sculpture trail and animal farm, and Heeley City Farm and environmental study centre. Recent regeneration includes the creation of the award-winning Peace Garden public square. Museums and galleries include Graves Art Gallery (19th- and 20th-century modern art), Turner Museum of Glass, Weston Park Museum, the Fire and Police Museum, the Kelham Island Museum and Traditional Heritage Museum of local history, and the Sheffield Bus Museum at Tinsley. Buildings of interest include the medieval cathedral, Sheffield Manor Lodge, where Mary Queen of Scots was held for 14 years, Bishop's House, the city's oldest surviving half-timbered house (with a museum), the remains of 12th-century Beauchief Abbey, the Victorian Birley Spa in Hackenthorpe, and the Abbeythorpe Industrial Hamlet, an 18th-century scythe works. The stunning Peak District National Park is a few miles away.

▲The Botanical Gardens

Destination Sheffield, 12 Norfolk Row, Sheffield, S1 2PA
Tel 0114 221 1900

BBC Radio Sheffield 104.1, 88.6 FM
Hallam 97.4 FM • **Galaxy** 105.6 FM
Magic 990, 1305, 1548 AM
Real Radio Yorkshire 107.7 FM

www.sheffield.gov.uk

★Do not miss

★**Hillsborough Walled and Wildlife Garden**, Middlewood Road, Hillsborough Park
★**Millennium Galleries**, Arundel Gate – art and design
★**Winter Garden**, Surrey Street – temperate glasshouse

Turner Museum of Glass B3
Union St.........B4
University Drama Studio B2
University of Sheffield (Tram Station)...B3
Upper Allen St... A3
Upper Hanover St..............B3
Upperthorpe Rd......... A2/A3
Verdon St....... A5
Victoria Quays ✦ .B5
Victoria Rd...... C2
Victoria St B3
Waingate B5
Watery St....... A3
Watson Rd...... C1
Wellesley Rd B2
Wellington St.... C3
West Bar........ A4
West Bar Green.. A4
West St.........B3
West St (Tram Station)...B4
Westbourne Rd.. C1
Western Bank B2
Western Rd A1
Weston Park B2
Weston Park Hospital B2
Weston Park Museum B2
Weston St........B2
Wharncliffe Rd .. C3
Whitham Rd......B1
Wicker A5
Wilkinson St B2
William St C3
Winter Garden✦ ..B4
Winter St B2
York St B4
Young St........ C4

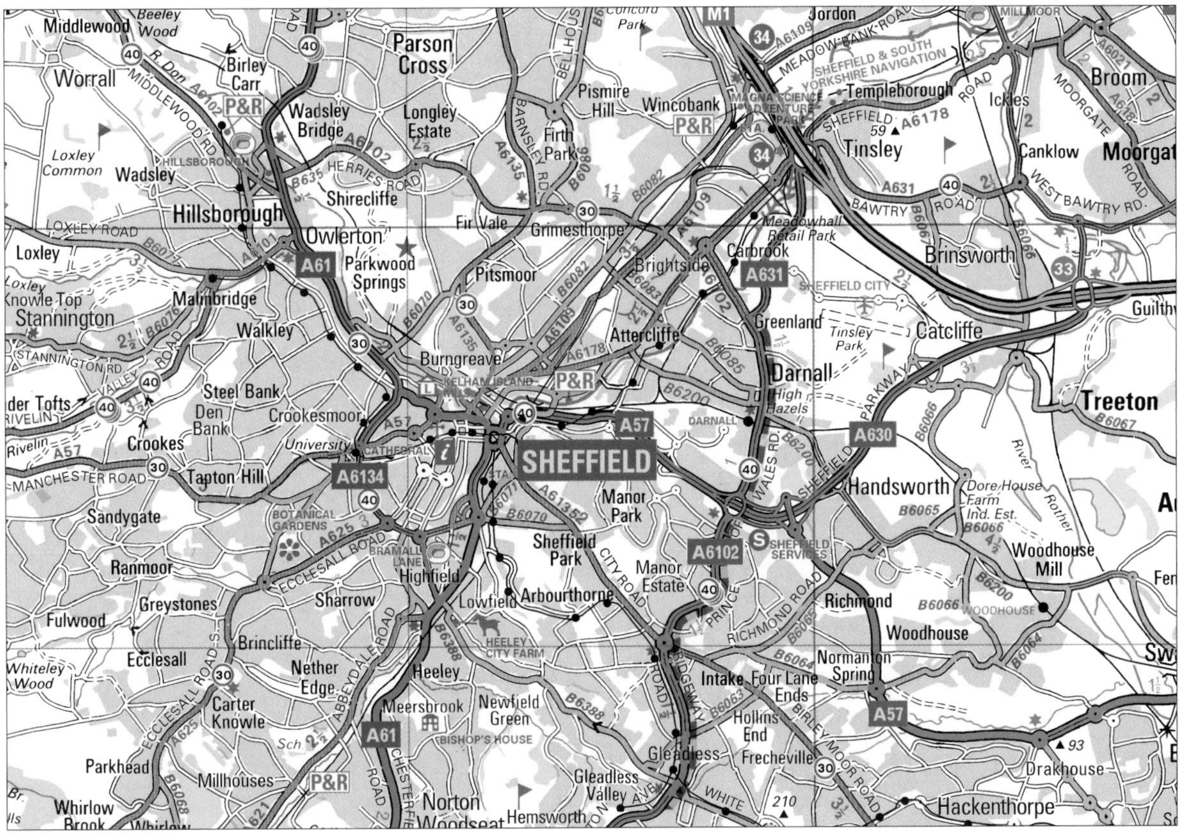

Southampton

A port of Saxon origins with some of the country's best-preserved medieval walls. It was through the Westgate that Henry V set out for Agincourt and the Pilgrim Fathers for America, while the Maritime Museum in a medieval warehouse charts Southampton's rich maritime history. Other sights include the Medieval Merchant's House, God's House Tower Museum of Archaeology, Hall of Aviation and the Millais and John Hansard art galleries. Shopping, from big retail stores to smaller independent outlets, is a high point and Ocean Village is one of the UK's biggest marina developments. Among nearby attractions are the New Forest and the ruins of 13th–century Netley Abbey.

▲*Queen Mary 2*

Southampton City Information, 9 Civic Centre Road, Southampton SO14 7FJ Tel 023 8083 3333

BBC Radio Solent 96.1 FM and 999 AM • **Capital Gold** 1447 AM **Ocean** 97.5FM • **Power** 103.2 FM **The Saint** 107.8 FM • **Wave** 105.2 FM

www.southampton.gov.uk

★Do not miss

★**Hall of Aviation**, Albert Road South
★**Maritime Museum**, Town Quay
★**Southampton City Art Gallery**, Civic Centre, Commercial Road
★**Titanic Trail** – city centre

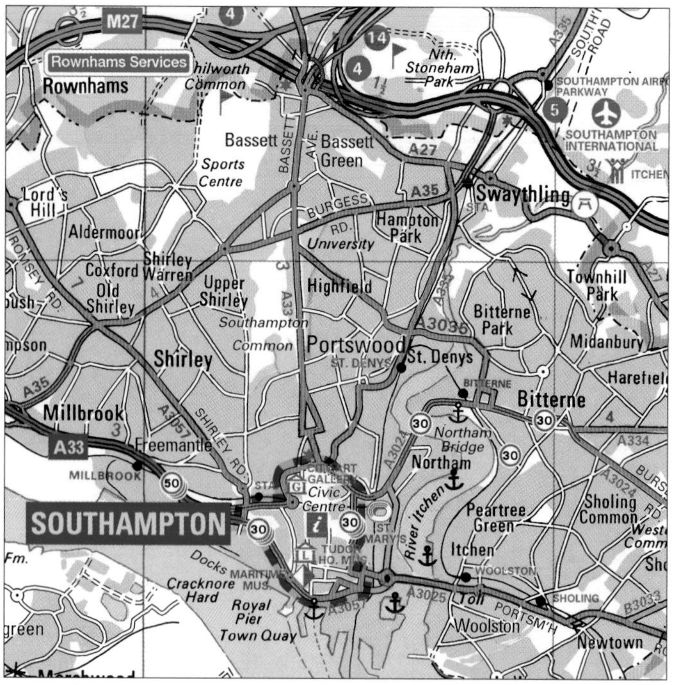

Southampton

- Above Bar St A2
- Albert Rd North B3
- Albert Rd South C3
- Anderson's Rd B3
- Argyle Rd A2
- Arundel Tower ✦ B1
- Bargate, The ✦ B2
- Bargate Centre B2
- BBC Regional Ctr A1
- Bedford Pl A1
- Belvidere Rd A3
- Bernard St C2
- Blechynden Terr A1
- Brazil Rd C3
- Brinton's Rd A2
- Britannia Rd A3
- Briton St C2
- Brunswick Pl A2
- Bugle St C1
- Canute Rd C3
- Castle Way C2
- Catchcold Twr ✦ B1
- Central Bridge C3
- Central Rd C2
- Channel Way C3
- Chapel Rd B3
- Cineworld C3
- City Art Gallery A1
- City College B3
- Civic Centre A1
- Civic Centre Rd A1
- Coach Station B1
- Commercial Rd A1
- Cumberland Pl A1
- Cunard Rd C2
- Derby Rd A3
- Devonshire Rd A1
- Dock Gate 4 C2
- Dock Gate 8 B1
- East Park A2
- East Park Terr A2
- East St B2
- East St Shopping Centre B2
- Endle St B3
- European Way C2
- Fire Station A2
- Floating Bridge Rd C3
- God's House Tower Museum of Archaeology C2
- Golden Gr A3
- Graham Rd A2
- Guildhall A1
- Hanover Bldgs B2
- Harbour Lights C3
- Harbour Pde B1
- Hartington Rd A3
- Havelock Rd A1
- Henstead Rd A1
- Herbert Walker Ave B1
- High St B2
- Hoglands Park B2
- Holy Rood (Rems), Merchant Navy Memorial B2
- Hospital A2
- Houndwell Pl B2
- Hythe Ferry C2
- Information Ctr A1
- Isle of Wight Ferry Terminal C1
- James St B3
- Java Rd C3
- Kingsland Market B2
- Kingsway A2
- Leisure World B1
- Library A1
- Lime St B2
- London Rd A2
- Marine Pde B3
- Maritime C1
- Marsh La B2
- Mayflower Memorial ✦ C1
- Mayflower Park C1
- Mayflower Theatre, The A1
- Medieval Merchant's House C1
- Melbourne St B3
- Millais A2
- Morris Rd A1
- Neptune Way C3
- New Rd A2
- Nichols Rd A3
- Northam Rd A3
- Ocean Dock C2
- Ocean Village Marina C3
- Ocean Way C3
- Odeon B1
- Ogle Rd B1
- Old Northam Rd A2
- Orchard La B2
- Oxford Ave A2
- Oxford St C2
- Palmerston Park A2
- Palmerston Rd A2
- Parsonage Rd A3
- Peel St A3
- Platform Rd C2
- Police Station A1
- Portland Terr B1
- Post Office A2/A3/B2
- Pound Tree Rd B2
- Quays Swimming & Diving Complex B1
- Queen's Park C2
- Queen's Peace Fountain ✦ A2
- Queen's Terr C2
- Queen's Way B2
- Radcliffe Rd A3
- Rochester St A3
- Royal Pier C1
- St Andrew's Rd A2
- St Mary St A2
- St Mary's B3
- St Mary's Leisure Centre A2
- St Mary's Pl B2
- St Mary's Rd A2
- St Mary's Stadium (Southampton F.C.) A3
- St Michael's C1
- Solent Sky C3
- South Front B2
- Southampton Central A1
- Southampton Solent University A2
- Southhampton Oceanography Centre ✦ C3
- SS Shieldhall C2
- Terminus Terr C2
- The Mall, Marlands A1
- The Polygon A1
- Threefield La B2
- Titanic Engineers' Memorial ✦ A2
- Town Quay C1
- Town Walls B2
- Tudor House C1
- Vincent's Walk B2
- West Gate C1
- West Marlands Rd A1
- West Park A1
- West Park Rd A1
- West Quay Rd B1
- West Quay Retail Park B1
- West Quay Shopping Ctr B1
- West Rd C2
- Western Esplanade B1

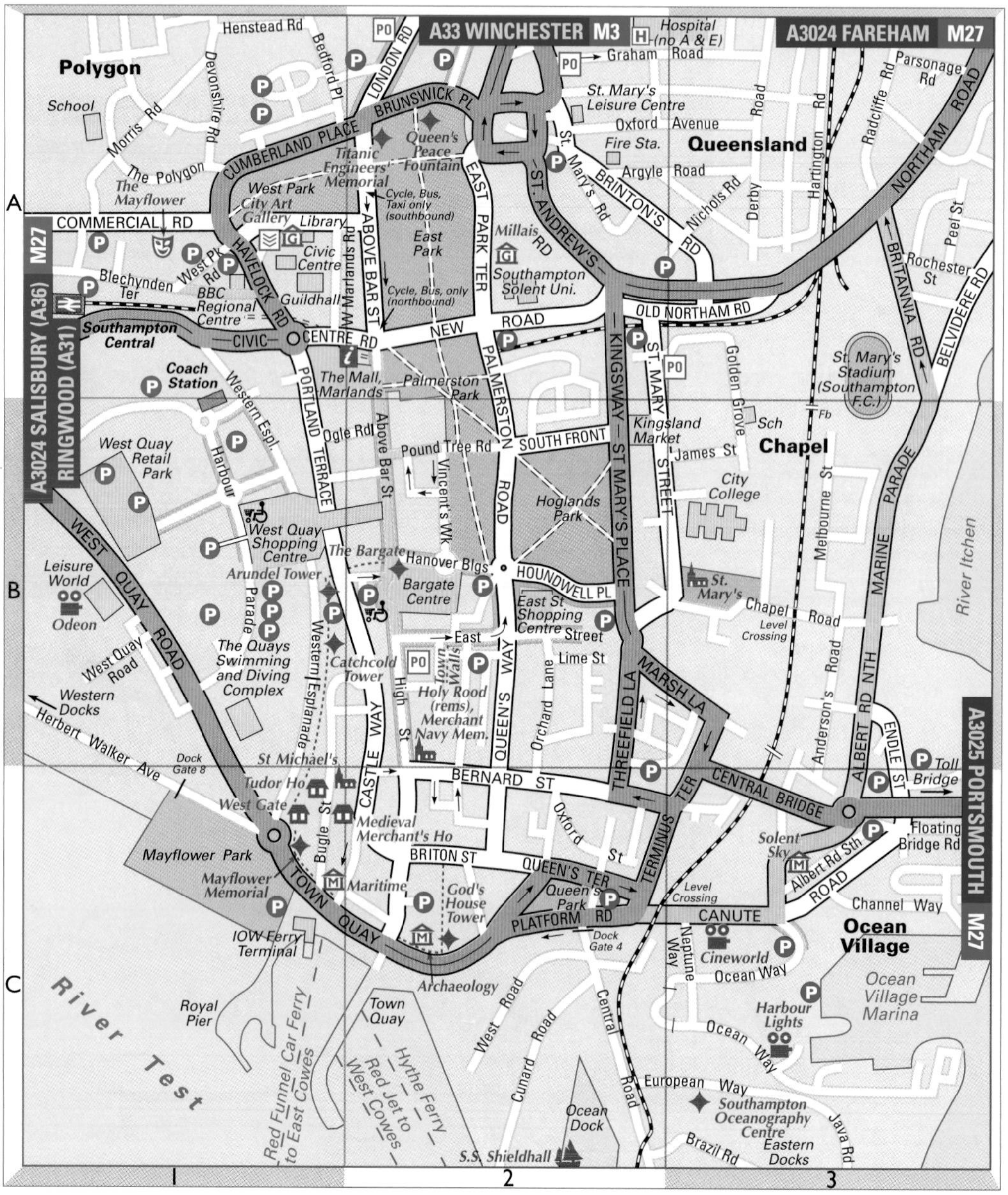

1/4 mile
1/4 1/2 km

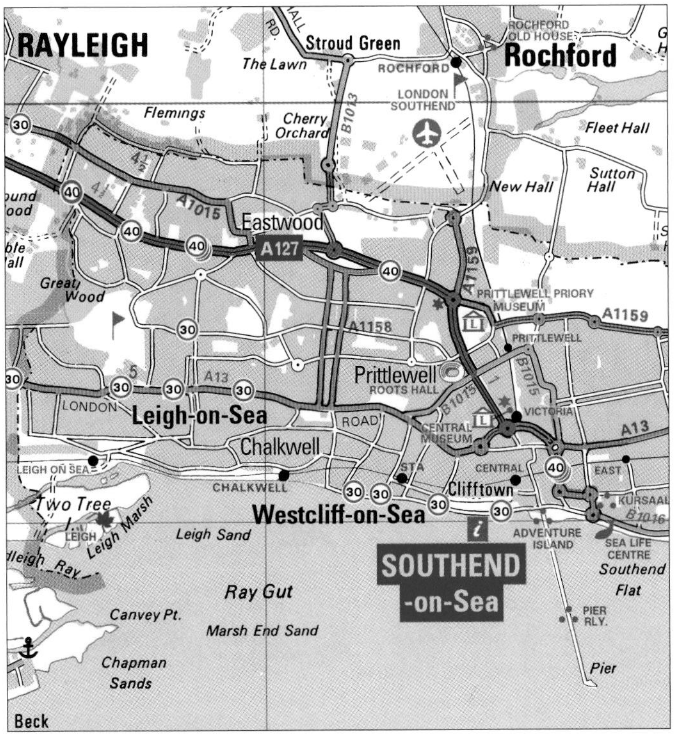

Southend-on-Sea

A traditional seaside centre on the Thames Estuary in Essex, on a site inhabited during the Stone Age, Bronze Age and early Iron Age, and successively settled by the Romans, Saxons and Danes – a history that is traced at Prittlewell Priory Museum. The closest resort to London, it boasts the world's longest pleasure pier (2360 yards), built in 1835, parts of which are shut following a fire in 2005 although attractions near the shore are open. The Golden Mile of leisure attractions includes Adventure Island themepark, the Kursaal with 10-pin bowling and other activities, and Never Never Land fantasy park, and the Central Museum including a planetarium. Just outside town are the 14th-century remains of Hadleigh Castle.

▲Southend beach huts

Southend Visitor Information Centre, The Pier Entrance, Southend Pier, Eastern Esplanade, Southend-on-Sea SS1 1EE Tel 01702 215620

BBC Essex 95.3 FM
Classic Gold Breeze 1431 AM
Essex 96.3, 102.6 FM

www.southend.gov.uk

★Do not miss

★**Jubilee Beach**, from Southend Pier to Thorpe Bay
★**Sealife Adventure**, Eastern Esplanade
★**Southend Pier**, Western Esplanade

Southend

Adventure Island ✦ C3
Albany Ave A1
Albert Rd C3
Alexandra Rd C2
Alexandra St C2
Art Gallery C1
Ashburnham Rd . . B2
Ave Rd B1
Avenue Terr B1
Balmoral Rd B1
Baltic Ave B3
Baxter Ave . . . A2/B2
Bircham Rd A2
Boscombe Rd B3
Boston Ave . . . A1/B2
Bournemouth Park Rd A3
Browning Ave . . . A3
Bus Station C3
Byron Ave A3
Cambridge Rd C1/C2
Canewdon Rd B1
Carnarvon Rd . . . A2
Central Ave A3
Chelmsford Ave . . A1
Chichester Rd B2
Church Rd C3
Civic Centre A2
Clarence Rd C2
Clarence St C2
Cliff Ave B1
Cliffs Pavilion . C1
Clifftown Parade . C2
Clifftown Rd C2
Colchester Rd . . . A1
College Way B2
County Court B3
Cromer Rd B3
Crowborough Rd . A2
Dryden Ave A3
East St A2
Elmer App B2
Elmer Ave B2
Gainsborough Dr A1
Gayton Rd A2
Glenhurst Rd A2
Gordon Pl B2
Gordon Rd B2
Grainger Rd A2
Greyhound Way . . A3
Guildford Rd B3
Hamlet Ct Rd B1
Hamlet Rd C1
Harcourt Ave A1
Hartington Rd . . . C3
Hastings Rd B3
Herbert Gr C3
Heygate Ave C3
High St B2/C2
Information Ctr C3
Kenway A2
Kilworth Ave B3
Lancaster Gdns . . . B3
Library B2
London Rd B1
Lucy Rd C3
MacDonald Ave . . A1
Magistrates Court A2
Maldon Rd A2
Marine Parade . . C3
Milton Rd B1
Milton St B2
Napier Ave B2
Never Never Land ✦ C2
North Ave A3
North Rd A1/B1
Odeon B2
Osborne Rd B1
Park Cres B1
Park Rd B1
Park St B1
Park Terr B1
Peter Pan's Playground ✦ . . C2
Pier Hill C3
Pleasant Rd C3
Police Station . A2
Post Office . B2/B3
Princes St B2
Queens Rd B2
Queensway B2/B3/C3
Rayleigh Ave A1
Redstock Rd A2
Rochford Ave A1
Royal Mews C2
Royal Terr C2
Royals Shopping Precinct C3
Ruskin Ave A3
St Ann's Rd B3
St Helen's Rd B1
St John's Rd B1
St Leonard's Rd . . C3
St Lukes Rd A3
St Vincent's Rd . . C1
Salisbury Ave . A1/B1
Scratton Rd C2
Shakespeare Dr . . A1
Short St A2
South Ave A3
Southchurch Rd . . B3
South East Essex College B2
Southend Central B2
Southend Pier Railway C3
Southend United F.C. A1
Southend Victoria B2
Stadium Rd A2
Stanfield Rd A2
Stanley Rd C3
Sutton Rd A3/B3
Swanage Rd B3
Sweyne Ave A1
Swimming Pool . . . B3
Sycamore Gr A3
Tennyson Ave A3
The Grove A3
Tickfield Ave A2
Tudor Rd A1
Tunbridge Rd A2
Tylers Ave B3
Tyrrel Dr B3
Vale Ave A2
Victoria Ave A2
Victoria Plaza Shopping Precinct B2
Warrior Sq B3
Wesley Rd C3
West Rd A1
West St A1
Westcliff Parade . C1
Western Espl C1
Weston Rd C2
Whitegate Rd B3
Wilson Rd C1
Wimborne Rd B3
York Rd C3

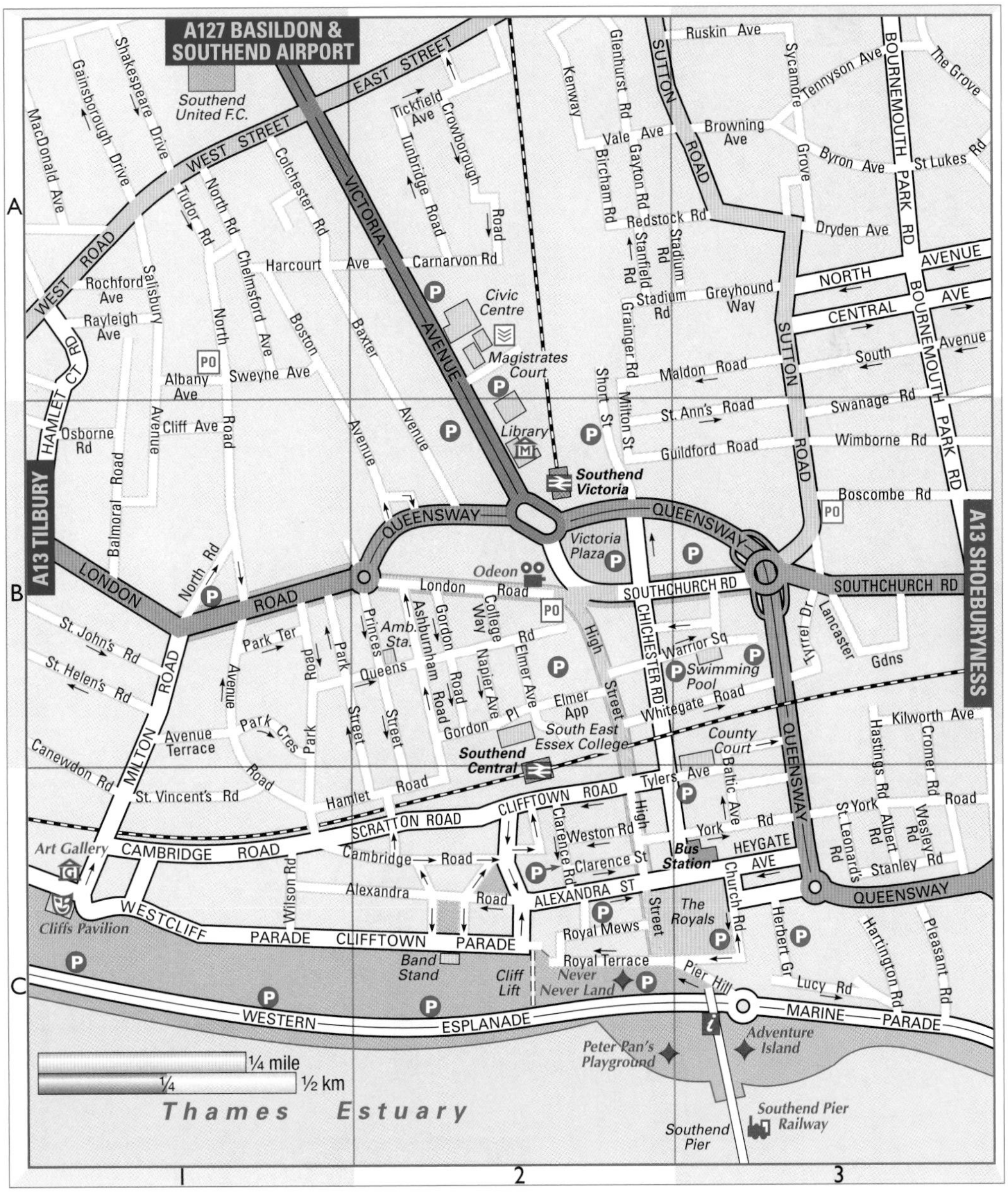

Stirling

A nucleus of Scottish heritage, with a large student population and good shopping amenities. Its superb castle, built during the reign of James VI, was a popular residence among Scottish monarchs. The Old Town has cobbled streets and some impressive architecture, including the medieval Church of the Holy Rude, where James VI was crowned and John Knox preached, and Argyll's Lodging, a restored 1570s mansion, while nearby ruined Cambuskenneth Abbey is where Robert the Bruce, victor of the nearby Battle of Bannockburn, held his parliament in 1326, and the National Wallace Memorial bears witness to William the Braveheart's battle for Scottish independence. This and other local history is charted in the Royal Burgh of Stirling Visitor Centre and the Smith Art Gallery and Museum. The city is well sited for visits to Loch Lomond and the Trossachs National Park, the Rob Roy & Trossachs Visitor Centre, and also handy for Gargunnock House and Garden, Blair Drummond Safari and Adventure Park, and the late-14th-century Doune Castle, used by Mary Queen of Scots.

★Do not miss

- ★**Bannockburn Heritage Centre**, Glasgow Road
- ★**Old Town Jail**, St John Street
- ★**Stirling Castle and Regimental Museum of the Argyll and Sutherland Highlanders**, Castle Wynd

▲Stirling Castle

Stirling Tourist Information Centre, Dumbarton Road, Stirling FK8 2QQ
Tel 01786 475019

BBC Radio Scotland 94.5 FM and 810 AM **Central** 103.1 FM
Xfm Scotland 106 FM

www.scottish.heartlands.org

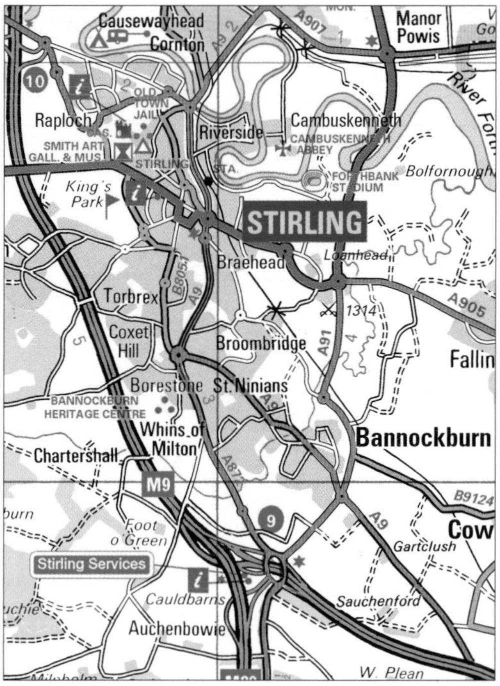

Stirling

Abbey Rd A3
Abbotsford Pl ... A3
Abercromby Pl .. C1
Albert Halls B1
Albert Pl......... B1
Alexandra Pl A3
Allan Park C2
Ambulance Station A2
AMF Ten Pin Bowling ✦ B2
Argyll Ave....... A3
Back O' Hill Industrial Estate A1
Back O' Hill Rd .. A1
Baker St B2
Ballengeich Pass A1
Balmoral Pl B1
Barn Rd B1
Barnton St B2
Bow St B1
Bruce St A2
Burghmuir Industrial Estate C2
Burghmuir Rd A2/B2/C2
Bus Station B2
Cambuskenneth Bridge......... A3
Carlton C2
Castle Ct......... B1
Causewayhead Rd A2
Cemetery A1/B1
Church of the Holy Rude B1
Clarendon Pl C1
Club House B1
Colquhoun St.... C3
Corn Exchange .. B2
Council Offices .. C2
Court............ B2
Cowane A2
Cowane St A2
Cowane's Hospital B1
Crawford Shopping Arcade B2
Crofthead Rd.... A1
Dean Cres A3
Douglas St A2
Drip Rd.......... A1
Drummond La ... C1
Drummond Pl ... C1
Drummond Pl La. C1
Dumbarton Rd... C2
Eastern Access Rd B2
Edward Ave A3
Edward Rd A2
Forrest Rd A2
Fort............. A1
Forth Cres B2
Forth St A2
Gladstone Pl C1
Glebe Ave....... C1
Glebe Cres C1
Glendevon Dr ... A1
Golf Course C1
Goosecroft Rd ... B2
Gowanhill....... A1
Greenwood Ave... B1
Harvey Wynd A1
Information Ctr A1/C2
Irvine Pl B2
James St A2
John St.......... B1
Kerse Rd........ C3
King's Knot ✦ B1
King's Park C1
King's Park Rd .. C1
Laurencecroft Rd A2
Leisure Pool B2
Library B2
Linden Ave C2
Lovers Wk A2
Lower Back Walk .B1
Lower Bridge St . A2
Lower Castlehill . A1
Mar Pl........... B1
Meadow Pl...... A3
Meadowforth Rd. C3
Middlemuir Rd .. C3
Millar Pl A3
Morris Terr....... B2
Mote Hill A1
Murray Pl B2
Nelson Pl C2
Old Town Jail.... B1
Orchard House Hospital (No A&E) A2
Park Terr........ C1
Phoenix Industrial Estate C3
Players Rd C3
Port St C2
Post Office A3/B1/B2/C2
Princes St B2
Queen St B2
Queen's Rd B1
Queenshaugh Dr. A3
Rainbow Slides ... B2
Ramsay Pl A2
Riverside Dr..... A3
Ronald Pl........ A1
Rosebery Pl A2
Royal Gardens B1
Royal Gdns....... B1
St Mary's Wynd ... B1
St Ninian's Rd ... C2
Scott St......... A2
Seaforth Pl....... B2
Shore Rd B2
Smith Art Gallery & Museum ... B1
Snowdon Pl C1
Snowdon Pl La .. C1
Spittal St B2
Springkerse Industrial Estate C3
Springkerse Rd .. C3
Stirling Business Centre......... C2
Stirling Castle . A1
Stirling County Rugby Football Club A3
Stirling Enterprise Park. .B3
Stirling Old Bridge......... A2
Stirling B2
Superstore A2
Sutherland Ave .. A3
TA Centre C3
Tannery La A2
Thistle Industrial Estate C3
Thistles Shopping Centre, The B2
Tollbooth, The ✦. .B1
Town Wall B1
Union St......... A2
Upper Back Walk .B1
Upper Bridge St . A1
Upper Castlehill .. B1
Upper Craigs C2
Victoria Pl C1
Victoria Rd....... B1
Victoria Sq.... B1/C1
Wallace St A2
Waverley Cres ... A3
Wellgreen Rd.... C2
Windsor Pl...... C1
YHA ▲.......... B1

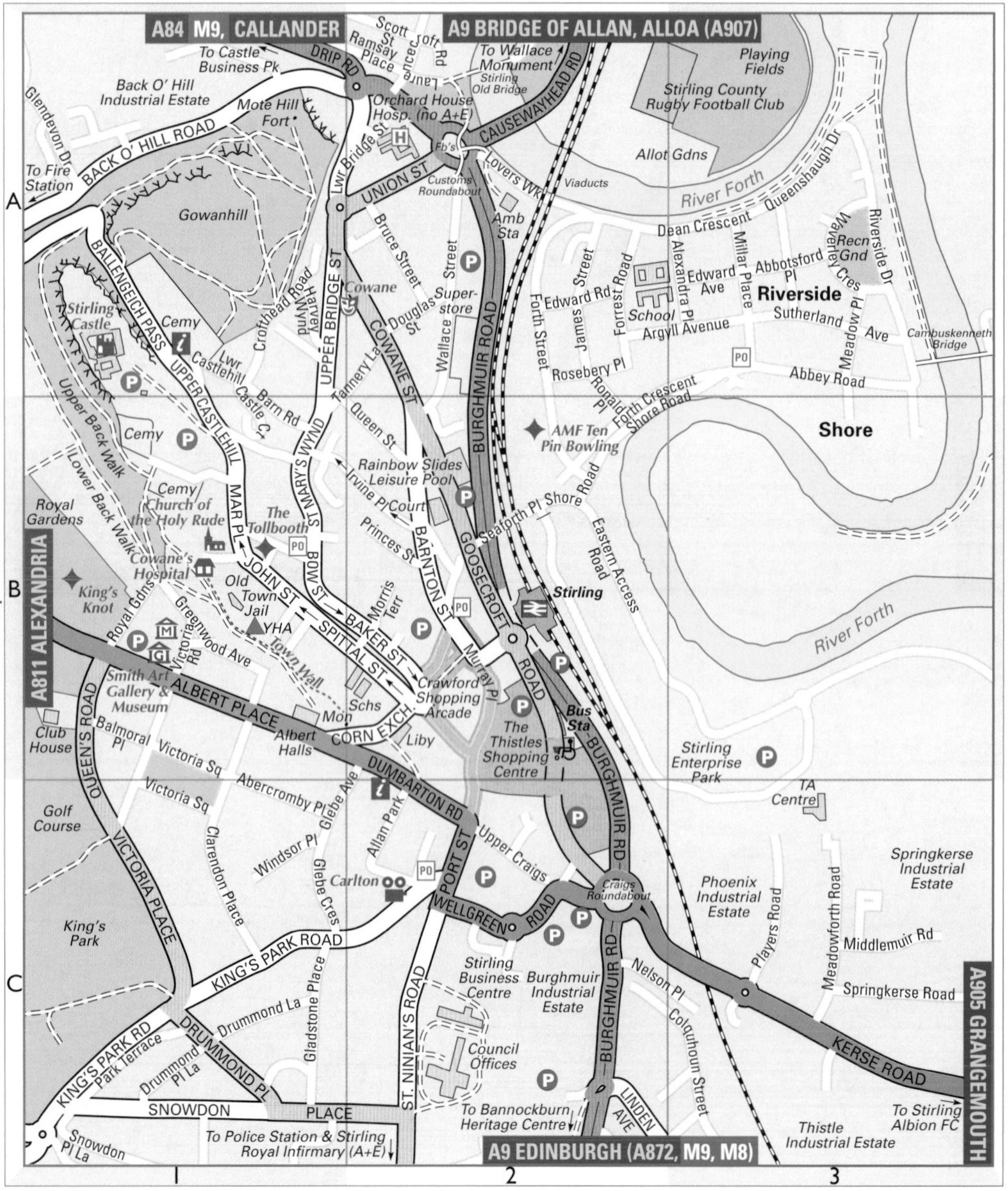

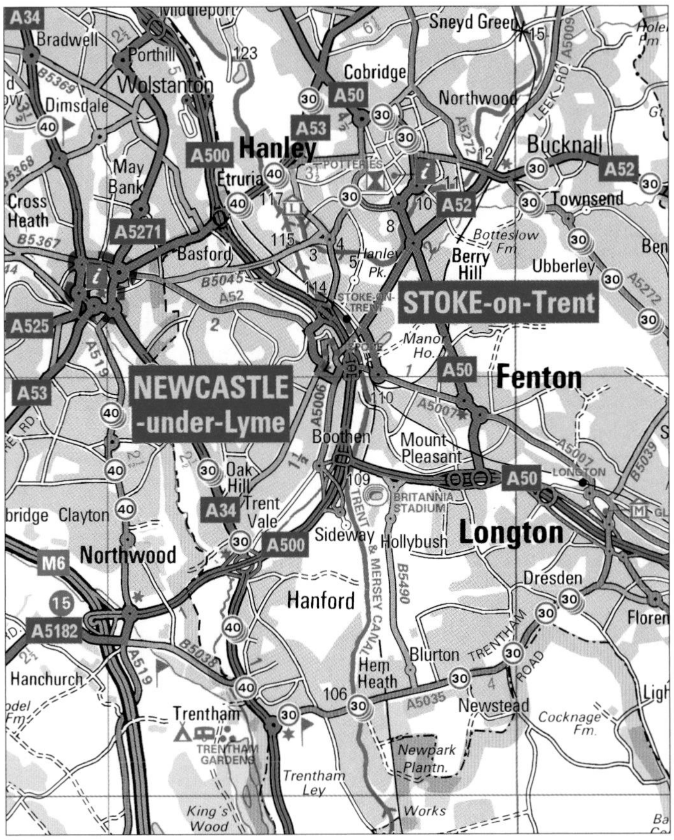

▲A bottle kiln

Stoke-on-Trent

Stoke is part of a city made up of six towns known collectively as The Potteries. The city is thus named as it is home to a host of world-renowned pottery manufacturers such as Aynsley, Portmeirion, Royal Doulton, Spode and Wedgwood. There are visitor centres, ceramic museums, and factory shops where you can buy direct from source. For your shopping requirements there are indoor and outdoor markets. Stoke is home to Staffordshire University and therefore a very vibrant town with its many theatres, pubs and restaurants. Festival Park has family attractions, including Waterworld theme park.

Stoke-on-Trent Tourist Information Centre, Victoria Hall, Cultural Quarter, Stoke-on-Trent City Centre ST1 3AD
Tel 01782 236000

BBC Radio Stoke 94.6 FM • **Signal 1** 102.6 FM • **Signal 2** 1170 AM

www.visitstoke.co.uk

★Do not miss

★**The Courtyards at Spode**, Church Street – visitor centre and factory tour

★**Churchill China**, Whielden Road – factory tour

★**Gladstone Pottery Museum**, Uttoxeter Road, Longton

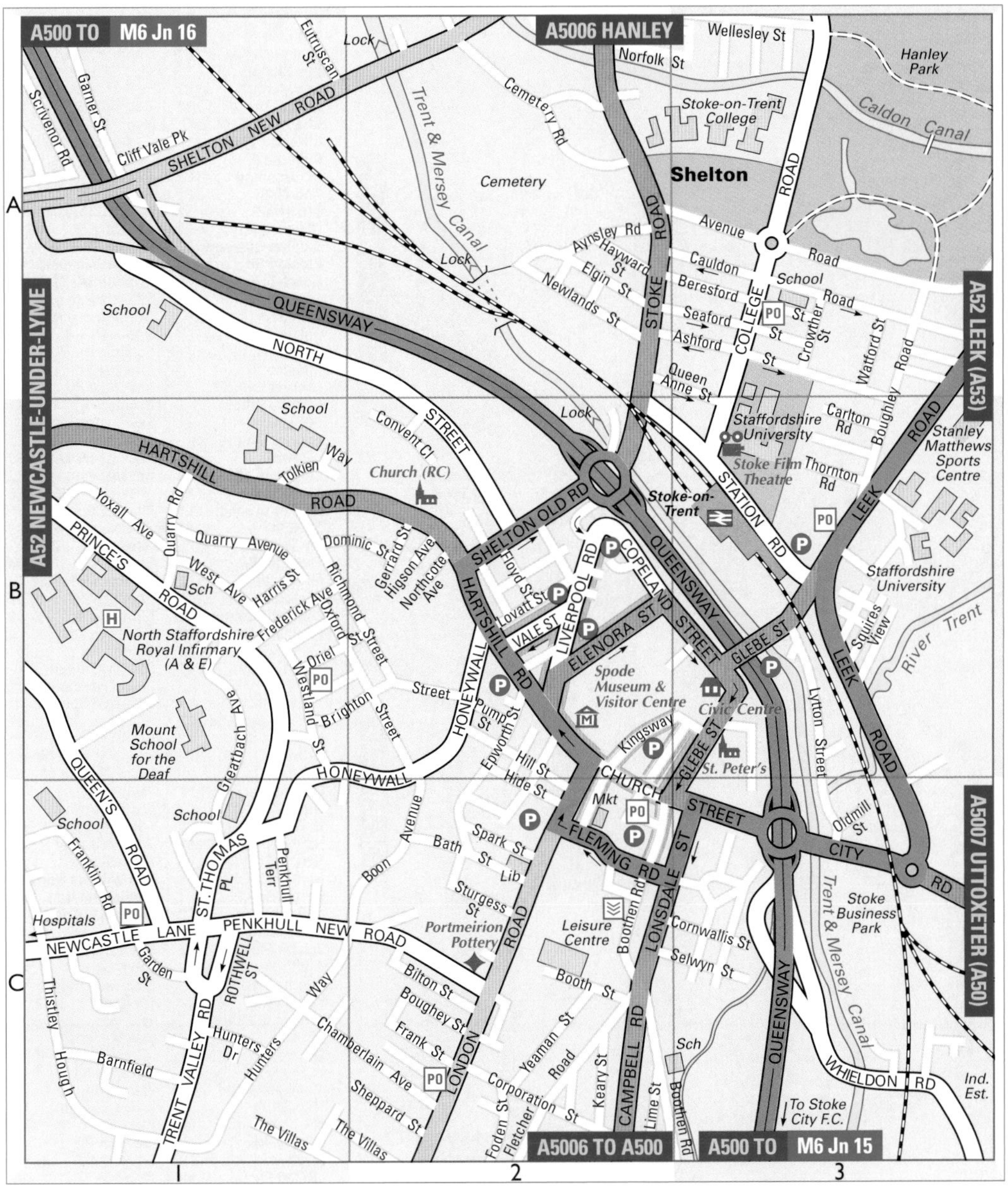

¼ mile
½ km

Stoke-on-Trent

Ashford St A3
Avenue Rd A3
Aynsley Rd A2
Barnfield C1
Bath St C2
Beresford St. A3
Bilton St C2
Boon Ave C2
Booth St C2
Boothen Rd . . C2/C3
Boughey St C2
Boughley Rd B3
Brighton St B1
Campbell Rd C2
Carlton Rd B3
Cauldon Rd A3
Cemetery A2
Cemetery Rd A2
Chamberlain Ave. C1
Church (RC) . . .B2
Church St. C2
City Rd C3
Civic Centre . . .B3
Cliff Vale Pk A1
College Rd A3
Convent Cl B2
Copeland St. B2
Cornwallis St C3
Corporation St . . C2
Crowther St A3
Dominic St B1
Elenora St B2
Elgin St. B2
Epworth St A3
Etruscan St A1
Fleming Rd C2
Fletcher Rd C2
Floyd St B2
Foden St. C2
Frank St C2
Franklin Rd C1
Frederick Ave B1
Garden St. C1
Garner St A1
Gerrard St B2
Glebe St B3
Greatbach Ave. . . .B1
Hanley Park A3
Harris St. B1
Hartshill Rd B1
Hayward St A2
Hide St B2
Higson Ave. B2
Hill St B2
Honeywall B2
Hunters Dr C1
Hunters Way C1
Keary St C2
Kingsway B2
Leek Rd B3
Leisure Centre. . . C2
Library C2
Lime St. C2
Liverpool Rd B2
London Rd C2
Lonsdale St C2
Lovatt St. B2
Lytton St. B3
Market C2
Mount School for the Deaf B1
Newcastle La. . . . C1
Newlands St. A2
Norfolk St. A2
North St A1/B2
North Staffordshire Royal Infirmary (A&E) B1
Northcote Ave B2
Oldmill St. C3
Oriel St. B1
Oxford St B1
Penkhull New Rd C1
Penkhull St C1
Police Station . C2
Portmeirion Pottery ✦. C2
Post Office . A3/B1/B3/C1/C2
Prince's Rd B1
Pump St B2
Quarry Ave B1
Quarry Rd. B1
Queen Anne St . . A3
Queen's Rd C1
Queensway A1/B2/C3
Richmond St B1
Rothwell St C1
St Peter's B3
St Thomas Pl C1
Scrivenor Rd A1
Seaford St A3
Selwyn St. C3
Shelton New Rd . A1
Shelton Old Rd . . .B2
Sheppard St. C2
Spark St C2
Spencer Rd B3
Spode Museum & Visitor Centre . .B2
Spode St C2
Squires View B3
Staffordshire Univ.B3
Stanley Matthews Sports Centre . . .B3
Station Rd B3
Stoke Business Park C3
Stoke Film Theatre B3
Stoke Rd. A2
Stoke-on-Trent College. A3
Stoke-on-Trent Station B3
Sturgess St C2
The Villas C1
Thistley Hough . . C1
Thornton Rd B3
Tolkien Way B1
Trent Valley Rd. . . C1
Vale St B2
Watford St A3
Wellesley St A3
West Ave. B1
Westland St B1
Yeaman St C2
Yoxall Ave. B1

Stratford-upon-Avon

Historic medieval market town most famous as the birthplace of William Shakespeare in 1564, boasting several sites associated with the playwright, including Mary Arden's House, childhood home of his mother; Hall's Croft, a Tudor house inhabited by his daughter Susanna; Nash's House/ New Place, a replica of an Elizabethan knot garden on the site of his retirement home; and his wife's pre-marital home. The Royal Shakespeare Company operates three venues here, including The Swan, a recreation of an Elizabethan galleried playouse, and there is a wide range of restaurants and specialist shops catering to theatregoers and tourists. Other sights include Harvard House, a largely 17th-century townhouse linked with the founder of Harvard University, the Shire Horse Centre and, a few miles away, the National Trust's Charlecote Park.

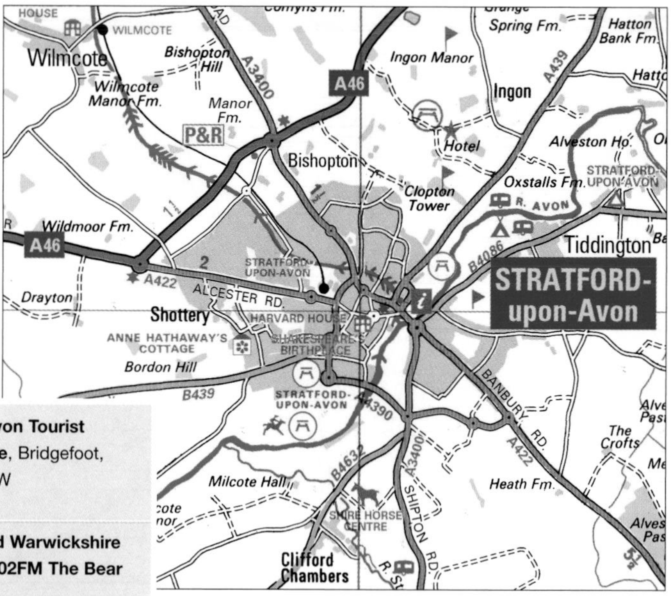

◀The Royal Shakespeare Theatre

Stratford-upon-Avon Tourist Information Centre, Bridgefoot, Stratford CV37 6GW
Tel 0870 160 7930

BBC Coventry and Warwickshire 94.8, 103.7 FM • **102FM The Bear** 102 FM

www.shakespeare-country.co.uk

★Do not miss

★**Anne Hathaway's Cottage**, Shottery
★**Shakespeare's Birthplace**, Henley Street
★**The Swan Theatre**, Waterside

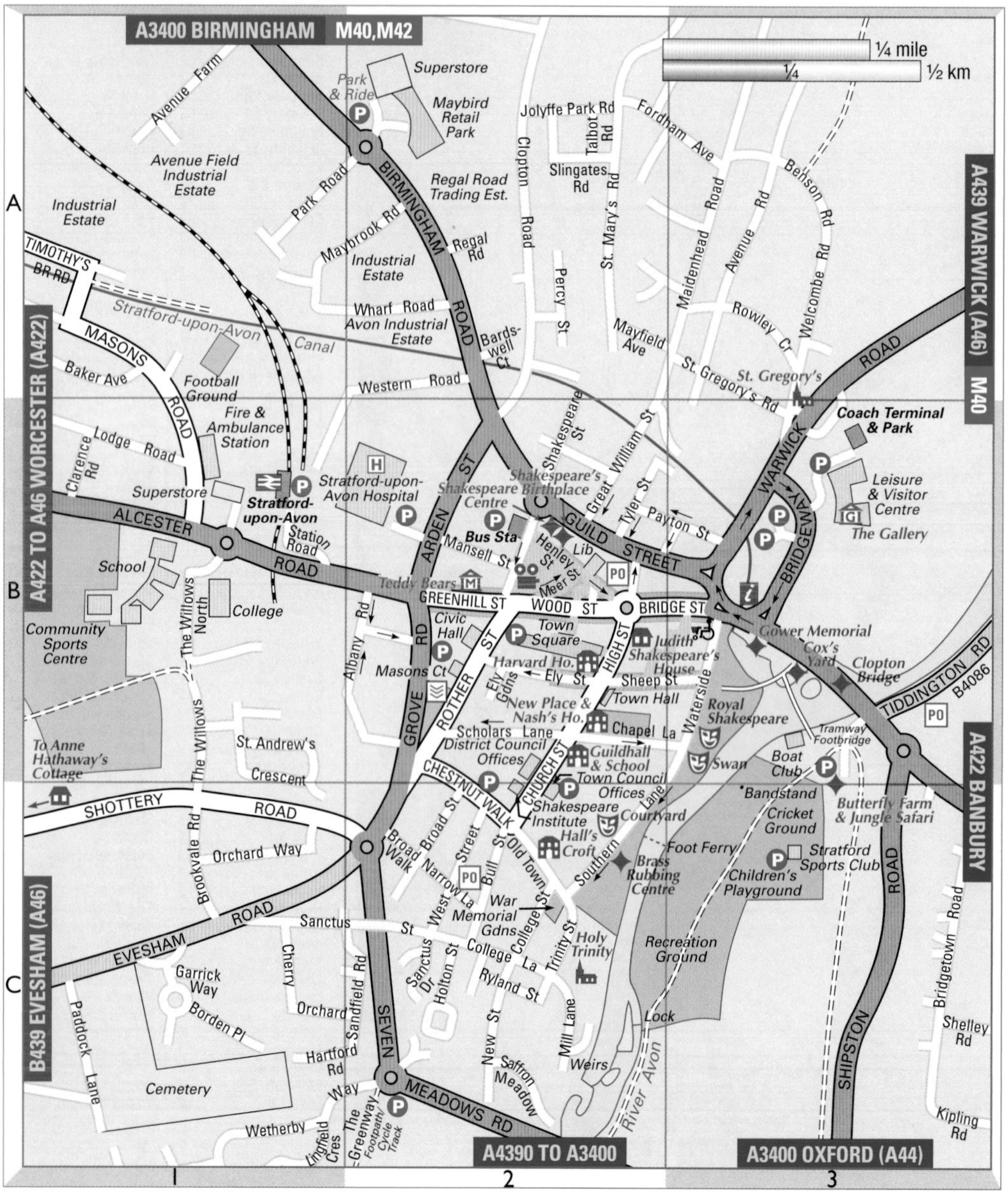

Stratford-upon-Avon

Albany Rd B1
Alcester Rd B1
Ambulance Stn . . . B1
Arden St B2
Avenue Farm A1
Avenue Field Ind Est A1
Avenue Rd A3
Avon Ind Est A2
Baker Ave A1
Bandstand C3
Benson Rd A3
Birmingham Rd . . A2
Boat Club B3
Borden Pl C1
Brass Rubbing Centre ✦ C2
Bridge St B2
Bridgetown Rd . . C3
Bridgeway B3
Broad St C2
Broad Walk C2
Brookvale Rd C1
Bull St C2
Butterfly Farm & Jungle Safari ✦ C3
Bus Station B2
Cemetery C1
Chapel La B2
Cherry Orchard . . C1
Chestnut Walk . . . B2
Children's Playground C3
Church St C2
Civic Hall B2
Clarence Rd B1
Clopton Bridge ✦ . B3
Clopton Rd A2
Coach Terminal & Park B3
College B1
College La C2
College St C2
Community Sports Centre . . . B1
Council Offices (District) B2
Council Offices (Town) B2
Courtyard C2
Cox's Yard ✦ B3
Cricket Ground . . C3
Ely Gdns B2
Ely St B2
Evesham Rd C1
Fire Station B1
Foot Ferry C3
Football Ground . . A1
Fordham Ave A2
Gallery, The B3
Garrick Way C1
Gower Memorial ✦ B3
Great William St . . B2
Greenhill St B2
Grove Rd B2
Guild St B2
Guildhall & Sch B2
Hall's Croft C2
Hartford Rd C1
Harvard House . B2
Henley St B2
High St B2
Holton St C2
Holy Trinity C2
Information Ctr . B3
Jolyffe Park Rd . . A2
Judith Shakespeare's House B2
Kipling Rd C3
Leisure & Visitor Centre B3
Library B2
Lodge Rd B1
Maidenhead Rd . . A3
Mansell St B2
Masons Court B2
Masons Rd A1
Maybird Retail Pk A2
Maybrook Rd A1
Mayfield Ave A2
Meer St B2
Mill La C2
Moat House Hotel . B3
Narrow La C2
New Place & Nash's House . B2
New St C2
Old Town C2
Orchard Way C1
Paddock La C1
Park Rd A1
Payton St B2
Percy St A2
Police Station B2
Post Office B2/B3/C2
Rec Grnd C2
Regal Rd A2
Regal Road Trading Estate A2
Rother St B2
Rowley Cr A3
Royal Shakespeare Theatre B3
Ryland St C2
Saffron Meadow . C2
St Andrew's Cr . . . B1
St Gregory's . . A3
St Gregory's Rd . . A3
St Mary's Rd A2
Sanctus Dr C2
Sanctus St C1
Sandfield Rd C2
Scholars La B2
Seven Meadows Rd C2
Shakespeare Ctr ✦ B2
Shakespeare Inst. C2
Shakespeare St . . . B2
Shakespeare's Birthplace ✦ B2
Sheep St B2
Shelley Rd C3
Shipston Rd C3
Shottery Rd C1
Slingates Rd A2
Southern La C2
Station Rd B1
Stratford-upon-Avon Hospital . B2
Stratford Sports Club B1
Stratford-upon-Avon Station . B1
Swan Theatre . . B3
Talbot Rd A2
Teddy Bears Museum B2
The Greenway . . . C1
The Willows B1
The Willows North B1
Tiddington Rd B3
Timothy's Bridge Rd A1
Town Hall B2
Town Sq B2
Tramway Bridge . . B3
Trinity St C2
Tyler St B2
War Memorial Gdns C2
Warwick Rd B3
Waterside B3
Welcombe Rd . . . A3
West St C2
Western Rd A2
Wharf Rd A2
Wood St B2

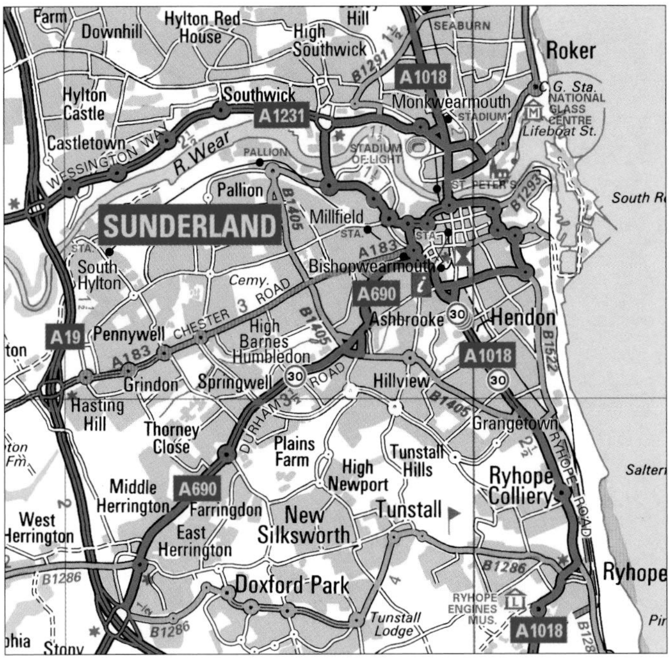

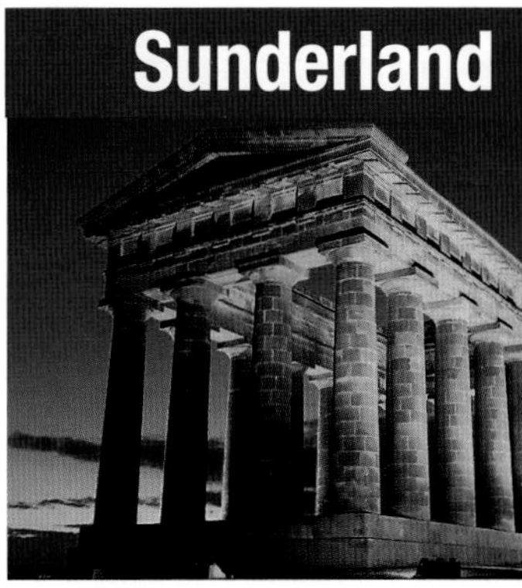

Sunderland

The port of Sunderland has a heritage going back over 800 years. By 1840 Sunderland was the biggest shipbuilding port in the world but by 1988 the last shipyard had closed. Meanwhile, location of a Nissan plant in Sunderland was a catalyst for new jobs in the automotive sector. The closure of the City's last coalmine, Wearmouth Colliery, in 1994 brought to an end the traditional industries. St Peter's Church founded in 674AD is one of the most important sites of early Christian history in England. Other places of interest include the Monkwearmouth Station Museum, Ryhope Engines Museum and Sunderland Museum and Winter Gardens. There's the beautiful fully restored Mowbray Park in the centre and Roker Beach on the coast. The Bridges Shopping centre boasts a wide selection of high street brands and there are many theatres, restaurants and pubs to choose from.

▲The Penshaw Monument

★Do not miss

★**National Glass Centre**, Liberty Way

★**Northern Gallery for Contemporary Art**, City Library and Arts Centre, Fawcett Street

★**St Peter's Church**, St Peter's Way

★**Penshaw Monument**, close to A183, 1.5 km west of junction with A19

Tourist Information Centre, 50 Fawcett Street, Sunderland SR1 1RF Tel 0191 553 2000

BBC Radio Newcastle 95.4 FM and 1458 AM • **Century** 101.8 FM **Galaxy** 105.3 FM • **Sun** 103.4 FM

www.sunderland.gov.uk

Sunderland

Albion Pl C2
Alliance Pl B1
Argyle St C2
Ashwood St C1
Athenaeum St B2
Azalea Terr C2
Beach St A1
Bede Theatre . . C3
Bedford St B2
Beechwood Terr . C1
Belvedere Rd C2
Blandford St B2
Borough Rd B3
Bridge Cr B2
Bridge St B2
Brooke St A2
Brougham St B2
Burdon Rd C2
Burn Park C1
Burn Park Rd C1
Carol St B1
Charles St A3
Chester Rd C1
Chester Terr B1
Church St A3
Cineworld B3
Civic Centre C2
Cork St B3
Coronation St B3
Cowan Terr C2
Crowtree Rd B2
Dame Dorothy St A2
Deptford Rd B1
Deptford Terr A1
Derby St C2
Derwent St C2
Dock St A3
Dundas St A2
Durham Rd C1
Easington St A2
Egerton St C3
Empire Theatre . B2
Farringdon Row . . B1
Fawcett St B2
Festival Park B2
Fox St C1
Foyle St B3
Frederick St B3
Gill Rd B2
Hanover Pl A1
Havelock Terr C1
Hay St A2
Headworth Sq B3
Hendon Rd B3
High St East B3
High St West . . B2/B3
Holmeside B2
Hylton Rd B1
Information Ctr . B2
John St B3
Kier Hardie Way . A2
Lambton St B3
Laura St C3
Lawrence St B3
Leisure Centre B2
Library & Arts Centre B3
Lily St B1
Lime St B1
Livingstone Rd . . . B2
Low Row B2
Matamba Terr B1
Millburn St B1
Millennium Way . A2
Minster B2
Monkwearmouth Station Museum A2
Mowbray Park . . . C3
Mowbray Rd C3
Murton St C3
Museum B3
National Glass Centre ✦ . A3
New Durham Rd . C1
Newcastle Rd . . . A2
Nile St B3
Norfolk St B3
North Bridge St . . A2
Otto Terr C1
Park La C2
Park Lane (Metro Station) . C2
Park Rd C2
Paul's Rd B3
Peel St C3
Police Station . . B2
Post Office B2
Priestly Cr A1
Queen St B2
Railway Row B1
Retail Park A1
Richmond St A2
Roker Ave A2
Royalty Theatre C1
Ryhope Rd C2
St Mary's Way B2
St Michael's Way . B2
St Peter's A3
St Peter's (Metro Station) . A2
St Peter's Way . . . A3
St Vincent St C3
Salem Rd C3
Salem St C3
Salisbury St C3
Sans St B3
Silkworth Row B1
Southwick Rd . . . A2
Stadium of Light (Sunderland A.F.C.) A2
Stadium Way A2
Stobart St A2
Stockton Rd C2
Suffolk St C3
Sunderland (Metro Station) . . B2
Sunderland ⇌ . . . B2
Sunderland St B3
Tatham St C3
Tavistock Pl B3
Technology Park . C1
The Bridges B2
The Royalty C1
Thelma St C1
Thomas St North . A2
Thornholme Rd . . C1
Toward Rd C3
Transport Interchange C2
Trimdon St Way . . . B1
Tunstall Rd C2
University . A3/B1/C2
University (Metro Station) . C1
University Library C1
Vaux Brewery Way A2
Villiers St B3
Villiers St South . . B3
Vine Pl C2
Violet St B1
Walton La B3
Waterworks Rd . . . B1
Wearmouth Bridge B2
Wellington La . . . A1
West Sunniside . . . B3
West Wear St B3
Westbourne Rd . . . B1
Western Hill C1
Wharncliffe B1
Whickham St A3
White House Rd . C3
Wilson St North . . A2
Winter Gdns C3
Wreath Quay A1

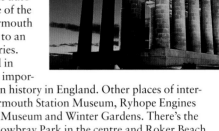

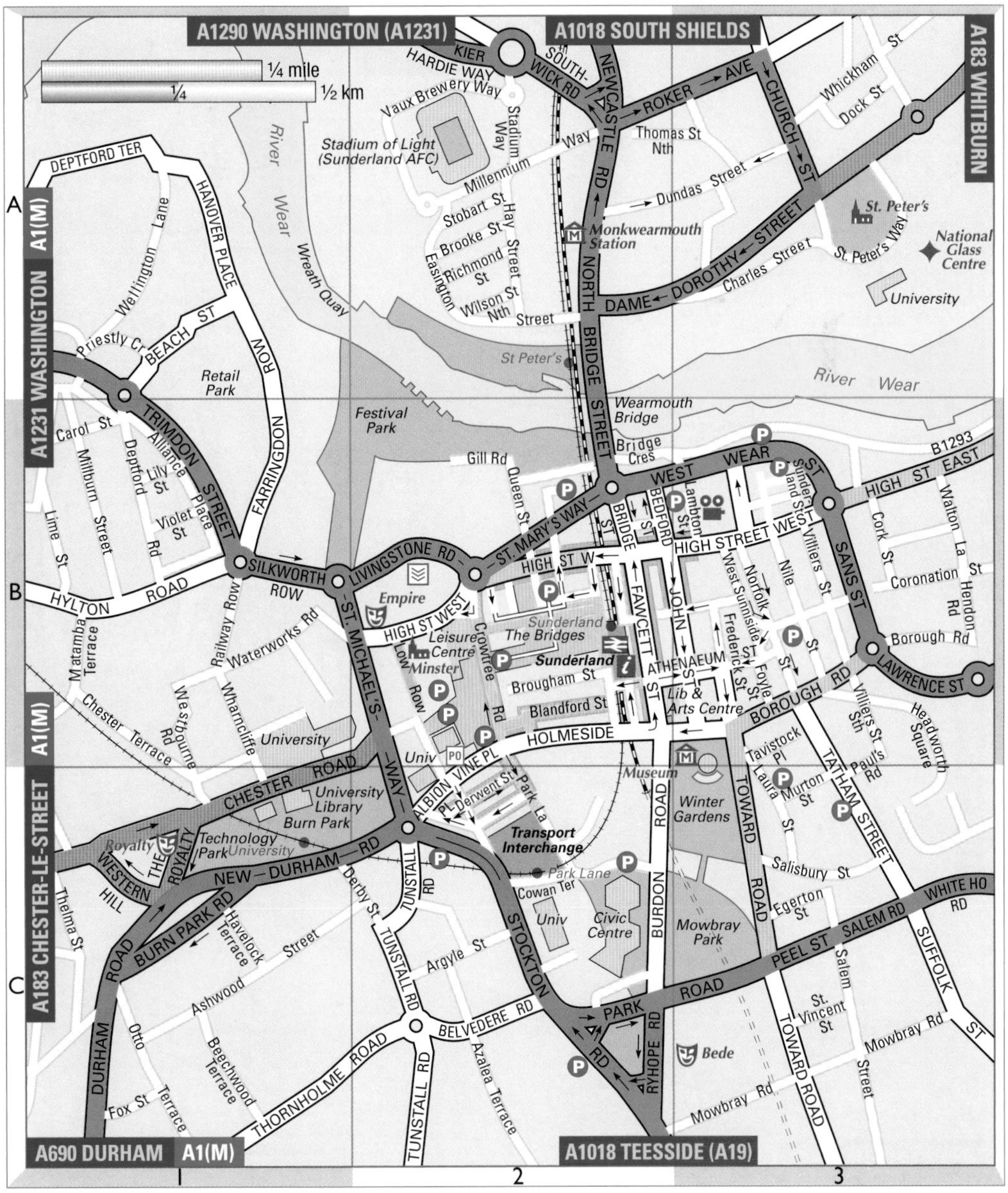

Swansea

▲Swansea's Maritime Quarter

Tourist Information Centre, Plymouth St, Swansea SA1 3QG Tel 01792 468321

BBC Radio Wales 93.9 FM • **Real Radio** 106.0 FM • **The Wave** 96.4 FM **Swansea Sound** 1170 AM

www.swansea.gov.uk

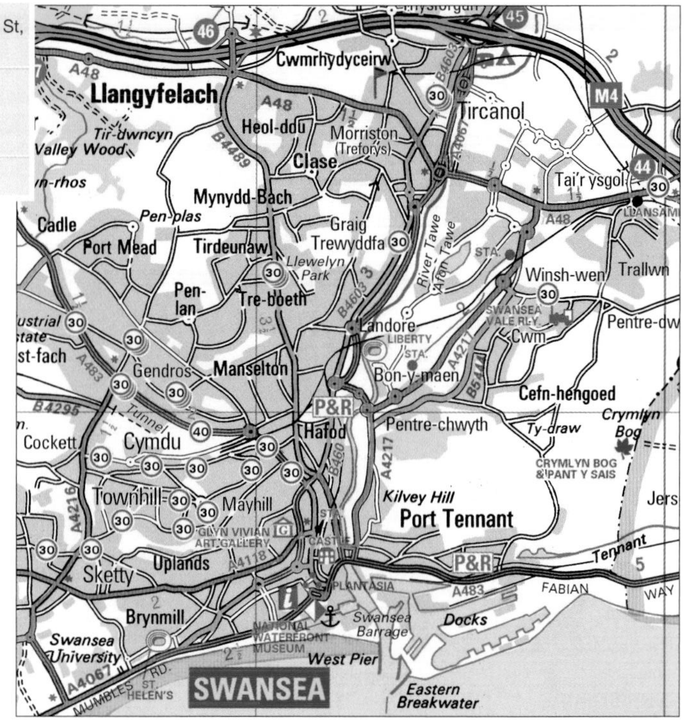

Swansea was founded in the 10th century by the Vikings and named after the Danish king Swein Forkbeard. Extensively bombed in WWII there remains little physical evidence of the city's history. Swansea was one of the major smelting centres of the Industrial Revolution, but now as a 21st-century city it focuses on its literary and maritime heritage with the Dylan Thomas Centre and National Waterfront Museum.

There is a wide array of shopping with both The Quadrant and St David's centres. There are also the Blue Flag beaches, Botanical Gardens – with Chyne Gardens, Singleton Botanical Garden and Plantasia, several theatres and a variety of pubs and restaurants.

★Do not miss

- ★**Glynn Vivian Art Gallery**, Alexandra Road – international fine art
- ★**Swansea Museum**, Victoria Road, The Maritime Quarter – local history
- ★**Plantasia**, Parc Tawe – hothouse garden with animals and plants

Swansea/ Abertawe

Adelaide St C3
Albert Row C3
Alexandra Rd B3
Argyle St C1
Baptist Well Pl A2
Beach St C1
Belle Vue Way B3
Berw Rd A1
Berwick Terr A2
Bond St C1
Brangwyn Concert Hall C1
Bridge St A3
Brookands Terr B1
Brunswick St C1
Bryn-Syfi Terr A2
Bryn-y-Mor Rd C1
Bullins La B1
Burrows Rd C1
Bus/Rail link A3
Bus Station C2
Cadfan Rd A1
Cadrawd Rd A1
Caer St B3
Carig Cr A1
Carlton Terr B2
Carmarthen Rd A3
Castle St B3
Catherine St C1
City & County of Swansea Offices (County Hall) C2
City & County of Swansea Offices (Guildhall) C1
Clarence St C2
Colbourne Terr A2
Constitution Hill B1
Court B3
Creidiol Rd A2
Cromwell St B2
Duke St B1
Dunvant Pl C2
Dyfatty Park A3
Dyfatty St A3
Dyfed Ave A1
Dylan Thomas Centre ✦ B3
Dylan Thomas C3
Eaton Cr C1
Eigen Cr A1
Elfed Rd A1
Emlyn Rd A1
Evans Terr A3
Fairfield Terr B1
Ffynone Dr B1
Ffynone Rd B1
Fire Station B3
Firm St A2
Fleet St C1
Francis St C1
Fullers Row B2
George St B2
Glamorgan St C2
Glyndwr Pl A1
Glynn Vivian B3
Graig Terr A3
Grand Theatre C2
Granogwen Rd A2
Guildhall Rd South C1
Gwent Rd A1
Gwynedd Ave A1
Hafod St A3
Hanover St B1
Harcourt St B2
Harries St A2
Heathfield B2
Henrietta St B1
Hewson St B2
High St A3/B3
High View A2
Hill St A2
Historic Ships Berth C3
HM Prison C2
Information Ctr C2
Islwyn Rd A1
King Edward's Rd C1
Law Courts C1
Library B3
Long Ridge A2
Madoc St C2
Mansel St B2
Maritime Quarter C3
Market B3
Mayhill Gdns B1
Mayhill Rd A1
Mega Bowl ✦ B3
Milton Terr A2
Mission Gallery C3
Montpellier Terr B1
Morfa Rd A3
Mount Pleasant B2
National Waterfront Museum C3
Nelson St C2
New Cut Rd A3
New St A3
Nicander Pde A2
Nicander Pl A2
Nicholl St B2
Norfolk St B2
North Hill Rd A2
Northampton La B2
Orchard St B3
Oxford St B2
Oystermouth Rd C1
Page St B2
Pant-y-Celyn Rd B1
Parc Tawe North B3
Parc Tawe Shopping & Leisure Ctr B3
Patti Pavilion C1
Paxton St C2
Penmaen Terr B1
Pen-y-Graig Rd A1
Phillips Pde C1
Picton Terr B2
Plantasia B3
Police Station B2
Post Office A1/A2/A3/B2/C1/C2/C3
Powys Ave A1
Primrose St B2
Princess Way B3
Promenade B2
Pryder Gdns A1
Quadrant Centre C2
Quay Park B3
Rhianfa La B1
Rhondda St B2
Richardson St C2
Rodney St C1
Rose Hill B1
Rosehill Terr B1
Russell St B1
St David's Sq C3
St Helen's Ave C1
St Helen's Cr C1
St Helen's Rd C1
St James Gdns B1
St James's Cr B1
St Mary's B3
Sea View Terr A3
Singleton St C2
South Dock C3
Stanley Pl B2
Strand B3
Swansea Castle B3
Swansea College Arts Centre C1
Swansea C3
Swansea A3
Taliesyn Rd B1
Tan y Marian Rd A1
Technical College B2
Tegid Rd A2
Teilo Cr A1
Terrace Rd B1/B2
The Kingsway B2
Tontine St A3
Tower of Eclipse ✦ C3
Townhill Rd A1
Tram Museum C3
Trawler Rd C3
Union St B2
Upper Strand A3
Vernon St A3
Victoria Quay C3
Victoria Rd B3
Vincent St C1
Walter Rd B1
Watkin St A2
Waun-Wen Rd A2
Wellington St C2
Westbury St C1
Western St C1
Westway C2
William St C2
Wind St B3
Woodlands Terr B1
YMCA B2
York St C3

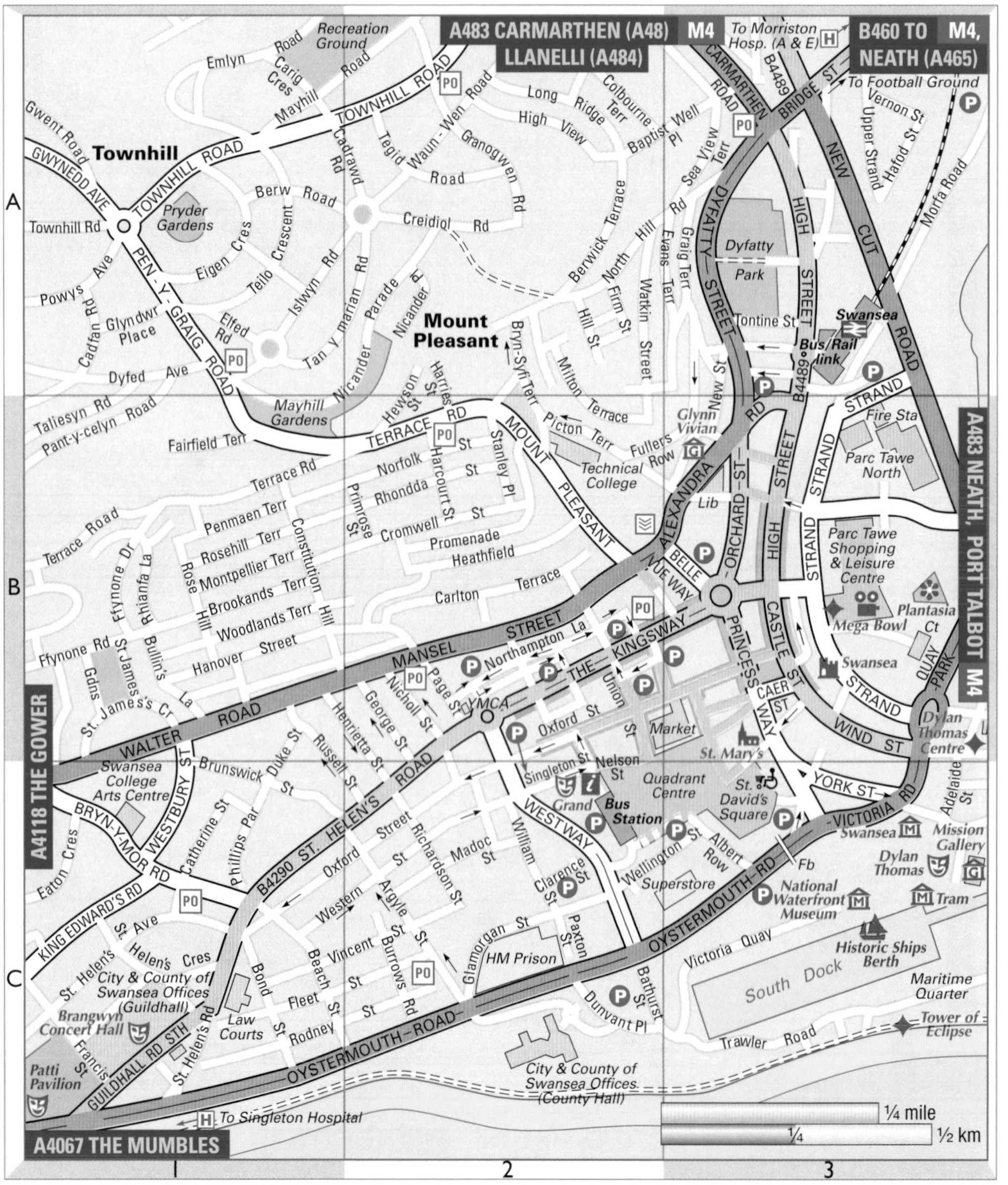

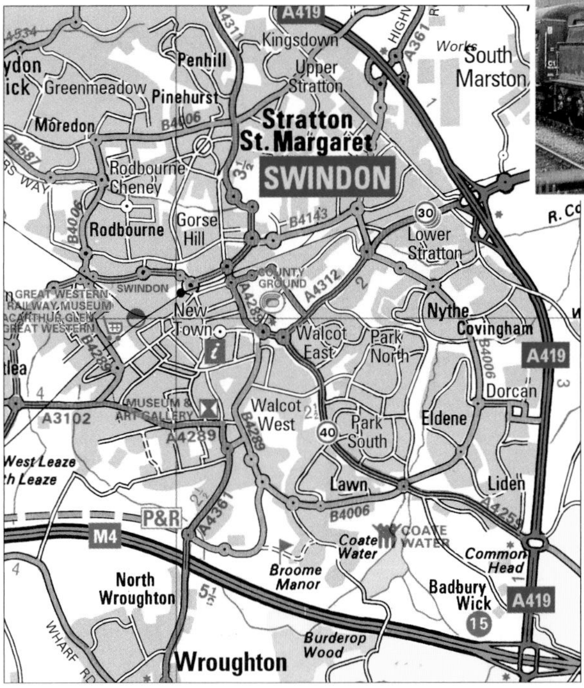

▲Swindon-built steam locomotive, *City of Truro*, the first to exceed 100mph

Swindon

A Saxon village that grew into a hilltop medieval market town and then into Wiltshire's biggest town with the arrival of the Great Western Railway in 1840 – the reconstructed Swindon and Cricklade Railway now offers steam-train trips. A thriving commercial centre, it has a number of small specialist shops in its Old Town and a designer clothes centre in restored railway buildings that also house the Great Western Railway museum. There's an important collection of 20th-century British works in its art gallery. Green spaces include Coate Water Country Park with its 56-acre lake, and, a few miles away, Barbury Castle, an Iron Age hillfort on the Ridgeway, surrounded by a 150-acre country park, Stanton Park, an area of 19th-century landscaped parkland.

★Do not miss

★**Lydiard House**, Park and Visitor Centre, Hook Street, Lydiard Tregoze

★**Swindon Museum and Art Gallery**, Bath Road

★**STEAM, Museum of the Great Western Railway**, Kemble Drive

Swindon Tourist Information Centre, 37 Regent St, Swindon SN1 1JL Tel 01793 530328

BBC Radio Wiltshire 103.5 FM
Classic Gold 936 and 1161 AM
GWR 97.2 and 102.2 FM

www.visitswindon.co.uk

Swindon

Albert St . . . C3
Albion St . . . C1
Alfred St . . . A2
Alvescot Rd . . . C3
Art Gallery & Museum . . . C3
Ashford Rd . . . C1
Aylesbury St . . . A2
Bath Rd . . . C2
Bathampton St . . . B1
Bathurst Rd . . . B3
Beatrice St . . . A2
Beckhampton St . . . B3
Bowood Rd . . . C1
Bristol St . . . B1
Broad St . . . A3
Brunel Arcade . . . B2
Brunel Plaza . . . B2
Brunswick St . . . C2
Bus Station . . . B2
Cambria Br Rd . . . B1
Cambria Pl . . . B1
Canal Walk . . . B2
Carfax St . . . B2
Carr St . . . B1
Cemetery . . . C1/C3
Chandler Cl . . . C3
Chapel . . . C1
Chester St . . . B1
Christ Church . . . C3
Church Pl . . . B1
Cirencester Way . . . A3
Clarence St . . . B2
Clifton St . . . C1
Cockleberry (r'about) . . . A2
Colbourne (r'about) . . . A3
Colbourne St . . . A3
College St . . . B2
Commercial Rd . . . B2
Corporation St . . . A2
Council Offices . . . B3
County Rd . . . A3
Courts . . . B2
Cricket Ground . . . A3
Cricklade St . . . C3
Crombey St . . . B1/C2
Cross St . . . C2
Curtis St . . . B1
Deacon St . . . C1
Designer Outlet (Great Western) . . . B1
Dixon St . . . C2
Dover St . . . C2
Dowling St . . . C2
Drove Rd . . . C3
Dryden St . . . C1
Durham St . . . C3
East St . . . B1
Eastcott Hill . . . C2
Eastcott Rd . . . C2
Edgeware Rd . . . B2
Elmina Rd . . . A3
Emlyn Sq . . . B1
Euclid St . . . B3
Exeter St . . . B1
Fairview . . . C1
Faringdon Rd . . . B1
Farnsby St . . . B1
Fire Station . . . B3
Fleet St . . . B2
Fleming Way . . . B2/B3
Florence St . . . A2
Gladstone St . . . A3
Gooch St . . . A2
Graham St . . . A3
Great Western Way . . . A1/A2
Groundwell Rd . . . B3
Hawksworth Way . . . A1
Haydon St . . . A2
Henry St . . . B2
Hillside Ave . . . C1
Holbrook Way . . . B2
Hunt St . . . C3
Hydro . . . B1
Hythe Rd . . . C2
Information Ctr . . . B2
Joseph St . . . C1
Kent Rd . . . C2
King William St . . . C2
Kingshill Rd . . . C1
Lansdown Rd . . . C2
Leicester St . . . B3
Library . . . B2
Lincoln St . . . B3
Little London . . . C3
London St . . . B1
Magic R'about . . . B3
Maidstone Rd . . . C2
Manchester Rd . . . A3
Market Hall . . . B2
Maxwell St . . . B1
Milford St . . . B2
Milton Rd . . . B1
Morse St . . . C2
Nat Monuments Record Centre . . . B1
Newcastle St . . . B3
Newcombe Dr . . . A1
Newcombe Trading Estate . . . A1
Newhall St . . . C2
North St . . . C2
North Star (r'about) . . . A1
North Star Ave . . . A1
Northampton St . . . B3
Oasis Leisure Ctr . . . A1
Ocotal Way . . . A3
Okus Rd . . . C1
Old Town . . . C3
Oxford St . . . B1
Park Lane . . . B1
Park Lane (r'about) . . . B1
Pembroke St . . . C2
Plymouth St . . . B3
Polaris House . . . A2
Polaris Way . . . A2
Police Station . . . B2
Ponting St . . . A2
Post Office . . . B1/B2/C1/C3
Poulton St . . . A3
Princes St . . . B2
Prospect Hill . . . C2
Prospect Pl . . . C2
Queen St . . . B2
Queen's Park . . . C3
Radnor St . . . C1
Railway Village . . . B1
Read St . . . C1
Reading St . . . B1
Regent St . . . B2
Retail Park . . . A2/A3/B3
Rosebery St . . . A3
St Mark's . . . B1
Salisbury St . . . A3
Savernake St . . . C2
Shelley St . . . C1
Sheppard St . . . B1
South St . . . C2
Southampton St . . . B3
Spring Gdns . . . B3
Stafford St . . . C2
Stanier St . . . C2
Station Rd . . . A2
Steam . . . B1
Swindon . . . A2
Swindon Coll . . . A2/C2
Swindon Rd . . . C2
Swindon Town F.C. . . . A3
TA Centre . . . B1
Tennyson St . . . B1
The Lawn . . . C3
The Nurseries . . . C1
The Parade . . . B2
The Park . . . B1
Theobald St . . . B1
Town Hall . . . B2
Transfer Bridges (r'about) . . . A3
Union St . . . C2
Upham Rd . . . C3
Victoria Rd . . . C3
Walcot Rd . . . B3
War Memorial . . . B2
Wells St . . . B3
Western St . . . C2
Westmorland Rd . . . B3
Whalebridge (r'about) . . . B2
Whitehead St . . . C1
Whitehouse Rd . . . A2
William St . . . C1
Wood St . . . C3
Wyvern . . . B2
York Rd . . . B3

¼ mile
¼ ½ km

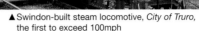

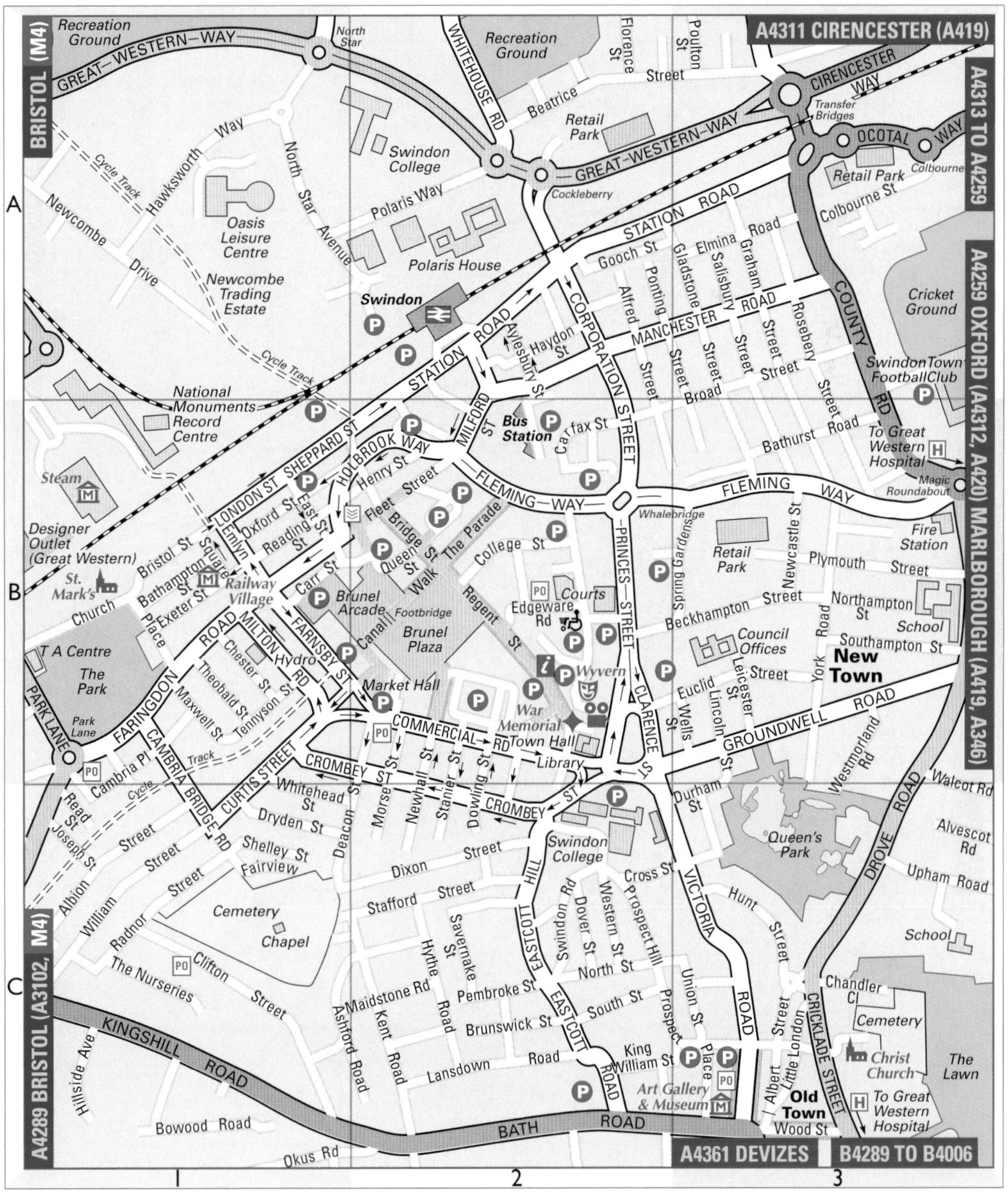

Taunton

Taunton Tourist Information Centre, Paul Street, Taunton TA1 3XZ
Tel 01823 336344

BBC Somerset Sound 1566 AM
Orchard 96.5, 102.6 FM

www.tauntondeane.gov.uk

★Do not miss

★**Hestercombe Gardens**, Cheddon Fitzpaine
★**Sheppy's Cider Farm**, Three Bridges, Bradford-on-Tone
★**Somerset Cricket Museum**, County Ground

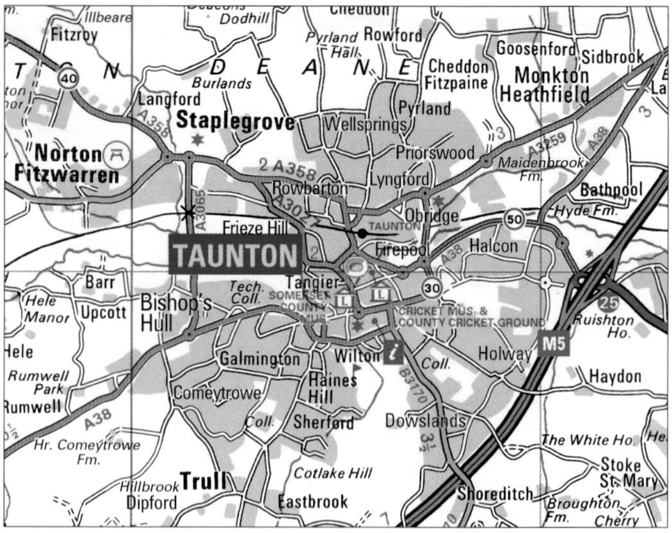

Somerset's county town, on the site of a Saxon fortress, with a pre-Conquest Saturday market. Buildings of historic interest include the Perpendicular St Mary Magdalene with its splendid tower, and a grammar school founded in 1522. Taunton has a tradition of brewing dating back as far as the Romans and continued by medieval monks; in the 20th century this was overtaken by cider-making. Somerset County Museum in historic Taunton Castle has a toy and doll collection, plus archeological artefacts, some from Roman times. There's a Monday antiques market with around 130 stalls and a good range of shops. Sights in the immediate vicinity include Bishops Lydeard Mill with its 2-tonne waterwheel, and Blazes Fire Museum about humans' relationship with fire.

▲ Taunton Castle

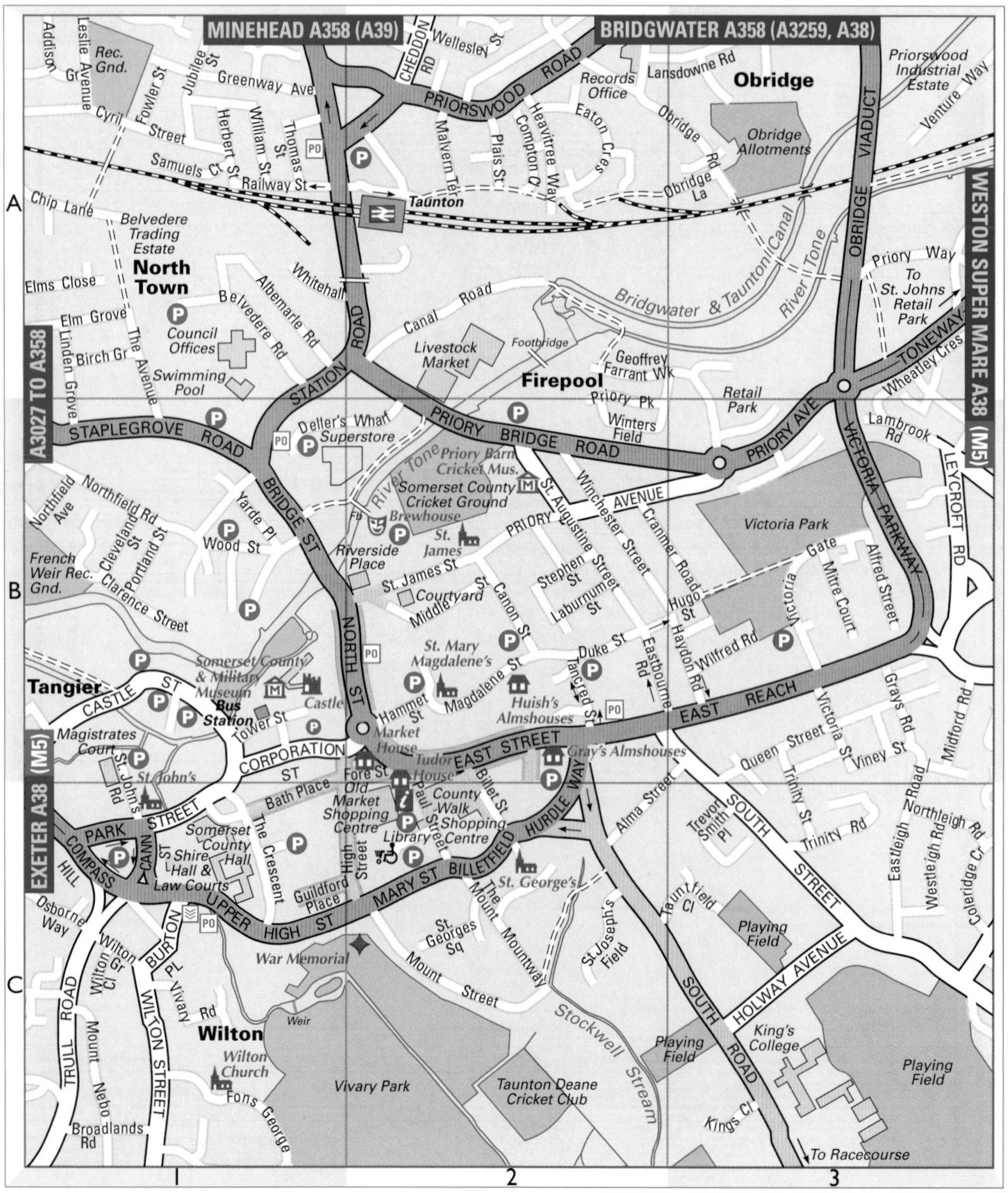

Taunton

Addison Gr A1
Albemarle Rd A1
Alfred St B3
Alma St C2
Bath Pl C1
Belvedere Rd A1
Billet St B2
Billetfield C2
Birch Gr A1
Brewhouse Theatre B2
Bridge St B1
Bridgwater & Taunton Canal A2
Broadlands Rd C1
Burton Pl C1
Bus Station B1
Canal Rd A2
Cann St C1
Canon St B2
Castle B1
Castle St B1
Cheddon Rd A2
Chip Lane A1
Clarence St B1
Cleveland St B1
Coleridge Cres C3
Compass Hill C1
Compton Cl A2
Corporation St B1
Council Offices A1
County Walk Shopping Ctr C2
Courtyard B2
Cranmer Rd B2
Cyril St A1
Deller's Wharf B1
Duke St B2
East Reach B3
East St B3
Eastbourne Rd B2
Eastleigh Rd C3
Eaton Cres A2
Elm Gr A1
Elms Cl A1
Fons George C1
Fore St B2
Fowler St A1
French Weir Rec Grnd B1
Geoffrey Farrant Wk A2
Gray's Almshouses B2
Grays Rd B3
Greenway Ave A1
Guildford Pl C1
Hammet St B2
Haydon Rd B3
Heavitree Way A2
Herbert St A1
High St C2
Holway Ave C3
Hugo St B3
Huish's Almshouses B2
Hurdle Way C2
Information Ctr C2
Jubilee St A1
King's College C3
Kings Cl C3
Laburnum St B2
Lambrook Rd B3
Lansdowne Rd A3
Leslie Ave A1
Leycroft Rd B3
Library C2
Linden Gr A1
Livestock Market A2
Magdalene St B2
Magistrates Court B1
Malvern Terr A2
Market House B2
Mary St C2
Middle St B2
Midford Rd B3
Mitre Court B3
Mount Nebo C1
Mount St C2
Mountway C2
North St B2
Northfield Ave B1
Northfield Rd B1
Northleigh Rd C3
Obridge Allotments A3
Obridge Lane A3
Obridge Rd A3
Obridge Viaduct A3
Old Market Shopping Ctr C2
Osborne Way C1
Park St C1
Paul St C2
Plais St A2
Playing Field C3
Police Station C1
Portland St B1
Post Office A1/B1/B2/C1
Priorswood Industrial Estate A3
Priorswood Rd A2
Priory Ave B2
Priory Barn Cricket Museum B2
Priory Bridge Rd B2
Priory Park A2
Priory Way A3
Queen St B3
Railway St A1
Records Office A2
Recreation Grd A1
Riverside Place B2
St Augustine St B2
St George's C2
St Georges Sq C2
St James B2
St.James St B2
St John's C1
St John's Rd B1
St Joseph's Field C2
St Mary Magdalene's B2
Samuels Ct A1
Shire Hall & Law Courts C1
Somerset County & Military Museum B1
Somerset County Cricket Grnd B2
Somerset County Hall C1
South Rd C3
South St C3
Staplegrove Rd B1
Station Rd A1
Stephen St B2
Swimming Pool A1
Tancred St B2
Tauntfield Cl C3
Taunton Dean Cricket Club C2
Taunton A2
The Avenue A1
The Crescent C1
The Mount C2
Thomas St A1
Toneway A3
Tower St B1
Trevor Smith Pl C3
Trinity Rd C3
Trinity St B3
Trull Rd C1
Tudor House B2
Upper High St C1
Venture Way A3
Victoria Gate B3
Victoria Park B3
Victoria St B3
Viney St B3
Vivary Park C2
Vivary Rd C1
War Memorial C1
Yarde Pl B1
Victoria Parkway B3
Wellesley St A2
Wheatley Cres A3
Whitehall A1
Wilfred Rd B3
William St A1
Wilton Church C1
Wilton Cl C1
Wilton Gr C1
Wilton St C1
Winchester St B2
Winters Field B2
Wood St B1
Yarde Pl B1

¼ mile
¼ ½ km

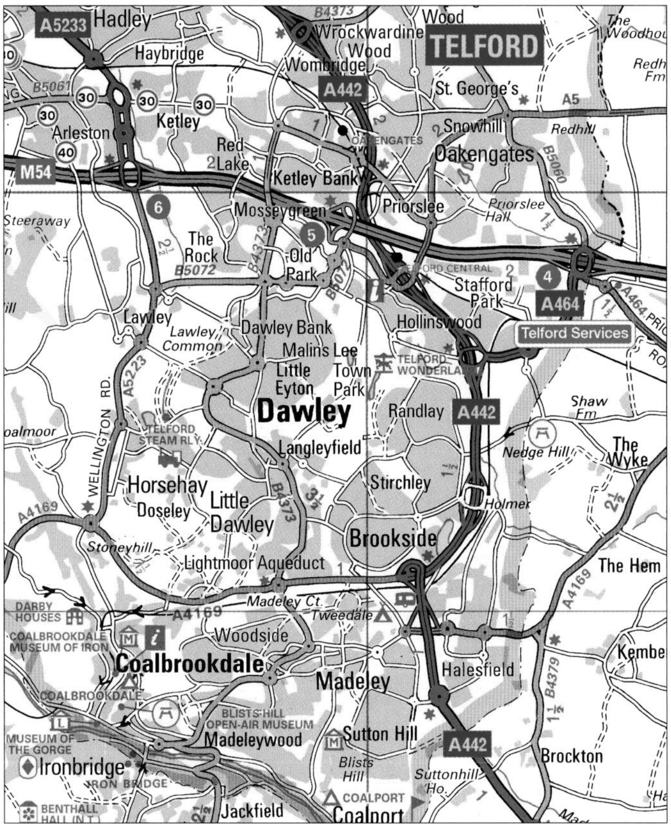

★Do not miss

★**Benthall Hall (National Trust)**, Benthall

★**Ironbridge Gorge Museums**, Ironbridge

★**Wonderland**, Telford Town Park – animated nursery rhymes and fairytales for children

Telford

▲The iron bridge at Ironbridge

A hi-tech New Town, named after civil engineer Thomas Telford and adjoining Ironbridge, the birthplace of the Industrial Revolution and site of the world's first cast-iron bridge, built to span the River Severn and now a UNESCO World Heritage Site with a total of nine museums about different aspects of the gorge, from ironwork to orchids. Family attractions in Telford include the 450-acre Town Park, Granville Country Park, and a steam railway. Nearby lie the ruined Augustinian 12th–13th-century Lilleshall Abbey, Wenlock Priory, Boscobel House, Weston Park (1671) with its Capability Brown landscaped gardens, and Cosford Aerospace Museum.

Telford Tourist Information Centre, Telford Shopping Centre, Telford TF3 4BX Tel 01952 238008

BBC Radio Shropshire 96 FM **Beacon** 103.1 FM • **Classic Gold** 1017 AM • **Telford** 107.4 FM

www.ironbridge.ws

Telford

Alma Ave C1
Amphitheatre. . . . C2
Bowling Alley B2
Brandsfarm Way . C3
Brunel Rd. B1
Bus Station B2
Buxton Rd C1
Castle Trading Estate A3
Central Park A2
Civic Offices. B2
Coach Central B2
Coachwell Cl B1
Colliers Way. A1
Courts. B2
Dale Acre Way. . . .B3
Darliston C3
Deepdale B3
Deercote B2
Dinthill C3
Doddington C3
Dodmoor Grange C3
Downemead. B3
Duffryn. B3
Dunsheath B3
Euston Way A3
Eyton Mound C1
Eyton Rd. C1
Forge Retail Park A1
Forgegate. A2
Grange Central . . .B2
Hall Park Way B1
Hinkshay Rd. C2
Hollinsworth Rd . A2
Holyhead Rd A3
Housing Trust. . . . A1
Ice Rink B2
Information Ctr .B2
Ironmasters Way. A2
Job Centre. B1
Land Registry B1
Lawn Central B2
Lawnswood C1
Library B2
Malinsgate B1
Matlock Ave. C1
Moor Rd. C1
Mount Rd C1
NFU Offices B1
Park Lane. A1
Police Station . .B1
Post Office B2
Priorslee Ave. . . . A3
Queen Elizabeth Ave C3
Queen Elizabeth Way. B1
Queensway. . . A2/B3
Rampart Way. . . . A2
Randlay Ave. C3
Randlay Wood. . . C3
Rhodes Ave C1
Royal Way B1
St Leonards Rd . . .B1
St Quentin Gate . .B2
Shifnal Rd A3
Sixth Ave A1
Southwater Way . .B1
Spout Lane. C1
Spout Mound. B1
Spout Way C1
Stafford Court B3
Stafford Park. B3
Stirchley Ave C3
Stone Row C1
Telford Bridge Retail Park. A1
Telford Central Station A3
Telford Centre, The B2
Telford International Ctr C2
Telford Way A3
Third Ave A2
Town Park C2
Town Park Visitor Centre. B2
Town Sports Club C2
Walker House B2
Wellswood Ave . . A2
West Centre Way. .B1
Withywood Drive C1
Woodhouse Central B2
Yates Way. A1

¼ mile
¼ ½ km

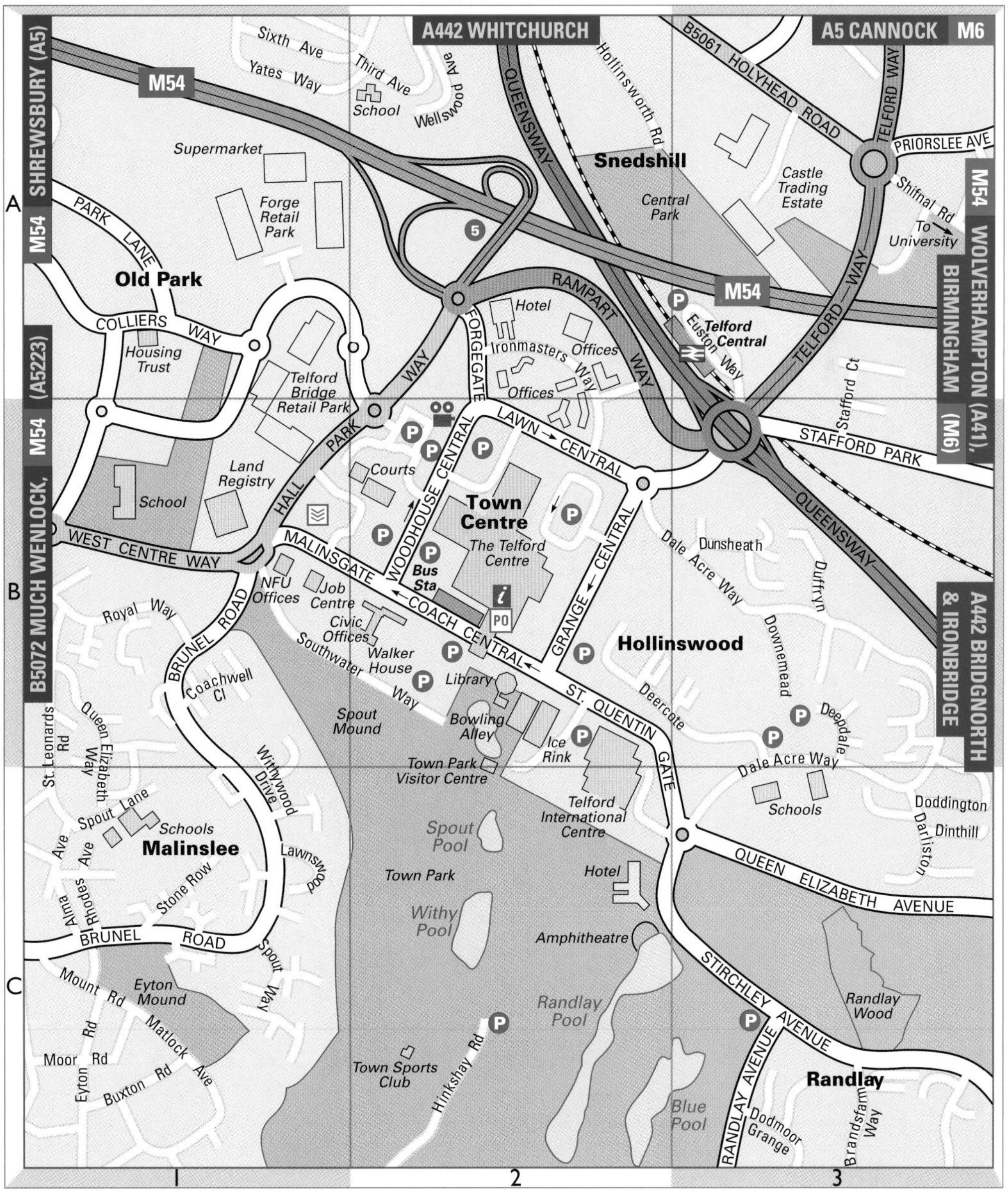

Torquay

▲Torquay at dusk

A stylish Torbay town with a palm-fringed seafront, handsome Victorian terraces and white Italian-style villas dating from its time as a fashionable 19th-century health and leisure resort, plus a modern marina. Attractions include a the new Aqualand aquarium; Babbacombe Model Village; Kent Cavern with its prehistoric remains; Bygones, a re-created Victorian street with shops, period rooms, and toys and models; and the Agatha Christie Trail revisiting sites associated with the crime writer, including a special exhibition in Torquay Museum. Among beaches are the award-winning Corbyn Sands, also the town is on the South West Coast Path. Nearby are the 14th–16th-century Compton Castle (National Trust), Plant World Gardens, Shaldon Wildlife Trust (a small-animal zoo) and Berry Head Country Park.

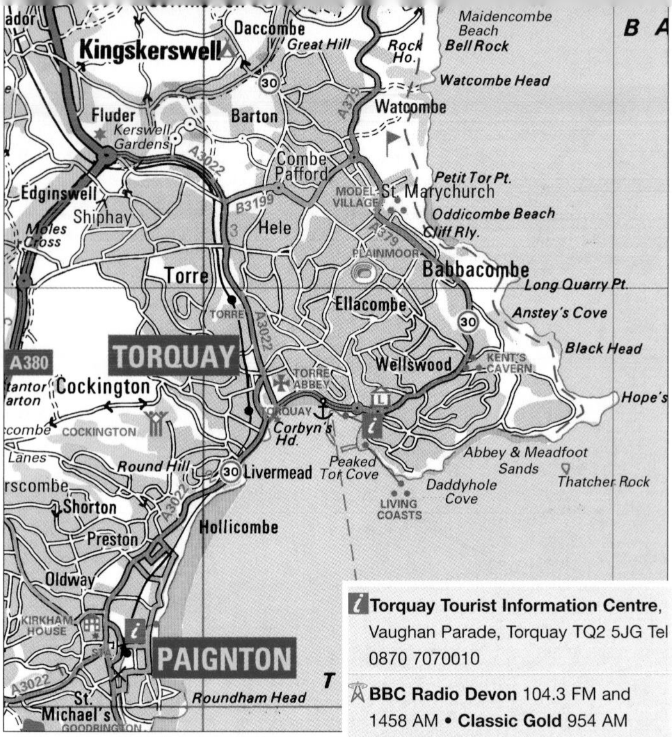

Torquay Tourist Information Centre, Vaughan Parade, Torquay TQ2 5JG Tel 0870 7070010

BBC Radio Devon 104.3 FM and 1458 AM • **Classic Gold** 954 AM **Gemini** 96.4 FM

www.torbay-online.co.uk

★Do not miss

★**Clifftop Railway**, Babbacombe to Oddicombe Beach
★**Cockington Court and Country Park**, Cockington
★**Torre Abbey and the Agatha Christie Memorial Room**, Kings Drive

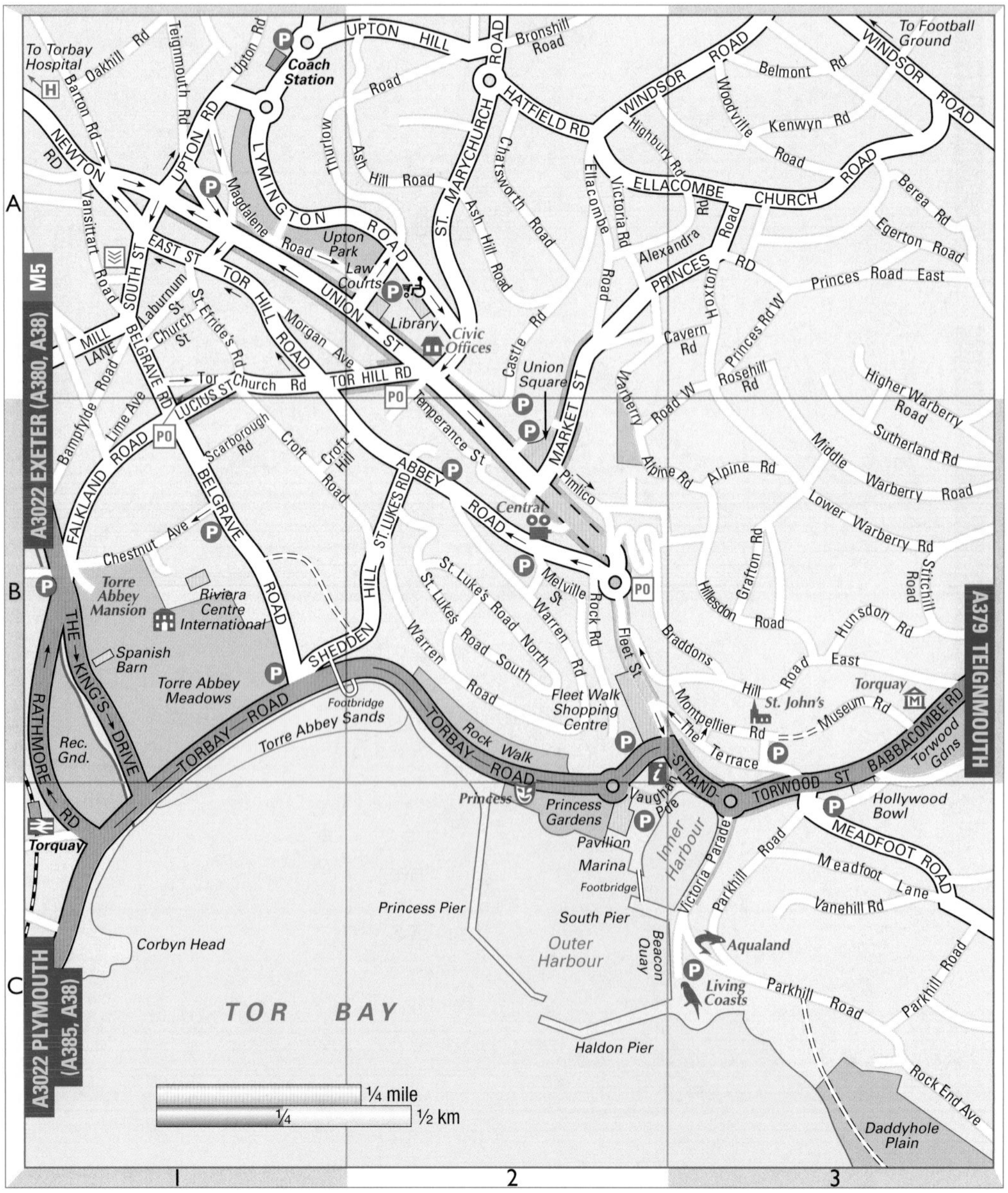

Torquay

Abbey Rd B2
Alexandra Rd A2
Alpine Rd B3
Aqualand C3
Ash Hill Rd A2
Babbacombe Rd B3
Bampfylde Rd B1
Barton Rd A1
Beacon Quay C2
Belgrave Rd . . A1/B1
Belmont Rd A3
Berea Rd A3
Braddons Hill Rd East B3
Bronshill Rd A2
Castle Rd A2
Cavern Rd A3
Central Cinema . . B2
Chatsworth Rd . . . A2
Chestnut Ave B1
Church St A1
Civic Offices . . A2
Coach Station . . . A1
Corbyn Head C1
Croft Hill B1
Croft Rd B1
Daddyhole Plain . C3
East St A1
Egerton Rd A3
Ellacombe Church Rd A3
Ellacombe Rd . . . A2
Falkland Rd B1
Fleet St B2
Fleet Walk Shopping Ctr . . . B2
Grafton Rd B3
Haldon Pier C2
Hatfield Rd A2
Highbury Rd A2
Higher Warberry Rd A3
Hillesdon Rd B3
Hollywood Bowl . C3
Hoxton Rd A3
Hunsdon Rd B3
Information Ctr . B2
Inner Harbour . . . C3
Kenwyn Rd A3
Laburnum St A1
Law Courts A2
Library A2
Lime Ave B1
Living Coasts . . C3
Lower Warberry Rd B3
Lucius St B1
Lymington Rd . . . A1
Magdalene Rd . . . A1
Marina C2
Market St B2
Meadfoot Lane . . C3
Meadfoot Rd . . . C3
Melville St B2
Middle Warberry Rd B3
Mill Lane A1
Montpellier Rd . . . B3
Morgan Ave A1
Museum Rd B3
Newton Rd A1
Oakhill Rd A1
Outer Harbour . . . C2
Parkhill Rd C3
Pavilion C2
Pimlico B2
Police Station . . A1
Post Office A2/B1/B2
Princes Rd A3
Princes Rd East . . A3
Princes Rd West . A3
Princess C2
Princess Gdns . . . C2
Princess Pier . . . C2
Rathmore Rd B1
Recreation Grnd . B1
Riviera Centre International . . . B1
Rock End Ave . . . C3
Rock Rd B2
Rock Walk B2
Rosehill Rd A3
St Efride's Rd . . . A1
St John's B3
St Luke's Rd B2
St Luke's Rd North B2
St Luke's Rd South B2
St Marychurch Rd A2
Scarborough Rd . B1
Shedden Hill B2
South Pier C2
South St A1
Spanish Barn B1
Stitchill Rd B3
Strand B3
Sutherland Rd . . . B3
Teignmouth Rd . . A1
Temperance St . . . B2
The King's Drive . B1
The Terrace B3
Thurlow Rd A1
Tor Bay B1
Tor Church Rd . . . A1
Tor Hill Rd A1
Torbay Rd B2
Torquay Museum B3
Torquay C1
Torre Abbey Mansion B1
Torre Abbey Meadows B1
Torre Abbey Sands B1
Torwood Gdns . . . B3
Torwood St C3
Union Square A2
Union St A1
Upton Hill A2
Upton Park A1
Upton Rd A1
Vanehill Rd C3
Vansittart Rd . . . A1
Vaughan Parade . C2
Victoria Parade . . C3
Victoria Rd A2
Warberry Rd West B2
Warren Rd B2
Windsor Rd . . A2/A3
Woodville Rd A3

Truro

In the 19th and 20th centuries Truro was a very busy port and prior to this a large mining and agricultural area. Today Truro is the centre of Cornwall for trade and commerce. Truro Cathedral was built on the site of the 16th century St Mary the Virgin Parish Church with work starting in 1880. There are many beautiful parks and gardens and the granite viaduct is a good piece of industrial architecture. As the county town it is a major shopping centre with small independent shops as well as department stores, high street names and a regular farmers' market. A wide variety of international cuisines is on offer, as well as a good selection of pubs. Nearby attractions include Trelissick Garden (National Trust).

▲Truro Cathedral

★Do not miss

★**Royal Cornwall Museum and Art Gallery**, River Street – Cornish history, art and mining heritage
★**Truro Cathedral**, St Mary's Street

Tourist Information Centre, Municipal Buildings, Boscawen Street, Truro TR1 2NE
Tel 01872 274555

BBC Radio Cornwall 103.9 FM and 630 AM • **Pirate FM** 102.8 FM

www.cornwall.gov.uk

Truro

Adelaide Ter. B1
Agar Rd B3
Arch Hill. C2
Arundell Pl. C2
Avondale Rd. B1
Back Quay B3
Barrack La C3
Barton Meadow. . A1
Benson Rd A2
Bishops Cl A2
Bosvean Gdns . . . B1
Bosvigo Gardens ✽ B1
Bosvigo La A1
Bosvigo Rd. B2
Broad St A3
Burley Cl. C3
Bus Station B3
Calenick St. B2
Campfield Hill . . . B3
Carclew St B3
Carew Rd A2
Carey Park B2
Carlyon Rd A2
Carvoza Rd. A3
Castle St. B2
Cathedral View . . A2
Chainwalk Dr. . . . A2
Chapel Hill B1
Charles St B2
City Hall B3
City Rd B2
Coinage Hall . . B3
Comprigney Hill . A1
Coosebean La A1
Copes Gdns A2
County Hall B1
Courtney Rd. A2
Crescent Rd B1
Crescent Rise . . . B1
Daniell Court. . . . C2
Daniell Rd C2
Daniell St C2
Daubuz Cl. A2
Dobbs La B1
Edward St. B2
Eliot Rd. A2
Elm Court. A3
Enys Cl A1
Enys Rd. A1
Fairmantle St. . . . B3
Falmouth Rd C2
Ferris Town B2
Fire Station B1
Frances St B2
George St. B2
Green Cl. C2
Green La. C1
Grenville Rd. A2
Hall For Cornwall B3
Hendra Rd A2
Hendra Vean A1
High Cross B3
Higher Newham La C3
Higher Trehaverne A2
Hillcrest Ave B1
Hospital B2
Hunkin Cl. A2
Hurland Rd. C3
Infirmary Hill B2
James Pl B3
Kenwyn Church Rd A1
Kenwyn Hill A1
Kenwyn Rd. A2
Kenwyn St B2
Kerris Gdns A1
King St B3
Lemon Quay. B3
Lemon Street Gallery B3
Library B1/B3
Malpas Rd B3
Market B3
Memorial Gdns . . . B3
Merrifield Close . B1
Mitchell Hill. A3
Moresk Cl. A3
Moresk Rd A3
Morlaix Ave C3
Nancemere Rd. . . A3
Newham Business Park . . C3
Newham Industrial Estate C3
Newham Rd C3
Northfield Dr C3
Oak Way A3
Pal's Terr A3
Park View C2
Pendarves Rd . . . A2
Plaza Cinema . . B3
Police Station . . B3
Post Office . B2/B3
Prince's St B3
Pydar St A2
Quay St. B3
Redannick Cres . . C2
Redannick La. . . . B2
Richard Lander Monument ✦. . . C2
Richmond Hill . . . B1
River St. B2
Rosedale Rd. A2
Royal Cornwall Museum B2
St Clement St . . . B3
St George's Rd . . A1
School La C2
Station Rd B1
Stokes Rd A2
Strangways Terr . C3
Tabernacle St . . . B3
The Avenue A3
The Crescent B1
The Leats B2
The Spires A2
Trehaverne La . . . A2
Tremayne Rd A2
Treseder's Gdns . A3
Treworder Rd. . . . B1
Treyew Rd B1
Truro Cathedral ✝. B3
Truro Harbour Office B3
Truro Station . B3
Union St B2
Upper School La . C2
Victoria Gdns B2
Waterfall Gdns . . . B2

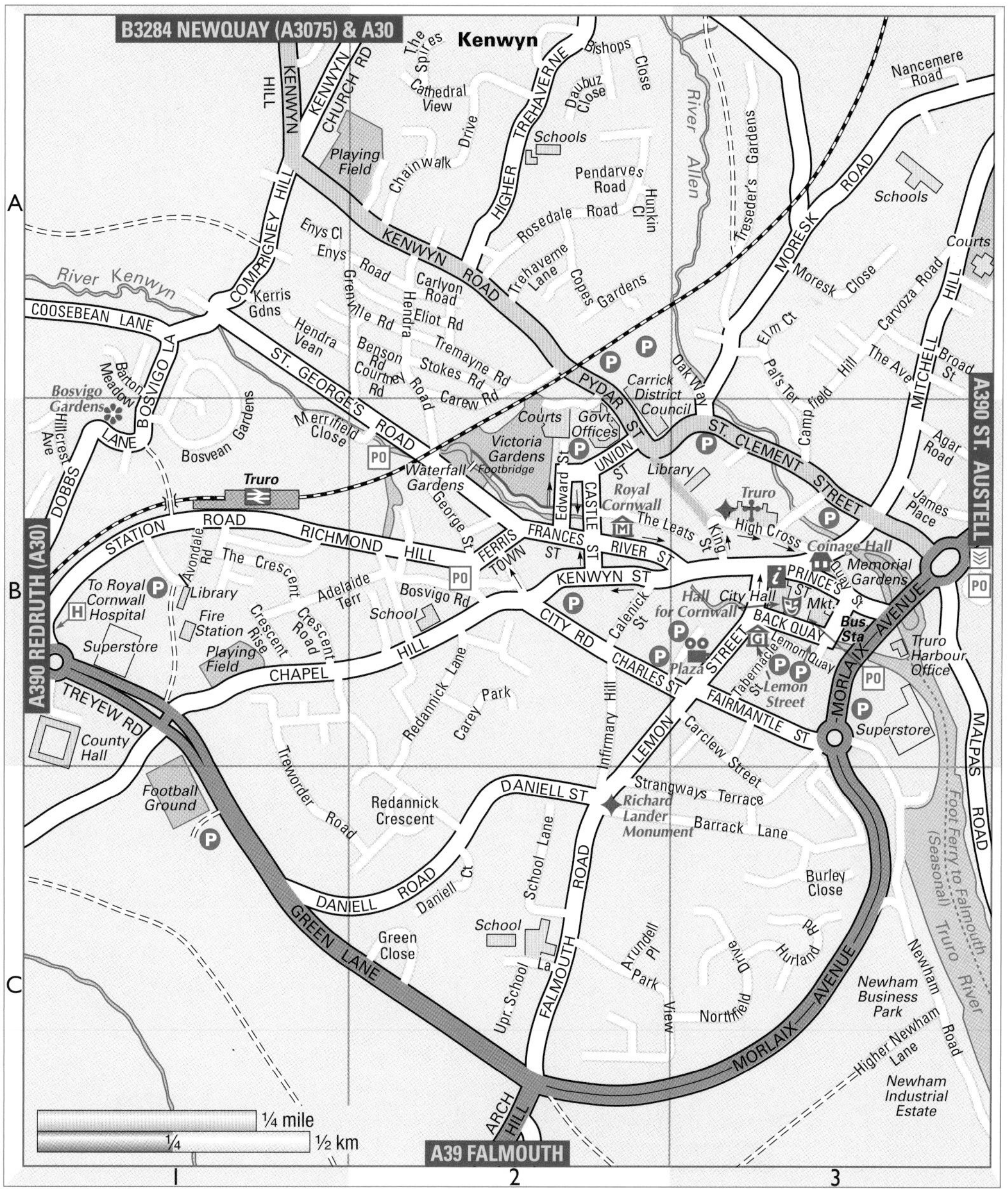

Wick

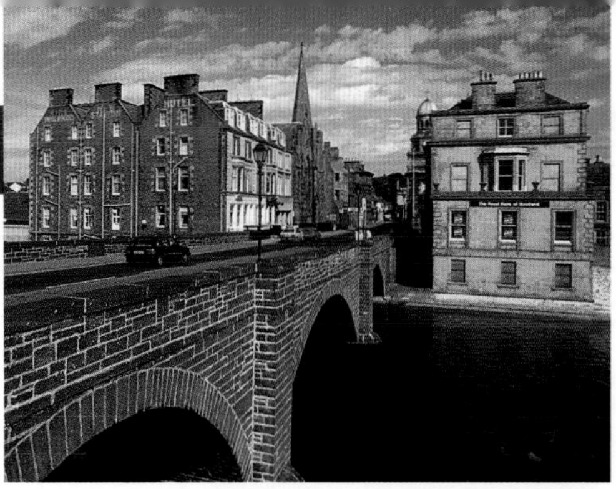

A Norse settlement on the far north-east coast of Scotland that became a royal burgh in 1589 and grew prosperous as a 19th-century herring 'boom town'. Of historical interest are the ruined castles of Girnigoe and Sinclair, separated by a rock-cut ravine, and clifftop Old Wick, one of the oldest remnants of a stone castle in Scotland, dating from the mid-12th century. Around Sinclair's Bay are two more ruined castles, Keiss and the Viking Bucholly, and a small museum on the history of the Norse settlers, while prehistoric remains in the area include the Cairn of Get, Hill O'Many Stanes and the Grey Cairns of Camster with their megaliths and stone circles. John O'Groats is 16 miles to the north.

▲View over the bridge to Wick

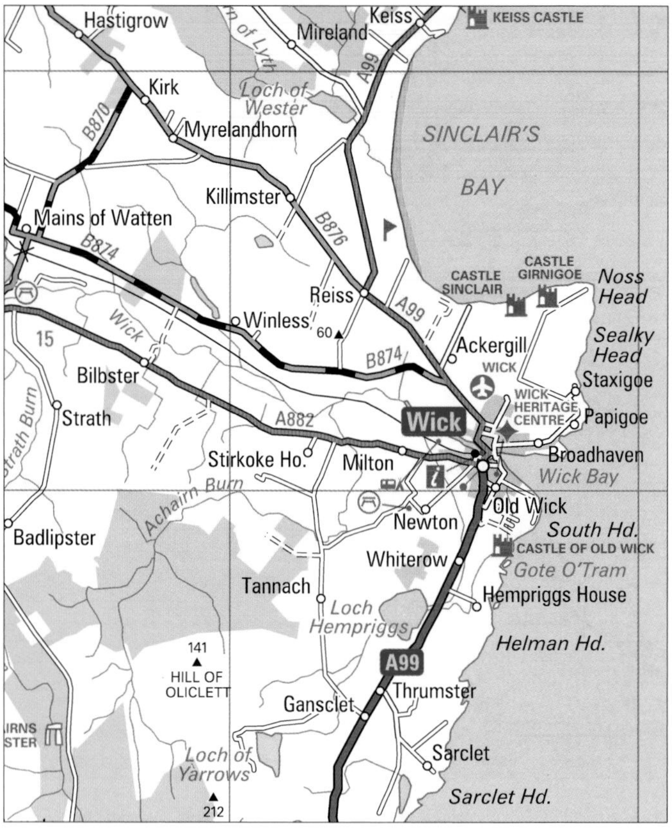

★Do not miss

★**Northlands Viking Centre**, Old School House, Auckengill

★**Wick Heritage Centre**, Bank Row

Wick Tourist Information Centre, Norseman Hotel, Riverside, Wick KW1 4NL Tel 0845 225 5121

BBC Radio Scotland 94.7 FM and 810 AM • **Caithness FM** 102.5 FM

www.caithness.org

¼ mile
¼ ½ km

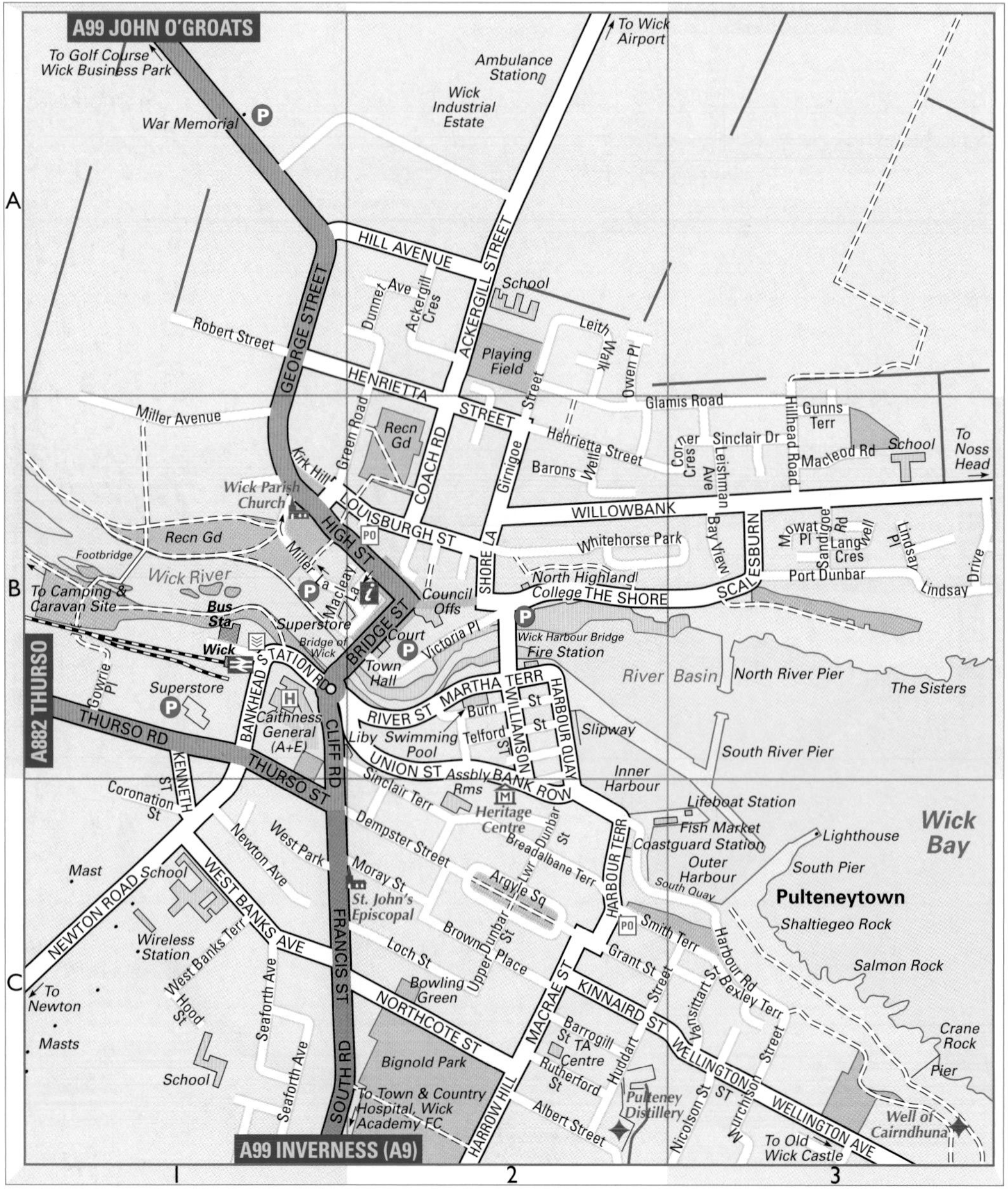

Wick

Ackergill Cres . . . A2
Ackergill St A2
Albert St. C2
Ambulance Stn . . A2
Argyle Sq C2
Assembly Rooms. C2
Bank Row. C2
Bankhead B1
Barons Well B2
Barrogill St C2
Bay View B3
Bexley Terr C3
Bignold Park C2
Bowling Green . . C2
Breadalbane Terr. C2
Bridge of Wick . . .B1
Bridge St B2
Brown Pl C2
Burn St. B2
Bus Station B1
Caithness General (A&E) B1
Cliff Rd B1
Coach Rd B2
Coastguard Stn . . C3
Corner Cres B3
Coronation St . . . C1
Council Offices . . .B2
Court. B2
Crane Rock C3
Dempster St. C2
Dunnet Ave A2
Fire Station B2
Fish Market C3
Francis St. C1
George St. A1
Girnigoe St B2
Glamis Rd. B2
Gowrie Pl B1
Grant St C2
Green Rd B2
Gunns Terr B3
Harbour Quay B2
Harbour Rd C3
Harbour Terr C2
Harrow Hill C2
Henrietta St. . A2/B2
Heritage Ctr . . C2
High St B2
Hill Ave A2
Hillhead Rd B3
Hood St C1
Huddart St C2
Information Ctr . .B2
Kenneth St. C1
Kinnaird St. C2
Kirk Hill B1
Langwell Cres B3
Leishman Ave B3
Leith Walk A2
Library B2
Lifeboat Stn. C3
Lighthouse. C3
Lindsay Dr B3
Lindsay Pl B3
Loch St. C2
Louisburgh St B2
Lower Dunbar St. C2
Macleay La. B1
Macleod Rd B3
MacRae St C2
Martha Terr B2
Miller Ave. B1
Miller La. B1
Moray St. C2
Mowat Pl B3
Murchison St. . . . C3
Newton Ave C1
Newton Rd C1
Nicolson St C3
North Highland College. B2
North River Pier . .B3
Northcote St C2
Owen Pl A2
Police Station . . .B1
Port Dunbar. B3
Post Office . B2/C2
Pulteney Distillery ✦ C2
River St. B2
Robert St A1
Rutherford St. . . . C2
St John's Episcopal C2
Sandigoe Rd B3
Scalesburn. B3
Seaforth Ave C1
Shore La. B2
Sinclair Dr B3
Sinclair Terr. C2
Smith Terr C3
South Pier C3
South Quay C3
South Rd C1
South River Pier . .B3
Station Rd B1
Swimming Pool. . .B2
TA Centre C2
Telford St B2
The Shore B2
Thurso Rd B1
Thurso St B1
Town Hall B2
Union St B2
Upper Dunbar St. C2
Vansittart St. C3
Victoria Pl B2
War Memorial . . . A1
Well of Cairndhuna ✦. . C3
Wellington Ave . . C3
Wellington St. . . . C3
West Banks Ave. . C1
West Banks Terr . C1
West Park. C1
Whitehorse Park. .B2
Wick Harbour Br. .B2
Wick Ind Est. A2
Wick Parish Church B1
Wick B1
Williamson St B2
Willowbank B2

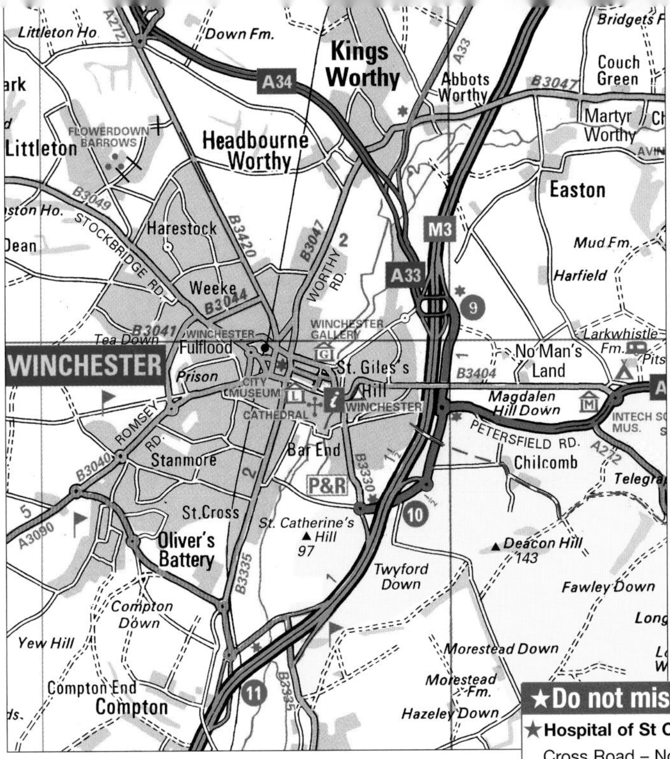

Winchester

▲Winchester Cathedral

England's ancient capital and the one-time seat of Alfred the Great, with a famous cathedral begun in 1079, attractive medieval streets and alleys full of one-off shops and boutiques. Of historic interest are Winchester City Mill, a working 1744 watermill; the remains of Winchester Castle and of Wolvesey Castle, the old bishops' palace; Winchester College, founded in 1382; City Museum; the Westgate fortified medieval gateway with its small museum; the Gurkha, Light Infantry, Royal Green Jackets, King's Royal Hussars, Royal Hampshire Regiment, Adjutant General's Corps museums in the Peninsula Barracks; and the Brooks Experience museum of Roman and medieval Winchester. INTECH is an interactive science and technology centre, while good green spaces include Queen Eleanor's Garden, a medieval herb garden. Nearby are Avington House and Park and Farley Mount Country Park, and the 100-mile South Downs Way of ancient routes and droveways runs from Winchester to Eastbourne.

Tourist Information Centre, Guildhall, The Broadway, Winchester SO23 9GH Tel 01962 840500

BBC Radio Solent 96.1 FM and 999 AM • **Win** 107.2 FM • **Capital Gold** 1557 AM • **Ocean** 96.7-97.5 FM • **Power** 103.2 FM

www.visitwinchester.co.uk

★Do not miss

★**Hospital of St Cross**, St Cross Road – Norman church, medieval hall

★**Winchester Cathedral**, The Close

★**Winchester Guildhall Gallery**, The Broadway

Winchester

Andover Rd A2
Andover Road Retail Park A2
Archery La C2
Arthur Rd A2
Bar End Rd C3
Beaufort Rd C2
Beggar's La B3
Bereweeke Ave .. A1
Bereweeke Rd ... A1
Boscobel Rd A2
Brassey Rd A2
Broadway B3
Brooks Shopping Ctr, The B3
Bus Station B3
Butter Cross ✦ ... B2
Canon St C2
Castle Wall ... C2/C3
Castle, King Arthur's Round Table .. B2
Cathedral ✝ C2
Cheriton Rd A1
Chesil St C3
Chesil Theatre . C3
Christchurch Rd . C1
City Museum .. B2
City Offices C3
City Rd B2
Clifton Rd B1
Clifton Terr B2
Close Wall ... C2/C3
Coach Park A2
Colebrook St C3
College St C2
College Walk C3
Compton Rd C2
County Council Offices B2
Cranworth Rd ... A2
Cromwell Rd C1
Culver Rd C2
Domum Rd C3
Durngate Pl B3
Eastgate St B3
Edgar Rd C2
Egbert Rd A2
Elm Rd B1
Fairfield Rd A1
Fire Station B3
Fordington Ave ... B1
Fordington Rd ... A1
Friarsgate B3
Gordon Rd B3
Greenhill Rd B1
Guildhall B3
HM Prison B1
Hatherley Rd A1
High St B2
Hillier Way A3
Hyde Abbey (Remains) ✝ ... A2
Hyde Abbey Rd ... B2
Hyde Cl A2
Hyde St A2
Information Ctr .. B3
Jewry St B2
John Stripe C1
King Alfred Pl ... A2
Kingsgate Arch .. C2
Kingsgate Rd C2
Kingsgate Park .. C2
Kingsgate St C2
Lankhills Rd A2
Library B2
Lower Brook St ... B3
Magdalen Hill B3
Market La B2
Mews La B1
Middle Brook St .. B3
Middle Rd B1
Military Museums B2
Milland Rd C3
Milverton Rd B1
Monks Rd A3
North Hill Cl A2
North Walls B2
North Walls Rec Grnd A3
Nuns Rd A3
Oram's Arbour B1
Owen's Rd A2
Parchment St B2
Park & Ride C3
Park Ave B3
Playing Field A1
Police H.Q. B1
Police Station .. B3
Portal Rd C3
Post Office . A2/B2/B3/C1/C2
Quarry Rd C3
Ranelagh Rd C1
River Park Leisure Centre ... B3
Romans' Rd C2
Romsey Rd B1
Royal Hampshire County (A&E) .. B1
St Cross Rd C2
St George's St B2
St Giles Hill C3
St James' La B1
St James' Terr B1
St James Villas .. C2
St John's B3
St John's St B3
St Michael's Rd ... C2
St Paul's Hill B1
St Peter St B2
St Swithun St C2
St Thomas St C2
Saxon Rd A2
School of Art B3
Screen Cinema .. B2
Sleepers Hill Rd . C1
Southgate St B2
Sparkford Rd C1
Staple Gdns B2
Station Rd B2
Step Terr B1
Stockbridge Rd .. A1
Stuart Cres C1
Sussex St B2
Swan Lane B2
Tanner St B3
The Square B2
The Weirs C3
Theatre Royal .. B2
Tower St B2
Town Hall C3
Union St B3
University of Winchester C1
Upper Brook St ... B2
Wales St B3
Water Lane B3
West End Terr B1
West Gate B2
Western Rd B1
Wharf Hill C3
Winchester Coll . C2
Winchester ... A2
Wolvesey Castle C3
Worthy Lane A2
Worthy Rd A2

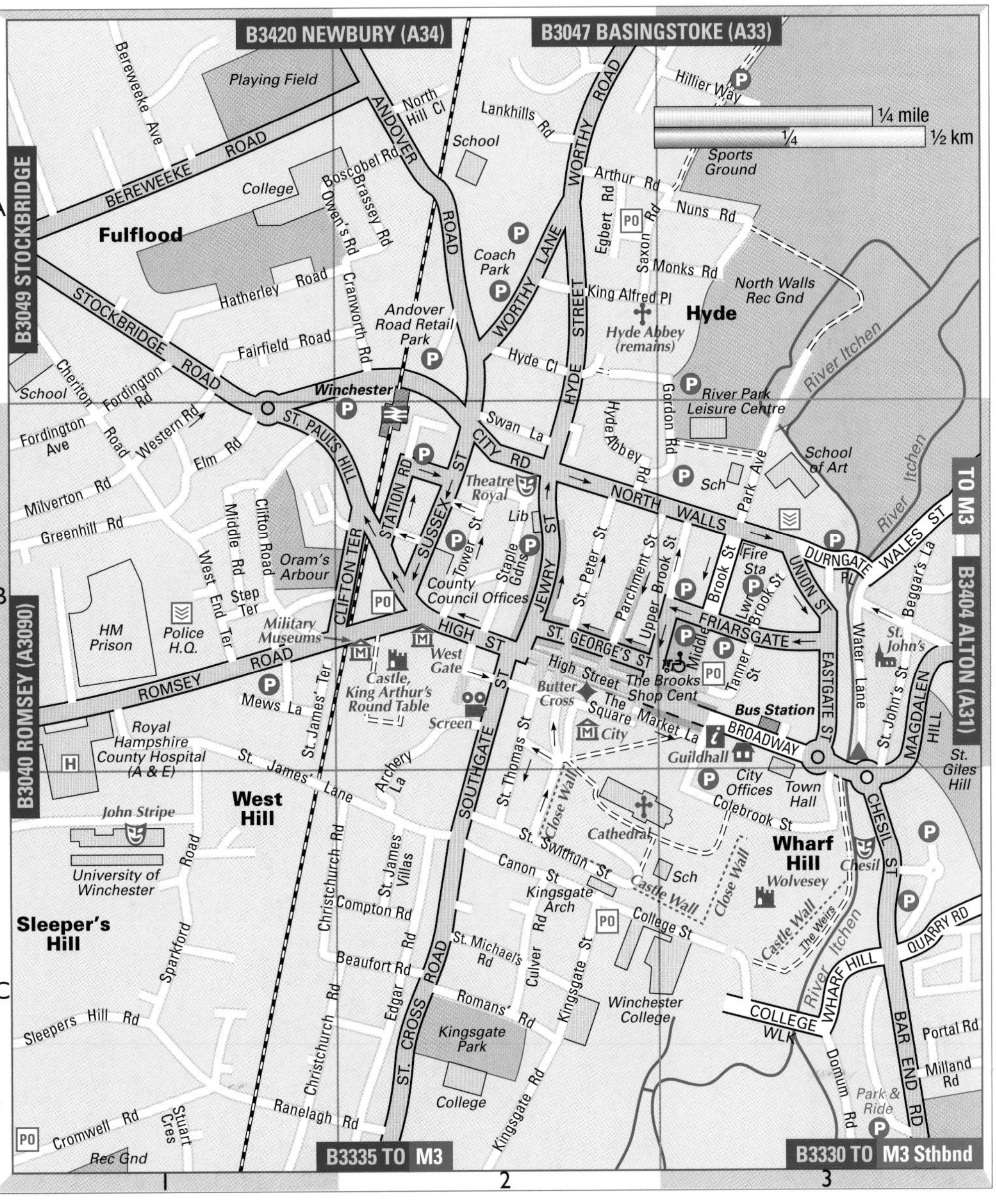

Windsor

A royal borough on the River Thames, with a large castle that has been a royal residence for more than 900 years (making it the world's oldest in continuous occupation) and that contains the beautiful St George's Chapel, where 10 monarchs are buried (including Henry VIII), Frogmore House, a favourite retreat of Queen Victoria, and a farm shop. Other attractions include Guildhall Island, the town centre with its narrow cobbled streets and 17th-century buildings, including Sir Christopher Wren's Guildhall and his house, now a hotel; the vast Windsor Great Park, containing Savill Garden, a 35-acre woodland garden; and Dorney Court, a fine Tudor house (limited opening). A few miles to the south is prestigious Ascot Racecourse, and to the southeast is Runnymede, where King John sealed the Magna Carta in 1215, now home to memorials to JFK and Air Force personnel who died in WWII.

▼Windsor Castle from The Home Park

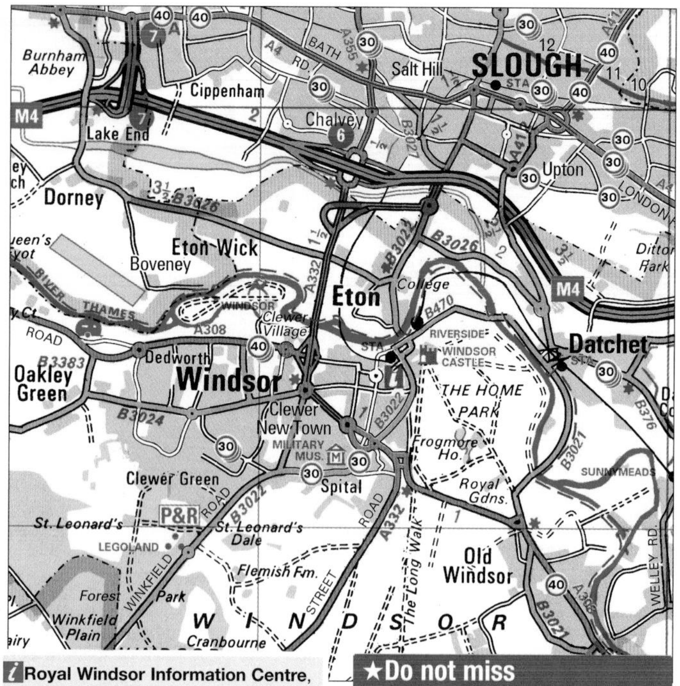

Royal Windsor Information Centre, Old Booking Hall, Windsor Royal Station, SL4 1PJ Tel 01753 743900

BBC Radio Berkshire 95.4, 104.1, 104.4 FM • **STAR** 106.6 FM

www.windsor.gov.uk

★**Do not miss**

★**Eton College**, Eton

★**Legoland Windsor**, Winkfield Road

★**Windsor Castle**, Thames Street

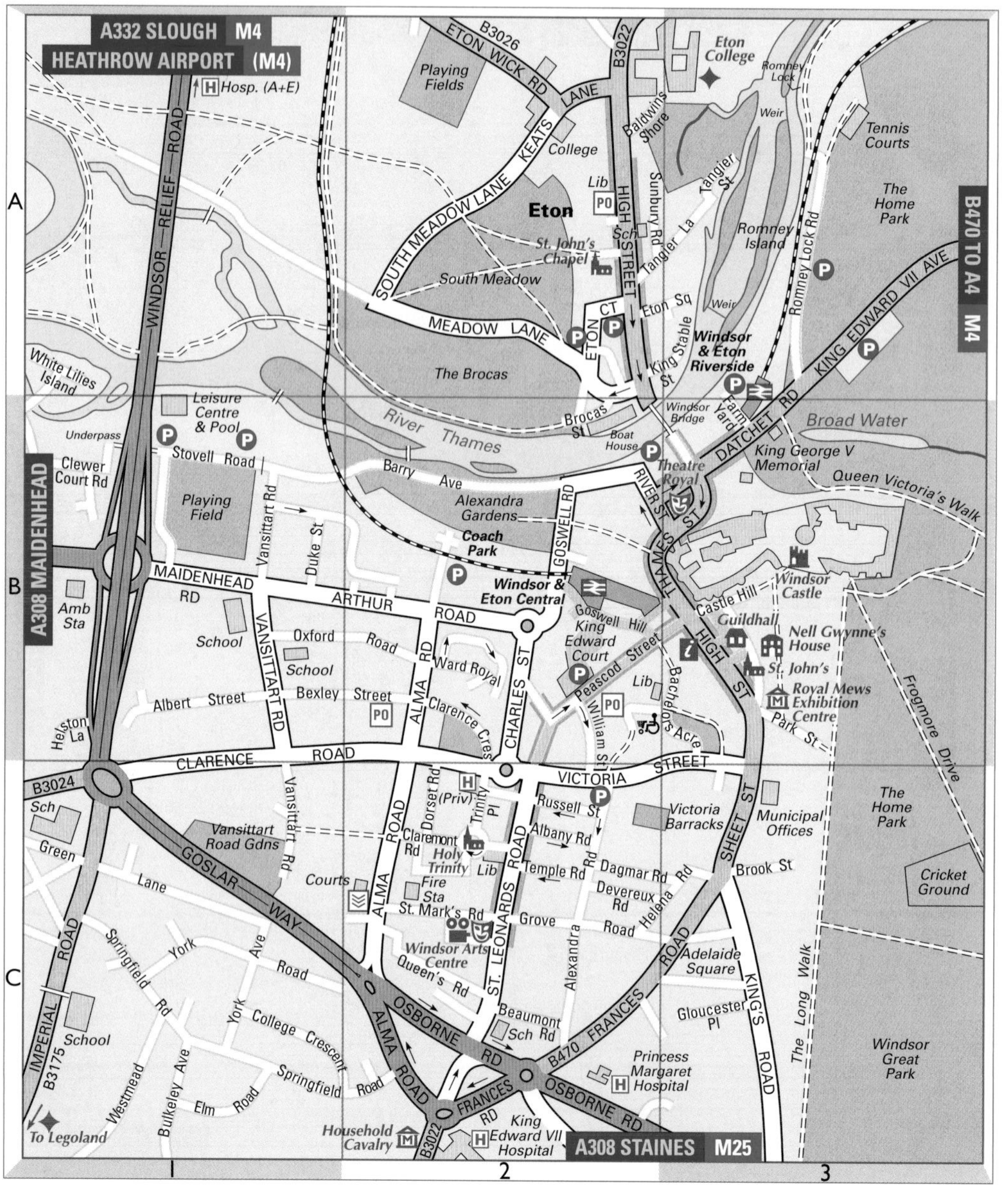

Windsor

Adelaide Sq C3
Albany Rd. C2
Albert St. B1
Alexandra Gdns. . .B2
Alexandra Rd. . . . C2
Alma Rd B2
Ambulance Stn . . .B1
Arthur Rd. B2
Bachelors Acre . . .B3
Barry Ave B2
Beaumont Rd. . . . C2
Bexley St B1
Boat House B2
Brocas St B2
Brook St. C3
Bulkeley Ave C1
Castle Hill B3
Charles St B2
Claremont Rd . . . C2
Clarence Cr B2
Clarence Rd. B1
Clewer Court Rd . .B1
Coach Park B2
College Cr C1
Courts. C2
Cricket Ground . . C3
Dagmar Rd. C2
Datchet Rd. B3
Devereux Rd C2
Dorset Rd. C2
Duke St. B1
Elm Rd C1
Eton College ✦. . A3
Eton Ct A2
Eton Sq. A2
Eton Wick Rd. . . . A2
Fire Station C2
Farm Yard. B3
Frances Rd. C2
Frogmore Dr B3
Gloucester Pl. . . . C3
Goslar Way. C1
Goswell Hill B2
Goswell Rd. B2
Green La. C1
Grove Rd C2
Guildhall B3
Helena Rd C2
Helston La B1
High St A2/B3
Holy Trinity C2
Hospital (Private) C2
Household Cavalry C2
Imperial Rd C1
Information Ctr . .B3
Keats La A2
King Edward Ct. . .B2
King Edward VII Ave A3
King Edward VII Hospital C2
King George V Memorial B3
King's Rd C3
King Stable St . . . A2
Leisure Ctr & Pool B1
Library C2
Maidenhead Rd. . .B1
Meadow La A2
Municipal Offices C3
Nell Gwynne's House B3
Osborne Rd C2
Oxford Rd. B1
Park St B3
Peascod St. B2
Police Station . C2
Post Office . . A2/B2
Princess Margaret Hospital C2
Queen Victoria's Walk B3
Queen's Rd C2
River St. B2
Romney Island. . . A3
Romney Lock. . . . A3
Romney Lock Rd. A3
Royal Mews Exhibition Ctr .B3
Russell St. C2
St John's B3
St John's Chapel A2
St Leonards Rd . . C2
St Mark's Rd C2
Sheet St C3
South Meadow . . A2
South Meadow La A2
Springfield Rd . . . C1
Stovell Rd. B1
Sunbury Rd A2
Tangier La A2
Tangier St. A3
Temple Rd C2
Thames St B3
The Brocas. A2
The Home Pk. A3/C3
The Long Walk . . C3
Theatre Royal . .B3
Trinity Pl. C2
Vansittart Rd . B1/C1
Vansittart Rd Gdns C1
Victoria Barracks C2
Victoria St C2
Ward Royal. B2
Westmead C1
White Lilies Island A1
William St B2
Windsor Arts Centre C2
Windsor Castle .B3
Windsor & Eton Central B2
Windsor & Eton Riverside . . . A3
Windsor Bridge. . .B3
Windsor Great Pk C3
Windsor Relief Rd A1
York Ave. C1
York Rd. C1

¼ mile
¼ ½ km

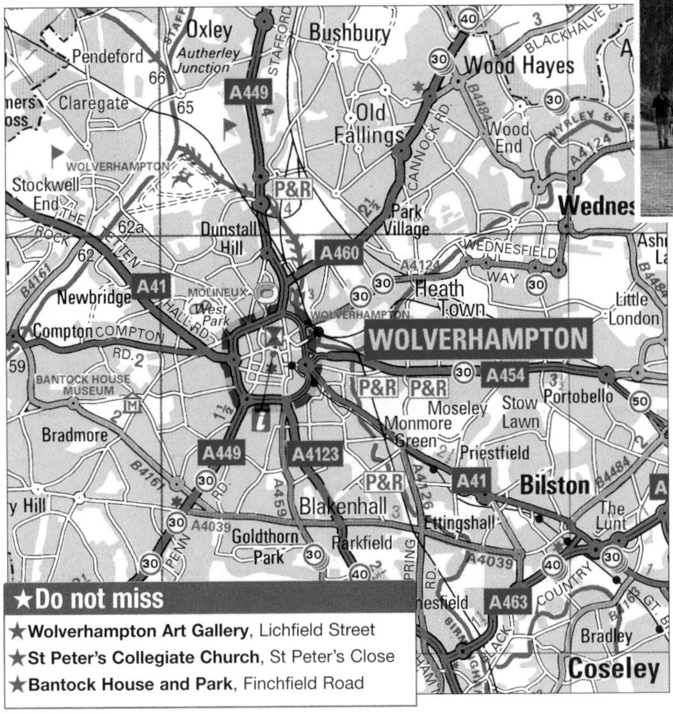

★Do not miss

★**Wolverhampton Art Gallery**, Lichfield Street

★**St Peter's Collegiate Church**, St Peter's Close

★**Bantock House and Park**, Finchfield Road

▲Broad Street canal basin

Wolverhampton

Tourist Information Centre, 18 Queen Square, Wolverhampton WV1 1TQ Tel 01902 556110

BBC WM 95.6 FM • **Beacon** 97.2 FM • **Classic Gold** 990 AM **Heart** 100.7 FM • **Saga** 105.7FM

www.wolverhampton.gov.uk

Wolverhampton has existed for over 1000 years and went from a wool-trade dominated town to a major centre of the Industrial Revolution. It is now a cultural centre with its galleries, museums and university, not to mention its football team Wolverhampton Wanderers. The Mander and Wulfrun shopping centres provide a wide range of shops and much of the city centre has been pedestrianised; Civic and Wulfrun halls are major concert venues for the Black Country; Light House Media Centre offers independent cinema; and the cosmopolitan population is reflected in the breadth of choice of bars, pubs and restaurants.

Wolverhampton

Albany Rd B1
Albion St B3
Alexandra St C1
Gallery B2
Ashland St C1
Austin St. A1
Badger Dr A3
Bailey St. B3
Bath Ave. B1
Bath Rd. B1
Bell St. C2
Berry St B3
Bilston Rd C3
Bilston St C3
Birmingham Canal A3
Bone Mill La A2
Bright St. A1
Burton Cres B3
Bus Station B3
Cambridge St . . . A3
Camp St B2
Cannock Rd A3
Castle St. C2
Chapel Ash. C1
Cherry St C1
Chester St A1
Church La. C2
Church St. C2
Civic Centre. B2
Clarence Rd B2
Cleveland Rd C2
Cleveland St C2
Clifton St C1
Coach Station B2
Compton Rd. B1
Corn Hill. B3
Coven St. A3
Craddock St. A1
Cross St North. . . A2
Crown & County Courts. C3
Crown St A2
Culwell St. B3
Dale St C1
Darlington St. . . . C1
Dartmouth St. . . . C3
Devon Rd A1
Drummond St B2
Dudley Rd. C2
Dudley St B2
Duke St. C3
Dunkley St B1
Dunstall Ave. A2
Dunstall Hill. A2
Dunstall Rd . . A1/A2
Evans St A1
Eye Infirmary H . C1
Fawdry St. A1
Field St. B3
Fire Station C1
Fiveways (r'about) A2
Fowler Playing Fields A3
Fox's La A2
Francis St. A2
Fryer St B3
Gloucester St. . . . A1
Gordon St. C3
Graiseley St C1
Grand B3
Granville St C3
Great Western St A2
Great Brickkiln St C1
Grimstone St B3
Gt. Hampton St . . A1
Harrow St. A1
Hilton St. A3
Horseley Fields . . . C3
Humber Rd C1
Jack Hayward Wy A2
Jameson St. A1
Jenner St C3
Kennedy Rd B3
Kimberley St C1
King St B2
Laburnum St C1
Lansdowne Rd. . . . B1
Leicester St A1
Lever St C3
Library C3
Lichfield St. B2
Lighthouse B3
Little's La B3
Lock St B3
Lord St C1
Lowe St A1
Lower Stafford St A2
Magistrates Court . B2
Mander Centre . . C2
Mander St C1
Market St B2
Market C2
Melbourne St. . . . C3
Merridale St C1
Middlecross. C3
Molineux St B2
Mostyn St. A1
New Hampton Rd East. A1
Nine Elms La A3
North Rd. A2
Oaks Cres. C1
Oxley St A2
Paget St A1
Park Ave. B1
Park Rd East A1
Park Rd West. B1
Paul St C2
Pelham St C1
Penn Rd C2
Piper's Row B3
Pitt St C2
Police Station . C3
Pool St C2
Poole St A3
Post Office . A1/A2/B2/B2/C2
Powlett St C3
Queen St B2
Raby St C3
Raglan St C1
Railway Dr B3
Red Hill St A2
Red Lion St B2
Retreat St. C1
Ring Rd. B2
Rugby St. A1
Russell St. C1
St Andrew's B1
St David's. B3
St George's C3
St James St C3
St John's C2
St John's C2
St John's Retail Park C2
St John's Square C2
St Mark's C1
St Marks Rd. C1
St Marks St C1
St Patrick's B2
St Peter's B2
St Peter's B2
Salisbury St C1
Salop St C2
School St C2
Sherwood St A2
Smestow St A3
Snowhill C2
Springfield Rd A3
Stafford St B2
Staveley Rd A1
Steelhouse La . . . C3
Stephenson St. . . C1
Stewart St C2
Sun St. B3
Sutherland Pl . . . C3
Tempest St. C2
Temple St. C2
Tettenhall Rd B1
The Maltings B2
The Royal (Metro) C3
Thomas St C2
Thornley St B2
Tower St. C2
Town Hall B2
University. B2
Upper Zoar St . . . C1
Vicarage Rd C3
Victoria St C2
Walpole St A1
Walsall St C3
Ward St. C3
Warwick St. C3
Water St. A3
Waterloo Rd. B2
Wednesfield Rd . . . B3
West Park (not A&E) H B1
West Park Swimming Pool. . B1
Wolverhampton St Georges (Metro) C2
Wharf St. C3
Whitmore Hill B2
Wolverhampton B3
Wolverhampton Wanderers Football Grnd (Molineux) . B2
Worcester St C2
Wulfrun Centre . . C2
Yarwell Cl. A3
York St C3
Zoar St C1

¼ mile
¼ ½ km

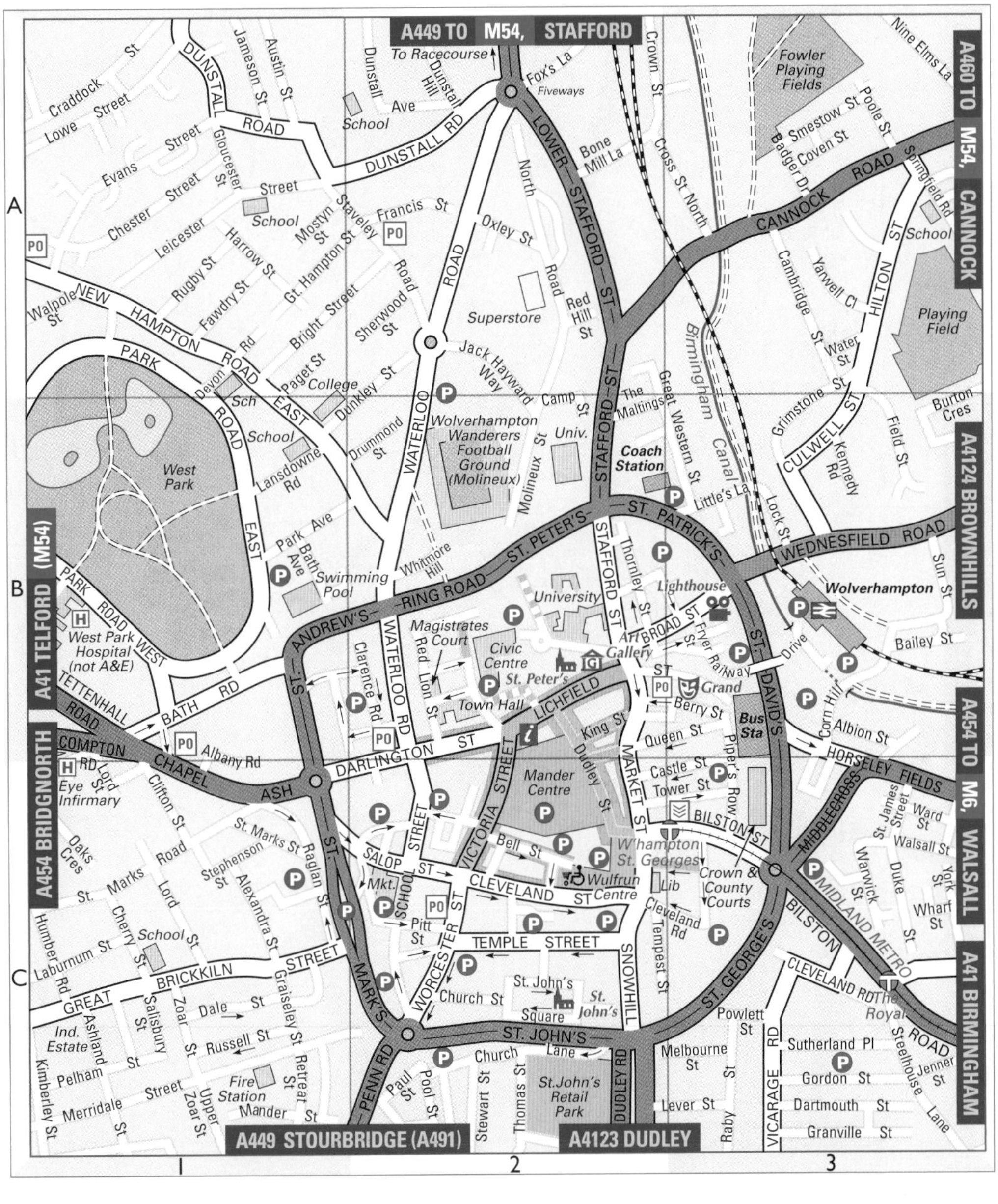

Worcester

▲Worcester Cathedral

★Do not miss

★**Worcester Cathedral**, College Green

★**Worcester City Art Gallery and Museum**, Foregate Street

★**The Greyfriars**, Friar Street – medieval merchant's house

Worcester is a beautiful cathedral city on the River Severn with a history going back over 1,000 years. The city played an important part in the Civil War and The Commandery museum honours this heritage. Other notable places of interest include the Worcester Guildhall; City Museum and Art Gallery; The Greyfriars; and Royal Worcester, the porcelain manufacturer, with a factory tour, visitor centre and museum. There's a good range of spectator sport with Worcester Racecourse, Worcestershire County Cricket Club and Worcester Rugby Club all centrally located. The Crown Gate Centre offers a variety of well known stores, or there are specialist shops off the pedestrianised High Street. For entertainment there is a choice of cinema and theatre and a good range of restaurants and pubs, with cider being prevalent as a speciality to nearby Herefordshire. Nearby green spaces include Worcester Woods Country Park and Spetchley Park Gardens.

The Guildhall, High Street, Worcester WR1 2EY
Tel 01905 726311

BBC Radio Worcester 104.0 FM and 738 AM • **Classic Hits** 1530 AM **Wyvern** 97.6, 102.8 FM

www.cityofworcester.gov.uk

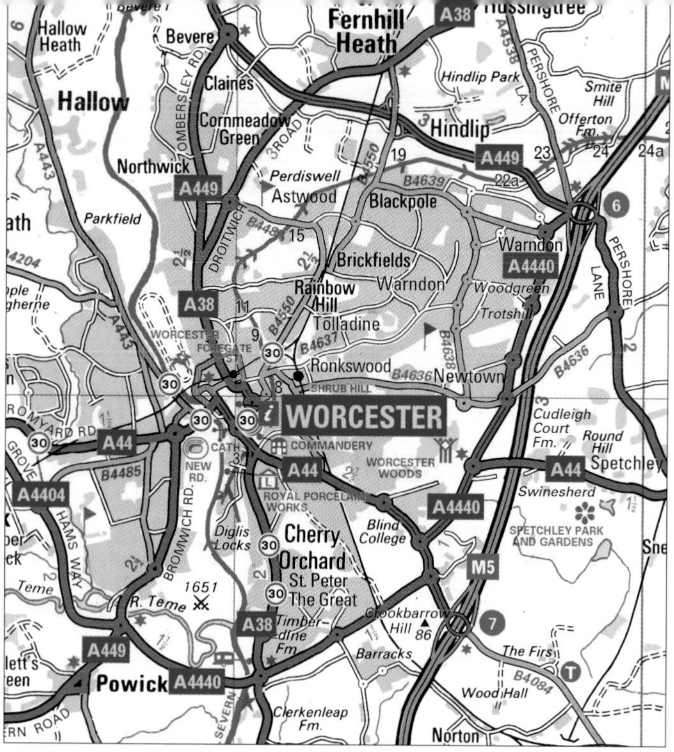

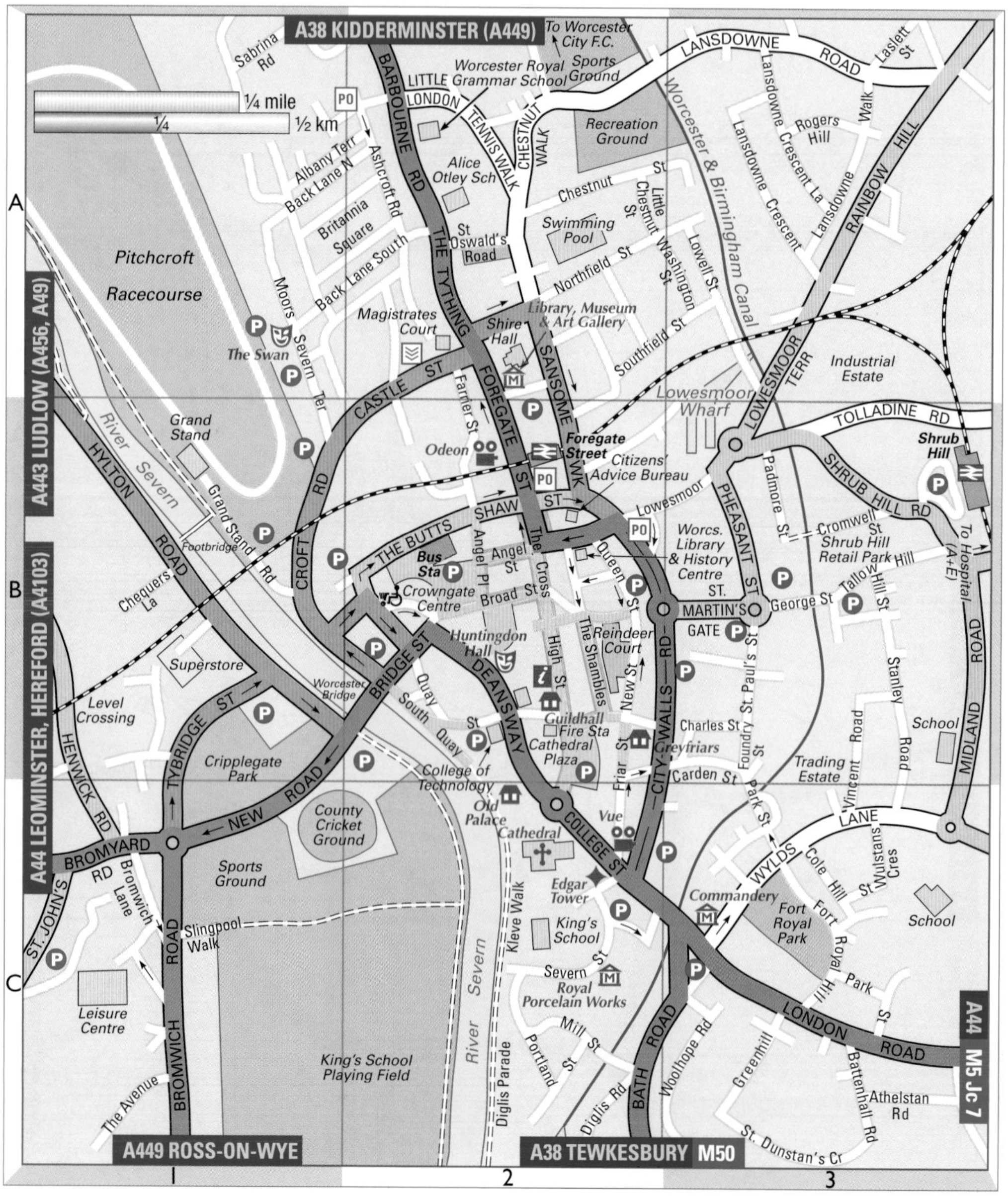

Worcester

Albany Terr. A1
Alice Otley Sch . . A2
Angel Pl B2
Angel St B2
Ashcroft Rd A2
Athelstan Rd C3
Back Lane North . A1
Back Lane South. A1
Barbourne Rd . . . A2
Bath Rd. C2
Battenhall Rd. . . . C3
Bridge St B2
Britannia Sq. A1
Broad St. B2
Bromwich La C1
Bromwich Rd. . . . C1
Bromyard Rd C1
Bus Station B2
Carden St. B3
Castle St. A2
Cathedral ✝. C2
Cathedral Plaza. . .B2
Charles St B3
Chequers La. B1
Chestnut St A2
Chestnut Walk. . . A2
Citizens' Advice Bureau B2
City Walls Rd B2
Cole Hill C3
Coll of Technology B2
College St C2
Commandery 🏛 . . C3
County Cricket Ground. C1
Cripplegate Park. .B1
Croft Rd B1
Cromwell St. B3
Crowngate Ctr. . . .B2
Deansway. B2
Diglis Pde C2
Diglis Rd. C2
Edgar Tower ✦ . . C2
Farrier St A2
Fire Station B2
Foregate St B2
Foregate St ⇌. . . .B2
Fort Royal Hill . . . C3
Fort Royal Park. . C3
Foundry St. B3
Friar St. C2
George St. B3
Grand Stand Rd. . .B1
Greenhill C3
Greyfriars 🏛 B2
Guildhall 🏛. B2
Henwick Rd B1
High St B2
Hill St B3
Huntingdon Hall 🎭. B2
Hylton Rd B1
Information Ctr ℹ.B2
King's School . . . C2
King's School Playing Field . . . C2
Kleve Walk. C2
Lansdowne Cr . . . A3
Lansdowne Rd. . . A3
Lansdowne Walk. A3
Laslett St A3
Leisure Centre. . . A3
Library, Museum & Art Gallery 🏛 . . A2
Little Chestnut St A2
Little London. . . . A2
London Rd C3
Lowell St A3
Lowesmoor B2
Lowesmoor Terr . A3
Lowesmoor Wharf A3
Magistrates Ct. . . A2
Midland Rd B3
Mill St. C2
Moors Severn Terr A1
New Rd. C1
New St B2
Northfield St A2
Odeon 🎥 B2
Old Palace 🏛 B2
Padmore St B3
Park St C3
Pheasant St B3
Pitchcroft Racecourse A1
Police Station 🏢. . A2
Portland St C2
Post Office PO. A1/A2/B2
Quay St. B2
Queen St B2
Rainbow Hill A3
Recreation Grnd . A2
Reindeer Court . . .B2
Rogers Hill. A3
Royal Worcester Factory Visitor Ctr & Mus 🏛. . . C2
Sabrina Rd A1
St Dunstan's Cr. . C3
St John's C1
St Martin's Gate . .B3
St Oswald's Rd . . A2
St Paul's St B3
St Wulstans Cr. . . C3
Sansome Walk. . . A2
Severn St C2
Shaw St B2
Shire Hall. A2
Shrub Hill ⇌. B3
Shrub Hill Retail Park B3
Shrub Hill Rd. B3
Slingpool Walk . . C1
South Quay B2
Southfield St A2
Sports Grnd . . A2/C1
Stanley Rd B3
Swan, The 🎭 A1
Swimming Pool. . A2
Tallow Hill B3
Tennis Walk A2
The Avenue C1
The Butts B2
The Cross. B2
The Shambles B2
The Tything A2
Tolladine Rd. B3
Tybridge St. B1
Vincent Rd B3
Vue Cinema 🎥. . . C2
Washington St. . . A3
Woolhope Rd. . . . C3
Worcester Br B2
Worcester Library & History Ctr B3
Worcester Royal Grammar Sch . . A2
Wylds La. C3

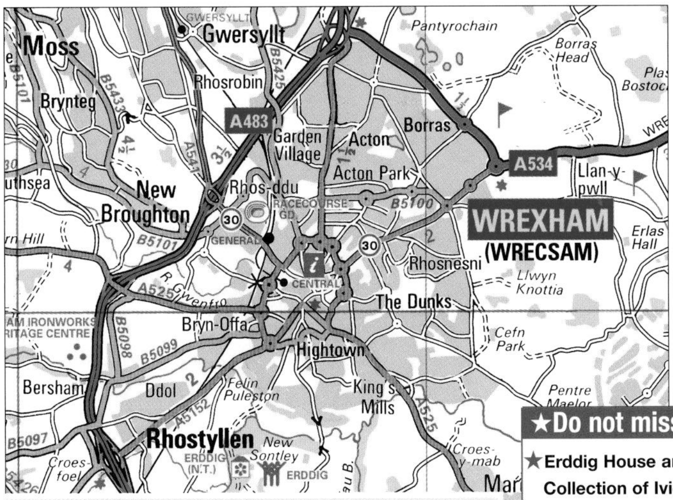

Wrexham Tourist Information Centre, Lambpit Street, Wrexham LL11 2RB Tel 01978 292015

BBC Radio Wales 95.4 FM
Classic Gold Marcher 1260 AM • **MFM** 103.4 FM

www.wrexham.gov.uk

★Do not miss

★**Erddig House and National Collection of Ivies** (National Trust; 1680s), south of town
★**Minera Lead Mines and Country Park**, Wern Road, Minera
★**Pontcysyllte Aqueduct** (Thomas Telford, 1795), Froncysyllte, near Cefn-mwar

Scenically situated between the Cheshire plains and the Welsh hills, Wrexham is home to the magnificent St Giles' Church, with a Perpendicular tower dubbed one of the 'seven wonders of Wales', the County Borough Museum in a former militia barracks, and a contemporary arts centre. Nearby attractions include Chirk Castle (National Trust); the picturesque village of Bangor-on-Dee with its part-medieval, part-17th-century bridge; the unspoilt Ceiriog Valley, described by Lloyd George as 'a little bit of heaven on earth' and traversed by the Offa's Dyke Path and the former Glyn Valley Tramway; Farmworld dairy farm and adventure park; and Alyn Waters and Ty Mawr country parks. The 5-mile waymarked Clywedog Trail explores the industrial heritage of the town, starting at Minera Lead Mines and taking in Nant Mill, Bersham Ironworks and Heritage Centre and the Erddig estate on its way to Wrexham.

Wrexham

▲Wrexham town centre

Wrexham/ Wrecsam

Abbot St . . . B2
Acton Rd . . . A3
Albert St . . . C3
Alexandra Rd . . . C1
Aran Rd . . . A3
Barnfield . . . C3
Bath Rd . . . C2
Beechley Rd . . . C3
Belgrave Rd . . . C2
Belle Vue Park . . . C2
Belle Vue Rd . . . C2
Belvedere Dr . . . A1
Bennion's Rd . . . C3
Berse Rd . . . A1
Bersham Rd . . . C1
Birch St . . . C3
Bodhyfryd . . . B3
Border Retail Park . . . B3
Bradley Rd . . . C2
Bright St . . . B1
Bron-y-Nant . . . B1
Brook St . . . C2
Bryn-y-Cabanau Rd . . . C3
Bury St . . . C3
Bus Station . . . B2
Butchers Market . . . B3
Citizens Advice Bureau . . . B2
Caia Rd . . . C3
Cambrian Ind Est . . . C3
Caxton Pl . . . B2
Cemetery . . . C1
Centenary Rd . . . C1
Chapel St . . . C2
Charles St . . . B3
Chester Rd . . . A3
Chester St . . . B3
Cilcen Gr . . . A3
Cobden Rd . . . B1
College of Art & Design . . . B2
Council Offices . . . B3
County 🏛 . . . B2
Crescent Rd . . . B3
Crispin La . . . A2
Croesnewyth Rd . . . B1
Cross St . . . A2
Cunliffe St . . . A2
Derby Rd . . . C3
DHS . . . B2
Dolydd Rd . . . B1
Duke St . . . B2
Eagles Meadow . . . C3
Earle St . . . C2
East Ave . . . A2
Edward St . . . C2
Egerton St . . . B2
Empress Rd . . . C1
Erddig Rd . . . C2
Fairy Rd . . . C2
Fire Station . . . B2
Foster Rd . . . A3
Foxwood Dr . . . C1
Garden Rd . . . A2
General Market . . . B3
Gerald St . . . B2
Gibson St . . . C1
Greenbank St . . . C3
Greenfield . . . A2
Grosvenor Rd . . . B2
Grove Park Rd . . . B3
Grove Park 🎭 . . . B2
Grove Rd . . . A3
Guildhall . . . B2
Haig Rd . . . C3
Hampden Rd . . . C2
Hazel Gr . . . A3
Henblas St . . . B3
High St . . . B3
Hightown Rd . . . C3
Hill St . . . B2
Holt Rd . . . B3
Holt St . . . B3
Hope St . . . B2
Huntroyde Ave . . . C3
Information Ctr ℹ . . . B3
Island Green Shopping Ctr . . . B2
Jubilee Rd . . . B2
King St . . . B2
Kingsmills Rd . . . C3
Lambpit St . . . B3
Law Courts . . . B3
Lawson Cl . . . A3
Lawson Rd . . . A3
Lea Rd . . . C2
Library & Arts Ctr . . . B2
Lilac Way . . . B1
Llys David Lord . . . B1
Lorne St . . . A2
Maesgwyn Rd . . . B1
Maesydre Rd . . . A3
Manley Rd . . . B3
Market St . . . B3
Mawddy Ave . . . A2
Mayville Ave . . . A2
Memorial Gall 🏛 . . . B2
Memorial Hall . . . B3
Mold Rd . . . A1
Mount St . . . C3
North East Wales Inst (N.E.W.I.) . . . A1
N.E.W.I. Sports Ctr . . . A1
Neville Cres . . . A3
New Rd . . . A2
North Wales Tennis Ctr . . . A1
Oak Dr . . . A3
Park Ave . . . A3
Park St . . . A2
Peel St . . . C1
Pentre Felin . . . C2
Pen-y-Bryn . . . C2
Penymaes Ave . . . A3
Peoples Market . . . B3
Percy St . . . C2
Plas Coch Retail Park . . . A1
Plas Coch Rd . . . A1
Police Station . . . B3
Poplar Rd . . . C2
Post Office PO . . . A2/B2/C2/C3
Powell Rd . . . B3
Poyser St . . . C2
Price's La . . . A2
Primose Way . . . B1
Princess St . . . C1
Queen St . . . B3
Queens Sq . . . B2
Regent St . . . B2
Rhosddu Rd . . . A2/B2
Rhosnesni La . . . A3
Rivulet Rd . . . C3
Ruabon Rd . . . C2
Ruthin Rd . . . C1/C2
St Giles ⛪ . . . C3
St Giles Way . . . C3
St James Ct . . . A2
St Mary's ✝ . . . B2
Salisbury Rd . . . C3
Salop Rd . . . C3
Smithfield Rd . . . C3
Sontley Rd . . . C2
Spring Rd . . . A2
Stanley St . . . C3
Stansty Rd . . . A2
Station Approach . . . B2
Studio 🎭 . . . B2/3
Talbot Rd . . . C2
Techniquest ✦ . . . A2
The Beeches . . . A3
The Pines . . . A3
Town Hill . . . C2
Trevor St . . . C2
Trinity St . . . B2
Tuttle St . . . C3
Vale Park . . . A1
Vernon St . . . B2
Vicarage Hill . . . B2
Victoria Rd . . . C2
Walnut St . . . A2
War Memorial . . . B3
Waterworld Swimming Baths ✦ . . . B3
Watery Rd . . . B1/B2
Wellington Rd . . . C2
Westminster Dr . . . A3
William Aston Hall 🎭 . . . A1
Windsor Rd . . . A1
Wrexham AFC . . . A1
Wrexham Central ⇌ . . . B2
Wrexham General ⇌ . . . B2
Wrexham Maelor (A&E) H . . . B1
Wrexham Technology Pk . . . B1
Wynn Ave . . . A2
Yale College . . . B3
Yale Gr . . . A3
Yorke St . . . C3

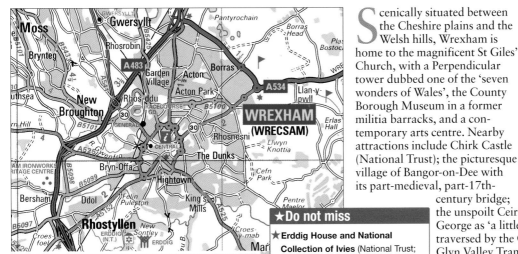

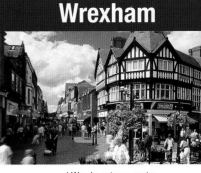

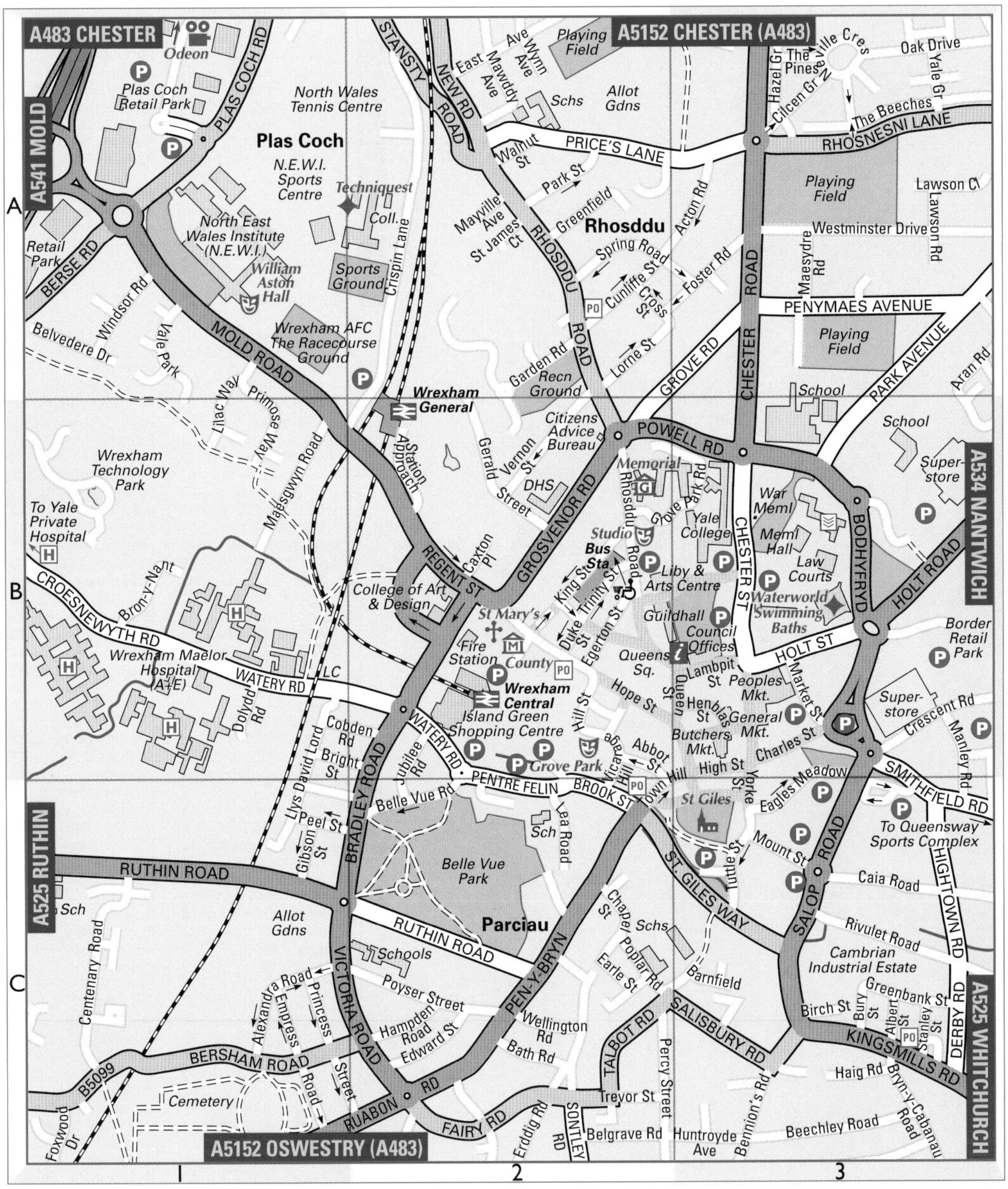

¼ mile
¼ ½ km

York

▲York Minster

An attractive city on the site of a major Roman settlement, subsequently occupied by the Anglo-Saxons, Vikings and Normans. The rebuilding of the Anglo-Saxon cathedral, which became York Minster (northern Europe's biggest medieval cathedral), began in the 11th century, and over the next 3 centuries York was transformed into the second largest city in the country. Its history can be explored in the Yorkshire Museum & Gardens; Treasurer's House; Barley Hall, a re-created medieval townhouse; Fairfax House, an 18th-century town-house with a furniture collection; the Micklegate Bar Museum; the Richard III Museum; the Regimental Museum; the Castle Museum; and the York Dungeon. Other attractions include the York Art Gallery, York Brewery, National Centre for Early Music with its festivals, York Maze (the world's largest, grown each summer) and York Model Railway.

Tourist Information Centre, De Grey Rooms, Exhibition Square, York YO1 7HB Tel 01904 550099

BBC Radio York 103.7 FM and 666 AM • **Galaxy** 105 FM **Minster** 104.7 FM

www.visityork.org

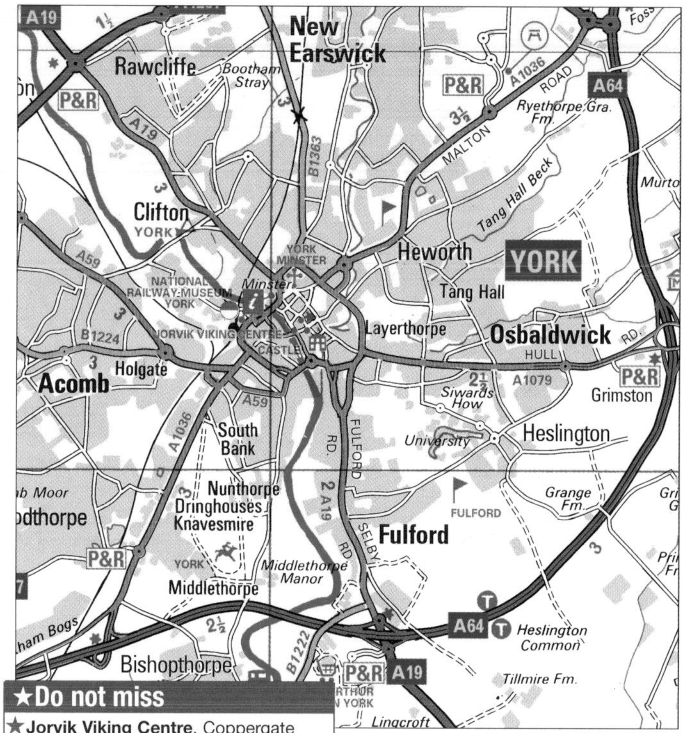

★Do not miss

★**Jorvik Viking Centre**, Coppergate

★**National Railway Museum**, Leeman Road

★**York Minster**, Minster Yard

¼ mile

½ km

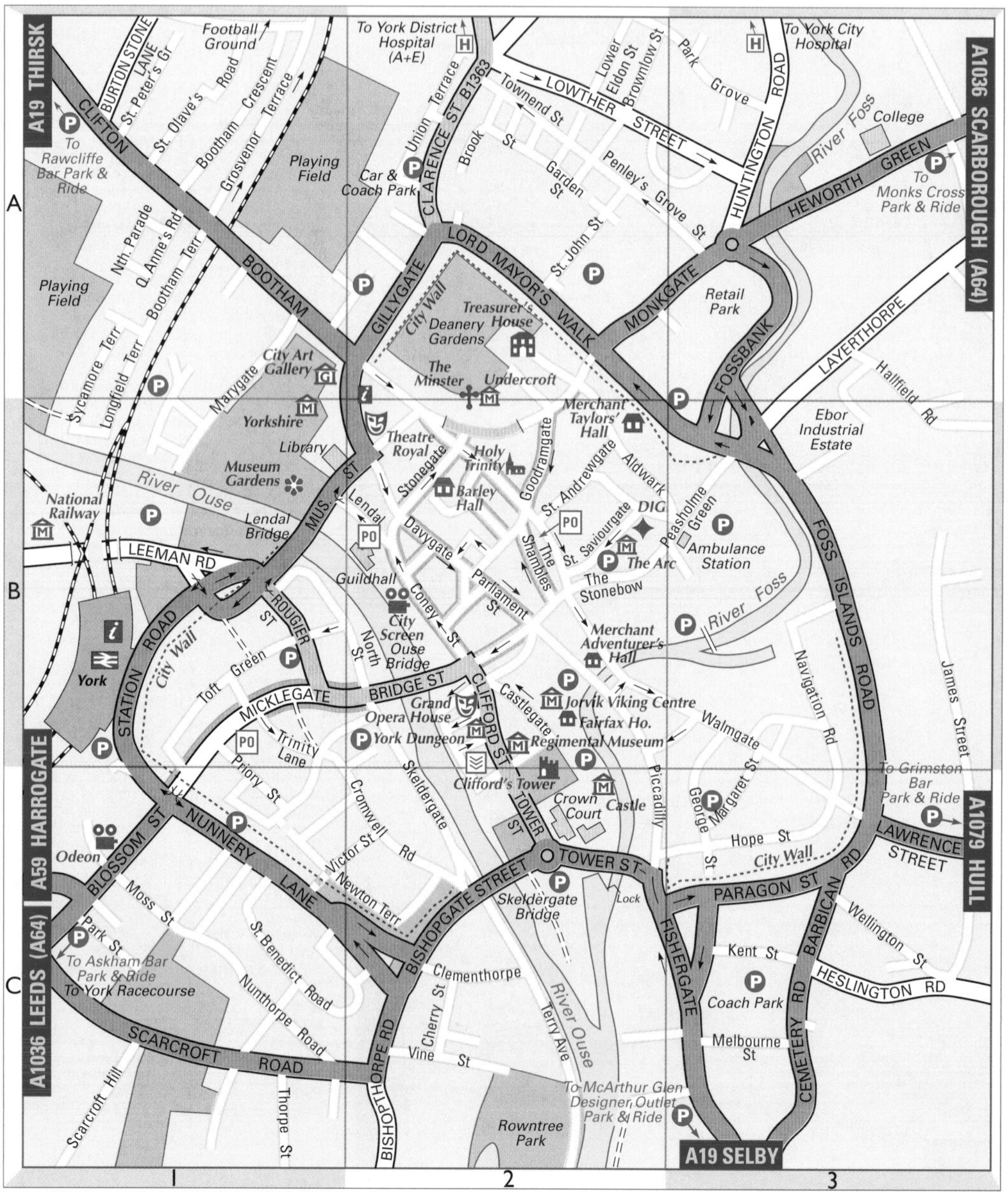

York

Aldwark B2
Ambulance Stn . . . B3
Arc Museum, The B2
Barbican Rd C3
Barley Hall B2
Bishopgate St . . . C2
Bishopthorpe Rd . C2
Blossom St C1
Bootham A1
Bootham Cr A1
Bootham Terr A1
Bridge St B2
Brook St A2
Brownlow St A2
Burton Stone La . A1
Castle Museum C2
Castlegate B2
Cemetery Rd C3
Cherry St C2
City Art Gallery A1
City Screen B2
City Wall . . A2/B1/C3
Clarence St A2
Clementhorpe . . . C2
Clifford St B2
Clifford's Tower B2
Clifton A1
Coach park . . A2/C3
Coney St B2
Cromwell Rd C2
Crown Court C2
Davygate B2
Deanery Gdns . . . A2
DIG ✦ B2
Ebor Ind Est B3
Fairfax House . B2
Fishergate C3
Foss Islands Rd . . . B3
Fossbank A3
Garden St A2
George St C3
Gillygate A2
Goodramgate B2
Grand Opera House B2
Grosvenor Terr . . . A1
Guildhall B2
Hallfield Rd A3
Heslington Rd . . . C3
Heworth Green . . A3
Holy Trinity B2
Hope St C3
Huntington Rd . . . A3
Information Ctr A2
James St B3
Jorvik Viking Centre B2
Kent St C3
Lawrence St C3
Layerthorpe A3
Leeman Rd B1
Lendal B2
Lendal Bridge B1
Library B1
Longfield Terr . . . A1
Lord Mayor's Wlk A2
Lower Eldon St . . A2
Lowther St A2
Margaret St C3
Marygate A1
Melbourne St C3
Merchant Adventurers' Hall B2
Merchant Taylors' Hall B2
Micklegate B1
Minster, The ✝ . . . A2
Monkgate A2
Moss St C1
Museum Gdns . . B1
Museum St B1
National Railway Museum B1
Navigation Rd B3
Newton Terr C2
North Pde A1
North St B2
Nunnery La C1
Nunthorpe Rd . . . C1
Odeon C1
Ouse Bridge B2
Paragon St C3
Park Gr A3
Park St C1
Parliament St B2
Peasholme Green . B3
Penley's Grove St A2
Piccadilly B2
Police Station . . B2
Post Office . B1/B2
Priory St B1
Queen Anne's Rd A1
Regimental Museum C2
Rowntree Park . . C2
St Andrewgate B2
St Benedict Rd . . C1
St John St A2
St Olave's Rd A1
St Peter's Gr A1
St Saviourgate B2
Scarcroft Hill C1
Scarcroft Rd C1
Skeldergate C2
Skeldergate Br . . C2
Station Rd B1
Stonegate B2
Sycamore Terr . . . A1
Terry Ave C2
The Shambles B2
The Stonebow B2
Theatre Royal . . B2
Thorpe St C1
Toft Green B1
Tower St C2
Townend St A2
Treasurer's House A2
Trinity La B1
Undercroft Museum A2
Union Terr A2
Victor St C2
Vine St C2
Walmgate B3
Wellington St C3
York Dungeon . B2
York Station . . B1
Yorkshire Museum B1

Abbreviations

Aberd C	**Aberdeen City**
Aberds	**Aberdeenshire**
Angl	**Isle of Anglesey**
Arg/Bute	**Argyll & Bute**
Bath/NE Som'set	**Bath & North East Somerset**
Beds	**Bedfordshire**
Bl Gwent	**Blaenau Gwent**
Blackb'n	**Blackburn with Darwen**
Blackp'l	**Blackpool**
Bournem'th	**Bournemouth**
Brackn'l	**Bracknell Forest**
Bridg	**Bridgend**
Brighton/Hove	**City of Brighton and Hove**
Bristol	**City and County of Bristol**
Bucks	**Buckinghamshire**
C/Edinb	**City of Edinburgh**
C/Glasg	**Glasgow City**
C/York	**City of York**
Caerph	**Caerphilly**
Cambs	**Cambridgeshire**
Card	**Cardiff**
Carms	**Carmarthenshire**
Ceredig'n	**Ceredigion**
Ches	**Cheshire**
Clack	**Clackmannanshire**
Cornw'l	**Cornwall**
Cumb	**Cumbria**
D'lington	**Darlington**
Denbs	**Denbighshire**
Derby	**Derbyshire**
Derby C	**Derby City**
Dumf/Gal	**Dumfries & Galloway**
Dundee C	**Dundee City**
E Ayrs	**East Ayrshire**
E Dunb	**East Dunbartonshire**
E Loth	**East Lothian**
E Renf	**East Renfrewshire**
ER Yorks	**East Riding of Yorkshire**
E Sussex	**East Sussex**
Falk	**Falkirk**
Flints	**Flintshire**
Glos	**Gloucestershire**
Gtr Man	**Greater Manchester**
Gwyn	**Gwynedd**
H'land	**Highland**
Hants	**Hampshire**
Hartlep'l	**Hartlepool**
Heref'd	**Herefordshire**
Herts	**Hertfordshire**
I/Man	**Isle of Man**
I/Scilly	**Isles of Scilly**
I/Wight	**Isle of Wight**
Invercl	**Inverclyde**
Kingston/Hull	**Kingston upon Hull**
Lancs	**Lancashire**
Leics	**Leicestershire**
Leics C	**Leicester City**
Lincs	**Lincolnshire**
London	**Greater London**
M/Keynes	**Milton Keynes**
Mersey	**Merseyside**
Merth Tyd	**Merthyr Tydfil**
Middlesbro	**Middlesbrough**
Midloth	**Midlothian**
Monmouths	**Monmouthshire**
N Ayrs	**North Ayrshire**
N Lanarks	**North Lanarkshire**
N Lincs	**North Lincolnshire**
N Som'set	**North Somerset**
N Yorks	**North Yorkshire**
NE Lincs	**North East Lincolnshire**
Neath P Talb	**Neath Port Talbot**
Newp	**City and County of Newport**
Northants	**Northamptonshire**
Northum	**Northumberland**
Nott'ham	**City of Nottingham**
Notts	**Nottinghamshire**
Oxon	**Oxfordshire**
Pembs	**Pembrokeshire**
Perth/Kinr	**Perth and Kinross**
Peterbro	**Peterborough**
Plym'th	**Plymouth**
Portsm'th	**Portsmouth**
Redcar/Clevel'd	**Redcar and Cleveland**
Renf	**Renfrewshire**
Rh Cyn Taff	**Rhondda Cynon Taff**
Rutl'd	**Rutland**
S'thampton	**Southampton**
S Ayrs	**South Ayrshire**
S Gloucs	**South Gloucestershire**
S Lanarks	**South Lanarkshire**
S Yorks	**South Yorkshire**
Scot Borders	**Scottish Borders**
Shetl'd	**Shetland**
Shrops	**Shropshire**
Som'set	**Somerset**
Southend	**Southend-on-Sea**
Staffs	**Staffordshire**
Stirl	**Stirling**
Stockton	**Stockton on Tees**
Stoke	**Stoke-on-Trent**
Swan	**Swansea**
Telford	**Telford and Wrekin**
Thurr'k	**Thurrock**
Torf	**Torfaen**
Tyne/Wear	**Tyne and Wear**
V/Glam	**Vale of Glamorgan**
W Berks	**West Berkshire**
W Dunb	**West Dunbartonshire**
W Isles	**Western Isles**
W Loth	**West Lothian**
W Midlands	**West Midlands**
W Sussex	**West Sussex**
W Yorks	**West Yorkshire**
Warwick	**Warwickshire**
Wilts	**Wiltshire**
Windsor	**Windsor and Maidenhead**
Worcs	**Worcestershire**
Wrex	**Wrexham**

A

Abbey Town *Cumb* **12** C2
Abbots Bromley *Staffs* **10** F6
Abbotsbury *Dorset* **5** M2
Aberaeron *Ceredig'n* **9** H5
Aberarth *Ceredig'n* **9** H5
Abercarn *Caerph* **9** M9
Aberchirder *Aberds* **21** H11
Abercrave *Powys* **9** L7
Aberdare *Rh Cyn Taff* **9** L7
Aberdaron *Gwyn* **8** E3
Aberdeen *Aberd C* **17** C11
Aberdour *Fife* **14** A7
Aberdulais *Neath P Talb* **9** L6
Aberdyfi *Gwyn* **8** G6
Aberfeldy *Perth/Kinr* **16** F6
Aberffraw *Angl* **8** C4
Aberfoyle *Stirl* **16** H4
Abergavenny *Monmouths* **9** L9
Abergele *Conwy* **8** C7
Abergwili *Carms* **9** K5
Abergwyngregyn *Gwyn* **8** C6
Abergynolwyn *Gwyn* **8** F6
Aberlady *E Loth* **15** A9
Abernethy *Perth/Kinr* **17** H7
Aberporth *Ceredig'n* **9** J4
Abersoch *Gwyn* **8** E4
Abersychan *Torf* **9** L9
Abertillery *Bl Gwent* **9** L9
Aberystwyth *Ceredig'n* **8** G5
Abingdon *Oxon* **4** G7
Abington *S Lanarks* **14** D6
Aboyne *Aberds* **17** D9
Accrington *Lancs* **12** J5
Acha *Arg/Bute* **18** F4
Achanalt *H'land* **20** G4
Achaphubuil *H'land* **18** E9
Acharacle *H'land* **18** E7
Achavanich *H'land* **21** C8
Achavraie *H'land* **20** E3
Achiemore *H'land* **20** B4
Achiltibuie *H'land* **20** E3
Achnacroish *Arg/Bute* **18** F8
Achnasheen *H'land* **20** H3
Achnashellach *H'land* **20** H3
Achosnich *H'land* **18** E6
Achriabhach *H'land* **18** E9
Acklam *N Yorks* **13** G10
Acle *Norfolk* **6** C9
Acomb *C/York* **13** H9
Acton Burnell *Shrops* **10** G3
Addingham *W Yorks* **12** H7
Adlington *Lancs* **10** B4
Adwick le Street *S Yorks* **11** B8
Affric Lodge *H'land* **16** B2
Ainsdale *Mersey* **10** B2
Aird *Arg/Bute* **19** H7
Aird Asaig Tairbeart = Tarbert *W Isles* **22** D3
Aird Uig *W Isles* **22** C3
Aird a Mhulaidh *W Isles* **22** D3
Airdrie *N Lanarks* **14** B5
Airor *H'land* **22** J6
Airth *Falk* **14** A6
Aisgill *Cumb* **12** F5
Aith *Shetl'd* **23** D2
Aith *Orkney* **23** B4
Akeley *Bucks* **4** E8
Albrighton *Shrops* **10** G5
Alcester *Warwick* **4** D5
Aldborough *N Yorks* **13** G9
Aldbourne *Wilts* **5** H6
Aldbrough *ER Yorks* **13** J13
Aldeburgh *Suffolk* **6** F10
Alderbury *Wilts* **5** K5
Alderley Edge *Ches* **10** D5
Aldermaston *W Berks* **5** H7
Aldershot *Hants* **7** L2
Aldridge *W Midlands* **10** G6
Aldsworth *Glos* **4** F5
Aldwick *W Sussex* **7** P2
Alexandria *W Dunb* **14** A3
Alford *Lincs* **11** D13
Alford *Aberds* **17** C9
Alfreton *Derby* **11** E8
Alfriston *E Sussex* **7** N5
Alkham *Kent* **7** L9
Allendale Town *Northum* **12** C6
Allenheads *Northum* **12** C6
Alloa *Clack* **16** J6
Allonby *Cumb* **12** C2
Almondsbury *S Gloucs* **5** G3
Alness *H'land* **20** G6
Alnmouth *Northum* **15** E13
Alnwick *Northum* **15** E12
Alphington *Devon* **3** F9
Alrewas *Staffs* **10** G6
Alsager *Ches* **10** E5
Alston *Cumb* **12** C5
Alt na h'Airbhe *H'land* **20** F3
Altanduino *H'land* **20** D7
Altarnun *Cornw'l* **2** G6
Altass *H'land* **20** E5
Althorne *Essex* **7** J7
Althorpe *N Lincs* **11** B10
Altnaharra *H'land* **20** D5
Alton *Hants* **5** K8
Alton *Staffs* **10** E6
Altrincham *Gtr Man* **10** C4
Alva *Clack* **16** J6
Alvechurch *Worcs* **4** C5
Alveley *Shrops* **10** H4
Alveston *S Gloucs* **5** G3
Alvie *H'land* **16** C6
Alwinton *Northum* **15** E11
Alyth *Perth/Kinr* **17** F8
Amble *Northum* **15** E13
Ambleside *Cumb* **12** E3
Ambrosden *Oxon* **4** F8
Amersham *Bucks* **7** J2
Amesbury *Wilts* **5** J5
Amlwch *Angl* **8** B5
Ammanford *Carms* **9** L6
Ampleforth *N Yorks* **13** G9
Ampthill *Beds* **6** G3
Amulree *Perth/Kinr* **16** G6
An t-Ob *W Isles* **22** E3
Ancaster *Lincs* **11** E10
Ancroft *Northum* **15** C11
Ancrum *Scot Borders* **15** D10
Andover *Hants* **5** J6
Andoversford *Glos* **4** F5
Andreas *I/Man* **13**
Angle *Pembs* **9** L2
Angmering *W Sussex* **7** N3
Annan *Dumf/Gal* **14** G7
Annbank *S Ayrs* **14** D4
Annfield Plain *Durham* **12** C7
Anstey *Leics* **11** G8
Anstruther *Fife* **17** H9
Appleby-in-Westmorland *Cumb* **12** D5
Applecross *H'land* **22** G6
Appledore *Kent* **7** M7
Appledore *Devon* **2** D7
Arbroath *Angus* **17** F10
Archiestown *Moray* **21** H9
Ardarroch *H'land* **20** H2
Ardbeg *Arg/Bute* **19** L6
Ardcharnich *H'land* **20** F3
Ardchyle *Stirl* **16** G4
Ardentinny *Arg/Bute* **14** A2
Ardersier *H'land* **20** H6
Ardessie *H'land* **20** F3
Ardgay *H'land* **20** F5
Ardhasig *W Isles* **22** D3
Ardingly *W Sussex* **7** M4
Ardleigh *Essex* **6** G8
Ardley *Oxon* **4** E7
Ardlui *Arg/Bute* **16** H3
Ardlussa *Arg/Bute* **19** J7
Ardnave *Arg/Bute* **19** K5
Ardrishaig *Arg/Bute* **19** J8
Ardrossan *N Ayrs* **14** C3
Ardtalnaig *Perth/Kinr* **16** G5
Ardvasar *H'land* **22** J6
Ardwell *Dumf/Gal* **14** H2
Ardwell *Moray* **17** B8
Arinagour *Arg/Bute* **18** F5
Arisaig *H'land* **18** D7
Armadale *H'land* **22** J6
Armadale *W Loth* **14** B6
Armathwaite *Cumb* **12** C4
Armitage *Staffs* **10** G6
Armthorpe *S Yorks* **11** B9
Arncliffe *N Yorks* **12** G6
Arncott *Oxon* **4** F8
Arnisdale *H'land* **18** C8
Arnold *Notts* **11** E8
Arnside *Cumb* **12** G4
Arreton *I/Wight* **5** M7
Arrochar *Arg/Bute* **16** H3
Arundel *W Sussex* **7** N3
Ascot *Windsor* **7** K2
Asfordby *Leics* **11** F9
Ash *Kent* **7** L9
Ash *Surrey* **7** L2
Ashbourne *Derby* **10** E6
Ashburton *Devon* **3** G8
Ashbury *Oxon* **5** G6
Ashby de-la-Zouch *Leics* **10** G7
Ashchurch *Glos* **4** E4
Ashford *Kent* **7** L8
Ashford *Derby* **10** D6
Ashingdon *Essex* **7** J7
Ashington *Northum* **15** F13
Ashley *Staffs* **10** F4
Ashton *Ches* **10** D3
Ashton Keynes *Wilts* **4** G5
Ashton Under Lyne *Gtr Man* **10** C5
Ashton under Hill *Worcs* **4** E5
Ashton-in-Makerfield *Gtr Man* **10** C3
Ashurst *Hants* **5** L6
Ashwater *Devon* **2** F6
Ashwell *Herts* **6** G4
Ashwick *Som'set* **5** J3
Askam-in-Furness *Cumb* **12** G3
Askern *S Yorks* **11** B8
Askrigg *N Yorks* **12** F6
Aslackby *Lincs* **11** F11
Aspatria *Cumb* **12** C2
Astwood Bank *Worcs* **4** C5
Atherstone *Warwick* **10** H7
Atherton *Gtr Man* **10** B4
Attleborough *Norfolk* **6** D8
Atworth *Wilts* **5** H4
Auchenblae *Aberds* **17** D10
Auchencairn *Dumf/Gal* **14** H5
Auchengray *S Lanarks* **14** C7
Auchertool *Fife* **17** J8
Auchinleck *E Ayrs* **14** D4
Auchronie *Angus* **17** D9
Auchterarder *Perth/Kinr* **16** H6
Auchterderran *Fife* **17** J8
Auchtermuchty *Fife* **17** H8
Auchtertyre *H'land* **18** B8
Audlem *Ches* **10** E4
Audley *Staffs* **10** E4
Auldearn *H'land* **21** H7
Aultbea *H'land* **20** F2
Austwick *N Yorks* **12** G5
Avebury *Wilts* **5** H5
Avening *Glos* **4** G4
Aveton Gifford *Devon* **3** H8
Aviemore *H'land* **16** C6
Avoch *H'land* **20** H6
Avonmouth *Bristol* **5** H2
Axbridge *Som'set* **3** C12
Axminster *Devon* **3** F11
Axmouth *Devon* **3** F11
Aylesbury *Bucks* **4** F9
Aylesford *Kent* **7** L6
Aylesham *Kent* **7** L9
Aylsham *Norfolk* **6** B8
Aynho *Northants* **4** E7
Ayr *S Ayrs* **14** D3
Aysgarth *N Yorks* **12** F6
Ayton *N Yorks* **13** F11
Ayton *Scot Borders* **15** B11

B

Bac *W Isles* **22** B5
Backwell *N Som'set* **3** B12
Bacton *Norfolk* **6** B9
Bacup *Lancs* **12** J6
Badenscoth *Aberds* **21** J11
Badenyon *Aberds* **17** C8
Badrallach *H'land* **20** F3
Bagh a Chaisteil = Castlebay *W Isles* **18** D2
Bagillt *Flints* **10** D2
Bagshot *Surrey* **7** K2
Baildon *W Yorks* **12** J7
Baile Ailein *W Isles* **22** C4
Bainbridge *N Yorks* **12** F6
Bainton *ER Yorks* **13** H11
Bakewell *Derby* **10** D7
Bala *Gwyn* **8** E7
Balbeggie *Perth/Kinr* **17** G7
Balblair *H'land* **20** G6
Balcombe *W Sussex* **7** M4
Balderton *Notts* **11** E10
Baldock *Herts* **6** G4
Balfour *Orkney* **23** C3
Balfron *Stirl* **14** A4
Balintore *H'land* **20** G7
Ballachulish *H'land* **18** F9
Ballantrae *S Ayrs* **14** F2
Ballasalla *I/Man* **13**
Ballater *Aberds* **17** D8
Ballaugh *I/Man* **13**
Ballinluig *Perth/Kinr* **16** F6
Balloch *H'land* **20** H6
Balloch *W Dunb* **14** A3
Ballochan *Aberds* **17** D9
Ballygrant *Arg/Bute* **19** K5
Balmaclellan *Dumf/Gal* **14** G5
Balmedie *Aberds* **17** C11
Balnapaling *H'land* **20** G6
Balquhidder *Stirl* **16** G4
Balsall *W Midlands* **10** J7
Balsham *Cambs* **6** F5
Baltasound *Shetl'd* **23** A4
Balvicar *Arg/Bute* **19** H7
Bamber Bridge *Lancs* **12** J4
Bamburgh *Northum* **15** D12
Bamford *Derby* **10** C7
Bampton *Devon* **3** D9
Bampton *Oxon* **4** F6
Banbury *Oxon* **4** D7
Banchory *Aberds* **17** D10
Banff *Aberds* **21** G11
Bangor *Gwyn* **8** C5
Bangor-is-y-coed *Wrex* **10** E2
Banham *Norfolk* **6** D8
Bankend *Dumf/Gal* **14** G7
Bankfoot *Perth/Kinr* **16** G7
Bankhead *Aberd C* **17** C11
Banks *Lancs* **12** J3
Bannockburn *Stirl* **16** J6
Banstead *Surrey* **7** L4
Banwell *N Som'set* **3** C11
Bar Hill *Cambs* **6** E4
Barabhas *W Isles* **22** B4
Barassie *S Ayrs* **14** D3
Barbon *Cumb* **12** F5
Bardney *Lincs* **11** D11
Barford *Warwick* **4** C6
Bargoed *Caerph* **9** L8
Bargrennan *Dumf/Gal* **14** G3
Barham *Kent* **7** L9
Barkway *Herts* **6** G4
Barlborough *Derby* **11** D8
Barlby *N Yorks* **13** J10
Barley *Herts* **6** G5
Barmby Moor *ER Yorks* **13** H10
Barmoor Castle *Northum* **15** D11
Barmouth *Gwyn* **8** F6
Barnard Castle *Durham* **12** E7
Barnet *London* **7** J4
Barnetby le Wold *N Lincs* **11** B11
Barnham *Suffolk* **6** E7
Barnhill *Moray* **21** H8
Barnoldswick *Lancs* **12** H6
Barnsley *S Yorks* **10** B7
Barnstaple *Devon* **3** D7
Barnt Green *Worcs* **4** C5
Barr *S Ayrs* **14** F3
Barrhead *E Renf* **14** C4
Barrhill *S Ayrs* **14** F3
Barrow upon Humber *N Lincs* **13** J12
Barrow-in-Furness *Cumb* **12** G2

Barrowford *Lancs* 12 J6
Barry *V/Glam* 9 N8
Barry *Angus* 17 G9
Barton *N Yorks* 13 E8
Barton upon Humber *N Lincs* 13 J12
Barton-le-Clay *Beds* 6 G3
Barwell *Leics* 11 H8
Baschurch *Shrops* 10 F3
Basildon *Essex* 7 J6
Basingstoke *Hants* 5 J8
Baslow *Derby* 10 D7
Baston *Lincs* 11 G11
Bath *Bath/NE Som'set* 5 H3
Bathford *Bath/NE Som'set* 5 H3
Bathgate *W Loth* 14 B6
Batley *W Yorks* 13 J8
Battle *E Sussex* 7 N6
Bawdeswell *Norfolk* 6 B8
Bawdsey *Suffolk* 6 F9
Bawtry *S Yorks* 11 C9
Bayston Hill *Shrops* 10 G3
Beachley *Glos* 4 G2
Beaconsfield *Bucks* 7 J2
Beadnell *Northum* 15 D13
Beaminster *Dorset* 3 E12
Bearsden *E Dunb* 14 B4
Bearsted *Kent* 7 L6
Beattock *Dumf/Gal* 14 E7
Beaufort *Bl Gwent* 9 L8
Beaulieu *Hants* 5 L6
Beauly *H'land* 20 H5
Beaumaris *Angl* 8 C5
Bebington *Mersey* 10 C2
Beccles *Suffolk* 6 D10
Beck Row *Suffolk* 6 E6
Beckermet *Cumb* 12 E2
Beckfoot *Cumb* 12 C2
Beckhampton *Wilts* 5 H5
Beckingham *Notts* 11 C9
Beckington *Som'set* 5 J4
Bedale *N Yorks* 13 F8
Beddgelert *Gwyn* 8 D5
Bedford *Beds* 6 F3
Bedlington *Northum* 15 F13
Bedwas *Caerph* 9 M8
Bedworth *Warwick* 10 H7
Beeford *ER Yorks* 13 H12
Beer *Devon* 3 F11
Beeston *Notts* 11 F8
Beeswing *Dumf/Gal* 14 G6
Begelly *Pembs* 9 L3
Beguildy *Powys* 9 H8
Beighton *S Yorks* 11 C8
Beith *N Ayrs* 14 C3
Belbroughton *Worcs* 10 J5
Belchford *Lincs* 11 D12
Belford *Northum* 15 D12
Bellingham *Northum* 15 F11
Bellsbank *E Ayrs* 14 E4
Bellshill *N Lanarks* 14 B5
Belmont *Blackb'n* 12 K5
Belmont *Shetl'd* 23 A3
Belper *Derby* 10 E7
Belsay *Northum* 12 B7
Beltinge *Kent* 7 K8
Belton *N Lincs* 11 B9
Belton *Norfolk* 6 C10
Bembridge *I/Wight* 5 M8
Benington *Lincs* 11 E12
Benllech *Angl* 8 B5
Benson *Oxon* 4 G8
Bentley *Hants* 5 J8
Bentley *S Yorks* 11 B8
Benwick *Cambs* 6 D4
Bere Alston *Devon* 2 G7
Bere Regis *Dorset* 5 M4
Berkeley *Glos* 4 G3
Berkhamsted *Herts* 7 H2
Berriedale *H'land* 21 D8
Berriew *Powys* 8 F8
Berrow *Som'set* 3 C11
Berwick *E Sussex* 7 N5
Berwick-upon-Tweed *Northum* 15 C11
Bethersden *Kent* 7 M7
Bethesda *Gwyn* 8 C6
Bettws Bledrws *Ceredig'n* 9 J6
Bettyhill *H'land* 20 B6
Betws *Bridg* 9 M7
Betws-y-Coed *Conwy* 8 D6
Beulah *Powys* 9 J7
Beverley *ER Yorks* 13 J12
Bewcastle *Cumb* 15 G9
Bewdley *Worcs* 10 J4
Bexhill *E Sussex* 7 N6
Bexley *London* 7 K5
Bibury *Glos* 4 F5
Bicester *Oxon* 4 E7
Bickington *Devon* 3 G8
Bicton *Shrops* 10 G3
Biddenden *Kent* 7 M7
Biddulph *Staffs* 10 E5
Bideford *Devon* 2 D7
Bidford-on-Avon *Warwick* 4 D5
Bigbury *Devon* 3 H8
Biggar *S Lanarks* 14 D7
Biggin Hill *London* 7 L5
Biggleswade *Beds* 6 F4
Bildeston *Suffolk* 6 F7
Billericay *Essex* 7 J6
Billesdon *Leics* 11 G9
Billingborough *Lincs* 11 F11
Billingham *Stockton* 13 D9
Billinghay *Lincs* 11 E11
Billingshurst *W Sussex* 7 M3
Bilston *W Midlands* 10 H5
Binbrook *Lincs* 11 C12
Bingham *Notts* 11 F9
Bingley *W Yorks* 12 J7
Birchgrove *Swan* 9 M6
Birchington *Kent* 7 K9
Birdlip *Glos* 4 F4
Birkdale *Mersey* 12 K3
Birkenhead *Mersey* 10 C2
Birmingham *W Midlands* 10 H6
Birtley *Tyne/Wear* 13 C8
Birtley *Northum* 12 B6
Bishop Auckland *Durham* 13 D8
Bishop Monkton *N Yorks* 13 G8
Bishop's Castle *Shrops* 8 G9
Bishop's Cleeve *Glos* 4 E4
Bishop's Frome *Heref'd* 4 D3
Bishop's Nympton *Devon* 3 D8
Bishop's Stortford *Herts* 6 G5
Bishop's Tawton *Devon* 3 D7
Bishop's Waltham *Hants* 5 L7
Bishopbriggs *E Dunb* 14 B5
Bishops Lydeard *Som'set* 3 D10
Bishopsteignton *Devon* 3 G9
Bishopstoke *Hants* 5 L7
Bishopston *Swan* 9 M5
Bitton *S Gloucs* 5 H3
Blaby *Leics* 11 H8
Blackburn *Blackb'n* 12 J5
Blackford *Perth/Kinr* 16 H6
Blackford *Cumb* 12 B3
Blackpool *Blackp'l* 12 J3
Blackridge *W Loth* 14 B6
Blackwall Tunnel *London* 7 J4
Blackwaterfoot *N Ayrs* 19 M8
Blackwood *S Lanarks* 14 C5
Blackwood *Caerph* 9 M8
Blaenau Ffestiniog *Gwyn* 8 D6
Blaenavon *Torf* 9 L9
Blagdon *N Som'set* 5 J2
Blaina *Bl Gwent* 9 L9
Blair Atholl *Perth/Kinr* 16 E6
Blairgowrie *Perth/Kinr* 17 F7
Blakeney *Norfolk* 6 A8
Blakeney *Glos* 4 F3
Blanchand *Northum* 12 C6
Blandford Forum *Dorset* 5 L4
Blaydon *Tyne/Wear* 12 B7
Bleadon *N Som'set* 3 C11
Blean *Kent* 7 K8
Bletchingdon *Oxon* 4 F7
Bletchley *M/Keynes* 4 E9
Blewbury *Oxon* 5 G7
Blidworth *Notts* 11 E9
Blisworth *Northants* 4 D8
Blockley *Glos* 4 E5
Blofield *Norfolk* 6 C9
Bloxham *Oxon* 4 E7
Blubberhouses *N Yorks* 12 H7
Blundeston *Suffolk* 6 D10
Blyth *Notts* 11 C9
Blyth *Northum* 15 F13
Blyth Bridge *Scot Borders* 14 C7
Blythburgh *Suffolk* 6 E10
Blythe Bridge *Staffs* 10 E5
Blyton *Lincs* 11 C10
Bo'ness *Falk* 14 A6
Boat of Garten *H'land* 16 C6
Boddam *Aberds* 21 H13
Boddam *Shetl'd* 23 F2
Bodedern *Angl* 8 C4
Bodenham *Heref'd* 4 D2
Bodiam *E Sussex* 7 M6
Bodinnick *Cornw'l* 2 H5
Bodmin *Cornw'l* 2 G5
Bognor Regis *W Sussex* 7 P2
Boldon *Tyne/Wear* 13 B8
Bollington *Ches* 10 D5
Bolney *W Sussex* 7 M4
Bolsover *Derby* 11 D8
Bolton *Gtr Man* 10 B4
Bolton Abbey *N Yorks* 12 H7
Bolton Bridge *N Yorks* 12 H7
Bolton by Bowland *Lancs* 12 H5
Bolton le Sands *Lancs* 12 G4
Bonarbridge *H'land* 20 F6
Bonby *N Lincs* 13 K11
Bonchester Bridge *Scot Borders* 15 E9
Bonchurch *I/Wight* 5 N7
Bonhill *W Dunb* 14 A3
Bonnybridge *Falk* 14 A6
Bonnyrigg *Midloth* 15 B8
Bonvilston *V/Glam* 9 N8
Boot *Cumb* 12 E2
Bootle *Cumb* 12 F2
Bootle *Mersey* 10 C2
Bordon *Hants* 5 K9
Borehamwood *Herts* 7 J4
Boreland *Dumf/Gal* 14 F7
Borgh *W Isles* 22 B4
Borgue *Dumf/Gal* 14 H5
Borough Green *Kent* 7 L6
Boroughbridge *N Yorks* 13 G8
Borrowdale *Cumb* 12 E3
Borth *Ceredig'n* 8 G6
Bosbury *Heref'd* 4 D3
Boscastle *Cornw'l* 2 F5
Bosham *W Sussex* 5 L9
Boston *Lincs* 11 E12
Boston Spa *W Yorks* 13 H9
Botesdale *Suffolk* 6 E8
Bothel *Cumb* 12 C2
Bothenhampton *Dorset* 3 F12
Botley *Oxon* 4 F7
Bottesford *Leics* 11 F10
Bottisham *Cambs* 6 E5
Botwnnog *Gwyn* 8 E4
Bourne *Lincs* 11 F11
Bourne End *Bucks* 7 J2
Bournemouth *Bournem'th* 5 M5
Bourton-on-the-Water *Glos* 4 E5
Bovey Tracey *Devon* 3 G9
Bow *Devon* 3 E8
Bowes *Durham* 12 E7
Bowmore *Arg/Bute* 19 L5
Bowness-on-Solway *Cumb* 12 B3
Bowness-on-Windermere *Cumb* 12 F4
Box *Wilts* 5 H4
Bozeat *Northants* 6 E2
Brabourne *Kent* 7 L8
Brabourne Lees *Kent* 7 M8
Bracadale *H'land* 22 H4
Bracebridge Heath *Lincs* 11 D10
Bracklesham *W Sussex* 5 M9
Brackley *Northants* 4 E7
Bracknell *Brackn'l* 7 K2
Braco *Perth/Kinr* 16 H6
Bradford *W Yorks* 12 J7
Bradford-on-Avon *Wilts* 5 H4
Brading *I/Wight* 5 M8
Bradpole *Dorset* 3 F12
Bradwell-on-Sea *Essex* 7 H8
Bradworthy *Devon* 2 E6
Brae *Shetl'd* 23 C2
Brae Roy Lodge *H'land* 16 D3
Braemar *Aberds* 17 D7
Braemore *H'land* 20 G3
Braemore *H'land* 21 D8
Brailsford *Derby* 10 E7
Braintree *Essex* 6 G6
Bramford *Suffolk* 6 F8
Bramhall *Gtr Man* 10 C5
Bramhope *W Yorks* 13 H8
Brampton *Cumb* 12 B4
Brampton *Cambs* 6 E4
Brancaster *Norfolk* 6 A6
Branderburgh *Moray* 21 G9
Brandon *Suffolk* 6 D6
Brandon *Durham* 13 C8
Branston *Lincs* 11 D11
Brantham *Suffolk* 6 G8
Bratton Fleming *Devon* 3 D8
Braunston *Northants* 4 C7
Braunton *Devon* 2 D7
Bray *Windsor* 7 K2
Breage *Cornw'l* 2 J3
Breakish *H'land* 22 H6
Bream *Glos* 4 F3
Breanais *W Isles* 22 C2
Brechfa *Carms* 9 K5
Brechin *Angus* 17 E10
Brecon *Powys* 9 K8
Brede *E Sussex* 7 N7
Bredenbury *Heref'd* 4 D3
Brent *London* 7 J4
Brentwood *Essex* 7 J6
Bretforton *Worcs* 4 D5
Brewood *Staffs* 10 G5
Bride *I/Man* 13
Bridestowe *Devon* 2 F7
Bridge *Kent* 7 L8
Bridge of Allan *Stirl* 16 J5
Bridge of Balgie *Perth/Kinr* 16 F4
Bridge of Cally *Perth/Kinr* 17 F7
Bridge of Don *Aberd C* 17 C11
Bridge of Earn *Perth/Kinr* 17 H7
Bridge of Orchy *Arg/Bute* 16 F3
Bridge of Weir *Renf* 14 B3
Bridgend *Arg/Bute* 19 K5
Bridgend *Bridg* 9 N7
Bridgnorth *Shrops* 10 H4
Bridgwater *Som'set* 3 D11
Bridlington *ER Yorks* 13 G12
Bridport *Dorset* 3 F12
Brierfield *Lancs* 12 J6
Brierley Hill *W Midlands* 10 H5
Brigg *N Lincs* 11 B11
Brighouse *W Yorks* 12 J7
Brighstone *I/Wight* 5 M7
Brightlingsea *Essex* 7 H8
Brighton *Brighton/Hove* 7 N4
Brigstock *Northants* 6 D2
Brill *Bucks* 4 F8
Brimfield *Heref'd* 4 C2
Brinklow *Warwick* 11 H8
Brinkworth *Wilts* 5 G5
Brinyan *Orkney* 23 B3
Bristol *Bristol* 5 H2
Briston *Norfolk* 6 B8
Briton Ferry *Neath P Talb* 9 M6
Brixham *Torbay* 3 H9
Brixton *Devon* 2 H7
Brixworth *Northants* 4 C8
Brize Norton *Oxon* 4 F6
Broad Chalke *Wilts* 5 K5
Broad Haven *Pembs* 9 L2
Broad Hinton *Wilts* 5 H5
Broadclyst *Devon* 3 F9
Broadford *H'land* 22 H6
Broadhembury *Devon* 3 E10
Broadmayne *Dorset* 5 M3
Broadstairs *Kent* 7 K10
Broadstone *Poole* 5 M4
Broadwas *Worcs* 4 D3
Broadway *Worcs* 4 E5
Broadwey *Dorset* 5 M3
Broadwindsor *Dorset* 3 E12
Brochel *H'land* 22 G5
Brockenhurst *Hants* 5 L6
Brockworth *Glos* 4 F4
Brocton *Staffs* 10 F5
Brodick *N Ayrs* 19 M9
Bromfield *Shrops* 10 J3
Bromham *Beds* 6 F2
Bromham *Wilts* 5 H4
Bromley *London* 7 K5
Bromley Green *Kent* 7 M8
Brompton *N Yorks* 13 F8
Brompton Regis *Som'set* 3 D9
Bromsgrove *Worcs* 4 C4
Bromyard *Heref'd* 4 D3
Brooke *Norfolk* 6 D9
Broomfield *Essex* 7 H6
Broomhaugh *Northum* 12 B7
Broomhill *Northum* 15 E13
Brora *H'land* 20 E7
Broseley *Shrops* 10 G4
Brothertoft *Lincs* 11 E12
Brotton *Redcar/Clevel'd* 13 D10
Brough *ER Yorks* 13 J11
Brough *H'land* 21 B9
Brough *Cumb* 12 E6
Broughton *Cumb* 12 D2
Broughton *Lancs* 12 J4
Broughton *Hants* 5 K6
Broughton *Scot Borders* 14 D7
Broughton *N Lincs* 11 B10
Broughton *Northants* 11 J10
Broughton Astley *Leics* 11 H8
Broughton-in-Furness *Cumb* 12 F3
Broughty Ferry *Dundee C* 17 G9
Brownhills *W Midlands* 10 G6
Broxburn *W Loth* 14 B7
Broxton *Ches* 10 E3
Bruichladdich *Arg/Bute* 19 K5
Brundall *Norfolk* 6 C9
Brunton *Northum* 12 B6
Brunton *Northum* 15 D13
Bruton *Som'set* 5 K3
Brymbo *Wrex* 8 D9
Brynamman *Carms* 9 L6
Bryncrug *Gwyn* 8 F6
Brynmawr *Bl Gwent* 9 L8
Brynsiencyn *Angl* 8 C5
Bubwith *ER Yorks* 13 J10
Buchlyvie *Stirl* 16 J4
Buck's Cross *Devon* 2 D6
Buckden *N Yorks* 12 G6
Buckden *Cambs* 6 E3
Buckfast *Devon* 3 G8
Buckfastleigh *Devon* 3 G8
Buckhaven *Fife* 17 J8
Buckie *Moray* 21 G10
Buckingham *Bucks* 4 E8
Buckland *Oxon* 4 G6
Buckland Brewer *Devon* 2 E7
Buckland Newton *Dorset* 5 L3
Buckley *Flints* 10 D2
Bucksburn *Aberd C* 17 C11
Bude *Cornw'l* 2 E5
Budleigh Salterton *Devon* 3 F10
Bugbrooke *Northants* 4 D8
Bugle *Cornw'l* 2 H5
Builth Wells *Powys* 9 J8
Bulford *Wilts* 5 J5
Bulkington *Warwick* 10 H7
Bulwell *Nott'ham* 11 E8
Bunbury *Ches* 10 E3
Bunessan *Arg/Bute* 18 G5
Bungay *Suffolk* 6 D9
Bunnahabhain *Arg/Bute* 19 K6
Buntingford *Herts* 6 G4
Bunwell *Norfolk* 6 D8
Burbage *Leics* 11 H8
Burbage *Derby* 10 D6
Burbage *Wilts* 5 H6
Bures *Suffolk* 6 G7
Burford *Oxon* 4 F6
Burgess Hill *W Sussex* 7 N4
Burgh le Marsh *Lincs* 11 D13
Burgh-by-Sands *Cumb* 12 C3
Burghclere *Hants* 5 H7
Burghead *Moray* 21 G8
Burghfield Common *W Berks* 5 H8
Burley *W Yorks* 12 H7
Burley *Hants* 5 L6
Burlton *Shrops* 10 F3
Burneside *Cumb* 12 F4
Burness *Orkney* 23 A4
Burnham *Bucks* 7 J2
Burnham Market *Norfolk* 6 A7
Burnham-on-Crouch *Essex* 7 J7
Burnham-on-Sea *Som'set* 3 C11
Burniston *N Yorks* 13 F12
Burnley *Lancs* 12 J6
Burnmouth *Scot Borders* 15 C11
Burntisland *Fife* 15 A8
Burntwood *Staffs* 10 G6
Burravoe *Shetl'd* 23 B3
Burrelton *Perth/Kinr* 17 G7
Burry Port *Carms* 9 L5
Burscough Bridge *Lancs* 10 B3
Burstwick *ER Yorks* 13 J13
Burton *Cumb* 12 G4
Burton Agnes *ER Yorks* 13 G12
Burton Bradstock *Dorset* 3 F12
Burton Fleming *ER Yorks* 13 G12
Burton Latimer *Northants* 6 E2
Burton Upon Trent *Staffs* 10 F7
Burton in Lonsdale *N Yorks* 12 G5
Burton upon Stather *N Lincs* 13 K11
Burwash *E Sussex* 7 M6
Burwell *Cambs* 6 E5
Burwick *Orkney* 23 D3
Bury *Gtr Man* 10 B5
Bury St. Edmunds *Suffolk* 6 E7
Bushey *Herts* 7 J3
Buttermere *Cumb* 12 E2
Buxted *E Sussex* 7 M5
Buxton *Derby* 10 D6
Byfield *Northants* 4 D7
Byfleet *Surrey* 7 K3
Bylchau *Conwy* 8 C7

C

Cabrach *Moray* 17 B8
Caenby Corner *Lincs* 11 C10
Caergwrle *Flints* 8 D9
Caerleon *Newp* 9 M9
Caernarfon *Gwyn* 8 C5
Caerphilly *Caerph* 9 M8
Caersws *Powys* 8 G8
Caerwent *Monmouths* 4 G2
Cairinis *W Isles* 22 G2
Cairndow *Arg/Bute* 16 H2
Cairnryan *Dumf/Gal* 14 G2
Caister-on-Sea *Norfolk* 6 C10
Caistor *Lincs* 11 B11
Calanais *W Isles* 22 C4
Caldbeck *Cumb* 12 C3
Calder Bridge *Cumb* 12 E2
Caldercruix *N Lanarks* 14 B6
Caldicot *Monmouths* 5 G2
Calfsound *Orkney* 23 B3
Calgary *Arg/Bute* 18 F5
Callander *Stirl* 16 H5
Callington *Cornw'l* 2 G6
Calne *Wilts* 5 H5
Calshot *Hants* 5 L7
Calstock *Cornw'l* 2 G7
Calverton *Notts* 11 E9
Cam *Glos* 4 G3
Camber *E Sussex* 7 N7
Camberley *Surrey* 7 K2
Cambo *Northum* 15 F12
Camborne *Cornw'l* 2 J3
Cambridge *Cambs* 6 F5
Camden *London* 7 J4
Camelford *Cornw'l* 2 F5
Cammachmore *Aberds* 17 D11
Campbeltown *Arg/Bute* 19 M7
Camrose *Pembs* 9 L2
Canisbay *H'land* 21 B9
Cannich *H'land* 20 J4
Cannington *Som'set* 3 D11
Cannock *Staffs* 10 G5
Canonbie *Dumf/Gal* 15 G8
Canterbury *Kent* 7 L8
Canvey *Essex* 7 J7
Caol *H'land* 18 E9
Caolas Stocinis *W Isles* 22 E3
Caoles *Arg/Bute* 18 F4
Capel *Surrey* 7 L3
Capel Curig *Conwy* 8 D6
Capel St. Mary *Suffolk* 6 G8
Carbis Bay *Cornw'l* 2 J2
Carbost *H'land* 22 H4
Carbost *H'land* 22 G5
Cardiff *Card* 9 N8
Cardigan *Ceredig'n* 9 J3
Cardington *Beds* 6 F3
Cardross *Arg/Bute* 14 B3
Cargill *Perth/Kinr* 17 G7
Carhampton *Som'set* 3 C10
Carisbrooke *I/Wight* 5 M7
Cark *Cumb* 12 G3
Carlabhagh *W Isles* 22 B3
Carleton Rode *Norfolk* 6 D8
Carlisle *Cumb* 12 C4
Carlops *Scot Borders* 14 C7
Carlton *Notts* 11 E9
Carlton *N Yorks* 13 J10
Carlton Colville *Suffolk* 6 D10
Carlton Miniott *N Yorks* 13 F9
Carlton-in-Lindrick *Notts* 11 C8
Carluke *S Lanarks* 14 C6
Carmarthen *Carms* 9 K5
Carmyllie *Angus* 17 F9
Carnachuin *H'land* 16 D6
Carnforth *Lancs* 12 G4
Carno *Powys* 8 G7
Carnoustie *Angus* 17 G9
Carnwath *S Lanarks* 14 C6
Carradale *Arg/Bute* 19 M8
Carrbridge *H'land* 16 B6
Carrick *Arg/Bute* 16 J3
Carronbridge *Dumf/Gal* 14 F6
Carsaig *Arg/Bute* 18 G6
Carsphairn *Dumf/Gal* 14 F4
Carstairs *S Lanarks* 14 C6
Carterton *Oxon* 4 F6
Cartmel *Cumb* 12 G3
Castle Acre *Norfolk* 6 C7
Castle Cary *Som'set* 5 K3
Castle Donington *Leics* 11 F8
Castle Douglas *Dumf/Gal* 14 G5
Castlebay = Bagh a Chaisteil *W Isles* 18 D2
Castleford *W Yorks* 13 J9
Castlemartin *Pembs* 9 M2
Castleside *Durham* 12 C7
Castleton *Derby* 10 C6
Castleton *N Yorks* 13 E10
Castletown *H'land* 21 B9
Castletown *I/Man* 13
Caston *Norfolk* 6 D7
Castor *Peterbro* 6 D3
Catcleugh *Northum* 15 E10
Caterham *Surrey* 7 L4
Caton *Lancs* 12 G4
Catrine *E Ayrs* 14 D4
Catsfield *E Sussex* 7 N6
Catterall *Lancs* 12 H4
Catterick *N Yorks* 13 F8
Catterick Camp *N Yorks* 12 F7
Catton *Northum* 12 C6
Caulkerbush *Dumf/Gal* 14 H6
Cawdor *H'land* 20 H7
Cawood *N Yorks* 13 J9
Cawston *Norfolk* 6 B8
Caythorpe *Lincs* 11 E10
Cefn-mawr *Wrex* 8 D9
Cemaes *Angl* 8 B4
Cemmaes Road *Powys* 8 F7
Cenarth *Carms* 9 J4
Ceres *Fife* 17 H9
Cerne Abbas *Dorset* 5 L3
Cerrigydrudion *Conwy* 8 D7
Chacewater *Cornw'l* 2 H3
Chaddesley Corbet *Worcs* 4 C4
Chadwell St. Mary *Thurr'k* 7 K6
Chagford *Devon* 3 F8
Chalfont St. Giles *Bucks* 7 J2
Chalford *Glos* 4 F4
Chalgrove *Oxon* 4 G8
Challacombe *Devon* 3 C8
Challock *Kent* 7 L8
Chandler's Ford *Hants* 5 K7
Channel Tunnel *Kent* 7 M8
Chapel St. Leonards *Lincs* 11 D13
Chapel en le Frith *Derby* 10 C6
Chapeltown *S Yorks* 10 C7
Chapeltown *S Lanarks* 14 C5
Chard *Som'set* 3 E11
Charing *Kent* 7 L7
Charlbury *Oxon* 4 F6
Charlestown of Aberlour *Moray* 21 H9
Charlton *Wilts* 5 G4
Charlton Horethorne *Som'set* 5 K3
Charlton Kings *Glos* 4 E4
Charlwood *Surrey* 7 L4
Charminster *Dorset* 5 M3
Charmouth *Dorset* 3 F11
Chartham *Kent* 7 L8
Chatham *Medway* 7 K6
Chathill *Northum* 15 D12
Chatteris *Cambs* 6 D4
Chatton *Northum* 15 D12
Chawleigh *Devon* 3 E8
Cheadle *Staffs* 10 E6
Cheadle *Gtr Man* 10 C5
Chedburgh *Suffolk* 6 F6
Cheddar *Som'set* 3 C12
Cheddleton *Staffs* 10 E5
Chellaston *Derby C* 10 F7
Chelmarsh *Shrops* 10 H4
Chelmsford *Essex* 7 H6
Cheltenham *Glos* 4 E4
Chepstow *Monmouths* 4 G2
Cherhill *Wilts* 5 H5
Cheriton *Hants* 5 K8
Cheriton Fitzpaine *Devon* 3 E9
Chertsey *Surrey* 7 K3
Chesham *Bucks* 7 H2
Cheshunt *Herts* 7 H4
Chester *Ches* 10 D2
Chester-le-Street *Durham* 13 C8
Chesterfield *Derby* 10 D7
Chew Magna *Bath/NE Som'set* 5 H2
Chewton Mendip *Som'set* 5 J2
Chichester *W Sussex* 5 L9
Chiddingfold *Surrey* 7 M2
Chideock *Dorset* 3 F12

Chigwell Essex 7 J5
Chilcompton Som'set 5 J3
Chilham Kent 7 L8
Chillington Devon 3 H8
Chilton Durham 13 D8
Chingford London 7 J4
Chinnor Oxon 4 F8
Chippenham Wilts 5 H4
Chipping Campden Glos 4 E5
Chipping Norton Oxon 4 E6
Chipping Ongar Essex 7 H5
Chipping Sodbury S Gloucs 5 G3
Chirbury Shrops 8 G9
Chirk Wrex 8 E9
Chirnside Scot Borders 15 C11
Chiseldon Swindon 5 H5
Chitterne Wilts 5 J4
Chobham Surrey 7 K2
Chollerton Northum 12 B6
Cholsey Oxon 5 G7
Chorley Lancs 12 K4
Chorleywood Herts 7 J3
Christchurch Dorset 5 M5
Christchurch Cambs 6 D5
Christow Devon 3 F9
Chudleigh Devon 3 G9
Chulmleigh Devon 3 E8
Church Stretton Shrops 10 H3
Church Village Rh Cyn Taff 9 M8
Churchdown Glos 4 E4
Churchill Oxon 4 E6
Churchstow Devon 3 H8
Chwilog Gwyn 8 E5
Cilgerran Pembs 9 J3
Cille Bhrighde W Isles 22 J1
Cilycwm Carms 9 K6
Cinderford Glos 4 F3
Cirencester Glos 4 F5
City London 7 J4
Clabhach Arg/Bute 18 F4
Clachan Arg/Bute 19 L7
Clachan H'land 22 H5
Clachan na Luib W Isles 22 F2
Clackmannan Clack 16 J6
Clacton-on-Sea Essex 7 H8
Cladich Arg/Bute 18 G9
Claggan H'land 18 F7
Claigan H'land 22 G4
Clanfield Hants 5 L8
Claonaig Arg/Bute 19 L8
Clapham Beds 6 F3
Clapham N Yorks 12 G5
Clare Suffolk 6 F6
Clashmore H'land 20 F6
Clavering Essex 6 G5
Claverley Shrops 10 H4
Clawton Devon 2 F6
Clay Cross Derby 10 D7
Claydon Suffolk 6 F8
Claypole Lincs 11 E10
Cleadale H'land 18 D6
Cleat Orkney 23 D3
Cleator Moor Cumb 12 E2
Cleethorpes NE Lincs 11 B12
Cleeve Prior Warwick 4 D5
Clehonger Heref'd 4 E2
Cleobury Mortimer Shrops 10 J4
Clevedon N Som'set 3 B12
Cleveleys Lancs 12 H3
Cley Norfolk 6 A8
Cliffe Medway 7 K6
Clifford Heref'd 9 J9
Clipston Northants 11 H9
Clitheroe Lancs 12 H5
Clive Shrops 10 F3
Clophill Beds 6 G3
Closeburn Dumf/Gal 14 F6
Cloughton N Yorks 13 F12
Clova Angus 17 E8
Clovelly Devon 2 D6
Clovenfords Scot Borders 15 D9
Clowne Derby 11 D8
Clun Shrops 8 G9
Clunbury Shrops 8 G9
Clunes H'land 16 D2
Clungunford Shrops 9 H9
Clutton Bath/NE Som'set 5 J3
Clydach Swan 9 L6
Clydebank W Dunb 14 B4
Clynnog-fawr Gwyn 8 D5
Clyro Powys 9 J9
Coalbrookdale Telford 10 G4
Coalburn S Lanarks 14 D6
Coalville Leics 11 G8
Coatbridge N Lanarks 14 B5
Cobham Surrey 7 L3
Cobham Kent 7 K6
Cock Bridge Aberds 17 C8
Cockburnspath Scot Borders 15 B10
Cockenzie E Loth 15 B9
Cockerham Lancs 12 H4
Cockermouth Cumb 12 D2
Cockfield Durham 12 D7
Cockfield Suffolk 6 F7
Cockshutt Shrops 10 F3
Coddenham Suffolk 6 F8
Codford St. Mary Wilts 5 J4
Coggeshall Essex 6 G7
Coignafearn Lodge H'land 16 C5
Coille Mhorgil H'land 18 C9
Coillore H'land 22 H4
Colby I/Man 13
Colchester Essex 6 G8
Cold Ashton S Gloucs 5 H3
Coldingham Scot Borders 15 B11
Coldstream Scot Borders 15 D11
Colebrooke Devon 3 F8
Coleford Glos 4 F2
Coleshill Warwick 10 H7
Colinton C/Edinb 15 B8
Colintraive Arg/Bute 19 K9
Collin Dumf/Gal 14 G7
Collingbourne Kingston Wilts 5 J6
Collingham W Yorks 13 H8
Collingham Notts 11 D10
Colmonel S Ayrs 14 F2
Colne Lancs 12 J6
Colpy Aberds 21 J11
Colsterworth Lincs 11 F10
Coltishall Norfolk 6 B9
Colwell Northum 12 B6
Colwich Staffs 10 F6
Colwyn Bay Conwy 8 C7
Colyton Devon 3 F11
Combe Martin Devon 3 C7
Comberton Cambs 6 F4
Combwich Som'set 3 C11
Compton W Sussex 5 L8
Compton W Berks 5 H7
Compton Martin Bath/NE Som'set 5 J2
Comrie Perth/Kinr 16 G5
Condover Shrops 10 G3
Congleton Ches 10 D5
Congresbury N Som'set 3 B12
Coningsby Lincs 11 E12
Conisbrough S Yorks 11 C8
Coniston Cumb 12 F3
Connah's Quay Flints 10 D2
Connel Arg/Bute 18 G8
Connel Park E Ayrs 14 E5
Cononbridge H'land 20 H5
Consett Durham 12 C7
Contin H'land 20 H5
Conwy Conwy 8 C6
Cookham Windsor 7 J2
Coolham W Sussex 7 M3
Coombe Bissett Wilts 5 K5
Copplestone Devon 3 E8
Coppull Lancs 10 B3
Copthorne W Sussex 7 M4
Corbridge Northum 12 B6
Corby Northants 6 D2
Corby Glen Lincs 11 F11
Corfe Castle Dorset 5 M4
Corfe Mullen Dorset 5 M4
Cornhill on Tweed Northum 15 D11
Corpach H'land 18 E9
Corran H'land 18 E9
Corrie N Ayrs 19 L9
Corringham Thurr'k 7 J6
Corringham Lincs 11 C10
Corris Gwyn 8 F6
Corsham Wilts 5 H4
Corsley Wilts 5 J4
Corsock Dumf/Gal 14 G5
Corton Suffolk 6 D10
Corwen Denbs 8 D8
Coseley W Midlands 10 H5
Cosham Portsm'th 5 L8
Costessey Norfolk 6 C8
Cotgrave Notts 11 F9
Cotherstone Durham 12 D7
Cottenham Cambs 6 E5
Cottered Herts 6 G4
Cottesmore Rutl'd 11 G10
Cottingham ER Yorks 13 J12
Coulags H'land 20 H2
Coulport Arg/Bute 14 A3
Countesthorpe Leics 11 H8
Coupar Angus Perth/Kinr 17 F8
Cove Arg/Bute 14 A3
Cove H'land 20 F2
Cove Bay Aberd C 17 C11
Coventry W Midlands 10 H7
Coverack Cornw'l 2 K3
Cowbit Lincs 11 G12
Cowbridge V/Glam 9 N7
Cowdenbeath Fife 17 J7
Cowes I/Wight 5 M7
Cowfold W Sussex 7 M4
Cowpen Northum 15 F13
Cowplain Hants 5 L8
Coxheath Kent 7 L6
Coylton S Ayrs 14 D4
Craggie H'land 20 J6
Crai Powys 9 K7
Craibstone Moray 21 H10
Craigellachie Moray 21 H9
Craighouse Arg/Bute 19 K6
Craigmore Arg/Bute 19 K9
Craignure Arg/Bute 18 G7
Craigtown H'land 21 C7
Crail Fife 17 H10
Cramlington Northum 13 B8
Cranborne Dorset 5 L5
Cranbrook Kent 7 M6
Cranleigh Surrey 7 M3
Cranmore Som'set 5 J3
Cranwell Lincs 11 E11
Crathie Aberds 17 D8
Craven Arms Shrops 10 H3
Crawford S Lanarks 14 D6
Crawfordjohn S Lanarks 14 D6
Crawley W Sussex 7 M4
Creag Ghoraidh W Isles 22 G2
Creake Norfolk 6 B7
Credenhill Heref'd 4 D2
Crediton Devon 3 F9
Creetown Dumf/Gal 14 H4
Cressage Shrops 10 G3
Cresselly Pembs 9 L3
Crewe Ches 10 E4
Crewkerne Som'set 3 E12
Crianlarich Stirl 16 G3
Criccieth Gwyn 8 E5
Crick Northants 4 C7
Crickhowell Powys 9 L9
Cricklade Wilts 4 G5
Crieff Perth/Kinr 16 G6
Crimond Aberds 21 H13
Crinan Arg/Bute 19 J7
Crocketford Dumf/Gal 14 G6
Croggan Arg/Bute 18 G7
Croglin Cumb 12 C4
Croick H'land 20 F5
Cromarty H'land 20 G6
Cromer Norfolk 6 A9
Cromor W Isles 22 C4
Crondall Hants 5 J8
Crook Durham 12 D7
Crookham Northum 15 D11
Crooklands Cumb 12 F4
Crosbost W Isles 22 C4
Crosby Cumb 12 C2
Crosby Ravensworth Cumb 12 E5
Cross-Hands Carms 9 L5
Crosshill S Ayrs 14 E3
Crossmichael Dumf/Gal 14 G5
Croston Lancs 12 K4
Crowborough E Sussex 7 M5
Crowland Lincs 11 G12
Crowle N Lincs 11 B9
Crowthorne Wokingham 5 H9
Croxton Kerrial Leics 11 F10
Croyde Devon 2 D7
Croydon London 7 K4
Cruden Bay Aberds 21 J13
Crudgington Telford 10 G4
Crymych Pembs 9 K3
Cuckfield W Sussex 7 M4
Cuddington Ches 10 D3
Cuddington Bucks 4 F8
Cudworth S Yorks 10 B7
Cuffley Herts 7 H4
Culgaith Cumb 12 D5
Culkein H'land 20 D3
Cullen Moray 21 G10
Cullicudden H'land 20 G6
Cullivoe Shetl'd 23 A3
Culloden H'land 20 H6
Cullompton Devon 3 E10
Culmazie Dumf/Gal 14 H3
Culmington Shrops 10 H3
Culmstock Devon 3 E10
Culrain H'land 20 F5
Culross Fife 14 A6
Cults Aberd C 17 C11
Cumbernauld N Lanarks 14 B5
Cuminestown Aberds 21 H12
Cummertrees Dumf/Gal 14 G7
Cumnock E Ayrs 14 D4
Cumnor Oxon 4 F7
Cumwhinton Cumb 12 C4
Cupar Fife 17 H8
Currie C/Edinb 14 B7
Curry Rivel Som'set 3 D11
Cwmafan Neath P Talb 9 M6
Cwmann Carms 9 J5
Cwmbran Torf 9 M9
Cwrt Gwyn 8 F6
Cymmer Neath P Talb 9 M7
Cynwyl Elfed Carms 9 K4

D

Dagenham London 7 J5
Dail bho Dheas W Isles 22 A5
Dailly S Ayrs 14 E3
Dalabrog W Isles 22 H1
Dalbeattie Dumf/Gal 14 G6
Dale Shetl'd 23 D1
Dale Pembs 9 L2
Dalguise Perth/Kinr 16 F6
Dalhalvaig H'land 20 C7
Dalkeith Midloth 15 B8
Dallas Moray 21 H8
Dalleagles E Ayrs 14 E4
Dalmally Arg/Bute 18 G9
Dalmellington E Ayrs 14 E4
Dalnaspidal Perth/Kinr 16 E5
Dalnessie H'land 20 E6
Dalry N Ayrs 14 C3
Dalry Dumf/Gal 14 F5
Dalrymple E Ayrs 14 E3
Dalston Cumb 12 C3
Dalton Dumf/Gal 14 G7
Dalton N Yorks 13 E8
Dalton-in-Furness Cumb 12 G3
Dalwhinnie H'land 16 D5
Damerham Hants 5 L5
Danbury Essex 7 H7
Darlington D'lington 13 E8
Dartford Kent 7 K5
Dartford Crossing Kent 7 K5
Dartington Devon 3 G8
Dartmouth Devon 3 H9
Darton S Yorks 10 B7
Darvel E Ayrs 14 D4
Darwen Blackb'n 12 J5
Daventry Northants 4 C7
Davington Dumf/Gal 15 E8
Dawlish Devon 3 G9
Deal Kent 7 L9
Dearham Cumb 12 D2
Dearne S Yorks 11 B8
Debenham Suffolk 6 E8
Deddington Oxon 4 E7
Deeping St. Nicholas Lincs 11 G12
Deerness Orkney 23 C3
Deganwy Conwy 8 C6
Delabole Cornw'l 2 F5
Delchirach Moray 21 J8
Delves Durham 12 C7
Denbigh Denbs 8 C8
Denby Dale W Yorks 10 B7
Denholm Scot Borders 15 E9
Denny Falk 14 A6
Dent Cumb 12 F5
Denton Lincs 11 F10
Denton Gtr Man 10 C5
Derby Derby C 10 F7
Dereham Norfolk 6 C7
Dersingham Norfolk 6 B6
Dervaig Arg/Bute 18 F6
Desborough Northants 11 H10
Desford Leics 11 G8
Devil's Bridge Ceredig'n 9 H6
Devizes Wilts 5 H5
Devonport Plym'th 2 H7
Dewsbury W Yorks 13 J8
Diabaig H'land 22 F6
Dibden Purlieu Hants 5 L7
Dickleborough Norfolk 6 D8
Didcot Oxon 5 G7
Digby Lincs 11 E11
Dinas Mawddwy Gwyn 8 F7
Dinas Powis V/Glam 9 N8
Dingwall H'land 20 H5
Dinnington S Yorks 11 C8
Dinton Wilts 5 K5
Dippen N Ayrs 19 M9
Dirleton E Loth 15 A9
Diss Norfolk 6 D8
Distington Cumb 12 D2
Ditchingham Norfolk 6 D9
Ditchling E Sussex 7 N4
Dittisham Devon 3 H9
Ditton Priors Shrops 10 H4
Dobwalls Cornw'l 2 G6
Docking Norfolk 6 B6
Dockray Cumb 12 D3
Doddinghurst Essex 7 J5
Doddington Cambs 6 D4
Doddington Northum 15 D11
Dolanog Powys 8 F8
Dolfor Powys 8 G8
Dolgarrog Conwy 8 C6
Dolgellau Gwyn 8 F6
Dollar Clack 16 J6
Dolphinton S Lanarks 14 C7
Dolton Devon 3 E7
Dolwyddelan Conwy 8 D6
Doncaster S Yorks 11 B8
Donhead St.Andrew Wilts 5 K4
Donington Lincs 11 F12
Donnington Telford 10 G4
Dorchester Oxon 4 G7
Dorchester Dorset 5 M3
Dores H'land 20 J6
Dorking Surrey 7 L3
Dornie H'land 18 B8
Dornoch H'land 20 F6
Dorridge W Midlands 10 J6
Dorstone Heref'd 9 J9
Douglas I/Man 13
Douglas S Lanarks 14 D6
Dounby Orkney 23 B2
Doune Stirl 16 H5
Dounreay H'land 21 B7
Dove Holes Derby 10 D6
Dover Kent 7 L9
Doveridge Derby 10 F6
Downham Cambs 6 D5
Downham Market Norfolk 6 C6
Downton Wilts 5 K5
Drayton Norfolk 6 C8
Dreghorn N Ayrs 14 D3
Drem E Loth 15 B9
Driffield ER Yorks 13 H12
Drigg Cumb 12 E2
Drimnin H'land 18 F6
Droitwich Spa Worcs 4 C4
Dronfield Derby 10 D7
Drongan E Ayrs 14 E4
Druid Denbs 8 D8
Drumbeg H'land 20 D3
Drumgask H'land 16 D5
Drumjohn Dumf/Gal 14 F4
Drummore Dumf/Gal 14 J2
Drumnadrochit H'land 20 J5
Drymen Stirl 14 A4
Drynoch H'land 22 H4
Duchally H'land 20 E4
Duddington Northants 6 C2
Dudley W Midlands 10 H5
Duffield Derby 10 E7
Dufftown Moray 21 J9
Dukinfield Gtr Man 10 C5
Dullingham Cambs 6 F6
Dulnain Bridge H'land 16 B6
Duloe Cornw'l 2 H6
Dulverton Som'set 3 D9
Dumbarton W Dunb 14 B4
Dumfries Dumf/Gal 14 G6
Dunans Arg/Bute 19 J9
Dunbar E Loth 15 B10
Dunbeath H'land 21 D8
Dunblane Stirl 16 H5
Duncansby H'land 21 B9
Dunchurch Warwick 4 C7
Dundee Dundee C 17 G8
Dundonald S Ayrs 14 D3
Dundrennan Dumf/Gal 14 H5
Dunecht Aberds 17 C10
Dunfermline Fife 14 A7
Dunino Fife 17 H9
Dunipace Falk 14 A6
Dunkeld Perth/Kinr 16 F7
Dunlop E Ayrs 14 C4
Dunnet H'land 21 B9
Dunning Perth/Kinr 16 H7
Dunnington C/York 13 H10
Dunoon Arg/Bute 19 K9
Dunragit Dumf/Gal 14 H2
Duns Scot Borders 15 C10
Dunsby Lincs 11 F11
Dunscore Dumf/Gal 14 F6
Dunsford Devon 3 F9
Dunstable Beds 6 G3
Dunster Som'set 3 C9
Dunston Staffs 10 G5
Dunsyre S Lanarks 14 C7
Dunure S Ayrs 14 E3
Dunvegan H'land 22 G4
Durham Durham 13 C8
Durness H'land 20 B5
Durrington Wilts 5 J5
Dursley Glos 4 G3
Dyce Aberd C 17 C11
Dykehead Angus 17 E8
Dymchurch Kent 7 M8
Dymock Glos 4 E3
Dysart Fife 17 J8
Dyserth Denbs 8 C8

E

Eaglescliffe Stockton 13 E9
Eaglesfield Dumf/Gal 15 G8
Eaglesham E Renf 14 C4
Eakring Notts 11 D9
Ealing London 7 J3
Earby Lancs 12 H6
Eardisley Heref'd 9 J9
Earith Cambs 6 E4
Earl Shilton Leics 11 H8
Earl Soham Suffolk 6 E9
Earl's Colne Essex 6 G7
Earls Barton Northants 4 C9
Earlsferry Fife 17 H9
Earlston Scot Borders 15 D9
Earsdon Tyne/Wear 13 B8
Easebourne W Sussex 7 M2
Easington Durham 13 C9
Easington ER Yorks 13 K13
Easington Colliery Durham 13 C9
Easingwold N Yorks 13 G9
East Bergholt Suffolk 6 G8
East Boldre Hants 5 M6
East Brent Som'set 3 C11
East Bridgford Notts 11 E9
East Calder W Loth 14 B7
East Cowes I/Wight 5 M7
East Cowton N Yorks 13 E8
East Dean E Sussex 7 P5
East Grinstead W Sussex 7 M5
East Harling Norfolk 6 D7
East Horsley Surrey 7 L3
East Ilsley W Berks 5 G7
East Kilbride S Lanarks 14 C5
East Leake Notts 11 F8
East Linton E Loth 15 B9
East Looe Cornw'l 2 H6
East Markham Notts 11 D9
East Norton Leics 11 G9
East Oakley Hants 5 J7
East Wemyss Fife 17 J8
East Wittering W Sussex 5 M9
East Witton N Yorks 12 F7
East Woodhay Hants 5 H7
Eastbourne E Sussex 7 P5
Eastchurch Kent 7 K8
Easter Skeld Shetl'd 23 D2
Eastfield N Yorks 13 F12
Eastleigh Hants 5 L7
Eastnor Heref'd 4 E3
Easton Northants 6 C3
Easton Dorset 5 N3
Easton-in-Gordano N Som'set 5 H2
Eastry Kent 7 L9
Eastwood Notts 11 E8
Eaton Leics 11 F9
Eaton Socon Cambs 6 F3
Ebberston N Yorks 13 F11
Ebbw Vale Bl Gwent 9 L8
Ecclaw Scot Borders 15 B10
Ecclefechan Dumf/Gal 14 G7
Eccleshall Staffs 10 F5
Echt Aberds 17 C10
Eckington Derby 11 D8
Eckington Worcs 4 D4
Edderton H'land 20 F6
Edenbridge Kent 7 L5
Edgmond Telford 10 G4
Edinburgh C/Edinb 15 B8
Edington Wilts 5 J4
Edmundbyers Durham 12 C7
Edwinstowe Notts 11 D9
Edzell Angus 17 E10
Egham Surrey 7 K3
Eglwyswrw Pembs 9 K3
Egremont Cumb 12 E2
Egton N Yorks 13 E11
Eilean Iarmain H'land 22 J6
Elan Village Powys 9 H7
Elgin Moray 21 G9
Elgol H'land 22 J5
Elham Kent 7 L8
Elie Fife 17 H9
Elishaw Northum 15 F11
Elland W Yorks 12 J7
Ellesmere Shrops 10 F3
Ellesmere Port Ches 10 D2
Ellington Northum 15 F13
Ellon Aberds 21 J12
Elmswell Suffolk 6 E7
Elphin H'land 20 E4
Elsdon Northum 15 F11
Elsenham Essex 6 G5
Elstead Surrey 7 L2
Elston Notts 11 E9
Elvanfoot S Lanarks 14 E6
Elveden Suffolk 6 E7
Elvington C/York 13 H10
Elworth Ches 10 D4
Ely Cambs 6 D5
Embleton Northum 15 D13
Embo H'land 20 F7
Empingham Rutl'd 6 C2
Emsworth Hants 5 L8
Enderby Leics 11 H8
Endon Staffs 10 E5
Enfield London 7 J4
Enstone Oxon 4 E6
Enterkinfoot Dumf/Gal 14 E6
Epping Essex 7 H5
Epsom Surrey 7 L4
Epworth N Lincs 11 B9
Eriboll H'land 20 C5
Errogie H'land 16 B4
Errol Perth/Kinr 17 G8
Erskine Renf 14 B4
Erskine Bridge Renf 14 B4
Escrick N Yorks 13 H10
Esh Winning Durham 12 C7
Esher Surrey 7 K3
Eskdalemuir Dumf/Gal 15 F8
Eston Redcar/Clevel'd 13 D9
Etchingham E Sussex 7 M6
Eton Windsor 7 K2
Ettington Warwick 4 D6
Etwall Derby 10 F7
Euxton Lancs 12 J4
Evanton H'land 20 G6
Evercreech Som'set 5 K3
Everleigh Wilts 5 J6
Evershot Dorset 5 L2
Evesham Worcs 4 D5
Ewell Surrey 7 K4
Ewhurst Surrey 7 L3
Ewyas Harold Heref'd 9 K9
Exbourne Devon 3 E7
Exeter Devon 3 F9
Exford Som'set 3 D9
Exminster Devon 3 F9
Exmouth Devon 3 F9
Exton Rutl'd 11 G10
Eyam Derby 10 D7
Eye Suffolk 6 E8
Eye Peterbro 6 C4
Eyemouth Scot Borders 15 B11
Eynsford Kent 7 K5
Eynsham Oxon 4 F7

F

Faddiley Ches 10 E3
Fairbourne Gwyn 8 F6
Fairford Glos 4 F5
Fairlie N Ayrs 14 C3
Fairlight E Sussex 7 N7
Fakenham Norfolk 6 B7
Fala Midloth 15 B9
Faldingworth Lincs 11 C11
Falkirk Falk 14 A6
Falkland Fife 17 H8
Falmer E Sussex 7 N4
Falmouth Cornw'l 2 J4
Falstone Northum 15 F10
Fareham Hants 5 L7
Faringdon Oxon 4 G6
Farnborough Hants 7 L2
Farnborough W Berks 5 G7
Farndon Ches 10 E3
Farnham Surrey 5 J9
Farnworth Gtr Man 10 B4
Farr H'land 20 J6
Fasag H'land 20 H2
Faslane Arg/Bute 16 J3
Fauldhouse W Loth 14 B6
Faversham Kent 7 K8
Fawley Hants 5 L7
Fazeley Staffs 10 G7
Fearn H'land 20 G7
Fearnan Perth/Kinr 16 F5
Feckenham Worcs 4 C5
Felixstowe Suffolk 6 G9
Felton Northum 15 E12
Feltwell Norfolk 6 D6
Fenny Bentley Derby 10 E6
Fenny Compton Warwick 4 D7
Fenny Stratford M/Keynes 6 G2
Fenwick E Ayrs 14 C4
Feock Cornw'l 2 J4
Feolin Ferry Arg/Bute 19 K6
Ferndown Dorset 5 L5
Ferness H'land 21 H7
Fernhurst W Sussex 7 M2
Fernilea H'land 22 H4
Ferryhill Durham 13 D8
Ferryside Carms 9 L4
Fettercairn Aberds 17 E10
Ffestiniog Gwyn 8 D6
Filby Norfolk 6 C10

Filey *N Yorks* 13 F12
Fillongley *Warwick* 10 H7
Filton *S Gloucs* 5 H3
Fincham *Norfolk* 6 C6
Finchingfield *Essex* 6 G6
Finchley *London* 7 J4
Findhorn *Moray* 21 G8
Findochty *Moray* 21 G10
Findon *W Sussex* 7 N3
Finedon *Northants* 6 E2
Finningley *S Yorks* 11 C9
Finstown *Orkney* 23 C2
Fintry *Stirl* 14 A5
Fionnphort *Arg/Bute* 18 G5
Fishbourne *I/Wight* 5 M7
Fishguard *Pembs* 9 K2
Fishnish *Arg/Bute* 18 F7
Fishtoft *Lincs* 11 E12
Flamborough *ER Yorks* 13 G13
Fleet *Hants* 5 J9
Fleetwood *Lancs* 12 H3
Flimby *Cumb* 12 D2
Flint *Flints* 10 D2
Flitwick *Beds* 6 G3
Flodden *Northum* 15 D11
Flookburgh *Cumb* 12 G3
Fochabers *Moray* 21 H9
Foel *Powys* 8 F8
Folkestone *Kent* 7 M9
Fontmell Magna *Dorset* 5 L4
Ford *Arg/Bute* 19 H8
Forden *Powys* 8 F9
Fordham *Cambs* 6 E6
Fordingbridge *Hants* 5 L5
Fordyce *Aberds* 21 G10
Forest Row *E Sussex* 7 M5
Forfar *Angus* 17 F9
Formby *Mersey* 10 B2
Forres *Moray* 21 H8
Forsinain *H'land* 21 C7
Forsinard *H'land* 20 C7
Fort Augustus *H'land* 16 C3
Fort William *H'land* 18 E9
Forth *S Lanarks* 14 C6
Forth Road Bridge *C/Edinb* 14 A7
Fortrie *Aberds* 21 H11
Fortrose *H'land* 20 H6
Fortuneswell *Dorset* 5 N3
Fothergill *Cumb* 12 D2
Fotheringhay *Northants* 6 D3
Foulden *Scot Borders* 15 C11
Foulsham *Norfolk* 6 B8
Fountainhall *Scot Borders* 15 C9
Fovant *Wilts* 5 K5
Fowey *Cornw'l* 2 H5
Fownhope *Heref'd* 4 E2
Foxdale *I/Man* 13
Foyers *H'land* 16 B4
Fraddon *Cornw'l* 2 H4
Framlingham *Suffolk* 6 E9
Frampton on Severn *Glos* 4 F3
Frant *E Sussex* 7 M5
Fraserburgh *Aberds* 21 G12
Freckleton *Lancs* 12 J4
Freethorpe *Norfolk* 6 C10
Fremington *Devon* 2 D7
Frensham *Surrey* 5 J9
Freshwater *I/Wight* 5 M6
Fressingfield *Suffolk* 6 E9
Freswick *H'land* 21 B9
Freuchie *Fife* 17 H8
Friday Bridge *Cambs* 6 C5
Fridaythorpe *ER Yorks* 13 G11
Frimley *Surrey* 7 L2
Frinton-on-Sea *Essex* 7 H9
Friockheim *Angus* 17 F9
Frizington *Cumb* 12 E2
Frodsham *Ches* 10 D3
Frome *Som'set* 5 J3
Frongoch *Gwyn* 8 E7
Froxfield *Wilts* 5 H6
Fulbourn *Cambs* 6 F5
Fulford *C/York* 13 H10
Fulwood *Lancs* 12 J4
Funzie *Shetl'd* 23 B4
Furnace *Arg/Bute* 19 H9
Fyfield *Essex* 7 H5
Fyvie *Aberds* 21 J11

G

Gaerwen *Angl* 8 C5
Gaick Lodge *H'land* 16 D5
Gailey *Staffs* 10 G5
Gainford *Durham* 12 E7
Gainsborough *Lincs* 11 C10
Gairloch *H'land* 20 G2
Gairlochy *H'land* 18 D9
Galashiels *Scot Borders* 15 D9
Galgate *Lancs* 12 H4
Galmisdale *H'land* 18 D6
Galmpton *Torbay* 3 H9
Galston *E Ayrs* 14 D4
Gamlingay *Cambs* 6 F4
Garbhallt *Arg/Bute* 19 J9
Garboldisham *Norfolk* 6 D8
Gardenstown *Aberds* 21 G12
Garelochhead *Arg/Bute* 16 J3
Garforth *W Yorks* 13 J9
Gargrave *N Yorks* 12 H6
Gargunnock *Stirl* 16 J5
Garlieston *Dumf/Gal* 14 H4
Garmouth *Moray* 21 G9
Garrow *Perth/Kinr* 16 F6
Garsdale Head *Cumb* 12 F5
Garstang *Lancs* 12 H4
Garston *Mersey* 10 C2
Garton-on-the-Wolds *ER Yorks* 13 G11
Garvald *E Loth* 15 B9
Garve *H'land* 20 G4
Gatehouse of Fleet *Dumf/Gal* 14 H4
Gateshead *Tyne/Wear* 13 B8
Gatley *Gtr Man* 10 C5
Gatwick Airport *Surrey* 7 L4
Gawthwaite *Cumb* 12 F3
Gaydon *Warwick* 4 D6
Gayton *Norfolk* 6 B6
Gaywood *Norfolk* 6 B6
Gearraidh na h-Aibhne *W Isles* 22 C4
Geary *H'land* 22 F4
Geddington *Northants* 6 D2
Gedney *Lincs* 11 F13
Georgeham *Devon* 2 D7
Gerrards Cross *Bucks* 7 J3
Gifford *E Loth* 15 B9
Giggleswick *N Yorks* 12 G6
Gillingham *Dorset* 5 K3
Gillingham *Medway* 7 K6
Gilmerton *Perth/Kinr* 16 G6
Gilsland *Northum* 15 G10
Gilwern *Monmouths* 9 L9
Giosla *W Isles* 22 C3
Girton *Cambs* 6 E5
Girvan *S Ayrs* 14 F2
Gisburn *Lancs* 12 H6
Gladestry *Powys* 9 J9
Glamis *Angus* 17 F8
Glanaman *Carms* 9 L6
Glanton *Northum* 15 E12
Glasbury *Powys* 9 K8
Glasgow *Glasg C* 14 B4
Glasserton *Dumf/Gal* 14 J4
Glasson *Lancs* 12 H4
Glastonbury *Som'set* 5 K2
Glemsford *Suffolk* 6 F7
Glenbarr *Arg/Bute* 19 M7
Glenborrodale *H'land* 18 E7
Glenbrittle *H'land* 22 H5
Glencaple *Dumf/Gal* 14 G6
Glencarse *Perth/Kinr* 17 G8
Glencoe *H'land* 18 F9
Glendoll Lodge *Angus* 17 E8
Gleneagles *Perth/Kinr* 16 H6
Glenelg *H'land* 18 C8
Glenfinnan *H'land* 18 D8
Glenluce *Dumf/Gal* 14 H3
Glenmaye *I/Man* 13
Glenmore Lodge *H'land* 16 C6
Glenprosen Lodge *Angus* 17 E8
Glenrothes *Fife* 17 H8
Glenstriven *Arg/Bute* 19 K9
Glentrool Village *Dumf/Gal* 14 G3
Glenwhilly *Dumf/Gal* 14 G2
Glinton *Peterbro* 6 C3
Glossop *Derby* 10 C6
Gloucester *Glos* 4 F4
Glusburn *N Yorks* 12 H7
Glyn Ceiriog *Wrex* 8 E8
Glyn Neath *Neath P Talb* 9 L7
Glyncorrwg *Neath P Talb* 9 M7
Glynde *E Sussex* 7 N5
Glyndyfrdwy *Denbs* 8 D8
Gnosall *Staffs* 10 F5
Goathland *N Yorks* 13 E11
Gobowen *Shrops* 8 E9
Godalming *Surrey* 7 L2
Godmanchester *Cambs* 6 E4
Godshill *I/Wight* 5 M7
Godstone *Surrey* 7 L4
Goldhanger *Essex* 7 H7
Golspie *H'land* 20 F7
Goodrich *Heref'd* 4 F2
Goodwick *Pembs* 9 K2
Goodwood *W Sussex* 7 N2
Goole *ER Yorks* 13 J10
Goonhavern *Cornw'l* 2 H3
Gordon *Scot Borders* 15 C10
Gorebridge *Midloth* 15 B8
Goring *Oxon* 5 G8
Goring-by-Sea *W Sussex* 7 N3
Gorleston-on-Sea *Norfolk* 6 C10
Gorran Haven *Cornw'l* 2 H5
Gorseinon *Swan* 9 M5
Gorslas *Carms* 9 L5
Gosberton *Lincs* 11 F12
Gosfield *Essex* 6 G6
Gosforth *Cumb* 12 E2
Gosport *Hants* 5 M8
Goswick *Northum* 15 C12
Gotham *Notts* 11 F8
Goudhurst *Kent* 7 M6
Gourdon *Aberds* 17 E11
Gourock *Inverclyde* 14 B3
Gowerton *Swan* 9 M5
Grabhair *W Isles* 22 D4
Grain *Medway* 7 K7
Grainthorpe *Lincs* 11 C12
Grampound *Cornw'l* 2 H4
Gramsdal *W Isles* 22 G2
Grange-over-Sands *Cumb* 12 G4
Grangemouth *Falk* 14 A6
Grantham *Lincs* 11 F10
Grantown-on-Spey *H'land* 16 B7
Grantshouse *Scot Borders* 15 B11
Grasby *Lincs* 11 B11
Grasmere *Cumb* 12 E3
Grassington *N Yorks* 12 G7
Grateley *Hants* 5 J6
Gravesend *Kent* 7 K6
Grayrigg *Cumb* 12 F4
Grays *Thurr'k* 7 K6
Grayshott *Hants* 5 K9
Great Ayton *N Yorks* 13 E9
Great Baddow *Essex* 7 H6
Great Badminton *S Gloucs* 5 G4
Great Barford *Beds* 6 F3
Great Bentley *Essex* 6 G8
Great Bridgeford *Staffs* 10 F5
Great Broughton *N Yorks* 13 E9
Great Chesterford *Essex* 6 F5
Great Clifton *Cumb* 12 D2
Great Dunmow *Essex* 6 G6
Great Eccleston *Lancs* 12 H4
Great Ellingham *Norfolk* 6 D8
Great Gidding *Cambs* 6 D3
Great Harwood *Lancs* 12 J5
Great Horwood *Bucks* 4 E8
Great Malvern *Worcs* 4 D3
Great Massingham *Norfolk* 6 B7
Great Missenden *Bucks* 7 H2
Great Oakley *Essex* 6 G9
Great Sampford *Essex* 6 G6
Great Shefford *W Berks* 5 H6
Great Shelford *Cambs* 6 F5
Great Somerford *Wilts* 5 G4
Great Staunton *Cambs* 6 E3
Great Torrington *Devon* 2 E7
Great Wakering *Essex* 7 J7
Great Waltham *Essex* 7 H6
Great Witley *Worcs* 4 C3
Great Yarmouth *Norfolk* 6 C10
Greatham *Hartlep'l* 13 D9
Greatstone-on-Sea *Kent* 7 M8
Green Hammerton *N Yorks* 13 H9
Greenhead *Northum* 15 G10
Greenholm *E Ayrs* 14 D4
Greenlaw *Scot Borders* 15 C10
Greenloaning *Perth/Kinr* 16 H6
Greenock *Inverclyde* 14 B3
Greenodd *Cumb* 12 F3
Greenway *Pembs* 9 K3
Greenwich *London* 7 K4
Gretna *Dumf/Gal* 15 G8
Gretna Green *Dumf/Gal* 15 G8
Gretton *Northants* 6 D2
Greystoke *Cumb* 12 D4
Grimsby *NE Lincs* 11 B12
Gritley *Orkney* 23 C3
Grizebeck *Cumb* 12 F3
Groby *Leics* 11 G8
Grove *Oxon* 4 G7
Grundisburgh *Suffolk* 6 F9
Guard Bridge *Fife* 17 H9
Guestling Green *E Sussex* 7 N7
Guildford *Surrey* 7 L3
Guildtown *Perth/Kinr* 17 G7
Guilsfield *Powys* 8 F9
Guisborough *Redcar/Clevel'd* 13 E10
Guiseley *W Yorks* 12 H7
Gullane *E Loth* 15 A9
Gunnerside *N Yorks* 12 F6
Gunnislake *Cornw'l* 2 G7
Gunnista *Shetl'd* 23 D3
Gutcher *Shetl'd* 23 B3
Gwalchmai *Angl* 8 C4
Gwaun-Cae-Gurwen *Neath P Talb* 9 L6
Gwbert-on-Sea *Ceredig'n* 9 J3
Gweek *Cornw'l* 2 J3
Gwennap *Cornw'l* 2 J3
Gwyddelwern *Denbs* 8 D8
Gwytherin *Conwy* 8 C7

H

Hackney *London* 7 J4
Hackthorpe *Cumb* 12 D4
Haddenham *Bucks* 4 F8
Haddenham *Cambs* 6 E5
Haddington *E Loth* 15 B9
Haddiscoe *Norfolk* 6 D10
Hadleigh *Suffolk* 6 F8
Hadleigh *Essex* 7 J7
Hadlow *Kent* 7 L6
Hadnall *Shrops* 10 F3
Hagworthingham *Lincs* 11 D12
Hailsham *E Sussex* 7 N5
Hainton *Lincs* 11 C11
Halberton *Devon* 3 E10
Halesowen *W Midlands* 10 H5
Halesworth *Suffolk* 6 E9
Halford *Warwick* 4 D6
Halifax *W Yorks* 12 J7
Halkirk *H'land* 21 C8
Halland *E Sussex* 7 N5
Hallow *Worcs* 4 D4
Hallworthy *Cornw'l* 2 F5
Halstead *Essex* 6 G7
Halton *Lancs* 12 G4
Haltwhistle *Northum* 15 G10
Halwill Junction *Devon* 2 F7
Hamble-le-Rice *Hants* 5 L7
Hambledon *Hants* 5 L8
Hambleton *N Yorks* 13 J9
Hambleton *Lancs* 12 H3
Hamerton *Cambs* 6 D3
Hamilton *S Lanarks* 14 C5
Hammersmith & Fulham *London* 7 K4
Hamnavoe *Shetl'd* 23 E2
Hamnavoe *Shetl'd* 23 C3
Hampstead Norreys *W Berks* 5 H7
Hampton in Arden *W Midlands* 10 H7
Hamstreet *Kent* 7 M8
Handcross *W Sussex* 7 M4
Hannington *Hants* 5 J7
Harbury *Warwick* 4 C6
Harby *Leics* 11 F9
Hardingstone *Northants* 4 D8
Harewood *W Yorks* 13 H8
Haringey *London* 7 J4
Harlech *Gwyn* 8 E5
Harleston *Norfolk* 6 D9
Harlow *Essex* 7 H5
Haroldswick *Shetl'd* 23 A4
Harpenden *Herts* 7 H3
Harrietfield *Perth/Kinr* 16 G6
Harrietsham *Kent* 7 L7
Harrington *Cumb* 12 D1
Harris *H'land* 18 D5
Harrogate *N Yorks* 13 H8
Harrold *Beds* 6 F2
Harrow *London* 7 J3
Harston *Cambs* 6 F5
Hartburn *Northum* 15 F12
Hartest *Suffolk* 6 F7
Hartfield *E Sussex* 7 M5
Harthill *N Lanarks* 14 B6
Hartington *Derby* 10 D6
Hartland *Devon* 2 D6
Hartlebury *Worcs* 4 C4
Hartlepool *Hartlep'l* 13 D9
Hartley *Kent* 7 K6
Hartley *Northum* 13 B8
Hartley Wintney *Hants* 5 J8
Hartpury *Glos* 4 E3
Hartshill *Warwick* 10 H7
Harvington *Worcs* 4 D5
Harwell *Oxon* 5 G7
Harwich *Essex* 6 G9
Harworth *Notts* 11 C9
Haselbury Plucknett *Som'set* 3 E12
Haslemere *Surrey* 7 M2
Haslingden *Lancs* 12 J5
Hassocks *W Sussex* 7 N4
Hastigrow *H'land* 21 B9
Hastings *E Sussex* 7 N7
Haswell *Durham* 13 C8
Hatch Beauchamp *Som'set* 3 E11
Hatfield *S Yorks* 11 B9
Hatfield *Herts* 7 H4
Hatfield Heath *Essex* 7 H5
Hatfield Peverel *Essex* 7 H7
Hatherleigh *Devon* 2 E7
Hathersage *Derby* 10 C7
Hatton *Derby* 10 F7
Hatton *Aberds* 21 J13
Haugh of Urr *Dumf/Gal* 14 G5
Haughley *Suffolk* 6 E8
Haughton *Staffs* 10 F5
Havant *Hants* 5 L8
Haverfordwest *Pembs* 9 L2
Haverhill *Suffolk* 6 F6
Haverigg *Cumb* 12 F2
Havering *London* 7 J5
Hawarden *Flints* 10 D2
Hawes *N Yorks* 12 F6
Hawick *Scot Borders* 15 E9
Hawkchurch *Devon* 3 F11
Hawkesbury Upton *S Gloucs* 5 G3
Hawkhurst *Kent* 7 M6
Hawkinge *Kent* 7 M9
Hawkshead *Cumb* 12 F3
Hawnby *N Yorks* 13 F9
Haworth *W Yorks* 12 J7
Hawsker *N Yorks* 13 E11
Haxby *C/York* 13 H10
Haxey *N Lincs* 11 B9
Hay-on-Wye *Powys* 9 J9
Haydon Bridge *Northum* 12 B6
Hayfield *Derby* 10 C6
Hayle *Cornw'l* 2 J2
Hayton *Cumb* 12 C4
Hayton *ER Yorks* 13 H11
Haywards Heath *W Sussex* 7 M4
Hazel Grove *Gtr Man* 10 C5
Hazlemere *Bucks* 7 J2
Heacham *Norfolk* 6 B6
Headcorn *Kent* 7 L7
Headley *Hants* 5 K9
Heanor *Derby* 11 E8
Heath End *Hants* 5 H7
Heathfield *E Sussex* 7 N5
Heathrow Airport *London* 7 K3
Hebburn *Tyne/Wear* 13 B8
Hebden Bridge *W Yorks* 12 J6
Heckington *Lincs* 11 E11
Hedge End *Hants* 5 L7
Hednesford *Staffs* 10 G6
Hedon *ER Yorks* 13 J12
Heighington *D'lington* 13 D8
Heilam *H'land* 20 B5
Helensburgh *Arg/Bute* 14 A3
Hellifield *N Yorks* 12 H6
Helmsdale *H'land* 21 E8
Helmsley *N Yorks* 13 F10
Helperby *N Yorks* 13 G9
Helpringham *Lincs* 11 E11
Helsby *Ches* 10 D3
Helston *Cornw'l* 2 J3
Hemel Hempstead *Herts* 7 H3
Hemingbrough *N Yorks* 13 J10
Hempnall *Norfolk* 6 D9
Hempton *Norfolk* 6 B7
Hemsby *Norfolk* 6 C10
Hemsworth *W Yorks* 11 B8
Hemyock *Devon* 3 E10
Henfield *W Sussex* 7 N4
Hengoed *Caerph* 9 M8
Henley-in-Arden *Warwick* 4 C5
Henley-on-Thames *Oxon* 5 G8
Henllan *Denbs* 8 C8
Henlow *Beds* 6 G3
Henstridge *Som'set* 5 L3
Herbrandston *Pembs* 9 L2
Hereford *Heref'd* 4 D2
Heriot *Scot Borders* 15 C9
Hermitage *W Berks* 5 H7
Herne Bay *Kent* 7 K8
Herstmonceux *E Sussex* 7 N6
Hertford *Herts* 7 H4
Hessle *Kingston/Hull* 13 J12
Heswall *Mersey* 10 C2
Hethersett *Norfolk* 6 C8
Hetton-le-Hole *Tyne/Wear* 13 C8
Hexham *Northum* 12 B6
Heybridge *Essex* 7 H7
Heysham *Lancs* 12 G4
Heytesbury *Wilts* 5 J4
Heywood *Gtr Man* 10 B5
Hibaldstow *N Lincs* 11 B10
High Bentham *N Yorks* 12 G5
High Bickington *Devon* 3 E7
High Ercall *Telford* 10 G4
High Hesket *Cumb* 12 C4
High Legh *Ches* 10 C4
High Wycombe *Bucks* 4 G9
Higham *Kent* 7 K6
Higham Ferrers *Northants* 6 E2
Highbridge *Som'set* 3 C11
Highclere *Hants* 5 J7
Highley *Shrops* 10 H4
Hightae *Dumf/Gal* 14 G7
Highworth *Swindon* 4 G6
Hilborough *Norfolk* 6 C7
Hildenborough *Kent* 7 L5
Hilgay *Norfolk* 6 D6
Hillingdon *London* 7 J3
Hillington *Norfolk* 6 B6
Hillswick *Shetl'd* 23 C2
Hilmarton *Wilts* 5 H5
Hilton *Derby* 10 F7
Hinckley *Leics* 11 H8
Hinderwell *N Yorks* 13 E11
Hindhead *Surrey* 7 M2
Hindley *Gtr Man* 10 B4
Hindon *Wilts* 5 K4
Hingham *Norfolk* 6 C8
Hinstock *Shrops* 10 F4
Hirwaun *Rh Cyn Taff* 9 L7
Histon *Cambs* 6 E5
Hitchin *Herts* 6 G3
Hockley *Essex* 7 J7
Hockliffe *Beds* 6 G2
Hoddesdon *Herts* 7 H4
Hodnet *Shrops* 10 F4
Hoff *Cumb* 12 E5
Holbeach *Lincs* 11 F12
Holbrook *Suffolk* 6 G8
Holbury *Hants* 5 L7
Holford *Som'set* 3 C10
Holkham *Norfolk* 6 A7
Holland-on-Sea *Essex* 7 H9
Hollandstoun *Orkney* 23 A4
Hollym *ER Yorks* 13 J13
Holme-on-Spalding-moor *ER Yorks* 13 J11
Holmer *Heref'd* 4 D2
Holmes Chapel *Ches* 10 D4
Holmfirth *W Yorks* 10 B6
Holsworthy *Devon* 2 E6
Holt *Wrex* 10 E3
Holt *Norfolk* 6 B8
Holyhead *Angl* 8 B4
Holywell *Flints* 8 C8
Honington *Lincs* 11 E10
Honiton *Devon* 3 F10
Hoo *Medway* 7 K6
Hook *Hants* 5 J8
Hook Norton *Oxon* 4 E6
Hope *Flints* 8 D9
Hope under Dinmore *Heref'd* 4 D2
Hopeman *Moray* 21 G8
Horam *E Sussex* 7 N5
Horden *Durham* 13 C9
Horley *Surrey* 7 L4
Horncastle *Lincs* 11 D12
Horndean *Hants* 5 L8
Horningsham *Wilts* 5 J4
Hornsea *ER Yorks* 13 H12
Horrabridge *Devon* 2 G7
Horringer *Suffolk* 6 E7
Horsey *Norfolk* 6 B10
Horsford *Norfolk* 6 C8
Horsforth *W Yorks* 13 J8
Horsham *W Sussex* 7 M3
Horsham St. Faith *Norfolk* 6 C9
Horsted Keynes *W Sussex* 7 M4
Horton *Som'set* 3 E11
Horton *Northants* 4 D9
Horton in Ribblesdale *N Yorks* 12 G6
Horwich *Gtr Man* 10 B4
Hoswick *Shetl'd* 23 E3
Houghton *Cumb* 12 C4
Houghton Regis *Beds* 6 G3
Houghton-le-Spring *Tyne/Wear* 13 C8
Hounslow *London* 7 K3
Hove *Brighton/Hove* 7 N4
Hoveton *Norfolk* 6 C9
Hovingham *N Yorks* 13 G10
Howden *ER Yorks* 13 J10
Howpasley *Scot Borders* 15 E8
Hoxne *Suffolk* 6 E8
Hoylake *Mersey* 10 C2
Hucknall *Notts* 11 E8
Huddersfield *W Yorks* 12 K7
Hugh Town *I/Scilly* 2 D3
Hulland Ward *Derby* 10 E7
Hullavington *Wilts* 5 G4
Hullbridge *Essex* 7 J7
Hulme End *Staffs* 10 E6
Humber Bridge *N Lincs* 13 J12
Humberston *NE Lincs* 11 B12
Humshaugh *Northum* 12 B6
Hundred House *Powys* 9 J8
Hungerford *W Berks* 5 H6
Hunmanby *N Yorks* 13 G12
Hunstanton *Norfolk* 6 A6
Hunterston *N Ayrs* 14 C2
Huntford *Scot Borders* 15 E10
Huntingdon *Cambs* 6 E4
Huntley *Glos* 4 F3
Huntly *Aberds* 21 H10
Hurlford *E Ayrs* 14 D4
Hurliness *Orkney* 23 D2
Hurn *Dorset* 5 M5
Hursley *Hants* 5 K7
Hurstbourne Tarrant *Hants* 5 J6
Hurstpierpoint *W Sussex* 7 N4
Hurworth-on-Tees *D'lington* 13 E8
Husbands Bosworth *Leics* 11 H9
Husinish *W Isles* 22 D2
Huttoft *Lincs* 11 D13
Hutton Cranswick *ER Yorks* 13 H12
Hutton Rudby *N Yorks* 13 E9
Hutton-le-Hole *N Yorks* 13 F10
Huyton *Mersey* 10 C3
Hyde *Gtr Man* 10 C5
Hynish *Arg/Bute* 18 G3
Hythe *Hants* 5 L7
Hythe *Kent* 7 M8

I

Ibsey *Hants* 5 L5
Ibstock *Leics* 10 G7
Icklingham *Suffolk* 6 E6
Idmiston *Wilts* 5 K6
Ilchester *Som'set* 5 K2
Ilderton *Northum* 15 D12
Ilfracombe *Devon* 2 C7
Ilkeston *Derby* 11 E8
Ilkley *W Yorks* 12 H7
Illogan *Cornw'l* 2 H3
Ilminster *Som'set* 3 E11
Immingham *NE Lincs* 11 B11
Inchnadamph *H'land* 20 D4
Inchture *Perth/Kinr* 17 G8
Ingatestone *Essex* 7 J6
Ingleton *N Yorks* 12 G5
Ingoldmells *Lincs* 11 D13
Ingram *Northum* 15 E12
Ingrave *Essex* 7 J6
Inkberrow *Worcs* 4 D5
Innellan *Arg/Bute* 19 K9
Innerleithen *Scot Borders* 15 D8
Innermessan *Dumf/Gal* 14 G2
Insch *Aberds* 17 B10
Instow *Devon* 2 D7
Inverallochy *Aberds* 21 G13
Inveran *H'land* 20 F5
Inveraray *Arg/Bute* 19 H9
Inverarity *Angus* 17 F9
Inverbervie *Aberds* 17 E11
Invergarry *H'land* 16 C3
Invergordon *H'land* 20 G6
Invergowrie *Dundee C* 17 G8
Inverie *H'land* 22 J6
Inverinate *H'land* 18 B8
Inverkeilor *Angus* 17 F10
Inverkeithing *Fife* 14 A7
Inverkirkaig *H'land* 20 D3
Inverlochlarig *Stirl* 16 H4
Invermoriston *H'land* 16 C4
Inverness *H'land* 20 H6
Inversnaid *Stirl* 16 H3
Inverurie *Aberds* 17 B10
Ipswich *Suffolk* 6 F8
Irchester *Northants* 6 E2
Irlam *Gtr Man* 10 C4
Ironbridge *Telford* 10 G4
Irthlingborough *Northants* 6 E2

Irvine *N Ayrs* 14 D3
Isbister *Shetl'd* 23 B2
Isle of Whithorn *Dumf/Gal* 14 J4
Isleham *Cambs* 6 E6
Islington *London* 7 J4
Islip *Oxon* 4 F7
Ivinghoe *Bucks* 7 H2
Ivybridge *Devon* 3 H8
Iwerne Minster *Dorset* 5 L4
Ixworth *Suffolk* 6 E7

J

Jamestown *W Dunb* 14 A3
Jarrow *Tyne/Wear* 13 B8
Jaywick *Essex* 7 H8
Jedburgh *Scot Borders* 15 D10
Jervaulx *N Yorks* 12 F7
John o'Groats *H'land* 21 B9
Johnshaven *Aberds* 17 E11
Johnston *Pembs* 9 L2
Johnstone *Renf* 14 B4

K

Kames *Arg/Bute* 19 K8
Kea *Cornw'l* 2 H3
Kedington *Suffolk* 6 F6
Keelby *Lincs* 11 B11
Keele *Staffs* 10 E5
Kegworth *Leics* 11 F8
Keighley *W Yorks* 12 H7
Keillmore *Arg/Bute* 19 J7
Keiss *H'land* 21 B9
Keith *Moray* 21 H10
Keld *N Yorks* 12 E6
Kellas *Moray* 21 H8
Kelsale *Suffolk* 6 E9
Kelsall *Ches* 10 D3
Kelso *Scot Borders* 15 D10
Keltneyburn *Perth/Kinr* 16 F5
Kelty *Fife* 17 J7
Kelvedon *Essex* 7 H7
Kelynack *Cornw'l* 2 J1
Kemble *Glos* 4 G5
Kemnay *Aberds* 17 C10
Kempsey *Worcs* 4 D4
Kempston *Beds* 6 F3
Kemsing *Kent* 7 L5
Kendal *Cumb* 12 F4
Kenilworth *Warwick* 4 C6
Kenmore *Perth/Kinr* 16 F5
Kennacraig *Arg/Bute* 19 K8
Kennethmont *Aberds* 17 B9
Kennford *Devon* 3 F9
Kenninghall *Norfolk* 6 D8
Kennington *Oxon* 4 F7
Kensington & Chelsea *London* 7 K4
Kentford *Suffolk* 6 E6
Kentisbeare *Devon* 3 E10
Kerry *Powys* 8 G8
Kerrysdale *H'land* 20 G2
Kershopefoot *Scot Borders* 15 F9
Kesgrave *Suffolk* 6 F9
Kessingland *Suffolk* 6 D10
Keswick *Cumb* 12 D3
Kettering *Northants* 11 J10
Kettletoft *Orkney* 23 B4
Kettlewell *N Yorks* 12 G6
Ketton *Rutl'd* 6 C2
Kew Br. *London* 7 K4
Kexby *Lincs* 11 C10
Keyingham *ER Yorks* 13 J13
Keymer *W Sussex* 7 N4
Keynsham *Bath/NE Som'set* 5 H3
Keysoe *Beds* 6 E3
Keyworth *Notts* 11 F9
Kibworth Beauchamp *Leics* 11 H9
Kidderminster *Worcs* 10 J5
Kidlington *Oxon* 4 F7
Kidsgrove *Staffs* 10 E5
Kidstones *N Yorks* 12 F6
Kidwelly *Carms* 9 L5
Kielder *Northum* 15 F10
Kilberry *Arg/Bute* 19 K7
Kilbirnie *N Ayrs* 14 C3
Kilbride *Arg/Bute* 18 G8
Kilcadzow *S Lanarks* 14 C6
Kilchattan *Arg/Bute* 19 L9
Kilchenzie *Arg/Bute* 19 M7
Kilchiaran *Arg/Bute* 19 K4
Kilchoan *H'land* 18 E6
Kilchrenan *Arg/Bute* 18 G9
Kilcreggan *Arg/Bute* 14 A3
Kildonan *H'land* 21 D7
Kilfinan *Arg/Bute* 19 K8
Kilham *ER Yorks* 13 G12
Kilkhampton *Cornw'l* 2 E6
Killamarsh *Derby* 11 C8
Killean *Arg/Bute* 19 L7
Killearn *Stirl* 14 A4
Killin *Stirl* 16 G4
Killinghall *N Yorks* 13 H8
Kilmacolm *Invercl* 14 B3
Kilmaluag *H'land* 22 F5
Kilmany *Fife* 17 G8
Kilmarnock *E Ayrs* 14 D4
Kilmartin *Arg/Bute* 19 J8
Kilmaurs *E Ayrs* 14 C4
Kilmelford *Arg/Bute* 19 H8
Kilmory *Arg/Bute* 19 K7
Kilmory *H'land* 18 E6
Kilmory *H'land* 18 C5
Kilmuir *H'land* 20 G6
Kilninver *Arg/Bute* 18 G8
Kilnsea *ER Yorks* 11 B13
Kilrenny *Fife* 17 H9
Kilsby *Northants* 4 C7
Kilsyth *N Lanarks* 14 B5
Kilwinning *N Ayrs* 14 C3
Kimbolton *Cambs* 6 E3
Kimpton *Herts* 7 H3
Kinbrace *H'land* 20 D7
Kinbuck *Stirl* 16 H5
Kincardine *Fife* 14 A6
Kincardine *H'land* 20 F6
Kincardine Bridge *Falk* 14 A6
Kincraig *H'land* 16 C6
Kineton *Warwick* 4 D6
King'S Lynn *Norfolk* 6 C6
King's Cliffe *Northants* 6 D3
King's Somborne *Hants* 5 K6
King's Sutton *Northants* 4 E7
King's Thorn *Heref'd* 4 E2
King's Worthy *Hants* 5 K7
Kingarth *Arg/Bute* 19 L9
Kinghorn *Fife* 15 A8
Kings Langley *Herts* 7 H3
Kingsbarns *Fife* 17 H9
Kingsbridge *Devon* 3 H8
Kingsbury *Warwick* 10 H7
Kingsclere *Hants* 5 J7
Kingsdown *Kent* 7 L9
Kingskerswell *Devon* 3 G9
Kingsland *Heref'd* 4 C2
Kingsley *Hants* 5 K8
Kingsley *Staffs* 10 E6
Kingsteignton *Devon* 3 G9
Kingston *Devon* 3 H8
Kingston *London* 7 K3
Kingston Bagpuize *Oxon* 4 G7
Kingston Upon Hull *Kingston/Hull* 13 J12
Kingswear *Devon* 3 H9
Kingswood *S Gloucs* 5 H3
Kington *Heref'd* 9 J9
Kingussie *H'land* 16 C5
Kinloch *H'land* 18 D5
Kinloch *H'land* 20 D4
Kinloch Rannoch *Perth/Kinr* 16 F5
Kinlochbervie *H'land* 20 C4
Kinlocheil *H'land* 18 D8
Kinlochewe *H'land* 20 G3
Kinlochleven *H'land* 18 E9
Kinlochmoidart *H'land* 18 E7
Kinloss *Moray* 21 G8
Kinmel Bay *Conwy* 8 B7
Kinross *Perth/Kinr* 17 H7
Kintarvie *W Isles* 22 D4
Kintore *Aberds* 17 C10
Kinuachdrachd *Arg/Bute* 19 J7
Kinver *Staffs* 10 H5
Kippax *W Yorks* 13 J9
Kippen *Stirl* 16 J5
Kirk Michael *I/Man* 13
Kirkabister *Shetl'd* 23 E3
Kirkbean *Dumf/Gal* 14 H6
Kirkbride *Cumb* 12 C3
Kirkburton *W Yorks* 10 B6
Kirkby *Mersey* 10 C3
Kirkby Lonsdale *Cumb* 12 G5
Kirkby Malzeard *N Yorks* 13 G8
Kirkby Stephen *Cumb* 12 E5
Kirkby Thore *Cumb* 12 D5
Kirkby-in-Ashfield *Notts* 11 E8
Kirkby-in-Furness *Cumb* 12 F3
Kirkbymoorside *N Yorks* 13 F10
Kirkcaldy *Fife* 17 J8
Kirkcolm *Dumf/Gal* 14 G2
Kirkconnel *Dumf/Gal* 14 E5
Kirkcowan *Dumf/Gal* 14 G3
Kirkcudbright *Dumf/Gal* 14 H5
Kirkham *Lancs* 12 J4
Kirkinner *Dumf/Gal* 14 H4
Kirkintilloch *E Dunb* 14 B5
Kirkland *Dumf/Gal* 14 F6
Kirkliston *C/Edinb* 14 B7
Kirkmichael *Perth/Kinr* 16 E7
Kirkmichael *S Ayrs* 14 E3
Kirknewton *Northum* 15 D11
Kirkoswald *S Ayrs* 14 E3
Kirkoswald *Cumb* 12 C4
Kirkpatrick Durham *Dumf/Gal* 14 G5
Kirkpatrick Fleming *Dumf/Gal* 15 G8
Kirkton of Glenisla *Angus* 17 E8
Kirkton of Largo *Fife* 17 H9
Kirkwall *Orkney* 23 C3
Kirkwhelpington *Northum* 15 F12
Kirriemuir *Angus* 17 F8
Kirtling *Cambs* 6 F6
Kirtlington *Oxon* 4 E7
Kirton *Lincs* 11 F12
Kirton in Lindsey *N Lincs* 11 B10
Knaresborough *N Yorks* 13 H8
Knayton *N Yorks* 13 F9
Knebworth *Herts* 6 G4
Knighton *Powys* 9 H9
Knott End-on-Sea *Lancs* 12 H3
Knottingley *W Yorks* 13 J9
Knowle *W Midlands* 10 J6
Knutsford *Ches* 10 D4
Kyle of Lochalsh *H'land* 22 H6
Kyleakin *H'land* 22 H6
Kylerhea *H'land* 22 H6
Kylestrome *H'land* 20 D4

L

Laceby *NE Lincs* 11 B12
Lacock *Wilts* 5 H4
Ladock *Cornw'l* 2 H4
Ladybank *Fife* 17 H8
Lagg *Arg/Bute* 19 K6
Laggan *H'land* 16 D5
Laggan *H'land* 16 D3
Laggan *Moray* 21 J9
Laide *H'land* 20 F2
Lairg *H'land* 20 E5
Lakenheath *Suffolk* 6 D6
Lamberhurst *Kent* 7 M6
Lambeth *London* 7 K4
Lambley *Northum* 12 C5
Lambourn *W Berks* 5 H6
Lamlash *N Ayrs* 19 M9
Lampeter *Ceredig'n* 9 J5
Lanark *S Lanarks* 14 C6
Lancaster *Lancs* 12 G4
Lanchester *Durham* 12 C7
Lancing *W Sussex* 7 N3
Landkey *Devon* 3 D7
Landrake *Cornw'l* 2 G6
Langford Budville *Som'set* 3 D10
Langham *Rutl'd* 11 G10
Langholm *Dumf/Gal* 15 F8
Langport *Som'set* 3 D12
Langsett *S Yorks* 10 B7
Langtoft *ER Yorks* 13 G12
Langtoft *Lincs* 11 G11
Langton Matravers *Dorset* 5 N4
Langtree *Devon* 2 E7
Langwathby *Cumb* 12 D4
Langwell *H'land* 20 E6
Lanivet *Cornw'l* 2 G5
Lapford *Devon* 3 E8
Larbert *Falk* 14 A6
Largs *N Ayrs* 14 C3
Larkhall *S Lanarks* 14 C5
Larkhill *Wilts* 5 J5
Lasswade *Midloth* 15 B8
Latchingdon *Essex* 7 H7
Latheron *H'land* 21 D9
Lauder *Scot Borders* 15 C9
Laugharne *Carms* 9 L4
Launceston *Cornw'l* 2 F6
Laurencekirk *Aberds* 17 E10
Laurieston *Dumf/Gal* 14 G5
Lavendon *M/Keynes* 6 F2
Lavenham *Suffolk* 6 F7
Lawers *Perth/Kinr* 16 G5
Laxey *I/Man* 13
Laxfield *Suffolk* 6 E9
Laxford Bridge *H'land* 20 C4
Laxton *Notts* 11 D9
Layer de la Haye *Essex* 6 G7
Lazonby *Cumb* 12 C4
Lea *Lincs* 11 C10
Leadburn *Midloth* 15 C8
Leaden Roding *Essex* 7 H6
Leadenham *Lincs* 11 E10
Leadgate *Durham* 12 C7
Leadhills *S Lanarks* 14 E6
Leasingham *Lincs* 11 E11
Leatherhead *Surrey* 7 L3
Lechlade-on-Thames *Glos* 4 G6
Ledbury *Heref'd* 4 E3
Ledmore *H'land* 20 E4
Lee-on-the-Solent *Hants* 5 L7
Leeds *W Yorks* 13 J8
Leedstown *Cornw'l* 2 J3
Leek *Staffs* 10 E5
Leeming Bar *N Yorks* 13 F8
Legbourne *Lincs* 11 C12
Leicester *Leics C* 11 G8
Leigh *Worcs* 4 D3
Leigh *Gtr Man* 10 B4
Leighton Buzzard *Beds* 6 G2
Leintwardine *Heref'd* 4 C2
Leiston *Suffolk* 6 E10
Leith *C/Edinb* 15 B8
Leitholm *Scot Borders* 15 C10
Lelant *Cornw'l* 2 J2
Lendalfoot *S Ayrs* 14 F2
Lenham *Kent* 7 L7
Lennoxtown *E Dunb* 14 B5
Leominster *Heref'd* 4 D2
Lephin *H'land* 22 G3
Lerwick *Shetl'd* 23 D3
Lesbury *Northum* 15 E13
Leslie *Fife* 17 H8
Lesmahagow *S Lanarks* 14 C6
Leswalt *Dumf/Gal* 14 G2
Letchworth *Herts* 6 G4
Letterston *Pembs* 9 K2
Lettoch *H'land* 21 J8
Leuchars *Fife* 17 G9
Leumrabhagh *W Isles* 22 D4
Leven *ER Yorks* 13 H12
Leven *Fife* 17 H8
Lewes *E Sussex* 7 N5
Lewisham *London* 7 K4
Lewiston *H'land* 16 B4
Leyburn *N Yorks* 12 F7
Leyland *Lancs* 12 J4
Leysdown-on-Sea *Kent* 7 K8
Lhanbryde *Moray* 21 G9
Liatrie *H'land* 20 J4
Lichfield *Staffs* 10 G6
Lidgate *Suffolk* 6 F6
Lifton *Devon* 2 F6
Lilleshall *Telford* 10 G4
Lincoln *Lincs* 11 D10
Lindale *Cumb* 12 F4
Lingfield *Surrey* 7 L4
Linkinhorne *Cornw'l* 2 G6
Linksness *Orkney* 23 C2
Linlithgow *W Loth* 14 B6
Linslade *Beds* 6 G2
Linton *Cambs* 6 F5
Liphook *Hants* 5 K9
Liskeard *Cornw'l* 2 G6
Liss *Hants* 5 K8
Lissett *ER Yorks* 13 H12
Litcham *Norfolk* 6 C7
Litherland *Mersey* 10 C2
Little Shelford *Cambs* 6 F5
Little Stukeley *Cambs* 6 E4
Little Walsingham *Norfolk* 6 B7
Littleborough *Gtr Man* 12 K6
Littlehampton *W Sussex* 7 N3
Littlemill *H'land* 21 H7
Littleport *Cambs* 6 D5
Littlestone-on-Sea *Kent* 7 M8
Liverpool *Mersey* 10 C2
Liverpool Airport *Mersey* 10 C3
Livingston *W Loth* 14 B7
Lizard *Cornw'l* 2 K3
Llanaber *Gwyn* 8 F5
Llanaelhaiarn *Gwyn* 8 D4
Llanafan-fawr *Powys* 9 J7
Llanarmon *Denbs* 8 D8
Llanarmon Dyffryn Ceiriog *Wrex* 8 E8
Llanarth *Ceredig'n* 9 J5
Llanarthne *Carms* 9 L5
Llanbadarn Fynydd *Powys* 9 H8
Llanbedr *Gwyn* 8 E5
Llanbedrog *Gwyn* 8 E4
Llanberis *Gwyn* 8 C5
Llanbister *Powys* 9 H8
Llanbrynmair *Powys* 8 F7
Llanddewi-Brefi *Ceredig'n* 9 J6
Llanddulas *Conwy* 8 C7
Llandeilo *Carms* 9 K6
Llandinam *Powys* 8 G8
Llandissilio *Pembs* 9 K3
Llandogo *Monmouths* 4 F2
Llandovery *Carms* 9 K6
Llandrillo *Denbs* 8 E8
Llandrindod Wells *Powys* 9 H8
Llandudno *Conwy* 8 B6
Llandybie *Carms* 9 L6
Llandyfriog *Ceredig'n* 9 J4
Llandygwydd *Ceredig'n* 9 J4
Llandyrnog *Denbs* 8 C8
Llandysul *Ceredig'n* 9 J5
Llanelidan *Denbs* 8 D8
Llanelli *Carms* 9 L5
Llanelltyd *Gwyn* 8 E6
Llanenddwyn *Gwyn* 8 E5
Llanerchymedd *Angl* 8 B5
Llanerfyl *Powys* 8 F8
Llanfaethlu *Angl* 8 B4
Llanfair Caereinion *Powys* 8 F8
Llanfair Talhaiarn *Conwy* 8 C7
Llanfairfechan *Conwy* 8 C6
Llanfairpwllgwngyll *Angl* 8 C5
Llanfechain *Powys* 8 E8
Llanfechell *Angl* 8 B4
Llanfihangel-ar-arth *Carms* 9 K5
Llanfrynach *Powys* 9 K8
Llanfyllin *Powys* 8 F8
Llangadfan *Powys* 8 F8
Llangadog *Carms* 9 K6
Llangammarch Wells *Powys* 9 J7
Llangefni *Angl* 8 C5
Llangeitho *Ceredig'n* 9 J6
Llangelynin *Gwyn* 8 F5
Llangennech *Carms* 9 L5
Llangernyw *Conwy* 8 C7
Llangoed *Angl* 8 C6
Llangollen *Denbs* 8 D9
Llangorse *Powys* 9 K8
Llangranog *Ceredig'n* 9 J4
Llangunllo *Powys* 9 H9
Llangurig *Powys* 8 G7
Llangwm *Conwy* 8 D7
Llangwm *Monmouths* 4 F2
Llangybi *Ceredig'n* 9 J6
Llangynidr *Powys* 9 L8
Llangynog *Powys* 8 E8
Llanharan *Rh Cyn Taff* 9 M7
Llanidloes *Powys* 8 G7
Llanilar *Ceredig'n* 9 H6
Llanllyfni *Gwyn* 8 D5
Llannor *Gwyn* 8 E4
Llanon *Ceredig'n* 9 H5
Llanpumsaint *Carms* 9 K5
Llanrhaeadr-ym-Mochnant *Powys* 8 E8
Llanrhian *Pembs* 9 K2
Llanrhidian *Swan* 9 M5
Llanrhystyd *Ceredig'n* 9 H5
Llanrug *Gwyn* 8 C5
Llanrwst *Conwy* 8 C6
Llansannan *Conwy* 8 C7
Llansawel *Carms* 9 K6
Llanstephan *Carms* 9 L4
Llanthony *Monmouths* 9 K9
Llantrisant *Rh Cyn Taff* 9 M8
Llantwit-Major *V/Glam* 9 N7
Llanuwchllyn *Gwyn* 8 E7
Llanvihangel Crucorney *Monmouths* 9 K9
Llanwddyn *Powys* 8 F8
Llanwenog *Ceredig'n* 9 J5
Llanwrda *Carms* 9 K6
Llanwrtyd Wells *Powys* 9 J7
Llanyblodwel *Shrops* 8 E9
Llanybydder *Carms* 9 J5
Llanymynech *Powys* 8 E9
Llanystumdwy *Gwyn* 8 E5
Llay *Wrex* 8 D9
Lledrod *Ceredig'n* 9 H6
Llithfaen *Gwyn* 8 D4
Llwyngwril *Gwyn* 8 F6
Llyswen *Powys* 9 K8
Loanhead *Midloth* 15 B8
Loch Baghasdail = Lochboisdale *W Isles* 22 J1
Loch nam Madadh = Lochmaddy *W Isles* 22 F2
Lochailort *H'land* 18 D7
Lochaline *H'land* 18 F7
Lochans *Dumf/Gal* 14 H2
Locharbriggs *Dumf/Gal* 14 F6
Lochboisdale = Loch Baghasdail *W Isles* 22 J1
Lochbuie *Arg/Bute* 18 G7
Lochcarron *H'land* 20 H2
Lochdon *Arg/Bute* 18 G7
Lochearnhead *Stirl* 16 G4
Lochgair *Arg/Bute* 19 J8
Lochgelly *Fife* 17 J7
Lochgilphead *Arg/Bute* 19 J8
Lochgoilhead *Arg/Bute* 16 H3
Lochinver *H'land* 20 D3
Lochmaben *Dumf/Gal* 14 F7
Lochmaddy = Loch nam Madadh *W Isles* 22 F2
Lochranza *N Ayrs* 19 L8
Lochwinnoch *Renf* 14 B3
Lockerbie *Dumf/Gal* 14 F7
Lockton *N Yorks* 13 F11
Loddiswell *Devon* 3 H8
Loddon *Norfolk* 6 D9
Loftus *Redcar/Clevel'd* 13 E10
Logan *E Ayrs* 14 D4
London *London* 7 J4
London Colney *Herts* 7 H3
Long Ashton *Bristol* 5 H2
Long Bennington *Lincs* 11 E10
Long Clawson *Leics* 11 F9
Long Compton *Warwick* 4 E6
Long Crendon *Bucks* 4 F8
Long Eaton *Derby* 11 F8
Long Itchington *Warwick* 4 C7
Long Melford *Suffolk* 6 F7
Long Preston *N Yorks* 12 H6
Long Stratton *Norfolk* 6 D8
Long Sutton *Lincs* 11 F13
Longbenton *Tyne/Wear* 13 B8
Longbridge Deverill *Wilts* 5 J4
Longdon *Worcs* 4 E4
Longford *Glos* 4 E4
Longforgan *Perth/Kinr* 17 G8
Longformacus *Scot Borders* 15 C10
Longframlington *Northum* 15 E12
Longhope *Orkney* 23 D2
Longhorsley *Northum* 15 F12
Longhoughton *Northum* 15 E13
Longnor *Staffs* 10 D6
Longridge *Lancs* 12 J5
Longside *Aberds* 21 H13
Longton *Lancs* 12 J4
Longtown *Cumb* 15 G8
Longtown *Heref'd* 9 K9
Loose *Kent* 7 L6
Lossiemouth *Moray* 21 G9
Lostock Gralam *Ches* 10 D4
Lostwithiel *Cornw'l* 2 H5
Loughborough *Leics* 11 F8
Loughor *Swan* 9 M5
Loughton *Essex* 7 J5
Louth *Lincs* 11 C12
Lowdham *Notts* 11 E9
Lower Beeding *W Sussex* 7 M4
Lower Killeyan *Arg/Bute* 19 L5
Lower Langford *N Som'set* 3 B12
Lower Mayland *Essex* 7 H7
Lower Shiplake *Oxon* 5 H8
Lowestoft *Suffolk* 6 D10
Lowick *Northum* 15 D12
Loxwood *W Sussex* 7 M3
Lubcroy *H'land* 20 E4
Lucker *Northum* 15 D12
Ludborough *Lincs* 11 C12
Ludford *Lincs* 11 C11
Ludgershall *Wilts* 5 J6
Ludgvan *Cornw'l* 2 J2
Ludham *Norfolk* 6 C9
Ludlow *Shrops* 10 J3
Lugton *E Ayrs* 14 C4
Lugwardine *Heref'd* 4 D2
Lumphanan *Aberds* 17 C9
Lumsden *Aberds* 17 B9
Luss *Arg/Bute* 16 J3
Lusta *H'land* 22 G4
Luton *Luton* 6 G3
Lutterworth *Leics* 11 H8
Lutton *Northants* 6 D3
Lybster *H'land* 21 D9
Lydd *Kent* 7 N8
Lydford *Devon* 2 F7
Lydham *Shrops* 8 G9
Lydney *Glos* 4 F3
Lyme Regis *Dorset* 3 F11
Lyminge *Kent* 7 L8
Lymington *Hants* 5 M6
Lymm *Warrington* 10 C4
Lympne *Kent* 7 M8
Lympstone *Devon* 3 F9
Lyndhurst *Hants* 5 L6
Lyneham *Wilts* 5 H5
Lyness *Orkney* 23 D2
Lynmouth *Devon* 3 C8
Lynton *Devon* 3 C8
Lytchett Minster *Dorset* 5 M4
Lytham St. Anne's *Lancs* 12 J3
Lythe *N Yorks* 13 E11

M

Mablethorpe *Lincs* 11 C13
Macclesfield *Ches* 10 D5
Macduff *Aberds* 21 G11
Machen *Caerph* 9 M9
Machrihanish *Arg/Bute* 19 N7
Machynlleth *Powys* 8 F6
Macmerry *E Loth* 15 B9
Madeley *Staffs* 10 E4
Madley *Heref'd* 4 E2
Maentwrog *Gwyn* 8 E6
Maesteg *Bridg* 9 M7
Maghull *Mersey* 10 B2
Magor *Monmouths* 5 G2
Maiden Bradley *Wilts* 5 K4
Maiden Newton *Dorset* 5 M2
Maidenhead *Windsor* 7 J2
Maidstone *Kent* 7 L6
Maldon *Essex* 7 H7
Malham *N Yorks* 12 G6
Mallaig *H'land* 18 D7
Mallwyd *Gwyn* 8 F7
Malmesbury *Wilts* 5 G4
Malpas *Ches* 10 E3
Maltby *S Yorks* 11 C8
Maltby le Marsh *Lincs* 11 C13
Malton *N Yorks* 13 G10
Manafon *Powys* 8 F8
Manby *Lincs* 11 C13
Manchester *Gtr Man* 10 C5
Manchester Airport *Gtr Man* 10 C5
Manea *Cambs* 6 D5
Mangotsfield *S Gloucs* 5 H3
Manningtree *Essex* 6 G8
Manorbier *Pembs* 9 M3
Mansfield *Notts* 11 D8
Mansfield Woodhouse *Notts* 11 D8
Manton *Rutl'd* 6 C2
Marazion *Cornw'l* 2 J2
March *Cambs* 6 D5
Marden *Heref'd* 4 D2
Marden *Kent* 7 L6
Mareham le Fen *Lincs* 11 D12
Maresfield *E Sussex* 7 M5
Marfleet *Kingston/Hull* 13 J12
Margam *Neath P Talb* 9 M6
Margate *Kent* 7 K9
Marham *Norfolk* 6 C6
Market Bosworth *Leics* 11 G8
Market Deeping *Lincs* 11 G11
Market Drayton *Shrops* 10 F4
Market Harborough *Leics* 11 H9
Market Lavington *Wilts* 5 J5
Market Rasen *Lincs* 11 C11
Market Warsop *Notts* 11 D8
Market Weighton *ER Yorks* 13 H11
Markfield *Leics* 11 G8
Markinch *Fife* 17 H8
Marks Tey *Essex* 6 G7
Markyate *Herts* 7 H3
Marlborough *Wilts* 5 H5
Marlborough *Devon* 3 J8
Marlow *Bucks* 5 G9
Marnhull *Dorset* 5 L3
Marple *Gtr Man* 10 C5
Marshchapel *Lincs* 11 B12
Marshfield *S Gloucs* 5 H3
Marske-by-the-Sea *Redcar/Clevel'd* 13 D10
Marston Magna *Som'set* 5 K2
Martham *Norfolk* 6 C10
Martin *Hants* 5 L5
Martley *Worcs* 4 C3
Martock *Som'set* 3 E12
Marton *Lincs* 11 C10
Mary Tavy *Devon* 2 G7
Marykirk *Aberds* 17 E10
Marypark *Moray* 21 J8
Maryport *Cumb* 12 D2
Marywell *Aberds* 17 D9
Marywell *Angus* 17 F10
Masham *N Yorks* 13 F8

Mathry Pembs 9 K2
Matlock Derby 10 D7
Mattishall Norfolk 6 C8
Mauchline E Ayrs 14 D4
Maud Aberds 21 H12
Maughold I/Man 13
Mawgan Cornw'l 2 J3
Maxwellheugh
Scot Borders 15 D10
Maybole S Ayrs 14 E3
Mayfield Staffs 10 E6
Mayfield E Sussex 7 M5
Mealabost W Isles 22 C5
Mealsgate Cumb 12 C3
Measham Leics 10 G7
Medstead Hants 5 K8
Meidrim Carms 9 L4
Meifod Powys 8 F8
Meigle Perth/Kinr 17 F8
Melbourn Cambs 6 F4
Melbourne Derby 10 F7
Melksham Wilts 5 H4
Mellon Charles H'land 20 F2
Mellor Lancs 12 J5
Melmerby Cumb 12 D5
Melrose Scot Borders 15 D9
Melsonby N Yorks 12 E7
Meltham W Yorks 10 B6
Melton Suffolk 6 F9
Melton Constable
Norfolk 6 B8
Melton Mowbray Leics 11 F9
Melvaig H'land 22 E6
Melvich H'land 20 B7
Menai Bridge Angl 8 C5
Mendlesham Suffolk 6 E8
Mennock Dumf/Gal 14 E6
Menston W Yorks 12 H7
Menstrie Clack 16 J6
Meonstoke Hants 5 L8
Meopham Kent 7 K6
Mere Wilts 5 K4
Mere Brow Lancs 12 K4
Meriden W Midlands 10 H7
Merriott Som'set 3 E12
Merthyr Tydfil
Merth Tyd 9 L8
Merton London 7 K4
Meshaw Devon 3 E8
Messingham N Lincs 11 B10
Metfield Suffolk 6 D9
Metheringham Lincs 11 D11
Methil Fife 17 H8
Methlick Aberds 21 J12
Methven Perth/Kinr 16 G7
Methwold Norfolk 6 D6
Mevagissey Cornw'l 2 H5
Mexborough S Yorks 11 B8
Mey H'land 21 B9
Micheldever Hants 5 J7
Michelmersh Hants 5 K6
Mickleover Derby C 10 F7
Mickleton Durham 12 D6
Mickleton Glos 4 D5
Mid Lavant W Sussex 5 L9
Mid Yell Shetl'd 23 B3
Midbea Orkney 23 A3
Middle Barton Oxon 4 E7
Middleham N Yorks 12 F7
Middlemarsh Dorset 5 L3
Middlesbrough
Middlesbro 13 D9
Middleton Norfolk 6 C6
Middleton Gtr Man 10 B5
Middleton Arg/Bute 18 F3
Middleton Cheney
Northants 4 D7
Middleton on the
Wolds ER Yorks 13 H11
Middleton-in-Teesdale
Durham 12 D6
Middleton-on-Sea
W Sussex 7 N2
Middlewich Ches 10 D4
Middlezoy Som'set 3 D11
Midhurst W Sussex 7 M2
Midsomer Norton
Bath/NE Som'set 5 J3
Milborne Port Som'set 5 L3
Mildenhall Suffolk 6 E6
Milford Surrey 7 L2
Milford Haven Pembs 9 L2
Milford on Sea Hants 5 M6
Millbrook Cornw'l 2 H7
Millom Cumb 12 F2
Millport N Ayrs 19 L9
Milnathort Perth/Kinr 17 H7
Milngavie E Dunb 14 B4
Milnthorpe Cumb 12 F4
Milovaig H'land 22 G3
Milton H'land 20 H4
Milton Abbot Devon 2 G6
Milton Keynes
M/Keynes 4 E9
Milverton Som'set 3 D10
Minchinhampton Glos 4 F4
Minehead Som'set 3 C9
Minera Wrex 8 D9
Minety Wilts 4 G5
Mingary H'land 18 E6
Minnigaff Dumf/Gal 14 G4
Minstead Hants 5 L6
Minster Kent 7 K7
Minster Kent 7 K9
Minsterley Shrops 8 F9
Mintlaw Aberds 21 H12
Mirfield W Yorks 12 K8
Misterton Notts 11 C9
Misterton Som'set 3 E12
Mistley Essex 6 G8
Mitchel Troy
Monmouths 4 F2
Mitcheldean Glos 4 F3
Modbury Devon 3 H8
Moelfre Angl 8 B5
Moffat Dumf/Gal 14 E7
Mold Flints 10 D2
Monar Lodge H'land 20 H3
Moniaive Dumf/Gal 14 F5
Monifieth Angus 17 G9
Monikie Angus 17 G9
Monkland Heref'd 4 D2
Monkokehampton
Devon 3 E7
Monkton S Ayrs 14 D3
Monmouth
Monmouths 4 F2
Montacute Som'set 3 E12
Montgomery Powys 8 G9
Montrose Angus 17 F10
Monymusk Aberds 17 C10
Morar H'land 18 D7
Morchard Bishop
Devon 3 E8
Mordiford Heref'd 4 E2
Morebattle
Scot Borders 15 D10
Morecambe Lancs 12 G4
Moreton-in-Marsh
Glos 4 E6
Moretonhampstead
Devon 3 F8
Morley W Yorks 13 J8
Morpeth Northum 15 F13
Mortehoe Devon 2 C7
Mortimer's Cross
Heref'd 4 C2
Morwenstow Cornw'l 2 E6
Mossley Gtr Man 10 B5
Mostyn Flints 8 C8
Motcombe Dorset 5 K4
Motherwell N Lanarks 14 C5
Mottisfont Hants 5 K6
Moulton Suffolk 6 E6
Moulton Lincs 11 F12
Moulton Northants 4 C9
Mountain Ash
Rh Cyn Taff 9 M8
Mountsorrel Leics 11 G8
Mousehole Cornw'l 2 J2
Mouswald Dumf/Gal 14 G7
Moy H'land 20 J6
Much Dewchurch
Heref'd 4 E2
Much Marcle Heref'd 4 E3
Much Wenlock Shrops 10 G4
Muchalls Aberds 17 D11
Muir of Ord H'land 20 H5
Muirdrum Angus 17 G9
Muirhead N Lanarks 14 B5
Muirkirk E Ayrs 14 D5
Muker N Yorks 12 F6
Mulben Moray 21 H9
Mullion Cornw'l 2 K3
Mundesley Norfolk 6 B9
Mundford Norfolk 6 D7
Munlochy H'land 20 H6
Murlaggan H'land 18 D9
Murton Durham 13 C9
Musbury Devon 3 F11
Musselburgh E Loth 15 B8
Muthill Perth/Kinr 16 H6
Mybster H'land 21 C8
Myddfai Carms 9 K6
Myddle Shrops 10 F3
Mydroilyn Ceredig'n 9 J5
Mynydd Isa Flints 10 D2

N

N. Queensferry Fife 14 A7
Nafferton ER Yorks 13 H12
Nailsea N Som'set 3 B12
Nailsworth Glos 4 G4
Nairn H'land 20 H7
Nannerch Flints 8 C8
Nantwich Ches 10 E4
Nappa N Yorks 12 H6
Narberth Pembs 9 L3
Narborough Leics 11 H8
Naseby Northants 11 J9
Navenby Lincs 11 E10
Neap Shetl'd 23 D3
Neath Neath P Talb 9 M6
Necton Norfolk 6 C7
Needham Market
Suffolk 6 F8
Needingworth Cambs 6 E4
Nefyn Gwyn 8 E4
Neilston E Renf 14 C4
Nelson Lancs 12 J6
Nenthead Cumb 12 C5
Neston Ches 10 D2
Nether Stowey
Som'set 3 D10
Netheravon Wilts 5 J5
Netherbury Dorset 3 F12
Netherton Northum 15 E11
Nethy Bridge H'land 16 B7
Netley Hants 5 L7
Nettlebed Oxon 5 G8
Nettleham Lincs 11 D11
Nettleton Lincs 11 C11
Nevern Pembs 9 J3
New Abbey Dumf/Gal 14 G6
New Aberdour Aberds 21 G12
New Alresford Hants 5 K8
New Buckenham
Norfolk 6 D8
New Clipstone Notts 11 D8
New Costessey
Norfolk 6 C8
New Cumnock E Ayrs 14 E5
New Deer Aberds 21 H12
New Earswick C/York 13 H10
New Edlington S Yorks 11 C8
New Galloway
Dumf/Gal 14 G5
New Holland N Lincs 13 J12
New Luce Dumf/Gal 14 G2
New Mills Derby 10 C6
New Milton Hants 5 M6
New Pitsligo Aberds 21 H12
New Quay Ceredig'n 9 J4
New Radnor Powys 9 H9
New Romney Kent 7 M8
New Rossington
S Yorks 11 C9
New Scone Perth/Kinr 17 G7
New Tredegar Caerph 9 L8
New Waltham
NE Lincs 11 B12
Newark-on-Trent Notts 11 E10
Newbiggin-by-the-Sea
Northum 15 F13
Newbigging S Lanarks 14 C7
Newborough Angl 8 C5
Newbridge Caerph 9 M9
Newbridge on Wye
Powys 9 J8
Newbrough Northum 12 B6
Newburgh Aberds 17 B11
Newburgh Fife 17 H8
Newburn Tyne/Wear 12 B7
Newbury W Berks 5 H7
Newby Bridge Cumb 12 F3
Newbyth Aberds 21 H12
Newcastle Shrops 8 G9
Newcastle Emlyn
Carms 9 J4
Newcastle-under-
Lyme Staffs 10 E5
Newcastle-Upon-Tyne
Tyne/Wear 13 B8
Newcastleton
Scot Borders 15 F9
Newchurch Powys 9 J9
Newdigate Surrey 7 L4
Newent Glos 4 E3
Newgale Pembs 9 K2
Newham London 7 J5
Newhaven E Sussex 7 N5
Newick E Sussex 7 M5
Newington Kent 7 M8
Newington Kent 7 K7
Newlyn Cornw'l 2 J2
Newmachar Aberds 17 C11
Newmarket Suffolk 6 E6
Newmarket W Isles 22 C5
Newmill Moray 21 H10
Newmilns E Ayrs 14 D4
Newnham Glos 4 F3
Newport Essex 6 G5
Newport Telford 10 F4
Newport Pembs 9 K3
Newport I/Wight 5 M7
Newport Newp 9 M9
Newport Pagnell
M/Keynes 6 F2
Newport-on-Tay Fife 17 G9
Newquay Cornw'l 2 G3
Newton Lancs 12 H5
Newton Abbot Devon 3 G9
Newton Arlosh Cumb 12 C2
Newton Aycliffe
Durham 13 D8
Newton Ferrers Devon 2 H7
Newton Mearns E Renf 14 C4
Newton Poppleford
Devon 3 F10
Newton St. Cyres
Devon 3 F9
Newton Stewart
Dumf/Gal 14 G4
Newton le Willows
Mersey 10 C3
Newtongrange Midloth 15 B8
Newtonhill Aberds 17 D11
Newtonmore H'land 16 D5
Newtown Heref'd 4 D3
Newtown Powys 8 G8
Newtown St. Boswells
Scot Borders 15 D9
Neyland Pembs 9 L2
Ninfield E Sussex 7 N6
Niton I/Wight 5 N7
Nordelph Norfolk 6 C5
Norham Northum 15 C11
Normanby le Wold
Lincs 11 C11
Normanton W Yorks 13 J9
North Baddesley
Hants 5 K6
North Berwick E Loth 15 A9
North Cerney Glos 4 F5
North Charlton
Northum 15 D12
North Elmham Norfolk 6 B7
North Ferriby ER Yorks 13 J11
North Frodingham
ER Yorks 13 H12
North Hill Cornw'l 2 G6
North Hykeham Lincs 11 D10
North Kessock H'land 20 H6
North Molton Devon 3 D8
North Newbald
ER Yorks 13 J11
North Petherton
Som'set 3 D11
North Somercotes
Lincs 11 C13
North Sunderland
Northum 15 D13
North Tawton Devon 3 E8
North Thoresby Lincs 11 C12
North Walsham
Norfolk 6 B9
North Wingfield Derby 11 D8
Northallerton N Yorks 13 F8
Northam Devon 2 D7
Northampton
Northants 4 C8
Northchapel W Sussex 7 M2
Northfleet Kent 7 K6
Northiam E Sussex 7 M7
Northleach Glos 4 F5
Northop Flints 10 D2
Northpunds Shetl'd 23 E3
Northrepps Norfolk 6 B9
Northwich Ches 10 D4
Northwold Norfolk 6 D6
Northwood I/Wight 5 M7
Northwood London 7 J3
Norton Glos 4 E4
Norton Suffolk 6 E7
Norton N Yorks 13 G10
Norton Worcs 4 D4
Norton Fitzwarren
Som'set 3 D10
Norwich Norfolk 6 C9
Norwick Shetl'd 23 A4
Nottingham Nott'ham 11 F8
Nuneaton Warwick 10 H7
Nunney Som'set 5 J3
Nutley E Sussex 7 M5
Nybster H'land 21 B9

O

Oadby Leics 11 G9
Oakdale Caerph 9 M8
Oakengates Telford 10 G4
Oakham Rutl'd 11 G10
Oban Arg/Bute 18 G8
Ochiltree E Ayrs 14 D4
Ockley Surrey 7 L3
Odie Orkney 23 B4
Odiham Hants 5 J8
Offord D'Arcy Cambs 6 E4
Ogbourne St. George
Wilts 5 H5
Okehampton Devon 3 F7
Old Basing Hants 5 J8
Old Bolingbroke Lincs 11 D12
Old Colwyn Conwy 8 C7
Old Deer Aberds 21 H12
Old Fletton Peterbro 6 D3
Old Leake Lincs 11 E12
Old Radnor Powys 9 J9
Oldbury S Gloucs 4 G3
Oldham Gtr Man 10 B5
Oldmeldrum Aberds 17 B11
Olgrinmore H'land 21 C8
Ollerton Notts 11 D9
Olney M/Keynes 6 F2
Ombersley Worcs 4 C4
Onchan I/Man 13
Onich H'land 18 E9
Ordhead Aberds 17 C10
Ordie Aberds 17 C9
Orford Suffolk 6 F10
Orleton Heref'd 4 C2
Ormesby St. Margaret
Norfolk 6 C10
Ormiston E Loth 15 B9
Ormskirk Lancs 10 B3
Orphir Orkney 23 C2
Orpington London 7 K5
Orton Cumb 12 E5
Osbournby Lincs 11 F11
Oskamull Arg/Bute 18 F6
Osmotherley N Yorks 13 F9
Ossett W Yorks 13 J8
Oswaldtwistle Lancs 12 J5
Oswestry Shrops 8 E9
Otford Kent 7 L5
Othery Som'set 3 D11
Otley W Yorks 12 H7
Otter Ferry Arg/Bute 19 J8
Otterburn Northum 15 F11
Otterton Devon 3 F10
Ottery St. Mary Devon 3 F10
Oulton Suffolk 6 D10
Oulton Broad Suffolk 6 D10
Oundle Northants 6 D3
Ousdale H'land 21 D8
Outwell Norfolk 6 C5
Over Cambs 6 E4
Over Wallop Hants 5 K6
Overbister Orkney 23 A4
Overseal Derby 10 G7
Overstrand Norfolk 6 A9
Overton Wrex 8 D9
Overton Hants 5 J7
Owston Ferry N Lincs 11 C10
Oxenholme Cumb 12 F4
Oxford Oxon 4 F7
Oxnam Scot Borders 15 E10
Oxted Surrey 7 L4
Oykel Bridge H'land 20 E4

P

Pabail W Isles 22 C5
Paddock Wood Kent 7 L6
Padiham Lancs 12 J6
Padstow Cornw'l 2 G4
Paibeil W Isles 22 F1
Paignton Torbay 3 G9
Pailton Warwick 11 H8
Painscastle Powys 9 J8
Painshawfield
Northum 12 C7
Painswick Glos 4 F4
Paisley Renf 14 B4
Palgrave Suffolk 6 E8
Palnackie Dumf/Gal 14 H6
Pangbourne W Berks 5 H8
Papworth Everard
Cambs 6 E4
Parkeston Essex 6 G9
Parkhurst I/Wight 5 M7
Parracombe Devon 3 C8
Partney Lincs 11 D13
Parton Cumb 12 D1
Pateley Bridge N Yorks 12 G7
Pathhead Midloth 15 B8
Patna E Ayrs 14 E4
Patrick Brompton
N Yorks 13 F8
Patrington ER Yorks 13 J13
Patterdale Cumb 12 E3
Paull ER Yorks 13 J12
Paulton
Bath/NE Som'set 5 J3
Peacehaven E Sussex 7 N5
Peak Forest Derby 10 D6
Peasedown St. John
Bath/NE Som'set 5 J3
Peasenhall Suffolk 6 E9
Peasmarsh E Sussex 7 M7
Peebles Scot Borders 15 C8
Peel I/Man 13
Pegswood Northum 15 F13
Pembrey Carms 9 L5
Pembridge Heref'd 4 D2
Pembroke Pembs 9 L2
Pembroke Dock
Pembs 9 L2
Pembury Kent 7 M6
Penally Pembs 9 M3
Penarth V/Glam 9 N8
Pencader Carms 9 K5
Pencoed Bridg 9 M7
Pendeen Cornw'l 2 J1
Penderyn Rh Cyn Taff 9 L7
Pendine Carms 9 L4
Penicuik Midloth 15 B8
Penistone S Yorks 10 B7
Penkridge Staffs 10 G5
Penmachno Conwy 8 D6
Penmaenmawr Conwy 8 C6
Pennan Aberds 21 G12
Pennyghael Arg/Bute 18 G6
Penpont Dumf/Gal 14 F6
Penrhyndeudraeth
Gwyn 8 E6
Penrith Cumb 12 D4
Penryn Cornw'l 2 J3
Pensford
Bath/NE Som'set 5 H3
Penshaw Tyne/Wear 13 C8
Penshurst Kent 7 L5
Pensilva Cornw'l 2 G6
Pentraeth Angl 8 C5
Pentrefoelas Conwy 8 D7
Penwortham Lancs 12 J4
Penybont Powys 9 H8
Penybontfawr Powys 8 E8
Penygroes Carms 9 L5
Penygroes Gwyn 8 D5
Penysarn Angl 8 B5
Penzance Cornw'l 2 J2
Perranporth Cornw'l 2 H3
Perranzabuloe Cornw'l 2 H3
Pershore Worcs 4 D4
Perth Perth/Kinr 17 G7
Peterborough Peterbro 6 D3
Peterchurch Heref'd 9 K9
Petercutler Aberd C 17 C11
Peterhead Aberds 21 H13
Peterlee Durham 13 C9
Petersfield Hants 5 K8
Petham Kent 7 L8
Petworth W Sussex 7 M2
Pevensey E Sussex 7 N6
Pewsey Wilts 5 H5
Pickering N Yorks 13 F10
Piddletrenthide Dorset 5 M3
Pidley Cambs 6 E4
Pierowall Orkney 23 A3
Pilling Lancs 12 H4
Pilton Som'set 5 J2
Pinchbeck Lincs 11 F12
Pinhoe Devon 3 F9
Pinmore Mains S Ayrs 14 F3
Pinwherry S Ayrs 14 F3
Pirbright Surrey 7 L2
Pirnmill N Ayrs 19 L8
Pitlochry Perth/Kinr 16 F6
Pittenweem Fife 17 H9
Plean Stirl 14 A6
Plockton H'land 22 H6
Pluckley Kent 7 L7
Plumpton Cumb 12 D4
Plymouth Plym'th 2 H7
Plympton Plym'th 2 H7
Plymstock Plym'th 2 H7
Pocklington ER Yorks 13 H11
Polegate E Sussex 7 N5
Polesworth Warwick 10 G7
Polloch H'land 18 E7
Polperro Cornw'l 2 H5
Polruan Cornw'l 2 H5
Polwarth Scot Borders 15 C10
Polzeath Cornw'l 2 G4
Pontardawe
Neath P Talb 9 L6
Pontardulais Swan 9 L5
Pontefract W Yorks 13 J9
Ponteland Northum 12 B7
Ponterwyd Ceredig'n 8 G6
Pontesbury Shrops 10 G3
Pontrhydfendigaid
Ceredig'n 9 H6
Pontrilas Heref'd 4 E2
Pontyates Carms 9 L5
Pontyberem Carms 9 L5
Pontycymer Bridg 9 M7
Pontypool Torf 9 L9
Pontypridd
Rh Cyn Taff 9 M8
Pool Cornw'l 2 H3
Poole Poole 5 M5
Poolewe H'land 20 G2
Pooley Bridge Cumb 12 D4
Porlock Som'set 3 C9
Port Askaig Arg/Bute 19 K6
Port Bannatyne
Arg/Bute 19 K9
Port Carlisle Cumb 12 B3
Port Charlotte
Arg/Bute 19 L5
Port Ellen Arg/Bute 19 L5
Port Erin I/Man 13
Port Eynon Swan 9 M5
Port Glasgow Invercl 14 B3
Port Henderson H'land 22 F6
Port Isaac Cornw'l 2 G4
Port Logan Dumf/Gal 14 H2
Port Nan Giuran
W Isles 22 C5
Port Nis W Isles 22 A5
Port St. Mary I/Man 13
Port Talbot
Neath P Talb 9 M6
Port William Dumf/Gal 14 H3
Portavadie Arg/Bute 19 K8
Portgordon Moray 21 G9
Porth Rh Cyn Taff 9 M8
Porthcawl Bridg 9 N7
Porthleven Cornw'l 2 J3
Porthmadog Gwyn 8 E5
Portishead N Som'set 3 B12
Portknockie Moray 21 G10
Portlethen Aberds 17 D11
Portmahomack H'land 21 F7
Portnacroish Arg/Bute 18 F8
Portnahaven Arg/Bute 19 L4
Porton Wilts 5 K5
Portpatrick Dumf/Gal 14 H2
Portreath Cornw'l 2 H3
Portree H'land 22 G5
Portskerra H'land 20 B7
Portslade-by-Sea
Brighton/Hove 7 N4
Portsmouth Portsm'th 5 M8
Portsoy Aberds 21 G10
Postbridge Devon 3 G8
Potter Heigham
Norfolk 6 C10
Potterne Wilts 5 J4
Potters Bar Herts 7 H4
Potterspury Northants 4 D8
Potton Beds 6 F4
Poulton-le-Fylde Lancs 12 J3
Poundstock Cornw'l 2 F5
Powick Worcs 4 D4
Poynton Ches 10 C5
Praa Sands Cornw'l 2 J2
Prees Shrops 10 F3
Preesall Lancs 12 H3
Presbury Ches 10 D5
Prescot Mersey 10 C3
Prestatyn Denbs 8 B8
Prestbury Glos 4 E4
Presteigne Powys 9 H9
Preston ER Yorks 13 J12
Preston Scot Borders 15 C10
Preston Kent 7 K9
Preston Lancs 12 J4
Preston Dorset 5 M3
Preston Candover
Hants 5 J8
Prestonpans E Loth 15 B8
Prestwich Gtr Man 10 B5
Prestwick S Ayrs 14 D3
Princes Risborough
Bucks 4 F9
Princetown Devon 3 G7
Probus Cornw'l 2 H4
Prudhoe Northum 12 B7
Pucklechurch
S Gloucs 5 H3
Puddletown Dorset 5 M3
Pudsey W Yorks 13 J8
Pulborough W Sussex 7 N3
Pulham Market Norfolk 6 D8
Pulham St. Mary
Norfolk 6 D9
Pumpsaint Carms 9 J6
Purfleet Thurr'k 7 K5
Purley W Berks 5 H8
Purley London 7 K4
Purton Wilts 5 G5
Puttenham Surrey 7 L2
Pwllheli Gwyn 8 E4
Pyle Bridg 9 M7

Q

Quadring Lincs 11 F12
Quainton Bucks 4 F8
Quedgeley Glos 4 F4
Queenborough Kent 7 K7
Queensbury W Yorks 12 J7
Queensferry C/Edinb 14 B7
Queensferry Flints 10 D2
Quorndon Leics 11 G8

R

Rackenford Devon 3 E9
Rackheath Norfolk 6 C9
Rackwick Orkney 23 D2
Radcliffe Gtr Man 10 B4
Radcliffe-on-Trent
Notts 11 F9

Radlett *Herts* **7** J3
Radley *Oxon* **4** G7
Radstock *Bath/NE Som'set* **5** J3
Radyr *Card* **9** M8
Raglan *Monmouths* **4** F2
Rainham *Medway* **7** K7
Rainworth *Notts* **11** E9
Rampside *Cumb* **12** G3
Ramsbottom *Gtr Man* **12** K5
Ramsbury *Wilts* **5** H6
Ramsey *Essex* **6** G9
Ramsey *I/Man* **13**
Ramsey *Cambs* **6** D4
Ramseycleuch *Scot Borders* **15** E8
Ramsgate *Kent* **7** K9
Rannoch Station *Perth/Kinr* **16** F4
Rapness *Orkney* **23** A3
Rathen *Aberds* **21** G13
Rattray *Perth/Kinr* **17** F7
Raunds *Northants* **6** E2
Ravenglass *Cumb* **12** F2
Ravenshead *Notts* **11** E8
Ravenstonedale *Cumb* **12** E5
Rawcliffe *C/York* **13** H9
Rawmarsh *S Yorks* **11** C8
Rawtenstall *Lancs* **12** J6
Rayleigh *Essex* **7** J7
Reading *Reading* **5** H8
Reay *H'land* **21** B7
Red Dial *Cumb* **12** C3
Red Point *H'land* **22** F6
Redbourn *Herts* **7** H3
Redbridge *London* **7** J5
Redcar *Redcar/Clevel'd* **13** D10
Redditch *Worcs* **4** C5
Redesmouth *Northum* **15** F11
Redhill *Surrey* **7** L4
Redland *Orkney* **23** B2
Redlynch *Wilts* **5** K6
Redmile *Leics* **11** F10
Redmire *N Yorks* **12** F7
Redruth *Cornw'l* **2** H3
Reedham *Norfolk* **6** C10
Reepham *Norfolk* **6** B8
Reeth *N Yorks* **12** F7
Reiff *H'land* **20** E2
Reigate *Surrey* **7** L4
Reiss *H'land* **21** C9
Renfrew *Renf* **14** B4
Rennington *Northum* **15** E13
Repton *Derby* **10** F7
Resolven *Neath P Talb* **9** L7
Reston *Scot Borders* **15** B11
Retford *Notts* **11** C9
Reydon *Suffolk* **6** E10
Rhayader *Powys* **9** H7
Rhewl *Denbs* **8** C8
Rhiconich *H'land* **20** C4
Rhiw *Gwyn* **8** E4
Rhondda *Rh Cyn Taff* **9** M7
Rhoose *V/Glam* **9** N8
Rhos-on-Sea *Conwy* **8** B7
Rhoslan *Gwyn* **8** D5
Rhosllanerchrugog *Wrex* **8** D9
Rhosneigr *Angl* **8** C4
Rhossili *Swan* **9** M5
Rhostryfan *Gwyn* **8** D5
Rhubodach *Arg/Bute* **19** K9
Rhuddlan *Denbs* **8** C8
Rhyd-Ddu *Gwyn* **8** D5
Rhyl *Denbs* **8** B8
Rhymney *Caerph* **9** L8
Rhynie *Aberds* **17** B9
Riccall *N Yorks* **13** J10
Richmond *N Yorks* **12** E7
Richmond *London* **7** K3
Rickmansworth *Herts* **7** J3
Ridsdale *Northum* **15** F11
Rievaulx *N Yorks* **13** F9
Rigside *S Lanarks* **14** D6
Rillington *N Yorks* **13** G11
Ringford *Dumf/Gal* **14** H5
Ringmer *E Sussex* **7** N5
Ringwood *Hants* **5** L5
Ripley *Derby* **11** E8
Ripley *N Yorks* **13** G8
Ripley *Surrey* **7** L3
Ripon *N Yorks* **13** G8
Ripponden *W Yorks* **12** J7
Risca *Caerph* **9** M9
Rishton *Lancs* **12** J5
Roade *Northants* **4** D8
Roadhead *Cumb* **15** G9
Roberton *Scot Borders* **15** E9
Robertsbridge *E Sussex* **7** M6
Robin Hood's Bay *N Yorks* **13** E11
Rocester *Staffs* **10** F6
Rochdale *Gtr Man* **10** B5
Roche *Cornw'l* **2** H4
Rochester *Medway* **7** K6
Rochester *Northum* **15** F11
Rochford *Essex* **7** J7
Rockcliffe *Cumb* **12** B3
Rockcliffe *Dumf/Gal* **14** H6
Rockingham *Northants* **11** H10
Rogart *H'land* **20** E6
Rogate *W Sussex* **5** K9
Roghadal *W Isles* **22** E3
Rolvenden *Kent* **7** M7
Romford *London* **7** J5
Romsey *Hants* **5** K6
Ropsley *Lincs* **11** F11
Rosedale Abbey *N Yorks* **13** F10
Rosehall *H'land* **20** E5
Rosehearty *Aberds* **21** G12
Rosemarket *Pembs* **9** L2
Rosemarkie *H'land* **20** H6
Roskhill *H'land* **22** G4
Roslin *Midloth* **15** B8
Rosneath *Arg/Bute* **14** A3
Ross *Northum* **15** D12
Ross-on-Wye *Heref'd* **4** E3
Rossett *Wrex* **8** D9
Rosyth *Fife* **14** A7
Rothbury *Northum* **15** E12
Rotherham *S Yorks* **11** C8
Rothes *Moray* **21** H9
Rothesay *Arg/Bute* **19** K9
Rothienorman *Aberds* **21** J11
Rothiesholm *Orkney* **23** B4
Rothwell *Northants* **11** H10
Rothwell *W Yorks* **13** J8
Rottal *Angus* **17** E8
Rottingdean *Brighton/Hove* **7** N4
Rowanburn *Dumf/Gal* **15** G9
Rowlands Gill *Tyne/Wear* **12** C7
Roxburgh *Scot Borders* **15** D10
Roxby *N Lincs* **13** K11
Royal Leamington Spa *Warwick* **4** C6
Royal Tunbridge Wells *Kent* **7** M5
Roybridge *H'land* **16** D3
Royston *Herts* **6** F4
Royston *S Yorks* **10** B7
Royton *Gtr Man* **10** B5
Ruabon *Wrex* **8** D9
Ruan Minor *Cornw'l* **2** K3
Ruardean *Glos* **4** F3
Rubery *Worcs* **10** J5
Rudston *ER Yorks* **13** G12
Rufford *Lancs* **12** K4
Rugby *Warwick* **11** J8
Rugeley *Staffs* **10** G6
Ruislip *London* **7** J3
Rumburgh *Suffolk* **6** D9
Rumney *Card* **9** N9
Runcorn *Halton* **10** C3
Rushden *Northants* **6** E2
Rushwick *Worcs* **4** D4
Ruskington *Lincs* **11** E11
Rutherglen *S Lanarks* **14** B5
Ruthin *Denbs* **8** D8
Ruthven *H'land* **16** D5
Ruthwell *Dumf/Gal* **14** G7
Ryal *Northum* **12** B7
Rydal *Cumb* **12** E3
Ryde *I/Wight* **5** M7
Rye *E Sussex* **7** M7
Ryhall *Rutl'd* **11** G11
Ryhope *Tyne/Wear* **13** C9
Ryton *Warwick* **10** J7

S

Sacriston *Durham* **13** C8
Saddell *Arg/Bute* **19** M7
Saffron Walden *Essex* **6** G5
Sageston *Pembs* **9** L3
St. Abb's *Scot Borders* **15** B11
St. Agnes *Cornw'l* **2** H3
St. Albans *Herts* **7** H3
St. Andrews *Fife* **17** H9
St. Ann's *Dumf/Gal* **14** F7
St. Arvans *Monmouths* **4** G2
St. Asaph *Denbs* **8** C8
St. Athan *V/Glam* **9** N8
St. Austell *Cornw'l* **2** H5
St. Bees *Cumb* **12** E1
St. Blazey *Cornw'l* **2** H5
St. Breward *Cornw'l* **2** G5
St. Briavels *Glos* **4** F2
St. Bride's Major *V/Glam* **9** N7
St. Buryan *Cornw'l* **2** J1
St. Clears *Carms* **9** L4
St. Columb Major *Cornw'l* **2** G4
St. Columb Minor *Cornw'l* **2** G4
St. Combs *Aberds* **21** G13
St. Cyrus *Aberds* **17** E10
St. David's *Pembs* **9** K1
St. Day *Cornw'l* **2** H3
St. Dennis *Cornw'l* **2** H4
St. Dogmaels *Pembs* **9** J3
St. Dominick *Cornw'l* **2** G6
St. Enoder *Cornw'l* **2** H4
St. Erth *Cornw'l* **2** J2
St. Fergus *Aberds* **21** H13
St. Fillans *Perth/Kinr* **16** G5
St. Germans *Cornw'l* **2** H6
St. Harmon *Powys* **9** H7
St. Helens *Mersey* **10** C3
St. Issey *Cornw'l* **2** G4
St. Ives *Cambs* **6** E4
St. Ives *Cornw'l* **2** H2
St. John's *I/Man* **13**
St. Johns Chapel *Durham* **12** D6
St. Just *Cornw'l* **2** J1
St. Keverne *Cornw'l* **2** J3
St. Leonards *E Sussex* **7** N7
St. Levan *Cornw'l* **2** J1
St. Mabyn *Cornw'l* **2** G5
St. Margaret's Hope *Orkney* **23** D3
St. Margaret's-at-Cliffe *Kent* **7** L9
St. Mary Bourne *Hants* **5** J7
St. Mary's *Orkney* **23** C3
St. Mary's Bay *Kent* **7** M8
St. Mawes *Cornw'l* **2** J4
St. Mellons *Card* **9** M9
St. Merryn *Cornw'l* **2** G4
St. Minver *Cornw'l* **2** G4
St. Monance *Fife* **17** H9
St. Neots *Cambs* **6** E3
St. Newlyn East *Cornw'l* **2** H4
St. Olaves *Norfolk* **6** C10
St. Osyth *Essex* **7** H8
St. Stephen *Cornw'l* **2** H4
St. Teath *Cornw'l* **2** G5
St. Tudy *Cornw'l* **2** G5
Salcombe *Devon* **3** J8
Sale *Gtr Man* **10** C4
Salen *H'land* **18** E7
Salen *Arg/Bute* **18** F6
Salford *Gtr Man* **10** C5
Salford Priors *Warwick* **4** D5
Saline *Fife* **16** J7
Salisbury *Wilts* **5** K5
Sallachy *H'land* **20** E5
Saltash *Cornw'l* **2** H7
Saltburn-by-the-Sea *Redcar/Clevel'd* **13** D10
Saltcoats *N Ayrs* **14** C3
Saltfleet *Lincs* **11** C13
Saltfleetby *Lincs* **11** C13
Saltwood *Kent* **7** M8
Sampford Courtenay *Devon* **3** E8
Sanaigmore *Arg/Bute* **19** K5
Sandbach *Ches* **10** D4
Sandbank *Arg/Bute* **19** K9
Sandgate *Kent* **7** M9
Sandhead *Dumf/Gal* **14** H2
Sandhurst *Brackn'l* **5** H9
Sandleigh *Oxon* **4** F7
Sandness *Shetl'd* **23** D1
Sandown *I/Wight* **5** M7
Sandringham *Norfolk* **6** B6
Sandwich *Kent* **7** L9
Sandy *Beds* **6** F3
Sanquhar *Dumf/Gal* **14** E5
Sarnau *Ceredig'n* **9** J4
Sarnesfield *Heref'd* **9** J9
Sarre *Kent* **7** K9
Satterthwaite *Cumb* **12** F3
Saundersfoot *Pembs* **9** L3
Sawbridgeworth *Herts* **7** H5
Sawston *Cambs* **6** F5
Sawtry *Cambs* **6** D3
Saxilby *Lincs* **11** D10
Saxlingham Nethergate *Norfolk* **6** D9
Saxmundham *Suffolk* **6** E9
Saxthorpe *Norfolk* **6** B8
Scalasaig *Arg/Bute* **19** J5
Scalby *N Yorks* **13** F12
Scalloway *Shetl'd* **23** E2
Scamblesby *Lincs* **11** D12
Scarborough *N Yorks* **13** F12
Scardoy *H'land* **20** H4
Scarinish *Arg/Bute* **18** F4
Scarning *Norfolk* **6** C7
Scole *Norfolk* **6** E8
Sconser *H'land* **22** H5
Scopwick *Lincs* **11** E11
Scorton *N Yorks* **13** E8
Scotch Corner *N Yorks* **13** E8
Scotter *Lincs* **11** B10
Scourie *H'land* **20** C3
Scousburgh *Shetl'd* **23** F2
Scrabster *H'land* **21** B8
Scremerston *Northum* **15** C12
Scunthorpe *N Lincs* **11** B10
Sea Palling *Norfolk* **6** B10
Seaford *E Sussex* **7** P5
Seaham *Durham* **13** C9
Seahouses *Northum* **15** D13
Seamer *N Yorks* **13** F12
Seascale *Cumb* **12** E2
Seaton *Cumb* **12** D2
Seaton *Devon* **3** F11
Seaton Delaval *Northum* **13** B8
Sebergham *Cumb* **12** C3
Sedbergh *Cumb* **12** F5
Sedgefield *Durham* **13** D8
Seend *Wilts* **5** H4
Selborne *Hants* **5** K8
Selby *N Yorks* **13** J10
Selkirk *Scot Borders* **15** D9
Sellafield *Cumb* **12** E2
Selsey *W Sussex* **5** M9
Sennen *Cornw'l* **2** J1
Sennybridge *Powys* **9** K7
Settle *N Yorks* **12** G6
Seven Sisters *Neath P Talb* **9** L7
Sevenoaks *Kent* **7** L5
Severn Beach *S Gloucs* **5** G2
Severn Stoke *Worcs* **4** D4
Sgarasta Mhor *W Isles* **22** E3
Shaftesbury *Dorset* **5** K4
Shalcombe *I/Wight* **5** M6
Shaldon *Devon* **3** G9
Shalford *Surrey* **7** L3
Shanklin *I/Wight* **5** M7
Shap *Cumb* **12** E4
Sharnbrook *Beds* **6** E2
Sharpness *Glos* **4** F3
Shawbury *Shrops* **10** F3
Shawford *Hants* **5** K7
Shebbear *Devon* **2** E7
Sheerness *Kent* **7** K7
Sheffield *S Yorks* **10** C7
Shefford *Beds* **6** G3
Sheigra *H'land* **20** B3
Shenfield *Essex* **7** J6
Shepherdswell *Kent* **7** L9
Shepley *W Yorks* **10** B6
Shepshed *Leics* **11** F8
Shepton Mallet *Som'set* **5** J3
Sherborne *Dorset* **5** L3
Sherborne St. John *Hants* **5** J8
Sherburn *N Yorks* **13** G11
Sherburn in Elmet *N Yorks* **13** J9
Shere *Surrey* **7** L3
Sherfield English *Hants* **5** K6
Sherfield on Lodden *Hants* **5** J8
Sheriff Hutton *N Yorks* **13** G10
Sheringham *Norfolk* **6** A8
Sherston *Wilts* **5** G4
Shiel Bridge *H'land* **18** C8
Shieldaig *H'land* **20** H2
Shifnal *Shrops* **10** G4
Shilbottle *Northum* **15** E13
Shildon *Durham* **13** D8
Shillingstone *Dorset* **5** L4
Shillington *Beds* **6** G3
Shinfield *Wokingham* **5** H8
Shipdham *Norfolk* **6** C7
Shipley *W Yorks* **12** J7
Shipston-on-Stour *Warwick* **4** E6
Shipton under Wychwood *Oxon* **4** F6
Shirebrook *Notts* **11** D8
Shoeburyness *Southend* **7** J7
Shoreham-by-Sea *W Sussex* **7** N4
Shorwell *I/Wight* **5** M7
Shotley Gate *Suffolk* **6** G9
Shottermill *Surrey* **7** M2
Shottisham *Suffolk* **6** F9
Shotts *N Lanarks* **14** B6
Shrewsbury *Shrops* **10** G3
Shrewton *Wilts* **5** J5
Shrivenham *Oxon* **5** G6
Siabost *W Isles* **22** B4
Sible Hedingham *Essex* **6** G6
Sibsey *Lincs* **11** E12
Sidbury *Devon* **3** F10
Sidford *Devon* **3** F10
Sidlesham *W Sussex* **5** M9
Sidmouth *Devon* **3** F10
Silloth *Cumb* **12** C2
Silsden *W Yorks* **12** H7
Silver End *Essex* **6** G7
Silverdale *Lancs* **12** G4
Silverstone *Northants* **4** D8
Silverton *Devon* **3** E9
Simonsbath *Som'set* **3** D8
Singleton *W Sussex* **5** L9
Sittingbourne *Kent* **7** K7
Sixpenny Handley *Dorset* **5** L5
Sizewell *Suffolk* **6** E10
Skegness *Lincs* **11** D13
Skellingthorpe *Lincs* **11** D10
Skelmersdale *Lancs* **10** B3
Skelmorlie *N Ayrs* **14** B2
Skelton *Redcar/Clevel'd* **13** E10
Skelton *Cumb* **12** D4
Skinburness *Cumb* **12** C2
Skipness *Arg/Bute* **19** L8
Skipsea *ER Yorks* **13** H12
Skipton *N Yorks* **12** H6
Skirlaugh *ER Yorks* **13** J12
Slaidburn *Lancs* **12** H5
Slaithwaite *W Yorks* **10** B6
Slaley *Northum* **12** C6
Slamannan *Falk* **14** B6
Sleaford *Lincs* **11** E11
Sledmere *ER Yorks* **13** G11
Sleights *N Yorks* **13** E11
Sligachan *H'land* **22** H5
Slough *Slough* **7** K2
Smailholm *Scot Borders* **15** D10
Smarden *Kent* **7** L7
Smethwick *W Midlands* **10** H6
Smithfield *Cumb* **15** G9
Snainton *N Yorks* **13** F11
Snaith *ER Yorks* **13** J10
Snape *Suffolk* **6** F9
Sneaton *N Yorks* **13** E11
Snettisham *Norfolk* **6** B6
Snodland *Kent* **7** K6
Soham *Cambs* **6** E5
Solas *W Isles* **22** F2
Solihull *W Midlands* **10** H6
Solva *Pembs* **9** K1
Somerby *Leics* **11** G9
Somercotes *Derby* **11** E8
Somersham *Cambs* **6** E4
Somerton *Som'set* **3** D12
Sonning *Wokingham* **5** H8
Sonning Common *Oxon* **5** H8
Sopley *Hants* **5** M5
Sorbie *Dumf/Gal* **14** H4
Sordale *H'land* **21** B8
Sorisdale *Arg/Bute* **18** E5
Sorn *E Ayrs* **14** D4
Sortat *H'land* **21** B9
Soulby *Cumb* **12** E5
South Anston *S Yorks* **11** C8
South Benfleet *Essex* **7** J6
South Brent *Devon* **3** H8
South Cave *ER Yorks* **13** J11
South Cerney *Glos* **4** G5
South Elkington *Lincs* **11** C12
South Harting *W Sussex* **5** L8
South Hayling *Hants* **5** M8
South Kelsey *Lincs* **11** C11
South Kirkby *W Yorks* **11** B8
South Molton *Devon* **3** D8
South Ockendon *Thurr'k* **7** J6
South Otterington *N Yorks* **13** F8
South Petherton *Som'set* **3** E12
South Petherwin *Cornw'l* **2** F6
South Shields *Tyne/Wear* **13** B8
South Tawton *Devon* **3** F8
South Walsham *Norfolk* **6** C9
South Warnborough *Hants* **5** J8
South Woodham Ferrers *Essex* **7** J7
South Wootton *Norfolk* **6** B6
South Zeal *Devon* **3** F8
Southam *Warwick* **4** C7
Southampton *S'thampton* **5** L7
Southborough *Kent* **7** L5
Southend *Arg/Bute* **19** N7
Southend-on-Sea *Southend* **7** J7
Southery *Norfolk* **6** D6
Southminster *Essex* **7** J7
Southport *Mersey* **12** K3
Southwark *London* **7** K4
Southwell *Notts* **11** E9
Southwick *W Sussex* **7** N4
Southwold *Suffolk* **6** E10
Sowerby *N Yorks* **13** F9
Sowerby Bridge *W Yorks* **12** J7
Spalding *Lincs* **11** F12
Spaldwick *Cambs* **6** E3
Sparkford *Som'set* **5** K3
Spean Bridge *H'land* **16** D3
Speke *Mersey* **10** C3
Spennymoor *Durham* **13** D8
Spilsby *Lincs* **11** D13
Spittal *Pembs* **9** K2
Spittal of Glenmuick *Aberds* **17** D8
Spittle of Glenshee *Perth/Kinr* **16** E7
Spixworth *Norfolk* **6** C9
Spofforth *N Yorks* **13** H8
Spott *E Loth* **15** B10
Spreyton *Devon* **3** F8
Sproatley *ER Yorks* **13** J12
Stadhampton *Oxon* **4** G8
Staffin *H'land* **22** F5
Stafford *Staffs* **10** F5
Staindrop *Durham* **12** D7
Staines *Surrey* **7** K3
Stainforth *S Yorks* **11** B9
Stainforth *N Yorks* **12** G6
Stainton *Lincs* **11** D11
Stainton *Middlesbro* **13** E9
Staintondale *N Yorks* **13** F11
Staithes *N Yorks* **13** E10
Stalbridge *Dorset* **5** L3
Stalham *Norfolk* **6** B9
Stallingborough *NE Lincs* **11** B11
Stalybridge *Gtr Man* **10** C5
Stamford *Lincs* **6** C3
Stamford Bridge *ER Yorks* **13** H10
Stamfordham *Northum* **12** B7
Standish *Gtr Man* **10** B3
Standlake *Oxon* **4** F6
Stanford le Hope *Thurr'k* **7** J6
Stanford on Teme *Worcs* **4** C3
Stanhope *Durham* **12** D6
Stanley *Durham* **13** C8
Stanley *Perth/Kinr* **17** G7
Stannington *Northum* **13** B8
Stansted Airport *Essex* **6** G5
Stansted Mountfitchet *Essex* **6** G5
Stanton *Suffolk* **6** E7
Stanton Harcourt *Oxon* **4** F7
Stanton St. John *Oxon* **4** F7
Stanway *Glos* **4** E5
Stanwix *Cumb* **12** C4
Stapleford *Notts* **11** F8
Staplehurst *Kent* **7** L6
Starcross *Devon* **3** F9
Staunton *Glos* **4** E3
Staunton on Wye *Heref'd* **9** J9
Staveley *Cumb* **12** F4
Staveley *Derby* **11** D8
Staxigoe *H'land* **21** C9
Staxton *N Yorks* **13** G12
Steeple Bumpstead *Essex* **6** F6
Steeple Claydon *Bucks* **4** E8
Stein *H'land* **22** G4
Stenhousemuir *Falk* **14** A6
Stevenage *Herts* **6** G4
Stevenston *N Ayrs* **14** C3
Stewarton *E Ayrs* **14** C4
Steyning *W Sussex* **7** N3
Stibb Cross *Devon* **2** E7
Stichill *Scot Borders* **15** D10
Stickford *Lincs* **11** D12
Stickney *Lincs* **11** E12
Stillington *N Yorks* **13** G9
Stilton *Cambs* **6** D3
Stirling *Stirl* **16** J5
Stobbs *Scot Borders* **15** E9
Stobo *Scot Borders* **14** D7
Stock *Essex* **7** J6
Stockbridge *Hants* **5** K6
Stockport *Gtr Man* **10** C5
Stocksbridge *S Yorks* **10** C7
Stockton *Warwick* **4** C7
Stockton-on-Tees *Stockton* **13** D9
Stoer *H'land* **20** D3
Stoke *Medway* **7** K7
Stoke Albany *Northants* **11** H10
Stoke Ferry *Norfolk* **6** D6
Stoke Fleming *Devon* **3** H9
Stoke Gabriel *Devon* **3** H9
Stoke Mandeville *Bucks* **4** F9
Stoke Poges *Bucks* **7** J2
Stoke Prior *Worcs* **4** C4
Stoke-on-Trent *Stoke* **10** E5
Stokenchurch *Bucks* **4** G8
Stokesley *N Yorks* **13** E9
Stone *Staffs* **10** F5
Stone *Bucks* **4** F8
Stone *Glos* **4** G3
Stonehaven *Aberds* **17** D11
Stonehouse *Glos* **4** F4
Stonehouse *S Lanarks* **14** C5
Stoneykirk *Dumf/Gal* **14** H2
Stonham Aspal *Suffolk* **6** F8
Stony Stratford *M/Keynes* **4** E9
Store *Orkney* **23** B4
Stornoway *W Isles* **22** C5
Storrington *W Sussex* **7** N3
Stotfold *Beds* **6** G4
Stourbridge *W Midlands* **10** H5
Stourpaine *Dorset* **5** L4
Stourport-on-Severn *Worcs* **4** C4
Stow *Scot Borders* **15** C9
Stow Bardolph *Norfolk* **6** C6
Stow-on-the-Wold *Glos* **4** E6
Stowmarket *Suffolk* **6** F8
Strachan *Aberds* **17** D10
Strachur *Arg/Bute* **19** H9
Stradbroke *Suffolk* **6** E9
Straiton *S Ayrs* **14** E3
Stranraer *Dumf/Gal* **14** G2
Stratford St. Mary *Suffolk* **6** G8
Stratford-upon-Avon *Warwick* **4** D6
Strathan *H'land* **20** B5
Strathaven *S Lanarks* **14** C5
Strathblane *Stirl* **14** B4
Strathdon *Aberds* **17** C8
Strathkanaird *H'land* **20** E3
Strathpeffer *H'land* **20** H5
Strathy *H'land* **20** B7
Strathyre *Stirl* **16** H4
Stratmiglo *Fife* **17** H8
Stratton *Glos* **4** F5
Stratton *Cornw'l* **2** E6
Stratton St. Margaret *Swindon* **5** G5
Streatley *W Berks* **5** G7
Street *Som'set* **3** D12
Strensall *C/York* **13** G10
Stretford *Gtr Man* **10** C5
Stretham *Cambs* **6** E5
Stretton *Rutl'd* **11** G10
Stretton *Warrington* **10** C4
Stretton *Staffs* **10** F7
Strichen *Aberds* **21** H12
Stromeferry *H'land* **20** J2
Stromemore *H'land* **20** J2
Stromness *Orkney* **23** C2
Stronachlachar *Stirl* **16** H4
Strone *Arg/Bute* **14** A2
Strontian *H'land* **18** E8
Stroud *Glos* **4** F4
Struy *H'land* **20** H4
Stubbington *Hants* **5** L7
Studland *Dorset* **5** M5
Studley *Warwick* **4** C5
Sturminster Marshall *Dorset* **5** M4
Sturminster Newton *Dorset* **5** L3
Sturry *Kent* **7** L8
Sturton *Lincs* **11** C10
Sudbury *Derby* **10** F6
Sudbury *Suffolk* **6** F7
Sulby *I/Man* **13**
Sullom *Shetl'd* **23** C2
Sully *V/Glam* **9** N8
Sunderland *Tyne/Wear* **13** C9
Sunk Island *ER Yorks* **13** K13
Sunninghill *Windsor* **7** K2
Sutterton *Lincs* **11** F12
Sutton *London* **7** K4
Sutton *Cambs* **6** D5
Sutton Bridge *Lincs* **11** F13
Sutton Coldfield *W Midlands* **10** H6
Sutton Courtenay *Oxon* **4** G7
Sutton Lane Ends *Ches* **10** D5
Sutton Scotney *Hants* **5** K7
Sutton Valence *Kent* **7** L7
Sutton-in-Ashfield *Notts* **11** D8
Sutton-on-Sea *Lincs* **11** C13
Sutton-on-Trent *Notts* **11** D9
Sutton-under-Whitestonecliffe *N Yorks* **13** F9
Swadlincote *Derby* **10** G7
Swaffham *Norfolk* **6** C7
Swalcliffe *Oxon* **4** E6
Swalecliffe *Kent* **7** K8

Swanage *Dorset* 5 N5
Swanley *Kent* 7 K5
Swansea *Swan* 9 M6
Sway *Hants* 5 M6
Swindon *Swindon* 5 G5
Swinefleet *ER Yorks* 13 J10
Swineshead *Lincs* 11 E12
Swinton *Gtr Man* 10 B4
Swinton *Scot Borders* 15 C11
Swinton *S Yorks* 11 C8
Symbister *Shetl'd* 23 C3
Symington *S Lanarks* 14 D6
Symonds Yat *Heref'd* 4 F2
Syresham *Northants* 4 D8
Syston *Leics* 11 G9

T

Tadcaster *N Yorks* 13 H9
Tadley *Hants* 5 H8
Tain *H'land* 20 F6
Tal-y-llyn *Gwyn* 8 F6
Talgarth *Powys* 9 K8
Talladale *H'land* 20 G2
Talley *Carms* 9 K6
Talsarnau *Gwyn* 8 E6
Talybont *Ceredig'n* 8 G6
Talysarn *Gwyn* 8 D5
Tamerton Foliot *Plym'th* 2 G7
Tamworth *Staffs* 10 G7
Tangmere *W Sussex* 7 N2
Tannadice *Angus* 17 F9
Tanworth-in-Arden *Warwick* 4 C5
Taobh Tuath *W Isles* 22 E2
Tarbert *Arg/Bute* 19 K8
Tarbert = Aird Asaig Tairbeart *W Isles* 22 D3
Tarbet *Arg/Bute* 16 H3
Tarbet *H'land* 18 D7
Tarbolton *S Ayrs* 14 D4
Tarland *Aberds* 17 C9
Tarleton *Lancs* 12 J4
Tarporley *Ches* 10 D3
Tarrant Hinton *Dorset* 5 L4
Tarskavaig *H'land* 22 J5
Tarves *Aberds* 21 J12
Tarvin *Ches* 10 D3
Tattenhall *Ches* 10 E3
Tattersett *Norfolk* 6 B7
Taunton *Som'set* 3 D11
Tavistock *Devon* 2 G7
Tay Bridge *Dundee C* 17 G9
Tayinloan *Arg/Bute* 19 L7
Taynuilt *Arg/Bute* 18 G9
Tayport *Fife* 17 G9
Teangue *H'land* 22 J6
Tebay *Cumb* 12 E5
Tedburn St Mary *Devon* 3 F9
Teignmouth *Devon* 3 G9
Telford *Telford* 10 G4
Temple Combe *Som'set* 5 K3
Temple Ewell *Kent* 7 L9
Temple Sowerby *Cumb* 12 D5
Templeton *Pembs* 9 L3
Tenbury Wells *Heref'd* 4 C2
Tenby *Pembs* 9 L3
Tenterden *Kent* 7 M7
Terrington *N Yorks* 13 G10
Terrington St. Clement *Norfolk* 6 B5
Tetbury *Glos* 4 G4
Tetney *Lincs* 11 B12
Tetsworth *Oxon* 4 F8
Teviothead *Scot Borders* 15 E9
Tewkesbury *Glos* 4 E4
Teynham *Kent* 7 K7
Thame *Oxon* 4 F8
Thatcham *W Berks* 5 H7
Thaxted *Essex* 6 G6
The Barony *Orkney* 23 B2
The Mumbles *Swan* 9 M6
Theale *W Berks* 5 H8
Thetford *Norfolk* 6 D7
Thirsk *N Yorks* 13 F9
Thornaby on Tees *Stockton* 13 E9
Thornbury *S Gloucs* 5 G3
Thorndon *Suffolk* 6 E8
Thorne *S Yorks* 11 B9
Thorney *Peterbro* 6 C4
Thornham *Norfolk* 6 A6
Thornhill *Dumf/Gal* 14 F6
Thornhill *Stirl* 16 H5
Thornthwaite *Cumb* 12 D3
Thornton *Lancs* 12 H3
Thornton-le-Dale *N Yorks* 13 F11
Thorpe *Norfolk* 6 C9
Thorpe-le-Soken *Essex* 6 G8
Thorverton *Devon* 3 E9
Thrapston *Northants* 6 E3
Three Legged Cross *Dorset* 5 L5
Threlkeld *Cumb* 12 D3
Threshfield *N Yorks* 12 G6
Thrumster *H'land* 21 C9
Thurcroft *S Yorks* 11 C8
Thurlby *Lincs* 11 G11
Thurlestone *Devon* 3 H8
Thurmaston *Leics* 11 G9
Thursby *Cumb* 12 C3
Thurso *H'land* 21 B8
Ticehurst *E Sussex* 7 M6
Tickhill *S Yorks* 11 C8
Tideswell *Derby* 10 D6
Tidworth *Wilts* 5 J6
Tighnabruaich *Arg/Bute* 19 K8
Tilbury *Thurr'k* 7 K6
Tillicoultry *Clack* 16 J6
Tillingham *Essex* 7 H8
Tilmanstone *Kent* 7 L9
Timberscombe *Som'set* 3 C9
Timsbury *Bath/NE Som'set* 5 J3
Tingewick *Bucks* 4 E8
Tintagel *Cornw'l* 2 F5
Tintern Parva *Monmouths* 4 F2
Tipton *W Midlands* 10 H5
Tiptree *Essex* 7 H7
Tisbury *Wilts* 5 K4
Titchfield *Hants* 5 L7
Tiverton *Devon* 3 E9
Tobermory *Arg/Bute* 18 F6
Toberonochy *Arg/Bute* 19 H7
Tobha Mor *W Isles* 22 H1
Toddington *Beds* 6 G3
Todmorden *W Yorks* 12 J6
Tolastadh bho Thuath *W Isles* 22 B5
Tollesbury *Essex* 7 H7
Tolob *Shetl'd* 23 F2
Tolpuddle *Dorset* 5 M3
Tomatin *H'land* 16 B6
Tomdoun *H'land* 18 C9
Tomintoul *Moray* 17 C7
Tomnavoulin *Moray* 17 B8
Tonbridge *Kent* 7 L5
Tondu *Bridg* 9 M7
Tong *Shrops* 10 G5
Tongue *H'land* 20 C5
Tonyrefail *Rh Cyn Taff* 9 M8
Topcliffe *N Yorks* 13 G9
Topsham *Devon* 3 F9
Torcross *Devon* 3 H9
Torness *H'land* 16 B4
Torphins *Aberds* 17 C10
Torpoint *Cornw'l* 2 H7
Torquay *Torbay* 3 G9
Torridon *H'land* 20 H2
Torroble *H'land* 20 E5
Torthorwald *Dumf/Gal* 14 G7
Torver *Cumb* 12 F3
Toscaig *H'land* 22 H6
Totland *I/Wight* 5 M6
Totley *S Yorks* 10 C7
Totnes *Devon* 3 H8
Totton *Hants* 5 L6
Tow Law *Durham* 12 D7
Towcester *Northants* 4 D8
Tower Hamlets *London* 7 J4
Town Yetholm *Scot Borders* 15 D11
Trafford Park *Gtr Man* 10 C4
Tranent *E Loth* 15 B9
Trawsfynydd *Gwyn* 8 E6
Trecastle *Powys* 9 K7
Tredegar *Bl Gwent* 9 L8
Trefeglwys *Powys* 8 G7
Trefnant *Denbs* 8 C8
Trefriw *Conwy* 8 C6
Tregaron *Ceredig'n* 9 H6
Tregony *Cornw'l* 2 H4
Tregynon *Powys* 8 G8
Treharris *Merth Tyd* 9 M8
Trelech *Carms* 9 K4
Tremadog *Gwyn* 8 E5
Trenance *Cornw'l* 2 G4
Trentham *Stoke* 10 E5
Treorchy *Rh Cyn Taff* 9 M7
Tresilian *Cornw'l* 2 H4
Tretower *Powys* 9 K8
Treuddyn *Flints* 8 D9
Trimdon *Durham* 13 D8
Trimley *Suffolk* 6 G9
Tring *Herts* 7 H2
Troon *S Ayrs* 14 D3
Troutbeck *Cumb* 12 E4
Trowbridge *Wilts* 5 J4
Trull *Som'set* 3 D11
Trumpington *Cambs* 6 F5
Trunch *Norfolk* 6 B9
Truro *Cornw'l* 2 H4
Tuddenham *Suffolk* 6 E6
Tudweiliog *Gwyn* 8 E4
Tullynessle *Aberds* 17 C9
Tummel Bridge *Perth/Kinr* 16 F5
Tunstall *Suffolk* 6 F9
Turnberry *S Ayrs* 14 E3
Turriff *Aberds* 21 H11
Turvey *Beds* 6 F2
Tutbury *Staffs* 10 F7
Tuxford *Notts* 11 D9
Twatt *Orkney* 23 B2
Tweedmouth *Northum* 15 C11
Tweedshaws *Scot Borders* 14 E7
Tweedsmuir *Scot Borders* 14 D7
Twenty *Lincs* 11 F11
Twyford *Leics* 11 G9
Twyford *Wokingham* 5 H9
Twyford *Hants* 5 K7
Ty'n-y-groes *Conwy* 8 C6
Tydd St. Giles *Cambs* 11 G13
Tydd St. Mary *Lincs* 11 G13
Tylorstown *Rh Cyn Taff* 9 M7
Tyndrum *Stirl* 16 G3
Tynemouth *Tyne/Wear* 13 B8
Tywardreath *Cornw'l* 2 H5
Tywyn *Gwyn* 8 F5

U

Uckfield *E Sussex* 7 M5
Uddingston *S Lanarks* 14 B5
Uffculme *Devon* 3 E10
Uffington *Oxon* 4 G6
Ufford *Suffolk* 6 F9
Ugborough *Devon* 3 H8
Uig *H'land* 22 F4
Ulbster *H'land* 21 C9
Ulceby *N Lincs* 13 K12
Ulceby Cross *Lincs* 11 D13
Uley *Glos* 4 G3
Ullapool *H'land* 20 F3
Ulsta *Shetl'd* 23 B3
Ulverston *Cumb* 12 G3
Unapool *H'land* 20 D4
Upavon *Wilts* 5 J5
Uphill *N Som'set* 3 C11
Upper Chapel *Powys* 9 J8
Upper Heyford *Oxon* 4 E7
Upper Hindhope *Scot Borders* 15 E10
Upper Poppleton *C/York* 13 H9
Upper Tean *Staffs* 10 F6
Uppingham *Rutl'd* 11 G10
Upton *Ches* 10 D3
Upton Snodsbury *Worcs* 4 D4
Upton upon Severn *Worcs* 4 D4
Upwey *Dorset* 5 M3
Urchfont *Wilts* 5 J5
Urmston *Gtr Man* 10 C4
Usk *Monmouths* 9 L9
Usselby *Lincs* 11 C11
Uttoxeter *Staffs* 10 F6
Uyeasound *Shetl'd* 23 A3

V

Valley *Angl* 8 C4
Veness *Orkney* 23 B3
Ventnor *I/Wight* 5 N7
Verwood *Dorset* 5 L5
Veryan *Cornw'l* 2 J4
Vickerstown *Cumb* 12 G2
Vidlin *Shetl'd* 23 C3
Virginia Water *Surrey* 7 K3
Voe *Shetl'd* 23 C2
Voy *Orkney* 23 C2

W

Waddesdon *Bucks* 4 F8
Waddingham *Lincs* 11 C10
Waddington *Lincs* 11 D10
Wadebridge *Cornw'l* 2 G4
Wadhurst *E Sussex* 7 M6
Wainfleet All Saints *Lincs* 11 D13
Wakefield *W Yorks* 13 J8
Walberswick *Suffolk* 6 E10
Walcott *Lincs* 11 E11
Walderslade *Medway* 7 K6
Waldron *E Sussex* 7 N5
Walford *Heref'd* 9 H9
Walkerburn *Scot Borders* 15 D8
Walkeringham *Notts* 11 C9
Wallasey *Mersey* 10 C2
Wallingford *Oxon* 5 G8
Walls *Shetl'd* 23 D2
Wallsend *Tyne/Wear* 13 B8
Walmer *Kent* 7 L9
Walpole *Norfolk* 11 G13
Walsall *W Midlands* 10 H6
Walsham le Willows *Suffolk* 6 E8
Walsoken *Cambs* 11 G13
Waltham *NE Lincs* 11 B12
Waltham Abbey *Essex* 7 H4
Waltham Forest *London* 7 J4
Waltham on the Wolds *Leics* 11 F10
Walton *Cumb* 15 G9
Walton-on-Thames *Surrey* 7 K3
Walton-on-the-Naze *Essex* 6 G9
Wanborough *Swindon* 5 G6
Wandsworth *London* 7 K4
Wangford *Suffolk* 6 E10
Wansford *Peterbro* 6 D3
Wantage *Oxon* 5 G7
Warboys *Cambs* 6 D4
Wardington *Oxon* 4 D7
Wardle *Ches* 10 E4
Ware *Herts* 7 H4
Wareham *Dorset* 5 M4
Wargrave *Wokingham* 5 H8
Wark *Northum* 12 B6
Warkworth *Northum* 15 E13
Warley *W Midlands* 10 H6
Warminster *Wilts* 5 J4
Warrington *Warrington* 10 C4
Warton *Lancs* 12 G4
Warwick *Warwick* 4 C6
Wasbister *Orkney* 23 B2
Washaway *Cornw'l* 2 G5
Washford *Som'set* 3 C10
Washingborough *Lincs* 11 D11
Washington *W Sussex* 7 N3
Washington *Tyne/Wear* 13 C8
Watchet *Som'set* 3 C10
Watchfield *Oxon* 4 G6
Waterbeach *Cambs* 6 E5
Waterhead *Angus* 17 E9
Waterhouses *Staffs* 10 E6
Wateringbury *Kent* 7 L6
Waterlooville *Hants* 5 L8
Watford *Herts* 7 J3
Wath upon Dearne *S Yorks* 11 C8
Watlington *Norfolk* 6 C6
Watlington *Oxon* 4 G8
Watten *H'land* 21 C9
Watton *Norfolk* 6 C7
Waunfawr *Gwyn* 8 D5
Weachyburn *Aberds* 21 H11
Wearhead *Durham* 12 D6
Weasenham *Norfolk* 6 B7
Weaverham *Ches* 10 D4
Weaverthorpe *N Yorks* 13 G11
Wedmore *Som'set* 3 C12
Wednesbury *W Midlands* 10 H5
Wednesfield *W Midlands* 10 G5
Weedon Bec *Northants* 4 C8
Weeley *Essex* 6 G8
Welbourn *Lincs* 11 E10
Weldon *Northants* 6 D2
Weldon *Northum* 15 F12
Welford *Northants* 11 H9
Welford *W Berks* 5 H7
Wellesbourne *Warwick* 4 D6
Wellingborough *Northants* 6 E2
Wellington *Som'set* 3 D10
Wellington *Telford* 10 G4
Wellow *Bath/NE Som'set* 5 J3
Wells *Som'set* 5 J2
Wells-next-the-Sea *Norfolk* 6 A7
Welney *Norfolk* 6 D5
Welshampton *Shrops* 10 F3
Welshpool *Powys* 8 F9
Welton *Lincs* 11 D11
Welwyn Garden City *Herts* 7 H4
Wem *Shrops* 10 F3
Wembury *Devon* 2 H7
Wemyss Bay *Invercl* 14 B2
Wendover *Bucks* 7 H2
Wensley *N Yorks* 12 F7
Wenvoe *V/Glam* 9 N8
Weobley *Heref'd* 4 D2
Werrington *Cornw'l* 2 F6
West Auckland *Durham* 12 D7
West Bergholt *Essex* 6 G7
West Bridgford *Notts* 11 F8
West Bromwich *W Midlands* 10 H6
West Burton *N Yorks* 12 F7
West Calder *W Loth* 14 B7
West Coker *Som'set* 5 L2
West Dean *Wilts* 5 K6
West End *Hants* 5 L7
West Felton *Shrops* 8 E9
West Grinstead *W Sussex* 7 M3
West Haddon *Northants* 4 C8
West Kilbride *N Ayrs* 14 C3
West Kingsdown *Kent* 7 K5
West Kirby *Mersey* 10 C2
West Linton *Scot Borders* 14 C7
West Looe *Cornw'l* 2 H6
West Lulworth *Dorset* 5 N4
West Malling *Kent* 7 L6
West Meon *Hants* 5 K8
West Mersea *Essex* 7 H8
West Moors *Dorset* 5 L5
West Rasen *Lincs* 11 C11
West Thorney *W Sussex* 5 L8
West Wellow *Hants* 5 L6
West Woodburn *Northum* 15 F11
Westbourne *W Sussex* 5 L8
Westbury *Shrops* 8 F9
Westbury *Wilts* 5 J4
Westbury-on-Severn *Glos* 4 F3
Westbury-sub-Mendip *Som'set* 5 J2
Westcott *Surrey* 7 L3
Westerham *Kent* 7 L5
Westfield *E Sussex* 7 N7
Westhill *Aberds* 17 C11
Westhoughton *Gtr Man* 10 B4
Westleton *Suffolk* 6 E10
Westminster *London* 7 J4
Weston *Staffs* 10 F5
Weston-super-Mare *N Som'set* 3 B11
Westonzoyland *Som'set* 3 D11
Westruther *Scot Borders* 15 C10
Westward Ho! *Devon* 2 D7
Wetheral *Cumb* 12 C4
Wetherby *W Yorks* 13 H9
Wetwang *ER Yorks* 13 H11
Weybourne *Norfolk* 6 A8
Weybridge *Surrey* 7 K3
Weyhill *Hants* 5 J6
Weymouth *Dorset* 5 N3
Whaley Bridge *Derby* 10 C6
Whalley *Lancs* 12 J5
Whalton *Northum* 15 F12
Whaplode *Lincs* 11 G12
Whatton *Notts* 11 F9
Whauphill *Dumf/Gal* 14 H3
Wheathampstead *Herts* 7 H3
Wheatley *Notts* 11 C9
Wheatley *Oxon* 4 F8
Wheatley Hill *Durham* 13 D8
Wheaton Aston *Staffs* 10 G5
Wheldrake *C/York* 13 H10
Whicham *Cumb* 12 F2
Whickham *Tyne/Wear* 13 B8
Whimple *Devon* 3 F10
Whipsnade *Beds* 7 H3
Whissendine *Rutl'd* 11 G10
Whitburn *W Loth* 14 B6
Whitby *N Yorks* 13 E11
Whitchurch *Shrops* 10 E3
Whitchurch *Bucks* 4 E9
Whitchurch *Bristol* 5 H3
Whitchurch *Devon* 2 G7
Whitchurch *Hants* 5 J7
Whitchurch *Heref'd* 4 F2
White Bridge *H'land* 16 C4
Whitehall *Orkney* 23 B4
Whitehaven *Cumb* 12 E1
Whitehouse *Arg/Bute* 19 K8
Whitekirk *E Loth* 15 A10
Whiteparish *Wilts* 5 K6
Whitfield *Kent* 7 L9
Whithorn *Dumf/Gal* 14 J4
Whitland *Carms* 9 L3
Whitley Bay *Tyne/Wear* 13 B8
Whitsome *Scot Borders* 15 C11
Whitstable *Kent* 7 K8
Whitstone *Cornw'l* 2 F6
Whittington *Derby* 10 D7
Whittington *Lancs* 12 G5
Whittington *Shrops* 8 E9
Whittington *Staffs* 10 G6
Whittlebury *Northants* 4 D8
Whittlesey *Cambs* 6 D4
Whittlesford *Cambs* 6 F5
Whitwell *Derby* 11 D8
Whitwell *I/Wight* 5 N7
Whitwick *Leics* 11 G8
Whitworth *Lancs* 12 K6
Whixley *N Yorks* 13 H9
Wick *H'land* 21 C9
Wick *S Gloucs* 5 H3
Wick *V/Glam* 9 N7
Wick *Wilts* 5 K5
Wicken *Cambs* 6 E5
Wickford *Essex* 7 J6
Wickham *Hants* 5 L7
Wickham Market *Suffolk* 6 F9
Wickwar *S Gloucs* 5 G3
Widdrington *Northum* 15 F13
Wide Open *Tyne/Wear* 13 B8
Widecombe in the Moor *Devon* 3 G8
Widemouth *Cornw'l* 2 E5
Widnes *Halton* 10 C3
Wigan *Gtr Man* 10 B3
Wigmore *Heref'd* 4 C2
Wigmore *Medway* 7 K7
Wigston *Leics* 11 H9
Wigton *Cumb* 12 C3
Wigtown *Dumf/Gal* 14 H4
Willand *Devon* 3 E10
Willaston *Ches* 10 D2
Willenhall *W Midlands* 10 G5
Willersley *Heref'd* 9 J9
Willesborough *Kent* 7 L8
Willingdon *E Sussex* 7 N6
Willington *Beds* 6 F3
Willington *Durham* 12 D7
Williton *Som'set* 3 C10
Willoughby *Lincs* 11 D13
Wilmington *Devon* 3 F11
Wilmslow *Ches* 10 C5
Wilnecote *Staffs* 10 G7
Wilton *Wilts* 5 K5
Wimblington *Cambs* 6 D5
Wimborne Minster *Dorset* 5 M5
Wincanton *Som'set* 5 K3
Winchcombe *Glos* 4 E5
Winchelsea *E Sussex* 7 N7
Winchester *Hants* 5 K7
Windermere *Cumb* 12 F4
Windsor *Windsor* 7 K2
Windygates *Fife* 17 H8
Wing *Bucks* 6 G2
Wingate *Durham* 13 D9
Wingham *Kent* 7 L9
Winkleigh *Devon* 3 E8
Winscombe *N Som'set* 3 C12
Winsford *Ches* 10 D4
Winslow *Bucks* 4 E8
Winster *Derby* 10 D7
Winston *Durham* 12 E7
Winterborne Stickland *Dorset* 5 L4
Winterbourne Abbas *Dorset* 5 M3
Winterton *N Lincs* 13 K11
Winterton *Norfolk* 6 B10
Wirksworth *Derby* 10 E7
Wisbech *Cambs* 11 G13
Wisbech St. Mary *Cambs* 6 C5
Wisborough Green *W Sussex* 7 M3
Wishaw *N Lanarks* 14 C6
Witchampton *Dorset* 5 L4
Witchford *Cambs* 6 E5
Witham *Essex* 7 H7
Witheridge *Devon* 3 E8
Withern *Lincs* 11 C13
Withernsea *ER Yorks* 13 J13
Withington *Glos* 4 F5
Witley *Surrey* 7 L2
Witnesham *Suffolk* 6 F8
Witney *Oxon* 4 F6
Wittersham *Kent* 7 M7
Wiveliscombe *Som'set* 3 D10
Wivelsfield *E Sussex* 7 M4
Wivenhoe *Essex* 6 G8
Wix *Essex* 6 G8
Woburn *Beds* 6 G2
Woburn Sands *M/Keynes* 6 G2
Woking *Surrey* 7 L3
Wokingham *Wokingham* 5 H9
Wolf's Castle *Pembs* 9 K2
Wollaston *Northants* 6 E2
Wolsingham *Durham* 12 D7
Wolverhampton *W Midlands* 10 H5
Wolverton *M/Keynes* 4 D9
Wolviston *Stockton* 13 D9
Wombwell *S Yorks* 10 B7
Wonersh *Surrey* 7 L3
Wonston *Hants* 5 K7
Woodbridge *Suffolk* 6 F9
Woodbury *Devon* 3 F10
Woodchester *Glos* 4 F4
Woodchurch *Kent* 7 M7
Woodcote *Oxon* 5 G8
Woodgreen *Hants* 5 L5
Woodhall Spa *Lincs* 11 D12
Woodhouse *S Yorks* 11 C8
Woodhouse Eaves *Leics* 11 G8
Woodley *Wokingham* 5 H8
Woodstock *Oxon* 4 F7
Woofferton *Shrops* 4 C2
Wookey *Som'set* 5 J2
Wookey Hole *Som'set* 5 J2
Wool *Dorset* 5 M4
Woolacombe *Devon* 2 C7
Woolavington *Som'set* 3 C11
Wooler *Northum* 15 D11
Woolwich *London* 7 K5
Woolwich Ferry *London* 7 K5
Wooperton *Northum* 15 D12
Woore *Shrops* 10 E4
Wootton Bassett *Wilts* 5 G5
Wootton Bridge *I/Wight* 5 M7
Wootton Wawen *Warwick* 4 C5
Worcester *Worcs* 4 D4
Worfield *Shrops* 10 H4
Workington *Cumb* 12 D1
Worksop *Notts* 11 D8
Wormit *Fife* 17 G8
Worsbrough *S Yorks* 10 B7
Wortham *Suffolk* 6 E8
Worthing *W Sussex* 7 N3
Wotton under Edge *Glos* 4 G3
Wragby *Lincs* 11 D11
Wrangle *Lincs* 11 E13
Wrea Green *Lancs* 12 J3
Wrentham *Suffolk* 6 D10
Wretham *Norfolk* 6 D7
Wrexham *Wrex* 8 D9
Writtle *Essex* 7 H6
Wroughton *Swindon* 5 G5
Wroxham *Norfolk* 6 C9
Wroxton *Oxon* 4 D7
Wyberton *Lincs* 11 E12
Wye *Kent* 7 L8
Wylye *Wilts* 5 K5
Wymondham *Leics* 11 G10
Wymondham *Norfolk* 6 C8

Y

Y Felinheli *Gwyn* 8 C5
Yalding *Kent* 7 L6
Yarcombe *Devon* 3 E11
Yardley Hastings *Northants* 4 D9
Yarm *Stockton* 13 E9
Yarmouth *I/Wight* 5 M6
Yarnton *Oxon* 4 F7
Yarrow *Scot Borders* 15 D8
Yate *S Gloucs* 5 G3
Yatton *N Som'set* 3 B12
Yaxley *Cambs* 6 D3
Yeadon *W Yorks* 12 H7
Yealmpton *Devon* 3 H7
Yelverton *Devon* 2 G7
Yeovil *Som'set* 5 L2
Yetminster *Dorset* 5 L2
York *C/York* 13 H9
Youlgreave *Derby* 10 D7
Yoxall *Staffs* 10 G6
Yoxford *Suffolk* 6 E10
Ysbyty Ifan *Conwy* 8 D7
Ysbyty Ystwyth *Ceredig'n* 9 H6
Ystalyfera *Neath P Talb* 9 L6
Ystradgynlais *Powys* 9 L6

Z

Zennor *Cornw'l* 2 J2

County and unitary authority boundaries

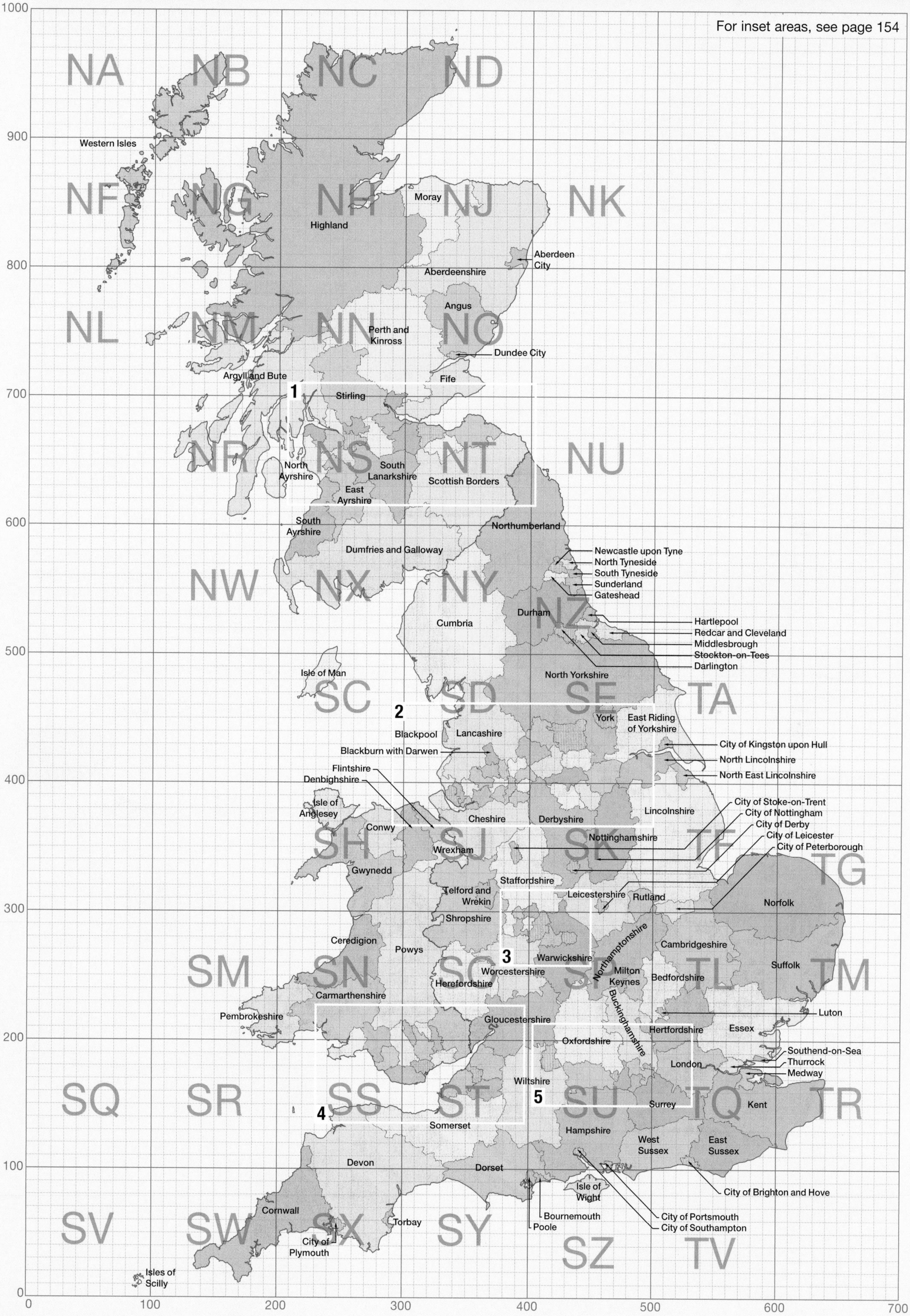

For inset areas, see page 154

1000

900

800

700

600

500

400

300

200

100

0   100   200   300   400   500   600   700

NA   NB   NC   ND

NF   NG   NH   NJ   NK

Western Isles

Moray

NL   NM   NN   NO

Highland

Aberdeenshire

Aberdeen City

Angus

Perth and Kinross

Dundee City

Argyll and Bute

Fife

1   Stirling

NR   NS   NT   NU

North Ayrshire

South Lanarkshire

Scottish Borders

East Ayrshire

South Ayrshire

Northumberland

NW   NX   NY   NZ

Dumfries and Galloway

Newcastle upon Tyne
North Tyneside
South Tyneside
Sunderland
Gateshead

Durham

Hartlepool
Redcar and Cleveland
Middlesbrough
Stockton-on-Tees
Darlington

Cumbria

Isle of Man

North Yorkshire

SC   SD   SE   TA

2   York

East Riding of Yorkshire

Blackpool

Lancashire

City of Kingston upon Hull
North Lincolnshire
North East Lincolnshire

Blackburn with Darwen

Flintshire
Denbighshire

Isle of Anglesey

Conwy

Cheshire

Derbyshire

Lincolnshire

City of Stoke-on-Trent
City of Nottingham
City of Derby
City of Leicester
City of Peterborough

SH   SJ   SK   TF   TG

Wrexham

Gwynedd

Nottinghamshire

Staffordshire

Telford and Wrekin

Leicestershire

Rutland

Norfolk

Shropshire

Ceredigion

Powys

3   Warwickshire

Cambridgeshire

SM   SN   SO   SP   TL   TM

Worcestershire

Northamptonshire

Milton Keynes

Bedfordshire

Suffolk

Carmarthenshire

Herefordshire

Buckinghamshire

Luton

Pembrokeshire

Gloucestershire

Hertfordshire

Essex

Oxfordshire

London

Southend-on-Sea
Thurrock
Medway

SQ   SR   SS   ST   SU   TQ   TR

Wiltshire

5

Surrey

Kent

4   Somerset

Hampshire

West Sussex

East Sussex

Devon

Dorset

City of Brighton and Hove

Cornwall

Torbay

SY

Isle of Wight

Bournemouth
Poole

City of Portsmouth
City of Southampton

City of Plymouth

SZ   TV

SV   SW   SX

Isles of Scilly

Unitary authority boundaries

Greater London

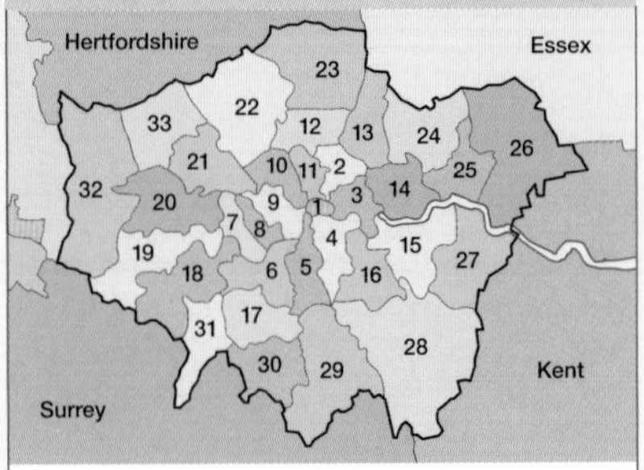

1 City and County of the City of London
2 Hackney
3 Tower Hamlets
4 Southwark
5 Lambeth
6 Wandsworth
7 Hammersmith and Fulham
8 Royal Borough of Kensington and Chelsea
9 City of Westminster
10 Camden
11 Islington
12 Haringey
13 Waltham Forest
14 Newham
15 Greenwich
16 Lewisham
17 Merton
18 Richmond upon Thames
19 Hounslow
20 Ealing
21 Brent
22 Barnet
23 Enfield
24 Redbridge
25 Barking and Dagenham
26 Havering
27 Bexley
28 Bromley
29 Croydon
30 Sutton
31 Kingston upon Thames
32 Hillingdon
33 Harrow

1 Central Scotland

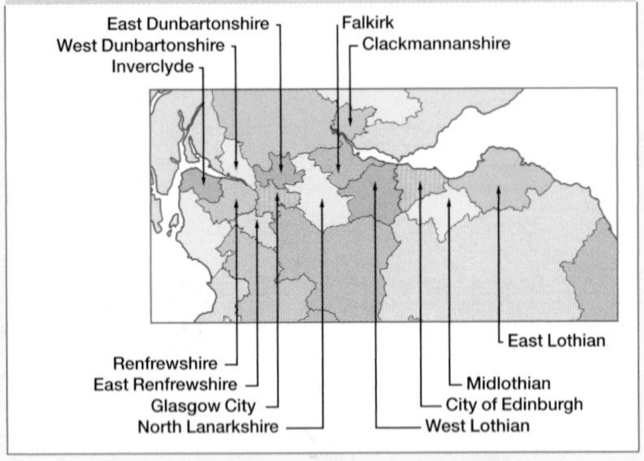

2 Northern England

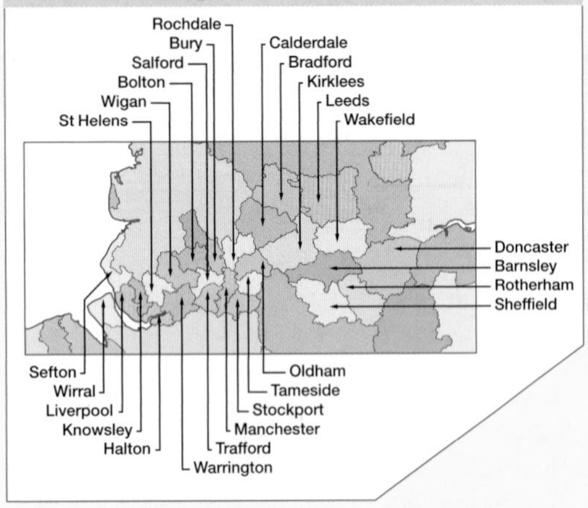

3 West Midlands

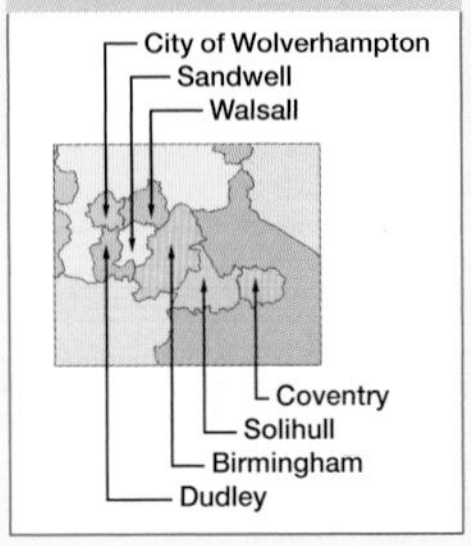

Ordnance Survey National Grid

The blue lines which divide the maps on pages 2 to 23 into squares for indexing match the Ordnance Survey National Grid. Each side of a grid square measures 20km on the ground. The blue grid lines on the boundaries map on page 153 also match the National Grid. These are at 10km intervals so the grid lines on pages 2-23 correspond to every other grid line on page 153.

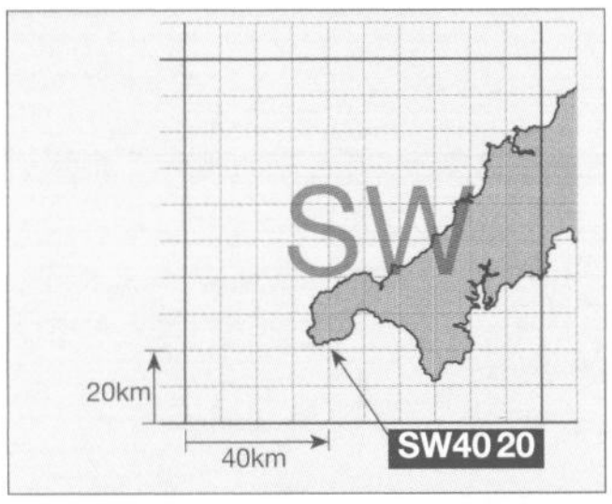

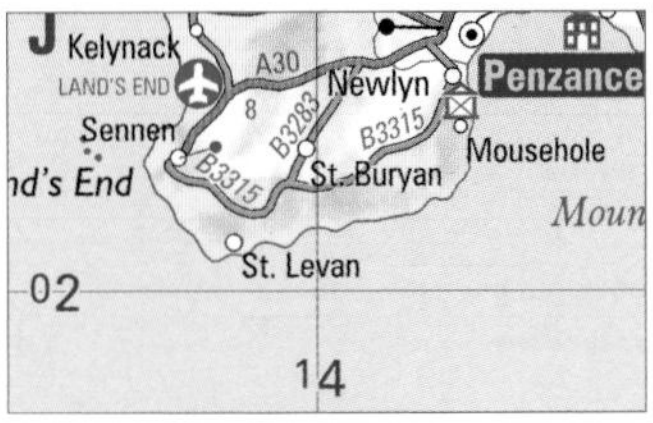

On pages 2 to 23, the National Grid 100km and 10km values are indicated on each grid line. The 100km values are shown in small type with the 10km values following in larger type. The corresponding 100km square letters may be found by referring to the map on page 153.

For example, the intersection SW4020 at the lower left corner of page 2 is 40km East and 20km North of the south-west corner of National Grid square SW.

Using GPS with Philip's mapping

Since Philip's maps are based on Ordnance Survey mapping, and rectified to the National Grid, they can be used with in-car or handheld GPS for locating identifiable waypoints such as road junctions, bridges, railways and farms, or assessing your position in relation to any of the features shown on the map.

On your receiver, choose British Grid as the location format and for map datum select Ordnance Survey (this may be described as Ord Srvy GB or similar, or more specifically as OSGB36). Your receiver will automatically convert the latitude/longitude co-ordinates transmitted by GPS into compatible National Grid data.

The positional accuracy of any particular feature is subject to the limitations of the original survey and the scale of mapping.

4 South Wales and Bristol area

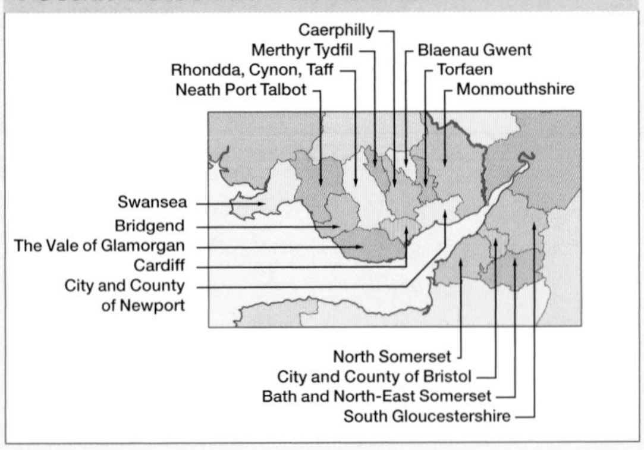

5 Thames Valley

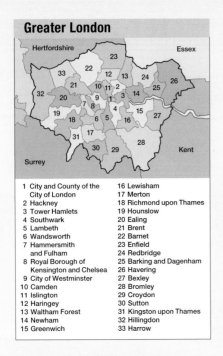

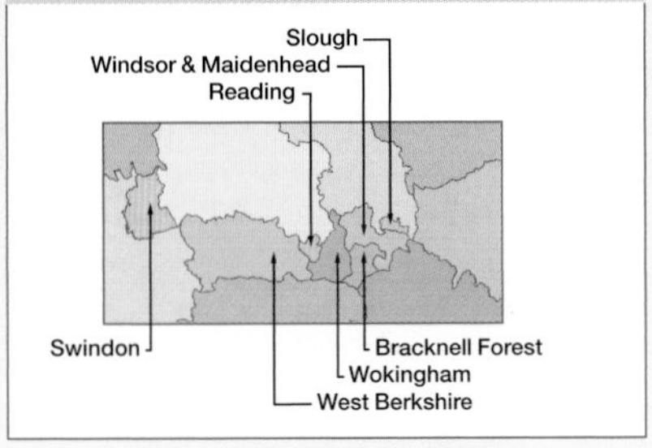